SAVING ABNORMAL

THE DISORDER OF

PSYCHIATRIC GENETICS

DANIEL R. BERGER II

ALETHIA
INTERNATIONAL
MINISTRIES.

Saving Abnormal: The Disorder of Psychiatric Genetics

Library of Congress Control Number: 2020904455

Trade Paperback ISBN: 978-0-9976077-8-9
Cover Artwork by: Priscilla Loewenthal
Edited by: Gail Berger

Unless otherwise noted, all Scripture references in this book are taken from the *English Standard Version*, copyright © 2001 by Crossway, Inc. Used by permission. All rights reserved.

Published by Alethia International Publications
Taylors, SC

www.drdanielberger.com

Printed in the United States of America

Dedicated to:

all people

who have suffered or died

under the influence and application of the

Kraepelinian genetic theory

of mental illness

ENDORSEMENTS

"Dr. Daniel Berger II is a detailed scholar and gifted writer. In *Saving Abnormal,* he elucidates the socio-political, philosophical, and unscientific underpinnings of the Kraepelinian genetic theory of mental illness. He does not stop at critique, but brings us to a biblical perspective and biblical hope. This is an excellent read for those interested in the roots of the *DSM* and psychiatric diagnoses." - **Dr. Jenn Chen, MABC, Psy.D., MAMFT, Adjunct Professor in Biblical Counseling for The Master's University, Former Clinical Instructor at The David Geffen School of Medicine at UCLA**

"In this important book, Dr. Berger clearly exposes what is said to be the 'science of psychiatric genetics' to be a philosophical approach — 'a religion' — rather than an empirically driven reality. From my own perspective, as both a seasoned professor of translational medicine and as an experimental biologist and geneticist, it seems that the field of 'psychiatric genetics,' in its essence, should be understood as a 'philosophy of psychiatric genetics.'

Despite the propaganda stating otherwise, we know very little about the human genome at both the molecular and functional levels. In the *OMIC*-era of genetics (e.g., genomic, transcriptome, methylome), we are still looking to identify genetic signature for valid diseases (e.g., cancer, Alzheimer's, and diabetes) and to understand the molecular determinants shaping the final product of genes and their functions. It is amazing that, while we fail even to quantitatively identify the cause and effect of measurable normal and organic-diseased phenotypes of humans, the whole array of psych-related professionals (e.g., psychiatrists, psychologists, neuro-psycho-biologists, pharmacists) rush to genetics in attempt to explain and justify their approaches and current treatments for most all mental, emotional, and behavioral struggles. Yet, as Dr. Berger exposes, many of the psychiatric constructs, which psychiatrists claim to be genetically caused, consist primarily of metaphysical phenomena, which cannot be approached within the scientific method. Moreover, simply correlating bodily systems does not validate the theory that the human genome somehow creates these phenomena.

One will also discover in Berger's important work that the genetic theory of mental illness has not helped people who are mentally struggling throughout its history. In fact, as is well-documented, the genetic theory of mental illness has consistently worsened humanity as a whole and societies in which it has been accepted. I encourage every physician, clinician, counselor, pastor, and social worker to consider the facts presented in *Saving Abnormal*." – **Dr. Shahriar**

Koochekpour, MD, PHD, Professor of Biology and Genetics, Cellular and Molecular Biologist, Translational Researcher on Cancer Drug Discovery and Targeted Therapy

"*Saving Abnormal* may literally save lives by giving hope and therapeutic approaches previously denied or hidden by the limitations of traditional psychiatry. Dr. Berger outlines the history of psychiatric constructs over the last several hundred years influencing today's treatments and failures. He goes well beyond the Neo-Kraepelinian bio-psycho–social model. I would dare to say he is speaking of surgery of the soul, which removes and repairs what is necessary for true healing. The double-edged scalpel of God's Word penetrates both sides of the dualistic model of man and the constructs of modern psychiatry which so easily entangles. Many fixed false beliefs may be removed by the truth in this book. Dr. Berger writes clearly with a great amount of academic research to show us a better way." **– Dr. Roy Hobbs, MD, FRCSP(C), FACS, Surgeon**

"In *Saving Abnormal,* Daniel Berger once again brings to the fore his intellectual excellence, impeccable scholarship, gracious heart, and passionate desire for the truth to be known. *Saving Abnormal* is a critically important and closeup view of the history of modern psychological theory, tracking its origins and following its trajectory as it blossomed from atheistic pseudoscience into the world-dominating religion that it is today. Daniel Berger demystifies the origins of racism, social injustice, and the never-ending reclassifications of 'mental illnesses.' Doctor? Therapist? Attorney? Judge? Social worker? Case worker? Been diagnosed with and medicated for a mental disorder? Love someone who has? This is a must-read book for you." – **Dr. Warren G. Lamb, Ph.D., Th.M., Director of Truth in Love Biblical Counseling and Training Center, Vice President of The International Association of Biblical Counselors, author of** *Behind the Veil: Exposing the Evil of Domestic Oppression*

"This is a must-read book for pastors and biblical counselors who want to understand the impact of reducing metaphysical issues to being explained and addressed through the doctrine of materialism. This mindset has influenced so many in the Christian Community, and it must stop. This book is masterful in educating us on the history, impact, and solutions to this issue. I truly appreciate the scholarship that went into writing this book. Thank you, Daniel, for your work."- **Dr. Nicolas Ellen Senior Pastor of Community of Faith Bible Church Houston, Texas, President of Expository Counseling Center LLC., Houston, Texas and Senior Professor of Biblical Counseling at the College of Biblical Studies Houston, Texas.**

"One of the most exciting times in a baseball game is the grand slam home run. It is even more exciting if it is a 'walk-off home run.' When it comes to writing books, Dr. Daniel Berger II has smashed a grand slam home run in what may well be his most critical book to date. While hoping, though, this is not Dr. Berger's "walk off" book, *Saving Abnormal* is perhaps one of the timeliest books of our day. It is informative. It is educational. It is undeniably factual, and it confronts a false belief system within the psychiatric world.

Many have assumed that the eugenics of Nazi Germany died with Hitler and his regime. But as Berger exposes, these assumptions are unfounded. The same philosophical underpinnings of the eugenics of the 30's and 40's has simply slid under the proverbial radar — disguised with new labeling. The core philosophy of the eugenics of the Nazis is alive and well. This book ought to be read by every psychiatrist, every psychologist, every psychotherapist, every neurologist, every Christian counselor, every biblical counselor, etc. It is a landmark book that addresses a critical mindset that has a grip on the psychiatric world, and readers would do well to ponder deeply the contents therein." - **Blake Shaw, Counseling Ministries Pastor at Grace Bible Church, Bozeman, MT**

"Have you wondered what "abnormal" is and why it needs saving? Dr. Daniel Berger walks the reader through an accurate yet disturbing history of psychiatry and the birth of abnormal. How was 'normal' decided? Even more perplexing is how did these 'normal' treatment providers inflict such inhumane treatments? Be cautioned, by reading this book you will be forced to re-evaluate your own, once seemingly foundational, beliefs of mental health. This is a book about faith; {spoiler alert} science is not foundational to the history of psychology. Science is nevertheless widely used as an antagonist to Christianity. Much like the successful marketing which insinuates that the field of psychiatry is supported by empirical scientific data, this is just one of many lies most of us have succumbed to believe. Dr. Berger gives the reader solid research through primarily secular sources to challenge these faulty presuppositional beliefs that we have accepted as sound science. Science is not opposed to faith, and psychiatry is not a science. *Saving Abnormal* is not just a rebuttal to humanistic psychiatry, it also provides a more reliable alternative. The genuine solution resides with our Creator – the One who makes all things, understands our fallen mental state, and provides the remedy through Jesus Christ." - **Greg M. Cintron, LMFT, MST, Marriage, Family and Child Therapist, Serving Combat Military and Sexual Trauma Victims, OIF Airborne Infantry Combat Medic, EMDR Provider**

"Dr. Daniel Berger's *Saving Abnormal* is solid wisdom, insight, and application bounded by two strong bookends of biblical discernment. The first bookend: don't be taken captive by empty and deceptive philosophy that depends on human tradition (Colossians 2:8). The second bookend: take every thought captive to make it obedient to Christ (2 Corinthians 10:5).

Saving Abnormal carefully, thoroughly, and objectively demonstrates how the current amalgamation of psychological thinking is based on theories and dogma that are designed to reduce human significance to genetic manipulation for a vague "greater good." As you read the book you discover this "greater good" is an ethical nightmare that is anything but good. There are no wild claims here. Instead you will find meticulous scholarship that challenges the direction modern psychology uses to evaluate our life-struggles and our state of mind.

The other bookend clearly and powerfully demonstrates how to take thoughts captive for Christ. This will equip you so that you will not be deceived by reasoning that has the appearance of wisdom but is, in fact, enslavement to a way of thinking that results in a life devoid of enduring moral principles. The only goal is an amoral pragmatism that has no connection to truly principled thought.

As Dr. Berger states, "If mankind was, in fact, created in the image of God, then understanding God's image is vital to understanding human nature and human phenomena." *Saving Abnormal* makes a compelling case for the sufficiency of Scripture in understanding and treating the wounded and hurting hearts of the 21st Century. *Saving Abnormal* is a must read to reclaim truth in a broken world for you and the people you love." **– Jay Younts, author and biblical counselor.**

"Daniel Berger has written a provocative volume that should anger and awaken every reader. *Saving Abnormal* exposes the hidden truths about psychiatry and its historical link with Nazism, evolution, alcoholism, and other philosophies that undermine the God-given dignity and value of all human life. Readers who seek to deny the truth presented in this book will be frustrated by their own inability to refute the preponderance of evidence exposing the deceptions of psychology and its pseudoscience. Conversely, readers seeking to know the truth should be disgusted by these same lies and thereby challenged to take action to transform their thinking and acceptance of common cultural norms. The content in this book elicits a response from every reader. Be prepared to never look at psychiatry the same way again!" – **Dr. Mark E. Shaw, Author of *The Heart of Addiction*, founder of The Addiction Connection**

"How does anyone find help and healing for a problem that is defined as a genetically fixed, inescapable mental illness? As is so often the case, the influence of a materialistic worldview has been so successfully infused into our society that it even permeates the very questions we ask. In a careful analysis of its history, Dr. Daniel Berger has masterfully revealed that every root, trunk and branch of modern psychiatry has been founded in a materialistic view of humanity and cultivated through the evolutionary ideals of the eugenics movement. It is my hope that every reader discovers the bankruptcy of the foundational presuppositions in psychiatric diagnoses. When it comes to providing real help to hurting people, your foundational ideas have enormous consequences. If this book doesn't change the way you counsel, read it again." - **Steve Ham, Senior Pastor, Hyde Park Baptist Church, Ohio.**

CONTENT

PART 1

PART 2

ACKNOWLEDGMENTS

This book was made possible by many friends, family, and professionals who sacrificed time and gave effort to read early drafts and offer me valuable feedback. Specifically, I would like to thank my wife, Oriana, my children, and my parents, Dan and Gail Berger, who are always supportive and helpful with each book that I author. I wish to also thank a group of professional medical researchers and physicians for their time and insight on this project: Dr. Shahriar Koochekpour, Dr. Anne Dryburgh, Dr. Peter Breggin, Dr. Mark Shaw, Steve Ham, Jay Younts, Eliezer Loewenthal, Dr. Julie Ganschow, Greg Cintron, Blake Shaw, Dr. Roy Hobbs, Dr. Nicolas Ellen, Dr. Josh Jones, Dr. Warren Lamb, Dr. Christopher Burman, and Dr. Jenn Chen.

DISCLAIMER

The material contained in this book is the result of years of experience, research, and professional interviews, but it is not intended in any way to be taken as medical advice. Rather, the views and material expressed in this book are written in order to provide truth and hope (a biblical phenomenology) to those who want to know more about the *false genetic theory* and begin to understand the foundation of their problems and, subsequently, the only remedy available. If you or someone under your care needs medical assistance, please see a licensed physician who can attend to your physical needs — especially as it relates to psychiatric withdrawal or counsel about psychotropic drug consumption.

ABBREVIATIONS

APA   American Psychiatric Association

DSM-IV   *Diagnostic & Statistical Manual of Mental Disorders IV*

DSM-5   *Diagnostic & Statistical Manual of Mental Disorders 5*

ESV   *English Standard Version of Scripture*

GWAS   Genome Wide Association Studies

HGP   Human Genome Project

ICD-10   *International Classification of Diseases 10*

JAMA   *Journal of the American Medical Association*

NEJM   *New England Journal of Medicine*

NIH   National Institutes of Health

NIMH   National Institute of Mental Health

OTHER BOOKS BY AUTHOR

CHAPTER 1

INTRODUCTION

"The idea that the social order is natural or inevitable, fixed by the will of God or the laws of nature (or, more recently, by the structure of one's genes) is not a new one."[1] *– Robert Proctor, Sandford Historian of Science*

"Who is John Galt?" This question was made famous by the atheist Ayn Rand in the opening of her classic book *Atlas Shrugged*.[2] Interestingly, historic records illuminate the significance of one particular John Galt, and his story, along with aspects of the biography of the "father of American psychiatry" Benjamin Rush, illuminates the field of modern psychiatry, its predominant genetic theory of mental illness, and the current worsening condition of individuals and society under the theory's application.

---

[1] Robert N. Proctor, *Racial Hygiene: Medicine Under the Nazis* (Cambridge, Massachusetts: Harvard University Press, 1988), 2.

[2] Ayn Rand, *Atlas Shrugged* (New York: Penguin Books, 1957), 11.

Moreover, the history of these two psychiatric figures both reveals a necessary and relevant philosophical discussion, as well as demands an inevitable choice between the two worldviews utilized by these two men to explain and approach the human soul/mind. How people fundamentally understand the human soul and its metaphysical human phenomena and, subsequently, how they attempt to resolve mental and behavioral struggles are some of the most important and urgent discussions in modern times.

On one hand, modern society is faced with a well-established but failed approach to human nature and human phenomena. Ironically, this currently championed perspective of mental health has served to worsen individuals and societies in which it has been accepted. On the other hand, a history of deliverance and hope — though still available and effective — has been minimized, ignored, and/or denied in order to sustain hope that the popular but failed approach to the soul will in the end both be validated and deliver on its propagated potential benefits. The time has come, though, to reconsider how impairing and destructive human mindsets, emotions, and behaviors are philosophically viewed and practically applied. Early American psychiatrists John Galt and Benjamin Rush provide a starting point in this discussion, one which inevitably leads to a choice of either genuine hope or continued harm.

Dr. John Galt

John Milton Galt II (1819-1862) was the first medical "superintendent" of the first free-standing mental hospital in America (first opened in 1773 and run by John Galt I).[3] While the Eastern Lunatic Asylum in Williamsburg, Virginia was officially declared to be a hospital (though more often referred to as "The Mad House"), it was for years less of a medical facility and more of a place of "legal [involuntary] confinement."[4] Before John Galt I assumed leadership, only "alienists"[5] or "keepers" of mental wards existed.[6] The keeper's job was to restrain, alienate, and confine — typically by brutal force and physical and chemical restraints, lest the insane bother, frighten, or threaten the general public. To be institutionalized in a mental ward in the early years of America meant that institutionalized individuals would be isolated from society, judged to be abnormal, and typically treated far worse than a farm animal.

Every keeper of the Eastern Lunatic Asylum since its opening and prior to John Galt II represented several generations in the Galt family. Based upon this consistent familial-behavioral pattern, a person might be tempted to suggest that for the Galt family, dealing with the insane was hereditary or genetic.

But John Galt II differed from most of the previous generations of alienists in his family in that he ushered into

[3] Mary A. Stephenson, "*The Eastern State Hospital at Williamsburg, Virginia,*" Colonial Williamsburg Digital Library (1950): https://research.history.org/DigitalLibrary/View/index.cfm?doc=ResearchReports%5CRR1078.xml.

[4] Ibid.

[5] Edward Shorter, *A History of Psychiatry: From the Era of the Asylum to the Age of the Prozac* (New York: John Wiley & Sons, 1997), 73.

[6] For definition of terms, see appendix A.

the American asylum a truly moral approach to the human soul.[7] It was in this new role that Galt would experiment, study intensely, and suggest and publish his theories of potential causes of insanity as well as ways in which the "insane" might be treated. Galt was a brilliant man who was well-traveled, religious, mastered over twenty languages,[8] and sought to establish his version of moral therapy in both America and other countries like Brazil and Russia.[9] In his most significant book, *The Treatment of Insanity*,[10] Galt discusses the clinical observations and common treatments by psychiatrists from around the world — providing a broad global perspective of psychiatric theory and treatments in the early to mid-1800s. Galt also notes in the book countless times how blood-letting,

[7] Galt's father (John I) and his brother (Alexander) both spoke of moral therapy and provided better conditions for those in their care. But these physicians still relied heavily on the coercive and biological approaches popular during their time. Likewise, historical revisionism is commonly utilized by some historians in claiming that Benjamin Rush introduced "moral therapy" into America (e.g., Marshall A. Ledger, "Benjamin Rush and 20 Years of Penn Psychiatry," *Penn Medicine* vol. XXIV (1) (Fall 2012): 29; https://www.penn medicine.org/news/-/media/ documents %20and%20audio/pr%20news/penn%20med%20 magazine/fall_ 2012_full_ issue_3.ashx). However, a cursory overview of Rush's approaches and biological attempts to treat insanity/mania yield a different conclusion. Rush certainly improved the daily living conditions in the mental wards he oversaw, though John Galt I (starting in 1773) preceded Rush (starting in 1781) in this effort.

[8] Granville L. Jones, "The history of the founding of the Eastern State Hospital of Virginia," *American Journal of Psychiatry* 110 (March 1954): 644.

[9] Wendy Gonaver, *The Peculiar Institution and the Making of Modern Psychiatry 1840-1880* (University of North Carolina Press, 2018), 14.

[10] John M. Galt, *The Treatment of Insanity* (New York: Harper and Brothers, 1846).

vomiting, showering, and drugging were common attempts at curing insanity during his day. For instance, Galt records one physician's approach:

> Mania — the cure rests chiefly in attention to the state of blood . . . First among pharmaceutical remedies stands vomiting. Etmuller asserts the cure to depend on strong vomits of antimony and hellebore.[11]

Galt also differed from his ancestors in that he arrived at a place of rejecting most of the barbaric but widely-accepted means of treatment so prevalent during his time.

One particular approach to insanity that Galt discusses in his book, however, greatly impacted his own conclusions in viewing and remedying madness, though the perspective was marginalized. That approach was in part made popular by French psychiatrist Philip Pinel, whom many historians claim was the first psychiatrist (1793).[12] In similar fashion to Galt, Pinel taught an altruistic approach to insanity referred to as "moral therapy." Though not as well known as Pinel, Galt would take his place in history as the leading advocate for a truly moral therapy in early America.

But Galt's attempt to revolutionize psychiatry in America also undermined the biological approach that the

[11] Ibid, preface A.

[12] Allen Frances, *Saving Normal: An Insider's Revolt against Diagnosis, DSM-5, Big Pharma, and the Medicalization of Ordinary Life* (New York: HarperCollins, 2013), 56; Jeffrey Lieberman and others note that Franz Anton Mesmer preceded Pinel and Benjamin Rush (*Shrinks: the Untold Story of Psychiatry* [New York: Little, Brown and Company, 2015], 27). Nonetheless, Pinel and Rush were some of the first psychiatrists who suggested different approaches to addressing the human soul.

influential Benjamin Rush had established well before Galt's time and which fellow American psychiatrists overwhelmingly embraced. One historian notes Galt's three pillars of revolution — two of which directly challenged the status quo in American psychiatry during that time:

> As Dr. Galt put it, three successive revolutions in psychiatry occurred in Williamsburg. The "First Revolution" was the Hospital's founding as a publicly supported facility exclusively for the care of the mentally ill. **The "Second Revolution" was the introduction of Moral Management therapy. This taught, as Dr. Galt said, that the mentally ill "differ from us in degree, but not in kind" and are entitled to human dignity.** . . . The "Third Revolution in Psychiatry" became clear in 1857, **when Dr. Galt was the first to advocate deinstitutionalization and community-based mental health care.** He wrote, "A large number of insane, instead of rusting out their lives in the confines of some vast asylum, should be placed... in the neighboring community... where any other class of persons than the insane collected together in such large numbers as is the case in some asylums, we are satisfied that the greatest disorder would be likely to ensue [emphasis added]."[13]

In a turn of events, this first supervisor of the first free-standing American state mental hospital concluded that treating people as normal who were mentally and behaviorally struggling rather than treating them as disordered/abnormal was the best treatment that they could receive. Moreover, Galt was convinced that deinstitutionalizing (as opposed to confinement and isolation) was vitally important to recovery. Galt was influenced into this "new" way of thinking through his

[13] "The History of Eastern State," (August 2019): http://www.esh.dbhds. virginia. gov/History.html.

own esteem for the Bible with its practical applications, his years of clinical experiments and observations, and through many of the principles of moral therapy taught by secular psychiatrist Philip Pinel. One historian remarks on Galt's paradigm shift:

> While in the past patients had been subjected to a series of brutal treatments (being plunged into cold water, "blistering" and drawing blood, electric shocks) **Galt implemented a policy of "moral" treatment, in line with developments taking place in Britain and France.** This limited the use of restraint and placed the emphasis on responding to the insane with respect and compassion [emphasis added].[14]

In *the Treatment of Insanity*, Galt writes on the efficacy of Pinel's moral approach, which produced its appeal:

> Visitors to the Salpetriere, witnessing the order and calmness which reign there, are struck with astonishment, and sometimes cry out with surprise, "But where are the mad?" They are ignorant that they thus pay the highest compliment to the institution, and that their question denotes the very remarkable difference between this and other hospitals, where the miserable insane are crowded together pell-mell and without any distinction; exasperated by the brutal rudeness of the attendants, and subject to the vain caprices and arbitrary orders of an unfit or negligent superior . . .[15]

Authors of the textbook *Abnormal Psychology* also note the success Pinel experienced in genuinely helping people

[14] The State of Virginia, "John M. Galt," (July 2019): http://xroads. virginia.edu/~MA05/havard/Galt/about_galt.htm.

[15] Galt, *The Treatment of Insanity*, 41.

recover who were set aside and stigmatized by society as disordered:

> Pinel's position was that the mentally ill were simply ordinary human beings who had been deprived of their reason by severe personal problems; to treat them like animals not only was inhumane but also impeded recovery . . . Based on the idea that the mentally ill were simply ordinary people with extraordinary problems, moral therapy aimed at restoring their "morale" by providing an environment in which they could discuss their difficulties, live in peace and engage in some useful employment. More than anything else, moral therapy aimed at treating patients like human beings. And apparently, this approach was extremely successful. Contemporary records show that during the first half of the nineteenth century, when moral therapy was the only treatment provided by mental hospitals in Europe and America, at least 70 percent of those hospitalized either improved or actually recovered [emphasis added].[16]

Historian James Jackson also records one of the key underlying beliefs that empowered moral therapy: "Pinel argued that, rather than treating mental illness with physical means, patients needed a mental approach to treatment."[17] True moral therapy, as both Galt and Pinel would champion, dismissed theories of biological explanations and manipulations and focused, instead, on

---

[16] Lauren B. Alloy, Joan Acocella, and Richard R. Bootzin, *Abnormal Psychology: Current Perspectives* 7th edition (New York: McGraw-Hill, 1996), 16-17.

[17] James W. Jackson, "Case Study of the Eastern State Hospital as Evidence of English Influence on American Ideas about Mental Illness," *University of Richmond UR Scholarship Repository* (December 15, 2015), 21; https://scholarship.richmond.edu/cgi/viewcontent.cgi?article=1000&context=jackson-award.

the metaphysical soul/psyche. These two pioneers also concluded that treating people who were mentally struggling as ordinary/normal was the best and most successful approach to helping them, and that what people needed to improve mentally was to be loved and dignified rather than viewed as abnormal/disordered and set aside.

Treating the human soul as metaphysical and moral consistently produced improvement in those who were struggling. Founding editor of *Penn Medicine*, Dr. Marshal Ledger, quotes historian Nancy Tomes in describing this age of psychiatry:

> As Tomes has noted, medical science in this period contributed little to the understanding of mental illness, but patient care improved nonetheless, "based less on any medical advances than on simple Christian charity and common sense."[18]

With the record of these positive results available,[19] one must ask why people who are struggling with even severe delusions or what have been framed as manic episodes are still today stigmatized as disordered and classified as abnormal and why many of the failed practices which Galt denounced are still administrated today under the guise of medicine? Why also is Christian faith and charity minimized or denied as healing the soul? These are

---

[18] Marshall A. Ledger, "Benjamin Rush and 20 Years of Penn Psychiatry," *Penn Medicine* vol. XXIV (1) (Fall 2012): 29; https://www.penn medicine.org/news/-/media/documents%20and%20audio/pr%20news/ penn%20med%20magazine/fall_2012_full_issue_3.ashx.

[19] "Interestingly, psychiatrists working in racially mixed asylums in colonial Asia championed cottage care in the early twentieth century with the same langue of liberty and progress that Galt had used" (Gonaver, *The Making of Modern Psychiatry*, 10).

questions that demand further exploration and solid answers.

Despite the overwhelming positive results that both Galt and Pinel accrued[20] and despite Galt's earnest efforts to deinstitutionalize the insane and to view them as ordinary people with intense problems, his empirically backed conclusions were rejected by influential politicians, by virtually every other psychiatrist, and by those who had invested financial interest in keeping madness as a medical and state-controlled issue. If Galt's ideas were popularized and implemented more broadly, then the expanding belief that approaching all of human nature from a strictly material perspective and that biological mechanisms and state-run institutions provided the best treatments available would have been undermined.

But there exists yet another reason that a great number of people rejected Galt's teachings and published empirical evidence — a reason that is the most significant, and that reason was the belief in and application of "race psychology." While the vast majority of psychiatrists and politicians endorsed slavery and propagated the construct of race, Galt consistently rejected the notion that some people are not morally equal to others. In fact, Galt's asylum was "the only U.S. institution to accept slaves and

[20] Galt records numerous people who "fully recovered" from their "insanity." The preaching from the Bible and corporate worship are also noted by Galt as being helpful to both calm and positively change the mind of those institutionalized (Galt, *The Treatment of Insanity*, 430-31). Galt also observed numerous asylums worldwide where both restraints and isolation were abolished and those patients under moral therapy were bettered. In Galt's view, the empirical evidence was overwhelming to prove the reliability and validity of treating people with dignity (Gonaver, *The Making of Modern Psychiatry*, 45-46).

free blacks as patients and to employ slaves as caregivers."[21] Psychiatrists' firm belief in the genetic or hereditary theory of mental illness placed Galt at the "unanimous objection of his peers."[22] In contrast to his fellow psychiatrists, Galt saw all people as valuable souls that were morally equal:

> Dr. Galt claimed to treat patients equally "without regard to race." In fact, he published no records as to the racial breakdown of the patient population. The mentally ill were another group suffering oppression at this time. Chaining and other forms of long-term restraint were common at Eastern Lunatic Asylum until the late 1830s, when Moral Management thinking [implemented by Galt] introduced the ideals of human dignity and least restraint.[23]

Member of the *Consortium for the History of Science, Technology, and Medicine* Wendy Gonaver observes,

> As a young man, John M. Galt had expressed reservations about slavery. He sought to avoid overt violence and permitted his enslaved staff a surprising degree of independent power. He advocated for mental health care without regard to race, the abolishment of physical restraints, and the opportunity for chronic patients to live and work with families in the community without stigma. Shunned by his fellow super-intendents for his views,

[21] Ibid., 1.

[22] Ibid.

[23] Sandy Kochersperger, "John Minson Galt II: a short history," *Eastern State Hospital Mental Heatlh Library* (accessed July 2019): http://www.oocities.org/sandy.kochersp/galt.html.

isolation yielded to despair once he found himself witness to the ghastly consequences of civil war.[24]

Galt rejected race/hereditary psychology — the most popular social construct of his day claimed to be scientifically based — and was therefore rejected himself by others in his profession and community. As many historians acknowledge in their records, the opposition and attacks toward Galt and his conclusions, based upon his years of clinical work and research, would lead him into depression,[25] and according to most historical records John Galt II committed suicide. One historian writes,

> Nobody agreed to what Galt said. The Hospital's Court of Directors prevented him to accomplish his plans to de-institutionalization his patients three times. This was most likely a factor of why Galt later succumbed to depression and committed suicide five years later in 1862.[26]

But most historians also acknowledge that Galt had many enemies both in politics and in psychiatry — especially those who held to racial psychology and despised that Galt strove to treat all men equally. Upon Galt's death, the Eastern Lunatic Asylum was immediately taken over by eugenic psychiatrists:

> The void created by Galt's death had created an opening for his professional adversaries, those colleagues who had never approved of his experiments with integrated and outpatient care, to influence the postwar reconstruction of

[24] Gonaver, *The Making of Modern Psychiatry*, 3.

[25] "The History of Eastern State,": http://www.esh.dbhds.virginia.gov/History.html.

[26] Unknown, "Dr. John Minson Galt and the Eastern State Insane Asylum" (July 2019): https://firstinsaneasylum.weebly.com/dr-john-minson-galt.html.

the asylum. Yet in implementing their vision of proper management, Northern reformers and their Southern allies actually hastened the end of moral therapy for African American patients. The Eastern Lunatic Asylum, which under John M. Galt might have offered a model for reconstruction governments to emulate, instead became an obscure and inconsequential institution.[27]

Once Galt's adversaries assumed full control, segregation was instituted and enforced at the Eastern Lunatic Asylum. Historian Wendy Gonaver relates that

> the Civil War affected everyone connected to the Eastern Lunatic Asylum and ultimately led to the creation of separate institutions for black and white patients.[28]

Clearly, there were many politicians and psychiatrists who did not like the fact that Galt — as with others like Pinel — provided empirical evidence that love and truth rather than medicine, stigma, and imposed social constructs were the best approach to treating mental, emotional, and behavioral struggles. Whether Galt's "overdose of laudanum" was self-inflicted or not may never be known. Yet, as with the fictional John Galt depicted in Ayn Rand's *Atlas Shrugged*, Dr. John M. Galt stood against institutionalism and was committed to practicing empathy no matter the cost involved.

Dr. Benjamin Rush

Although John Galt II would have revolutionized American psychiatry if allowed, there is little known about

---

[27] Gonaver, *The Making of Modern Psychiatry*, 145-46.

[28] Ibid., 145.

him today in history books on mental illness or psychiatry. Instead, another American psychiatrist, Dr. Benjamin Rush (1746-1813) — whom Galt's views opposed — is highly honored, and it is largely upon Rush's original core ideas that much of today's popular psychiatric theory depends:

> The origins of American psychiatry are traditionally traced to Benjamin Rush, one of the signers of the Declaration of Independence. He is considered a Founding Father of the United States, and through the sepia mists of time he has acquired another paternal appellation: Father of American Psychiatry.[29]

Historian and Pulitzer Prize winner David McCullough writes of Rush's significance in the history of psychiatry and his introduction of materialism into academia as an approach to the human mind/soul:

> In November of 1812, Rush sent [John] Adams a first copy of what he considered his most important work, *Medical Inquiries and Observations upon the Diseases of the Mind*. For years Rush had been investigating the causes of and remedies for madness and other "diseases" of the mind. "The subjects of them have hitherto been enveloped in mystery," he wrote to Adams. **"I have endeavored to bring them down to the level of all other diseases of the human body, and to show that the mind and body are moved by the same causes and subject to the same laws."** He expected to be chastised by his fellow physicians. "But time, I hope, will do my opinions justice. I believe them to be true and calculated to lessen some of the greatest evils of human life. If they are not, I shall console myself of having aimed well and erred honestly. **The book was to become the standard American guide for mental illnesses, and in later years, Rush would**

---

[29] Lieberman, *Shrinks*, 61.

become known as the father of American psychiatry [emphasis added].[30]

Former president of the American Psychiatric Association, John Oldham also acknowledges the importance and ongoing influence of both Rush's theory of a material soul and his publishing of the first textbook of psychiatry:

> Benjamin Rush was a major, major figure in the history of psychiatry and usually is referred to as the "Father of American Psychiatry." He is widely recognized for his work. On the wall [of psychiatric history] is the first real textbook of psychiatry, called *Medical Inquiries and Observations, Upon Diseases of the Mind*. It was the standard textbook in psychiatry for decades.[31]

It is upon Rush's original theory that not only American psychiatry is principally established, but also the global modern psychiatric genetic field.

After his son's first attempt at suicide,[32] Rush began to theorize more urgently about the concept of mental illness and material explanations of the soul and human morality — likely as an attempt to explain his son's unfortunate struggles and eventual demise. Historian Stephen Fried remarks on how the mental difficulties of his

---

[30] David McCullough, *American Presidents: John Adams, Mornings on Horseback, Truman, and the Course of Human Events* (New York: Simon and Schuster, 2001), 609.

[31] Drew Ramsey and John M. Oldham, "A Brief History of American Psychiatry: From a Founding Father to Dr. Anonymous," *Medscape Psychiatry* (November 7, 2019): https://www.medscape.com/viewarticle/917451?nlid=132561_424&src=WNL_mdplsfeat_191112_mscpedit_psyc&uac=264124BV&spon=12&impID=2164621&faf=1.

[32] Ibid.

son John "inspired" Rush to write his psychiatric theory: *Medical Inquiries and Observations, Upon Diseases of the Mind*:

> Rush's eldest child, Lt. John Rush, a navy surgeon he had hoped would take over his practice, descended into mental illness, triggered in apart by a tragic duel. He would spend the rest of his life in his father's care, and his situation would inspire Rush's last and most influential book, the first American volume on "diseases of the mind."[33]

Dr. Oldham also comments about Rush:

> [His son's attempted suicide] turned his interest onto the field of mental health and mental illness. He was widely regarded as a very revered expert and compassionate physician who really moved away from the early pre-colonial myths—demons and witchcraft—**to focus in on the medical nature of the brain and the mind, and to treat it as a part of the body that we needed to understand more about** [emphasis added].[34]

But unlike Oldham's assertion, Rush was not entirely revered or compassionate, nor was he honored because he accomplished anything of value concerning medically approaching the mind, proved his theory of a material soul/mind, or had success in treating mental struggles with biological treatments. In fact, when it came to attempting to explain and treat the mind, both Rush's theories and methods were themselves maddening. Rush likely had altruistic intentions in attempting to reduce humanity to only a material existence, but his teachings, social constructs, and suggested remedies would

---

[33] Stephen Fried, *Rush: Revolution, Madness, and the Visionary Doctor who became a Founding Father* 1st edition (NY: Random House, 2018), 7.

[34] Ramsey and Oldham, "A Brief History of American Psychiatry."

consistently prove to be destructive both in his own time and thereafter. For example, Rush proposed that

> having rejected the abdominal viscera, the nerves, and the mind, as the primary seats of madness, I shall now deliver an opinion, which I have long believed and taught in my lectures, and that is, that the cause of madness is seated primarily in the blood-vessels of the brain, and that it depends upon the same kind of morbid and irregular actions that constitutes other arterial diseases.[35]

Rush's theories were not only absurd, his treatments were also barbaric. Historians Lucy Ozarin and Dilip Ramchandam — writing for the American Psychiatric Association — remark about Rush that

> Rush's practice of psychiatry was based on bleeding, purging, and the use of the tranquilizer chair and gyrator. By 1844 these practices were considered erroneous and abandoned. Rush, however, was the first American to study mental disorder in a systematic manner, and he is considered the father of American Psychiatry.[36]

The significance of developing a psychiatric system of disorders will be discussed in the chapters to come, but merely approaching human struggles in a systematic way is not in itself worthy of honor. In actuality, academic psychiatrists esteem Rush for his material theory of the soul, his hereditary concept of madness, his creation of psychiatric constructs, and his theory of biological treatments — though his actual treatments have widely been

[35] Benjamin Rush, *Medical Inquiries and Observations Upon the Diseases of the Mind* ed. (Philadelphia: Grigg and Elliot, 1835), 15.

[36] Lucy D. Ozarin and Dilip Ramchandam (ed.). "History Notes: The Official Seal of the APA," *Psychiatric News.* American Psychiatric Association (April 17, 1998).

rejected. Former American Psychiatric Association president-elect, Jeffrey Lieberman, also recognizes the absurdity of Rush's biological treatments:

> Between the nauseating spinning chairs and the constant evacuation of bowels [and the bleeding patients out], one guesses that a psychiatric ward in Rush's hospital could be a very messy place.[37]

Rush's proposed remedies were so harmful that many people died as a result of being treated under his care.[38]

In contrast to Galt and Pinel, Rush believed that terror/fear and not "moral therapy" was one of the most effective approaches to madness. He asserts, "Terror acts powerfully upon the body, through the medium of the mind, and should be employed in the cure of madness."[39] Rush is also quoted by Galt as advising physicians that when being respectful and truthful fail to help, then more drastic and abusive measures are required to treat mania:

> Be always dignified. Never laugh at or with them. Be truthful. Meet them with respect. Act kindly towards them in their presence. **If these measures fail, coercion is necessary. Tranquilizing chair. Strait waistcoat. Pour cold water down their sleeves. The shower-bath for fifteen or twenty minutes. Threaten them with death.** Chains seldom, and the whip never required. Twenty to

---

[37] Lieberman, *Shrinks*, 63.

[38] Robert L. North, "Benjamin Rush, MD: Assassin or Beloved Healer?" *Proceedings Baylor University Medical Center* vol. 13 (1) (January, 2000): 49. doi:10.1080/08998280.2000.

[39] Rush, *Medical Inquiries and Observations*, 209.

forty ounces of blood, unless fainting occur previously . . .
. Solitude. Darkness [emphasis added].[40]

According to Rush's thinking (as observed in many of his practices and inventions), the best way to treat a perceived abnormality was to create an abnormal environment and impose abnormal and destructive physical treatments upon the individual's body. The exception to this reality was Rush's implementing the policy that patients in his hospital should have orderly living quarters and work—what would later in history be developed into "occupational therapy."

To be fair, Rush did seem to have a sincere desire to help those under his care, and he drastically improved the conditions of patients once confined to chains and held in unlivable conditions. Many historians regard these improvements and his care for his patients as equaling "moral therapy." But Rush even regarded morality as a physical issue, and missed the point that genuine moral therapy rested upon the belief that mankind was a metaphysical soul with a physical body. With the exceptions of isolation, tranquilizers, occupational therapy, and confinement against one's will, none of Rush's other proposed psychiatric treatments stood the test of time.

In addition to his material explanation of the soul and his biological approach or medical model, another of Rush's theories would not only prosper in the United States, it would come to dominate psychiatry worldwide. *Race psychology*—or as it would also become known as: *hereditary madness, eugenics,* and the *genetic theory of mental illness*—

---

[40] Benjamin Rush quoted by Galt, *The Treatment of Insanity*, 81.

coupled with materialism is likely Rush's most notable contribution to psychiatry.

Rush regularly proposed the misguided and racist idea that blacks were "disordered" or "diseased" as evidenced in their skin color. He writes that

> the big lip, and flat nose so universal among the negros, are symptoms of the leprosy. I have more than once seen them in the Pennsylvania hospital. The wooly heads of the negros cannot be accounted for from climate, diet, state of society, or bilious diseases . . . Wool is peculiar to the negro . . . However, by the same token, whites should not intermarry with them, for this would tend to infect posterity with the disorder.[41]

In this same text, Rush also clearly articulates his genetic/hereditary theory of madness — including his most known psychiatric construct, what he referred to as "alcoholism" and "consumption"[42]:

> The tumors in the throat in the Cretins who inhabit the Alps, are transmitted from father to son, through a long succession of generations. **Madness and consumption in like manner are hereditary in many families, both of which occupy parts of the body** [emphasis added].[43]

[41] Benjamin Rush, "Observations Intended to Favour a Supposition That the Black Color of the Negroes Is Derived from the Leprosy," *Transactions of the American Philosophical Society* (June 17, 1797), 293. https://digitalcollections. nypl.org/items/ac54c7c0-1628-0134-e13b-00505686a51c#/?uuid=ac953040-1628-0134-fd20-00505686a51c.

[42] Rush described the state of alcoholism as a "temporary fit of madness" (Benjamin Rush, *Inquiry into the Effects of Ardent Spirits Upon the Human Body and Mind,* originally published in 1785 [1943], 323).

[43] Rush, "Observations Intended," 294.

Historian Daniel Boorstin offers further insight in Rush's hereditary approach:

> When asked to account for the duration of the Negro's color through long centuries, Rush answered that leprosy was of all diseases the most permanently inherited. According to Rush, the fact that in the eighteenth-century Negroes seldom infected others with the disease could not be held against his theory.[44]"

Hereditary negritude," as Rush coined the term, along with "hereditary madness" and "hereditary alcoholism" are some of the first recorded assertions of the foundational concepts of psychiatric eugenics in America.[45] In fact, Rush suggests as potential treatments for the disorder of "negritude" the very treatments for insanity so popular during his day and the same treatments that Galt denounced. Rush states,

> Depletion, whether by bleeding, purging, or abstinence, has been often observed to lessen black color in negros. The effects of the above remedies in curing the common leprosy, satisfy me that they might be used with advantage in the state of leprosy which I conceive to exist in the skin of the negros. A similar change in the color of

---

[44] Daniel J. Boorstin, *The Lost World of Thomas Jefferson* (Chicago: University of Chicago Press, 1993), 90.

[45] Rush stated his motive as proving the biblical account of creation and the idea of one singular race: "Curing the disease . . . . Rush argues it would make [negros] happier and strengthen the claim that all people are descended from one original couple" (The New York Public Library: https://digitalcollections.nypl.org/items/ac54c7c0-1628-0134-e13b-00505686a51c#/?uuid=acd74720-1628-0134-9602-00505686a51c).

the negros, though of a more temporary nature, has often been observed in them from the influence of fear.[46]

Rush believed that if his theorized medical disorder of "negritude" could be cured — that is that blacks could be transformed into being white, then blacks could be happy. It was upon forming a wrong view of normalcy and ignoring the life context of slavery — a false anthropological starting point focused on differentials — that Rush constructed his racist hereditary/genetic theory. Boorstin remarks,

> Through this whole argument ran the assumption (the more significant because not explicitly vowed) that the norm of the color of a healthy member of the human species was white . . . . One of his final arguments for redoubling the effort to perfect a cure was that the Negro might have the happiness of wearing the proper white color of the human skin.[47]

Physicians at The University of Pennsylvania Medical School, where Rush taught and was an influential figure, warn of Rush's "scientific" eugenic theory being repeated today:

> Much as medicine and science have moved beyond the bloodletting and purging favored by Benjamin Rush 200 years ago, it behooves today's doctors and scientists to make sure eugenics remains an illegitimate science.[48]

---

[46] Benjamin Rush, "Observations Intended," 296.

[47] Daniel J. Boorstin, *The Lost World of Thomas Jefferson* (Chicago: University of Chicago Press, 1993), 92.

[48] Penn Medicine's Department of Communications, "Psychiatry and Eugenics," *Penn Medicine News* (October 23, 2012): https://www.pennmedicine.org/news/news-blog/2012/october/ psychiatry-and-eugenics.

It is important to recognize that Rush was not merely the father of American psychiatry, he was also the informal father of psychiatric eugenics. Historian Christopher Willoughby, writing for *The Oxford University Press* under grant from the *National Science Foundation*, comments,

> Throughout the eighteenth century, physicians and scientists in Europe and the United States discussed and attempted to define racial difference. **In the 1790s, however, Benjamin Rush, a founding father and early medical professor at the University of Pennsylvania, introduced racial difference into the curriculum of US medical schools.** Rush taught his students that blackness was a form of leprosy that physicians would learn to cure eventually. **By constructing a national future free of black Americans, Rush defined the country's destiny as all white. Thus, within a few decades after the founding of the United States' first medical school, physicians began to carve out their position as experts on racial difference** [emphasis added].[49]

Dr. Seema Yasmin noted in 2020 how the history of racism in medicine has largely been ignored or denied — enabling oppression to continue:

> We must be acutely aware that racism is baked into our medical institutions, and that we teach racist medicine every time we choose to exclude a history of the concept of race in our medical curricula. **By not challenging the construct of race and its continued misuse in medicine,**

---

[49] Christopher Willoughby, "Racist Medicine: A History of Race and Health," *The Oxford University Press* (September 12, 2017): https://blog.oup.com/2017/09/racist-medicine-history-race-health/.

we perpetuate a system of oppression [emphasis added].[50]

Though many historians portray Francis Galton as the father of eugenics, it is Benjamin Rush (almost a century before Galton) who theorized and promoted the genetic/hereditary theory of mental illness based upon "racial" differences.

Many of Rush's teachings—including his views concerning alcoholism, hereditary madness, criminal degeneracy, and people of color—would be observed in the Nazi psychiatric institutes in Germany over a century later as key constructs.[51] If Rush had known the extent of damage his psychiatric theory would produce over the next two centuries, he would surely not have shared it publicly.

From the start, psychiatry and the eugenic theory in the United States have not been separate issues. So much so that some historians note "that slavery and ideas about race

[50] Seema Yasmin, "How Medicine Perpetuates the Fallacy of Race," *Medscape Psychiatry* (March 11, 2020): https://www.medscape.com/view article/926549?nlid=134510_424&src=WNL_mdplsfeat_200317_mscpedit_psyc &uac=264124BV&spon=12&impID=2315032&faf=1#vp_1.

[51] "Director of the Kaiser Wilhelm Institute for Anthropology, Human Heredity, and Eugenics from 1927 to 1942, [Eugen] Fischer authored a 1913 study of the Mischlinge (racially mixed) children of Dutch men and Hottentot women in German southwest Africa. Fischer opposed 'racial mixing,' arguing that "negro blood" was of 'lesser value' and that mixing it with 'white blood' would bring about the demise of European culture" (United States Holocaust Memorial Museum, "Deadly Medicine: Creating the Master Race," *HMM Online*: https://www.ushmm.org/exhibition/deadly-medicine/ profiles/). See also, Richard C. Lewontin, Steven Rose, and Leon J. Kamin, *Not in Our Genes: Biology, Ideology, and Human Nature 2nd edition* (Chicago: Haymarket Books, 2017), 207.

were fundamental to early psychiatry."[52] Other psychiatrists confirm the same sobering reality:

> Although cultural categories such as gender and race are pertinent to every illness, the many-stranded Western cultural associations that link gender and race to madness have had an especially profound influence on psychiatry. As forms of otherness, madness and blackness, for example, and madness and the feminine have both been entwined in cultural tropes that influence diagnosis, perceptions of mental health, and aspects of psychiatric treatment.[53]

In similar fashion, professors of psychiatry and anthropology at the King's College London and Guy's Hospital, Roland Littlewood and Maurice Lipsedge, acknowledge this undisputed fact in their book:

> We shall have a look at racism itself and see that not only have medicine and psychiatry invariably been associated with it, but that they have provided it with some of its most powerful arguments . . . . the relations between black people and white medicine [have] been the most characteristic of the association between science and social control.[54]

Today, many people regularly overlook the true history and significance of Benjamin Rush when it comes to psychiatric theory, since historians often present only positive facts about Rush — highlighting the good that he clearly did during his life in the areas of politics and valid

---

[52] Gonaver, *The Making of Modern Psychiatry*, 4.

[53] *Philosophy of Psychiatry: A Companion* edited by Jennifer Radden (New York: Oxford University Press, 2014), 11.

[54] Roland Littlewood and Maurice Lipsedge, *Aliens and Alienists: Ethnic Minorities and Psychiatry*, 3rd edition (London: Taylor and Francis, 1997), 25-26.

fields of medicine.[55] Historian David Barton comments on this reality: "too many biographers [of Rush] today substitute their own opinions for the actual words of the subject."[56] Others miss or deny the truth that Rush was regularly conflicted in what he said and did, thus concentrating on only one aspect of his life. For example, Rush was well known as an advocate for ending slavery, while at the same time, he purchased and owned slaves.[57] Historian Vanessa Jackson discusses the "irony" of Rush's life:

> Benjamin Rush, MD, signer of the Declaration of Independence, Dean of the Medical School at the University of Pennsylvania and the "Father of American Psychiatry," described Negroes as suffering from an affliction called Negritude, which was thought to be a

[55] For example, in 1897, *The Journal of the American Medical Association* (*JAMA*) published an article about Rush, which highlighted his contributions to medicine without any mention of his horrific theories and practices. The author concludes the article by stating that, "In this great historic city one of its most honored names in medical and political history, Dr. Benjamin Rush, was the pioneer psychiatrist and *neuriatirst* (if you will permit the coinage of this word) of the century . . . . Rush's record might be further extended, but enough has been said to name him among the immortals in medicine and philanthropy as he is among statesmen" (Speech at the annual *American Medical Association* conference presented by C. H. Hughes, "Neurological Progress in America," (June 1-4, 1897), published in *JAMA: Medical Literature of the Period* edited by John B. Hamilton (Chicago, American Medical Association Press, August 1897): 315-16.

[56] David Barton, *Benjamin Rush: Signer of the Declaration of Independence* (Aledo, TX: Wallbuilders, 1999), 5.

[57] Clayborne Carson, *African American Lives* (New York: Pearson Longman, 2005), 119. His contradictory behavior has led many historians to assert that Rush had a "contradiction in his character" (North, "Benjamin Rush, MD: assassin or beloved healer?" *Proceedings Baylor University Medical Center* vol. 13 [1] [2000]: 45-9. doi:10.1080/08998280.2000.11927641).

mild form of leprosy. The only cure for the disorder was to become white . . . . The irony of Dr. Rush's medical observations was that he was a leading mental health reformer and co-founder of the first anti-slavery society in America.[58]

Similarly, historian and professor of journalism, Stephen Fried, states,

Rush had been controversial in many ways. He was referred to as "the American Hippocrates," sometimes as a compliment but other times as an insult to his outsized ego. He openly criticized powerful slave owners—even during the ten years after the war when he owned a slave himself.[59]

Likewise, historians regularly present Rush as a "devout Christian,"[60] since he attended a Presbyterian or Episcopalian church most of his life, spoke highly and often of the Bible, and clearly wrote and taught from the Calvinistic perspective he grew up learning. But while Rush did not abandon all of the biblical principles he had been taught, he would eventually accept doctrines which opposed Scripture, such as universalism.[61] Rush himself stated,

---

[58] Vanessa Jackson, "An Early History: African American Mental Health," *University of Dayton* (March 20, 2002): 4. Available from: http://academic. udayton.edu/health/01status/mental01.htm.

[59] Fried, *Rush: Revolution, Madness, and the Visionary Doctor*, 9.

[60] Helen Thompson, "Meet the Doctor Who Convinced America to Sober Up," *Smithsonian Online* (July 6, 2015): https://www.smithsonian mag.com/ smart-news/how-colonial-doctor-changed-medical-views-alcohol-180955813/.

[61] Carl Binger, *Revolutionary Doctor: Benjamin Rush, 1746-1813* (New York: W. W. Norton and Company, 1966), 297.

At Dr. Finley's school, I was more fully instructed in those principles by means of the Westminster catechism. I retained them without any affection for them until about the year 1780. I then read for the first time Fletcher's controversy with the Calvinists, in favor of the universality of the atonement. This prepared my mind to admit the doctrine of universal salvation, which was then preached in our city by the Rev. Mr. Winchester. It embraced and reconciled my ancient Calvinistical [sic] and my newly adopted Arminian principles. From that time I have never doubted upon the subject of the salvation of all men. My conviction of the truth of this doctrine was derived from reading the works of Stonehouse, Seigvolk, White, Chauncey and Winchester, and afterwards from an attentive perusal of the Scriptures.[62]

Historian Donald D'Elia points out Rush's change in theology, "His early Calvinism notwithstanding, Rush later embraced the loving heresy of universal salvation."[63] Fried also quotes Rush as stating that Rush "would rather have the 'opinions of Confucius or Mahomed inculcated upon our youth, than see them grow up wholly devoid of a system of religious principles.'"[64] Rush certainly was religious and regularly utilized biblical principles in his decision making and political life. But in grievous ways, Rush also opposed the Scripture he claimed to believe.

[62] Benjamin Rush, *A Memorial containing Travels Through Life or Sunday Incidents in the Life of Dr. Benjamin Rush written by Benjamin Rush*, complied by Louis Alexander Biddle (Philadelphia, PA: Ivy Leaf, 1905), 125.

[63] Donald J. D'Elia for Penn State University Press, "The Republican Theology of Benjamin Rush," *Pennsylvania History: A Journal of Mid-Atlantic Studies* vol. 33 (2) (April 1966): 188. Full text available at: https://journals.psu.edu/phj/article/download/23146/22915.

[64] Fried, *Rush: Revolution, Madness, and the Visionary Doctor*, 281-82.

Most prominent among his unbiblical teachings were his theory of the material soul and his ideas of morality. In fact, Rush's theory of "diseases of the mind" (or "mental illnesses") was an attempt to replace the biblical and then widely accepted and historical concept of insanity/madness that existed prior to the American Revolution.[65] Likewise, his theory attempted to replace biblical dualism with materialism in explaining distressful and impairing phenomena of human nature and behaviors Scripture deemed to be immoral. Upon hearing Rush explain his new theory of the physical mind and physical causes to metaphysical phenomena, Rush's good friend, John Adams, would write to Rush: "You will be accused of materialism and consequently of Atheism."[66] Rush was about to introduce a new worldview, which was antithetical to fundamental doctrines contained in Scripture.

Stephen Fried remarks on a speech that Rush delivered to the American Philosophical Society entitled: "An Inquiry into the Influence of Physical Causes on the Moral Faculty."

> Rush began by defining the "moral faculty" as the "power in the human mind of distinguishing and choosing good and evil . . . virtue or vice." He then laid out the crux of his argument: that there were "physical causes" for many actions that had previously been viewed through the prism of morality and will. Much of what was labeled

---

[65] For further study on how historic madness became mental illness, see Daniel R. Berger II, *The Insanity of Madness: Defining Mental Illness* (Taylors, SC: Alethia International Publications, 2018).

[66] A Letter from John Adams to Benjamin Rush, (November 14, 1812): https://founders.archives.gov.

immorality could, in fact, be a manifestation of physical illness — requiring medical treatment, and prayers that the medical treatment worked.[67]

The speech would eventually be published into a pamphlet, and in it Rush would set forth teachings that were clearly antithetical to Scripture:

> If physical causes influence morals . . . may they not also influence religion and principles and opinions? — I answer in the affirmative, and I have authority, from the records of physic, as well as from my own observations, to declare, that religious melancholy and madness, in all their variety of species, yield with more facility to medicine, than simply to polemical discourses or causistical advice."[68]

To make matters worse, much of Rush's new worldview was based upon a faulty interpretation of Scripture. For example, he writes as support for his medical model:

> To the cases that have been mentioned, I shall only add, that, Nebuchadnezzar was cured of his pride by means of solitude and vegetable diet. Saul was cured of his evil spirit, by means of David's harp, and St. Paul expressly says, "I keep my body under, and bring it into subjection, lest that by any means, when I have preach to others, I myself should be cast-away." But I will go one step further, and add, in favour of divine influence upon the moral principle, that in those extraordinary cases, where bad men are suddenly reformed without the instrumentality of physical, moral or rational causes, I believe that the organization of those arts of the body, in

---

[67] Fried, *Rush: Revolution, Madness, and the Visionary Doctor*, 274.

[68] Benjamin Rush, *An Inquiry into the Influence of Physical Causes on the Moral Faculty* (Philadelphia, PA: The American Philosophical Society, February 1786), 23; PDF available from: https://collections.nlm.nih.gov/ ext/mhl/57020900R/PDF/57020900R.pdf.

which the faculties of the mind are seated, undergoes physical change, and hence the expression of a "new creature." St. Paul was suddenly transformed from a persecutor into a man of a gentle and amiable spirit. The manner in which this change was effected upon his mind, he tells us in the following words: "Neither circumcision availeth any," which is made use of in the Scriptures to denote this change is proper in literal, as well as figurative sense. It is probably the beginning of that perfect renovation of the human body, which is predicted by St. Paul in the following words: "For our conversation is in heaven, from whence we look for the Savior, who shall change our vile bodies, that they may be fashioned according to his own glorious body."[69]

In this specific publication, Rush's understanding of the Bible and the Holy Spirit's work of conversion and progressive sanctification were twisted into supposed evidence for a material soul. In Rush's view, biblical change was presented as the result of physical manipulation and not through the work of the Holy Spirit.

This belief would birth the concept of "mental illness." Psychiatrists Roland Littlewood and Maurice Lipsedge comment:

> The new concept of mental illness developed as part of the ideology of the French and American revolutions . . . . Benjamin Rush described 'revolutiona' — a hypochrondriacal illness found during the American revolutionary war among people excessively concerned with property, prestige and social changes: inflation was the major cause. Mental illness was blamed on the French

[69] Ibid, 18-19.

Revolution by conservative alienists, while radicals emphasized the psychopathology of the monarch.[70]

Mental illness was never discovered; it was created as a construct with categories and descriptive labels (e.g., "hypochrondriacal illness") by reframing human nature and human phenomena to fit into one's faith/worldview.

Rush had not formed his theory based upon empirical evidence or discovered actual diseases of the mind. Instead, he set out to make all available evidence — including Scripture — fit into his belief system and personal experiences. Dr. Charles Caldwell, who was employed as a professor at Penn Medical School with Rush, wrote about Rush in his own autobiography,

> Instead of making them the groundwork of his doctrines, **he allowed his doctrines to be too often the controllers and modifiers of them.** This I do not allege that he did by design; **he did it through the delusion thrown around him by his inordinate devotedness to theory and hypothesis.** For of theory and hypothesis, his fancy was a hotbed – I say his fancy, not his intellect deliberately exercised [emphasis added].[71]

One of Rush's most profound contradictions was quite possibly the fact that he was a signer on the Declaration of Independence, which championed equality and freedom.

---

[70] Roland Littlewood and Maurice Lipsedge, *Aliens and Alienists: Ethnic Minorities and Psychiatry*, 3rd edition (London: Taylor and Francis, 1997), 33.

[71] Charles Caldwell quoted by Marshall A. Ledger, "Benjamin Rush and 20 Years of Penn Psychiatry," *Penn Medicine* (Fall 2012): 28; https://www.penn medicine.org/news/-/media/documents%20and%20audio/pr%20news/ penn%20med%20magazine/fall_2012_full_issue_3.ashx.

The founding fathers of the United States of America penned and affirmed their belief that truths were

> self-evident; that all men are created equal; that they are endowed by their creator with certain unalienable rights; that among these are life, liberty, and the pursuit of happiness.

In many areas of Rush's life, he championed liberty and unalienable rights (e.g., women's rights). But when it pertained to psychiatry, Rush did not see the perceived mentally disordered as equal, and neither would psychiatrists for centuries to come.

With the notion that some individual's souls/minds are disordered while most of humanity 's minds are not, come the inevitable removal of a person's unalienable rights and the stigma of being categorized as abnormal. In being categorized and labeled as mentally abnormal, a person's life, liberty, and happiness are regularly diminished and sometimes eradicated.

Although Rush's eugenics/genetic theory is often minimized or even denied based upon selected aspects of his life (e.g., that he was a leader in the antislavery movement), race psychology and the "hereditary disorder" theory both became widely accepted in psychiatry and eventually in the general population. The genetic theory, hereditary madness, or race psychology, as it was also once called, became so prevalent in early America that "the colored population" was diagnosed on many US censuses to be mostly insane/mentally ill:

> In many towns, all the colored population are stated to be insane; in very many others, two-thirds, one third, one-

fourth or one-tenth of this ill-starred race are reported to be thus afflicted.[72]

Among the suggested psychiatric remedies for what many like Rush falsely perceived to be a genetic disorder in blacks was slavery and whipping. A former director of NIMH and three professors from Harvard Medical School note this sad reality in their book *Mental Health, Racism, and Sexism*:

> How does racism influence basic definitions of mental illness? Dominant racial groups may construct definitions of mental illness that justify their superiority or the subjugated group's inferiority. If behavior that is more common in one racial group is described as abnormal, then members of that group will more often be considered abnormal. In the history of mental illness in the United States, race has been the basis for the claims not only of excess incidence, but also of relatively limited incidence. The well-known example in the United States was the theory that African slaves were not subject to depressive disorders (Prudhomme and Musto 1973). **Although genetics was the main basis for explaining the lower incidence of depression in African Americans, this construction also bolstered the notion that the living conditions of slaves** (lacking as they were in the need to make decisions and therefore lacking in the burdens of conflict) **were really beneficial rather than oppressive** [emphasis added].[73]

Former APA president-elect Jeffrey Lieberman also remarks on the troubling history of race psychology/the genetic theory as recorded in many of the past US censuses:

[72] Lieberman, *Shrinks*, 90.

[73] Patricia Perri Rieker, Bernard M. Kramer, and Bertram Brown, *Mental Health, Racism, and Sexism,* ed. Charles Willie (New York: University of Pittsburgh Press, 2013), 6-7.

More troubling was the fact that the results of this census were used to defend slavery: Since the reported rates of insanity and idiocy among African Americans in the Northern states were much higher than in the Southern states, advocates of slavery argued that slavery had mental health benefits.[74]

Lieberman rightly denounces this ideology as applied in early America. But sadly, both the genetic theory of mental illness and the biological means to treat human nature proposed by many American psychiatrists in the early and mid-1800s remain premier components to biological psychiatrists' very existence. It is upon the misguided teachings of Benjamin Rush contained in his publications[75] and the development of race psychology that American psychiatry and abnormal psychology are founded — a point that will be developed further in the chapters that follow.

CHOOSING A WORLDVIEW

In contrast to the vast majority of others in his day, John Galt II not only rejected race psychology, but he also claimed to be a Christian who believed that truth and love were fundamental laws to approaching all of human nature and that basing relationships on God's relationship with mankind was fundamental to implementing Galt's concept of moral therapy. Historian Wendy Gonaver records Galt's

---

[74] Lieberman, *Shrinks*, 90.

[75] U.S. National Library of Medicine, "Diseases of the Mind: Highlights of American Psychiatry through 1900 (Benjamin Rush, M.D. (1749-1813): "The Father of American Psychiatry) *The History of Medicine Online*: https://www.nlm.nih.gov/hmd/diseases/benjamin.html.

influence over the Medical Superintendents of American Institutions that he helped to found:

> Members of the Association for Medical Superintendents of American Institutions stressed that the role of the superintendent in implementing moral therapy was of paramount importance to the quality of an asylum. **This emphasis reflected a hierarchical, paternalistic conception of morality that was partly derived from mainstream practices of authority drawn from Euro-Christian notions of God's relationship to human beings** [emphasis added].[76]

Galt's idea of moral therapy was based upon biblical theology and anthropology, and he not only attempted to live godly in relation to all those under his supervision but also saw the reading of Scripture as therapeutic. Galt quotes George Chandler, who shared Galt's views:

> The perusal of the Scriptures tends wholly to good, for therein is written the law of love and kindness, justice and truth, and therein is taught nothing that vitiates the conscience, injures the health, or deranges the mind.[77]

Galt also wrote in The Eastern Lunatic Asylum Annual Report,

> In connection with this subject we would remark that the book most read and desired by the patients is the Bible . . . . There are many who peruse the Bible as a daily exercise, and there would probably be more if there were a greater number of copies.[78]

---

[76] Gonaver, *The Making of Modern Psychiatry*, 51.

[77] George Chandler quoted by John Galt in: *Essays on Asylums for Person of Unsound Mind* (Richmond, VA: Ritchies and Dunnavant, 1853), 12.

[78] John Galt, *The Eastern Lunatic Asylum Annual Report* (1844), 30-31.

Galt found that the Bible positively influenced the mind of most of his patients who desired help.

As previously noted, but worth emphasizing, Galt saw two important approaches to people in distress which were antithetical to the very core of the eugenics theory that he denounced but that were fundamental to helping people with mental, emotional, and behavioral struggles. First, when Galt stated that people may "differ from us in degree, but not in kind,"[79] he was expressing his disapproval and rejection of the key underlying philosophy of all genetic theories of mental illness. Galt believed, as God declared in the Bible, that the souls of all men are created morally equal; all people struggle with depravity and fragility. Therefore, the idea that some people who were troubled, deceived, distressed, or behaving in persistently destructive ways that could not be so easily explained were degenerates while all others were "normal" was not acceptable to him.

Additionally, Galt came to realize that psychiatrists' common practice of isolating or alienating people from their communities and from those that love them — whether by physically removing them from society or by chemical or surgical means — created abnormal circumstances that caused further struggle and worse mental conditions. In the end, Galt concluded that what was abnormal was not the individuals who struggled, but rather, what was truly disordered were both the accepted materialistic psychiatric theories about those who were struggling as well as the accepted biological treatments. Galt suggested that, "life in

[79] "The History of Eastern State,": http://www.esh.dbhds. virginia.gov/History.html.

the asylum [should be] as sane, orderly, and pleasant as possible... to emphasize the patients' sanity rather than their insanity as a means of curing them."[80] If false fixed beliefs and unhealthy relationships are the root problems, so he rationalized, then truth/reality, love, and discipline provide the remedy. Understanding a person's relationships with both God and fellow mankind most often explains a person's "madness."

Though a tragedy, Rush's eldest son's "mental illness" validates Galt's perspective. There were a series of traumatic events in John's life that accumulated and heavily impacted his relationship with his father and weighed heavily upon his soul.

One event was what his father called a "public disgrace," in which John had broken his university's policies and was withdrawn from Princeton University.[81] Upon returning home, Rush made John agree to and sign a document stating that he would forfeit what appeared to be his inheritance if he broke that formal agreement and behaved poorly again.[82] The fear of losing his inheritance and control over his father's estate, would be observed later in John's delusions of "inheriting a large estate in New Orleans."[83] More troubling was John's perceived failure to

---

[80] John Galt II quoted by Shomer S. Zwelling, *Quest for a Cure: The Public Hospital in Williamsburg, 1773-1885* (Williamsburg, VA: Colonial Williamsburg Foundation, 1985), 32.

[81] Benjamin Rush in a letter to J. M. Duffin, *University of Pennsylvania Archives:* www.archives.upeen.edu/WestPhila1777/.

[82] Fried, *Rush: Revolution, Madness, and the Visionary Doctor*, 340.

[83] Ibid., 448.

please his father. John described himself as "the degenerate son of an eminent and respectful father, as a failure to the fair reputation of his brothers and in short . . . as a blackguard."[84] It is clear that Rush had high hopes for his eldest son, and John seemed to hopelessly believe that he could not meet those expectations or follow in his father's very large footsteps. The constant falling short of his father's wishes for him weighed on John throughout his life.

But a much more traumatic event occurred that would "send him into madness." In 1807, John was called out by his close friend, Turner, to settle a petty dispute in a duel. Upon John's killing Turner that day, Rush's eldest son "suffered some sort of breakdown" and was never the same.[85]

Rush would write to John Adams that "My eldest son John, since his unfortunate duel, has lost his health."[86] E.T. Carlson and J.L Wollock also comment,

> Benjamin Rush saw the cause of John's illness much more in the circumstances of his life and behavior . . . . As Rush said, "The distress and remorse which followed this even deprived him of his reason." Benjamin Rush announced

[84] J. Jefferson Looney and Ruth L. Woodward, *Princetonians, 1791-1794* (Princeton, NJ: Princeton University Press, 1991), 435.

[85] E.T. Carlson and J.L. Wollock, "Benjamin Rush and His Insane Son," *The History of Medicine and Behavioral Sciences* vol. 51 (11) (December 1975): 1314.

[86] Benjamin Rush in a letter to John Adams, *Founders Online* (July 26, 1809): https://founders.archives.gov.

quite early that the unfortunate duel was the cause of his son's insanity. [87]

The staff at the psychiatric ward where John Rush would be held for some time agreed that "John's duel was the 'sole cause' of his condition."[88] Guilt, deep sorrow, unfulfilled hopes and dreams, and broken relationships had led Benjamin Rush's son into a state of despair. Yet unfortunately, John was subjected to horrific physical treatments for the remainder of his life in accordance with his father's belief that manipulating the body could cure "insanity."

The history of John Rush's "insanity" undermines the hereditary theory that Rush propagated. Doctors Eric Carlson and Jeffrey Wollock discuss this point:

> Causation of an illness, therefore, was to be found in the organization of the body, its responsiveness, and the types and strengths of stimuli in the environment, including all types of psychological factors. Rush believed, for example, in the role of heredity, and even reported almost simultaneous and similar emotional illness in a pair of separated twins. **If we look for hereditary factors in the Rush family, we find no evidence for any previous clear-cut mental illness** . . . [emphasis added].[89]

Though the philosophies that Rush introduced are still upheld and applied today, they failed to properly explain or to help Rush's own son's mental turmoil.

---

[87] Carlson and Wollock, "Benjamin Rush and His Insane Son,": 1325.

[88] Fried, *Rush: Revolution, Madness, and the Visionary Doctor*, 447.

[89] Carlson and Wollock, "Benjamin Rush and His Insane Son,": 1324.

Labeling some people as abnormal/degenerates and placing them in conditions and under treatments which are abnormal (e.g., solitary confinement, beating, bleeding out, shocking, drugging, etc.) is incredibly destructive. Galt realized that the psychiatric eugenic construct — both in theory and practice — created abnormal and hopeless people out of normal broken and fragile souls. Unlike the vast majority of other psychiatrists of his day, Galt saw many people recover from their mental turmoil within his compassionate approach.

It is important to note that eugenics — even in its early years — should be understood not principally as ethnic differences or impairing mindsets or behaviors. Rather, eugenics is primarily concerned with developing and enforcing social and descriptive constructs, which both create the degenerates — those who are selected as categorically abnormal or "unhealthy" and set aside — and establish the healthy — those who are judged to be of good, normal, or healthy stock.

Though in the early years of America, ethnicity/skin color was clearly an established social construct, race psychology/eugenics is not limited to physical appearances or even objective biology. The morality of society typically determines the social and descriptive constructs created, and both the diagnostic system and how various people fit into the imposed categories depends entirely upon the shared moral standard established by a social authority or society as a whole. Skin color, habits, cognition, socio-economic classes, religion, ethnicity, habitual behavior, and virtually any human phenomena can be constructed into an alleged mental disorder. Eugenics is primarily about creating constructs

41

which differentiate between groups of people and ascribe biological (most often genetic) causes to those established differences.

Eugenics or the genetic theory of mental illness is a worldview that sees all aspects of human nature (physical, metaphysical, and even social/relational) as either normal or abnormal. There certainly are biological causes to valid diseases, but eugenics is a theory that claims biological causes for perceived undesirable traits and human phenomena rather than for valid illnesses. The truth is, however, that there exists a clear distinction between valid genetic and neurological disorders (such as Down Syndrome and Alzheimer's disease) versus a psychiatric construct (like Schizophrenia or Bipolar I). Dr. Lieberman explains,

> The discovery that some mental disorders had a recognizable biological basis — while others did not — led to the establishment of two distinct disciplines. Physicians who specialized exclusively in disorders with an observable neural stamp [e.g., Alzheimer's] become known as neurologists. **Those who dealt with the invisible disorders of the mind became known as psychiatrists** [emphasis added].[90]

In valid medicine, there exist many genetic variances within the human genome that can and do produce physical defects. But in psychiatry, genetic variances are only speculated to cause mental, emotional, and behavioral struggles. That which is invisible, as Lieberman notes, is not approachable within science, and as will be observed in this book, that reality makes the genetic theory of mental illness purely conjecture. Furthermore, the reality that the

[90] Lieberman, *Shrinks*, 26.

metaphysical nature of humanity cannot be approached utilizing the scientific method makes psychiatry the ideal "authority" to design social and descriptive constructs (e.g., race) which determine who is diagnosed as fit and who is categorized as disordered within an alleged medical and scientific framework.

One cannot separate the modern genetic theory of mental illness from its genesis in Rush's five main psychiatric doctrines: (1) material explanations of the soul/mind and morality, (2) hereditary madness, (3) race psychology, (4) proposed physical remedies, and (5) his many social and descriptive constructs compiled into a diagnostic system (e.g., alcoholism).[91] The genetic theory is not simply a minor theory in psychiatry; the genetic theory of mental illness is the necessary theory to assert psychiatry as a legitimate medical field and to present the metaphysical soul and its phenomena as an approachable organ that can be accessed using the scientific method and as a by-product of the human genome and nervous system. This vital psychiatric belief is inseparable from the history of psychiatry, and as historian Stephen Fried notes, Rush is a central figure in the paradigm's development:

> [Rush's] 1786 speech also provided the groundwork for his most lasting contribution to medicine: fusing his ideas about equality and republicanism with clinical work, he declared that mental illness and addiction were medical conditions and deserved to be treated as such. **At Pennsylvania Hospital he enacted this philosophy, laying the foundation for the development of**

---

[91] Arribas-Ayloon, Bartlett, and Lewis, *Psychiatric Genetics*, 7.

psychiatry, clinical psychology, and addiction medicine [emphasis added].[92]

This philosophy, worldview, or phenomenology must be examined thoroughly, and the last 200+ years provide a wealth of empirical data to study.

As previously discussed but important to develop further at this point, Rush is most known for his viewing the metaphysical soul (including faith and theology) as physical or as a product of biology. In his last published book, *Medical Inquiries and Observations upon the Diseases of the Mind*,[93] Rush laid out his materialistic theory of the mind—a faith that would become the basis of modern psychiatry:[94]

> Before I proceed to consider the diseases of the mind, I shall briefly mention its different faculties and operations. Its faculties are: Understanding, Memory, Imagination, Passions, the principle of Faith, Will, the Moral faculty, Conscience, and the sense of Deity. Its principal operations, after sensation, are: Perception, Association, Judgment, Reasoning and Volition. All its subordinate operations, which are known by the names of Attention, Reflection, Contemplation, Wit, Consciousness, and the like, are nothing but modifications of the five principal operations that have been mentioned.[95]

After making it clear that his definition of the mind was in effect the spiritual or metaphysical nature of mankind,

[92] Fried, *Rush: Revolution, Madness, and the Visionary Doctor*, 6.

[93] Rush, *Medical Inquiries and Observations Upon the Diseases of the Mind* (Philadelphia: Kimber and Richardson, 1812).

[94] McCullough, *American Presidents*, 609.

[95] Rush, *Medical Inquiries*, 8.

Rush then explains his biological approach to mankind's metaphysical reality:

> All the operations in the mind are the effects of motions previously excited in the brain, and every idea and thought appears to depend upon a motion peculiar to itself. In a sound state of the mind, these motions are regular . . . . In inquiring into the causes of the diseases of the mind, and the remedies that are proper to relieve them, I shall employ the term derangement, to signify the disease of all the faculties of the mind . . . . **By derangement in the understanding, I mean every departure of the mind in its perceptions, judgments, and reasonings, from its natural and habitual order; accompanied with corresponding actions** [emphasis added].[96]

Rush assumed that a standard of normal for the spiritual/metaphysical nature existed and that this suggested standard of normal represented mental health. Moreover, Rush saw any deviance from this presumed standard as both caused by the body and equaling a medical disorder. In his view, it was not just skin color that was caused by biological processes; it was every aspect of human nature including one's faith, personality, moral character, and behavior. Any human tendency, phenomena, or behavior which deviated from what Rush viewed to be orderly was considered to be a "mental disorder."

Clearly, Rush viewed the metaphysical nature of humanity as if it were biologically caused, and he accepted the eugenic notion that some people were not normal — their minds had allegedly departed from their "natural and habitual order." But this reductionistic belief — still

[96] Ibid., 9.

foundational to psychiatric theory today — requires that an objective standard of normal first be established and that empirical evidence then be supplied to affirm that the brain produces the mind or that they are one in the same. Yet, the "mind-brain" connection remains a mystery within scientific exploration.[97]

After Rush's death, his eugenics views/race psychology would flourish in the United States. Samuel Cartwright (1793-1863), for example, was a psychiatrist who theorized about an alleged mental illness that he called "Drapetomania," which he suggested caused slaves "an insane desire to run away."[98] And though Galt's book is about treatments of insanity from around the world, he also documents numerous cases of other psychiatrists utilizing the phrase "hereditary insanity" and the technique of "bloodletting" — showing the eugenic perspective's global acceptance after Rush.[99]

Teaching at the prestigious University of Pennsylvania Hospital had provided Rush with the opportunity to propagate his harmful theories on a large scale. One respected medical historian Percy Ashburn comments on Rush's impact on American medicine:

---

[97] Ronald Pies, "Can We Salvage the Bio-psycho-social Model?" *Psychiatric Times Online* (January 22, 2020): https://www.psychiatrictimes.com/couch-crisis/can-we-salvage-biopsychosocial-model/page/0/1.

[98] Proctor, *Racial Hygiene*, 13.

[99] E.g., "She had also strong hereditary predisposition to insanity, her mother being insane at the time of her birth" (Rush quoted by Galt, *The Treatment of Insanity*, 81).

By virtue of his social and professional prominence, his position as teacher and his facile pen Benjamin Rush had more influence upon American medicine and was more potent in propagation and long perpetuation of medical errors than any man of his day. To him, more than any other man in America, was due the great vogue of vomits, purging, and especially of bleeding, salivation and blistering, which blackened the record of medicine and afflicted the sick almost to the time of the Civil War.[100]

Professor of medicine Robert North also reflects on the influence of Dr. Rush:

Benjamin Rush has been hailed as "the American Sydenham," "the Pennsylvania Hippocrates," the "father of modern psychiatry," and the founder of American medicine. The American Medical Association erected a statue of him in Washington, DC, the only physician so honored. A medical school is named after him. He was a prolific and facile writer and a very influential teacher. **Yet, the only enduring mark he has left on the history of American medicine is his embarrassing, obdurate, messianic insistence, in the face of all factual evidence to the contrary,** on the curative powers of heroic depletion therapy. **Rush's thinking was rooted in an unscientific revelation as to the unitary nature of disease, which he never questioned.** He viewed nature as a treacherous adversary to be fought on the battleground of his patients' bodies. **It is hard to imagine philosophies more radically at variance with those of Hippocrates and Sydenham** [emphasis added].[101]

---

[100] Percy Moreau Ashburn, *A History of the Medical Department of the United States Army* (Boston: Houghton Mifflin and Co, 1929). Quoted in Williams G. *The Age of Agony* (Chicago: Academy Chicago Publishers, 1996), 204.

[101] Robert L. North, "Benjamin Rush, MD: Assassin or Beloved Healer?" *Proceedings Baylor University Medical Center* vol. 13 (1) (January, 2000): 49. doi:10.1080/08998280.2000.

Rush's philosophies, which oppose those of Hippocrates and Sydenham, will be more fully addressed in the chapters to come. Significantly, his philosophies so influenced American psychiatry that in 1890 the American Psychiatric Association chose to commemorate Rush by making him the central feature of its logo — as one who best represents its vision and cause; [102] the "Father of American psychiatry."

Today's bio-psycho-social psychiatry is born out of Rush's creation of biological psychiatry and his insistence upon "alienism." Professors of psychiatry and anthropology at the King's College London and Guy's Hospital, Roland Littlewood and Maurice Lipsedge, wrote a book entitled *Aliens and Alienists: Ethnic Minorities and Psychiatry* to discuss the undisputed history and racial prejudices that still exist today:

> **The modern psychiatrist is a descendant, not of the psychoanalyst, but of the nineteenth-century mental asylum keeper.** As treatment for physical illness became increasingly effective, the mentally ill — incurable — were lodged in large purpose-built hospitals. **Each was governed by the superintendent, a paternalistic figure whose popular image has been described as both divine and satanic: divine because of his power over the sick and satanic because of his demonic knowledge.** The physical coercion of the pre-psychiatric era was replaced by moral authority: the ideal psychiatrist, like the ideal colonial official or plantation owner, was a 'father to his children'. Cures could occasionally be effected by his 'presence' . . . . Only a third of American psychiatrists would however 'admit blacks to close kinship by

---

[102] Lieberman, *Shrinks,* 70.

marriage'. Psychiatric treatment in America is related to the doctor's political opinions [emphasis added].[103]

Modern psychiatry claims to be moral and altruistic, but as these prominent psychiatrists acknowledge, Rush's eugenic beliefs and many of his practices still dominate society. Chemical alienation may have replaced physical isolation and blood-letting, but the underlying philosophies and approaches, as well as the demoralizing effects, remain the same.

But along with teaching unscientific techniques that have been said by contemporary critics of Rush to be "one of those great discoveries which have contributed to the depopulation of the earth"[104] (introducing psychiatric eugenics into American medicine), Rush also introduced the construct of "alcoholism" as a disease entity:

> Many historians argue that Rush's philosophy ultimately shaped how Western doctors treat alcoholism today. Rush was, according to Green, one of the first doctors to talk about alcoholism as a progressive disease, and one of the first people to suggest that in order to kick the habit, addicts should go away somewhere to sober up.[105]

Essentially, Rush believed that any mental, emotional, behavioral, or social problem that involved the mind or body in some way could be constructed into a psychiatric

[103] Roland Littlewood and Maurice Lipsedge, *Aliens and Alienists: Ethnic Minorities and Psychiatry*, 3rd edition (London: Taylor and Francis, 1997), 10-11.

[104] William Cobbett, quoted by Robert L. North, "Benjamin Rush, MD: Assassin or Beloved Healer?"

[105] Thompson, "Meet the Doctor."

disorder, and alcoholism would become his most famous descriptive construct.[106]

But just as the attempted suicide of Rush's own son "inspired" him to explain his son's spiritual struggle within a medical paradigm,[107] the death of his good friend President John Adam's son, Charles, several years before John's taking his own life, likely encouraged Rush's further development of the construct of "alcoholism" — as a medical explanation to a destructive and sad phenomenon his friend's family experienced.[108]

Rush's hereditarian/biological approach to human nature spread globally after his death, and it became the dominant theory of modern American psychiatry virtually at the point of Galt's death and at the emancipation of American slaves:

> **The displacement of environmental etiologies and moral treatment by hereditarianism and somatic approaches after the Civil War occurred at the moment when African Americans and women made important legal gains toward autonomy.** Thus they obtained ownership of and moral authority over their bodies, only to discover that **medicine considered these bodies fundamentally flawed** [emphasis added].[109]

Upon the acceptance of Rush's hereditary theory, psychiatrists successfully instituted a social construct and

[106] Stefan Kuhl, *The Nazi Connection: Eugenics, American Racism, and German National Socialism* (New York: Oxford University Press, 1994), 20.

[107] Fried, *Rush: Revolution, Madness, and the Visionary Doctor*, 7.

[108] Ibid.

[109] Gonaver, *The Making of Modern Psychiatry*, 8.

subsequent system whereby degenerates could be created and psychiatrists would be considered relevant to explaining and treating the soul/mind. *Penn Medicine News* reports on Rush's and his contemporaries' influence over American psychiatry and the following generations of psychiatrists who would receive his eugenics teachings decades after he was deceased:

> **In Marshall Ledger's forthcoming "Benjamin Rush and 200 Years of Penn Psychiatry," we discover that at least one Penn doctor supported eugenics as well.** Charles W. Burr, an 1886 alumnus of Penn's medical school . . . Burr was appointed professor of mental diseases in 1901, and (as Ledger explains) "with that title the Department of Psychiatry came into being, although with the old terminology." Burr was described by a Penn colleague as "conservative." That may be putting it mildly.
> In "Government Should Undertake Prevention of Insanity," printed in *The New York Times* in 1913, Burr called for "segregation of the defective classes," including government-imposed lifetime confinement in institutions. **In his opinion piece, Burr spent nearly half his space discussing undesirable immigrants, then cautioned against "the intermarriage of races as far apart as the negro and the Caucasian . . . . It leads to degeneracy." Whether Burr's favorable view of eugenics was instilled and nurtured by his illustrious predecessors is not known.** What is known is that Burr became president of the Eugenics Research Association in 1925 [emphasis added].[110]

"Defective classes" and "degeneracy" are key terms and philosophies of the early eugenics' movement, and they are concepts/philosophies that are still foundational to today's psychiatric theory of genetics. Granted, the terms have

---

[110] Penn Medicine's Department of Communications, "Psychiatry and Eugenics," *Penn Medicine News* (October 23, 2012): https://www.pennmedicine.org/news/news-blog/2012/october/psychiatry-and-eugenics.

changed over time from *hereditary madness*, to *race psychology*, to *racial hygiene*, to *eugenics*, and now currently to *psychiatric genetics*, but the underlying philosophies, goals, and practices of this theory of human nature remain the same.

From its conception, eugenics has been foundational to American psychiatry, and by the mid-1800s hereditary madness or psychiatric genetics was the most prominent psychiatric approach to explain and deal with the human soul:

> Prior to 1812 [the year before Rush's death], hereditary transmission had appeared mainly in footnotes and short discussions. Alienists [psychiatrists] had only mentioned 'hereditary influence," but after 1812 it assumes a central explanatory role.[111]

As will be discussed, the genetic theory of mental illness and subjecting people to abnormal circumstances because they are deemed to be abnormal is not a history of successes and discoveries — even in modern times. Instead, the genetic theory is a history of atrocities, failed theories, unethical psychiatric experiments, damaging treatments, and possibly most troubling, the creating of alleged degenerates. Psychiatrist and historian Edward Shorter describes the age of the Asylum:

> The rise of the asylum is the story of good intentions gone bad. That the dreams of the early psychiatrists failed is unquestionable. By World War I, asylums had become vast warehouses for the chronically insane and demented. Yet whether the failure of the asylum lay in the nature of the enterprise itself is a matter of controversy. Some argue that the asylum failed because it was overwhelmed by the

---

[111] Arribas-Ayloon, Bartlett, and Lewis, *Psychiatric Genetics*, 25.

ever-rising numbers of psychiatric patients in the
nineteenth century. Others maintain that many people
admitted to the asylum had no psychiatric illness and
were confined merely because they were social misfits
and outcasts, inconvenient rather than ill.[112]

The employment of asylums is just one of the many failures
accumulated in the history of psychiatric eugenics under
the claims of altruism, scientific advancement, and
medicine.

Despite the failure to validate the theory for over two
centuries now, psychiatry relies heavily on the genetic
theory of mental illness to sustain its presence and
influence over many societies. It is not merely marketing
the idea that genes or other biological explanations cause
mental illness, but rather, it is the creating of degenerates
that is essential to maintain the construct and psychiatry's
relevance. Without an accepted construct that creates
people who are viewed to be disordered/abnormal—"a
defective class," both modern psychiatry and the mental
health paradigm it has imposed upon society cease to exist.
Influencers in psychiatry must create and save abnormal,
and the genetic theory of mental illness for the last two
centuries has been one of psychiatry's best hopes to ensure
its continued existence, acceptance, and influence.

[112] Edward Shorter, *A History of Psychiatry*, 33.

Today, though racism still exists within psychiatry,[113] people's ethnicity is not the biological basis or the social construct which psychiatrists and psychologists endorse as their primary system of degeneration. Instead, people's impairing, unwanted, or destructive mindsets, emotions, and behaviors (all human phenomena viewed negatively) are constructed into alleged biological defects, and people who are distressed or impaired in a persistent way are categorized as mentally disordered and said to be genetically defective.[114]

In the preface of his published pamphlet, *An Inquiry into the Influence of Physical Causes Upon the Moral Faculty*, Benjamin Rush wrote the following about his "radical new ideas" concerning morality and a material explanation to human nature and human phenomena:

> Those who come after me upon this subject will find a way open for extensive and important observations, and will probably enjoy with more certainty than the author the fruits of their labors . . . If these new ideas have the same operation on the mind of the reader that they had upon the mind of the author, they will at first be doubted,

[113] Steven Starks, "Working with African American/Black Patients," The *American Psychiatric Association* (February 2020): https://www.psychiatry.org/psychiatrists/cultural-competency/education/best-practice-highlights/best-practice-highlights-for-working-with-african-american-patients?fbclid=IwAR0e0yedfsVDHrgr5TuufbUTi8bRtI_s_sPBKximxYbfUP-cWhH5uUodFd0.

[114] American Psychiatric Association, *Diagnostic and Statistical Manual of Mental Disorders*, 5th ed. (Washington, DC: American Psychiatric Publishing, 2013), 20. Hereafter referred to as the *DSM-5*.

afterwards believed, and finally, they will be propagated.[115]

Rush's philosophies of psychiatry were believed, propagated worldwide, and most are still upheld today despite their failure to deliver humanity from the soul's vexation.

Early American society was faced with a choice between accepting the dualistic moral therapy of Galt or trusting in the fledgling eugenics theory of Rush. Currently in America, the freedom to choose an approach to the metaphysical nature (the mind/soul) is still available, but likely not for long if society continues saving abnormal at the expense of losing human morality, dignity, and the biblical view of human nature that declares all men to be morally equal and equally in need of deliverance and mental restoration.

---

[115] Benjamin Rush, *An Inquiry into the Influence of Physical Causes on the Moral Faculty* (Philadelphia, PA: The American Philosophical Society, February 1786), preface.

CHAPTER 2

THE HISTORY OF PSYCHIATRIC GENETICS

Without a historical understanding of psychiatric genetics, we would fail to recognize the ways in which distant problems and controversies have shaped its social and epistemic organization. We would fail to appreciate the field's remarkable stability and resilience in spite of its failures and criticism. In short, we need the past as a way to understand the present.[116]*- Michael Arribas-Ayloon, Andrew Bartlett, and Jamie Lewis, socio-genomic researchers*

To understand modern psychiatric genetics, one must first discover its relatively short history. As discussed in the previous chapter, Benjamin Rush's elements of eugenic thought (a material soul/the biological approach, hereditary madness, and race psychology) would become mainstream within American psychiatry. But by the mid-1800s, the eugenics/hereditary theory of mental illness had gained wide global acceptance among psychiatrists, psychologists (philosophers), and many in the health industry. Most prominent among them were German

---

[116] Michael Arribas-Ayloon, Andrew Bartlett, and Jamie Lewis, *Psychiatric Genetics: From Hereditary Madness to Big Biology* (Vanderbilt, New York: Routledge, 2019), 6.

psychologists and psychiatrists, who by the late 1800s were leading the way in eugenics — many of whom would profoundly impact not only the development of psychiatric genetics but also world history. There are also key historical figures, however, who further developed the principle concepts of the eugenic theory upon which German and American genetics would be formally founded. These men also require attention, as one cannot accurately understand or morally approach modern psychiatric genetics without first studying its origins and foundational philosophies.

UNDERSTANDING THE GENETIC THEORY

Before eugenicists can be identified and their philosophies studied, a definition and understanding of eugenics must first be established. *Eugenics* (derived from the Greek word *eugenes*) is regularly defined as "good/healthy stock" or "good/healthy genes." *Merriam Webster's Dictionary*, for example, defines eugenics as

> the practice or advocacy of controlled selective breeding of human populations (as by sterilization) to improve the population's genetic composition.[117]

While eugenics is typically perceived to be about differences in ethnicity or between "races," some of the key phrases to these concepts are "controlled selection," "degeneration," and "genetic composition." These terms apply to the construct of race, but they are by no means

---

[117] "Eugenics," https://www.merriam-webster.com/dictionary/ eugenics. Accessed July 18, 2019.

limited to biological features or just one social construct. In fact, the medical definition of eugenics focuses on what is allegedly normal and abnormal within the human genome:

> A pseudoscience with the stated aim of improving the genetic constitution of the human species by selective breading. Eugenics is from a Greek word meaning "normal genes." . . . It is important to note that no experiment in eugenics has ever been shown to result in measurable improvements in human health.[118]

Eugenics is about establishing alleged normal genes and normal human nature and, consequently, creating abnormal from these perceived standards. As this medical definition acknowledges, eugenics is not a field that provides healing.

Whether it is referred to as race psychology, racial hygiene, hereditary theory, or the genetic theory of mental illness, selecting or diagnosing some people as abnormal/disordered and attributing such variances to genetic causes is fundamental to eugenics. Eugenics, then, is not merely about advancing humanity as is often portrayed — what is regularly referred to as "positive eugenics." But also, and just as important to the field, eugenics is about creating, identifying, and approaching perceived degenerates — referred to as "negative eugenics." Positive and negative eugenics are two sides of the same philosophical coin, and one cannot exist without the other. Another medical dictionary acknowledges this concept in their definition of eugenics:

[118] William C. Shiel, "Medical Definition of Eugenics," *MedicineNet* (August 17, 2019): https://www.medicinenet. com/script/main/art.asp? articlekey=3335.

The study or practice of trying to improve the human race by encouraging the breeding of those with desired characteristics (positive eugenics) or by discouraging the breeding of those whose characteristics are deemed undesirable (negative eugenics). **The concept implies that there exists some person or institution capable of making such decisions.** It also implies possible grave interference with human rights. For these reasons, the principles, which have long been successfully applied to domestic animals, have never been adopted for humans except by despots such as Adolf Hitler [emphasis added].[119]

As recognized, eugenics demands an established authority to determine what is considered to be "healthy" and "unhealthy."

In negative eugenics, the "treatment" of alleged degenerates or the disordered includes restraints, confinement, lobotomy, isolation/segregation, sterilization, electric shock, psychopharmaceutic drugs, abortion, and sometimes far worse measures, as in the case of euthanasia. But negative eugenics was not and still is not limited to the Asylum Era or to Nazi Germany:

Negative eugenics aimed at preventing the transmission of "unworthy" genes. The most frequently adopted policy was the sterilization of women considered undesirable to produce offspring. Mentally ill and disabled persons were soon subjected to compulsory sterilization. This policy was first adopted on a larger scale in a compulsory sterilization of congenitally deaf people following Graham Bell's (1847–1922) — from 1912 to 1918 chairman

---

119 "Eugenics," *Miller-Keane Encyclopedia and Dictionary of Medicine, Nursing, and Allied Health,* Seventh Edition (January 7, 2020): https://medical-dictionary.thefreedictionary.com/eugenics.

of the board of scientific advisers to the Eugenics Record Office associated with Cold Spring Harbor Laboratory in New York—hereditary theory. In the early 20th century, eugenics inspired laws and initiatives pursuing the compulsory sterilization of mentally ill and disabled individuals, and/or persons with hereditary diseases were enacted in 33 federal states of the United States—the legislation was upheld by the US Supreme Court in 1927—the Scandinavian countries, and Switzerland [sic].[120]

According to eugenic thinking, by eliminating proposed bad genes, good genes can be genetically inherited, which theoretically applies to all aspects of human nature and not merely to race or somatic features. Stanford professor Robert Proctor explains how positive eugenics is not only about ethnicity:

> The ideology of racial hygiene, at least before the mid-twenties, was in this sense less racialist than nationalist or meritocratic, less concerned with the comparison of one race against another than with discovering principles of improving the human race in general.[121]

Professor of Biology at the University of Sand Diego, Laura Rivard, comments on how the first people targeted within the formalized and government-controlled eugenic movement in America (and in Nazi Germany as well) were both the alleged mentally ill and racial groups:

> The eugenics movement began in the U.S. in the late 19th century . . . . Committees were convened to offer solutions to the problem of the growing number of

120 Heinz Haefner, "Comment on E.F. Torrey and R.H. Yolken: "Psychiatric Genocide: Nazi Attempts to Eradicate Schizophrenia."

121 Robert N. Proctor, *Racial Hygiene: Medicine Under the Nazis* (Cambridge, Massachusetts: Harvard University Press, 1988), 20.

"undesirables" in the U.S. population. Stricter immigration rules were enacted, but the most ominous resolution was a plan to sterilize "unfit" individuals to prevent them from passing on their negative traits. During the 20th century, a total of 33 states had sterilization programs in place. **While at first sterilization efforts targeted mentally ill people exclusively, later the traits deemed serious enough to warrant sterilization included alcoholism, criminality chronic poverty, blindness, deafness, feeble-mindedness, and promiscuity. It was also not uncommon for African American women to be sterilized during other medical procedures without consent.** Most people subjected to these sterilizations had no choice, and because the program was run by the government, they had little chance of escaping the procedure. It is thought that around 65,000 Americans were sterilized during this time period.[122]

At its core, eugenics is an attempt to declare all of human nature and human phenomena — physical traits, personalities, habits, mindsets, emotions, beliefs, and behaviors, etc. — within a strictly medical and scientific framework and to classify all these features and characteristics as either acceptable or undesirable — as healthy or unhealthy. This attempt to medicalize human phenomena demands a biological/scientific explanation and theorizes about biological solutions.

It is important to emphasize that psychiatric genetics is different than natural/physical genetics in that psychiatric genetics seeks to explain the metaphysical psyche/soul/mind/consciousness within a genetic framework:

Psychiatric genetics was established as a scientific discipline in the early 20th century. **The intention was to**

122 Laura Rivard, "Introduction to Eugenics," *Genetics Generation* (2015): https://knowgenetics.org/history-of-eugenics/.

provide evidence for the inheritance of mental illnesses.
This was to open up new paths in prevention, since
therapeutic options at the time were meagre.[123]

Eugenicists must frame human social and mental problems
within a material stricture, or else, they cannot claim
human phenomena as inherited or claim a position of
authority over matters of human nature.

Essentially, two main goals exist in psychiatric genetics: to
prove the construct of mental illness as a medical/scientific
field by providing empirical evidence that thus far is
elusive, and to attempt the discovery of a reliable and valid
medical treatment for mental, emotional, and behavioral
struggles, which can better the human race while
eliminating disorders (positive and negative). Psychiatrists
believe, accordingly, that by proving their biological
approach to the human soul, they can save individuals,
societies, and eventually all of humanity.

Also essential to psychiatric eugenics is to declare
impairing, distressful, and undesirable mindsets and
behavior as abnormalities and to blame said differences
upon genetic and neurological causes — whether or not
objective evidence exists to do so. In the abstract of an
article published in the journal of *The History of Psychiatry*,
the author describes this sobering reality:

> Eugenics, the attempt to improve the genetic quality of
> the human species by 'better breeding,' developed as a
> worldwide movement between 1900 and 1940. It was

[123] Gundula Kösters, Holger Steinberg, Kenneth Clifford Kirkby, Hubertus
Himmerich' "Ernst Rüdin 's Unpublished 19922-1925 Study "Inheritance of
Manic-Depressive Insanity": Genetic Research Findings Subordinated to
Eugenic Ideology," *PLOS Genetics* (November 6, 2015): https://journals.plos.
org/plosgenetics/article?id=10.1371/journal.pgen.1005524.

particularly prominent in the United States, Britain and Germany, and in those countries was based on the then-new science of Mendelian genetics. Eugenicists developed research programs to determine the degree in which traits such as Huntington's chorea, blindness, deafness, mental retardation (feeblemindedness), intelligence, alcoholism, schizophrenia, manic depression, rebelliousness, nomadism, prostitution and feeble inhibition were genetically determined.[124]

These eugenic research programs are still fully functioning today but under the nomenclature of psychiatric genetics. Professor of Biology Garland Allen also imparts,

> Eugenics in most western countries in the first four decades of the 20th century was based on the idea that genes control most human phenotypic traits, everything from physical features such as polydactyly and eye colour to physiological conditions such as the A-B-O blood groups to mental and personality traits such as "feeblemindedness," alcoholism [one of Benjamin Rush's social constructs] and pauperism. In assessing the development of the eugenics movement—its rise and decline between 1900 and 1950—it is important to recognise that its naïve assumptions and often flawed methodologies were openly criticised at the time by scientists and nonscientists alike . . . . It was not the case that nearly everyone in the early 20th century accepted eugenic conclusions as the latest, cutting-edge science. There are lessons from this historical approach for dealing

[124] G.E. Allen, "The Social and Economic Origins of Genetic Determinism: A Case History of the American Eugenics Movement, 1900-1940 and its Lessons for Today," *Genetica* vol. 99 (2-3) (1997): 77-88: https://www.ncbi.nlm.nih.gov/pubmed/9463076.

with similar naïve claims about genetics today [emphasis added].[125]

When it comes to issues of human nature as framed within the construct of mental illness, eugenics is fundamentally about one group of people with social authority selecting another group of people and declaring them to be either defective/disordered/degenerate/abnormal or healthy/normal/of good genetic stock. According to this approach, deciding who is viewed as mentally healthy and who is categorized as mentally ill is based upon the authority's moral predisposition — how the authority interprets and explains mental, emotional, social, and behavioral struggles — and whether or not the established authority subjectively attributes said struggles to physical causes.

In order for eugenic selection to occur, a social or descriptive construct and system of categorization must be created, widely accepted in society as a field of medicine, and deemed to be reliable and valid. This process of establishing a system of selection also enables the designer(s) both authority and control. As the construct grows in acceptance, more people can either self-identify with its description or be selected by authority figures as defective. If people become convinced that objective evidence and altruistic motives uphold the system, then they are more likely to submit themselves to diagnostic scrutiny.

It is also helpful to understand that psychiatric eugenics — or "genetics" as it is now called — is an anthropology based

[125] Allen, "Eugenics and Modern Biology."

upon social Darwinianism and the belief that humanity is normally advancing and evolutionary concepts of natural selection are occurring. Psychiatry is a necessary profession for evolutionists to attempt explaining all of human nature — including such things as metaphysical mindsets and emotions — within a strictly biological/evolutionary framework. Whereas the neurologist and geneticist treat valid physical maladies, the psychiatrist constructs invisible syndromes (based upon observable symptoms) to explain impairing and distressful aspects of human nature. In creating these constructs and medical labels, "disorders" are proposed to be genetic defects/valid disease entities. "Psychiatric disorders," then, represent categories of "mentally ill" — the diagnostic system of negative eugenics.

Psychiatric eugenics has three available approaches to those diagnosed as disordered: 1) people who are allegedly mentally or physically defective can be treated if possible, 2) they can be physically or chemically prevented from passing on their genetic code (e.g., abortion, sterilization, isolation, and castration), or 3) alleged degenerates can be eliminated altogether for the alleged betterment of their families and society. Throughout its history, psychiatric geneticists have employed all of these methods to address people whom they diagnose to be abnormal — those said to be a threat to themselves, their families, their communities, and the human race in general. In fact, psychiatrists have even categorized historical figures as mentally disordered who threatened the ideologies of psychiatry[126] and who have exposed its pseudoscience.[127]

For decades, psychiatric genetics/eugenics has been widely claimed to be an altruistic and scientific field, but to hold to this belief system about human nature requires that presuppositional philosophies first be accepted, though behind every conceived human philosophy is a fallible person. Therefore, because some of the fallible people in the history of psychiatric genetics provided underlying theory while others were key figures in experimentation, propagation, and application, it is profitable to examine them to better understand the genetic theory of mental illness.

The Scientists of Old

Although the psychiatrist Benjamin Rush (1746-1813) was noted in chapter one as an American whose proposed ideas of hereditary madness, a material explanation of the soul, physical remedies, the development of psychiatric constructs, and race psychology are still held today, three other prominent historical figures in the history of the genetic theory of mental illness were also strong advocates for race psychology/eugenics. Each of these eugenicists promoted the genetic theory as objective science, which

---

[126] Evan D. Murray, Miles G. Cunningham, and Bruce H. Price, "The Role of Psychotic Disorders in Religious History Considered," *Journal of Neuropsychiatry and Clinical Neurosciences* 24 (2012): 410-26.

[127] "Antipsychiatrist" is a term that psychiatrists regularly utilize to mark or categorize anyone who disagrees with popular psychiatric beliefs or who exposes psychiatric claims of validity to be conjecture.

paved the way for psychiatric genetics to bring about the Holocaust in Nazi Germany under the guise of formal science and medicine. These three men (in addition to Rush) are: Charles Darwin (1809-1882), Augustin Morel (1809-1873), and Francis Galton (1822-1911).

Charles Darwin

Charles Darwin was not a psychiatrist, but he is arguably one of the most influential philosophers in the fields of modern science, medicine, and anthropology. While Darwin is most known for his theory of evolution, he also asserted and promoted race psychology/eugenics in his book *The Descent of Man:*

> Be enquired whether man, like so many other animals, has given rise to varieties and sub-races, differing but slightly from each other, or to races differing so much that they must be **classed as doubtful species . . . the civilized races of man will almost certainly exterminate, and replace throughout the world the saved races.**[128]

In Darwin's view, differences — if deemed by an established authority to be so — could result in people being viewed as "doubtful species." Darwin, like Benjamin Rush, held to race psychology, and this hereditary theory would lead biological scientists to search for the human soul within the body and eventually within the human genome. Dr. Bruce Lipton shares his own discovery:

> How did we get to the widespread and often-cited notion that genes "control" biology? In the *Origin of Species*, Darwin suggested that "hereditary" factors were passed

[128] Charles Darwin, *The Descent of Man, and Selection in Relation to Sex* (London: John Murray, 1871), 9-10; 201.

on from generation to generation, controlling the traits of the offspring. **Darwin's influence was so great that scientists myopically focused on identifying that hereditary material which, they thought, controlled life.**[129]

Harvard geneticist, Richard Lewontin also states about Darwin and his theory of evolution:

> Despite its claims to be above society, science, like the Church before it, is a supremely social institution, reflecting and reinforcing the dominant values and views of society that teach historical epoch. Sometimes the source in social experiences of a scientific theory and the way in which that scientific theory is a direct translation of social experiences are completely evident, even at a detailed level. The most famous case is Darwin's theory of evolution by natural selection . . . . He claimed that there was a universal struggle for existence because more organisms were born than could survive and reproduce, and that in the course of that struggle for existence, those organisms who were more efficient, better designed, cleverer, and generally better built for the struggle would leave more offspring than the inferior kinds. As a consequence of this victory in the struggle for existence, evolutionary change occurred.[130]

[129] Bruce H. Lipton, *The Biology of Belief: Unleashing the Power of Consciousness, Matter and Miracles* (New York: Hay House, 2005), 30.

[130] Richard C. Lewontin, *Biology as Ideology: The Doctrine of DNA* (New York: HarperCollins Publishers, 1991), 9.

For Darwin, it was important to create a system whereby strong people or healthy genomes and unhealthy people could be differentiated. Darwin had his own eugenics theory which he called "pangenesis,"[131] and this theory's key concept was hereditary struggle versus strength. The "healthy" should procreate and advance evolution, whereas the weak or defective should not survive, unless the weakness or abnormality can be biologically corrected or prevented. It is on this ideology that psychiatry was created as a field of anthropology within the fields of medicine and philosophy.

As with Rush, Darwin's influence in shaping psychiatry and in propagating the genetic/ hereditary/eugenic theory of mental illness is undeniable. Professor of psychiatry at the University of Cape Town, South Africa Dan Stein

Figure 1 - The International Congress of Eugenics' Logo, 1921

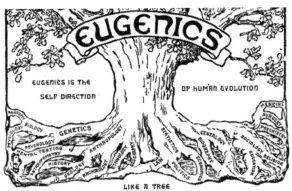

states,

> Darwin's seminal publications in the nineteenth century
> laid the foundation for an evolutionary approach to
> psychology and psychiatry. Advances in 20th century

[131] Proctor, *Racial Hygiene*, 32.

evolutionary theory facilitated the development of evolutionary psychology and psychiatry as recognized areas of scientific investigation.[132]

Stein comments further on the evolutionary theory and psychiatry's reliance upon each other in establishing psychiatric genetics:

> In this century, advances in understanding the molecular basis of evolution, of the mind, and of psychopathology, offer the possibility of an integrated approach to understanding the proximal (psychobiological) and distal (evolutionary) mechanisms of interest to psychiatry and psychopharmacology. **There is, for example, growing interest in the question of whether specific genetic variants mediate psychobiological processes that have evolutionary value in specific contexts, and of the implications of this for understanding the vulnerability to psychopathology and for considering the advantages and limitations of pharmacotherapy. The evolutionary value, and gene-environmental mediation, of early life programming is potentially a particularly rich area of investigation.** Although evolutionary approaches to psychology and to medicine face important conceptual and methodological challenges, current work is increasingly sophisticated, and may prove to be an important foundational discipline for clinicians and researchers in psychiatry and psychopharmacology.[133]

As Stein also acknowledges, both proposed psychiatric etiologies and suggested psychotropic treatments are based in eugenics. Other biological psychiatrists note how

---

[132] Dan J. Stein, "Evolutionary Theory, Psychiatry, & psycho-pharmacology," *Progress in Neuropsychopharmacology and Biological Psychiatry* 30 (5) (July, 2006): 766; https://www.ncbi.nlm.nih.gov/pubmed/16580111.

[133] Ibid.

psychiatry is founded upon Darwin's theory of natural selection:

> Darwin's theory of evolution, and in particular one of its mechanisms, natural selection, is being used as the explanatory cornerstone of many unsolved problems in human biology and human affairs. Psychiatry is an example of that. Darwinian psychiatry's main proponents endorse the adaptationist program to carry out their project to implement an evolutionary psychiatry . . . . [134]

Similarly, professor of psychiatry Martin Brune remarks on how the creation of degenerates/inferiors in Nazi Germany was largely based upon beliefs about material origins:

> Evolutionary theory has had a major impact on psychiatry since the middle of the 19th century. During the Nazi regime psychiatry supported compulsory sterilization and euthanasia of physically and mentally ill and subsequently the killing of "inferior" races by borrowing scientifically invalid conclusions from evolutionary biology.[135]

Though Darwin was not a psychiatrist, without the evolutionary theory, which insists that the world and all of human nature are only materially caused and thus materially explained, psychiatric genetics would likely not

[134] B. Dubrovsky, "Evolutionary Psychiatry. Adaptationist and Nonadaptationist Conceptualizations," *Progress in Neuropsychopharmacology and Biological Psychiatry* 26 (1) (January, 2002): 1-19; https://www.ncbi.nlm.nih.gov/pubmed/11853097.

[135] Martin Brune, "Evolutionary Fallacies of Nazi Psychiatry. Implications for Current Research," *Perspectives in Biology and Medicine* 44 (3) (Summer 2001): 426-33; https://www.ncbi.nlm.nih.gov/pubmed/11482011.

exist: "Evolution is a pivotal concept in biology with relevant applications in psychiatry."[136]

Psychiatry needed the ideas of selection and materialism contained in the Darwinian concept of "natural [materialism] selection [positive or negative]," and conversely, the evolutionary theory needed psychiatry to formalize a system of selection and to explain and apply the vital belief in individual degeneracy — the negative/undesirable metaphysical aspects of human nature that theorists cannot otherwise explain within their secular worldview.

Augustin Morel

In addition to Darwin, another influential, historic scientist was the French psychiatrist Benedict Augustin Morel, as historian of medicine and neuroscience Frank Stahnisch records:

> This proto-eugenic view had been around in the European discussion since the time of Vienna-born French psychiatrist Bénédict Augustin Morel (1809-1873), **who had postulated the existence of an original healthy and moral state of human society and diagnosed a subsequent deterioration as a consequence of people's germ material alteration.**[137]

---

[136] T. Baptista, E. Aldana, F. Angeles, S. Beaulieu, "Evolution Theory: an overview of its applications in psychiatry," *Psychopathology* 41 (1) (2008): 17.

[137] Frank W. Stahnisch, "The Early Eugenics Movement and Emerging Professional Psychiatry: Conceptual Transfers and Personal Relationships between Germany and North America, 1880s to 1930s," *CBMH* Vol. 31 (1) (2014): 17-40: https://pdfs.semanticscholar.org/ 8855/29ed3162bfbdf659 cba36ae3b1566c9a06b5.pdf."

Whereas Darwin concentrated on racial differences, Morel regularly focused on moral variances. Yet, both suggested a system of perceived healthy people and perceived unhealthy degenerates based upon a selected social or descriptive construct and genetic/hereditary explanations:

> Degeneration: a reversion to a more primitive type of behavior . . . . According to Morel (1857), mental disorders are the result of "hereditary degeneration."[138]

Morel understood that in order to have a deviance or a proposed degeneration (a theorized regression to a previously evolved mental state), there must be an established social norm. By accepting the Darwinian idea of natural selection, Morel proposed that normal people are morally/mentally healthy. Thus, the concept of "mental hygiene" rather than "racial hygiene" was introduced.

In accordance with the Darwinian theory of natural selection, Morel was able to introduce *hereditary degeneration* as a medical concept — a foundational principle of psychiatry. Stanisch writes,

> **Morel's highly influential volume was fully dedicated to the psychiatric and social problem of "degeneration."** His book — the Traité des dégénérescences physiques, intellectuelles et morales de l'espèce humaine et de ces causes qui produisent ces variétés maladives (1857/8)63 — **was very well received by the emerging field of clinical and brain psychiatry, as its protagonists believed that it would help prove that mental diseases had a somatic basis.** However, it is interesting to note that not only clinical psychiatrists but a number of related approaches were also influenced by the broader scientific context of degeneration theories (theories de dégénérescence) and

---

[138] Philip Lawrence Harriman, *Dictionary of Psychology* (New York: The Citadel Press, 1947), 98.

early eugenics thought within academic European psychiatry, especially among those individuals who worked with psychiatric patients at the same time.[139]

Stahnisch continues,

> French-Austrian psychiatrist Bénédict Augustin Morel's (1809-1873) *Traité des dégénérescences physiques, intellectuelles et morales de l'espèce humaine* (1857) **was fully dedicated to the social problem of "degeneration" and it became very attractive to German-speaking psychiatrists during the latter half of the 19th century.** [Several psychiatrists] integrated Morel's approach and searched for the somatic and morphological alterations in the human brain; **a perspective of research that Ernst Rüdin (1874-1952) at Munich further prolonged into a thorough analysis of hereditary influences on mental health.**[140]

The *Encyclopaedia Britannica* recognizes this important psychiatric belief:

> Morel saw mental deficiency as the end stage of a process of mental degeneration that included mental illness. He articulated his theory of mental illness in *Traité des maladies mentales* (1860; *"A Treatise on Mental Illness"*), in which he coined the term *demence-precoce* to refer to mental degeneration.[141]

Both Rush's and Morel's shared belief in mental degenerationism would become a vital tenet of psychiatric eugenics. As also noted, prominent psychiatrists thereafter (e.g., Emil Kraepelin and Ernst Rüdin) would rely heavily

---

[139] Stahnisch, "The Early Eugenics Movement."

[140] Ibid.

[141] Editors of Encyclopaedia Britannica, "Benedict Augustin Morel," *Encyclopaedia Britannica* (updated March 16, 2019): https://www.britannica.com/biography/Benedict-Augustin-Morel.

on the genetic theory of individual/hereditary degenerationism. In fact, Emil Kraepelin would utilize Morel's concept of *demence precoce* in creating the psychiatric construct viewed in Nazi eugenics as a specific form of mental degeneracy known as *dementia praecox* and eventually as *schizophrenia*. From its conception, the psychiatric construct of schizophrenia has not been a separate concept from the philosophy of individual degeneracy, which is fundamental to the eugenic theory.

It was upon these evolutionary theories that modern psychiatry was born and became a necessary field to both sustain evolutionary theory and to attempt dismissing God as the intelligent designer of human nature. Haefner points out this reality:

> These theories and discoveries dramatically advanced knowledge on the human species and led beyond the previously embraced belief of man's creation by God.[142]

At its core, the eugenics theory asserts humanity as the supreme architect, moral judge of what is acceptable, and savior of its own future.

Though the genetic theory of mental illness is an important aspect of the larger theory of Darwinian evolution, the genetic theory attempts to dismiss the theory of natural selection by transferring the selection from theorized chance to being governed by intelligent beings. Whereas Darwin had suggested that nature selects the strongest to survive, psychiatric geneticists believed that they had

---

[142] Heinz Haefner, "Comment on E.F. Torrey and R.H. Yolken: 'Psychiatric Genocide: Nazi attempts to eradicate schizophrenia'" *Schizophrenia Bulletin* vol. 36 1 (2010): 26-32.

"replaced the evolutionary forces of selection."[143] In an article published in the *American Journal of Psychiatry* in 1942, psychiatrist Foster Kennedy proposes

> three things we may lay rough hands on, with little enough knowledge how to do it: man's life now, his reproduction of himself, and his evolution, which is the way he is to go. There are indeed many feebleminded people not easily recognizable at first sight in the social world . . . . Were we to try to sterilize all the abnormal, I am sure that we would defeat the evolution of the higher life.[144]

Susan Bachrach, writing for the *NEJM*, agrees:

> Proponents of eugenics in the early 20th century argued that modern medicine interfered with Darwinian natural selection by keeping the weak alive; that mentally retarded and ill persons were reproducing at a much faster rate than valuable, productive persons; and that costs were escalating for maintaining "defectives" in special homes, hospitals, schools, and prisons.[145]

Humanity's attempt to alter or change theorized natural selection reveals that the asserted bio-evolutionary processes are not the determiner or architect of humanity that many evolutionists insist they are. Since its conception, most psychiatrists have taken the moral responsibility upon themselves to isolate or eliminate the weak or

[143] Robert Jay Lifton, *The Nazi Doctors: Medical Killing and the Psychology of Genocide* (New York: Basic Books, 1986), 143.

[144] American Psychiatric Association, "Defective: Education, Sterilization, Euthanasia," *American Journal of Psychiatry* vol. 99 (1) (1942): 13.

[145] Susan Bachrach, "In the Name of Public Health — Nazi Racial Hygiene," *New England Journal of Medicine* 351 (2004): 417-420, DOI:10.1056/NEJMp0481 36.

"defectives," to control society with social and descriptive constructs, and to uphold at all costs the theory of evolution, which maintains that mankind is merely amoral genomes wandering through the universe attempting to strengthen and survive.

Francis Galton

As with Rush, Darwin, and Morel, Francis Galton (1822-1911) — another prominent psychologist and philosopher — not only endorsed the idea of eugenics, but is also referred to as the father of eugenics. Most historians present Galton as the figurehead, since he first suggested the term *eugenics* — a word that eventually replaced popular phrases such as "race psychology" and "hereditary madness":

> The term eugenics was first coined by Darwin's cousin, Francis Galton, in 1883. The eugenic movement gained public popularity across Europe and North America at the end of the Victorian era, fueled by the concept of 'social Darwinism' and public fear of a decline in the number of ideal citizens.[146]

Using propaganda, eugenicists — accepting Galton's formalized genetic theory as scientific — began to convince many people to believe in individual degenerationism:

> The eugenics movement — first called so by Francis Galton (1822–1911), . . . set out to prevent the alleged accumulation of unfit genotypes. Attempts to breed healthier, stronger, and wiser human beings by

---

[146] E. Wittmann, "To What Extent were Ideas and Beliefs about Eugenics Held in Nazi Germany Shared in Britain and the United States Prior to the Second World War?" *Vesalius* (1) (June 10, 2004): 16-9; https://www.ncbi.nlm.nih.gov/pubmed/15386878.

promoting the spread of "good" genes were propagated as positive eugenics.[147]

Eugenics was not limited to Germany; the eugenic movement was worldwide.[148] Moreover, it was Rush (America), Darwin (United Kingdom), and Morel (France) rather than Galton who introduced and popularized the concepts globally on which the field of eugenics was formally recognized as "science."

However, though eugenics was a globally accepted anthropology, claimed to fall within scientific study by the early 1900s, the movement needed a global figurehead, physical headquarters, and scientific research facilities to prove its reliability and validity. Eugenicists also needed people who were perceived to be categorical degenerates in order to study and on which to apply their theory. Pre-Nazi Germany provided the genetic theory of mental illness with all that Rush's, Darwin's, Morel's, and Galton's combined ideas needed to flourish.

The Nazis

The major development of the formal field of psychiatric genetics — in philosophy, experimentation, and systematic

[147] Haefner, "Comment on E.F. Torrey." See also R.D. Strous, 'Psychiatric genocide: reflections and responsibilities' *Schizophrenia Bulletin* Advance access publication on February 4, 2010; doi:10.1093/schbul/sbq003)." *Schizophrenia Bulletin* vol. 36 (3) (2010): 450-4; doi:10.1093/schbul/sbq034.

[148] Robert A. Wilson, "Eugenics Never Went Away," *AEON* (June 5, 2018): https://aeon.co/essays/eugenics-today-where-eugenic-sterilisation-continues-now?utm_source=Aeon+Newsletter&utm_ campaign=574e66bb0c-EMAIL_ CAMPAIGN_2018_06_06_11_10&utm_ medium=email&utm_term=0_411a82 e59d-574e66bb0c-69588105.

application—occurred primarily both in Germany and in the United States. It is impossible, then, to separate eugenics and psychiatric genetics as if they were distinct ideologies or to objectively separate the field into different countries. Volker Roelcke, German historian of medicine at the Max Planck Institute, remarks,

> The development of genetics, in particular psychiatric genetics, is inextricably associated with eugenics and its funding by philanthropic or state institutions.[149]

As will be developed further in the next chapter, it was primarily psychiatrists—experimenting and attempting to prove their genetic theory of mental illness—who would initiate and draft legislature responsible for ushering in the Holocaust as well as creating the field of modern-day psychiatric genetics. Renowned psychiatrists E. Fuller Torrey and Robert Yolken assert,

> The sterilization and murder of hundreds of thousands of patients with schizophrenia and other psychiatric disorders in Nazi Germany between 1934 and 1945 was the greatest criminal act in the history of psychiatry. . . . **It was also based on what are now known to be erroneous genetic theories and had no apparent long-term effect on the subsequent incidence of schizophrenia** [emphasis added].[150]

---

[149] Volker Roelcke, "Mentalities and Sterilization Laws in Europe During the 1930s. Eugenics, Genetics, and Politics in a Historic Context," *Der Nervenarzt* [*The Neurologist*] 73 (11) (November 2002): 1019; https://www.ncbi.nlm.nih.gov/pubmed/12430043.

[150] E. Fuller Torrey and Robert H Yolken, "Psychiatric Genocide: Nazi attempts to eradicate schizophrenia." *Schizophrenia Bulletin* vol. 36,1 (2010): 26-32. doi:10.1093/schbul/sbp097.

Even in the prestigious *Schizophrenia Bulletin* it is acknowledged that historians rightly discern the cause of the Holocaust to rest squarely upon the psychiatric genetic theory:

> Susser and Smith write that **Hitler's systematic killing of 6 million Jews "was in fact developed and piloted" by the murder of mental patients.** Nasierowski, too, describes how the killing of the mentally ill preceded the Holocaust and the gas chambers in the concentration camp . . . [emphasis added].[151]

Likewise, Stanford professor of history Robert Proctor describes how psychiatrists and other medical researchers led the way for their eugenic theory to be ushered into Germany:

> Biomedical scientists [led by psychiatrists] played an active, even leading role in the initiation, administration, and execution of Nazi racial programs. In this sense the case can be made that science (especially biomedical science) under the Nazis cannot simply be seen in terms of a fundamentally "passive" or "apolitical" scientific community responding to purely external political forces; on the contrary, there is strong evidence that scientists actively designed and administered central aspects of National Socialist racial policy [e.g., psychiatrist Ernst Rüdin].[152]

The Holocaust was not merely one of the most horrific psychiatric experiments gone wrong; it is, more specifically, the genetic theory of mental illness — both positive and negative aspects — being fully carried out under the banner of science and medicine and eventually

---

[151] Haefner, "Comment on E.F. Torrey."

[152] Proctor, *Racial Hygiene*, 6.

with government cooperative funding. In fact, the eugenic scientists — psychiatrists and biological psychologists — involved in the Holocaust were not passive influences nor were they manipulated into participating; they were the primary architects and energy behind the eugenics theory long before the political system of national socialism was implemented. Dr. Proctor offers insight:

> Nazi racial science is probably most often associated with the medical experiments performed on so-called lower races. Testimony presented at the Nuremberg and Buchenwald trials documented the involvement of **German physicians** in a series of brutal and often "terminal experiments" . . . . **The ideological structure we associate with National Socialism was deeply embedded in the philosophy and institutional structure of German biomedical science [psychology and psychiatry] long before the beginning of the euthanasia program in 1939 — and to a certain extent, even before 1933.** The published record of the German medical profession makes it clear that many intellectuals cooperated fully in Nazi racial programs, and that many of the social and intellectual foundations for these programs were laid long before the rise of Hitler to power.[153]

In *A Sign for Cain*, psychiatrist Fredric Wertham forthrightly lays the blame for psychiatry's activities during the Holocaust squarely upon his own profession:

> The tragedy is that the psychiatrists did not have to have an order. **They acted on their own.** They were not carrying out a death sentence pronounced by someone else. **They were the legislators who laid down the rules for deciding who was to die; they were the administrators who worked out the procedures, provided the patients and places, and decided the methods of killing; they pronounced a sentence of life**

[153] Ibid., 6.

**or death in every individual case; they were the
executioners** who carried out or - without being coerced
to do so - surrendered their patients to be killed in other
institutions; they supervised and often watched the slow
deaths [emphasis added].[154]

Professor of psychiatry at the University of Tel Aviv Rael
Strous concurs:

> Psychiatrists, along with many other physicians,
> facilitated the resolution of many of the regime's
> ideological and practical challenges, rather than taking a
> passive or even active stance of resistance. Psychiatrists
> played a prominent and central role in two categories of
> the crimes against humanity, namely sterilization and
> euthanasia. It was psychiatrists (many of whom were
> senior professors in academia) who sat on planning
> committees for both processes and who provided the
> theoretical backing for what transpired. It was
> psychiatrists who reported their patients to the authorities
> and coordinated their transfer from all over Germany to
> gas chambers situated on the premises of the six
> psychiatric institutions: Brandenburg, Grafeneck,
> Hartheim, Sonnenstein, Bernburg, and Hadamar [2,3]. It
> was psychiatrists who coordinated the "channeling" of
> patients on arrival into specially modified rooms where
> gassing took place. It was psychiatrists who saw to the
> killing of the patients (initially using carbon monoxide
> and later, starvation and injection). Finally, it was
> psychiatrists who faked causes of death on certificates
> sent to these patients' next of kin. It has been estimated
> that over 200,000 individuals with mental disorders of all
> subtypes were put to death in this manner. Much of this

---

[154] Fredric Wertham, *A Sign for Cain* (New York: Paperback Library, 1969),
161.

process took place before the plan to annihilate the Jews, Gypsies and homosexuals of Europe.[155]

Strous further reveals that

> Hitler never gave the order to kill patients with mental illness. He only permitted it in a letter written in October 1939 and backdated to September 1, 1939. Psychiatrists were therefore never ordered to facilitate the process or carry out the murder of mentally ill . . . they were empowered to do so. Activity by psychiatrists and psychiatric institutions thus constituted the connection between euthanasia and the larger scale annihilation of Jews and other "undesirables" such as homosexuals in what came to be known as the Holocaust.[156]

The fact that Nazi ideologies and legislation were largely born out of the psychiatric genetic theory (e.g., individual degeneracy) of mental illness is well supported.[157]

Although eugenics likely began in the late 1700s/early 1800s with psychiatrists such as Benjamin Rush and Augustin Morel, modern psychiatric eugenics (the genetic theory of mental illness) finds its substantive origin in pre-Nazi Germany and in the United States. As this book exposes, many psychiatric eugenicists were international constituents of and compliant with one another. Many of these psychiatrists and psychologists lived and traveled between countries — discussing and propagating shared

---

[155] Rael D. Strous, "Psychiatry During the Nazi Era: Ethical Lessons for the Modern Professional," *Annals of General Psychiatry* vol. 6 (8) (February 27, 2007): doi:10.1186/1744-859X-6-8.

[156] Ibid.

[157] This historic fact will be discussed in the next chapter.

theories and developing new ones. Historian of medicine Frank W. Stahnisch writes,

> Taking these preliminary considerations into account, it would be totally artificial to analyze the scientific versions of eugenics discourse in Germany and in the US separately.[158]

Dr. Peter Breggin concurs that America and Germany were unified in their eugenics vision and that it was at times the United States that led the way for Germany to follow:

> In summary, many psychiatric and public health officials in the west fully supported the eugenics program in Nazi Germany, including involuntary sterilization and castration, and California provided a eugenical model for planners in Germany. **A few American authorities openly supported euthanasia itself, including the prestigious** *American Journal of Psychiatry.*[159]

In 1942, articles were published by the American Psychiatric Association (APA) which discussed in earnest whether the "feebleminded" (people with valid biological impairments) should be euthanized or not:

> If euthanasia is to become at some distant day an available procedure, enabling legislation will be required. The story of sterilization will doubtless be repeated on an extended scale. But legislation may be expected to follow only upon the spread and strength of public opinion, and the nucleus of that opinion should be the attitude of those most nearly concerned — the parents of the candidates for the contemplated procedure. It is in the evaluation and

---

[158] Stahnisch, "The Early Eugenics Movement," pdf.

[159] Peter Breggin, Psychiatry's Role in the Holocaust," *International Journal of Risk and Safety in Medicine* 4 (1993), 141.

melioration of this parental attitude that the interest of the psychiatrist in the whole question must center.[160]

It was not only German psychiatrists who proposed euthanasia and discussed the need for political support. In the same journal entry, Dr. Kennedy argues that the parents' desire to keep their afflicted child alive should itself be considered and approached as a delusion or a problem of "mental hygiene":

> That is precisely the psychiatric problem this overlength discussion has been trying to get at, namely, the "fondness" of the parents of an idiot and their "want" that he should be kept alive. It is this parental state of mind that we believe deserves study — the extent to which it exists, in fact and not merely as a generalization of opinion, what underlying factors such as those set forth above are discoverable, **whether it can be assessed as healthy or morbid, and whether in the latter case it is modifiable by exposure to mental hygiene principles** [emphasis added].[161]

In America by the 1930s, as in Germany, *racial hygiene* had been replaced with the broader eugenic concept of *mental hygiene*, and this worldview was held to in America apart from socialism. Despite political differences, psychiatry was globally unified upon the genetic theory — to the point of supporting sterilization and euthanasia. Renowned German historian Volker Roelcke relates,

> The article describes the emergence of research programs, institutions and activities of the early protagonists in the field of psychiatric genetics: Ernst Rüdin in Munich, Eliot Slater in London, Franz Kallmann in New York and Erik

---

[160] Foster Kennedy, "Euthanasia," *American Journal of Psychiatry* vol. 99 (1942): 143.

[161] Ibid.

Essen-Möller in Lund. During the 1930s and well into the Nazi period, the last three had been research fellows at the German Research Institute for Psychiatry in Munich. **It is documented that there was a continuous mutual exchange of scientific ideas and practices between these actors, and that in all four contexts there were intrinsic relations between eugenic motivations and genetic research, but with specific national adaptations** [emphasis added].[162]

It is likely that many people today are unfamiliar with the history of German eugenics, but it is also likely that most Americans are far more ignorant of the history of psychiatric eugenics within their own country.

The eugenics theory of mental illness was so important to psychiatrists worldwide that racial and national boundaries were set aside for the belief in and development toward established shared goals. It is best, therefore, to view eugenics in the late 1800s and especially in the early 1900s and beyond as a unified movement that had limited divide between nations.

To understand the current genetic theory, then, it is imperative to examine the key figures who together formalized the modern psychiatric genetic theory of mental illness over several decades. This task requires that German psychiatrists — who were considered to be leading authorities in psychiatric genetics and some of whom are still revered as key figures — be examined in a chapter dedicated exclusively to them. Understanding the "field"

---

[162] Volker Roelcke, "Eugenic Concerns, Scientific Practices: International Relations in the Establishment of Psychiatric Genetics in Germany, Britain, the USA and Scandinavia, C. 1920-60," *The History of Psychiatry* Vol. 30 (1) (March 2019): 19: DOI: 10.1177/0957154X18808666.

of psychiatric genetics — not just recognizing historic figures who introduced key theoretical concepts — requires that the architects and their tenets of faith be identified and understood together in toto.

CHAPTER 3

THE ARCHITECTS OF PSYCHIATRIC GENETICS

"The lineage of the effort to find genetic predispositions runs back through the eugenic thinking of the 1930s and 1920s, with its belief in genes for criminal degeneracy, sexual profligacy, alcoholism, and every other type of activity disapproved of by bourgeois society. It is deeply embedded in today's deterministic ideology. Only thus can we account of the extraordinary repetitive perseverance and uncritical nature of research into the genetics of schizophrenia."[163] – Geneticist Richard Lewontin, Neuroscientist Steven Rose, and Psychologist Leon Kamin

The history of the genetic theory of mental illness is certainly important. But one cannot fully understand psychiatric eugenics without also examining the key figures involved in shaping theory, and furthermore, these men's specific underlying philosophies, which are still prominent beliefs today. Yet, much of this important history has been excluded from academia and hidden from public knowledge. Psychiatrist Peter Breggin remarks on this fact:

---

[163] Richard C. Lewontin, Steven Rose, and Leon J. Kamin, *Not in Our Genes: Biology, Ideology, and Human Nature 2nd edition* (Chicago: Haymarket Books, 2017), 207.

psychiatrists suffer from the repression of painful memories as much as anyone else does. Genetic psychiatrists not only must repress the lessons of Nazi Germany, they have to forget about the lessons of their own research, which ultimately has undermined their position. As a result, the history of genetics is largely expurgated from reviews on the subject.[164]

Clinical psychiatrist Paul Minot concurs: "Psychiatry is so ashamed of its history that it has deleted much of it."[165] In the *International Review of Psychiatry*, other psychiatrists also comment:

> **Reviewing the history of psychiatric genetics is a difficult task**, since — in contrast to genetic research into most other disorders — it cannot simply be done by chronologically listing methodological achievements and major findings. Instead, it necessitates a comprehensive assessment of how the aetiological concept of mental disorders has developed since as early as the world of ancient Greece. **Furthermore, it has to touch upon the sensitive issue of the eugenic movement that was closely linked to the study of heredity in mental disorders in the first half of the 20th century and, in Nazi Germany, led to the systematic mass murder of psychiatric patients** [emphasis added].[166]

Clearly, there exists a need to examine this history more thoroughly. In this chapter, the principle figures of

[164] Breggin, *Toxic Psychiatry*, 107.

165 Paul Minot, "My Insecure Profession," *Straight Talk Psychiatry* (August 31, 2019): https://www.youtube.com/watch?time_continue=2&v=Wz4lHXG4sw4&feature=emb_logo, 10:20-25.

[166] T. G. Schulze, H. Fangerau, P. Propping, "From Degeneration to Genetic Susceptibility, From Eugenics to Genethics, From Bezugsziffer to LOD score: The History of Psychiatric Genetics," *International Review of Psychiatry* (4) (November 16, 2004): 246-59.

psychiatric genetics will be discovered and their teachings traced through generations of psychiatrists, and in the next chapter, their precise philosophical beliefs and corresponding system will be examined more thoroughly.[167]

Wilhelm Wundt

Widely regarded as the father of modern psychology, experimental psychology, and abnormal psychology, Wilhelm Wundt (1832-1920) is clearly one of the most famous and influential figures in the history of psychology and psychiatry.[168] Wundt not only coined the term "psychologist," he also helped to shape the beliefs and approaches to the human psyche/soul of arguably the two most influential psychiatrists in history: Sigmund Freud and Emil Kraepelin. It might also be helpful to recognize that Wundt was a biologist as well as a psychologist/philosopher, which explains why Wundt's education and corresponding theories of the human psyche/soul were ideal for psychiatric eugenics to develop into a flourishing field.

In fact, it was under the teaching of Wilhelm Wundt that abnormal psychology and thus psychiatry would gain significant traction, and human thought, morality, and the metaphysical soul would be conceived as a scientifically observable and measurable phenomena rather than as

167 Appendix B is a list of key psychiatric figures throughout history and each of their most significant contributions to the psychiatric eugenic theory.

168 Saul McLeod, "Wilhelm Wundt," *Simply Psychology Online*, 2008, https://www.simplypsychology.org/wundt.html.

principally studies in religion or philosophy. Authors of one abnormal psychology textbook explain:

> In 1879, Wilhelm Wundt, a professor of psychology at the University of Leipzig, Germany, established a laboratory for the scientific study of psychology—that is, the application of scientific experimentation, with precise methods of measurement and control, to human thought and behavior. **The opening of Wundt's laboratory is often cited as the beginning of modern psychology. It was also a critical step in the development of abnormal psychology, for the methods taught by Wundt were soon applied to abnormal as well as normal behavior** [emphasis added].[169]

Under Wundt's leadership, identifying—some might say creating—mental abnormality began to be considered a scientific and biological endeavor. Professor of clinical psychology Jonathan Shedler also offers insight into Wundt's historical significance:

> Psychology has its own concepts and methods. Wilhelm Wundt established the first experimental psychology laboratory in 1879, studying mental life scientifically at a time when bloodletting was still common medical practice.[170]

In theory, Wundt reframed all of human nature apart from the traditional religious view of Scripture and within an experimental approach. His insistence that all mindsets, emotions, and behaviors be considered and treated within

---

[169] Lauren B. Alloy, Joan Acocella, and Richard R. Bootzin, *Abnormal Psychology: Current Perspectives* 7th edition (New York: McGraw-Hill, 1996), 19.

[170] Jonathan Shedler, "It's Time for Psychology to Lead, Not Follow: Psychotherapy is not a medical treatment," *Psychology Today Online* (October 27, 2019): https://www.psychologytoday.com/us/blog/psychologically-minded/201910/it-s-time-psychology-lead-not-follow.

scientific strictures was based upon his rejection of traditional Christian values and religion.

Wundt not only despised religion, he often claimed religious philosophers as fit for the asylum. For example, in a letter to his student Emil Kraepelin, Wundt said of the revered German philosopher Gustav Teichmuller (1832-1888),

> Recently I read the preface to *Philosophy of Religion* by your colleague Teichmuller. I thought I could skip the rest afterwards . . . . Generally speaking this philosopher's declamations rather give the impression that he will be ready for your asylum in the near future.[171]

In Wundt's mind, psychology could be the field of study that replaced both religion and philosophy as best explaining human existence — as a new humanistic religion.

Ironically, in order to establish this new perspective, Wundt needed to apply and propagate a philosophy in accordance with social Darwinianism, referred to as materialism, scientism, reductionism, or positivism.[172] As previously stated, Wundt did not create psychology; he redefined it within an evolutionary framework:

> [In] 1879, German psychologist Wilhelm Wundt redefines psychology from its original meaning, "study of the soul," to the modern concept of man as a stimulus-response

---

[171] H. Steinberg and M. C. Angermeyer, "Emil Kraepelin's years at Dorpat as professor of psychiatry in nineteenth-century Russia," *History of Psychiatry* 12, (47) (2001): 304.

[172] *Materialism* is the philosophy which claims that human nature consists only of a physical nature, and which can presumably be approached fully within scientific strictures.

animal who can be controlled . . . . At the University of Leipzig, Wundt founds the first psychological laboratory to study the physiological activity of the brain. **Psychologists from around the world flock to Germany to learn this new concept of man as animal rather than a body and soul** [emphasis added].[173]

While others before him, such as the influential Benjamin Rush, believed and promoted materialism, it is with Wundt that secular psychologists and psychiatrists globally and in unison began to dogmatically promote the metaphysical soul as a product of the physical nature rather than as a distinct spiritual reality. In place of *dualism*, materialism or reductionism became the common secular belief concerning human nature. Wundt writes in his textbook *Introduction to Psychology* that

> the Cartesian [spiritual; metaphysical] soul can no longer exist in the face of our present-day physiological knowledge of the physical substratum of our mental life. And metaphysical monism in these two forms, which try to combine soul and body substance into one unity, would shut out the possibility of any knowledge of our physical life. Therefore, in contradistinction to this metaphysical concept of a mind-substance, we set up the concept of the actuality of mind.[174]

Though no objective basis exists for Wundt's belief and redefining of the soul, his accepted perspective enabled all human phenomena to be theoretically presupposed as scientific and somatic. As Wundt also correctly realized,

[173] Colbe Mazzarella, "Psychiatry's Little-known Role in Creating the Holocaust," *The New Boston Post* (February 9, 2018): https://newbostonpost .com/2018/02/09/psychiatrys-little-known-role-in-creating-the-holocaust/.

[174] Wilhelm Wundt, *Introduction to Psychology* reprint (London: George Allen and Unwin, LTD, 1912), 192.

accepting the traditional dualistic understanding of human nature was antithetical to his reductionistic approach to the human soul. Thus, Wundt introduced into psychology the idea of "mental science" or "actuality of mind":

> The name "mental science" has only the right to exist, so long as these departments of learning are based upon the facts of psychology — the mental science in the most general sense of the term. Now when would a historian, philologist, or jurist make use of any other means to understand some phenomenon or of any other arguments to prove some statement than those which spring from immediate facts of mental life? Why then should the standpoint of psychology be in absolute contradiction to the standpoints of its most nearly related science? [175]

But Wundt — as with biological psychologists and psychiatrists today — needed a physical explanation for mental processes and human phenomena experienced in the soul, and race psychology/eugenics/genetic theory seemed to him to be the best foundation on which to also explain the immaterial psyche.

Following his rationale, if it could be proven that the differences in which people think, believe, act, and feel — not just their ethnicity and physical features — are all caused by genetic variances or other biological etiologies, then "mental science" could be validated and the evolutionary process controlled through scientific observation and manipulation. But as Wundt also acknowledged, this new "psychology" largely depended upon society's acceptance of the social construct of race:

> Psychology must not only strive to become a useful basis for the other mental sciences, but it must also turn again

[175] Ibid., 194.

to the **historical science,** in order to obtain an understanding for the more highly developed mental processes. **Racial psychology is the clearest proof of this latter. It is one of the newest of the mental sciences and depends absolutely on these relations between psychology and the historical sciences. It is the first transition from psychology to the other mental sciences** [emphasis added].[176]

Wundt went to the extent of asserting that *Racial Psychology* or *Race Psychology* was the important anthropological connection between all other "mental sciences." Psychology, then, is the pursuit to prove and uphold at all cost Wundt's theory of mental sciences ("psychology") by explaining human nature and human phenomena within the restriction of humanistic and materialistic faith.

Wundt's biological concept of psychology — founded on the evolutionary theory of hereditary differences first promoted by men like Rush, Darwin, Galton, and Morel — would not only become the basis of Nazi eugenics, but its principal tenets are still widely held today. Prominent Harvard geneticist Richard Lewontin explains how the same perspective guides modern genetics:

> Genes make individuals and individuals make society, and so genes make society. If one society is different from another, that is because the genes of the individuals in one society are different from those in another. Different races are thought to be genetically different in how aggressive or creative or musical they are. Indeed, culture as a whole

---

[176] Ibid., 194-95.

is seen as made up of little bits and pieces of cultural brig-
a-brac [sic], what some sociobiologists call *culturgens*.[177]

Whether it is physical or metaphysical characteristics, differences within race psychology and subsequent so-called mental sciences are explained as differences in genetic constitution. Along this line of reasoning, if these clearly somatic differences between ethnic groups could be proven as hereditary and perceived as lower evolutionary quality, then surely other cultural, mental, social, and phenomenological variances could also be framed as genetic abnormalities.

As with contemporary views such as "culturgens," Wundt's concept of "cultural psychology" or *Völkerpsychologie* (*Völk*; people; culture; race)[178] relied on created social and descriptive constructs about mindsets, emotions, behaviors, and human phenomena. These constructs were said to "underpin the general development of human societies and the creation of joint intellectual results that are of generally recognised value."[179] Without the creation of descriptive constructs (e.g. schizophrenia), metaphysical differences (e.g., a person's beliefs, motives, or consciousness) cannot be explained within a scientific framework or attributed to biological causes such as the genes. Wundt's idea of mental sciences permitted the construct of mental hygiene and not just racial hygiene to be viewed as a legitimate study and a valid understanding

[177] Richard C. Lewontin, *Biology as Ideology: The Doctrine of DNA* (New York: HarperCollins Publishers, 1991), 14.

[178] Wundt, *An Introduction to Psychology*, 84.

[179] Wilhelm Wundt, *Völkerpsychologie*, 3rd ed. vol. 1 (Leipzig: W. Engelmann, 1911), 1.

of the psyche/soul (psychology). In truth, *Völkerpsychologie* was a formal seemingly scientific system that enabled social authorities to control ideas of anthropology and phenomenology.

This process also allowed biological and observable human phenomena (e.g., trauma) to be combined with metaphysical phenomena (e.g., stress) into constructs, which were then claimed as medical entities in and of themselves. The physical phenomena (e.g., somatic changes, experiences, and outward behavior) could be approached using the scientific method, but the metaphysical "symptoms" (e.g., cognition, motives, desires, and consciousness) could not. Thus, social and descriptive psychiatric constructs depended upon lumping observable somatic changes and behaviors into constructs with metaphysical mindsets and emotions which formed the core of the alleged categorical disorder. Wundt writes,

> Given its position between the natural sciences and the humanities, psychology really does have a great wealth of methodological tools. While, on the one hand, there are the experimental methods, on the other hand, objective works and products in cultural development [constructs] (*Objektivationen des menschlichen Geistes*) also offer up abundant material for comparative psychological analysis.[180]

The field of psychiatry provided the opportunity to frame human nature into descriptive constructs and at the same time to present them as best explained within a medical model. In order to sell this view, the field was split into two separate groups. On one hand, psychiatrists like Louis Alzheimer, who studied under Emil Kraepelin, discovered

---

[180] Wilhelm Wundt, *Logik* vol. 3, 4th ed. (1921), 51.

a legitimate neurological disease with observable biological markers on the brain. Thus, the field of neurology was established. On the other hand, however, psychiatrists invented constructs to describe all impairing and distressful aspects of human nature, which they theorized to also be sourced in biological causes but for which no biological cause had ever been found. Geneticist Richard Lewontin, neuroscientist Steven Rose, and clinical psychologist Leon Kamin explain,

> At an earlier time, psychiatrists and neurologists chose to distinguish between "organic" and "functional" nervous disorders. In organic disorders there was something obviously and demonstrably wrong with the brain. There might be a lesion, or the aftermath of a stroke with the brain. By contrast "functional" disorders—schizophrenia, the depressions, paranoia, and so on—were disorders of the mind, which could not be attributed to any obvious brain damage.[181]

In late 2019, chair of the *DSM-IV* and professor of psychiatry at Duke University, Allen Frances, acknowledged this clear division:

> Psychiatry and Neurology are no closer now than when [they] parted ways 200 years ago: 1) Neuroscience so far hasn't helped psych patients, 2) Patients in 2 specialties present different needs and challenges, 3) Neurologists and psychiatrists have different personality.[182]

---

[181] Lewontin, Rose, Kamin, *Not in Our Genes*, 173.

[182] Allen Frances, *Twitter* (November 18, 2019): https://twitter.com/AllenFrancesMD/status/1196419043885899777.

Editor-in-Chief Emeritus of the *Psychiatric Times*, Ronald Pies, agrees with Frances while still claiming that suggested mental disorder is sourced in the brain:

> We have other reasons to believe that the discourse of psychiatry differs fundamentally from that of neurology, notwithstanding the common substrate of these two disciplines (i.e., the human brain). The discourse of psychiatry, notwithstanding its burgeoning interest in neuroscience, remains grounded in human subjectivity and existential concerns. This applies not only to psychotherapy but to psychiatry as a whole. Psychiatry has always been, and essentially remains, a discourse of interlacing and multilayered meanings. Neurology is fundamentally a discourse of neuroanatomical and neurophysiological relationships.[183]

Michael Fitzgerald, writing for the Royal College of Psychiatrists, also comments on this division:

> The separation of neurology from psychiatry has led to a separation of the brain from the mind [dualism] – the physical from the mental – which has been unhelpful for both disciplines.[184]

Clinical psychologist Michael Arribas-Ayloon, sociologist Andrew Bartlett, and social genomic researcher Jamie Lewis also comment on psychiatrists' transformation of the theory of heredity into explaining the moral nature of humanity from a materialistic perspective:

> It was the alienists who promoted a new division between 'physical' (physiological) and 'moral' (psychological)

[183] Ronald Pies, "Why Psychiatry and Neurology Cannot Simply Merge," *The Journal of Neuropsychiatry and Clinical Neurosciences* vol. 17 (3) (August 2005): 305.

[184] Michael Fitzgerald, "Do Psychiatry and Neurology Need a Close Partnership or a merger?" *BJ Psychiatric Bulletin* vol. 39 (3) (June 2015): 106.

heredity. The obstacle they faced was developing a style of reasoning where a taxonomy of moral symptoms was dependent on the body's constitution, thus implicating hereditary transmission.[185]

Psychiatry, a unique "medical field" since the days of Benjamin Rush, has sought to explain the metaphysical mind ("consciousness"), emotions, phenomena, and observable behavior through a strictly biological and hereditary framework. Eugenics, as it would become known as, was the approach that first enabled psychiatry's transformation from psychiatrists being perceived as alienists or keepers to being viewed as scientists and physicians who insist upon the "medical treatment of the soul."[186]

The belief that some people deviate from the established social and descriptive norms is referred to as *individual* or *hereditary degeneration* — a critical concept to abnormal psychology and psychiatry that will be developed further in the next chapter. Without constructs about the soul/psyche/mind that frame mindsets, emotions, and moral behaviors as abnormalities, there could be no proposed abnormal genes or "dysfunction." Eugenics, then, is fully dependent upon cultural/race/volk/ descriptive psychology, with biological psychiatry now dominating the field.

If all of human nature — especially mindsets, emotions, and behaviors which are distressful or threaten individuals and

[185] Michael Arribas-Ayloon, Andrew Bartlett, and Jamie Lewis, *Psychiatric Genetics: From Hereditary Madness to Big Biology* (Vanderbilt, New York: Routledge, 2019), 23-24.

[186] Lieberman, *Shrinks*, 26-27.

society — can be described and categorized into medical constructs, then allegedly medicine and science and not morality determine both the standard of normal and abnormal (mentally healthy and mentally ill). Harvard geneticist Richard Lewontin conveys this supposition:

> A medical model of all human variation makes a medical model of normality, including social normality, and dictates that we preemptively or through subsequent corrective therapy bring into line anyone who deviates from that norm.[187]

Within such thinking, if depression is a medical issue, then happiness and hope are too. If distress is a disease, then peace of mind is a health concern . . . Psychiatry represents the most powerful race/cultural/volk/abnormal psychology that exists, since psychiatrists have "successfully" constructed a widely accepted medical system from which to identify, explain, and treat alleged degenerates or disordered. It is a moral system that continues to expand, as all of human nature can be described and categorized as acceptable or not.

Race psychology (eugenics) is a vital worldview to secularists, since it is an attempt to sustain the evolutionary theory, identifies and studies alleged degenerations from observable somatic differences, and bases all human nature upon theorized measurable, inherited, and biological causes. By creating and applying social and descriptive constructs, any physical or metaphysical variance or characteristic of human nature can be viewed as healthy or unhealthy. As established in the first two chapters, *race* is one of the premier historic examples of how social

---

[187] Lewontin, *Biology as Ideology*, 65.

constructs can be created through differences and how these social constructs have historically enabled social control:

> Within psychology, race is generally accepted as a social construct that is shaped by power structures and prevailing norms; yet historically, the field included an essentialist view of race interpreting racial differences as fixed.[188]

When a person or group of people assert or are granted authority to decide which human variances concerning the human soul/consciousness/psyche are theoretically normal and which are abnormal, he/she is applying what has historically been called "race/racial or cultural psychology." But for the last two hundred years, race has also been viewed as genetically fixed between groups of people.[189] These two tenets (unacceptable differences and hereditary fixity) are key to eugenics.

Wundt's greatest contributions to psychiatric eugenics were his transforming the metaphysical soul into a theoretical scientific field and introducing volk/cultural/descriptive psychology as a seemingly legitimate science based upon race psychology. These two contributions

---

[188] Kira Hudson Banks and Richard Harvey, "Race," Oxford Bibliographies," *Oxford Bibliographies* (March 29, 2017): DOI: 10.1093/OBO/9780199828340-0137.

[189] "Research suggests that there is more genetic variation within groups than across groups, leaving the argument that race is purely a scientific construct debunked. Therefore, examining how the field of psychology has and continues to navigate the construct of race, and how individuals perceive and experience race, discrimination, and racism, is of great importance." Kira Hudson Banks and Richard Harvey, "Race," Oxford Bibliographies," *Oxford Bibliographies* (March 29, 2017): DOI: 10.1093/OBO/9780199828340-0137.

would enable one of Wundt's students, Emil Kraepelin, to develop the currently accepted construct of mental disorders still widely held in America and much of the developed world.

Emil Kraepelin

Though likely not the most known disciple of Wilhelm Wundt, Emil Kraepelin (1856-1926) is arguably the most significant. One psychiatric journal recognizes Wundt's and Kraepelin's important relationship:

> Wilhelm Wundt, a well-known psychologist, philosopher and physiologist who met Kraepelin there, became a particularly influential person in Kraepelin's life. Kraepelin worked with enthusiasm in Wundt's laboratory in Leipzig where his dedication to scientific research became obvious. As a result of spending most of his time in the laboratory, he lost his position as a physician because of neglect of clinical work.[190]

Kraepelin is known today as the father of modern psychiatry, biopsychiatry, psychopharmacology, the statistical or quantitative genetic approach, and the current mental health and diagnostic system in America.[191] Historians of science at the Max Planck Institute of

---

[190] Andreas Ebert and Karl-Jürgen Bär, "Emil Kraepelin: A Pioneer of Scientific Understanding of Psychiatry and Psychopharmacology," *Indian Journal of Psychiatry* 52 (2) (Apr-Jun 2010): 191-92; http://www.ncbi.nlm.nih.gov/pmc/articles/PMC2927892/.

[191] See Daniel Berger, *Mental Illness: The Necessity for Faith and Authority* (Taylors, SC: Alethia International Publications, 2014), 62-70. See also Elliot Valenstein, *Blaming the Brain: The Truth about Drugs and Mental Health* (New York: Basic Books, 1998), 10.

Psychiatry, Matthias Weber and Eric Engstrom, report in the *Encyclopedia of Clinical Psychology*,

> Emil Kraepelin (1856-1926) was a German clinical psychiatrist best known for his division of endogenous psychoses into two forms: dementia praecox [schizophrenia] and manic-depressive illness [Bipolar I]. He became one of the most influential psychiatrists in the first quarter of the twentieth century. More recently he has inspired the work of so-called neo-Kraepelians, who have ascribed to him paradigmatic status as a new, post-Freudian "father" of clinical psychiatry, the *DSM*, and quantitative methodologies.[192]

Psychiatrist and historian Edward Shorter remarks of Kraepelin, "It is Kraepelin, not Freud, who is the central figure in the history of psychiatry,"[193] and most every educated psychiatrist agrees.[194]

But Kraepelin is not merely the most influential or central figure in the history of mental illness; he is also predominantly responsible for systematizing and popularizing the modern theory of psychiatric genetics:

> Psychiatric genetics emerges from the interplay and convergence of clinical, statistical, and laboratory styles of

[192] Eric J. Engstrom and Matthias M. Weber, "Emil Kraepelin (1856-1926)," *The Encyclopedia of Clinical Psychology* (2015): DOI: 10.1002/9781118625392.wb ecp090.

[193] Edward Shorter, *A History of Psychiatry: From the Era of the Asylum to the Age of the Prozac* (New York: John Wiley & Sons, 1997), 100.

[194] "Although Kraepelin was born [over] 160 years ago, his works have still been cited with a frequency, which makes him one of the most influential psychiatrists of all times" (Juri Allik and Erki Tammiksaar, "Who was Emil Kraepelin and Why do we Remember Him 160 Years Later?" *TRAMES*, 20 [4] [2016]: 317; DOI: 10.3176/tr.2016.4.01).

reasoning in the early twentieth century when Emil Kraepelin became the director of the German Institute for Psychiatric Research in Munich. The Institute itself was a clinic, hospital and laboratory, which established the conditions for Ernst Rüdin to conduct the first family study of schizophrenia in 1916.[195]

Historian of psychiatry Richard Noll comments on how influential Kraepelin's creation of "dementia praecox" — what is today referred to as *schizophrenia* — was to the psychiatric eugenics/genetics movement:

> Dementia praecox had been a diagnosis of hopelessness from its creation . . . . by World War I Kraepelin's term, if not his actual diagnostic criteria or prognostic fatalism, had gained general acceptance, and dementia praecox was identified as the primary mental health problem to be addressed in the asylum practices of alienists, in laboratory research in psychiatry, in the eugenics movement, in the mental hygiene movement, and in the courts through its infiltration into medical jurisprudence.[196]

One of the most significant contributions Kraepelin made to the genetic theory is his creation of a formal and statistical classification and diagnostic system of alleged degenerations or abnormalities. Kraepelin's system was so widely accepted that it became the basis for both the American Psychiatric Association's *Diagnostic and Statistical Manual (DSM)*[197] and the World Health Organization's

[195] Arribas-Ayloon, Bartlett, and Lewis, *Psychiatric Genetics*, 7.

[196] Richard Noll, *American Madness: The Rise and Fall of Dementia Praecox* (Harvard University Press, 2011), 3-4.

[197] Walter Coville, Timothy Costello, and Fabian Rouke, *Abnormal Psychology: Mental Illness Types, Causes, and Treatment* (New York: Barnes and Noble, 1960), 8-9.

International Classification of Diseases (ICD).[198] Molecular
psychiatrist Jaak Panksepp submits,

> Kraepelin's original taxonomy described the outlines of
> major psychiatric categories still accepted today. His
> textbooks had clear descriptions of syndromes that we
> now recognize as schizophrenia, various phobias,
> depression, and anxiety disorders with their links to
> obsessions and compulsions. The modern standard
> classification schemes, ever since the *DSM*-1 of 1951, have
> clearly followed the Kraepelinian outline.[199]

As many historians note, Kraepelin's statistical approach
was not separate from the eugenic theory:

> Kraepelin was an advocate for eugenics, as he believed
> certain groups of people were genetically predisposed to
> mental disorders . . . . Although few people are aware of
> his influence, Kraepelin's work is at the foundation of all
> diagnostic measures used in psychology today, including
> the American Psychiatric Association's Diagnostic and
> Statistical Manual of Mental Disorders (*DSM*) and the
> World Health Organization's International Classification
> of Diseases (*ICD*). Kraepelin also pioneered research in
> psychopharmacology [emphasis added].[200]

Though Kraepelin is known for his brain dysfunction
theory, his psychopharmacology theory, and his genetic
and neurological theory of mental illness, his most
influential contributions to psychiatry were to create

---

[198] Allen Frances, *Saving Normal: An Insider's Revolt against Diagnosis, DSM-5, Big Pharma, and the Medicalization of Ordinary Life* (New York: HarperCollins, 2013), 59. See also, Shorter, *History of Psychiatry*, 106.

[199] Jaak Panksepp, ed., *Textbook of Biological Psychiatry* (New York: John Wiley and Sons, 2004), 17.

[200] "Emil Kraepelin (1856-1926)," http://www.goodtherapy.org/famous-psychologists/emil-kraepelin.html.

disease entities (psychiatric constructs) out of normal but impairing mental struggles, to attribute them to genetic or hereditary causes, and to provide a seemingly reliable statistical system from which to determine/diagnose these suggested degenerates.

Without proposing disease entities to explain undesirable or disturbing human phenomena, there would likely be no societal acceptance of suggested degenerates based upon common mindsets, emotions, and behaviors, and without degenerates, there would be no need for psychiatrists or the study of abnormal psychology. Beyond this fact, however, is the reality that without the creation of a defective or unhealthy class of people and proposed physical causes for individuals' degeneracy, eugenics does not exist. Whereas Wundt had framed abnormal and cultural/social/volk psychologies within a scientific paradigm, Kraepelin had created the specific social and descriptive constructs and subsequent diagnostic system to apply and seemingly legitimize these beliefs as scientific.

Prior to Kraepelin, there existed no standardized apparatus or system that was either widely accepted among psychiatrists or which seemed to validate the eugenics/ hereditary theory of mental illness as empirically sound. Arribas-Ayloon, Bartlett, and Lewis explicate,

> Before the nineteenth century, there was no arrangement for thinking that human heredity was a biological concept with explanatory force. Medical discourse was preoccupied with hereditary as a description of a family trait or a disease transmitted from one generation to another. **To acquire the status of a scientific entity, the concept of 'heredity' required the stabilization of a domain of production, a domain that had special relevance for psychiatry. For heredity to become a self-**

sufficient cause of mental illness, it required a system of relations that existed in and around the asylum apparatus. Indeed, Foucault (2008) observes that psychiatric power comes to establish itself in a mode of questioning about family history.[201]

The premise of eugenics is that all of human nature is caused by genetic material (even if there is no biological markers or valid pathology) and that undesirable qualities of human nature represent diseases/disorders/abnormalities. It is primarily upon Kraepelin's creation of a system of diseases—his diagnostic and statistical system—that many people still view themselves as abnormal, disordered, or as part of the "unhealthy class":

> The concepts embodied in Kraepelin's classification system did not originate with him, but he was the first to synthesize them into a workable model that could be used to diagnose and treat mental patients. His classification was particularly influential during the early 20th century.[202]

In addition to the construct of race, Kraepelin added the construct of the metaphysical soul (and its metaphysical phenomena) as a medically approachable and biological organ within a formal system of selection. Under Kraepelin's theory, "mental hygiene" became an accepted medical concern in Germany. All those who were deemed mentally and socially inferior—not just racially inferior—could be viewed within the eugenics paradigm.

---

[201] Arribas-Ayloon, Bartlett, and Lewis, *Psychiatric Genetics*, 19.

[202] Editors, "Emil Kraepelin: German Psychiatrist," *Encyclopedia Britannica* (July 20, 1998): https://www.britannica.com/biography/Emil-Kraepelin.

Indeed, Kraepelin had created a system of mental abnormalities within a medical setting and seemingly within a scientific framework; he had taken eugenics and formalized it into the field of psychiatric genetics and provided psychiatry with the ability to subjectively create categories of abnormal.

Coupled with the fact that "Germany became the world leader in psychiatry during the nineteenth century,"[203] Kraepelinianism became known and eventually accepted worldwide. Kraepelin's social construct and system of selection (diagnoses) had offered psychiatrists the potential power over society to theoretically determine those who were normal and those who were disordered. One abnormal textbook states,

> Among Wundt's students was the German researcher Emil Kraepelin (1856-1926), who eventually established his own psychological laboratory, **devoted primarily to the study of psychopathology, or abnormal psychology**. . . . In all, experimental abnormal psychology made substantial strides in the first two decades of the century. Thereafter, it fell behind somewhat, as a result of the rising popularity of psychodynamic theory [Freudianism], which, at least in its early years, did not lend itself to experimental study. But in the 1950s the experimental branch of abnormal psychology [Kraepelinian theory] once again become influential and productive, and it has remained so, providing some of the most important current findings in the field.[204]

Abnormal psychology is actually the assertion and study of perceived mental, emotional, and behavioral degeneration.

[203] Shorter, *A History of Psychiatry*, 35.

[204] Alloy, Acocella, & Bootzin, *Abnormal Psychology*, 19.

The authors of *Abnormal Psychology: Current Perspectives* explain this "biogenic viewpoint":

> It was Kraepelin, the founder of experimental abnormal psychology, who first placed the medical model in the forefront of European psychiatric theory. In his *Textbook of Psychiatry* (1883/1923), Kraepelin not only argued for the central role of brain pathology in mental disturbance but furnished psychiatry with its first comprehensive classification system, based on the biogenic viewpoint. He claimed that mental illness, like physical illness, could be classified into separate pathologies, each of which had a different organic cause and could be recognized by a distinct cluster of symptoms, called a syndrome.[205]

Like valid biological diseases, metaphysical human struggles could not only be counted as diseases within the biogenic worldview, but also as disorders that were genetically/hereditarily caused. One author in the *Journal of Medical History* records when eugenics under the leadership of Emil Kraepelin in pre-Nazi Germany gained its "scientific" platform:

> The founding of the German Research Institute for Psychiatry and its Genealogic-Demographic Department (Genealogisch-Demographische Abteilung; GDA) in 1918 gave the world the first institutional platform for the field of psychiatric genetics. The years between the two World Wars saw the GDA grow in importance with much international respect.[206]

---

[205] Ibid., 20.

[206] A. Cottebrune, "On the Track of "Franz Josef Kallmann (1897-1965) and the Transfer of Psychiatric-Genetic Scientific Concept from National Socialist Germany to the U.S.A." *Medizinehistorisches Journal [Journal of Medical History]*, Vol 44 (3-4) (2009), 296.

In 1924, The Kaiser Wilhelm Institute of Psychiatry and the GDA would be combined under the leadership of Kraepelin's premier disciple, Ernst Rüdin:

> The Kaiser-Wilhelm Institute of Psychiatry in Munich had been established in 1917 as the German Institute for Psychiatric Research by the eminent psychiatrist, Prof. Emil Kraepelin. A major benefactor of the Munich institute was the American-born Jewish philanthropist, and at one time a patient of Kraepelin's, James Loeb. **The Munich psychiatric institute became the first and foremost psychiatric research institute in the world.** In 1924 the institute joined with the Kaiser-Wilhelm research organization [under the direction of Ernst Rüdin]. The building of the new institute, which opened in 1928, was the first major construction project of the KWG to be financed by a grant from the medical division of the Rockefeller Foundation.[207]

German psychiatry, the worldwide leader in eugenics under Ernst Rüdin, continued to be heavily funded by American philanthropists:

> Underlying the close working relationship between America and Germany was the extensive financial support of American Foundations for the establishment of eugenic research in Germany. The main supporter was the Rockefeller Foundation in New York. It financed the research of German racial hygienist Agnes Bluhm on hereditary and alcoholism in early 1920 [under Kraepelin's guidance]. . . . The Rockefeller Foundation played the central role in establishing and sponsoring major eugenic institutes in Germany, including the Kaiser Wilhelm Institute of Psychiatry and the Kaiser Wilhelm Institute for Anthropology, Eugenics, and Human Heredity. In 1918, German psychiatrist Emil Kraepelin

---

[207] William E. Seidelman, *Science and Inhumanity: The Kaiser-Wilhelm/Max Planck Society revised* (2001), 2-3; https://www.doew.at/cms/download/b1c46/en_seidelman_max_planck_society.pdf.

founded the institute for Psychiatry in Munich, which was taken over by the Kaiser Wilhelm Society in 1924. The Department for Genealogy and Demography was headed by Ernst Rüdin, later director of the Institute for Psychiatry. This department — the core of the Institute — concentrated on locating the genetic and neurological basis of traits such as criminal propensity and mental disease.[208]

Eugenics had found a global leader in Kraepelin and thereafter Rüdin, a global center in Germany, and financial support from wealthy American donors.

Kraepelin's Degenerates

Kraepelin is likely best known for his suggested degenerate categories of *Schizophrenia* (premature dementia) and *Bipolar* (affective psychosis). But he also emphasized and included in his diagnostic system of degeneracy one of the first proposed hereditary disorders attributed to Benjamin Rush, "alcoholism":

> The first anti-alcohol study, however, was published by Kraepelin only at the end of the 19th century (Kraepelin 1899). Since the beginning of the 20th century, his regular studies on the damage of alcohol on the mental health of a person appeared, several of them were published in the proceedings of the Basel temperance society founded by Bunge (Kraepelin 1987: 234–238). As a result, these two

---

[208] Stefan Kuhl, *The Nazi Connection: Eugenics, American Racism, and German National Socialism* (New York: Oxford University Press, 1994), 20.

abstainers began to communicate with each other (Kraepelin 1987: 71).[209]

Kraepelin also theorized about other "mental diseases" such as homosexuality[210] — an alleged form of degeneracy that remained in the *DSM-II* until the LGBT movement insisted that the American Psychiatric Association (APA) cease categorizing them as abnormal/disordered in the *DSM-III*.[211]

In addition to creating and heavily influencing the *DSM* disorders still used today, there exists other darker proposed degeneracies that are far too often excluded in Kraepelin's legacy. Sadly, the psychiatric notion that the Jews, Gypsies, Blacks, other minorities, and any opponents of German ideologies were degenerates/"mentally ill" began its wide acceptance with Emil Kraepelin. Psychiatrists Andreas Ebert and Karl-Jürgen Bär disclose this selectivity in one psychiatric journal:

> One of the most problematical issues about Kraepelin is his generalization of psychiatric findings to social and political contexts. For example, socialists and opponents of World War I were judged to be mentally ill by him. **He**

[209] Juri Allik and Erki Tammiksaar, "Who was Emil Kraepelin and Why do we Remember Him 160 Years Later?" *TRAMES*, 20 (4) (2016): 322: DOI: 10.3176/tr.2016.4.01.

[210] Florian Mildenberger, "Kraepelin and the 'Urnings': Male Homosexuality in Psychiatric Discourse," *The History of Psychiatry* vol. 18 (3) (September 1, 2007): https://doi.org/10.1177%2F0957154X07079796.

[211] Lloyd L. Sederer and Jack Drescher in accordance with Columbia University Psychiatry, "The 'Checkered' History of Psychiatry's Views on Homosexuality," *Medscape Psychiatry* (December 3, 2019): https://www.medscape.com/viewarticle/921143?nlid=132938_424&src=WNL_mdplsfeat_19 1210_mscpedit_psyc&uac=264124BV&spon=12&impID=2199579&faf=1.

also theorized about frequent genetic predispositions for psychiatric disorders in Jews [emphasis added].[212]

Furthermore, Kraepelin himself clearly pronounced and promoted his adherence to race psychology:

> I also regarded the growing danger that Judaism posed to the future of our folk as a matter of great concern. On a number of occasions, the Semitic race has demonstrated a tendency to forge ahead for the sake of superficial advantage rather than for inner gratification . . . . I noted with concern that the influence wielded by Jews in the science far outweighed the proportion they represent of the population, this was disastrous, because once again the ambition for success and recognition took precedence over the search for truth and knowledge. Although I entertained personal relations with numerous Jews, and held some in great esteem, I could only regard them as the salt of the earth, which perhaps was necessary for the development of our own abilities. Any dominant influence of the Jewish spirit on German science, such as sadly came to be increasingly evident, seemed to me to pose a very grave danger indeed . . . .[213]

In Kraepelin's mind, both racial and mental hygiene were psychiatric approaches that would address these theorized degenerates. Professors of psychiatry Burkhart Bruckner and Julian Schwarz reveal that

[212] Andreas Ebert and Karl-Jürgen Bär, "Emil Kraepelin: A Pioneer of Scientific Understanding of Psychiatry and Psychopharmacology," *Indian Journal of Psychiatry* 52, no. 2 (Apr-Jun 2010): 191-92; http://www.ncbi.nlm.nih.gov/pmc/articles/PMC2927892/.

[213] Emil Kraepelin translated by Eric J. Engstrom, Wolfgang Burgmair, and Matthias M. Weber, "Emil Kraepelin's 'Self-Assessment': clinical autography in historical context," *History of Psychiatry*, 13 (49) (2002): 089–098; https://doi.org/10.1177/0957154X0201304905.

Kraepelin held explicitly ethno-nationalist (so-called "völkisch") views . . . . After the year 1900, Kraepelin increasingly addressed the issue of population policy. Just like Morel before him, he claimed that psychiatric institutions should serve eugenic purposes in preventing "numerous diseased persons from reproducing their worrying properties," as stated in a lecture on the psychiatric tasks of the state (*Die psychiatrischen Aufgaben des Staates*, 1900: 17). In the 1909 edition of his textbook, he warned against a "serious threat to our race" due to the "struggle for existence" in the urbanized [sic] industrial society with its "potential impact on the human breed" "if the unquestionable effects of these conditions are reflected in the hereditary properties of large sections of the population" (1909: 198 ff) . . . . Kraepelin's political views became more radical during WWI, probably in reaction to the enormous losses of German soldiers and the resulting "völkisch" fears.[214]

In an article published in the *American Journal of Psychiatry*, Drs. Rael Strous and Annette and Lewis Opler write,

Kraepelin was an ardent proponent of eugenics and of "degeneration theory," which propagated that the Aryan race was degenerating into higher rates of mental illness and other conditions due to various undesirables in its midst. In a 1919 paper titled "Psychiatric Observations on Contemporary Issues," Kraepelin proclaimed that "dreamers, poets, swindlers and Jews" possess "distinctly hysterical traits" and fall outside the bounds of normality, adding that Jews exhibit "frequent psychopathic disposition." These tendencies, he noted, are most importantly accompanied by "their harping criticism, their rhetorical and theatrical abilities, and their doggedness and determination." Kraepelin also stated that "the preponderant influence of the Jewish spirit on

[214] Burkhart Bruckner and Julian Schwarz, "Emil Kraepelin (1856-1926)," *Biographical Archive of Psychiatry* (2015): https://www.researchgate.net/publication/284045219_Biographical_entry_-_Emil_Kraepelin_1856-1926.

German science, as is unfortunately wielded ever more intensely, appeared to me to be a serious danger."[215]

Without question, it was Kraepelin who was the principle force in developing the philosophical seeds of psychiatric eugenic thought in pre-Nazi Germany. The article continues on to reveal that it was Kraepelin's theory/phenomenology that ushered in eugenic euthanasia:

> Kraepelin was clearly guilty of profound boundary violations, allowing his clinical work and academic pursuits to be influenced by a right-wing socio-political agenda—**an agenda that led psychiatrists, for the first time, to exterminate their patients during the Nazi era . . . . Kraepelin contributed fundamentally to the ideological basis of racial hygiene in Germany. Gaupp proclaimed that Kraepelin's work "comprised nothing less than the foundation of all Nazi racial hygiene laws." Kraepelin is neither a generative forefather nor a great icon, as history looks at his views. Kraepelin may be the father of psychiatric eugenics;** however, we dispute declaring him the forefather of a field dedicated to the ethical caring and management of long-suffering individuals striving to recover and reclaim meaningful roles and functions [emphasis added].[216]

The true "Father of Nazi Eugenics" was not Kraepelin's premiere disciple, Ernst Rüdin, as many historians have asserted. Rather, the true author of Nazi Eugenics was the prejudiced psychiatrist, Emil Kraepelin, who used Rüdin, Alfred Hoche, and Paul Nitsche — among many other psychiatrists and physicians — to carry on his ideology and

---

[215] Rael D. Strous, Annette A Opler, and Lewis A. Opler, "Reflections on 'Emil Kraepelin: Icon and Reality,'" *American Journal of Psychiatry* 173 (3) (March 2016), 301.

[216] Ibid.

to dominate German medicine and psychiatry globally thereafter:

> The historical or real Kraepelin is not the icon created by the neo-Kraepelinians. While it is important to know about Kraepelin's work in experimental psychology, we question why there is [typically] no mention of Kraepelin's work promoting eugenics, racism, and anti-Semitism. Kraepelin died in 1926, before the rise to power of the Third Reich, but he mentored three prominent Nazi psychiatrists: Robert Gaupp (1870–1953), Paul Nitsche (1876- 1948), and Ernst Rüdin (1874–1952). Gaupp echoed the thoughts of Kraepelin when he wrote that he felt wrong caring for "his patients, when people of 'full value' were starving to death in the world outside." Nitsche was the director of the Sonnenstein hospital where tens of thousands of mentally ill were killed under the guise of mercy killing (euthanasia), and he later headed the entire T4 euthanasia program. Rüdin, president of the Society of German Neurologists and Psychiatrists, was author of the 1933 "Law for the Prevention of Hereditarily Diseased Offspring" and was referred to as the "Reichsführer for Sterilization [emphasis added]."[217]

Psychologist Philip Yanos attests to the influence upon Germany that Kraepelin's psychiatric eugenics ideology had:

> Psychology and psychiatry also contributed to the actions of the eugenic movement with regard to mental illness. In the early 20th century, German psychiatrist Emil Kraepelin revolutionized psychiatry by drawing a distinction between the two main forms of what had been until then simply called insanity-manic-depressive psychosis (now called bipolar I disorder) and dementia praecox (now called schizophrenia). Although he died before the beginning of the Third Reich, Kraepelin's assertion that dementia praecox had an inevitably hopeless and

[217] Ibid., 300.

deteriorating course provided cover for the Nazi regime's decision to enact their "euthanasia" program.[218]

Kraepelin was a prominent character in constructing the idea of mental illness, in creating constructs of perceived abnormalities which enable the eugenic theory, and in authoring the statistical approach and philosophical blueprint of eugenics that brought about the Holocaust. As troubling as these facts are, most of today's "mental health systems" in developed countries are "Kraepelinian." In reality, Kraepelin is the true father of Nazi eugenics/genetics, though his chosen successor, Ernst Rüdin, would earn the historic title by applying Kraepelin's genetic theory.

Ernst Rüdin

As with Wundt, Kraepelin passed on his genetic theory of mental illness to his adherents. One of Kraepelin's premiere disciples, the individual who was hired by Kraepelin to research and to advance Wundt's and Kraepelin's genetic theory of mental illness at the *Deutsche Forschungsanstalt für Psychiatrie* (DFA), and who would become known in history as the father of Nazi Eugenics was Ernst Rüdin (1874-1952). Head of the history archive at the German Max Planck Institute of Psychiatry, Matthias Weber, remarks,

> The "Deutsche Forschungsanstalt für Psychiatrie" (DFA) in Munich, one of the most important research institutes

---

[218] Philip Yanos, "The Long Shadow of the Eugenics Movement: Its Influence Persists," *Psychology Today Online* (June 02, 2018): https://www.psychologytoday.com/us/blog/written/201806/the-long-shadow-the-eugenics-movement.

in the field of theoretical and clinical psychiatry was founded in 1917 by Emil Kraepelin. Its financial existence between the World Wars was guaranteed by enormous donations from the Jewish American James Loeb. The scientific work done by Walther Spielmeyer (neuropathology), Felix Plaut (serology), Kurt Schneider (clinical psychiatry) and Ernst Rüdin (psychiatric genetics) earned the DFA the reputation as an international center for psychiatry and neurology [emphasis added].[219]

Professor of psychiatry at the University of Toronto, William Seidelman also discusses the system which Kraepelin established and in which Rüdin would become instrumental:

> Three of its institutes that were beneficiaries of the Rockefeller Foundation [Psychiatry (Munich); Brain Research (Berlin-Buch); Anthropology, Genetics, Eugenics (Berlin-Dahlem)] played an important role in the development, implementation and exploitation of the racial programs of the Third Reich including murderous experiments and the exploitation of the dead. Kaiser-Wilhelm scientists joined with the Nazi state in pursuit of the goal of improving the people's health (Volksgesundheit), the major emphasis being on eugenic and racial purification . . . . Rüdin joined Kraepelin when he moved from Heidelberg to Munich in 1903. In 1909 Rüdin succeeded Alzheimer as senior physician at the Munich psychiatric hospital. In Munich, Rüdin led the genealogical/Demographic research department of the Kraepelin Institute. The focus of Rüdin's research was on the inheritance of psychiatric disorders.[220]

---

[219] Matthias M. Weber, "A Research Institute for Psychiatry . . . . The development of the German Research Institution of Psychiatry in Munich between 1917 and 1945," *Sudhoffs Archive* 75 (1) (February 1991): 74.

[220] Seidelman, *Science and Inhumanity*, pdf.

The three institutions which played important roles in the German racial and mental hygiene movement paralleled the three tenets of Kraepelin's theory of mental illness (brain dysfunction, genetics, psychopharmacology), with Rüdin acting as the driving force behind the three research centers. Historians Jay Joseph and Norbert Wetzel explain,

> Ernst Rüdin (1874–1952) was the founder of psychiatric genetics and was also a founder of the German racial hygiene movement . . . . **Rüdin developed the psychiatric genetics field in the early twentieth century. During that period he was working with the founder of modern psychiatry Emil Kraepelin**, first in Heidelberg, and then following Kraepelin to Munich in 1907 (Weber, 1996). **Rüdin and his racial hygienicist [sic] colleagues were tireless advocates of programs aimed against the carriers of a presumed "hereditary taint" (erbliche Belastung) well before the Nazi seizure of power in 1933.** Lacking any family or twin studies, **Rüdin called for the eugenic sterilization of chronic alcoholics as early as 1903, which "marked the beginning of a life-long crusade for sterilization of the degenerate"** (Weindling, 1989, p. 186) [emphasis added].[221]

The "alcoholic," which Benjamin Rush had proposed over a century before and about which Kraepelin had spent a great deal of time studying and theorizing, would begin Rüdin's life-long mission to sterilize all people who fit into Kraepelin's psychiatric system of degenerates. Seidelman notes that

> in 1928 Rüdin became director of a "greatly expanded" genealogical department of what had become the Kaiser-Wilhelm Institute of Psychiatry. **In 1931 he ascended to the leadership of the world's preeminent psychiatric**

---

[221] Jay Joseph and Norbert A. Wetzel, "Ernst Rüdin : Hitler's Racial Hygiene Mastermind," *Journal of the History of Biology* vol. 46 (1) (February 2013): 1-2; https://doi.org/10.1007/s10739-012-9344-6.

research institute. Rüdin built on Kraepelin's relationship with the Rockefeller Foundation and James Loeb [emphasis added].[222]

Rüdin was carefully selected by Kraepelin to carry out genetic studies, to prove Kraepelin's theory of mental illness, and to eventually establish and apply Kraepelin's diagnostic system of disorders (alleged degenerates) — a control mechanism which enabled eugenics to be practically applied in Germany:

> Ernst Rüdin (1874-1952) was one of the major representatives of German psychiatry, genetics, and eugenics in the first half of the twentieth century. Born in Switzerland, he was influenced early on by his brother-in-law Alfred Ploetz, who propagated the ideas of social Darwinism and "racial hygiene" in Germany after 1890. **Rüdin began his career in psychiatry at Emil Kraepelin's clinic in Munich, where he developed the concept of "empirical genetic prognosis" of mental disorders.** He published his first results on the genetics of schizophrenia in 1916. From 1917-1945 Rüdin was director of the Genealogical-Demographic Department at the German Institute for Psychiatric Research, which Kraepelin had founded [emphasis added].[223]

Other historians submit that

> Emil Kraepelin is the principal figure of this new alignment who stabilizes psychiatric nosology and sets the foundations for a science of heredity. When Kraepelin famously split psychosis into its affective and non-affective features, **Rüdin selected the stable clinical features of 'schizophrenia' as the object of his family study** . . . All the methodological innovations of Rüdin's study belong to a network of production that formed

[222] Seidelman, *Science and Inhumanity,* pdf.

[223] Weber, "Ernst Rüdin, 1874-1952," 323-31:

around Kraepelin's 'research institute not unlike the
methodological diversity of contemporary
'multidisciplinary' research centers, the Munich Institute
assembled clinical, statistical and laboratory styles of
reasoning around large patient populations [emphasis
added].[224]

The rationale and applications of Ernst Rüdin cannot be
understood properly apart from Emil Kraepelin's genetic
mental hygiene paradigm. Moreover, the "science of
heredity risk" and "genetic risk scores" cannot be
considered without its eugenic foundation.

Rüdin's Degenerates

As with all eugenicists, Rüdin needed degenerates. If
disordered people do not exist, then neither does eugenics,
and since Kraepelin's system was now academically and
financially backed and soon to be government supported,
Rüdin was well positioned to make an impact on his
society. What Rüdin needed for experimentation was live
souls, bodies, and body parts, and in theory, these
necessities must be supplied by categorical degenerates.

Rüdin spoke often of identifying, preventing, and
eventually eliminating those he viewed as genetically
tainted. In 1933, he stated,

> Every day we recognize more clearly that many of these
> cases though superficially regarded as normal show some
> minor **deviation from normality** by which the type may
> be recognized. **The chief task of scientific geneticists co-
> operating with clinicians in the near future is the
> discovery of these symptomatic deviations with the**

[224] Arribas-Ayloon, Bartlett, and Lewis, *Psychiatric Genetics*, 11.

object of facilitating the detection of the carrier. This still leaves a considerable group of persons who show no abnormality suggestive of their being carriers, but who, as relatives of insane patients, are, nevertheless, suspect in regard to the normality of their offspring [emphasis added].[225]

Rüdin also wrote,

> My experience has led me to the conclusion that systematic and careful propaganda should be undertaken where sterilization is advisable. Such propaganda should, of course, be gradual and should be directed in the first instance at the medical directors in institutions and schools, medical officers of health, and finally at private practitioners . . . . Where sterilization would become operative amongst the most degenerate group in the community.[226]

It was through Rüdin's inherited and propagated psychiatric vision that other medical directors (e.g., neurologists, pediatricians, gynecologists, etc.) embraced eugenics. Rüdin was not merely governing German psychiatry; he was deliberately gaining control of all German medicine and convincing physicians to accept Kraepelin's psychiatric genetic theory. As historian Stefan Kuhl notes, "Rüdin was the leading figure in eugenics across all medical fields — 'the chairman of the IFEO

---

[225] Ernst Rüdin, "Eugenic Sterilization: An Urgent Need" *Birth Control Review* (April 1933): 102; https://lifedynamics.com/app/uploads/2015/09/1933-04-April.pdf. https://newbostonpost.com/2018/02/09/psychiatrys-little-known-role-in-creating-the-holocaust/.

[226] Ibid.

[International Federation of Eugenic Organizations] committee on race psychiatry.'"[227]

Despite the fact that many before him, including Benjamin Rush, Wilhelm Wundt, and Emil Kraepelin, proposed and experimented to prove the psychiatric genetic theory of mental illness, it was Rüdin who became known as the historic Father:

> **Ernst Rüdin (1874–1952) has been credited as the originator of modern psychiatric human genetics** on the basis of his research aiming to establish inheritance estimates, that is the risk of a relative developing the same disease as the index patient, which he termed the *"empirische Erbprognose"* ("empirical heredity prognosis") [emphasis added].[228]

Furthermore, it was Rüdin's rule over German medicine during the Nazi era that granted him the historic designation as "the Father of Nazi Eugenics." Rüdin's research helped to solidify his place in history, as the Holocaust was arguably the largest psychiatric experiment ever recorded. It was also the realization of Kraepelin's original desire to apply his genetic theory of mental illness:

> Rüdin, who acknowledged the "eminent" Kraepelin as his teacher and collaborator, wrote that "thanks to Hitler, has

---

[227] Stefan Kuhl, *The Nazi Connection: Eugenics, American Racism, and German National Socialism* (New York: Oxford University Press, 1994), 27-28.

[228] Gundula Kösters, Holger Steinberg, Kenneth Clifford Kirkby, Hubertus Himmerich' "Ernst Rüdin's Unpublished 19922-1925 Study "Inheritance of Manic-Depressive Insanity": Genetic Research Findings Subordinated to Eugenic Ideology," *PLOS Genetics* (November 6, 2015): https://journals.plos.org/plosgenetics/article?id=10.1371/journal.pgen.1005524.

our 30-year-long dream of translating racial hygiene into action finally become a reality."[229]

As John Read and Jeffrey Mason point out, sterilization was among some of Kraepelin's endorsed treatments, which Rüdin would eventually apply:

> The inventors of schizophrenia paved the way. In 1913, Kraepelin, writing about "dementia praecox," had stated "Lomer has, it is true, proposed as a heroic profilactic measure bilateral castration as early as possible, but scarcely anyone will be found who will have the courage to follow him."[230]

Rüdin's twin studies, though now discredited, are likely the most famous psychiatric research conducted to prove a genetic basis for Kraepelin's idea of schizophrenia (dementia praecox), and these studies remain alleged evidence claimed to validate modern psychiatric genetics. For example, in the book *Psychiatric Genetics, a Primer for Clinical and Basic Scientists*, the International Society of Psychiatric Genetics suggests that

> the twin family design is one of the most powerful study designs in genetic epidemiology because it yields estimates of heritability, but also permits evaluation of mutigenerational patterns of expression of genetic and environmental risk factors.[231]

---

[229] Strous, Opler, & Opler, "Reflections on 'Emil Kraepelin," 300.

[230] Emil Kraepelin, quoted by John Read and Jeffrey Masson, *Models of Madness: Psychological, Social, and Biological Approaches* edited by John Read, Richard Bentall, and Loren Mosher (Philadelphia: Routledge, 2004), 35.

[231] Alison K. Merikangas and Kathleen R. Merikangas, *Psychiatric Genetics: A Primer for Clinicians and Basic Scientists* edited by Thomas G. Schulze and Francis J. McMahon (New York: Oxford University Press, 2018), 11.

The Holocaust was not primarily a politics-driven exercise, but a psychiatric experiment to prove Kraepelinianism and to attempt dealing with Kraepelin's suggested degenerates.

Under the administration of Rüdin, the perceived disordered were not simply categorized within Kraepelin's system, they were experimented on, "treated," sterilized, and then eventually exterminated. People were euthanized in order to both supply researchers with body parts[232] as well as to allegedly preserve the "good stock" by eliminating the perceived bad human genomes. Both negative and positive eugenics motivated virtually all that occurred in the Holocaust. German historian at the Max Plank Institute, Mathias Weber, records:

> After a short interruption from 1925-1928, Rüdin returned to Munich and enlarged the department. After 1933 the National Socialist government and party endorsed Rüdin's work by supplying financial and manpower support. **Nazi health policy required a scientific basis to justify its actions, and Rüdin's ideas corresponded partially with this kind of thinking. In 1934 he prepared the official commentary on the "Law for the Prevention of Genetically Diseased Offspring."** The connections of Rüdin's department to National Socialism can be understood as one of the main reasons for the critical attitude towards psychiatric genetics in Germany after 1945.[233]

Other historians elaborate on how Rüdin was the primary author of Nazi law and not merely one of Hitler's "yes men." The laws put in place were written by the most

---

[232] Seidelman, *Science and Inhumanity*, pdf.

[233] Weber, "Ernst Rüdin, 1874-1952," 323-31.

powerful psychiatrist in Germany in accordance with his ardent belief in Kraepelinian eugenics:

> **The 1933 Sterilization Law established diagnostic categories for enforced sterilization. Two of the categories were for psychiatric conditions first characterized by Kraepelin and investigated by Rüdin, namely schizophrenia and manic-depressive disorder.** An estimated 400,000 German citizens qualified for sterilization under the law. This goal was achieved. The Kaiser Wilhelm Institute of Psychiatry under Rüdin became a major academic eugenic center during the Hitler period. It was to the psychiatric institute that doctors and the courts turned for an "expert" opinion on eugenic matters. It can be assumed that Rüdin, as an architect of the sterilization law, did not support appeals against sterilizations ordered by the court. Rüdin was such an avid proponent of eugenic sterilization that his colleagues nicknamed him "Reichsfuhrer for Sterilization" [emphasis added].[234]

It is not that Rüdin just permitted or went along with the practice of sterilization and euthanasia. Rather, he ensured their implementation:

> Throughout his long career he played a major role in promoting eugenic ideas and policies in Germany, including helping formulate the 1933 Nazi eugenic sterilization law and other governmental policies directed against the alleged carriers of genetic defects. In the 1940s Rüdin supported the killing of children and mental patients under a Nazi program euphemistically called "Euthanasia."[235]

[234] Seidelman, *Science and Inhumanity,* pdf.

[235] Joseph & Wetzel, "Ernst Rüdin: Hitler's Racial Hygiene Mastermind," 1-2.

It is important to recognize that Rüdin was one of the primary figures in implementing these psychiatric eugenic "treatments" and supplying the body parts for medical experiments.[236]

Nazi Euthanasia was first promoted by psychiatrists such as Ernst Rüdin and Alfred Hoche, but eventually also by many physicians in all branches of medicine under Rüdin's leadership. The fact that euthanasia was a psychiatric concept explains why the practice was first applied to the perceived "mentally ill" and "feeble-minded." Psychiatrist and former full-time consultant for the National Institute of Mental Health (NIMH), Peter Breggin, comments,

> A number of historians have pointed out that the scientific bureaucratization of murder was a unique quality of the holocaust; but none seem to have given credit to the source. **Bureaucratic, scientific killing was invented and first implemented by organized psychiatry.** This is one reason why physicians Mitscherlich, Alexander and Ivy each separately declared that **psychiatry was key to the holocaust and that the tragedy might not have happened without the initial euthanasia program** [emphasis added].[237]

---

[236] "The neuropathologist Dr. Julius Hallervorden (1882-1965), who directed famed Kaiser-Wilhelm Institute of Brain Research (KWIBR) in Berlin-Buch seized the opportunity afforded by the murder of psychiatric patients at Brandenburg to acquire hundreds of brain specimens for what was probably the foremost neuropathological collection in the world. Renamed the Max Planck Institute for Brain Research (MPIBR), the institute and its neuropathological collection were relocated from Berlin-Buch to Frankfurt" (William E. Seidelman, "The Holocaust: Medicine and Murder in the Third Reich," *Dimensions: Journal of Holocaust Studies*, Vol 13 [1] [1999]: https://www. jewish virtuallibrary.org/medicine-and-murder-in-the-third-reich).

[237] Peter Breggin, Psychiatry's Role in the Holocaust," *International Journal of Risk and Safety in Medicine* 4 (1993), 142.

Psychiatrist Rael Strous affirms this sordid history:

> For the first time in history, psychiatrists during the Nazi
> era sought to systematically exterminate their patients.
> However, little has been published from this dark period
> analyzing what may be learned for clinical and research
> psychiatry. At each stage in the murderous process lay a
> series of unethical and heinous practices, with many
> psychiatrists demonstrating a profound commitment to
> the atrocities, playing central, pivotal roles critical to the
> success of Nazi policy . . . . Psychiatry during this period
> provides a most horrifying example of how science may
> be perverted by external forces. It thus becomes crucial to
> include the Nazi era psychiatry experience in ethics
> training as an example of proper practice gone awry.[238]

Additionally, Psychiatrists E. Fuller Torrey and Robert
Yolken relate that

> the idea of killing the patients in psychiatric hospitals first
> surfaced prominently in 1920 in a publication by Karl
> Binding, a lawyer, and Alfred Hoche, a psychiatrist.
> Entitled *Permission for the Destruction of Life Unworthy of
> Life*, the tract posed the question: "Is there human life
> which has so far forfeited the character of something
> entitled to enjoy the protection of the law, that its
> prolongation represents a perpetual loss of value, both for
> its bearer and for society as a whole?" The authors'
> answer was clearly affirmative and described such
> individuals as being "mentally dead" and "on an
> intellectual level which we only encounter way down in

---

[238] Rael D. Strous, "Psychiatry During the Nazi Era: Ethical Lessons for the
Modern Professional," *Annals of General Psychiatry* vol. 6 (8) (February 27, 2007):
doi:10.1186/1744-859X-6-8.

the animal kingdom." The authors emphasized the economic burden of such individuals to Germany.[239]

German historian Volker Roelcke notes that Ernst Rüdin was the underlying financial and philosophical force behind the murderous experiments on children in Heidelberg by psychiatrists such as Julius Deussen.[240] Like other Nazi psychiatrists, Carl Schneider, professor and Chairman of the Department of Psychiatry of the University of Heidelberg and who served under Rüdin's leadership,

> used the Nazis' euthanasia program for his own depraved research. Schneider conducted psychological assessments of children he knew were doomed to die, and had their brains collected and dissected after they were murdered.[241]

Roelcke also denounces the attempt by some historians to "whitewash" Rüdin's and fellow psychiatrists' reputations:

> Ernst Rüdin (1874-1952), director of the Deutsche Forschungsanstalt für Psychiatrie in Munich, was one of the leading psychiatrists in Nazi Germany . . . a general evaluation of the historical sources on the systematic killing of patients clearly shows that due to the fragmentary character of the evidence, any exculpation of particular individuals or institutions is premature to date. Furthermore, the reevaluation of already known archival material and new documents presented here proves that

---

[239] E. Fuller Torrey and Robert H. Yolken, "Psychiatric genocide: Nazi attempts to eradicate schizophrenia." *Schizophrenia Bulletin* vol. 36 (1) (2010): 26-32; doi:10.1093/schbul/sbp097.

[240] A. Abbott, "German Science Begins to Cure its Historical Amnesia," *Nature* 403 (2000): 474–475.

[241] Seidelman, "The Holocaust: Medicine and Murder in the Third Reich."

Rüdin had a genuine interest in research which on the one hand made profitable use of the killings, and on the other hand was aimed at formulating scientific criteria for the systematic selection and "euthanasia" of those supposedly unworthy to live.[242]

Roelcke offers further insight into Rüdin's advancement of euthanasia:

> Julius Deussen (1906-1970), since 1939 head of the department for hereditary psychology at the Deutsche Forschungsanstalt, was also a close co-worker of Carl Schneider (1891-1946) at the University of Heidelberg. He coordinated the research on children carried through in the context of the "euthanasia" programme [sic] between 1943 and 1945. This research sought to systematically correlate clinical and laboratory findings with the histopathological data of the victims' brains. From the beginning, it included the killing of the patients. Central elements of the research programme had been formulated by Deussen already in Munich. Rüdin supported the activities of Deussen in Heidelberg and repeatedly pointed out that they were of importance for the health and population policy of the Nazi regime.[243]

In *The American Journal of Psychiatry,* published by the American Psychiatric Association, Psychiatrist Rael Strous reveals,

> The euthanasia program became the Nazi regime's first campaign of mass murder against specific populations whom it considered inferior and threatening to the well-being of the Aryan race and **the first time in history where psychiatrists sought out to systematically**

[242] Volker Roelcke, M. Rotzoll, and G Hohendorf, "Hereditary psychological research in the context of 'euthanasia': new documents and aspects on Carl Schneider, Julius Deussen and Ernst Rüdin ," *Fortschritte der Neurologie and Psychiatrie* 66 (7): 331.

[243] Ibid., 331-32.

exterminate their patients, with several prominent psychiatrists playing central roles . . . . The Hadamar Psychiatric Institute near Wiesbaden, Germany, code-named "Facility-E," was refashioned for use as a psychiatry euthanasia facility in November 1940 . . . . In August 1942, after a short break, the facility again functioned as a euthanasia center, using lethal medication doses or starvation. After removal of various organs for medical research, the bodies were buried in mass graves located on the hospital grounds. The killing center remained operational until its liberation by American troops on March 26, 1945. **Operation-T4 claimed approximately 200,000 lives. Psychiatric euthanasia institutions served as training centers for the Schutzstaffel (SS) who used the experience to construct larger killing centers (Auschwitz, Treblinka, etc.).** The psychiatrist Dr. Imfried Eberl, Treblinka's first commandant and the only physician to command a death camp, established the facility following his experience as superintendent of Brandenburg Psychiatry Hospital [emphasis added].[244]

Another psychiatrist discusses "operation-T4":

The 1933 Sterilization Law to which Rüdin contributed and in which the Kaiser Wilhelm Psychiatry Institute participated established the basis for the Nazi programs of selection and eugenic and racial purification. These programs included the killing of handicapped children and the T-4 *Aktion* for the murder of adults in psychiatric institutions . . . It was also revealed at that time that the Max Planck Institute of Psychiatry had in its collection brain specimens from children murdered in the child "euthanasia" program. These specimens came from children murdered at Eglfing-Haar; a psychiatric institution near Munich [emphasis added].[245]

---

[244] Strous, "Nazi Euthanasia of the Mentally Ill at Hadamar."

[245] Seidelman, *Science and Inhumanity*, pdf.

Many academic psychiatrists and historians today do admit the horrific historic origins of the psychiatric genetic theory and Rüdin's true character. Psychiatric genetics was the underlying enabler and force behind the Holocaust, and Rüdin was the figurehead and driving force in the Nazi eugenics/mental and racial hygiene movement. Former professor of psychiatry at Harvard University Robert Lifton remarks,

> The predominant medical presence in the Nazi sterilization program was Dr. Ernst Rüdin, a Swiss-born psychiatrist of international renown. Originally a student of Emil Kraepelin . . . "the aim of his life" was to establish the genetic basis for psychiatric conditions, and that "he was not so much a fanatical Nazi as a fanatical geneticist" [emphasis added].[246]

Similarly, renowned psychiatrists E. Fuller Torrey and Robert Yolken write,

> In 1933, Rüdin was one of the guiding forces behind the passage of Germany's first compulsory sterilization law, called "the law for the prevention of progeny with hereditary defects." Its initial target was individuals with mental retardation, schizophrenia, manic-depressive disorder, epilepsy, Huntington chorea, hereditary blindness and deafness, hereditary alcoholism, and "grave bodily malformation." Hitler had become chancellor 6 months earlier. The majority of the targeted individuals were in psychiatric hospitals, which had become massively overcrowded, thereby forcing the discharge of some patients to make room for more admissions. Patients with schizophrenia who were scheduled for discharge were deemed to be of high

---

[246] Robert Jay Lifton, *The Nazi Doctors: Medical Killing and the Psychology of Genocide* (New York: Basic Books, 1986), 27-28.

priority for sterilization in order to prevent them from producing offspring.[247]

Peter Breggin also conveys this aspect of Rüdin's true biography:

> How objective was this scientist? How unbiased were his motivations? When Hitler came to power, Rüdin was ready for him. **It was Rüdin who influenced Hitler, not Hitler who influenced Rüdin. The psychiatrist became the architect** and official interpreter of the first legislation establishing the Nazi eugenics program that led to the castration and sterilization of tens of thousands of individuals accused of being schizophrenic, retarded, epileptic, or in some other way physically or mentally "defective" [emphasis added].[248]

By claiming that theorized genetic predispositions in degenerates were fixed, psychiatrists convinced an entire nation to eliminate the "defective." The Holocaust was not primarily driven by national socialism, but by the Kraepelinian psychiatric genetic theory practically applied by Ernst Rüdin and those under his authority.[249] In fact, as psychiatrist Robert Jay Lifton records, the Germans declared "national socialism as 'nothing but applied

---

[247] Torrey & Yolken, "Psychiatric Genocide:" 26-32.

[248] Peter R. Breggin, *Toxic Psychiatry* (New York: St. Martin's Press, 1991), 102.

[249] Philip Yanos, "The Long Shadow of the Eugenics Movement: Its Influence Persists," *Psychology Today Online* (June 02, 2018): https://www.psychologytoday.com/us/blog/written/201806/the-long-shadow-the-eugenics-movement.

biology.'"[250] The application of Nazi Socialism was the product of the medical model.

Rüdin's Science

Rüdin had not only accepted Kraepelin's theory of eugenics, he also had provided eugenics with specific research methods, which are still utilized today within the field of psychiatric genetics:

> This historical review introduces a series of papers abstracting, reanalyzing and commenting upon family studies of schizophrenia conducted by Ernst Rüdin and his geneologic-demographic department in Munich. **These studies, which pioneered many of the methods still critical to psychiatric genetics, are little known in the anglophonic world.** Starting with a study of schizophrenia in siblings, members of the Rüdin school expanded to study a wide range of relationships (including grandchildren and nieces/nephews) and disorders (including affective illness, obsessive-compulsive disorder, epilepsy and personality disorders) [emphasis added].[251]

William Seidelman states,

> The focus of Rüdin's research was on the inheritance of psychiatric disorders. His 1916 paper on that subject is

[250] Robert Lifton, *Nazi Doctors: Medical Killing and the Psychology of Genocide* (New York: Basic Books, 1986), 129.

[251] E. Zerbin-Rüdin and Kenneth S. Kendler, "Ernst Rüdin (1874-1952) and his genealogical-demographic department in Munich (1917-1986): An Introduction to their family studies of Schizophrenia," *American Journal of Medical Genetics* 67 (4) (July 1996): 332; https://www.ncbi.nlm.nih.gov/pub med/8837698.

considered a classic that continues to be cited in the
literature on the genetics of schizophrenia.[252]

Most academic psychiatrists and historians recognize that
the history of psychiatric genetics places Rüdin and
Kraepelin's construct of schizophrenia front and central:

> The history of psychiatric genetics is informed by this
> paper, which serves to review the legacy of German
> psychiatric genetics and its antecedents during the
> twentieth century. It also serves as an introduction to two
> new annotated abstracts of basic research papers on
> family studies of schizophrenia by Ernst Rüdin in 1916
> and by Bruno Schulz in 1932 . . .[253]

Historian of medicine Paul Weindling relates how the
Holocaust was a massive psychiatric genetic experiment to
both prove Kraepelinianism as scientifically valid and to
eliminate perceived unhealthy stock who were diagnosed
within psychiatry to be genetically defective:

> The physiological experiments were construed as studies
> in the physiology of death, and poison gas experiments
> were pilot studies for the extermination camps. **The
> taking of thousands of brains from euthanasia victims
> showed how medical research was linked to the
> psychiatric killings.** The experimental X-ray sterilizations
> and other efforts to make women infertile bridged
> sterilization and the Holocaust. The prosecutors claimed –
> with much justice given the massive scale of Nazi

---

[252] Seidelman, *Science and Inhumanity*, pdf.

[253] Bertelsen A. Gottesman II, "Legacy of German Psychiatric Genetics:
Hindsight is Always 20/20," *American Journal of Medical Genetics* 67 (4) (July
1996): 317; https://www.ncbi.nlm.nih.gov/pub med/8837696.

euthanasia – that there were half a million victims of medical abuses under Nazism [emphasis added].[254]

One medical journal however, reports that Rüdin never did arrive at conclusive scientific discovery to prove the psychiatric genetic theory:

> Applying modern study designs and statistical methods, the German psychiatrist Ernst Rüdin (1874–1952) found lower inheritance of affective disorders than anticipated. He surmised that external factors were also important in their development. From the vantage point of the present, his results were sound. However, this major study, titled "On the Inheritance of Manic-Depressive Insanity", though developed as a manuscript, was never published. **The question arises whether Rüdin doubted his own scientific methods and hence results, or if he was influenced by his ideological views and the expectations of the scientific community and German society. Whilst withholding his results, he continued to promote prevention of assumed hereditary mental illnesses by prohibition of marriage or sterilization** [emphasis added].[255]

While psychiatric genetics was the philosophical engine behind the Holocaust, Rüdin himself never based his decisions on objective empirical evidence. Instead, it was fear and propaganda, produced by conjecture, which enabled eugenics' social acceptance:

> In the early 20th century, there were few therapeutic options for mental illness and asylum numbers were rising. This pessimistic outlook favoured the rise of the eugenics movement. Heredity was assumed to be the principal cause of mental illness. Politicians, scientists and

[254] Weindling, *Nazi Medicine*, 6.

[255] Kösters, Steinberg, Kirkby, & Himmerich' "Ernst Rüdin 's Unpublished 1922-1925 Study "Inheritance of Manic-Depressive Insanity."

clinicians in North America and Europe called for compulsory sterilisation of the mentally ill. **Psychiatric genetic research aimed to prove a Mendelian mode of inheritance as a scientific justification for these measures. Ernst Rüdin's seminal 1916 epidemiological study on inheritance of dementia praecox featured large, systematically ascertained samples and statistical analyses. Rüdin's 1922-1925 study on the inheritance of "manic-depressive insanity" was completed in manuscript form, but never published. It failed to prove a pattern of Mendelian inheritance, counter to the tenets of eugenics of which Rüdin was a prominent proponent.** It appears he withheld the study from publication, unable to reconcile this contradiction, thus subordinating his carefully derived scientific findings to his ideological preoccupations. Instead, Rüdin continued to promote prevention of assumed hereditary mental illnesses by prohibition of marriage or sterilisation and was influential in the introduction by the National Socialist regime of the 1933 "Law for the Prevention of Hereditarily Diseased Offspring" (Gesetz zur Verhütung erbkranken Nachwuchses) [emphasis added].[256]

The Kraepelinian theory of mental illness — the ideology on which the Holocaust was initiated and empowered and on which psychiatric genetics exists — has never been scientifically justified.

Franz Josef Kallmann

Although most historians present Rüdin as the key figure in implementing Kraepelin's theory and ushering in Nazi eugenics, it was another prominent psychiatrist who not only passionately embraced eugenics, but who also assured that eugenics was both continued after Rüdin's death and

---

[256] Ibid.

that the worldview would eventually be embraced as the fundamental approach to mental struggles in the United States. That man is the father of American psychiatric eugenics, Franz Josef Kallmann (1897-1965). Several psychiatric historians note Rüdin's and Kallmann's unified vision and friendship:

> The systematic sterilization and killing of individuals with schizophrenia in Nazi Germany from 1934 to 1945 was influenced by several factors. **Perhaps, of greatest importance was a belief that schizophrenia was a simple Mendelian inherited disease, passed down from generation to generation. In Germany, this theory was promoted by Drs Ernst Rüdin and Franz Kallmann, among others.**[257]

What may be of surprise to some is that Kallmann was Jewish, yet working with and supporting the eugenics theory within Germany. Furthermore, as many historians acknowledge, Kallmann was often more passionate about eugenics and sterilization of perceived degenerates than even Rüdin was:

> When the National Socialist state was created in 1933, an exodus of anti-Nazi elite began. However, some researchers who were forced to leave Germany approved Nazi eugenic politics, even as Jews. **One of them was the psychiatrist Franz Josef Kallmann, a researcher on schizophrenia, who demanded an even more radical sterilization policy than the Nazis.**[258]

What is also worth noting in Rüdin and Kallmann's friendship and partnership at the DFA is that Nazi eugenics was not originally focused primarily on ethnicity.

---

[257] Torrey & Yolken, "Psychiatric Genocide."

[258] Mildenberger, "On the Track of "Scientific Pursuit," 183.

The degeneration theory was a psychiatric theory that first focused on the perceived mentally ill and expanded thereafter to include political opponents and minorities. Apparently, those in authority could progressively expand the construct of eugenics to fit any group of people they selected to categorize as disordered/defective. But as observed previously, the list of degenerates was based upon Kraepelin's original theory, and history reveals a clear progression through his list.

When the perceived mentally disordered had been mostly eliminated by Rüdin and Kallmann within the asylums, the eugenic experiments were not complete. The Alliance for Human Research Protection describes the process that the German "healing profession" followed in their experiments:

> Germany's medical leaders set in motion the downward spiral of medicine from its lofty heights as a healing profession that values the individual person, to a profession obsessed with racial hygiene and obsessed with demonstrating Aryan superiority by denigrating other segments of humanity as inferior subhuman. **Medical doctors first classified mentally disabled children and adults as genetically inferior, followed by Jews and gypsies.** The designation "inferior" was not merely humiliating, it escalated methodically into industrialized mass murder and genocide [emphasis added].[259]

Rüdin and his constituents were systematically working through Kraepelin's diagnostic list of the alleged

---

[259] The Alliance for Human Research Protection "1932-1945: Doctors and Academics Perverted Medicine and Science in Nazi Germany," *AHRP Online* (accessed August 10, 2019): https://ahrp.org/1932-1945-doctors-academics-perverted-medicine-science-in-nazi-germany/.

disordered in order to eliminate the genetically defective ("genocide"). While the Jewish people rightfully receive the most attention in historic reviews due to the millions who were euthanized, the list of alleged degenerates was much broader.

There might also be another reason why the Jewish people and other ethnic groups were targeted later. As already touched on but worth examining further, the two primary sources of funding during the first solution of the Holocaust were the Rockefeller Foundation –which "was established in 1913 by John D. Rockefeller 'to promote the well-being of mankind throughout the world'"[260] – and the Jewish philanthropist, James Loeb, who had been a patient of Kraepelin and who, before his death, "bequeathed $1,000,000 to the Munich institute" as a final gift.[261] In a sad twist of fate, Kraepelin's prominence and the Holocaust's philosophical engine were largely funded by the generous gifts of a Jewish patient and an American foundation. But the cessation of these donors' funding was likely the catalyst for Rüdin's utilizing Kraepelin's full list of degenerates:

> In 1935 the Rockefeller Foundation withheld funding for genealogical and demographic research at the Munich institute. In 1940 the executors of the Loeb estate also ceased payment to the institute. Desperate for support Rüdin turned to the SS terror organization for salvation. In 1939 the world's first and foremost psychiatric research institute came under the influence, if not the control, of

[260] "The Rockefeller Foundation Archives" https://rockarch.org/collections/rf/: accessed August 14, 2019.

[261] Seidelman, *Science and Inhumanity*, pdf.

the SS and its research organization, the notorious *Ahnenerbe*.[262]

The defunding of German eugenics by the Loeb estate not only prompted Rüdin to turn to the SS, but it would also cause other geneticists like Otmar Von Vershuer, who under Rüdin's leadership had become a "noted expert on the genetics of twins" and who trained murderers like Josef Mengele,[263] to include the Jewish people into the diagnostic category as Kraepelin had first asserted. When psychiatrists ran out of degenerates in the asylums for experimentation and elimination and money ran out from their gracious donors, eugenicists, now under the control of the SS, were forced to turn their attention to the categorized social and racial degenerates as well. The United States Holocaust Memorial Museum recounts about Vershuer:

> In 1927, he recommended the forced sterilization of the "mentally and morally subnormal." Once a member of an ultra-nationalist paramilitary Frelkorps unit of World War I veterans, Vershcuer typified those academics whose interest in Germany's "national regeneration" provided motivation for their research.[264]

It was Vershuer, serving in the SS, who many historians say first proposed the "final solution" — a suggestion that would force Rüdin's co-eugenicist, Jewish psychiatrist Josef Franz Kallmann, to flee Nazi Germany. This fact is why Kallmann passionately participated only in the first half of

---

[262] Seidelman, Science and Inhumanity, pdf.

[263] Ibid.

[264] The United States Holocaust Memorial Museum, "Deadly Medicine: Creating the Master Race," *HMM Online* (accessed August 10, 2019): https://www.ushmm.org/exhibition/deadly-medicine/profiles/.

the Holocaust experiments — especially in the twin studies. Kallmann also gave a significant eugenic speech in 1935 on sterilization. But a year later, before the final phase ("the final solution"), Kallmann was forced to escape to the United States where, despite his previous experience, he would continue his eugenic vision:

> **Kallmann, a Berlin psychiatrist who had been a student of Rüdin,** studied schizophrenia in twins and also believed that the disease was transmitted by a recessive gene. In a 1935 speech, Kallmann advocated the examination of all relatives of individuals with schizophrenia to identify nonaffected carriers, which he believed could be done by noting "minor anomalies," and then the compulsory sterilization of such individuals. **A year later, Kallmann emigrated to New York, where he continued his twin research and later became one of the founders of the American Society of Human Genetics** [emphasis added].[265]

Sadly, before his departure, Kallmann's 1935 eugenic speech in Germany prompted the sterilization and eventual slaughter of those targeted and their families, including children whose bodies were divided and distributed for various medical experiments:

> In 1935, a young protégé of Ernst Rüdin's, Dr Franz J. Kallman, presented a paper at the Berlin International Congress for Population Science, in which he argued for the sterilization of even the apparently healthy relatives of those with schizophrenia, along with the patients themselves, to eliminate defective genes. Kallmann's genetic studies were used partly to justify the murder of patients, many of them children. The killing of children with mental and physical disabilities was carried out in so-called Specialized Children's Departments. Information on these children was sent to Berlin, where it

---

[265] Torrey & Yolken, "Psychiatric Genocide."

was reviewed by a panel of 3 medical experts who decided whether a particular child was to be killed.[266]

As Torrey and Yoken acknowledge, Kallmann did not denounce eugenics. Instead, Kallmann became the father of the modern American psychiatric eugenics movement, founded the American Society of Human Genetics, and established the precise experimental approach to psychiatric genetics that Rüdin and he had developed at the GDA in accordance with the Kraepelinian theory:

> The close collaboration between the GDA's [Genealogic-Demographic Department or *Genealogisch-Demographische Abteilung;* GDA)] protagonist Ernst Rüdin and the National Socialist regime was certainly not an inhibiting factor for the worldwide recognition of the eugenic research conducted in Munich. **Around the mid-1930s, the German psychiatrist émigré Franz Josef Kallmann brought the field of study which had been put into practice in Munich to the United States. He fought an uphill battle to be accepted by the North American scientific community, but finally he was able to establish himself as the main researcher in the field of psychiatric genetics** [emphasis added].[267]

Moreover, Kallmann and Rüdin continued to collaborate and maintained their friendship even after the war had ended:

> [Kallmann] co-operated closely with the German Research Foundation for Psychiatry in Munich and its leader, Ernst Rüdin. From Rüdin he received help in leaving Germany

---

[266] Mary V. Seeman, "Psychiatry in the Nazi Era," *Canadian Journal of Psychiatry* Vol. 50 (4) (March 2005): 222.

[267] Anne Cottebrune, "Franz Josef Kallmann (1897-1965) and the transfer of psychiatric-genetic scientific concepts from national socialist Germany to the U.S.A," *Medizinhistoriches Journal* 44 (3-4) (January 2009): 296.

and finding a job in USA, and Rüdin's assistant, Theo Lang, delivered data-material from Munich to New York. After 1945 Rüdin got a denazification certificate from Kallmann who already co-operated again with Lang.[268]

The alleged purpose of a "denazification certificate," which Rüdin received from Kallmann, was "to lead the Germans to a fundamental revision of their recent political philosophy."[269] But if the underlying philosophy was psychiatric rather than primarily political, and Kallmann simply relocated the core of the theory to the United States, then denazification has never truly occurred. As observed in both the history of Kallmann and Rüdin, the psychiatric theory of eugenics which had led to the Holocaust had been entirely overlooked in "de-nazifying the world." Kallmann and Rüdin never abandoned support for each other or their faith in both Kraepelin's genetic theory of mental illness, his psychiatric constructs, and his statistical approach.

Despite Kallmann's close ties with Rüdin and Nazi Germany, he along with his followers would eventually convince the American Psychiatric Association to accept eugenics as the primary theory and approach to mental struggles in America. Of course, this accomplishment was not an easy task, and for obvious reasons after WWII,

---

[268] Mildenberger, "On the Track of 'Scientific Pursuit,'" *Medizinhistoriches Journal (Journal of Medical History)* vol. 37 (2) (2002): 183; https://www.ncbi.nlm.nih.gov/pubmed/12522917.

[269] Noland Norgaard, "Eisenhower Claims 50 Years Needed to Tre-Educate Nazis," *Oregon Statesman* (October 13, 1945), 2.

psychiatrists were skeptical about eugenics in the United States.

Ironically, psychiatrists were not primarily skeptical because of the fact that eugenics had been the driving force behind the Holocaust. Instead, they were hesitant because of the popularity of another Jewish psychiatrist who had studied under Wilhelm Wundt, who despised Emil Kraepelin, and who also was forced to flee from Germany to the United States. That influential person was Sigmund Freud, the man who championed the psychoanalytic approach that he had developed in Germany while under Wundt's watchful eye. This theory opposed Kallmann's work:

> Interestingly enough, the fact that [Kallmann's] kind of research [eugenics] had been heavily supported by the National Socialist regime was not a barrier to his acceptance. The fact that it took him a long time to establish the field of eugenics in the U.S.A. is better explained by the psychoanalytic research methods at the time, which gave hereditary transmission short shrift. At the New York State Psychiatric Institute he was able to continue his research, including the examination of race-hygienic motifs, **where he designed a research program that was directly based on concepts and methods from Ernst Rüdin's team of researchers in Munich.**[270]

It must be made clear, though, that Kallmann had not brought merely some elements of Kraepelin's eugenics paradigm to the United States. Rather, Kallmann had convinced American psychiatrists and eventually society in general to embrace the precise eugenics paradigm he was taught and endorsed while in Nazi Germany:

---

[270] Cottebrune, "Franz Josef Kallmann," 296.

The only deviation from the original research was in terms of the use of eugenic prophylaxis where he aligned his research in the context of North American democracy in the post-war era. However, **the eugenic goal of elimination of certain categories of peoples remained unchanged**.[271]

It was Kallmann's efforts that assured that American psychiatrists in the early 1960s into the 1970s both embraced Kraepelinianism and denounced Freudianism, but it would be the psychiatrists and pharmaceutical companies working in unison who promoted the eugenics theory and convinced many Americans that they were individually disordered. Kallmann's approach, which the APA accepted, had not changed in the least upon entering the United States:

> Kallmann called for coercive state interventions for eugenic intervention, including both sterilization and the prevention of marriage. Kallmann was aware of the comparison between his proposals and those being implemented in Germany. He had only recently left Germany, where he had proposed such sweeping sterilization measures that even the Nazis considered them too extreme. These measures included the same ones he advocated in *Eugenical News* after his arrival in America.[272]

In 1938 in the *Eugenical News,* while living in America, Kallmann argued that a system be put in place to both identify and prevent genetic disorders from continuing. Of course, just as it had been in Nazi Germany, sterilization

[271] Ibid.

[272] Breggin, "Psychiatry's Role in the Holocaust," 139-40.

was front and center to his plan. Kallmann would assert in 1938 that

> satisfactory eugenic success in the heredity-circle of schizophrenia cannot be secured without systematic preventive measures among the tainted children and siblings of schizophrenics. Especially inadvisable are the marriages of schizoid eccentrics and borderline cases, when contracted with individuals who either manifest certain symptoms of a schizophrenic taint themselves or prove to belong to a strongly tainted family.[273]

As previously noted, to prove Kraepelin's created psychiatric construct of schizophrenia and eugenics, Kraepelinians have historically focused on conducting twin studies and claimed their results as empirical evidence.[274] In the 1920s twin studies became a central feature of Ernst Rüdin's propaganda and his primary hope of finding a genetic link to alleged schizophrenia that would validate the speculative eugenic faith.

Hans Luxenburger, working under Ernst Rüdin in the German Research Institute of psychiatry in Munich, was another prominent psychiatric researcher who focused on twin studies.[275] But Luxenburger's reputation was rightfully tarnished by his association with Ernst Rüdin

---

[273] Franz Josef Kallmann, "Heredity, reproduction and eugenic procedure in the field of schizophrenia," *Eugenical News* 23 (1938): 113.

[274] Benjamin Rush is one of the first to theoretically link the hereditary theory with twins. For further study on the genetic theory, see Jay Joseph, *The Gene Illusion: Genetic Research in Psychology and Psychiatry under the Microscope* (New York: Algora Publishing, 2004).

[275] Shorter, *History of Psychiatry*, 241.

and his staunch defense of Nazi eugenics.[276] Because of these connections, Luxenburg's research was marginalized. But Kallmann's move from Nazi Germany to the United States because of the final solution enabled US psychiatrists to embrace his genetic theory as if it were an ideology apart from eugenics. In fact, a majority of American psychiatrists fully accepted Kallmann's research conclusions, goals, and exact methods from his days in Kraepelin's research institute in Munich. Historian and professor of psychiatry Edward Shorter comments,

> In 1929, Kallmann became involved in the large-scale studies that Rüdin and Luxenburger were undertaking, and as an extension of that work moved to the Herzberge Mental Hospital in Berlin where he did a family study of all blood relatives of schizophrenics admitted to the hospital 30 years previously . . . . In the early 1940s, Kallmann decided to apply his tremendous energy to a twin study of all patients in public asylums in New York State . . . . These findings were such a solid index of organicity in schizophrenia that, when they were presented in 1950 at the First World Congress of Psychiatry in Paris, they caused a sensation. Kallmann had written in an unvarnished manner about the Mendelian inheritance of schizophrenia (meaning a single locus in the DNA). . . . it was by now apparent that schizophrenia and manic-depressive illness were heavily genetic in nature.[277]

Much of Kallmann's evidence recorded in his books and research is not from experiments conducted in the US, but from research conducted in Nazi Germany:

> [Kallmann] collaborated with Ernst Rüdin (1874-1952), investigating sibling inheritance of schizophrenia and

[276] Ibid.

[277] Ibid., 243-44.

becoming a protagonist of genetic research on psychiatric conditions. In 1936, Kallmann was forced to immigrate to the USA where he published *The Genetics of Schizophrenia* (1938), based on data he had gathered from the district pathological institutes of Berlin's public health department. Kallmann resumed his role as an international player in biological psychiatry and genetics, becoming president (1952) of the American Society of Human Genetics and Director of the New York State Psychiatric Institute in 1955.[278]

Kallmann was the perfect candidate to carry on Kraepelin's legacy and eugenic psychiatric research. In the *Journal of Medical History* in an article entitled "On the Track of 'Franz Josef Kallmann' (1897-1965) and the Transfer of Psychiatric-Genetic Scientific Concept from National Socialist Germany to the U.S.A.," this reality is noted.[279] Others note the same historic facts:

In 1936, Kallmann was forced to immigrate to the USA where he published *The Genetics of Schizophrenia* (1938), based on data he had gathered from the district pathological institutes of Berlin's public health department. Kallmann resumed his role as an international player in biological psychiatry and genetics, becoming president (1952) of the American Society of Human Genetics and Director of the New York State Psychiatric Institute in 1955. **While his work was well received by geneticists, the idea of genetic differences barely took hold in American psychiatry, largely because of émigré psychoanalysts who dominated American clinical psychiatry until the 1960s and established a philosophical direction in which genetics**

[278] S. Pow and F.W. Stahnisch, "Eugenics Ideals, Racial Hygiene, and the Emigration Process of German-American Nuerogeneticist Franz Josef Kallmann (1897-1965)," *Journal of the History of the Neurosciences* (3) (July-September 2016): 253; https://doi.org/10.1080/ 0964704X.2016.1187486.

[279] Cottebrune, "On the Track of "Franz Josef Kallmann," 296.

played no significant role, being regarded as dangerous in light of Nazi medical atrocities. After all, medical scientists in Nazi Germany had been among the **social protagonists of racial hygiene which, under the aegis of Nazi philosophies, replaced medical genetics as the basis for the ideals and application of eugenics** [emphasis added].[280]

Over time, Kallmann not only successfully persuaded fellow psychiatrists to transfer their faith in Freud to faith in Kraepelin, but he also furthered faith in psychiatric genetics globally.

Despite the optimism, however, Kallmann's research failed to find any validating evidence, and it only produced correlations that can be explained otherwise. As some historians who "do not treat the genetics of psychiatric disorders as something inherently false and unsavory"[281] recognize, "the literature of twin and adoption studies is a pliable resource rather than a static canon of universal validity."[282] Harvard geneticist Richard Lewontin, neuroscientist Steven Rose, and clinical psychologist Leon Kamin also state about Kallmann's scientific work that

> [the] views of the future president of the American Society for Human Genetics are so bloodcurdling that one can sympathize with the efforts of present-day geneticists to misrepresent or to suppress them. They have not, however, suppressed the mountains of published statistics with which Kallmann attempted to prove that schizophrenia (like tuberculosis and homosexuality) was a hereditary form of degeneracy.

[280] Pow & Stahnisch, "Eugenics Ideals, Racial Hygiene . . ."

[281] Arribas-Ayloon, Bartlett, & Lewis, *Psychiatric Genetics*, 11.

[282] Ibid., 12.

> Those figures are presented to students in today's
> textbooks as the fruits of impartial science . . . Kallmann's
> figures cannot be regarded seriously [emphasis added].[283]

Beginning with Kraepelin, passing through Rüdin, and primarily arriving in the US through Kallmann, the purely speculative genetic theory of mental illness and schizophrenia in particular has been the central theme of modern eugenics. One medical journal records this sobering history without naming Rüdin's disciples specifically:

> Rüdin's concept of an empirical heredity prognosis served
> as a methodological model for many subsequent studies
> at the DFA, known as the Munich School. European and
> American scientists, some of whom had been fellows of
> the Genealogic-Demographic Department (GDA) of the
> DFA, used Rüdin's research methodology in psychiatric
> genetic studies.[284]

Kallmann not only transferred Kraepelinianism from Nazi psychiatric institutes to the American psychiatric Association, but he also seemingly provided the illusive so-called empirical evidence for scientists and psychiatrists alike to place full faith in the genetic theory of mental illness as valid science. Lewontin, Rose, and Kamin explain:

> Perhaps the chief harm brought about by Kallmann's
> deluge of incredible and poorly documented data was to
> create a climate in which the findings of subsequent

---

[283] Richard C. Lewontin, Steven Rose, and Leon J. Kamin, *Not in Our Genes: Biology, Ideology, and Human Nature 2nd edition* (Chicago: Haymarket Books, 2017), 209.

[284] Kosters, Steinberg, Kirkby, & Himmerich, "Ernst Rüdin 's Unpublished 1922-1925 Study "Inheritence of Manic-Depressive Insanity."

workers seemed so reasonable and moderate that they escaped serious critical scrutiny. **Thus, Kallmann's data have faded from the body of acceptable evidence, but the belief for which he was largely responsible — that a genetic basis for schizophrenia has been clearly established — still remains powerful in and out of science** [emphasis added].[285]

Lewontin, Rose, and Kamin comment further on how academic psychiatrists and geneticists regularly present a false narrative about Kallmann's character and work in order to not expose the psychiatric genetic theory of schizophrenia as being eugenics:

> The particular genetic theory espoused by Kallmann [the single recessive gene theory] has made it possible for latter-day psychiatric geneticists to attempt a spectacular rewriting of their history. Thus, in a recent textbook the following note appears: "Kallmann's theory was apparently not based solely on his data. His widow has indicated that Kallmann advocated a recessive model because he could then argue convincingly against the use of sterilization to eliminate the gene. As a Jewish refugee, Kallmann was very sensitive to this issue and afraid of the possible social consequences of his own research."[286]

But Lewontin, Rose, and Kamin confront this clear attempt to white-wash Kallmann's image:

> The picture of Kallmann as a bleeding-heart protector of schizophrenics, adjusting his scientific theories to mirror his compassion, is grotesquely false.[287]

[285] Lewontin, Rose, & Kamin, *Not in Our Genes,* 212-13.

[286] Ibid., 208.

[287] Ibid.

Today, thanks in large part to Kallmann and a false historical narrative taught about him and his predecessors, the mental health system in America and much of the developed world is at its core the same Kraepelinian eugenic paradigm constructed in Nazi Germany.

Adolf Meyer

There is yet another famous American psychiatrist who played a significant role in introducing Kraepelinianism (the eugenics theory) into the APA prior to WWI. In 1896, the soon-to-be president of the American Psychiatric Association, Adolf Meyer, visited Germany to study under Emil Kraepelin and left embracing German "biological psychiatry." Meyer accepted Kraepelin's classificatory system, but he still believed that Freud's psychoanalysis was the best clinical approach to address these issues.

While it was chiefly Kallmann who established Kraepelinianism as the primary psychiatric clinical and research theory in the APA post-WW2, Meyer was the first American psychiatrist to introduce the Kraepelinian construct and diagnostic system into American psychiatry:

> Adapted from the methods of Emil Kraepelin, [Meyer's] clinical system represented his attempt to harmonize the methods and expectations of scientific medicine with a biological view of mind.[288]

Meyer was so influenced by Kraepelin that he shifted his attention from neurology to psychiatry:

---

[288] S. D. Lamb, *Pathologist of the Mind: Adolf Meyer and the Origins of American Psychiatry* (Baltimore: Johns Hopkins University Press, 2014), 22.

[Meyer] worked persistently to implement new clinical methods based on the work of the German clinical psychiatrist Emil Kraepelin. These efforts garnered him repute as a scientific reformer, an accomplished neuropathologist and clinician, and a leader within the emerging field of psychiatry. His motivations were twofold and interrelated. First, he experienced a reorientation of his own scientific interests away from brain research (what he called comparative neurology) and toward work with **mentally disordered patients** (something he distinguished as psychiatry). **Meyer's reform impulse was fueled by a passionate conviction that if the problems of the asylum patients were essentially medical** (upon which alienists and their critics agreed), psychiatrists must approach those problems using the investigational methods of pathology [the study and diagnosis of disease], **the only basis upon which medicine could claim to be scientific.**[289]

If psychiatry was to be considered as a scientific and medical endeavor, then a physical cause and an objective diagnostic system were needed. But since psychiatrists created mental/social disorders rather than discovering objective biological diseases, claiming hereditary/biological causes — and eventually specific genes — made psychiatry seem like a legitimate medical field. Kraepelin's proposal that psychopharmacology — or as he called it *pharmacopsychology*[290] — be a potential remedy to fix defective genes, while at the same time serving as a behavioral control mechanism to deal with degenerates, only added to the aura of mental and racial hygiene truly falling under the auspices of the medical and scientific fields. If physicians prescribed drugs for social and

[289] Ibid., 27.

[290] Elliot Valenstein, *Blaming the Brain: The Truth about Drugs and Mental Health* (New York: Basic Books, 1998), 10.

descriptive constructs framed as diseases, then society would be more likely to consider the human struggles being addressed as objective biological abnormalities which require a medicine man. Meyer contributed greatly to American psychiatrists' eventual embrace of Kraepelinianism by insisting without evidence on its scientific validity and reliability.

But there also exists another significant and often overlooked contribution that Adolf Meyer made in the eventual American acceptance of Kraepelinian eugenics. Being the "the most recognizable, authoritative, and influential psychiatrist in the United States," Adolf Meyer successfully convinced the Rockefeller Foundation to fund the development of a psychiatric diagnostic book based upon Kraepelin's original statistical diagnostic system. That book would come to be known as the *Diagnostic and Statistical Manuel of Mental Disorders* (the *DSM*),[291] and it has enabled the Kraepelin's degenerative statistical approach and his many psychiatric constructs to flourish even today.

Meyer had embraced Kraepelin's theory while studying in Germany under Emil Kraepelin's tutelage, and it is likely that Meyer's relationship with both the Rockefeller Foundation and Kraepelin led to the Rockefeller Foundation's funding of German psychiatry between World Wars I and II. While the process of creating an American psychiatric classification system began in the early 1900s in a joint effort by the APA and the National

[291] Lamb, *Pathologist of the Mind: Adolf Meyer*, 1-2.

Committee for Mental Hygiene, the *DSM* would come later.[292]

Meyer—one of Kraepelin's first American disciples—paved the way for Kraepelinianism to be accepted in the United States by insisting that the theory was scientifically sound and establishing a diagnostic system to determine degeneracy based upon Kraepelin's own model. When Kallmann formalized the eugenics theory in America and presented what he claimed to be empirical evidence to validate Kraepelinianism as a mental science (late 1950s), the APA began to denounce Freudianism in favor of this seemingly new field of psychiatric genetics. By the late 1960s, the APA realized that the *DSM* needed to be revised in order to have a more "scientific approach," but in reality, it reflected the APA's switch from Freudianism to Kraepelinianism.[293] Historian and psychiatrist Ed Shorter writes,

> The current Diagnostic and Statistical Manual of Mental Disorders *(DSM)-5* arose from a tradition filled with haphazard science and politically driven choices. The nosology of modern psychiatry began with the German classifiers of the late 19th century, especially Emil Kraepelin. Psychoanalysis then blotted out the classificatory vision for the next half-century, and most of this European psychopathological science failed to cross the Atlantic. The *DSM* series was a homegrown American product, beginning with Medical 203 in 1945, then guided by psychoanalytic insights through *DSM-I* in 1952 and

[292] Edward Shorter, "The History of Nosology and the Rise of the Diagnostic and Statistical Manual of Mental Disorders," *Dialogues in Clinical Neuroscience* 17 (1) (March 2015): 59.

[293] "By the late 1960s, the great swing from psychoanalysis to biology was in full course" (Shorter, "The History of Nosology," 61).

DSM-II in 1968. In 1980, *DSM-III* represented a massive "turning of the page" in nosology, and it had the effect of steering psychoanalysis toward the exit in psychiatry and the beginning of a reconciliation of psychiatry with the rest of medicine. With the advent of *DSM-5*, however, questions are starting to be asked about whether this massive venture is on the right track.[294]

Though Meyer died before the *DSM* became fully Kraepelinian, his relationship with Kraepelinwas instrumental in its creation.

Also significant is that the term *mental hygiene*—derived from acceptance of Kraepelinianism—was coined by Adolf Meyer, "the Dean of American Psychiatry" in the early 1900s.[295] *Mental health*, as *mental hygiene* is now called, is a Kraepelinian eugenic concept that classifies alleged disordered people according to established social and descriptive constructs, prescribes controlling psychotropic drugs to allegedly manage degeneracy, and blames said abnormalities on genetic/biological causes. The nomenclature has changed, but the eugenics theory that creates categorical degenerates—alleged disordered people—remains the same.

Simply changing the name from eugenics to psychiatric genetics does not mystically provide ethical guidelines or moral integrity. Likewise, changing nomenclature also does not erase the horrific history or hide the underlying philosophies.

[294] Ibid., 59.

[295] Lamb, *Pathologist of the Mind: Adolf Meyer*, 1.

Other Significant Kraepelinians

There are other significant psychiatrists who not only held to Kraepelinian eugenics but also spread the belief abroad. The two most prominent of these Kraepelinian disciples were Alfred Ploetz and Eliot Slater.

Alfred Ploetz

Alfred Ploetz was married to Pauline Rüdin, the sister of Ernst Rüdin,[296] and like the Rüdins, Ploetz was an ardent eugenicist:

> He soon married Pauline Rüdin (1866-1942)—the sister of Ernst Rüdin (1874-1952)— who was likewise trained as a medical doctor. During the very same year and in a state of emotional and professional uncertainty, Ploetz and his wife emigrated to Springfield, Massachusetts in the United States. Cultivating his eugenic ideals, Ploetz became caught up in ongoing post-Civil War debates about "breeding" and creating better U. S. citizens as a means of healing the societal wounds . . . . Having practiced as a physician, Ploetz began to feel a great disillusionment with the limits of both American social reform politics and with contemporary medical research practice as well. Now Ploetz was also forced to confront the fact that despite many attempts, social-Darwinist and proto-eugenic thought had not made much practical progress in North America. He came to accept a belief, common among American eugenicists of the time, that modern society was a sickened entity. Ploetz later put forward an image widespread in pathological theory of human society as "a body made up of cells" (in 1904), and

---

[296] "Alfred Ploetz," *Revolvy Online*: https://www.revolvy. com/page/ Alfred-Ploetz.

pointed out that the health of the social organism relied on the health of its individual members.[297]

There are some historians who believe that Ploetz preceded Kraepelin in forming modern psychiatric eugenics, since "racial hygiene" (much like Meyer's "mental hygiene") became a common term (1895) used by German psychiatrists. However, as already noted, the eugenic theory — not the formal field — was ushered in by Rush and Morel even before Ploetz. Nonetheless, Ploetz was a eugenic figure in both America and in Germany:

> Ploetz's book introduced the term "Racial Hygiene" (Rassenhygiene) to the German medical readership, before leading German psychiatrists — such as Emil Kraepelin (1856-1926) in Munich, Alois Alzheimer (1864-1915) in Frankfurt am Main, or Robert Sommer (1864-1937) in Giessen — hopped on the same bandwagon in the 1910s and 1920s. But where Galton had focused on rather general questions and the research applications of psychiatry-related eugenics by describing instances of social deprivation and general distribution of mental illness, the new eugenic psychiatrists sought distinct forms of "treatment" (such as alcohol moderation, the prevention of venereal diseases, and early eugenics marriage counselling programs in the general practices of psychiatrists and neurologists) . . . .[298]

---

[297] Frank W. Stahnisch, "The Early Eugenics Movement and Emerging Professional Psychiatry: Conceptual Transfers and Personal Relationships between Germany and North America, 1880s to 1930s," *CBMH* Vol. 31 (1) (2014): 18; https://pdfs.semanticscholar.org/8855/ 29ed3162bfbdf659cb a36ae3b1566c9a06b5.pdf.

[298] Ibid.

Undeniably, Ploetz, Kraepelin, Rüdin, Meyers, and all prominent psychiatrists were "the new eugenic psychiatrists."

Eliot Slater

Just as Rüdin and Kallmann had continued Kraepelin's eugenic legacy within the medical field, so too did Eliot Slater postwar after WW2—though Kallmann and Slater did so under the new medical name of *psychiatric genetics* and outside of Germany:

> In the UK, the physical origins of psychiatric genetics were humble to say the least. Peter McGuffin (2017; 124) describes the first dedicated unit as 'a make-shift post-war prefabricated building, affectionately known by staff as the "hut." . . . It was here that the German-trained psychiatrist, Eliot Slater, established the first Medical Research Counsel (MRC) Psychiatric Genetics Unit in 1959.[299]

Slater regularly published articles in the *Eugenics Review*, highlighting his psychiatric perspective.[300] As previously noted, the field of psychiatric genetics had begun in formal theory and physical location under Emil Kraepelin and was first physically located in Nazi Germany. It was then under the leadership of psychiatrist Ernst Rüdin that experimentation and practical application took full effect. Clinical psychologist Jay Joseph, who has researched and

---

[299] Arribas-Ayloon, Bartlett, & Lewis, *Psychiatric Genetics*, 1.

300 Eliot Slater, "A note on Jewish-Christian intermarriage." *The Eugenics Review* vol. 39 (1) (1947): 17-21.

written extensively on the Kraepelinian construct of schizophrenia and its presumed genetic etiology, submits,

> The psychiatric genetics field was founded in Germany in the early part of the 20th century. German "Munich School" psychiatric geneticists in the interwar period performed family and twin studies in an attempt to establish the genetic basis of psychiatric disorders and socially disapproved behavior (such as criminality). Their primary goal was to promote the eugenic program (called "racial hygiene" in Germany) of curbing the reproduction of people they viewed as carrying the "hereditary taint of mental illness," by sterilization or other means. It is important to note that eugenic theories, laws, and practices, which harmed millions of people, were backed by a false set of claims (premises) based on very bad "science" and on the social prejudices of the economically powerful, who helped fund and support the eugenics movement. Eugenicists claimed that hereditary influences on human behavior are very important, and that environmental influences on human behavior are relatively unimportant.[301]

Whereas Eliot Slater had been trained in Germany under Ernst Rüdin and then established psychiatric genetics in Britain, Frans Joseph Kallmann had done the same in America. Dr. Anne Cotterbrune of the University of Giessen relates how the transfer of Kraepelinianism from Nazi Germany to US and British psychiatry occurred:

> The early protagonists which today are considered the **founding-fathers of this field** in Britain and the USA, Eliot Slater and Franz Kallmann, both had been research fellows at the Munich GDA in the mid-1930s which at that time was directed by Ernst Rüdin. Rüdin was perceived as the leading personality in the field internationally; at the same time, he was one of the protagonists of the German movement of eugenics and racial hygiene, and

[301] Joseph, *Schizophrenia and Genetics*, introduction.

after the Nazi-takeover in 1933 closely co-operated with the regime in regard to health and racial policies. **The contribution documents that not only Rüdin, but also Kallmann and Slater throughout their career in medical genetics until the 1960s were motivated by eugenic ideas, and engaged in eugenic organisations, - however, with different consequences, and in different political contexts** [emphasis added].[302]

By the mid-1900s, the "majority of European psychiatrists had embraced Kraepelin's classifications."[303] Though slower to embrace Kraepelin's eugenics theory, American psychiatrists eventually established the Kraepelinian construct as authoritative in the 1960-70s. One thing remained consistent globally within Kraepelinianism and spanning across periods of time: no one was being cured, which left people, families, and societies feeling hopeless.

The "science" of psychiatric genetics was formed upon the "scientists" and their presuppositional faith. While it is certainly an inconvenient truth for modern day academic psychiatrists, eugenics, does, indeed, represent the true basis and substance of modern psychiatric genetics.

[302] Volker Roelcke, "The establishment of Psychiatric Genetics in Germany, Great Britain and the USA, ca. 1910-1960. To the inseparable history of eugenics and human genetics," *Act Historica Leopoldina* (48) (2007): 173; https://www.ncbi.nlm.nih.gov/pubmed/18447192.

[303] Lieberman, *Shrinks*, 95-96.

CHAPTER 4

THE PHILOSOPHIES OF PSYCHIATRIC GENETICS

"It seems necessary to conclude that the inherent, basic principles of psychiatry were not only consistent with Nazi totalitarian and racist aims, but anticipated, encouraged and paved the way for Hitler's eugenical and euthanasia programs. Without psychiatry, the holocaust would probably not have taken place."[304] *- Peter Breggin, professor of psychiatry and former consultant for the NIMH*

If denazification genuinely occurred post WW2, then the underlying eugenics philosophies — the basic principles of Kraepelinian psychiatry — should have been identified and denounced and not merely the political policies that Rüdin penned. Philosophical approaches or styles of reasoning are fundamental to what is often referred to as "science," and these presuppositional beliefs best explain a person's or society's moral behavior.

In fact, psychiatry is primarily a philosophical field about human nature and human phenomena, which explains why there exists numerous books fully dedicated to a

---

[304] Peter Breggin, "Psychiatry's Role in the Holocaust," *International Journal of Risk and Safety in Medicine* 4 (1993): 147.

philosophy of psychiatry, commonly referred to as
phenomenology. Whether it is *The Oxford Handbook of
Philosophy and Psychiatry* or the *Philosophical Issues in
Psychiatry: Explanation, Phenomenology, and Nosology,*[305]
more and more psychiatrists are both admitting the field's
true nature to be philosophical and attempting to present
new theory according to better established philosophy.

The "bio-psycho-social" model or "neo-Kraepelinian"
paradigm is currently the most widely accepted
phenomenology, a worldview that undergirds psychiatric
genetics. In the *Philosophy of Psychiatry: A Companion*,
numerous psychiatrists, philosophers, and psychologists
discuss how modern-day psychiatry is philosophy-driven:

> Psychiatry still cleaves to its traditional self-conception as
> a biological science and medical subspecialty, however,
> and one purpose of this book is to expose the
> philosophical presuppositions within psychiatry and to
> spotlight the need for philosophical approaches to this
> branch of medicine.[306]

Neo-Kraepelinianism/the biological approach to the soul
has specific doctrines that must be carefully examined and
better understood.

If the genetic theory of mental illness is truly scientific —
meaning that the field is objective, validated, and reliable, it
still requires that fundamental beliefs be held in order to
approach and interpret data and to guard against deceitful

---

[305] Kenneth S. Kendler & Josef Parnas, *Philosophical Issues in Psychiatry:
Explanation, Phenomenology, and Nosology* (Johns Hopkins University Press,
2008).

[306] *Philosophy of Psychiatry: A Companion* edited by Jennifer Radden (New
York: Oxford University Press, 2014), 4.

and immoral applications.[307] In truth, there is no approach to the natural world or to phenomena that does not stem from a presuppositional faith. Acclaimed Harvard geneticist Richard Lewontin explains,

> We think science is objective. Science has brought us all kinds of good things . . . . At the same time, science, like other productive activities, like the state, the family, sport, is a social institution completely integrated into and influenced by the structure of all our other social institutions. **The problems that science deals with, the ideas that it uses in investigating those problems, even the so-called scientific results that come out of scientific investigation, are all deeply influenced by predispositions that derive from the society in which we live.** Scientists do not begin life as scientists, after all, but as social beings immersed in a family, a state, a productive structure, and **they view nature through a lens that has been molded by their social experience** [emphasis added].[308]

Moreover, the Bible declared centuries ago that approaches to the natural world require presuppositional faith. Hebrews 11:3, for example, states, "By faith we understand that the universe was created by the Word of God, so that what is seen was not made out of things that are visible." The secular field of psychology (abnormal, cultural, descriptive, clinical, race, or otherwise), as Wundt described it, is no different, and a comprehensive

---

[307] Christopher Lane, "The Truth about Medical PR," *Psychology Today* (November 14, 2019): https://www.psychologytoday.com/us/blog/side-effects/201911/the-truth-about-medical-pr?fbclid=IwAR3NFoWPNIUqs-a9zPDfQuL6xrt6sTH54E-7kQ63AiwkJ6DgSGAMRxzpDT0.

[308] Richard C. Lewontin, *Biology as Ideology: The Doctrine of DNA* (New York: HarperCollins Publishers, 1991), 3.

understanding of the field requires the underlying metaphysical faith first be recognized and understood.

Wilhelm Wundt himself recognized that, "all psychological investigation extrapolates from metaphysical [spiritual] presuppositions."[309] Acclaimed Psychiatrist Karl Jaspers also understood that

> **there are not objective relationships of body and psyche but have only been deduced.** They are plausible and the time of onset and cessation of the trouble seems to indicate a possible connection and, in many cases, a certain one. Yet all this is still very far away from phenomena genuinely expressing an objective unity of body and psyche . . . . A vast inextricable confusion is created from obvious empirical facts, which are extremely difficult to isolate and grasp clearly. **Patterns of possible experiences, of understandable connections with somatic phenomena, are mixed up with speculative metaphysical and cosmic interpretations.** What emerges as true is only the general, indefinite reminder that the occurrence of a body-psyche relationship and all the facts that demonstrate it cannot be even approximately exhausted by our customary simple schemata and most certainly cannot be sufficiently comprehended in this way. There is no scientific value in this psychotherapeutically nourished, fantastic configuration, justified though it may be as a negative kind of appeal against being too satisfied with the simplicities of psychological causation [emphasis added].[310]

Similarly, former president of the Royal College of Psychiatrists, Andrew Sims, writes that

[309] Wilhelm Wundt: *System der Philosophie* 1 (1919), preface ix.

310 Karl Jaspers, *General Psychopathology*, Vol. 1 & 2 (Baltimore, MD: Johns Hopkins University Press; 1997 first published in 1959), 244-46.

objective assessments are necessarily subjectively value-laden in what the observer chooses to measure; and this subjective aspect can be made more precise and reliable. There are always value judgments associated with both subjective and objective assessments. The process of making scientific evaluation consists of various states . . . . 'There is no such thing as an unprejudiced observation' (Karl Popper).'[311]

Others, such as renowned secular psychiatric geneticist Kenneth Kendler and psychiatric phenomenologist Joseph Parnas agree and identify why psychiatrists and all people within the mental health field must study and rely heavily on presuppositional philosophical assumptions:

First, the commonsense idea that good clinicians and scientists see the world as it truly is just by attending to the facts is mistaken. **Our perceptions of the world are influenced by our theoretical conceptions of it, and in no fields is this more true than psychiatry** . . . . Human behavior and experience are so stunningly complex that if we didn't have preconceived categories [e.g., mentally healthy versus disordered] — places to put things, including symptoms (such as hallucinations, anxiety), syndromes [constructs] (say, bulimia, dementia), and processes (for example, transference, acting out) — we would be overwhelmed and helpless. **But it is not only in our categories that we bring strong a priori assumptions. You cannot work in the field of mental health without having some set of beliefs — examined or otherwise — about the nature of causal processes, about what constitutes a "good explanation," or about the relative value of symptom-based assessments versus deeper characterizations of psychopathological processes. So, whether you like it or not, you have a set of tacitly operating philosophical concepts and beliefs that you**

[311] Andrew Sims, Is Faith Delusion? Why Religion is Good for Your Health (London: Continuum, 2009), 146.

**use to organize your views about the nature of
psychiatric illness and its treatment** [emphasis added].[312]

Pseudoscience and objective studies of the natural world both require foundational faith, and whether the genetic theory of mental illness is valid science or pseudo-science, there exist underlying philosophies which must first be embraced if the field is to be upheld.

Whereas in the previous chapter, the specific psychiatrists who have shaped the field of psychiatric genetics were introduced along with an overview of their shared moral value system/worldview, this chapter presents the underlying philosophical doctrines of that worldview in order to better illuminate the true nature of psychiatric eugenics. If eugenicists' foundational tenets of faith have not been rejected, then eugenics — whether or not the field maintains the same name — remains a destructive social influence that must be eliminated.

Individual Degenerationism

In 2013, chair of the *DSM-IV* task force and former head of psychiatry at Duke University Medical School, Allen Frances, wrote a book that was widely accepted by American culture and many medical professionals. The title of his book is *Saving Normal: an insider's revolt against out-of-control psychiatric diagnosis, DSM-5, big pharma, and the medicalization of ordinary life*. Unquestionably, Frances is to be commended for speaking out against the corruption and dangerous position of psychiatry at this stage in history. Yet, though there exist many valid points of

---

[312] Kendler & Parnas, Philosophical Issues in Psychiatry, 1-2.

concern that Frances raises in the book, there is an underlying philosophy contained in the main title *Saving Normal*, which Frances further discusses throughout the work. That philosophy is *individual degenerationism* — the first and one of the most powerful tenets of the eugenics theory past and present.

In fact, to suggest the notion that normal must be saved implies that categories of mental abnormality exist, and as Frances' book acknowledges, the scope and categories of alleged psychiatric abnormalities continues to increase rapidly as the existing powers create and tweak social and descriptive constructs and frame human phenomena into types or categories of perceived disorders.

Worth also noting is that the subtitle of Frances' book addresses many of the very issues that Emil Kraepelin's eugenic theory proposed, which Rüdin and Kallmann implemented, and which will be explored further in this chapter: psychiatric diagnoses (cultural, descriptive, and abnormal psychologies), *DSM-5* (a standardized system of categorization), psychopharmacology, and medicalizing "ordinary life" (medicalizing all of human nature and creating and treating perceived degenerates). The philosophies and subsequent problems found in psychiatric eugenics in the 1800-1900s remain the same issues embedded in modern psychiatric genetics. Though the previous chapters have highlighted how key figures established individual degenerationism as fundamental to their approaches to the human soul/mind/consciousness, the philosophy itself needs closer examination.

Of all psychiatric beliefs, *Individual Degenerationism* and *materialism* are the most prominent. Degeneration is likely a term with which many are not familiar. The word is often used in older psychology and psychiatry textbooks, but it typically only appears in reference to validated neurological diseases such as Alzheimer's Disease. In these cases, physical diseases are categorized as "neurodegenerative diseases."[313] But when used in reference to social and descriptive constructs that are said to be "mental disorders" (e.g., schizophrenia, alcoholism, or ADHD), hereditary or individual degenerationism is a clear indication of the historic eugenic theory.

It is also important to consider that modern psychiatrists have replaced the phrase *hereditary degeneration* with the concepts of *genetic disorder, dysfunction,* or *abnormality*. Despite the change in nomenclature, the underlying philosophy and application remain the same. *Disorder* is defined as "lack of order; to disturb the regular or normal functions of; an abnormal physical or mental condition."[314] When it comes to the mind, emotions, or moral behaviors, the phrase "psychiatric disorders" signals the fact that the philosophy of individual degeneracy is being utilized to qualify a social or descriptive construct. Without creating and saving abnormal within a medical framework, Kraepelinian psychiatry cannot be sustained as a legitimate approach to human nature and phenomena, let alone a medical field.

It cannot be overemphasized that *Individual degeneration* or *hereditary degeneration* is a critical philosophy to abnormal psychology and psychiatry, and as observed in chapter two, the philosophy is socially supported by the acceptance

[313] Alloy, Acocella, and Bootzin, *Abnormal Psychology*, 418-20.

[314] "Disorder," *Merriam Webster's Dictionary* (accessed August 25, 2019): https://www.merriam-webster.com/dictionary/disorder.

of the evolutionary theory. Psychiatrist and historian Heinz Haefner of the Schizophrenia Research Unit at the Central Institute of Mental Health records,

> There are 2 psychological factors worth mentioning that influenced the way social Darwinism was adopted and incorporated in psychiatry. In the wake of the Industrial Revolution, countries with existing systems of psychiatric care experienced a massive increase in admissions to asylums for the insane. For example, in Germany, the number of asylums rose from 93 to 233 and that of their inmates from 47 228 to 239 583 in the period from 1880 to 1913. **In the light of the theory of evolution and B.A. Morel's (1809–1873) theory of degeneration, this was seen as a sign of a massive increase in mental disorder resulting from a "genetic decadence" of the population** [emphasis added].[315]

Haefner also asserts that

> the history of ideas shows that social Darwinism in the educated classes and the doctrine of degeneration in psychiatry widely influenced thinking prior to World War II. Psychiatrists, lacking effective treatment for steadily growing numbers of the mentally ill, were susceptible to these ideologies. In a first step, several countries introduced compulsory sterilization as a genetic means of preventing diseases believed to be hereditary. Hitler's megalomaniac idea of creating a new human species by steering human evolution through the elimination of "unfit" genes in the mentally ill and inferior races led to the breach of human rights.[316]

---

[315] Heinz Haefner, "Comment on E.F. Torrey and R.H. Yolken: "Psychiatric genocide: Nazi attempts to eradicate schizophrenia," *Schizophrenia Bulletin* vol. 36 (1) (2010): 26-32.

[316] Ibid.

Similarly, Frank Stahnisch relates how accepting "natural selection" in social Darwinianism leads also to accepting the eugenic philosophy of individual degenerationism—a fact which explains why Emil Kraepelin embraced individual/hereditary degenerationism as key to his paradigm:

> Because they saw the Darwinian process of "natural selection" decelerated or even stopped in postwar Germany, physicians and anthropologists such as Ploetz came to perceive the health situation of the German people as "badly hurt in mind or body." Rüdin and Hoche had further launched severe polemics against the social welfare programs before the Weimar Republic, but now became more agitated: in a Kraepelinian vein, Rüdin and Hoche saw welfare programs as unwarranted expenditures because they would secure the longevity of "low value" populations. The resulting increase in the numbers of the psychiatrically and neurologically ill would lead "to an unacceptable burden for the welfare state, especially as so little is currently known about the treatment and long-term development of these conditions." Their critique was also applied to the National Pension Law designed to meet the needs of the army of war-injured veterans returning back from the fronts in 1918.[317]

The philosophy of individual degenerationism suggests that "normal people" are mentally healthy—a standard that has never been objectively established[318]—and think

---

[317] Frank W. Stahnisch, "The Early Eugenics Movement and Emerging Professional Psychiatry: Conceptual Transfers and Personal Relationships between Germany and North America, 1880s to 1930s," *CBMH* Vol. 31 (1) (2014): 18; https://pdfs.semanticscholar.org/8855/29 ed3162bfbdf659cba36ae3b1566c9a06b5.pdf.

[318] Daniel R. Berger II, *Mental Illness: The Necessity for Faith and Authority* (Taylors, SC: Alethia International Publications, 2016).

and behave in a productive and beneficial manner rather than in a maladaptive or impairing way. When people are said to be disordered or abnormal within Kraepelinianism, they are theorized to have reverted to a more primitive form of "evolutionary adaptation" as a result of claimed organic pathologies in their genes.[319] At its basic level, individual degenerationism is negative eugenics, which seeks to identify and categorize the mentally unhealthy and thereafter approach them.

The original psychiatric diagnostic system was Kraepelin's, and individual degeneration was undoubtedly the key philosophy on which he constructed his genetic theory of mental illness prior to World War I:

> **This argument was likewise taken up and prominently reformulated in Kraepelin's famous article "On Degeneration"** (Zur Entartungsfrage), which appeared in the influential Zentralblatt fuer Nervenheilkunde, Psychiatrie und gerichtliche Psychopathologie in 1908. Long before the war, Kraepelin argued that the etiology of neurasthenia and related mental disorders depended on the general conditions of modern life. **These views about nervous degeneration by the doyen of German psychiatry became so powerful that they even impacted approaches in social medicine and psychoanalysis later in the Weimar Republic.** It was clear for Kraepelin that the war-traumatized had not become ill due to the external conditions of industrialized warfare, **but because the nervous degenerate dispositions, which these individuals had since birth,** had given rise to their "nervous diseases [emphasis added].[320]

---

[319] Philip Lawrence Harriman, *Dictionary of Psychology* (New York: The Citadel Press, 1947), 98.

[320] Stahnisch, "The Early Eugenics Movement," 18.

It was Kraepelin who popularized the psychiatric idea that "individuals" could have an inherited mental "degenerate disposition." By combining the teachings of Rush, Morel, Darwin, Galton, and Wundt into a system of categorization that could be practically applied as a medical model to both diagnose and treat problems of human nature, Kraepelin convinced the world that his construct of individual hereditary madness should be embraced and applied just as the construct of race was upheld.

Even before Kraepelin, however, individual degeneration has been a critical tenet of faith in sustaining the eugenic construct of mental illness/diseases of the mind. Professors of psychology Castellano Turner and Bernard Kramer convey how differences in perceived races were from the beginning framed as degeneracy by psychiatrists—leading to specific theories of mental degeneracy:

> Racism may have several impacts on the effort to understand the origins of mental illness. To the extent that racist thought explains abnormality as deriving from fundamental differences between racial groups, one would expect that such thought would lead eventually to theories of mental illness as based on genetic inferiority of an entire population. **In this general way of thinking about differences between people, superiority and inferiority play critical roles. Abnormal behavior or mental aberrations might well be considered as expressions of genetic inferiority** [emphasis added].[321]

Individual degenerationism is naturally a part of race psychology, since the social construct of race was created to establish a hierarchy of ethnic groups based upon proposed physical and mental differentials. Professors of

[321] Castellano B. Turner and Bernard M. Kramer, *Mental Health, Racism, and Sexism*, ed. Charles Willie (New York: University of Pittsburgh Press, 2013), 7.

psychiatry Roland Littlewood and Maurice Lipsedge tell how creating categorical individual degenerates (mentally abnormal) is an attempt to justify and defend one's own presuppositional anthropology and dearly held identity:

> However we conceive of our group, whether a class, a nation, or a race, we define it by those we exclude from it. These outsiders are perceived as different from ourselves. They may have different languages, different customs or beliefs. They may look different. We may even regard them as sick or as sub-human. However we define them we perceive them as an undifferentiated mass with no individual variations. Outsiders always pose a threat to the status quo. Even if they are not physically dangerous, they are threatening simply because they are different. Their apartness is dangerous. It questions our tendency to see our society as the natural society and ourselves as the measure of normality. **To admit a valid alternative is already to question the inevitability of our type of world. We forget that the outsiders are part of our definition of ourselves. To confirm our own identity we push the outsiders even further away. By reducing their humanity we emphasize our own** [emphasis added].[322]

While many try to disown the mindsets, emotions, and behaviors they either cannot explain within evolutionary theory or find repulsive and destructive, setting people aside as abnormal, based upon their immaterial nature, highlights the destructive, normal, and yet deceived human tendency to maintain one's own false anthropological beliefs by controlling the identities of others. Within psychiatry, those deemed inferior by those who establish themselves as superior are not merely

---

[322] Roland Littlewood and Maurice Lipsedge, *Aliens and Alienists: Ethnic Minorities and Psychiatry*, 3rd edition (London: Taylor and Francis, 1997), 27.

viewed as different but as categorically and genetically disordered.

It is worth reiterating that individual hereditary/genetic degeneration was an essential doctrine to psychiatric eugenics both in Nazi Germany and in the United States. The issue of race purification by purging was one of the most popular social constructs of German psychiatrists in the first half of the 20th century for multiple reasons:

> The concept of **racial hygiene had deep roots in Germany**. In the late 19th and early 20th centuries, growing numbers of medical and public health professionals decried Germany's declining birth rate and the **perceived biologic "degeneration" of the nation and proposed reforms to improve the quantity and quality of the population . . . . But in return for accepting the persecution of Jews as a source of biologic degeneration**, many in the medical community welcomed the new emphasis on biology and heredity, increased research funding, and new career opportunities — including openings created by the purge of Jews and leftists from the medical and public health fields.[323]

Still today, many modern health care professionals and much of society view psychiatry as the authority in abnormal-descriptive psychology. This belief is due in large part to the creation of the field of psychiatry from a need to determine individual or "hereditary degenerates"[324] within evolutionary social and anthropological theories. The philosophy of individual

---

[323] Susan Bachrach, "In the Name of Public Health — Nazi Racial Hygiene," *New England Journal of Medicine* 351 (2004): 417-420; DOI: 10.1056/NEJMp048136.

[324] Philip Lawrence Harriman, *Dictionary of Psychology* (New York: The Citadel Press, 1947), 98.

degenerationism (the "neo-Kraepelinian model") remains the premiere theory in formal psychiatric genetics today:

> Formal genetic psychiatry was established in the early 20th century at a time of therapeutic nihilism, when psychiatry was strongly influenced by the theory of hereditary degeneration. This combined with economic considerations, led to a change of emphasis from healing to prevention of the more severe types of psychiatric illness. This was reflected in the popularity of the eugenics movement, which advocated measures such as restrictions on marriage or sterilization to prevent inherited disease. **A key aim of psychiatric genetic research was to provide scientific evidence that severe mental illnesses were inherited, thus strengthening the case for eugenic measures** [emphasis added].[325]

Though many terms, figureheads, social and descriptive constructs, and physical locations have changed, the principle goals of psychiatric genetics have remained the same.

Not only is it important to understand what individual degenerationism is, where it originated and was formalized, and why it is so important to Darwinian faith, but also it is helpful to be able to recognize when the philosophy is being applied. Individual degenerationism exists when people are devalued, set aside as spoiled ("stigmatized"), tainted, said to be mentally abnormal, and/or approached as soulless animals or machines:

---

[325] Gundula Kösters, Holger Steinberg, Kenneth Clifford Kirkby, Hubertus Himmerich' "Ernst Rüdin 's Unpublished 19922-1925 Study "Inheritance of Manic-Depressive Insanity": Genetic Research Findings Subordinated to Eugenic Ideology," *PLOS Genetics* (November 6, 2015): https://journals.plos.org/plosgenetics/article?id=10.1371/journal.pgen.1005524.

The idea had already plagued philosophers such as Rousseau, who considered the civilization of man as going against human nature, and eventually **"sparked over" to the medical sciences in the late 19th and early 20th century. At that time, human "self-domestication" appealed to psychiatry, because it served as a causal explanation for the alleged degeneration of the *"erbgut"* (genetic material) of entire populations and the presumed increase of mental disorders.** Consequently, Social Darwinists emphasized preventing procreation by people of "lower genetic value" and positively selecting favorable traits in others [emphasis added].[326]

It is also important to be able to discern how psychiatrists determine and control alleged degenerates, the perceived disordered, or the categorical abnormal in order to identify individual degeneracy and reject its application in society. There are several key factors that reveal Kraepelinian eugenics' ongoing influence that require further attention.

An Accepted Construct

Whether it is constructs of race, social variances, economic status, behaviors, mental processes, distresses, or a combination of these "branches of psychology," descriptive and social constructs are key to enabling eugenics and individual degenerationism. In fact, it is the construct — or as Wundt called it: *volke*/cultural psychology — that is said to be a disease, dysfunction, or syndrome caused by genetic defects. Today, some scientists call this

---

[326] M. Brune, "On Human Self-Domestication, Psychiatry, and Eugenics," *Philosophies, Ethics, and Humanities in Medicine* 5 (2) (October 2007): 21; https://www.ncbi.nlm.nih.gov/pubmed/17919321.

Kraepelinian approach "social constructivism" or the "bio-psycho-social" model:

> This distinction applies in the context of theorizing about psychiatry. Consider the claim that some mental disorders depend on social norms – that reference to social norms is relevant in an explanation for why a patient suffers from a mental disorder. Social norms may have a causal impact on the development of disorders, and facts about social norms may ground, in the non-causal sense, facts about disorders . . . . one may subscribe to social constructivism concerning mental disorders themselves, such as schizophrenia, PTSD, or dissociative identity disorder.[327]

Allen Frances contends in his book *Saving Normal* that the entire modern psychiatric system built upon Kraepelin's original system is cultural/race and descriptive psychology:

> **Our classification of mental disorders is no more than a collection of fallible and limited constructs that seeks but never finds the truth** — but this remains our best current way of communicating about, treating, and researching mental disorders [emphasis added].[328]

Psychiatric constructs must be centered on perceived abnormality, deviance, degeneracy, or dysfunction and not only on ideas about cultural or human nature. In this light, revered professor of psychiatry at Johns Hopkins University Medical School, Jerome Frank, once said that "psychotherapy may be the only treatment that creates the

---

[327] Raphael van Riel, "What Is Constructionism in Psychiatry? From Social Causes to Psychiatric Classification." *Frontiers in Psychiatry* vol. 7 (57) (April 18, 2016): doi:10.3389/fpsyt.2016.00057.

[328] Allen Frances, Saving Normal: An Insider's Revolt against Out-of-Control Psychiatric Diagnosis, DSM-5, Big Pharma, and the Medicalization of Ordinary Life (New York: HarperCollins, 2013), 21.

illness it treats."[329] Yale trained psychiatric epidemiologist Allan Horwitz also remarks,

> The harmful component of the HD [Harmful Dysfunction] analysis stipulates that only conditions that are harmful can be mental disorders. **When dysfunctions are also socially disvalued, and therefore harmful, they are mental disorders. Because social values always at least partially determine what conditions are harmful, concepts of mental disorders are to some degree intrinsically relative to particular times and places** . . . . In addition, the HD view provides the grounds for critiquing mental health practices. The failure to perform an evolutionarily designed function is a necessary condition that sets limits on the legitimate use of the concept of mental disorder. A condition that is not a dysfunction is not a disorder . . . . **Cultural values and social interests, not nature, set the borders between definitions of normality and pathology that are found in any particular time and place** [emphasis added].[330]

Additionally, numerous psychiatrists of the World Psychiatric Association write,

> In view of current controversies about **how to conceptualize and categorize psychiatric disorders,** which is currently occurring as the *DSM-5* and *ICD-11* are taking shape, it is likely that psychiatric nosology will need a reshuffling of categories. **We suggest that it is worth considering a reclassification of disorders according to the evolutionary significance of behavior that is expressed in malfunctioning ways, given conditions germane to modern environments compared to ancestral ones.** Several conceptualizations have been

[329] Mark Hubble, Barry Duncan, and Scott Miller, *The Heart and Soul of Change: What Works in Therapy* (Washington, D.C.: American Psychological Association, 1999), 2.

[330] Allan V. Horwitz, *The Oxford Handbook of Philosophy of Social Science* (Oxford Press, 2012): DOI: 10.1093/oxfordhb/9780195392753 .013.0023.

published in the recent past, including the "harmful dysfunction analysis" and an "evolutionary taxonomy of treatable conditions," but none of them satisfactorily addresses the problem of reductionism. **Accordingly, historical aspects of psychiatric nosology and findings from neuroscience have been proven difficult to reconcile, and similar obstacles will arise for any attempt to develop a psychopathological system based on insights from evolutionary theory. In any event, if such a prospect shall be successful at all, it would need to involve analyses by researchers with expertise in evolutionary social sciences** [emphasis added].[331]

Individual degenerationism and evolutionary belief are dependent upon each other. The American Psychiatric Association likewise stated in the *DSM-IV*:

> **The boundaries between normality and pathology** [alleged biological degeneracy; mental abnormality] **vary across cultures for specific types of behaviors.** Thresholds of tolerance for specific symptoms or behaviors differ across cultures, social settings, and families. Hence, the level at which an experience becomes problematic or pathological will differ. **The judgment that a given behavior is abnormal and requires clinical attention depends on cultural norms that are internalized by the individual and applied by others around them, including family members and clinicians** [emphasis added].[332]

Simply by describing and classifying undesirable, impairing, or seemingly unexplainable aspects of human

---

[331] Martin Brüne, Jay Belsky, Horacio FaBrega, Jay r. FeierMan, Paul gilBert, kalMan glantz, JosePH PoliMeni, JoHn s. Price, Julio sanJuan, roger sullivan, alFonso troisi, Daniel r. Wilson, "The Crisis of Psychiatry — insights and prospects from evolutionary theory," *World Psychiatry* 11 (1) (February 2012): 57.

[332] APA, *DSM-IV*, 14.

nature, Psychiatrists like Rush and Kraepelin have created a system of degeneracy which could be claimed to fall within the fields of science and medicine.

Perceived dysfunctional mindsets, emotions, behaviors, political views, religions, social economic classes, and supposed "lesser races" all became disorders classified as hereditary degenerations in Nazi Germany. *Baker's Encyclopedia of Psychology and Counseling* imparts,

> In psychiatry the descriptive approach is most commonly associated with the work of Emil Kraepelin . . . . Kraepelin's classification of psychopathologies was in essence a descriptive approach. His assumption was that groups of symptoms that occur regularly together should be regarded as a specific psychopathology ["syndromes," or constructs]. This approach remains in the current classifications of mental disorders, *DSM*.[333]

Sadly, as acknowledged, the American mental health system of classification contained in the *DSM* is still the Kraepelinian approach. Professor of History at the University of Houston Hannah Decker expresses how the *DSM-III* redirected American psychiatry back toward Kraepelin's descriptive psychology:

> The contents of the third edition of the American Psychiatric Association's *Diagnostic and Statistical Manual of Mental Disorders (DSM-III)* can only be understood by studying aspects of the last one hundred years of psychiatric history. This paper deals with: (1) three aspects of Kraepelinian psychiatry — descriptive psychiatry, Kraepelin's devotion to empirical research and his inability always to carry it through, and his anti-psychoanalytic stance; (2) the optimistic yet troubled state

---

[333] David G. Benner and Peter C. Hill, *Baker Encyclopedia of Psychology and Counseling* 2nd ed. (Grand Rapids: Baker Books, 1999), 342.

of American psychiatry in the period 1946 to 1974; (3) the
work of the so-called 'neo-Kraepelinians.'[334]

Kraepelin did not discover diseases, he merely took existing descriptions of troubling human nature and recast them as forms of degeneracy. Today, the *DSM* enables Kraepelin's approach to continue. Other psychiatrists and philosophers submit that

> the influence of the *DSM*s is nowhere more evident than in the discussion of psychopathology; indeed, the category of psychopathology itself, defined as the symptom expression of a disorder or disease in the individual, derives from these classifications.[335]

It is important to restate that the mindsets, emotions, and behaviors (the "symptoms" or phenomena which are described) that constitute the various psychiatric constructs in the *DSM-5* are real, but the constructs/disorders/syndromes (a compilation of symptoms), which psychiatrists assert to be valid disease concepts, are not validated realities approachable within scientific methods. These constructs simply describe features and phenomena of human nature within a formalized and controlled system according to evolutionary belief.

The Construct of Schizophrenia

The most famous construct, and one which has been historically central to sustaining psychiatric eugenics and

---

[334] Hannah S. Decker, "How Kraepelinian was Kraepelin? How Kraepelinian are the neo-Kraepelinians? From Emil Kraepelin to *DSM-III*," *History of Psychiatry* 71 (3) (September 18, 2007): 337.

[335] Radden, Philosophy of Psychiatry, 8.

concepts of mental hereditary degeneration, is the construct of schizophrenia. The influential Dr. Frances comments on the true nature of the construct of schizophrenia:

> Schizophrenia is a useful construct — not myth, not disease. **It is a description of a particular set of psychiatric problems, not an explanation of their cause.** Someday we will have a much more accurate understanding and more precise ways of describing these same problems. But for now, schizophrenia is very valuable in our day-to-day work. **And so are the other *DSM* disorders. It is good to know and use the *DSM* definitions, but not to reify** [to regard them as fact] **or worship them** [emphasis added].[336]

According to other psychiatrists, such as the prominent Peter Breggin, psychiatric constructs are formally accepted cultural descriptions and not material realities:

> Is there such a thing as schizophrenia? Yes and no. Yes, there are people who think irrationally at times and who attribute their problems to seemingly inappropriate causes, such as extraterrestrials or voices in the air. Yes, there are people who think they are God or the devil and repeat the claim no matter how much trouble it gets them into. **But no, these people are not biologically defective or inherently different from the rest of us. They are not afflicted with a brain disorder or disease** [emphasis added].[337]

Considered by most psychiatrists over the last several centuries to be one of the leading psychiatric researchers on the construct of schizophrenia, Sir Robin Murray declares,

---

[336] Frances, *Saving Normal*, 21.

[337] Peter R. Breggin, *Toxic Psychiatry* (New York: St. Martin's Press, 1991), 45.

> **I expect to see the end of the concept of schizophrenia soon. Already the evidence that it is a discrete entity rather than just the severe end of psychosis has been fatally undermined.** Furthermore, the syndrome is already beginning to breakdown, for example, into those cases caused by copy number variations, drug abuse, social adversity, etc. Presumably this process will accelerate, and the term schizophrenia will be confined to history, like 'dropsy' [emphasis added].[338]

Others, such as clinical psychologist John Read, insist that the psychiatric label "schizophrenia" is a "scientifically meaningless and socially devastating label."[339] To accept the descriptive label as objective is to also accept the cultural beliefs which created the label, and in the case of the constructs of schizophrenia and bipolar, there is likely no deeper Kraepelinian faith. In fact, even today, one would have a difficult time attempting to separate the Kraepelinian construct of schizophrenia from Nazi eugenics.

A diagnosis of "schizophrenia" is devastating and stigmatizing, because the construct—developed by Kraepelin as *"dementia praecox"* (premature dementia)—is historically a cultural label that classifies people as hereditary/individual degenerates and pronounces them hopeless. Schizophrenia was not a discovered disease; it was a construct created on evolutionary beliefs in attempt to explain why individuals can be given over to deceitful

---

[338] Robin M. Murray, "Mistakes I Have Made in My Research Career," *Schizophrenia Bulletin* (December, 2016): doi: 10.1093/schbul/sbw165.

[339] John Read and Jeffrey Masson, *Models of Madness: Psychological, Social, and Biological Approaches* edited by John Read, Richard Bentall, and Loren Mosher (Routledge, 2004), 34.

thinking (e.g., delusions and hallucinations). Historian of medicine and psychiatry Richard Noll reports,

> In 1896 German psychiatrist Emil Kraepelin proposed a classification of mental diseases based on this new fundamental medical principle, and described *dementia praecox* as a psychotic process that began in the decade after puberty with a distinctive course and outcome [sic]. Mental deterioration, weakness and defect worsened and became permanent. It was a hopeless diagnosis. **But Kraepelin argued that dementia praecox, as well as other major mental diseases that he created, would one day be found to be rooted in natural, biological disease processes. This claim, in part, made Kraepelinian classification attractive to American alienists who desired to retain their status as physicians.** There is a co-dependency of the psychiatric profession and a biological disease concept that persists today [emphasis added].[340]

As Noll describes, maintaining that psychiatric constructs have biological basis is essential to claiming them as diseases entities. Thus, eugenics/genetics/hereditary became an attractive hypothesis. To claim that defective genes cause schizophrenia assumes that schizophrenia is a disease rather than the social and descriptive construct that it truly is. When a "psychiatric disorder" or "mental disorder" is spoken of, one should understand that these ideas are descriptive constructs rather than valid diseases,[341] and moreover, that these constructs which

---

[340] "The Rise and Fall of American Madness," *Harvard University Press* (January 30, 2012): https://harvardpress.typepad. com/hup_publicity/2012 /01/the-rise-and-fall-of-american-madness.html.

[341] There are several valid neurological diseases listed as mental disorders in the *DSM-5*. Alzheimer's disease, for example, should not be considered as a mental disorder.

claim genetic causation expose the eugenic philosophy of hereditary/individual degenerationism.

The Criteria for Construction

Since concepts of degeneracy/abnormality are foundational to every psychiatric construct, it is also imperative that the criteria for determining a constructed psychiatric disorder be examined. Professor of sociology Jerome Wakefield—who the World Psychiatric Association claims "has done more in the last decade or so to clarify and analyze the concept of mental disorder,"[342] defined a mental/psychiatric disorder as that which

> lies on the boundary between [1] the given natural world and the [2] constructed social world; a disorder exists when **the failure** of a person's internal mechanisms to perform their functions **as designed by nature** impinges harmfully on the person's well-being **as defined by social values** [emphasis added].[343]

Wakefield notes that two preceding requirements are allegedly necessary to determine not only who is perceived to be abnormal/disordered, but also to discover if any abnormality exists at all. The first is a compliance or conformity to a "design." For Wakefield—an evolutionist— his proposed designer is nature itself (e.g., natural selection).

[342] Derek Bolton, "The Usefulness of Wakefield's Definition for the Diagnostic Manuals," *World Psychiatry (WPA)* 6 (3) (2007): 164.

[343] Jerome C. Wakefield, "The Concept of Mental Disorder," *American Psychologist* 47 (1992): 373.

Evolutionary psychiatric geneticists believe that the human genome, passing through the mystical processes of evolution and environments, is the designer. For others, such as Christians, however, the Creator God determines the standard of conformity for the soul/psyche, human phenomena, and outworking moral behavior. These distinctions reveal that social constructs related to the soul/psyche are formed primarily on presuppositional beliefs in origins rather than on objective discoveries in the natural world. Accepting or rejecting individual degeneracy of the soul, then, is based upon an individual's and society's anthropological views — their moral faith.

Wakefield's proposed design is based upon evolutionary anthropology and phenomenology, and according to Darwinian theory upon which Kraepelinianism (eugenics) is founded, the belief that humanity is constantly evolving or "adapting." But if, in fact, Darwinian evolution were true, then everyone is on an evolutionary continuum, and the standard "design of nature" could never be realized. If, however, no objective standard exists in evolution, then neither do degenerates — that is unless social values become the only true standard of normalcy.

Wakefield's second criterion is a falling short of "values," and this requirement reveals the true singular evolutionary criterion for determining psychiatric disorders. For Wakefield and most evolutionists, these values are determined by an established social authority and change over time and across cultures. One abnormal psychology textbook notes:

> The problem of mental disorder is probably as old as man. Recorded history reports a broad range of interpretations of abnormal behavior and methods for its alleviation or eradication, which have generally reflected

the degree of enlightenment and the trends of religious, philosophical, and social beliefs and practices of the times.[344]

In many cultures around the world, whose values still rest outside of Kraepelinianism, human phenomena such as what is termed as psychosis/schizophrenia are not viewed as degeneracy, but as spiritual enlightenment. In the 2016 documentary, *CRAZYWISE*, for example, the producers reveal how many cultures esteem and elevate to positions of leadership those who experience the human phenomena framed within neo-Kraepelinianism as psychosis:[345]

> When a young person experiences a frightening break from reality, Western experts usually label it a "first-episode psychosis" while some psychologists and cultures define it as a "spiritual awakening." The documentary CRAZYWISE reveals remarkably effective treatment approaches and a survivor led movement challenging a mental health system in crisis.[346]

Social and descriptive constructs about human nature and human phenomena must be created and marketed as medical issues if the metaphysical soul/psyche is to be viewed as a scientific endeavor. This transforming of race and other cultural and descriptive psychologies into a formally published medical model of mental illness

---

[344] Walter Coville, Timothy Costello, and Fabian Rouke, *Abnormal Psychology: Mental Illness Types, Causes, and Treatment* (New York: Barnes and Noble, 1960), 11.

[345] CRAZYWISE: https://crazywisefilm.com.

[346] Victoria Maxwell, "Crazywise," *Psychology Today* (January 27, 2015): https://www.psychologytoday.com/us/blog/crazy-life/201501/crazywise.

(eugenics) with formal constructs was arguably Kraepelin's most powerful influence on psychiatry.

Creating Constructs

Within evolutionary thinking, whoever obtains the most social power and influence has the privilege/responsibility to determine normalcy according to personal or societal chosen values/morality. Though altruism and the natural world might be claimed as the guiding moral value, eugenics (cultural genetic values) is the true underlying guide. In a society where physicians and scientists are primary figures of authority in determining perceived normal and abnormal mental states according to their values, constructs can be framed within a medical model and presented as a validated disease concept that are not questioned. Psychiatrist Peter Breggin states this precise occurrence in the Holocaust:

> The third principle concerns the application of medical "diagnosis" to psychological, spiritual, social and political problems. The use of diagnoses establishes a hierarchy of superior (allegedly normal) and inferior (allegedly mentally ill) people. It "medicalizes" human conflict, permitting "treatment" of the victims. This fit Nazi ideology and paved the way for "selections" in extermination centers.[347]

Eugenics requires that social constructs, which describe perceived negative, impairing, or harmful aspects of human nature, be developed by an established authority within a medical framework and applied to social reform.

---

[347] Peter Breggin, "Psychiatry's Role in the Holocaust," 143.

The notion that mass shootings are a form of mental illness provides one illustration of how constructs are created and degenerates made. Many people in society today have mentally constructed violence and mass shootings into a psychiatric disorder, while others, based upon their moral values, disagree. In late 2019, The American Psychiatric Association asserted themselves as "a leader in confronting the problem of gun violence" and began "calling gun violence a public health problem in need of immediate action."[348] In 2019, Editor-in-Chief Emeritus of the *Psychiatric Times,* Ronald Pies, and current Editor-in-Chief, James Knoll, discussed this topic:

> In the wake of the horrific mass public shootings in El Paso and Dayton, the public dialogue has turned to focus more squarely on mental illness. **Many are unable to fathom how a human being could commit such acts without being under the influence of some powerful "alien" force.** An example of a recent question posed to us by the media was: *"Psychiatrists say that violence and mass killing are not closely linked to mental illness. But can we agree that shooting 20 strangers more or less at random is not normal, rational behavior?"* [emphasis added][349]

If one believes that normal is not evil, then degeneracy (something apart from perceived healthy human nature) seems like the logical explanation of all evil within a

---

[348] Liza H. Gold, "Gun Violence and Medical Professional Organizations: Political Business as Usual?" *Psychiatric Times* vol. 36 (11) (November 25, 2019): https://www.psychiatrictimes.com/forensic-psychiatry/gun-violence-and-medical-professional-organizations-political-business-usual.

[349] James L. Knoll IV and Ronald W. Pies, "Cruel, Immoral Behavior Is Not a Mental Illness," *Psychiatric Times Online* (August 19, 2019): https://www.psychiatrictimes.com/couch-crisis/cruel-immoral-behavior-not-mental-illness?rememberme=1&elq_mid=8335& elq_cid=893295&GUID=31158D64-F01A-4DEA-AC1A-D3CE843FC9BC.

biological/evolutionary worldview. Knoll and Pies continue,

> It may be more comforting to believe that some "disease of the mind" took over and caused someone to commit an unspeakable act than to recognize that "sane" persons are quite capable of violent and sadistic behavior. Sadly, the ancient problem of *homo sapiens* choosing to act in a supremely selfish and violent manner has always been with us. Do we advance our understanding by labeling such behavior "mental illness," and calling for greater scrutiny of "mentally troubled" individuals? As psychiatrists, we think not, even as we acknowledge the problem of untreated psychiatric illness. Another way of posing the question is to ask — *Does immoral, callous, cruel, and supremely selfish behaviors constitute a mental illness?* These socially deviant traits appear in those with and without mental illness, and are widespread in the general population. Are there some perpetrators suffering from a genuine psychotic disorder who remain mentally organized enough to carry out these attacks? Of course, but they are a minority.[350]

While the mindsets, emotions, and behaviors may be the same in alleged normal and abnormal people, it is the established authority who determines the construct and how the construct is interpreted and applied. John Read and Jeffrey Masson explain,

> Some might argue that what happened in Germany 60 years ago has nothing to do with how biological psychiatry operates today. We document these awful events, however, precisely because they so clearly illustrate, again, the three themes present throughout the history of the treatment of people considered mad: (1) social control in the interests of the powerful, (2) damaging and violent 'treatments', and (3) the ability of

[350] Ibid.

193

experts to generate theories camouflaging what is really happening.[351]

What this discussion about gun violence and mental disorders also exposes is that established social and descriptive constructs shape how society interprets and approaches moral behavior — viewed as either mental degeneracy or evil, as sick or sinful. Knoll and Pies reveal how easy but futile it is to take an individual, social, or behavioral problem and create a psychiatric construct/diagnosis:

> Even if psychiatrists were to create a dubious diagnosis called "Mass Shooting Disorder," it would be utterly useless. The diagnostic criteria for "MSD" would be so broad and nonspecific that "diagnosing" would be meaningless . . . . Further, there are no diagnostic criteria that would allow one to reliably "flag" an individual. Factors such as poor stress tolerance, impulse control problems, substance abuse, hopelessness, desperation, and social isolation also occur in those *without* mental illness diagnoses.[352]

For psychiatrists to create degenerates and claim genetic etiologies, they must develop descriptive constructs framed as medical/biological illnesses. Yet, if the American Psychiatric Association chose in the future to create a Mass Shooting Disorder (MSD), then by simply formally describing recognizable behavior as symptoms and blaming said symptoms on biological causes, they could create a social construct or "syndrome," which would likely be accepted by much of society as describing the

---

[351] John Read and Jeffrey Masson, *Models of Madness: Psychological, Social, and Biological Approaches* edited by John Read, Richard Bentall, and Loren Mosher (Routledge, 2004), 35.

[352] Knoll IV & Pies, "Cruel, Immoral Behavior Is Not a Mental Illness."

human phenomenon. Added to this belief and descriptive construct would likely be both psychiatric geneticists' endless search for a defective gene or group of genes theorized to be responsible for MSD and the prescribing of a psychotropic drug to control established violent symptoms. Bipolar, Borderline Personality, Anxiety, Schizophrenia, Pedophiliac, ADHD, and most every other classified psychiatric construct simply describes aspects of human nature that are troubling or not explainable within the evolutionary worldview.

Another factor to consider in the reality that psychiatric disorders are social and descriptive constructs is that not only are these constructs shaped by cultural beliefs, but ironically, society is heavily influenced by the constructs it accepts as valid and reliable. Psychiatrist Leon Eisenberg conveys this social reality: "Human sciences are beset by a paradox: what is believed to be true about behaviour affects the very behaviour which it purports to explain."[353] What is also fascinating is that a direct correlation exists between the rise of specific diagnoses and their media promotion and public discussion:

> Borch-Jacobsen identifies a whole boatload of psychological disorders that appear and disappear as specific medical and psychiatric theories and treatments gain or lose popularity. He devotes a chapter to depression, a condition he says was relatively rare until a recent upsurge. He notes that the rise in depression corresponds with the introduction of antidepressant medications in the 1960s, with the number of depression diagnoses skyrocketing as more targeted medications appeared in the late 1980s. "This is clearly not a

[353] Leon Eisenberg, "The Social Construction of Mental Illness," *Psychological Medicine* 18 (1988): 2.

coincidence," says Borch-Jacobsen. "Far from arriving on the market to treat a previously existing psychiatric disorder, these new drugs actually promoted it. Modern, Western depression, we might say, is a side effect of antidepressants."[354]

In a small study conducted by psychiatrists at John Hopkins, the same human tendency was observed with the construct of schizophrenia:

> Because we've shined a spotlight in recent years on emerging and early signs of psychosis, diagnosis of schizophrenia is like a new fad, and it's a problem especially for those who are not schizophrenia specialists because symptoms can be complex and misleading.[355]

In the same manner, suicide rates have been known for decades to increase within communities and in accordance with continued public dialogue following one completed suicide.[356] Benjamin Rush wrote in 1786 that "suicidal thinking might be contagious, often propagated by means of newspapers."[357] These "copycat suicides" reveal how

[354] Nancy Joseph, "Mental Illness as a Social Construct," *University of Washington* (July 2010): https://artsci.washington.edu/news/2010-07/mental-illness-social-construct.

[355] Krista Baker quoted by Johns Hopkins Medicine, "Study suggests overdiagnosis of Schizophrenia," *Science News* (April 22, 2019): https://www.sciencedaily .com/releases/2019/04/190422090842.htm.

[356] J. Leo, "Could Suicide Be Contagious?" *Time Magazine* (February 1986): 59.

[357] Benjamin Rush, *An Inquiry into the Influence of Physical Causes on the Moral Faculty* (February 1786), 22.

intimate relationships and public discourse can shape thinking and behavior.[358]

In addition, constructs of mental degeneracy and suicide now being advertised on television and presented in shows and in movies are influential, and people tend to identify/self-diagnose with the established and marketed description of their problems.

In many ways, a clinician teaches those under his/her care to view themselves through his/her belief system about human phenomena (phenomenology) by accepting a psychiatric diagnosis. This type of "medicine" (rather a form of discipleship) creates a reality through self-fulfilling prophecy and a faith in what each construct represents:

> To recognize that scientific theories are inventions of the imagination is to enhance rather than to diminish their grandeur. It is, however, their very success in introducing order into the chaos of appearance that makes it easy to mistake them for reality itself. For the clinician as scientist, the problem is compounded: **the more he is believed, the more his prophecies become self-fulfilling. Accounts of disease, through the expectations they arouse, impact on the course of disease.** If professional ideology influences society, it also profoundly reflects the values of the society in which it is embedded . . . . **theories of behaviour are not simply statements about the connections between 'facts,' they are statements which change 'facts' and have profound moral implications for the role of human agency in the cause, persistence and cure of mental disorders** [emphasis added].[359]

---

[358] Leo, "Could Suicide Be Contagious?" 59.

[359] Eisenberg, "The Social Construction of Mental Illness," 9.

Clinicians who tell people what to expect when they receive a diagnosis—what the APA refers to as "predictive validators,"[360] should expect those people who place their faith in the constructed diagnostic system to live accordingly. While clinicians may sincerely wish to help those who come to them, they are in actuality restricting hurting people to a fabricated system of beliefs that creates individual degenerates rather than heals mental and behavioral struggles. Eugenics is not merely a controlling diagnostic system; it is a new faith for individuals to establish identity and for societies to interpret human nature and their own phenomena/experiences.

Diagnostic System

Once the descriptive social construct has been established—whether or not empirical evidence exists to support its acceptance, then a corresponding and formal diagnostic system—a standardized means of selection—must also follow. Those who are diagnosed, categorized, or selected as disordered (as a degenerate) are entered into the neo-eugenics system. In an article entitled, "Eugenics Never Went Away," Robert Wilson writes,

> Eugenics survivors are those who have lived through eugenic interventions, which typically begin with being categorised as less than fully human – as 'feeble-minded', as belonging to a racialised ethnic group assumed to be inferior, or as having a medical condition, such as epilepsy, presumed to be heritable. That categorisation enters them into a eugenics pipeline. The ongoing eugenic sterilisation of people with disabilities, prisoners, poor people, people from certain racialised ethnic groups and

[360] APA, DSM-5, 20.

indigenous people (especially women) affects precisely the same sorts of people explicitly targeted by eugenics before 1945. These sterilisations are not a reminder of a eugenics past. They result from continuing and new eugenics pipelines. And they bring that feeling of eugenics ever closer [emphasis added].[361]

In Nazi Germany, it was psychiatrists who were viewed as the "experts" in diagnosing/selecting those who they judged to be disordered:

> From late 1933 on, doctors at mental hospitals and homes for the mentally disabled had to fill in a questionnaire for each chronically mentally ill or disabled patient no longer fully fit for work. **The questionnaires were then submitted to psychiatrists chosen as experts.** The list included patients with schizophrenia, epilepsy, mental retardation, final states of neurological diseases, mentally ill criminals, and all psychiatric patients interned for more than 5 years. The experts drew a red cross on the questionnaires of those patients they selected for being killed. Several professors of psychiatry served as such experts, for example, Prof. Werner Heyde (Würzburg), Prof. Max de Crinis (Berlin), Prof. Karl Schneider (Heidelberg), and Prof. Paul Nitsche (Head of the Public Mental Hospital Pirna-Sonnenstein, successor to Heyde as the "Medical Director of the Euthanasia Program"). Schneider and De Crinis committed suicide after the war [emphasis added].[362]

---

[361] Robert A. Wilson, "Eugenics Never Went Away," *AEON* (June 5, 2018): https://aeon.co/essays/eugenics-today-where-eugenic-sterilisation-continues-now?utm_source=Aeon+Newsletter&utm_ campaign=574e66bb0c-EMAIL_ CAMPAIGN_2018_06_06_11_10&utm_medium=email&utm_term=0_411a82 e59d-574e66bb0c-69588105.

[362] Heinz Haefner, "Comment on E.F. Torrey and R.H. Yolken: 'Psychiatric genocide: Nazi attempts to eradicate schizophrenia,'" *Schizophrenia Bulletin* vol. 36 (1) (2010): 26-32.

Similarly, psychiatrist Rael Strous highlights both how psychiatrists' significant influence during the Holocaust is largely hidden and how psychiatric selection was based upon Darwinian theory that naturally led to a eugenic diagnostic system:

> While it would be expected that the involvement of psychiatrists in such a profound manner would be well-known in the field, this is not the case. Little has been published on the subject in mainstream psychiatry journals and even less is part of the formal education process for medical students and psychiatry residents. Several reasons may be proposed for this. First, it remains an embarrassment for the field that so many senior members – professors, department heads and internationally known figures – were so intimately involved. Second, many of those involved continued to practice and conduct research long after the war and were protected by colleagues. **Third, and arguably most important, what psychiatrists did was based upon a paradigm shift in how patients and mental illness were viewed. Activities of psychiatrists became much of a value judgment in how they "read" the community and principles of neo-Darwinism with subsequent consideration of racial hygiene** [emphasis added].[363]

Peter Breggin likewise points out that one of the major factors which both the Holocaust and modern psychiatry share is the diagnostic system:

> **There is still another principle, usually unstated, that is critical to psychiatry and to the holocaust alike. It is** *selection.* A number of writers have emphasized the role of doctors in "selecting" patients for death. Lifton's *Nazi Doctors* describes the use of this euphemism at Auschwitz and makes clear that the so-called selections were made

[363] Rael D. Strous, "Psychiatry During the Nazi Era: Ethical Lessons for the Modern Professional," *Annals of General Psychiatry* vol. 6 (8) (February 27, 2007): doi:10.1186/1744-859X-6-8.

by medical doctors. The term "selection" was intended to invest murder with medical respectability. Selection took place in the extermination camps the moment victims alighted from the railroad cars, the more healthy and physically able being sent to slave labor and the remainder to the gas chambers. It also took place throughout life in Auschwitz, including on the medical wards.[364]

The word *Diagnoses* "means 'discernment' or 'knowing the difference between' one thing and another."[365] In psychiatry, the *DSM-5* represents this formal attempt to establish a line of demarcation—a clinical standard of both selecting abnormal people over normal and discerning in which perceived category of degeneracy they should be classified.[366] Historian and philosopher Michel Foucault also expresses how selection is key to psychiatry:

> Without being named as such, **selection has always been intrinsic to psychiatry and is found at its very origins during the industrial revolution,** when urban centers became flooded with homeless people. Institutional psychiatry initially developed during the early industrial revolution as a method of removing homeless people from urban streets for indefinite incarceration in the newly created state mental hospitals.[367]

[364] Breggin, "Psychiatry's Role in the Holocaust," 143.

[365] Ronald Pies, "Positivism, Humanism, and the Case for Psychiatric Diagnosis," *Psychiatric Times Online* 31, no. 7 (July 1, 2014): http://www.psychiatrictimes.com/couch-crisis/positivism-humanism-and-case-psychiatric-diagnosis/page/0/1.

[366] As will be observed in chapter six, there is no significant differential between most of the "severe" classifications of disorders.

[367] Michel Foucault, *Madness and Civilization* (New York: Vintage, 1973), 39.

Worth restating is that Kraepelin provided the most widely accepted psychiatric/psychological eugenic system of selection, complete with social and descriptive constructs, on which the American Psychiatric Association's (APA) *Diagnostic and Statistical Manual* (the *DSM*) would be largely based. Former APA president Jeffrey Lieberman remarks on how Kraepelin established the ideal eugenic system for distinguishing between alleged mental degenerates and those perceived as healthy:

> Kraepelin, on the contrary [to Freud], drew a sharp boundary between mental health and mental illness. This bright dividing line, along with his system of classifying disorders based on their symptoms and time-course of the illness, ran entirely counter to the psychoanalytic conception of mental disease.[368]

By describing human struggle in a systemized and descriptive way and naming this list with medical-sounding nomenclature, Kraepelin gained social control and authority for psychiatry. But moreover, Kraepelin provided a formal diagnostic system of mental hygiene/health. Lieberman records as well how Kraepelin's original construct is still utilized and considered just as desirous as when Kraepelin first created his eugenics paradigm:

> Despite the initial resistance to Kraepelin's novel proposal, his classification system was eventually accepted by the majority of European psychiatrists, and by the 1890s it had become the first common language used by European psychiatrists of all theoretical bents to discuss the psychoses. To help explain his classification system, Kraepelin wrote portraits of prototypical cases for each diagnosis, derived from his own experiences with

---

[368] Lieberman, *Shrinks*, 96.

patients. These vivid portraits became a pedagogical device that influenced generations of European psychiatrists and are as compelling today as when he wrote them more than a century ago.[369]

Significantly, it is not simply that the genetic theory was born out of Kraepelinianism. Rather, the current genetic theory and diagnostic system of alleged mental illnesses is fully Kraepelinian and is adversely affecting modern society in similar ways as it did in twentieth-century Germany. Clinical psychologists John Read and Jeffrey Masson assert that

> the genetic theories that still dominate psychiatry today provided the motivation, and the camouflage, for what happened. It was psychiatrists who developed the theory that undesirable behaviors are genetically transmitted. It was this theory that was used to justify compulsory sterilization and murder.[370]

Despite its changes, the psychiatric genetic theory remains centered upon the philosophy of degeneracy—creating, maintaining, explaining, and attempting to deal with the perceived mentally abnormal within a controlled but fluid diagnostic system.

Claimed as Science

For psychiatric eugenics to exist, eugenicists must claim science as the basis for the descriptive constructs and corresponding diagnostic system, and thereafter, the

[369] Ibid., 94.

[370] John Read and Jeffrey Masson, *Models of Madness: Psychological, Social, and Biological Approaches* edited by John Read, Richard Bentall, and Loren Mosher (Routledge, 2004), 35.

narrative must be accepted by society on that premise. In Nazi Germany, just as today, undesirable mindsets, emotions, and behaviors were viewed as social constructs, identifying people as degenerates while claiming to be scientifically sound. Furthering this belief in scientism was the large sums of invested money which funded ongoing clinical and laboratory research to both prove the theory and to potentially discover a remedy for perceived genetic disorders.

In Nazi Germany, the three main constructs of degeneracy that Kraepelin proposed were social (religious, economic, and political) status, mental hygiene/health, and racial hygiene. Kraepelin also claimed these constructs to be scientifically based, which provided worldwide justification for their acceptance:

> [by the late 1800s early 1900s] The shame of hereditary stigma accompanied a diagnosis of insanity, because much of middle-class America was horrified by any hint of "degeneration" in the familial line and its potential to weaken the genetic health of future generations . . . . **Concurrently, the ideas and methods of the German clinician Emil Kraepelin moved to the center of American psychiatry. Kraepelin had demonstrated that psychiatry was not only viable as a clinical science but could be fruitful in each of its three consecutive spheres: research, training, and practical innovation.** Calls sounded within the medical community at every opportunity for the creation of institutions modeled on the university clinics that Kraepelin had established in Heidelberg and later Munich.[371]

---

[371] S. D. Lamb, Pathologist of the Mind: Adolf Meyer and the Origins of American Psychiatry (Baltimore: Johns Hopkins University Press, 2014), 100.

Kraepelinianism not only dominated German psychiatry, it ruled over all fields of medicine in Germany. While eugenics has consistently been claimed as both scientific and medicinal, creating alleged degenerates out of subjective and fallible social and descriptive constructs is not primarily a scientific endeavor. This reality prompted Harvard geneticist Richard Lewontin to discern,

> What appears to us in the mystical guise of pure science and objective knowledge about nature turns out, underneath, to be political, economic, and social ideology.[372]

The term "hereditary madness" has today been replaced with theorized genetically caused mental illness; instead of claiming that constructs are inherited or run in the family, the eugenics field seems to be more scientifically legitimate, as psychiatrists now claim that specific genes, a large group of genes, or the entire genome are responsible for specific psychiatric constructs ("disorders").

Likewise, the discovery of valid genetic diseases (those with proven pathology and biological markers) has increased faith that psychiatric constructs are also caused by degeneration in the human genome, and this reality will someday be proven. Professor of molecular biological psychology at Columbia University Samuel Barondes explains,

> Scientists have learned to go beyond vaguely defined "inherited inclinations" to their very specific and tangible underpinnings — the genes themselves. Since the discovery of DNA, a powerful technology has been

[372] Richard C. Lewontin, *Biology as Ideology: The Doctrine of DNA* (New York: HarperCollins Publishers, 1991), 57.

developed to scrutinize exact differences in the genes of individual people and to relate them to many attributes, such as vulnerabilities to various diseases. **Now this same approach is being applied to hunt for DNA variations that play a role in "the affliction[s] of insanity." —** afflictions that once seemed so heavily influenced by life experiences that genetic studies didn't seem very worthwhile [emphasis added].[373]

Though human genes are approachable within the scientific method to some degree, the fluid psychiatric constructs genes are claimed to create are not tangible realities approachable within a scientific framework. In valid genetic diseases that exist biologically, however, the scrutiny of individual genes can be both reliable and valid. But in attempting to approach metaphysical social and descriptive constructs using the scientific method, it is impossible to claim validity and reliability. Despite this fact, eugenicists/geneticists still make the claim that psychiatric genetics is valid science (a claim that will be explored further in the next two chapters).

Individual degenerationism is the philosophy which the entire psychiatric claim of scientific pursuit and corresponding attempts to discover genetic variances rests upon. "Hereditary madness," "mental hygiene," or "psychiatric disorders" (however one chooses to call them) do not exist without dogmatically asserting individual degeneration. If there is no human mental, emotional or behavioral abnormality — though a person is clearly struggling in his/her soul and in distress, then eugenicists

---

[373] Samuel H. Barondes, *Mood Genes: Hunting for Origins of Mania and Depression* (New York: Oxford Press, 1998), 1.

cannot objectively classify anyone as mentally ill. Consequently, psychiatry would cease to exist.

Creating and maintaining concepts of abnormality within a pseudo-scientific framework are vital to psychiatry. Jerome Wakefield along with psychiatric epidemiologist Allan Horwitz submit that the entire premise of individual degeneration rests on psychiatrists' descriptive and social constructs/syndromes and that "these symptom-based definitions" must be viewed as disorders for the neo-Kraepelinian theory to be sustained:

> The fact that these **symptom-based definitions** are the foundation of the entire mental health research and treatment enterprise makes their validity critically important. Psychiatric research and treatment are like an upside-down pyramid, **and the *DSM* definitions of mental disorders that determine who is counted as disordered are the one small point on which the soundness of the entire pyramid rests** [emphasis added].[374]

Though holding that human distresses and impairments that comprise psychiatric constructs are abnormalities is essential to psychiatric theory, there does not exist a scientific basis for this belief. For example, an article published in the *Journal of Psychiatric Research* in 2019 exposed that there is no scientific value or objective validity to any of the diagnostic categories or published definitions in the *DSM-5*. Professor Peter Kinderman at the University of Liverpool expresses his concern:

---

[374] Allan Horwitz and Jerome Wakefield, The Loss of Sadness: How Psychiatry Transformed Normal Sorrow into Depressive Disorder (New York: Oxford, 2007), 7-8.

This study provides yet more evidence that the
biomedical diagnostic approach in psychiatry is not fit for
purpose. Diagnoses frequently and uncritically reported
as real illnesses are in fact made on the basis of internally
inconsistent, confused, and contradictory patterns of
largely arbitrary criteria. The diagnostic system wrongly
assumes that all distress results from disorder, and relies
heavily on subjective judgments about what is normal.[375]

As Kinderman recognizes, it is not only that science is
lacking to validate psychiatric constructs; it is also that no
science exists to validate the presuppositional belief that
persistent human distress and deep impairing falsehood
must be viewed as mental degeneration/disorder.

If creating and sustaining constructs of abnormality
(individual degenerationism) are vital to psychiatry's
existence and abnormality (psychiatric disorders) is a
deviance from an established norm, then it may come as a
surprise for many to learn that within formal psychiatry,
no standard of normalcy exists.[376] The World Psychiatric
Association, however, realizes that to continue insisting
that people with persistent mental problems are
degenerates or disordered requires that objective standards
of normalcy first be established. As already stated, but
worth reiterating, this task is impossible within
evolutionary thinking:

> To establish that a condition is a *disorder in* the sense of
> Wakefield's analysis, we would have to establish, or at
> least have a consensus about, whether it arose because of
> or at least involved *"failure of a natural mental or behavioural*

[375] University of Liverpool, "Psychiatric Diagnosis 'Scientifically
Meaningless.'" *ScienceDaily* 8 (July 2019): www.sciencedaily.com
/releases/2019/07/190708131152.htm.

[376] Berger, Mental Illness: The Necessity for Faith and Authority.

mechanism to function as designed in evolution." But as opposed to what? Behavioural scientists working in an evolutionary theoretic framework have suggested that *failure of function* in Wakefield's sense as a pathway to harmful conditions can be contrasted with, for instance, evolutionary design/current environment mismatch, or maladaptive learning. **If these are the kinds of intended contrasts, we need to wait until the science has been done to establish which types or sub-types of problems are "genuine disorders" in the sense of Wakefield's analysis, and which are not.** And in the meantime, during what might be a long wait, we would need *another name for* the problems, not *disorder* (which in this scenario we are interpreting in Wakefield's sense), but perhaps, for instance, *mental health problems,* the criteria for which would have to be reliable enough for us to do meaningful, generalizable research [their own emphasis].[377]

As the World Psychiatric Association rightly acknowledges, calling people degenerates/disorderly without having an objective standard of normal function is neither scientifically valid, practically reliable, or remotely altruistic. Instead, it exposes the subjective eugenics philosophy of degenerationism.

Moreover, Wakefield's idea of "function" requires purpose, and if evolution were true, then the claim that people individually and corporately have purpose or are designed negates the evolutionary theory that asserts chance as explaining human nature. Simply stated, if there is a failure of function, then human nature has a purpose according to a design, and a design with purpose reveals a rational intellectual designer. If psychiatrists insist that their rationale be accepted, then they make themselves out to be the standard of normalcy and the moral gatekeepers of

[377] Derek Bolton, "The Usefulness of Wakefield's Definition for the Diagnostic Manuals," *World Psychiatry (WPA)* 6 (3) (2007): 164-65.

selection and individual purpose. In essence, whoever decides "failure of function" within evolutionary thinking also declares themselves to be the moral authority over human nature.

In humanistic thinking, that authority is said to be mankind—especially those in the medical field, and in accordance with this reasoning, a degenerate is anyone who does not perfectly conform to the designer's intentions, fit into fellow humanity's expectations, or fulfill one's own pursuits, desires, and perceived purposes. If life does not go according to one's desires, for example, and deep impairing sorrow and persistent hopelessness result, then degeneracy can be assumed and explained as a psychiatric construct (e.g., Major Depressive Disorder). As several psychologists realize, such a standard, if consistently applied, positions everyone as degenerates:

> Since the ideal is difficult to achieve, most people are seen as being poorly adjusted at least part of the time. One may strive to achieve the ideal, but one seldom makes it. In light of such theories, many people may judge themselves to be abnormal, or at least in need of psychological treatment, even though they have no obvious [psychiatric] symptoms.[378]

This "harmful dysfunction" (HD) concept also assumes that mindsets, emotions, and behaviors that are harmful must be viewed as dysfunction or abnormalities if they are subjectively judged to be severe. Harmful dysfunction is another way to assert individual degeneracy, and it is also an attempt to medicalize the metaphysical/spiritual nature:

[378] Lauren B. Alloy, Joan Acocella, and Richard R. Bootzin, *Abnormal Psychology: Current Perspectives* 7th edition (New York: McGraw-Hill, 1996), 7.

The HD analysis views psychological dysfunctions as conceptually equivalent to physical dysfunctions. Just as the heart is designed to pump blood, the lungs to breath, or the kidneys to process waste, evolution designed psychological processes of cognition, motivation, emotion, and the like to operate in certain ways: Fear emerges in response to danger, sadness to loss, anger to inequity, and so forth. **A mental disorder exists when some psychological mechanism is unable to perform its natural function, that is, the function that evolution designed it to do. Dysfunctions, which can lie in the hardware of the brain or the software of the mind, exist when psychological processes either arise in contexts they are not designed for** (e.g., fear in the absence of danger or sadness without loss) or fail to emerge in contexts when they ought to arise (serious danger or loss) [emphasis added].[379]

But as psychiatrist Allan Horwitz elucidates, "psychological" and valid medical dysfunction are two different things:

There is a major difference, however, between mental and physical dysfunctions. Mental dysfunctions are inherently *contextual*. In contrast to physical organs, which do not turn off and on but which operate continuously, psychological mechanisms are designed to be triggered in certain contexts and not to emerge in the absence of appropriate triggers. Both cultural and subjective systems of meaning influence what contexts are and therefore what normal responses to them should be. This means that the determination of what an appropriate or inappropriate context for the emergence of an emotion is

[379] Allan V. Horwitz, *The Oxford Handbook of Philosophy of Social Science* (Oxford Press: November, 2012): DOI: 10.1093/oxfordhb/9780195392753 .013.0023.

much more difficult to detect for psychological (p. 566) than for physical functioning.[380]

The humanistic evolutionary argument assumes both that there is a measurable standard of and purpose for human nature/consciousness and that persistent human distress, impairment (e.g., anxiety and sorrow), and falsehood (e.g., delusions) amount to a dysfunction from the designed purpose. Moreover, this line of reasoning also sees the purpose as genetically inherited and reliably reproduced. Ironically, this worldview becomes less of an evolutionary theory and more of an explanation that an intelligent designer created all of human nature and holds people accountable to the consistent and intended created design.

As previously mentioned, what has been called *degeneration* historically in psychiatric eugenics is now referred to as *disordered* within psychiatric genetics, just as what was once marketed as mental hygiene is now framed as mental health. Yet, the underlying psychiatric philosophy concerning human nature remains the same:

> A mental disorder is a syndrome characterized by clinically significant disturbance in an individual's cognition, emotional regulation, or behavior that reflects a dysfunction in the psychological, biological, or developmental processes underlying mental functioning. Mental disorders are usually associated with significant distress or disability in social, occupational, or other important activities.[381]

The APA insists that the following three elements are required to have a "mental disorder:" 1) a syndrome (based

---

[380] Horwitz, "The Oxford Handbook of Philosophy of Social Science."

[381] APA, *DSM-5*, 20.

upon observable symptoms; a descriptive construct), 2) "clinically significant disturbance" or significant distress or impairment, and 3) claimed biological causes (though by definition and in contrast to valid neurological diseases, no solid empirical evidence exists to validate "mental" disorders). It is important to recognize that these are the fundamental elements of eugenics framed as disorders.

Moreover, these criteria are entirely dependent upon one's subjective presuppositional beliefs. The American Psychiatric Association does admit in the *DSM-5* that determining whether someone is abnormal within their diagnostic system is not objective science:

> In the absence of clear biological markers or clinically useful measurements of severity for many mental disorders, it has not been possible to completely separate normal and **pathological symptoms expressions** ["phenotypes"] contained in diagnostic criteria.[382]

There do not exist objective biological markers or objective standards of severity on which diagnoses are made. The historian of psychiatry and mental illness, Andrew Scull, reports similar realisms:

> Notwithstanding periodic breathless proclamations to the contrary, the roots of schizophrenia or of major depression remain wrapped in mystery and confusion. And with no X-rays, no MRIs, no PET scans, no laboratory tests that allow us to proclaim unambiguously that this person is mad, that person sane, **the boundaries between**

---

[382] Ibid., 21.

Reason and Unreason remain shifting and uncertain, contested and controversial [emphasis added].[383]

Director of Forensic Psychiatry at SUNY upstate Medical University in Syracuse New York James Knoll and Editor in Chief Emeritus of the *Psychiatric Times* Ronald Pies also admit:

> The concept of mental disorder, like many other concepts in medicine and science, lacks a consistent operational definition that covers all situations . . . . It is highly unsatisfying to entertain the notion that severe selfishness, resentment and desire for infamy are simply a part of the broad range of human nature. But such traits have been with us since the dawn of our species.[384]

Likewise, former president of the American Psychiatric Association Jeffrey Lieberman confesses that the very definition of mental disorder includes the foundational concept that no biological explanation exists — though the desire and pursuit to prove that one does exist remains a constant concern:

> Psychiatry originated as a medical specialty that took as its province a set of maladies that, by their very definition, had no identifiable physical cause. Appropriately, the term "psychiatry" — coined by the German physician Johann Christian Reil in 1808 — literally means "medical treatment of the soul."[385]

Despite the reality that proposed mental disorders are metaphysical constructs, which explain mostly tangible but

[383] Andrew Scull, *Madness in Civilization: A Cultural History of Insanity* (New Jersey: Princeton University Press, 2015), 15.

[384] Knoll IV & Pies, "Cruel, Immoral Behavior Is Not a Mental Illness."

[385] Jeffrey A. Lieberman, *Shrinks*, 26-27.

non-physical aspects of human nature, psychiatry must insist that its created disorders are biologically caused. Still, psychiatrists continue to claim "risk factors" allegedly correlate to genes in attempt to validate their categories of degeneracy, while at the same time, they admit that genes and risk factors are not incontrovertible evidence:

> Approaches to validating diagnostic criteria for discreate categorical mental disorders have included the following types of evidence: [1] antecedent validators (similar genetic markers, family traits, temperament, and environmental exposure), [2] concurrent validators (similar neural substrates, biomarkers, emotional and cognitive processing, and symptom similarity), and [3] predictive validators (similar clinical course and treatment response) . . . . **Until incontrovertible etiological or pathophysiological mechanisms are identified to fully validate specific disorders or disorder spectra, the most important standard for the *DSM-5* disorder criteria will be their clinical utility for the assessment of clinical course** and treatment response of individuals grouped by a given set of diagnostic criteria.[386]

Though the APA admits that psychiatric constructs are not yet validated, it persists that the constructs should be utilized to know how to treat people and how to address the expectations of the diagnosed individual and his/her family. These alleged criteria for determining what should be considered to be a legitimate psychiatric disease are based upon Emil Kraepelin's theory:

> [Eli] Robins was influenced by Emil Kraepelin, the late 19th century German psychiatrist who taught that "diagnosis is prognosis," that the course of illness tells you which symptoms represent different diseases . . . With his colleague Samuel Guze, Robins articulated four

[386] APA, *DSM-5*, 20.

other diagnostic validators that, along with symptoms, should be used to identify if groups of patients differ from each other enough to justify seeing them as having different diagnoses (their article focused on schizophrenia, but they later applied these principles to all diagnoses). Those validators are shown [as] (1. Symptoms, 2. Course of Illness, 3. Genetics, and 4. Treatment Effects). The most important is course of illness, Kraepelin's key criterion.[387]

But alleged psychiatric disorders are also said to be "heterogenous"; that is, they are fluid syndromic concepts.[388] Course of alleged illness, suggested genes, and proposed treatment effects are all based upon the presuppositional idea that symptoms equal a form of valid mental degeneracy. But as psychiatrist Nassir Ghaemi relates, these criteria are not reliable validators of psychiatric constructs. He comments on "treatment responses": "This is by far the weakest validator of a diagnosis, because drugs are nonspecific [they are not treating actual diseases but causing specific effects]. Yet many clinicians focus a lot on this factor."[389]

Despite this reality, the American Psychiatric Association claims that the *DSM-5* contains a "method for allegedly

[387] "Classic Study of the Month," *The Psychiatry Letter* (January 2015): https://www.psychiatryletter.com/classic-study-jan-2015.html.

[388] Till F. M. Andlauer, Bertram Muller-Myhsok, and Stephan Ripke, *Psychiatric Genetics: A Primer for Clinicians and Basic Scientists* edited by Thomas G. Schulze and Francis J. McMahon (New York: Oxford University Press, 2018), 57-58.

[389] Nassir Ghaemi, "Was Kraepelin Right?" *The Psychiatry Letter* (October 6, 2019): https://www.psychiatryletter.net/post/was-kraepelin-right.

achieving diagnostic validity in psychiatric illness."[390] Returning the construct of schizophrenia as one example, the elements claimed as validating the diagnosis as a real biological disorder reflect the same criteria listed in the *DSM-5*. In one journal entry published in the *American Journal of Psychiatry*, psychiatrists note 5 phases for this method: "clinical description [a descriptive construct], laboratory study ["scientific experiments"], exclusion of other disorders [application of the diagnostic system], follow-up study [medical practice], family study [hereditary/genetic theory]."[391] These elements not only resemble the *DSM-5*, they also reflect the original theory of Emil Kraepelin's eugenics, which Rüdin attempted to prove through experimentation carried out in Nazi Germany. It is not merely that the eugenics theory must have a system of selection—a diagnostic system, but also that the system relies on the belief that the invisible disease is familial/hereditary as noted in this said list of alleged validating factors.

Upon realizing that there is no science to the labels, categories, and system of the *DSM-5* psychiatric disorders patterned after Kraepelin's original eugenics system and specific social constructs, Professor of psychology John Read stated in 2019 in the journal *Science Daily* that

> perhaps it is time we stopped pretending that medical-sounding labels contribute anything to our understanding

[390] Eli Robins and Samuel B. Guze "Establishment of Diagnostic Validity in Psychiatric Illness: Its Application to Schizophrenia," *The American Journal of Psychiatry* (April 1, 2006): https://doi.org/10.1176/ajp.126.7.983.

[391] Ibid.

of the complex causes of human distress or of what kind
of help we need when distressed.[392]

Psychiatrist, biomedical researcher, and director of
translational medicine-neuroscience at Novartis Institutes
Nassir Ghaemi, who is a principle figure within
psychopharmacology, contends:

> **By diagnosing patients within the *DSM* strictures only,
> we practice non-scientifically; we use hundreds of
> made-up labels for professional purposes, without
> really getting at the reality of what is wrong with the
> patient.** Sometimes those patients have diseases; we don't
> know what they are. Sometimes they don't have diseases;
> we don't know when that is. And, because the whole
> process is "pragmatic" and made-up, we make no gradual
> progress in identifying when diseases are present, and
> when they are not, and what the causes of those diseases
> (or non-disease conditions) might be [emphasis
> added].[393]

Former APA president elect John Oldham agrees:

> The *DSM* is a diagnostic manual that the APA has been
> the leader in developing, and it's not just used in this
> country; it's used worldwide. **The labels in the *DSM* are
> not based on hard science alone.** We use all of the
> research we've got. we use all of the clinical wisdom
> we've got. **But it's a language. It's a way we can talk to
> each other.** We know pretty much what we're talking
> about by using the same terms, but there is nothing

---

[392] University of Liverpool, "Psychiatric Diagnosis 'Scientifically
Meaningless.'" *ScienceDaily* 8 (July 2019): www.sciencedaily.com
/releases/2019/07/190708131152.htm.

[393] Nassir Ghaemi, "One Step Back, Two Steps Forward: The Solution to
DSM and drugs?" *Medscape Psychiatry Online* (January 15, 2013): http://boards.
medscape.com/forums/?128@@.2a37df02! comment=1&cat=All.

specific [about it] that is absolutely gospel [emphasis added].[394]

Drew Ramsey, professor of psychiatry at the University of Columbia, similarly expresses,

That frustrates the public in a certain way — that this is a "language" for us to frame up how individuals are struggling and how to understand what parts of their personality could be at play. **But in some ways, how else would we do that when we don't know exactly what these disorders are, from a biological basis?** What do you think Benjamin Rush would have thought about this [emphasis added]? [395]

The entire premise and system on which the eugenics theory of mental illness rests — determining who is a degenerate and who is not — has been shown to be a subjective belief system marketed as scientifically sound and medicinal in nature. Regrettably, it is a descriptive moral system to which millions of people worldwide ascribe and submit.

There is no scientific discovery or valid disease entity within this paradigm; only descriptive, cultural, genetic, and abnormal psychology are being posited. In truth, psychiatry is less of a healing art and more of an attempt to sustain materialism and evolutionary theory by creating

---

[394] John M. Oldham and Drew Ramsey, "A Brief History of American Psychiatry: From a Founding Father to Dr. Anonymous," *Medscape Psychiatry* (November 7, 2019): https://www.medscape.com/viewarticle/917451?nlid=132561_424&src=WNL_mdplsfeat_191112_mscpedit_psyc&uac=264124BV&spon=12&impID=2164621&faf=1.

[395] Drew Ramsey, Ibid.

categorical abnormalities without any validating evidence to do so.

Within neo-Kraepelinianism/the bio-psycho-social model, descriptive constructs are formed based on the speculative claim that genes cause mental impairment and distress and that persistent impairment and distress equal disorder/ degeneration. If persistent mental and behavioral impairment and distress as well as deep deceit, however, are normal rather than abnormal, then degenerationism, eugenics, and biological psychiatry become invalidated — even harmful — social concepts.

Medical Nomenclature

Many of the original descriptive constructs of Nazi Germany have changed names over the last decades, but they are substantively still Kraepelin's diagnostic categories. Schizophrenia, bipolar, and alcoholism — a few of the most important psychiatric constructs — remain the foundation of the modern genetic theory. But even before Kraepelin, psychiatrists had discovered that assigning medical nomenclature to metaphysical human struggles and distresses enabled their control over society.

As previously related, in the late 1700s Benjamin Rush significantly helped to establish the psychiatric practice of describing impairing human behavior within a medical framework, creating a medical label, and publishing the construct as a syndrome/disorder in a book claimed to be medical. Professor of clinical psychology Jonathan Shedler highlights how psychiatrists' utilization of the term "disorder" to qualify descriptive constructs enables the human phenomena listed to be viewed as medical issues:

> Psychiatric diagnoses are categorically different because
> they are merely descriptive, not explanatory. They sound
> like medical diseases, especially with the ominously-
> appended disorder, but they aren't.[396]

Just as genetic/hereditary degeneracy was applied in Nazi
psychiatric genetics, *disorder* has been instituted in modern
times. Eugenics is a belief system about undesirable or
threatening human nature framed as a medical issue.

As Lewontin, Rose, and Kamin assert, the medical model of
mental illness through both naming, categorizing, and
diagnosing perceived degeneracy enables a "state
apparatus" to control people perceived to be a threat to
themselves, their family, or society:

> It would be a mistake, however, to see the coercive use of
> psychiatry as merely a cynical attempt to suppress
> dissidents while pretending to help them, like the
> mystifying term "protective custody" introduced by
> fascist regimes in the 1930s to mean imprisonment or
> commitment to a concentration camp. **The labeling of
> social dissidents as mad is but one aspect of a general
> attempt to understand and cope with social deviance . . .**
> . If, in addition, their thoughts and behavior threaten the
> very basis of society, the simple possibility of treating
> their madness medically becomes a social imperative. **The
> medical model of deviance then provides even the most
> cynical state apparatus with a legitimate tool to control**

---

[396] Jonathan Shedler, "A Psychiatric Diagnosis Is Not a Disease:
Doublethink makes for bad Treatment," *Psychology Today* (July 27, 2019):
https://www.psychologytoday.com/us/blog/psychologically-
minded/201907/psychiatric-diagnosis-is-not-disease?fbclid=IwAR0HB
vie7R1uPUC0XpB2MFws4UinQMKb7mDJRwxmnV23SbugqUPQWnRIeqo.

the behavior of individuals before they cohere as a dangerous social group [emphasis added].[397]

This fact is why so many in American society are calling out to government officials to reform mental health care in hope that such problems as mass shootings and gun control will be resolved through mental hygiene. Editor-in-Chief of the *Psychiatric Times* James Knoll IV shares how societal fear of mass shootings and belief in mental illness as causative has encouraged much of society to turn to psychiatry for answers:

> In recent times, we have seen a significant reduction in National Institute of Mental Health funding of psychiatric research, as well as a prominent former editor of the *New England Journal of Medicine* make inaccurate and disparaging comments about psychiatry. But suddenly, in the wake of highly publicized mass shootings and deceptive correlations of mental illness with gun violence, the national dialogue has changed.[398]

Whether it was psychiatric eugenics of old or modern psychiatric genetics, dealing with categorically-created degenerates under the guise of genetic and neurological

---

[397] Lewontin, Rose, *Kamin, Not in Our Genes*, 168.

[398] James L. Knoll IV, "The Return of the Alienist," *Medscape Psychiatry* (May 10, 2013): https://www.medscape.com/viewarticle/803662_2.

medicine for the alleged good of the people is a shared theme.[399]

Individual degenerationism, then, is a concept based entirely upon evolutionary thinking that normal people do not struggle mentally, emotionally, or behaviorally in a persistent and impairing way (according to what a humanistic task force establishes as normal or according to ideas of self-actualization). When people are unable within their own genetic makeup and self-ability/self-actualization to fix their mental, emotional, and behavioral struggles, then a proposed biological cause is blamed. Eugenics, and thus individual degeneration, requires the following: a descriptive and social construct to establish normal from asserting abnormal, a diagnostic system to determine who is disordered and who is "healthy," a medical framework to both claim biological etiologies and attempt to treat the alleged degenerate, and a group of scientists and physicians to claim authority and devotion to establishing and upholding the altruistic claim of the "greatest good for the greatest number."

---

[399] "By explicitly formulating a psychopathology and neurology-based degeneration hypothesis, both Rüdin (as the director of the Demographic Study Unit at the German Research Institute for Psychiatry in Munich serving as a major research hub for German, North American, and Scandinavian mental hygienists and eugenicists) and Hoche (as Director of the Clinic of Psychiatry at the University of Freiburg) continued Kraepelin's eugenic and racial anthropological legacy" (Stahnisch, "The Early Eugenics Movement," 18).

Materialism

In addition to individual degenerationism, eugenics depends heavily upon the philosophy of materialism[400] — a belief that all human nature consists of, is created through, is explained by, and is potentially remedied through biological/material causes. In accordance, materialists view science as the only means of truly understanding and approaching "bad" or destructive mindsets, emotions, and behaviors.

Franz Anton Mesmer — said by some historians to be the very first psychiatrist[401] — held to material explanations of the soul. In fact, as former APA president, Jeffrey Lieberman notes, Mesmer is considered to be the first psychiatrist because of his materialistic faith:

> In the 1770s [Mesmer] rejected the prevailing religious and moral accounts of mental illness in favor of a physiological explanation, making him arguably the world's first psychiatrist.[402]

For a psychiatrist to be influential in modern times requires that he or she assume a "physiological explanation" of human nature and all human phenomena — a position that opposes biblical anthropology.

Psychiatrist Benjamin Rush, the father of American race psychology, of American hereditary madness, of the

---

[400] Materialism is also known as reductionism and scientism.

[401] Other prominent psychiatrists (e.g., Allen Frances) believe that Philippe Pinel was the first psychiatrist (*Saving Normal*, 56).

[402] Lieberman, *Shrinks*, 27.

medical model of mental illness, and of American psychiatry, who remains the face of the American Psychiatric Association's official seal, also held to the same materialistic beliefs as Mesmer did. Rush wrote in his book, *Medical Inquiries and Observations Upon the Diseases of the Mind*,

> I have endeavored to bring them ["diseases of the mind"] down to the level of all other diseases of the human body, and to show that the mind and body are moved by the same causes and subject to the same laws.[403]

It was upon Rush and Mesmer's reductionistic belief and clearly stated hope that modern psychiatry and its many constructed disorders would be founded.[404] While Mesmer was likely the first to suggest the reductionist definition and approach to the soul, it would be Rush's teachings in America that would allow its widespread acceptance.[405]

[403] Benjamin Rush, quoted by David McCullough, American Presidents: John Adams, Mornings on Horseback, Truman, and the Course of Human Events (New York: Simon and Schuster, 2001), 609.

[404] Ibid.

[405] Mesmer lost influence as he was revealed to be a fraud. Allan H. Ropper, "Two Centuries of Neurology and Psychiatry in the *Journal*," *New England Journal of Medicine* 367 (July 5, 2012): 58-65.

Rush regularly used the term "phrenetic predisposition"[406] to describe his materialistic approach to human nature. Rush's phrenetic predisposition was a philosophy that would first lead to the pseudoscience of phrenology[407] (see

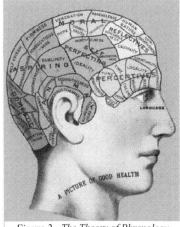

Figure 1), thereafter identified as the field of formal biological psychiatry. Phrenologists taught that every facet of man (including faith, personality, emotions, desires, motives, character, etc.) was determined by specific areas of a person's skull and brain. Phrenology principally taught that "the brain is the organ of the mind"[408] — a belief still upheld by many biological

Figure 2 - The Theory of Phrenology

psychiatrists. In fact, phrenology forms the basic approach

[406] Benjamin Rush, *Medical Inquiries and Observations Upon the Diseases of the Mind* ed. (Philadelphia: Grigg and Elliot, 1835), 25.

[407] "The close approximation of Dr. Rush's remarks to the doctrines of Phrenology, will be easily recognized. In many details he differs from, and falls short of the views of Phrenologists, but in the general conclusion maintained by him, that physical causes influence the moral faculty, the coincidence is complete" (George Combe writing in the foreword of a reprint of *An Inquiry into the Influence of Physical Causes of the Faculty* (Philadelphia, PA: Haswell, Barrington, and Haswell, 1839), 3-4; Available from: https://collections.nlm.nih.gov/ext/mhl/57020900R/PDF/57020900R.pdf.

[408] Kara Rogers, "Phrenology: Pseudoscientific Practice," *Encyclopaedia Britannica* (May 1, 2018): https://www.britannica.com/topic/phrenology.

to modern psychiatry,[409] as historian of science John Van
Wyhe imparts,

> Phrenology was a science of character divination, faculty
> psychology, theory of brain and what the 19th-century
> phrenologists called "the only true science of mind."[410]

Not only was Rush's phrenetic predisposition a forerunner
to phrenology and psychiatry that laid a theory of a
material soul,[411] but it was also reflective of individual
degenerationism and another philosophy yet to be
discussed: *biodeterminism*. In many ways, psychiatrists have
transformed "phrenetic predisposition" first into
"hereditary risk" and then into "genetic predisposition."
Today, psychiatric materialists have shifted their etiological
theories from primarily the human brain to the human
genome, though psychiatrists still consider the "social
brain" to be a major part of the material/eugenic
explanation of the soul.[412]

---

[409] "Though a flawed science that gave way to fantism, phrenology, we
could say, was the midwife to modern psychiatry" (Group for the
Advancement of Psychiatry, "The History of Psychiatry 19th Century,"
[October 5, 2017]: https://m.youtube.com/watch?feature=youtu.be
&v=TFoJ0b4v3hY: 3:52-5:14).

410 John Van Wyhe, *The History of Phrenology on the Web* (2011):
http://www.historyofphrenology.org.uk/overview.htm.

411 Franz Joseph Gall also taught phrenic hereditary principles around the
same time as Rush (1758-1828) (Ibid).

[412] Douglas A. Kramer, "Remembering: A Gentleman and a Psychiatrist,"
Psychiatric Times Online (December 9, 2019): https://www.psychiatrictimes.
com/couch-crisis/remembering-gentleman-and-psychiatrist?rememberme=
1&elq_mid=10030&elq_cid=893295&GUID=31158D64-F01A-4DEA-AC1A-
D3CE843FC9BC.

In addition to Rush, other early psychiatrists like Augustin Morel and Pierre Cabanis (1802) also taught that physiological-hereditary causes explained all of human nature.[413] By the time Emil Kraepelin proposed his formal system of suggested mental science and brain dysfunction, materialism was widespread.

Despite the fact that many biological psychologists/ psychiatrists since Mesmer and Rush believed and taught that "disordered" mental processes and bad behavior arose out of the body and thus were hereditarily caused, some historians credit Wilhelm Wundt as the first to propagate materialism within modern psychology:

> The beginning of materialistic psychology and psychiatry was Wundt's claim that man had no soul. As soon as psychology and psychiatry defined themselves to be the study of man's soulless brain activities, it seemed logical to think of humans as animals, disposing of the unwanted [degenerates] in any "efficient" way.[414]

Though Wundt did not conceive the reductionistic model, his significant influence in propagating the belief is undeniable, for it is largely upon Wundt's "sciences of the mind" that Kraepelin was inspired to devise his eugenic paradigm under the guise of science and medicine.

Wundt influenced many people with his beliefs, besides Kraepelin. But it was clearly German psychiatry that would

[413] Michael Arribas-Ayloon, Andrew Bartlett, and Jamie Lewis, *Psychiatric Genetics: From Hereditary Madness to Big Biology* (Vanderbilt, New York: Routledge, 2019), 25.

[414] Colbe Mazzarella, "Psychiatry's Little-known Role in Creating the Holocaust," *The New Boston Post* (February 9, 2018): https://newbostonpost.com/2018/02/09/psychiatrys-little-known-role-in-creating-the-holocaust/.

popularize a formal system of classification, a humanistic philosophical phenomenology of human nature, and a common psychiatric language on which Kraepelinianism would be accepted worldwide. Historian Ed Shorter relates:

> After the mid-19th century, the classification of psychiatric illnesses belonged to the Germans, and by the 1920s, German was the international language of psychiatry. The German primacy was initiated with the publication of the second edition of Berlin psychiatrist Wilhelm Griesinger's textbook in 1861 (the principal means of conveying new ideas in psychiatry, in those days, was in textbooks rather than articles). **Griesinger argued that the brain represented the basis of psychiatric illness, and thus initiated a long tradition of biological thinking in psychiatry** . . . . The German whose figure towers over us, even today, in the *DSM* series is Kraepelin, professor of psychiatry before World War I: first in Heidelberg, then in Munich. A series of editions of Kraepelin's textbooks, which started to attract world attention with the fourth edition in 1893 and concluded with the great eighth edition, published in its five volumes between 1909 and 1915, grew to be anticipated with the same rapt attention that awaits new editions of the *DSM* today.[415]

Materialism—the biological perspective on which the medical model exists—was a fundamental doctrine leading to the acceptance of eugenics not only in Germany, but also globally across all medical and scientific fields. Historian of medicine Frank Stahnisch explains how psychiatric eugenics depends heavily upon the doctrine of materialism, is antithetical to the biblical concept of

---

[415] Edward Shorter, "The History of Nosology and the Rise of the Diagnostic and Statistical Manual of Mental Disorders," *Dialogues in Clinical Neuroscience* vol. 17 (1) (March 2015): 60-61.

dualism, and is the practical means of transforming Wundt's new material concept of the soul into a working social model:

> Eugenic discourses at the turn from the 19th to the 20th century had remarkably widespread attraction not only to medical doctors or biological and social scientists. **Eugenic programs promised to give a biological redefinition of human morality and particularly of the modern soul. This prospect likewise accounted for the fact that professional psychiatrists felt attracted by the specific implications that eugenic thought had for questions of diagnosis and psychiatric treatment** [emphasis added].[416]

If mental, emotional, and behavioral issues were to be accepted as biologically caused, then the belief in dualism (that human nature consists of both a spiritual and physical reality) had to be rejected. *Baker's Encyclopedia of Psychology and Counseling* submits that

> Descartes' importance for psychology lies in his promulgation of a dualistic view of the person, in which the true self is viewed as an immaterial soul that is distinct from the body. Though his position is widely rejected in the twentieth century, Descartes' formulation of the mind/body problem continues to be a starting place for contemporary discussions of the issue.[417]

Since Descartes' time, there has existed a conflict between materialism and dualism that is often incorrectly framed as Christianity (religion) versus science, since Scripture teaches the psychosomatic nature of humanity. Dualism, though, is equally as "scientific" as materialism, but

[416] Stahnisch, "The Early Eugenics Movement," 18.

[417] David G. Benner and Peter C. Hill, *Baker Encyclopedia of Psychology and Counseling* 2nd ed. (Grand Rapids: Baker Books, 1999), 342.

dualism simply recognizes that not all of human nature can unnecessarily be forced/reduced into a materialistic explanation or exploration. Psychiatric faith and the Christian doctrine are opposing worldviews because they hold to opposing beliefs about human origins, the true nature of the human soul/psyche, and human phenomena. Former president of the Royal College of Psychiatrists Andrew Sims identifies this conflict:

> The unhealthy situation in which psychiatry denies the significance, and even existence, of soul or spirit has led religious people to have a profound distrust of psychiatry and been disastrous for all those involved.[418]

Materialism is an attempt to dismiss and replace necessary faith in God with faith in man's wisdom to explain and remedy human nature as discovered in the natural world.

The logic followed is that if science cannot approach a reality or "appearances of reality," then human nature and phenomena must not be real unless they can be explained through descriptive constructs and theoretically related to the body. Geneticist Richard Lewontin states precisely why humanistic geneticists must fully commit to materialism:

> It is not that the methods of and institutions of science somehow compel us to accept a material explanation of the phenomenal world, but on the contrary, **that we are forced by our a *priori adherence* to material causes to create an apparatus of investigation and a set of concepts that produce material explanations**, no matter how counterintuitive, no matter how mystifying to the uninitiated. **Moreover, that materialism is absolute, for**

---

[418] Andrew Sims, Is Faith Delusion? Why Religion is Good for Your Health (London: Continuum, 2009), 2.

we cannot allow a Divine Foot in the door [emphasis added].[419]

On the surface, it may appear that reductionism is a scientifically sound and objective approach to humanity. But in truth, materialism/reductionism is merely faith in scientism. The genetic theory — no matter how illogical and empirically invalidated — is vitally necessary for evolutionists and biological psychiatrists to sustain belief in materialism over dualism and, moreover, to sustain psychiatry itself. Director of the Institute of Psychiatric Phenomics and Genomics (IPPG) in München, Germany Thomas Schulze and psychiatrist Kristina Adorjan assert,

> The quest to understand and treat psychiatric illness not by serendipity but through a rigorous scientific approach was too important to be discarded. **Giving up genetic approaches would have amounted to denying the medical model of psychiatry** [emphasis added].[420]

Dr. Peter Breggin also discloses,

> Why psychiatrists themselves would favor biochemical and genetic theories is no secret. Their entire professional identity depends on this ideology, and in the case of researchers, their funding can be totally dependent on it. . . . Leaders in psychiatry, nearly one and all, have long declared that mental disorders are physical in origin. The claim has been made loudly and with determination since psychiatrists first appeared on the world stage. After all, we psychiatrists are physicians. **Why would we want to make any other claim, when any other claim would**

---

[419] Lewontin, "Billions and Billions of Demons."

[420] Thomas Schulze and Kristina Adorjan, "Psychiatric Genetics," *Psychiatric Times Online* vol. 35 (8) (August 23, 2018): http://www.psychiatric times.com/genetic-disorders/psychiatric-genetics-2018-genomic-revolution-friendly-data-sharing-and-global-partnerships.

make irrelevant all our years of medical studies, invalidate our basic philosophies of life, undermine our authority in the field, and threaten our power to treat mental patients against their will [emphasis added]?[421]

Furthermore, accepting materialism over dualism enables the eugenic construct of mental hygiene/health to allegedly exist as a medical field.

One might also consider that society's acceptance of materialism depends upon a eugenic-like paradigm being established in order to replace biblical concepts of morality and human fragility. Much of what Scripture presents as good and bad, eugenics presents as healthy and unhealthy — claiming physical causes to morality. If the metaphysical realities of the soul, human phenomena, and relationships cannot be framed within a positive and negative system, then people who deny God as the Creator cannot relate, and chaos would inevitably ensue. Social scientists Arribas-Ayloon, Bartlett, and Lewis discuss how eugenics is a new moral system grounded in materialism:

> With materialistic approaches gaining favor among physicians in the late eighteenth century, the medical concepts of 'temperament' and 'constitution' began to frame moral qualities on physiological grounds. **Pierre Cabanis (1802) argued that all mental phenomena were based on a physical, organic structure; temperamental features are not only transmitted from parent to children but modified by environmental circumstances such as 'education, weather or diet.' This is a crucial consideration for the hygienist program that now**

---

[421] Breggin, *Toxic Psychiatry*, 94; 108.

entered theoretical and ideological debates in post-revolutionary France [emphasis added].[422]

The reality is that the philosophies of materialism and individual degenerationism are interdependent upon each other, working together to sustain psychiatric eugenics. Materialism—approaching man as merely evolved masses of dirt or as animals without moral souls—is foundational to treating people as soulless objects and creating categories of mental and social degeneracy:

> The materialist analysis of the kind of scientific socialism—which many of the above physicians, anthropologists, and psychiatrists had shared in their utopian pretensions—recognized political struggles and social contradictions mainly in terms of economic relations. By contrast, the eugenicist critique of modern society—as argued by Forel and Ploetz— increasingly perceived social ills in terms of the sickly, **degenerate, or moribund strains in the "social body" of Western cultures. The healthy and natural body, as it came to be idealized in eugenic discourse, could only be achieved by undoing civilization's ill effects, an undertaking in which psychiatrists like Kraepelin, Alzheimer, or Rüdin in Germany, Adolph Meyer (1866-1950) at Johns Hopkins University and G. Alder Blumer (1857-1940) at the State Asylum in South Dakota in the United States, along with Charles Kirk Clarke (1857-1924) from the Toronto General Hospital in Canada, were eager to come forward with clinical and public health solutions. The related trope of "degeneracy" of the mind and the brain** often referred to the cramped housing conditions in major industrialized cities, poor diet of the urban proletariat, which became a class of those who could not cope with the strains of modern industrialism, as well as

---

[422] Arribas-Ayloon, Bartlett, & Lewis, *Psychiatric Genetics*, 25.

to money-marriages, aristocratic inbreeding, and the physical inactivity of the idle rich [emphasis added].[423]

As historian Frank Stahnisch acknowledges, degenerationism and materialism have been key connected psychiatric concepts in the United States and Britain, as well as in pre-Nazi Germany. Lewontin, Rose, and Kamin also consider individual degenerationism's and materialism's mutual dependency:

> When a small number of people display a deviant, and presumably undesirable, trait [degeneracy], the reductionist program [materialism] prescribes an alteration in the gene or genes that are thought to determine the trait [biodeterminism]. **If a defective gene is the ultimate cause of a deviant behavior, then an alteration in the gene cures the deviance.** Since, in fact, no one has ever actually located any gene or genes for criminal violence, schizophrenia, or paranoid delusions, the treatment offered is at the level of anatomy or biochemistry; that is, at the level of the primary effect of the supposed genes. Nevertheless, **genetic manipulation remains the ultimate goal of reductionist determinism** [emphasis added].[424]

In addition, psychiatrists, writing in one psychiatric journal, discuss issues present today in psychiatry that were foundational to Nazi eugenics:

> Nazi psychiatry raises questions about medical ethics, stigma and mental illness, scientific "fashions," psychiatry's relations with government, and psychiatrists' perceived core business. Psychiatric resistance to future similar threats should be based on commemoration, broad-based education and reflection on **cultural values,** strong partnerships between psychiatrists and patients,

[423] Stahnisch, "The Early Eugenics Movement," 18.

[424] Lewontin, Rose, *Kamin, Not in Our Genes*, 173.

and willingness to question publicly policies and attitudes that disadvantage and stigmatize groups. The principle fundamental to all these practices is an orientation to people as subjects rather than objects [emphasis added].[425]

But if some people are viewed as less than people — as degenerates, deviants, disordered, or monsters — and all of human nature is reduced to material explanations and considered to have the same moral value as say a cockroach, then atrocities against humanity are inevitable and should be expected.

After a series of appalling crimes committed by American citizens in 2018, psychiatrist Robert Berezin highlighted the psychiatric approaches of hereditary degenerationism and materialism in an article published in the *Psychiatric Times*:

> I don't know anything about the formative years of Larry Nassar and the elder Turpins, or what traumas they may have entailed. But I do know that their characters were founded in sadomasochism. **They represent the extremes of moral monsters.** The harm they have done to children is unconscionable. They have passed it on to these children ("the sins of the father"). **What about the rest of us who are not monsters?** We need to look to ourselves to provide the best loving environment for our children [emphasis added].[426]

---

[425] M. Dudley and F. Gale, "Psychiatrists as a Moral Community? Psychiatry under the Nazis and its Contemporary Relevance," *Australian and New Zealand Journal of Psychiatry* 36 (5) (October 2002): 585-94; http://www.ncbi.nlm.nih.gov/pubmed/12225440.

[426] Robert Berezin, "Reflections on the 'Moral Monsters' Dominating the News," *Medscape Psychiatry Online* (February 1, 2018): https://www.medscape.com/viewarticle/891927#vp_2. Accessed August 24, 2019.

In the same article, however, Berezin also notes that true care and help come not from treating people according to Kraepelinianism but by seeing "psychiatric problems and symptoms" as "human problems":

> Finally, we need to address the responsibility of the helping professions. Psychiatry has lost its way and has become a distribution center for psychiatric drugs. It needs to face that psychiatric problems and symptoms are human problems, no more and no less, derived from the formation of our characters as we adapt to our emotional environment.[427]

Clinical psychologist Philip Yanos maintains that

> in today's public discourse, the use of terms like "animals" and "apes" to refer to members of historically marginalized racial and ethnic groups strikes a painful chord. **In a related manner (though evoking less public outrage), terms like "monsters" and "sickos" are tossed about to refer to people with mental illnesses. These terms are particularly hurtful because they call up the distant memory of the eugenics movement, which gained prominence in the United States and elsewhere in the early 20th century, and eventually contributed to the atrocities of the Nazi Holocaust .... Today, eugenic ideas live on in coded statements like those quoted above, that reduce members of entire groups to less-than-human statuses.** Though we might now be inclined to see these statements as nothing more than private opinions, in the early 20th century, these ideas had a very real impact on social policy that caused a tremendous amount of damage in the world. We should remain

---

[427] Ibid.

vigilant regarding the possibility of their reemergence [emphasis added].[428]

How one views people, as material and bio-determined monsters or as struggling and moral souls, determines how a person philosophically and practically approaches others in need.

Though already stated, it must be made clear that the philosophy of materialism, which undergirds the neo-Kraepelinian genetic theory of mental illness so rigidly held today, is an antithetical belief to dualism. To accept neo-Kraepelinianism is to embrace materialism. Authors of *The Oxford Handbook of Philosophy and Psychiatry leave no doubt:*

> The American Psychiatric Association in particular anticipated the launch of the *DSM* revision process with a publication setting out its Research Agenda for *DSM-V* (Kupher et al. 2002). In their introduction the editors of the Research Agenda, David Kupfer, Michael First, and Daryl Regier, who went on to become leaders of the *DSM-5* review, **argued that progress in the sciences of psychiatry required "an as yet unknown paradigm shift"** (p. xix) .... The particular conceptual issues they cover, moreover, show a considerable degree of overlap with the issues covered in this handbook. There is an extensive discussion on how the concept of "mental disorder" and related concepts such as "illness" and "diseases" should be defined [individual degeneracy]; and **in just the first three pages of the chapter problems are raised respectively in the philosophy of science (core concerns include "validity" and "reliability"), in the philosophy of mind ("Cartesian dualism" is explicitly**

[428] Philip Yanos, "The Long Shadow of the Eugenics Movement: Its Influence Persists," *Psychology Today Online* (June 02, 2018): https://www.psychologytoday.com/us/blog/written/201806/the-long-shadow-the-eugenics-movement.

rejected), and philosophical value theory (values being taken to differentiate what they call "sociopolitical" from "biomedical" models of disorder) [emphasis added].[429]

Individual degenerationism and materialism are two of the narrow-minded philosophies which produced the psychiatric eugenic system and which sustain the system's key theory of "mental disorder" being caused by faulty genes or hereditary risks. While the APA acknowledges the need for a paradigm shift to occur, they "explicitly reject Cartesian dualism," which has been reliable in healing the souls of many throughout history.

Genetic Determinism

As with individual degenerationism and materialism, *genetic determinism* or *bio-determinism* is a philosophy which undergirds psychiatric eugenics. Genetic determinism, defined, is "the attempt to reduce the whole of biology to the physical sciences, with the behavior of organisms being shaped largely by their genetic constitution."[430] Relying on materialism, genetic determinism holds that all of human nature is determined or caused by an individual's genome. More specifically, the philosophy asserts that inherited genes predispose a person's personality, character,

---

[429] Nasir Ghaemi, Thomas Fuchs, et. al., edited by K.W.M. Fulford, Martin Davies Richard G.T. Gipps, George Graham, John Z. Sadler, Giovanni Stanghellini, and Tim Thornton, *The Oxford Handbook of Philosophy and Psychiatry* (Oxford University Press, 2015), 9.

[430] Angus John Clarke, *Emery and Rimoin's Principles and Practice of Medical Genetics* sixth edition, edited by David Rimoin, Red Pyeritz, and Bruce Korf (Academic Press, 2013), 1-40.

behaviors, beliefs, and perceived forms of mental degeneracy. Belief in the philosophy is sustained by the notion that genes are immutable or "fixed." Phrases like "hereditary risk" and "genetic predisposition" are common ways in which the philosophy is applied in modern day. The theories seem to be more advanced, but they are the same Darwinian positions accepted in Nazi Germany. Neuroscientists Steve and Hilary Rose describe the philosophy of bio-determinism:

> Within this framework new forms of biological determinism have arisen. Not of course the old Social Darwinism, which provided a biologised defense of the prevailing social hierarchies of Victorian society, but modern and seemingly more sophisticated forms, powered by this vast expansion of biological and particularly genetic, knowledge and technology.[431]

While the eugenics theory has become more accepted as a valid theory due to technologic advancements and changes in nomenclature, bio/genetic determinism and bio/genetic probabilism continue to uphold the evolutionary concept of natural selection:

> On the one hand, it claims, our biology is our destiny, written in our genes by the shaping forces of human evolution through natural selection and random mutation. . . . This second strand, of biological fatalism, however, runs alongside and interacts with the Promethean claims of these promised genetic technologies. This strand is above all part of a **struggle**

---

[431] Steve Rose and Hilary Rose eds., *Alas, Poor Darwin: The Case against Evolutionary Psychology* (London: Vintage Publishing, 2001), 1-3.

about how we should conceive of human nature and human society and culture [emphasis added].[432]

The psychiatric genetic theory is at its foundational level a theory of human origins, anthropology, phenomenology, and sociology.

As geneticist Richard Lewontin also discusses, bio-determinists have introduced many names, such as "sociobiology," that reflect genetic determinism without directly revealing the belief:

> The most modern form of naturalistic human nature ideology is called sociobiology. It emerged onto the public scene about 15 years ago and has since become the ruling justifying theory for the permanence of society as we know it. It is an evolutionary and a genetic theory that uses the entire theoretical apparatus of modern evolutionary biology . . . . Sociobiology is the latest and most mystified attempt to convince people that human life is pretty much what it has to be and perhaps even out to be.[433]

Most mainstream psychiatrists prefer the term "bio-psycho-social"[434] over the broader idea of sociobiology or neo-Kraepelinianism to accommodate their theory of the soul, but faith in bio-determinism is vital to psychiatric genetics. Richard Lewontin expresses how the genetic theory of mental illness is part of a new humanistic gospel

[432] Ibid.

[433] Richard C. Lewontin, *Biology as Ideology: The Doctrine of DNA* (New York: HarperCollins Publishers, 1991), 89.

[434] Ronald W. Pies, "Debunking the Two Chemical Imbalance Myths, Again," *Psychiatric Times* (April 30, 2019): https://www. psychiatrictimes.com/ depression/debunking-two-chemical-imbalance-myths-again/page/0/1.

that denies God's providence in exchange for belief in the human genome's sovereignty:

> As evolutionary theory has developed over the last one hundred years and become technologically and scientifically sophisticated, as vague notions of inheritance have become converted into a very precise theory of the structure and function of DNA, so the evolutionary view of human nature has developed a modern, scientific-sounding apparatus that makes it seem every bit as unchallengeable as the theories of divine providence seemed in an earlier age.[435]

Bio-determinism is a humanistic gospel that blames human fragility and depravity on "mother nature's selection" rather than on the fall of Adam and Eve. It is a doctrine that denies God's sovereignty in exchange for faith in the human genome.

In order to theoretically shift responsibility for humanity's consciousness and outworking behavior to natural selection, geneticists must embrace the philosophies of individual degeneration and materialism, which together depend upon bio/genetic determinism. In theory, accepting these beliefs removes responsibility for moral mindsets, emotions, and behaviors from the individual. Former NIMH consultant and professor of psychiatry Peter Breggin remarks,

> It's understandable that parents would prefer to think of their children as genetically defective rather than as resentful, rebellious, misunderstood, or even abused. But it's harder to see why people in despair would want to see themselves as innately defective, as some patients do. One reason is that they typically feel helpless. Genetic and biochemical theories confirm that helplessness and

[435] Lewontin, *Biology as Ideology*, 88-89.

alleviate the need to overcome it. Often they feel frightened by the seemingly primitive impulses stirring within them, and genetic or biochemical theories help to explain those impulses away. Frequently they feel guilty about their passions and their problems—and especially about their resentment toward their parents—and biopsychiatry relieves them of facing these personal conflicts.[436]

Genetic determinism—the theory that who a person truly is at his/her core is fixed and predetermined by his/her inherited genome—is not a scientific concept, but a tenet of evolutionary anthropology which is antithetical to the creation account. If genes are fixed, so the reasoning goes, then so too are personalities, ways of thinking, beliefs, motives, emotions, and moral behavioral patterns.

Utilitarianism

There is also a fourth philosophy, *utilitarianism*, that undergirds faith in evolution, humanism, and eugenics. If human nature is only material and an amoral product of evolution, the logic must then follow that no moral or objective truth exists apart from what evolution insists is true. If this assertion is verifiable, then no objective truth can exist apart from the established authorities' interpretation of the natural world according to their presuppositional moral belief of what is best for the majority.

In order to declare objective truth, as psychiatric geneticists insist that they do, there must be an authoritative claim made upon an interpretation of the natural world.

[436] Breggin, *Toxic Psychiatry*, 94.

Historically, psychiatrists have found that there exists strength in numbers and in the guiding principle of the "greatest good for the greatest number."

If a group rather than an individual declares something to be true, then people are often more willing to accept a perceived authority's opinion. Large groups, especially in medicine and science, by nature thwart questioning of popular opinion and establish seemingly agreed-upon thought as objective truth. This reality is exactly why the American Psychiatric Association once believed Freudianism to be scientific and accepted it for decades as the premier theory of mental illness. But now, most Kraepelinians rightfully view psychoanalysis as a delusion.

The ability to change constructs as an authority wills or society demands is key to psychiatry. Sociologists Herb Kutchins and Stuart Kirk write,

> First, you must appreciate that the notion of mental disorder is what social scientists call a construct. Constructs are abstract concepts of something that is not real in the physical sense that a spoon or motorcycle or cat can be seen and touched. **Constructs are shared ideas, supported by general agreement. . . . Mental illness is a construct.** . . . The category itself is an invention, a creation. It may be a good and useful invention, or it may be a confusing one. *DSM* is a compendium of constructs. **And like a large and popular mutual fund, *DSM's* holdings are constantly changing as the managers' estimates and beliefs about the value of those holdings change** . . . . The constant revising provides the illusion that knowledge is changing rapidly [emphasis added].[437]

---

[437] Herb Kutchins and Stuart A. Kirk, Making Us Crazy: DSM: The Psychiatric Bible and the Creation of Mental Disorders (New York: Free Press, 1997), 22-25.

The philosophy that many people should decide what is right for the claimed good of the majority is referred to as utilitarianism, and it is a vital tenet of the APA's ongoing acceptance in society as the highest authority on the metaphysical nature of humanity. Utilitarianism is the *epistemology* (the rule or measure of how one determines what is true in life) of secular psychiatry and psychology.[438]

Likewise, utilitarianism is a vital philosophy on which psychiatric constructs — and thus degenerates — are created. Allen Frances writes in his book *Saving Normal* that utilitarianism, based upon individual and corporal morals or "values," is fundamental to modern psychiatry's determining who is perceived as a degenerate:

> Utilitarianism provided the first, and remains the only practical philosophic guidance on how and where to set a boundary between "normal" and "mental disorder." The guiding assumptions are that "normal" has no universal meaning and can never be defined with precision by the spinning wheels of philosophical deduction — it is very much in the eye of the beholder and is changeable over time, place, and cultures . . . . [Utilitarianists] always seek the "greatest good for the greatest number." Make decisions depending on what measurably works best.[439]

While Frances acknowledges that the philosophy of utilitarianism is foundational to creating psychiatric constructs, he attempts to deny that creating psychiatric constructs requires the spinning wheels of philosophical deduction — what the established APA task force perceives

---

[438] David Woodruff Smith, "Phenomenology," *Sandford Encyclopedia of Philosophy* (Summer Edition, 2018): https://plato.stanford.edu/entries/phenomenology/.

[439] Frances, *Saving Normal*, 5.

"works best." In a later paragraph, Frances does, however, admit that utilitarianism is the APA's true epistemology or guiding moral system:

> Granted that, in the wrong hands, utilitarianism can be **blind to good values and twisted by bad ones**, it still remains the best or only **philosophical guide** when we embark on the difficult task of setting boundaries between the mentally "normal" and the mentally "abnormal." This is the approach we used in *DSM-IV* [emphasis added].[440]

What Frances fails to see is that declaring some people to be abnormal/disordered based upon constructed subjective syndromes is in itself a twisted value system. On the other hand, Frances does rightly concede that utilitarianism was a key philosophy that enabled the Holocaust:

> There are also undeniable uncertainties in being a practical utilitarian, and even worse there are **dangerous value land mines.** "The greatest good for the greatest number" sounds great on paper, but how do you measure the quantities and **how do you decide what's the good?** It is no accident that utilitarianism is currently least popular in Germany, where Hitler gave it such an enduringly bad name. During World War II, it was statistically normal for the German population to act in barbaric ways that would be deemed decidedly abnormal before or since — all justified at the time on utilitarian grounds as necessary to provide for the greatest good of the master race [emphasis added].[441]

Psychiatric eugenics, which theoretically creates the alleged mentally disordered, has not philosophically changed over

[440] Ibid.

[441] Ibid.

time, and it even now remains a philosophy that is practically applied according to one's moral values.

Without changing the foundational moral values that guide anthropologies and their necessary practical fields, human atrocities will continue to occur. The notion that teaching future physicians or society at large "medical ethics" will protect society from future barbaric and unethical practices was greatly disproven by Nazi psychiatrists' tragic application of Kraepelinianism. Writing in the *Annals of General Psychiatry*, Rael Strous relates,

> Several reports have been published that extol the virtues of medical ethics training in psychiatry residency training programs. However, while the importance of such training programs is well recognized, so was the importance of medical ethics acknowledged in Germany in the 1930's. **In fact, Germany possessed one of the most advanced and sophisticated codes of medical ethics in the world in existence from 1931.** Some have even suggested that in certain aspects it was stricter than the subsequent Nuremberg Code or Helsinki Accord [emphasis added].[442]

As observed in Nazi Germany, ethical codes established upon a faulty worldview will always fail to protect humanity—even if the majority of medical professionals agree otherwise. Dr. Strous further expounds,

> Doctors in general and psychiatrists in particular who were involved in the euthanasia program were not morally blind or devoid of the power of moral reflection . . . . The example of Nazi psychiatry is a prime illustration of how ethics training without a focus on history is

---

[442] Rael D. Strous, "Psychiatry During the Nazi Era: Ethical Lessons for the Modern Professional," *Annals of General Psychiatry* vol. 6 (8) (February 27, 2007): doi:10.1186/1744-859X-6-8.

useless; where policy, even though existing, can be disregarded in the most grotesque fashion.[443]

Both the history and philosophy of psychiatric eugenics are vitally important to understand and denounce. The atrocities and mistreatment of people who are mentally and behaviorally struggling will continue under Kraepelinian faith and its "altruistic" and "medical" applications unless foundational faith is radically changed, a genuine paradigm shift occurs in anthropology, phenomenology, and thereafter in the field of medicine, and history is considered markedly relevant.

Astoundingly, the underlying Kraepelinian worldview, which ushered in the Holocaust, has not been abandoned. The theory of psychiatric genetics — mental health/the medical model/Nazi eugenics/the biopsychosocial model/neo-Kraepelinianism — remains the dominant value/belief system governing the utilitarian approach of the APA today, the entire mental health system in America, and much of the developed world.

More sobering still, the United States government (e.g., NIH, NIMH, FDA, and the Human Genome Project, etc.) and most major educational institutions in America fully support and propagate faith in Kraepelinianism — forming a utilitarian perspective that is difficult to counter even with empirical facts. Most medical journals write from a bio-psycho-social perspective and have convinced many physicians that Kraepelinianism is an altruistic and scientifically validated theory. Just as it was in Nazi Germany, there exists a global eugenic culture in the modern world, which can be observed in the

---

[443] Ibid.

interconnectivity and codependency of universities, medical facilities and journals, pharmaceutical companies, research centers, news agencies, and existing governments.

The continued propagation of the neo-Kraepelinian faith primarily occurs within academia. Government and pharmaceutical grants are regularly issued today to universities in pursuit of proving the Kraepelinian paradigm and potentially finding remedies for human nature within the reductionistic worldview. In Nazi Germany, psychiatrists — via Kraepelin and Rüdin — led the medical and scientific communities into the eugenics worldview by utilizing a parallel utilitarian approach.

Today, research and global efforts to produce "scientific discoveries," as it relates to the human psyche/soul, are at an all-time high. Yet, no significant changes have occurred within Kraepelinianism or have been validated by the extensive research, though influential notable figures like Jeffrey Lieberman continue to admonish fellow psychiatrists "to become leaders of change":

> Psychiatrists can view health care reform as leading to an inevitable change from the status quo and worrisome loss of autonomy. Alternatively, they can recognize that psychiatrists are well positioned to participate in and direct new health care initiatives — to become leaders of change, rather than siloed providers outside the mainstream of modern health care. We are the most highly trained, knowledgeable, and best positioned of all health care specialists to determine and provide (or at least oversee) the care of people with mental disorders . . . . There is a historic and exciting opportunity for psychiatrists to influence the future of medical care and occupy our rightful position in the field of medicine. Our nation is still at the beginning of the reform process, and we have the ability to influence its direction, but not if we choose to sit on the sidelines. It is important for

psychiatrists to stay involved, not only in practice settings, but as APA members at the local and district branch levels. Step up and make your thoughts known to health care and government leaders; most are willing to listen if we offer ideas and solutions. The health care reform process is under way; the world will be changing around us. If psychiatrists are engaged in influencing that change — if we take a more active role — then we are more likely to be satisfied with the end result. This may be our most important role of all.[444]

Lieberman and fellow Columbia University psychiatrist Grant Mitchell's statement could have been written by Ernst Rüdin in the early 1900s in pre-Nazi Germany. Instead, it was published in modern North America.

Nazi eugenics in Kraepelin's day fully resembles the psychiatric approach and narrative, the cultural environment, and even the political temperature of today. While socialism may still be denounced by many in America, the underlying philosophical approach of Kraepelinian eugenics remains and has gained widespread acceptance.

What remains to be realized in modern America is a fear-based panic that will cause people to demand mental health reform and political regulations for the good of the people — though such a demand has already been initiated. In many ways, eugenics leads to the eventual institution of socialism so that full control can be attained. With the increase of mass shootings, political divide over eugenics

---

[444] Grant Mitchell and Jeffrey Lieberman, "The Role of Psychiatrists in the Brave New World of Health Care," *Psychiatric News* (March 31, 2014): https://doi.org/10.1176/appi.pn.2014.4a22.

issues (e.g., abortion[445]), and created racial and moral tension, this next step in eugenics' evolvement may not be too far in the distant future for America.

No matter what one's view of psychiatric genetics/ eugenics may be, every approach to human nature and human phenomenology requires a presuppositional faith:

> The "reality" of the natural world is subordinate to beliefs about it, and there is no way of adjudicating between the claims to truth made by one group of scientists compared with those made by another. What Wilson, Dawkins, or Trivers write about sociobiology reflects their interests in advancing their own social position. What we write reflects ours.[446]

The undeniable truth is that a person's or group's faith and interests shape their "scientific" approaches and conclusions. Individual degenerationism, materialism, genetic determinism, and utilitarianism all explain why the eugenics theory continues to thrive around the world under the concept of psychiatric genetics and why mental

---

[445] "Abortions (preventions) — 1933 — Psychiatrist Ernst Rüdin uses compulsory sterilization laws in the United States as a model for Germany's Law for the Prevention of Genetically Diseased Offspring. This law allows for the forced sterilization of individuals with physical and mental disabilities. The magazine Margaret Sanger [of Planned Parenthood] founded publishes his article, "Eugenical Sterilization, an Urgent Need," and Hitler gives him a medal as a "pathfinder in the field of hereditary hygiene" (Colbe Mazzarella, "Psychiatry's Little-known Role in Creating the Holocaust," *The New Boston Post* (February 9, 2018): https://newbostonpost.com/2018/ 02/09/psychiatrys-little-known-role-in-creating-the-holocaust/. For further study on how abortion is a practical application of eugenics, see Daniel R. Berger II, "How to Understand the Fallacy of the Pro-Abortion Agenda," *RickThomas.net* (July 2019): https://rickthomas.net/how-to-understand-the-fallacy-of-the-pro-abortion-agenda/.

[446] Lewontin, Rose, Kamin, *Not in Our Genes*, 77-78.

hygiene is now accepted as mental health. These foundational beliefs must be embraced if humanism[447] and evolutionary theories of origin are to be sustained.

But as long as these beliefs are held and practically applied in society, eugenics has not been eliminated. In fact, it is also helpful to understand how these philosophies work together and are interdependent. Denouncing all but one philosophical pillar of eugenics will inevitably return society to adopting them all.

Combining these philosophies together leads to the creation of and acceptance of constructs of mental illness. The sociobiology, bio-psycho-social, neo-Kraepelinian theory requires that any human mindset, emotion, or behavior (or combination thereof into a construct/syndrome) which cannot be explained as morally acceptable within the restricted and integrated philosophies of materialism, bio-determinism, and humanism be framed as inherited individual degeneration. All human phenomena within this religion must be filtered through these eugenic philosophies.

One should consider that the genetic theory of mental illness or bio-psycho-social perspective is not principally about pathology but about anthropology and phenomenology; it is a religion or worldview.

Dr. Nassir Ghaemi, who is an adjunct professor of psychiatry at Harvard Medical School and Tufts University and who directs early drug discovery at Novartis Institutes for Biomedical Research (one of the largest distributers of

---

[447] Humanism is the belief that mankind is the highest value, the greatest good, the judge of what is true, and the sovereign of all life in the universe.

psychopharmacology), explains how the biopsychosocial model is a postmodern worldview that is not based upon science but upon relativism:

> I think the problem goes beyond the issue of whether it was a model in a scientific sense, as opposed to a more general approach to a worldview. The key problem, if I were to simplify it in one sentence, is that the **BPS model for the past half century has served as a postmodernist excuse for eclecticism. Let me explain this sentence . . . . Postmodernism (PM), in my usage, is a philosophy, rooted in Schopenhauer and Nietzsche**, and expressed most clearly later by Heidegger and Foucault. **It rejects the Enlightenment heritage in its claim that science can replace religion as the source of independent truths.** (There is more to it; but let's focus on this point). PM in this classic form is relativistic and critical (or cynical) about science in general, and psychiatry in particular (the target of much of Foucault's ire). If PM is accepted, there are two options: nothing is true—nihilism; or anything can be true—eclecticism. That is how the BPS model has played out in the past half century. **Mental health clinicians do whatever they like, and they claim support for that anarchy in the BPS approach** [emphasis added].[448]

If the bio-psycho-social model is accepted, then those who socially control what is perceived to be true about the soul's nature and phenomena can never be wrong in their assertions of truth. Ironically, within this philosophical framework, empirical science is rejected rather than upheld. As Ghaemi notes, this worldview is a newly constructed faith, which is denied as being religious in

[448] S. Nassir Ghaemi, "The Postmodern Assumptions of Biopsychosocial Approach," *Psychiatric Times* (January 27, 2020): https://www.psychiatrictimes.com/couch-crisis/postmodern-assumptions-biopsychosocial-approach?rememberme=1&elq_mid=10664&elq_cid=893295&GUID=31158D64-F01A-4DEA-AC1A-D3CE843FC9BC.

nature while being upheld in attempt to replace other religions.

Essentially, the bio-psycho-social perspective is an approach to the human soul/mind which attempts to convince people of three things: 1) that human character, moral behavior, and metaphysical phenomena are born out of the material nature and predetermined by evolutionary processes and environments, 2) that science (including medicine) and scientists alone are best equipped to both explain and save humanity from all impairment and distress, and 3) that truth is relative, not objective, and determined by humanity. These secular goals directly attack God's gracious character and good will.

Psychiatric genetics is simply the new title of the old Kraepelinian eugenic faith, which creates individual degenerates by establishing social and descriptive constructs and claiming them as genetic diseases that threaten individuals, families, and societies. Neo-Kraepelinianism is the "new" big humanistic theory and hope. Yet, as Nassir Ghaemi transparently acknowledges, "In psychiatry, the lesson of history runs, big theories mean big trouble."[449] The Kraepelinian theory that governs the modern mental health system has historically only produced worsening conditions in every society where it has been embraced. The bio-psycho-social model is not a faith/worldview/phenomenology that restores individual soul's to health.

[449] Nasir Ghaemi, Thomas Fuchs, et. al., edited by K.W.M. Fulford, Martin Davies Richard G.T. Gipps, George Graham, John Z. Sadler, Giovanni Stanghellini, and Tim Thornton, *The Oxford Handbook of Philosophy and Psychiatry* (Oxford University Press, 2015), 3.

CHAPTER 5
THE SCIENCE OF PSYCHIATRIC GENETICS (1)

The words "science" and "scientific," which we all revere and freely use to endorse our pet beliefs, are ambiguous and have at times been used to sanction man's inhumanity to man.[450] – *Zbigniew J. Lipowski, psychiatrist*

In early 2016, psychiatric geneticists declared with enthusiastic triumph that the precise gene which causes schizophrenia had likely been identified.[451] What seemed to be the validation of Kraepelin's version of the eugenics theory — at least as reported, quickly turned out to be another false alarm. As scientist Michael Balter reports in the journal *Scientific American* (2017), "Gene studies were supposed to reveal the disorder's roots. That didn't

---

[450] Zbigniew J. Lipowski, "Psychiatry: Mindless or Brainless, Both or Neither?" *Canadian Journal of Psychiatry* 34 (3) (1989): 250.

[451] Rachel Rettner, "'Schizophrenia Gene' Discovery Sheds Light on Possible Cause," *Scientific American* (January 28, 2016): https://www.scientific american.com/article/schizophrenia-gene-discovery-sheds-light-on-possible-cause/.

happen."[452] Renowned geneticist Steven McCarroll[453] had promised to deliver concrete scientific evidence of a genetic etiology for the construct of schizophrenia. But in an article published in *Nature*, McCarroll and his constituents reveal that there only exists "a set of genetic variations that are strongly associated with the risk of developing schizophrenia."[454] Despite their dogmatic belief that schizophrenia is a disease entity, McCarroll, along with the *Schizophrenia Working Group of the Psychiatric Genomics Consortium*, admits that "schizophrenia is a heritable brain illness with unknow pathogenic mechanisms."[455] In other words, only correlations exist which "associate" human behavioral patterns within a strictly genetic theoretical framework. A true "path" from proposed psychiatric symptoms to genetic causes has never been discovered, and yet, based upon published claims, many people dogmatically believe that mental, emotional, and behavioral struggles are genetically based.

[452] Michael Balter, "Schizophrenia's Unyielding Mysteries," *Scientific American Online* Vol. 28 (4) (May 2017): https://www.scientificamerican.com/article/schizophrenia-rsquo-s-unyielding-mysteries/.

[453] McCarrol is the assistant professor in the Department of Genetics at Harvard Medical School, is the Director of Genetics at the Broad Institute of MIT's and Harvard's Stanley Center for Psychiatric Research, and is considered by many to be one of the leading experts on genetic theory and experimentation.

[454] Schizophrenia Working Group of the Psychiatric Genomics Consortium (Steven A. McCarroll, Mark J. Daly, Michael C. Carroll, and Beth Stevens, et al.), "Schizophrenia Risk from Complex Variation of Complement Component 4," *Nature* 530 (February 11, 2016): 177.

[455] Ibid.

Clinical psychologist and researcher Richard Bental and Professor of Health and Social Sciences David Pilgrim comment on the grand claims so often made within the psychiatric genetic field:

> Last year, researchers at the University of Cardiff claimed to have discovered the "Rosetta Stone gene" for schizophrenia. This year, geneticists at Harvard University claimed in an article in the *New York Times* that they had completed "a landmark study that provides the first rigorously tested insight into the biology behind any common psychiatric disorder." In London, a research group at the Sanger Institute announced their discovery that a gene called SETD1A was the "strongest single gene conclusively implicated in schizophrenia." But are these claims warranted? Close inspection of the relevant studies suggests not. The Rosetta Stone gene study was carried out with mice and the gene involved, DISC1, was found not to be linked to schizophrenia in a comprehensive 2012 review of patient studies. In the Harvard research, the genetic effect was very small, but this was exaggerated by the way the authors interpreted their findings. And the SETD1A gene was found in only 10 out of nearly 8,000 patients, seven of whom also suffered from learning difficulties. In fact, when looked at in the round, molecular genetic research simply does not support the standard "genes for schizophrenia" story that makes good copy for journalists.[456]

In late 2019, professors of psychiatry Caleb Gardner at Cambridge University and Arthur Kleinman at Harvard University proposed that

> we are facing the stark limitations of biologic treatments, while finding less and less time to work with patients on difficult problems. Ironically, although these limitations

---

[456] Richard Bentall and David Pilgrim, "There Are No 'Schizophrenia Genes': Here's Why," *The Conversation* (April 8, 2016): https://theconversation.com/there-are-no-schizophrenia-genes-heres-why-57294.

are widely recognized by experts in the field, the prevailing message to the public and the rest of medicine remains that the solution to psychological problems involves matching the "right" diagnosis with the "right" medication. Consequently, **psychiatric diagnoses and medications proliferate under the banner of scientific medicine, though there is no comprehensive biologic understanding of either the causes or the treatments of psychiatric disorders** [emphasis added].[457]

Adjunct professor of psychiatry at Tufts University and Harvard University Medical Schools and director of translational medicine-neuroscience at Novartis Institutes of biomedical research Nassir Ghaemi agrees:

> The problem with this view is that genetic research has completely failed in the past two generations in psychiatry. For over 30 years, researchers have assiduously looked for "the" genes for major depressive disorder (MDD), bipolar illness, schizophrenia, anxiety conditions, personality disorders - and come up empty.[458]

While researchers' claims are never validated, the false narrative the published articles and the widespread news coverage present is further engrained into society's thinking. Faith in Kraepelinianism (including Kraepelin's constructs of schizophrenia and bipolar, the genetic theory, the diagnostic system, the statistical approach, psychopharmacology, etc.) is deepened by each publicized

457 Caleb Gardner and Arthur Kleinman, "Medicine and the Mind — The Consequences of Psychiatry's Identity Crisis," *New England Journal of Medicine* vol. 381 (October 31, 2019): DOI: 10.1056/NEJMp1910603.

458 Nassir Ghaemi, "The Genetic Fallacy in Psychiatry," *Medscape Psychiatry* (August 5, 2013): http://boards.medscape.com/ forums/?128@@.2a590550! comment=1.

false claim that the illusive, yet dogmatically insisted upon, schizophrenia gene(s) has been found.

But publicly announcing the discovery of an alleged schizophrenia gene(s) and furthering faith that the genetic theory is scientifically valid is nothing new. In fact, propagating eugenics to the public as empirically sound without concrete evidence has been a consistent historical strategy in maintaining the false anthropology. Medical Historian Paul Lombardo with the Center for Biomedical Ethics at the University of Virginia explains:

> The eugenicists were successful in fueling public fear about the growing "army of idiots and imbeciles" graphically depicted in their pedigree charts. Their success was the result of a finely crafted educational program — propaganda that reduced science to simplistic terms. **The tendency to oversimplify concepts of genetic causation and the rush to amplify the significance of research findings through the popular media is also apparent today. What begins as publicity has the potential to be transformed into propaganda**. Although many in the scientific community are understandably reluctant to revisit the abuses of the past, that community must confront the history of eugenics as a necessary antidote to the genetic hype that surrounds us [emphasis added].[459]

Professor of biology Garland Allen expresses how a public narrative — even echoing the same narratives of Nazi Germany — is necessary to continue belief in the eugenics theory:

---

[459] Paul A. Lombardo, "Pedigrees, Propaganda, and Paranoia: Family Studies in a Historical Context," *Journal of Continuing Education in the Health Professions* Vol. 21 (4) (Fall 2001): 247; https://www.ncbi.nlm.nih.gov/pubmed/11803769.

Eugenicists were also active in the political arena, lobbying in the United States for immigration restriction and compulsory sterilization laws for those deemed genetically unfit; in Britain they lobbied for incarceration of genetically unfit and in Germany for sterilization and eventually euthanasia. In all these countries one of the major arguments was that of efficiency: that it was inefficient to allow genetic defects to be multiplied and then have to try and deal with the consequences of state care for the offspring. National socialists called genetically defective individuals "useless eaters' and argued for sterilization or euthanasia on economic grounds. Similar arguments appeared in the United States and Britain as well.[460]

Allen then points out that not much has changed within modern times:

At the present time (1997) much research and publicity is being given to claims about a genetic basis for all the same behaviors (alcoholism, manic depression, etc.), again in an economic context — care for people with such diseases is costing too much. There is an important lesson to learn from the past: genetic arguments are put forward to mask the true — social and economic — causes of human behavioral defects.[461]

Since most people will never take the time to understand the language, details, or history of the field of psychiatric genetics let alone ever observe or understand the intricacies of an actual human gene, much of society has accepted in blind faith the speculative theory as proven fact:

[460] Garland E. Allen, "The Social and Economic Origins of Genetic Determinism: A Case History of the American Eugenics Movement, 1900-1940 and its Lessons for Today," *Genetica* vol. 99 (2-3) (1997): 77-88; https://www.ncbi. nlm.nih.gov/pubmed/9463076.

[461] Ibid.

Much of the new knowledge from genetics, molecular biology, and the neurosciences is esoteric [only understood by those in the field]. But its cultural impact is already running ahead of the science. People begin to see themselves not as wholes with a moral center but the result of the combined action of parts for which they have little responsibility.[462]

Psychiatric eugenics must continue to publicly proclaim itself as scientifically based and as falling within valid medicine in order to be accepted. But the science of psychiatric genetics consists more of strategically attempting to prove and sustain Kraepelin's construct than of objectively desiring to discover empirical knowledge or providing a valid remedy for those in need.

When closely examined, the alleged science is not difficult to understand, and moreover, it becomes apparent that the genetic theory of mental illness can never be objectively proven utilizing the scientific method. What is difficult to know, however, are the intricacies of genes themselves. Yet, the alleged science of the mind — the vital point on which claims of "mental disorder" rest — and not merely the confounding science of the genes remains a mystery to secularists. In fact, as stated in this chapter and those to follow, further knowledge of the genome does nothing to explain or to help approach the human soul. Still, just as with the biblical concept of delivering grace, which allows broken people to find deliverance and intimately know the one true God, secularists have established the knowledge of the human genome as a replacement theory. Geneticist Richard Lewontin purports,

[462] Alun Anderson, "Are you a machine of many parts?," *The World in 1999, The Economist* (1999): 109ff.

For biology, this [genetic] worldview has resulted in a
particular picture of organisms and their total life activity.
Living beings are seen as being determined by internal
factors, the genes. Our genes and the DNA molecules that
make them up are the modern form of grace, and in this
view we will understand what we are when we know
what our genes are made of. The world outside us poses
certain problems, which we do not create but only
experience as objects.[463]

From this perspective, the hope for humanity is built on
human wisdom produced by geneticists whose logic is that
if only the body can be fully understood, then mankind can
be delivered from all evil and distress. Upon this
conjecture, the search for Kraepelin's psychiatric unicorn,
marketed today as schizophrenia, continues.

The Reality

It is imperative to recall throughout the next two chapters
that the science of psychiatric genetics cannot be separated
from its foundational philosophical assumptions (as
established in Part I, chapter 4). All science is first and
foremost faith-based, as it attempts to explain the natural
world in accordance with one's learned worldview. Famed
biological psychiatrist Kenneth Kendler addresses this
issue to fellow psychiatrists:

Whether you like it or not, you have a set of tacitly
operating philosophical concepts and beliefs that you use
to organize your views about the nature of psychiatric
illness and its treatment. You can leave these assumptions
unexamined, or you can take as critical an approach to
these fundamental questions as you should to the

[463] Richard C. Lewontin, *Biology as Ideology: The Doctrine of DNA* (New
York: HarperCollins Publishers, 1991), 13.

differential diagnosis or treatment planning of your patients. Thus, your choice is between following an implicit philosophical framework — which could be wrong, or overly simplistic, or at least misrepresent key aspect of our clinical and research world . . . .[464]

Similarly, Lewontin, Rose, and Kamin remark on this sobering reality:

The sorry history of this century of insistence on the iron nature of **biological determination of criminality and degeneracy** [individual degeneration], leading to the growth of the eugenics movement, sterilization laws, and the race science of Nazi Germany has frequently been told. It is not our purpose here to retrace that history. Rather, we are concerned with the way in which the **philosophy of reductionism** [materialism], and its intimate intertwining with **biological determinism, developed into the modern synthesis of sociobiology and molecular biology** [emphasis added].[465]

Molecular psychiatry and psychiatric genetics, while claimed to be legitimate fields of science and medicine, are the new ways to pronounce and sustain the old faith in individual degeneracy, materialism, and biological/genetic determinism. Historian Edwin Black shares his own understanding:

Only after the truth about Nazi extermination became known did the American eugenics movement fade. **American eugenic institutions rushed to change their names from eugenics to genetics.** With its new identity, the remnant eugenics movement reinvented itself and helped establish the modern, enlightened human genetic

[464] Kenneth S. Kendler edited by Kenneth S. Kendler & Josef Parnas, *Philosophical Issues in Psychiatry: Explanation, Phenomenology, and Nosology* (Johns Hopkins University Press, 2008), 2-3.

[465] Lewontin, Rose, *Kamin, Not in Our Genes*, 57.

revolution. **Although the rhetoric and the organizational names had changed, the laws and mindsets were left in place** [emphasis added].[466]

The word *eugenics* is correctly thought of with disdain — as a false belief, a moral crime, and as pseudoscience, although some of its original empowering social and descriptive constructs (e.g., schizophrenia, alcoholism, and bipolar), foundational goals, and damaging applications remain practically unchanged. These concepts are today propagated with terms such as "Polygenic Risk Scores."[467] The University of Pennsylvania Medical School relates that

> after World War II, the word *eugenics* acquired its current bad odor. Modern geneticists are loath to accept any association with the movement. Yet the fact remains that eugenics was considered legitimate science by influential academics and intellectuals irrespective of their other political views."[468]

Another article, published in the *NEJM*, suggests that the horror of the psychiatric eugenic experiment (the Holocaust) exposed eugenics to be a pseudoscience: "Globally, the Holocaust helped to discredit eugenics, and the term itself became taboo in the scientific

---

[466] Edwin Black, *War against the Weak: Eugenics and America's Campaign to Create a Master Race* (New York: Four Walls Eight Windows, 2003), preface xvii-iii.

467 Alicia R. Martin, Mark J. Daly, Elise B. Robinson, Steven E. Hyman, and Benjamin M. Neale, "Predicting Polygenic Risk of Psychiatric Disorders," *Biological Psychiatry* vol. 86 (2) (July 15, 2019): 97-109; https://doi.org/10.1016/j.biopsych.2018.12.015.

[468] Penn Medicine's Department of Communications, "Psychiatry and Eugenics," *Penn Medicine News* (October 23, 2012): https://www.penn medicine.org/news/news-blog/2012/october/psychiatry-and-eugenics.

community."[469] But in reality, the Holocaust did not discredit eugenics in many people's minds. Rather, it caused many to demand that the concept of psychiatric eugenics remain but with the perception of new ethical guidelines and without its original name or sordid "scientific" history:

> We argue that psychiatric genetics has not only propelled our understanding of mental disorders but has significantly benefited genetic research into other complex disorders through the development of methodologically robust approaches (e.g., systematic phenotype characterization, methods to control for ascertainment biases, age-correction). Given the recent reasons for new optimism, i.e., the identification of susceptibility genes for psychiatric phenotypes, a continued methodologically sound approach is needed more than ever to guarantee robust results. **Finally, psychiatric genetic research should never again be performed in an environment void of ethical standards.**[470]

Furthermore, professor of biology Garland Allen cautions:

> From this history, I think two important conclusions emerge. The first is that it is important for knowledgeable geneticists to examine claims about the inheritance of this or that trait (especially complex behavioural, personality and mental traits) when they are publicised today. We have been treated for several decades at the end of the 20th century to a barrage of claims about the genetic basis of a multitude of human complex behaviours, from I.Q. to

[469] Susan Bachrach, "In the Name of Public Health — Nazi Racial Hygiene," *New England Journal of Medicine* 351 (2004): 417-420; DOI: 10.1056/NEJMp 048136.

[470] T.G. Schulze, H. Fangerau, P. Propping, "From Degeneration to Genetic Susceptibility, From Eugenics to Genethics, From Bezugsziffer to LOD score: The History of Psychiatric Genetics," *International Review of Psychiatry* (4) (November 16, 2004): 246-59.

criminality, aggressiveness, alcoholism, shyness, sexual orientation, manic depression, bipolar disorder and attention-deficit hyperactivity disorder — even "religiosity." Many of these claims have not held up to careful scrutiny, and all have been criticised for the same faults for which the older eugenic studies were found guilty. Since claims about the genetic basis of such characteristics can have serious medical consequences — pharmacogenomics and drug treatment — it is important that the scientific accuracy of the various claims should be clearly delineated and exposed.[471]

The continued call for ethical standards and honesty by so many contemporary geneticists, who wish to ensure that history does not repeat itself, is an acknowledgement of the dark genesis of psychiatric genetics.

What most people miss in this discussion is that eugenics/the genetic theory of mental illness is a faulty ethical standard to begin with and is based upon philosophies which demand that degenerates be created, they be sustained within a medical framework, and the process be hidden under the façade of science. Volker Roelcke, professor at the Institute of Medicine at the University of Lubeck, comments on the true history of psychiatric genetics development:

> Eugenics and the practice of sterilisation are constitutively linked to scientific justifications, just as - complementarily - the development of genetics, in particular psychiatric

471 Garland E. Allen, "Eugenics and Modern Biology: Critiques of Eugenics, 1910-1945," *Annals of Human Genetics* vol. 75 (2011): 324; doi: 10.1111/j.1469-1809.2011.00649.x.

genetics, is inextricably associated with eugenics and its
funding by philanthropic or state institutions.[472]

Simply by claiming a theory as scientific and subjecting it
to controlled studies within a strict presuppositional faith
does not transform conjecture into valid science no matter
how long the narrative is sustained and no matter how
great the number of believers may grow. Historian Paul
Weindling discusses the expectation (faith) that science
could seemingly deliver humanity from all its problems:

> The history of eugenics has become a classic arena for
> examining how the interplay of culture, social interests
> and social structures affects the advancement of science.
> At the same time eugenics demonstrates how in the first
> half of the twentieth century, the expectation arose that
> science could offer the solution of social problems; for
> biology intruded into many areas of social policy during
> the 1920s and 30s. Historians of science have been struck
> by the coincidence between the rise of genetics and
> eugenics after 1900.[473]

Weindling also highlights the many "sciences" that not
only define eugenics but expose it to be Kraepelinianism:

> Genetics underpinned techniques of family
> reconstruction, which were deployed for the screening of
> population groups. Areas of social policy such as the
> prediction of potential intriguing problems concerning the
> extent to which genetic research was motivated by

---

[472] Volker Roelcke, "Mentalities and Sterlization Laws in Europe During
the 1930s. Eugenics, Genetics, and Politics in a Historic Context," *Der
Nervenarzt* 73 (11) (November 2002): 1019; https://www.ncbi.nlm.nih.gov/
pubmed/12430043.

[473] Paul Weindling, "The 'Sonderweg' of German Eugenics: Nationalism
and Scientific Internationalism," *The British Journal of the History of Science* vol.
22 (3) ((September 1989): 321; https://www.jstor.org/stable/
4026899?seq=1#page_scan_tab_contents.

eugenic ideals, particularly in the field of human genetics. At the same time, it is important to recognize that eugenics was a heterogenous agglomeration of sciences: in addition to genetics, a prominent place was taken by anthropology, clinical medicine, statistics, and psychology. These diverse constituents were welded together by cultural and social movements peculiar to respective national contexts.[474]

The combination of the fields of genetics, anthropology, clinical medicine, phenomenology, statistics, and psychology was the foundation to Wundt's "sciences of the mind" upon which Kraepelin formed his "medical model" of mental disorders. But it is likely that most people would not recognize that the exact same genetic studies and theories conducted and held in Nazi Germany are being conducted and propagated today as "new ground-breaking" discovery. The sciences that Weindling describes as constituting eugenics and as "welded together," however, perfectly describe modern psychiatry and its current phenomenological and statistical approaches wrapped in the genetic theory of mental illness.

With the exception of technological advancements, a de-emphasis on the construct of race, and the removal of intentional sterilization and euthanasia backed by law, the eugenics theory remains virtually unchanged. Likewise, the underlying philosophies, theories, practices, and "utopian dreams" of evolving or perfecting humankind remain central to the neo-Kraepelinian vision even today:

> Over the past six decades, the science of human heredity has advanced greatly, from knowledge of the operation of DNA to the mapping of the human genome. Such progress holds great promise for medical advances but

[474] Ibid.

also **inspires new, utopian visions of perfecting humankind. The history of Nazi racial-hygiene policies and eugenics reminds us of the importance of maintaining democratic checks and balances in the application of biomedical research and of always guarding against the use of genetics for the purpose of discriminating against persons or groups** [emphasis added].[475]

As long as the anthropology is accepted which sets forth the idea that people are only material objects and that some people are degenerates because they persistently struggle in their souls in a way that contradicts evolutionary theory, then discrimination and stigmatization will remain — as the perceived abnormal are a threat to themselves, society, and eugenicists' "utopian vision." As psychiatrist and historian Volker Roelcke reveals in one journal abstract, psychiatry has been and still is central to the eugenics' bio-psycho-social model:

> Three widely shared assumptions are fundamentally challenged by the historical evidence: (1) that medical atrocities were imposed from "above" by Nazi politicians on apolitical physicians; (2) that mass sterilisations and patient killings had nothing to do with contemporary state of the art medical reasoning and practice; (3) that ethically unacceptable research on psychiatric patients had nothing to do with contemporary state of the art biomedical sciences. It is argued that the structural findings on these issues of Nazi medicine are not specific to Germany and the period between 1933 and 1945; rather the underlying features were the extreme manifestations

[475] Bachrach, "In the Name of Public Health."

of some problematic potentials implicit in modern medicine in general.[476]

It was not political policy or even socialism that caused the Holocaust, though legislation certainly enabled its full application. Instead, the acceptance of the underlying philosophies which still sustain the façade of science within the modern genetic theory of mental illness is fully responsible. These false philosophies and scientific bases fuel the continued conjecture, which psychiatric geneticists consistently claim as empirical science. In truth, the alleged science of psychiatric genetics is not driven by objective fact but by presuppositional faith—a faith which demands that all human nature and phenomena be interpreted and approached through the philosophies of materialism, individual degenerationism, biodeterminism, and humanism, and which is said to be validated by utilitarian agreement upon these tenets of faith.

The Theory

Many people are unaware or outright deny that the bio-psycho-social model is neo-Kraepelinianism. Still others reject the notion that psychiatric disorders (e.g., schizophrenia, major depression, and ADHD) are strictly social and descriptive constructs, and they especially despise any reference to the Kraepelinian model's true sordid history. At the same time, Kraepelinian theorists/disciples insist that though no empirical evidence exists to show physiological causes, mental disorders or

[476] Volker Roelcke, "Psychiatry During National Socialism: Historical Knowledge and Some Implications," *Neurology Psychiatry and Brain Research* 22 (92) (April, 2016): http://dx.doi.org/10.1016/j.npbr.2016.01.006.

psychiatric syndromes will one day be scientifically proven as valid disease entities with biological markers and objective pathologies — equaling physical hereditary diseases and governed by the same laws of nature.[477] As presented in chapter one, this hypothesis was the precise desire of Benjamin Rush.[478] Psychiatrist Niall McLaren reiterates the reasoning:

> The major alternative is summarised in the aphorism, variously attributed to Benjamin Rush and Henry Maudsley, that "All Mental Disorder is Brain Disorder." That is, it relies on the physicalist notion that the behavior or properties of a higher-order entity can be reduced to and thus fully explained by the behavior or properties of the lower-order entities of which it is composed. In brief, biological reductionism argues that for every mental disorder, there is a physical disorder of the brain which is both necessary and sufficient for that mental disorder (necessary means that the mental disorder won't appear without the underlying physical disorder, while sufficient means that every time the physical disorder is present, the mental disorder will also be present). It says that a full understanding of the brain will explain all there is to know about mental disorder, with no questions left unanswered...[479]

Psychiatric genetics is a philosophical theory and not a valid study fully approachable in fields of science. There

---

[477] David McCullough, *American Presidents: John Adams, Mornings on Horseback, Truman, and the Course of Human Events* (New York: Simon and Schuster, 2001), 609.

[478] Ibid.

[479] Niall McLaren, "Pies' Polemic and the Question of Theories in Psychiatry, Again," *Mad in America* (September, 4, 2019): https://www.madinamerica.com/2019/09/pies-polemic-and-the-question-of-theories-in-psychiatry-again/.

certainly are physical elements that can be studied and approached using the scientific method (e.g., genes, the brain, and outward manifestations of behavior), but these elements can neither be proven as causative nor be considered as the core of alleged categorized disorders. Within neo-Kraepelinian faith, the physical elements must be elevated to theoretically explain in full the human phenomena. But such speculative explanation is not empirically based; it is philosophically driven.[480]

Like Rush, the reductionistic perspective upon which all psychiatric genetic theory is founded would also become the shared dream of German psychiatrists like Karl Ludwig Kahlbaum (1850s) and thereafter Emil Kraepelin. Heavily influenced by Kahlbaum's theories of *psychosis* ("a condition of the soul")[481] and *catatonia*,[482] Wilhelm Wundt's "mental (soul/psyche) sciences," and Benjamin Rush's "diseases of the mind," Kraepelin postulated specific types of degeneracy based upon clinical observations, framed them as diseases (e.g., schizophrenia and bipolar disorders), and desired to scientifically discover valid pathologies to prove the eugenics theory:

[480] Kenneth S. Kendler edited by Kenneth S. Kendler & Josef Parnas, *Philosophical Issues in Psychiatry: Explanation, Phenomenology, and Nosology* (Johns Hopkins University Press, 2008), 2-3.

[481] The term psychosis is another German term reflecting materialistic beliefs about the soul. See M. Dominic Beer, "Psychosis: From Mental Disorder to Disease Concept," *History of Psychiatry* 6 (22) (June 1, 1995): 177–200.

[482] Michael Alan Taylor and Max Fink, "Catatonia in Psychiatric Classification: A Home of Its Own," *The American Journal of Psychiatry* vol. 160 (7) (July 1, 2003): 1233; https://doi.org/10.1176/appi.ajp.160.7.1233.

Emil Kraepelin is one of the most renowned figures of psychiatry . . . . Kraepelin ranks among the great clinical medicine forerunners who followed in Kahlbaum's footsteps. For him, the foremost task of scientific psychiatry was to circumscribe pathological entities.[483]

Upon this dream—to prove a biological and thus hereditary cause of theorized degeneracy and specifically a pathology for schizophrenia (*premature dementia*)—the alleged science of psychiatric genetics was pursued. In modern times, the theory seems to have advanced from the hereditary assertions of Rush to the introduction of Kraepelin's scientific and medical system of genetic and hereditary degeneracy, but in actuality, it has not.

The psychiatric genetic theory is not only based upon the tradition of materialistic psychiatric belief but also largely based upon the hope that with the discovery of valid genetic diseases, psychiatric constructs will, too, someday be validated as true disease entities:

There are many human conditions that are clearly pathological and that can be said to have a unitary genetic cause. As far as is known, cystic fibrosis and Huntington's chorea occur in people carrying the relevant mutant gene irrespective of diet, occupation, social class, or education. Such disorders are rare . . . . **These disorders provide the model on which the program of medical genetics is built, and they provide the human interest drama on which books like *Mapping our Genes and Genome* are built** [emphasis added].[484]

[483] M. Geraud, "Emil Kraepelin: A Pioneer of Modern Psychiatry on the occasion of the hundred and fiftieth anniversary of his birth," *L'Encephale* 33 (4) (September 2007): 561; https://www.ncbi.nlm.nih.gov/pubmed/18033143.

[484] Richard C. Lewontin, *Biology as Ideology: The Doctrine of DNA* (New York: HarperCollins Publishers, 1991), 65.

German geneticist Peter Propping shares the same perspective:

> The false doctrine of eugenics and its practical application by the Nazi regime paved the way for the development of a prevailing anxiety in society that psychiatric genetics might lead to stigmatisation or even a revitalization of eugenics. **The major challenge for the field, however, stems from the attitudes of fellow geneticists who doubt that genetics can ever contribute to an understanding of brain function and mental disease. Whereas genetically complex traits are being successfully pinned down to the molecular level in other fields of medicine, psychiatric genetics still awaits a major breakthrough** [emphasis added].[485]

Psychiatric geneticists (neo-eugenicists) already claim to be a field as valid as legitimate branches of medicine. However, psychiatric genetics is not even remotely the same. Psychiatric constructs have no distinguishing biological markers or legitimate pathologies, and most contain core metaphysical symptoms/phenomena (e.g., sorrow, guilt, delusions, fear, stress, etc.) that cannot be approached utilizing the traditional scientific method.[486] By

---

[485] Peter Propping, "The Biography of Psychiatric Genetics: From early achievements to Historical Burden, form an Anxious Society to Critical Geneticists," *American Journal of American Genetics: Neuropsychiatric Genetics* 136B (1) (July 5, 2005): 2; https://www.ncbi.nlm.nih.gov/pubmed/15924298.

[486] Alicia R. Martin, Mark J. Daly, Elise B. Robinson, Steven E. Hyman, and Benjamin M. Neale, "Predicting Polygenic Risk of Psychiatric Disorders," *Biological Psychiatry* vol. 86 (2) (July 15, 2019): 97-109; https://doi.org/10.1016/j.biopsych.2018.12.015.

their precise definition, psychiatric disorders are invisible and have "no identifiable physical cause."[487]

Moreover, the psychiatric constructs themselves — since they are social and descriptive ideas and not physiological realities — also rest outside of scientific investigation, can be altered at will, and vary across time, culture, and established authorities. Still, the promise that psychiatric eugenics will eventually be authenticated in the same way as valid fields of genetic medicine is the faith that sustains psychiatric genetics.

If, however, there is no objective physical means to approach social constructs, how can the genetic theory be claimed as valid and reliable, as scientifically sound, or as able to objectively prove genetic etiologies of constructed psychiatric disorders? Over the course of the last one hundred years, billions of dollars have been poured into science laboratories searching for a genetic cause of mental disorder — attempting to prove Rush's, Morel's and Kraepelin's shared belief. Yet, the core problems and unanswered questions within the theory remain unchanged.

Since the days of Kraepelin, no alleged psychiatric disorder has been more scrutinized and asserted as scientifically validated and caused by hereditary/genetics than Kraepelin's construct of schizophrenia (dementia praecox). It is helpful, then, to examine the alleged science of psychiatric genetics, primarily utilizing the premier

---

[487] Jeffrey A. Lieberman, *Shrinks: the Untold Story of Psychiatry* (New York: Little, Brown and Company, 2015), 26-27.

eugenic construct of schizophrenia which ignited the Holocaust.

The Correlations

In medicine, establishing, discovering, and studying correlations is the foundational scientific approach to proving causation/*etiology*.[488] More specifically, the process of discovering the biological "path" from symptoms to cause is referred to as *pathology*, and key in attempting to establish a causation/etiology in the pathology of a particular disease is identifying correlations. If scientists do not at least have hypothesized correlations with which to work, then they cannot form and test hypotheses of potential causation by utilizing the scientific method. Richard Lewontin remarks on this important fact: "For the geneticist, it is the correlation that indicates the role of genes; the heritability predicts nothing about changes in the group average from generation to generation."[489]

Proving causation requires first that at least two human phenomena be identified as correlating, and thereafter that one or more of those correlates be shown as the cause and the other(s) as the effect. It is important, therefore, to realize the correlates that have historically been suggested, identified, and studied within psychiatric theory. The history of psychiatric genetic correlations can be divided into four basic timeframes or stages in the development of theory. These stages begin with race and heredity and

---

[488] "etiology" is the medical nomenclature to express the study of causes.

[489] Lewontin, *Biology as Ideology*, 34.

arrive at today's version, which is exposed in its utilized terms of phenotypes, endophenotypes, and genotypes. This current stage will receive its own treatment in the next chapter.

Correlates #1: Race and Heredity

The historic beginning of psychiatric genetics, as introduced in chapters 1 and 2, was established in race psychology.[490] But, further, it is helpful to understand within the discussion of correlates why race was the first social construct within eugenics.

Whereas the scientific method requires that objects of study be observable, measurable, and repeatable, eugenics requires that differentials be identified and a diagnostic system of positives and negatives be established within a statistical framework based on these variances. Since clear observable and measurable physical differences exist between ethnic groups, minorities became an easy target for creating "scientifically demonstrated" forms of degeneracy or mental illness based upon race and genetic psychologies and founded upon evolutionary belief. Just as physical and ethnic differences have often enabled prejudices toward groups of people, subsequent constructs of perceived abnormality, which describe other human phenomena, have also been claimed as hereditary or genetic.

Of course, as most educated scientists today realize, ethnic differences are not forms of degeneracy, so the basis of the

---

[490] Wendy Gonaver, *The Peculiar Institution and the Making of Modern Psychiatry 1840-1880* (University of North Carolina Press, 2018), 4.

eugenic or race theory was faulty from the beginning. University of Massachusetts professors of psychology Castellano Turner and Bernard Kramer impart how psychiatric degeneracy began by the correlation of physical differences in minorities with presumed genetic defects:

> The history of racism has also intersected in several ways with the history of mental health care. For example, a prominent explanation of mental illness has been that of genetic predisposition in some racial stocks. During the several surges of immigration to the United States, a dominant claim was made that the new immigrants would bring inferior stock. An alleged indication of such inferiority was the presumed "scientifically demonstrated" prevalence of mental inferiority and mental illness in that population (Chase 1977). During the 1940s and 1950s the focus shifted to a belief that African Americans suffer from mental illness as a "mark of oppression" (Kardiner and Ovesey 1951).[491]

They later state,

> How does racism influence basic definitions of mental illness? Dominant racial groups may construct definitions of mental illness that justify their superiority or the subjugated groups' inferiority. **If behavior that is more common in one racial group is described as abnormal, then members of that group will more often be considered abnormal. In the history of mental illness in the United States, race has been the basis for claims not only of excess incidence, but also of relatively limited incidence** [emphasis added].[492]

Professors of psychiatry Roland Littlewood and Maurice Lipsedge point out that the alleged psychiatric correlations

---

[491] Castellano B. Turner and Bernard M. Kramer, *Mental Health, Racism, and Sexism*, ed. Charles Willie (New York: University of Pittsburgh Press, 2013), 5.

[492] Ibid., 6-7.

between race and heredity were not scientifically founded but represented a control mechanism:

> Projection is a mechanism, not an explanation . . . . As we shall see, the rhetoric of the American War of Independence had to advocate freedom for the white settlers and deny it to the black slaves. **This was achieved by ascribing to blacks a different biology. This solved the immediate contradiction, legitimated their exploitation and provided a model for the later theory of eugenics which was directed at the problem of the poor white and the mentally ill** [emphasis added].[493]

Seema Yasmin also discusses this reality in an article published in *Medscape Psychiatry,*

> There is no reason to believe that any single genetic trait is uniformly and exclusively distributed in the entire population. Race is not a proxy for genetics, and any effort to ascribe such is shallow and lacking in understanding. **The social construction of race dates back to at least the 18th century when German scientist Johann Friedrich Blumenbach published a book called *On the Natural Variety of Mankind.*** Blumenbach is credited with inventing one of the first race-based classifications, and in his book he listed five categories, including Ethiopian (the black race) and Caucasian (the white race). Blumenbach's system was useful to white Americans during the American Revolution. They used this "science" to maintain that whites possessed innate qualities that made them superior and that allowed them to justifiably enslave black people. **The social construction of race is also demonstrated by the**

---

[493] Roland Littlewood and Maurice Lipsedge, *Aliens and Alienists: Ethnic Minorities and Psychiatry*, 3rd edition (London: Taylor and Francis, 1997), 29.

convenient manipulation of racial categories over time to suit those in power [emphasis added].[494]

Yasmin continues in the article to disclose,

In a study of 350 mandatory preclinical lecture slides presented at an Ivy League medical school, race was mentioned in 102 slides. In 96% of those slides, race was presented as a biological phenomenon. **Medicine, obsessed with its evidence and gold standards, has accepted a made-up thing as a natural phenomenon. Not lazily or accidentally, but purposefully, because as physicians we hold power over the bodies of the voiceless and vulnerable, and it makes sense that those who yield power, any power, are trained to perpetuate the beliefs that uphold the dominant culture . . . . race continues to be misconstrued as a surrogate marker for genetic ancestry, and upholding race as a biological phenomenon in medicine will enable this misconception to be taught to future generations of healthcare providers** [emphasis added].[495]

As these psychiatrists and physicians reiterate, the eugenics model was founded upon the control mechanism of race psychology. Sadly, it is a foundation that continues the perpetuation of manmade constructs which categorize some people as disordered and is still utilized in forming

---

[494] Seema Yasmin, "How Medicine Perpetuates the Fallacy of Race," *Medscape Psychiatry* (March 11, 2020): https://www.medscape.com/view article/926549?nlid=134510_424&src=WNL_mdplsfeat_200317_mscpedit_psyc &uac=264124BV&spon=12&impID=2315032&faf=1#vp_1.

[495] Ibid.

and conducting research on the construct of schizophrenia.[496]

Not only has the theory of different human races been proven to be a Darwinian social construct without empirical evidence to support it, but also there is no significant genetic variance between alleged races to sustain racism (the belief that different races exist within the one human race) as if it were valid science. Geneticist Richard Lewontin recognizes that

> there is in general a great deal less difference genetically between races than one might suppose from the superficial cues we all use in distinguishing races. Skin color, hair form, and nose shape are certainly influenced by genes, but we do not know how many such genes there are, or how they work . . . . So we have no reason *a priori* to think that there would be any genetic differentiation between racial groups in characteristics such as behavior, temperament, and intelligence. Nor is there an iota of evidence that social classes differ in any way in their genes except insofar as ethnic origins, or race may be used as a form of economic discrimination. **The nonsense propagated by ideologues of biological determinism that the lower classes are biologically inferior to the upper classes, that all the good things in European culture come from the Nordic groups, is precisely nonsense. It is meant to legitimate the structures of inequality in our society by putting a biological gloss on them and by propagating the continual confusion between what may be influenced**

[496] Harvard Medical School, "Sex, genes and vulnerability: Researchers pinpoint genes behind sex biases in autoimmune disorders, schizophrenia," *ScienceDaily* (May 11, 2020): www.sciencedaily.com/releases/2020/05/200511112602.htm

**by genes and what may be changed by social and
environmental alterations** [emphasis added].[497]

Neuroscientist Carl Hart agrees that the philosophies of
inherited degeneracy and biodeterminism are fundamental
to racism:

> So many people have misused and diluted the term that
> its perniciousness gets lost. Racism is the belief that social
> and cultural differences between groups are inherited and
> immutable, making some groups inalterably superior to
> others.[498]

The American Anthropological Association also asserts,

> From its inception, this modern concept of "race" was
> modeled after an ancient theorem of the Great Chain of
> Being, which posited natural categories on a hierarchy
> established by God or nature. Thus "race" was a mode of
> classification linked specifically to peoples in the colonial
> situation. It subsumed a growing ideology of inequality
> devised to rationalize European attitudes and treatment
> of the conquered and enslaved peoples. Proponents of
> slavery in particular during the 19th century used "race"
> to justify the retention of slavery. **The ideology
> magnified the differences among Europeans, Africans,
> and Indians, established a rigid hierarchy of socially
> exclusive categories underscored and bolstered unequal
> rank and status differences, and provided the**

---

[497] Turner and Kramer, *Mental Health, Racism, and Sexism*, 6-7.

[498] Carl Hart, *High Price: A Neuroscientist's Journey of Self Discovery That
Challenges Everything You Know about Drugs and Society* (New York: Harper,
2013), 14.

rationalization that the inequality was natural or God-given [emphasis added].[499]

Correlating the social construct of race with the theory of inherited genes established psychiatric eugenics — the theory of genetic/hereditary degeneracy. But it is important to reaffirm the truth that psychiatric eugenics has never been dependent upon maintaining the social construct of race, but only in sustaining the belief in evolved-hereditary-individual degeneracy. Nonetheless, race and heredity formed the basic "scientific" correlates of psychiatric genetics — a pseudoscience from the field's conception.

Correlates #2: Genes and the Soul

Once the social construct of race was believed to be correlated with the human genome and pronounced to be scientifically sound within the psychiatric perspective, more constructs could be added or eventually subtracted from the eugenic theory. This development, occurring in accordance with Wundt's new concept of "mental sciences,"[500] would enable the construct of race to be either replaced altogether or new constructs to be added to it, all the while still maintaining the philosophies that undergird psychiatric eugenics. As long as two potential correlates existed — one of them being genes or heredity and the other

[499] "AAA Statement on 'Race,'" *American Anthropological Association*: http://www.americananthro.org/Connect WithAAA/Content.aspx?Item Number=2583. Accessed August 20, 2019.

[500] Wilhelm Wundt, *An Introduction to Psychology reprint* (London: George Allen and Unwin, LTD, 1912), 194-95.

a cultural/social or descriptive construct that was undesirable, impairing, or seemingly unexplainable – then eugenics could be sustained. Moreover, as long as theories were agreed upon by the scientific and medical communities and were scrutinized in clinics and research facilities, then eugenics could be claimed as science and faith in the field could spread. Though a common mistake, it is an error to assume that eugenics is primarily based upon race psychology rather than upon differentials or perceived individual degeneracy.

As also established in previous chapters, Emil Kraepelin maintained the construct of racial hygiene, but added the constructs of mental hygiene and economic and political social classes. Kraepelin's additions had created a formal and practical system for Wundt's *Völkerpsychologie*[501] whereby limitless constructs which described human nature and the soul's phenomena could be theoretically correlated to the human genome – though during Kraepelin's life, the ability to closely examine genes and neurons did not exist, and Kraepelin was not primarily interested in studying the body.[502]

Thanks in large part to the global acceptance of Rush, Wundt, and Kraepelin's redefinition of the human soul/psyche, materialists worldwide began to dogmatically proclaim a correlation between the human genome and the human soul. Despite this shift in eugenic belief, hereditary madness (individual degenerationism)

---

[501] Ibid., 84.

[502] Edward Shorter, "The History of Nosology and the Rise of the Diagnostic and Statistical Manual of Mental Disorders," *Dialogues in Clinical Neuroscience* 17 (1) (March 2015): 59.

was theorized to be genetically caused without any validating genetic studies ever having been done. Instead, both twin and familial studies — as Benjamin Rush and Francis Galton had first suggested[503] — became the dominant attempt to prove a correlation between the immaterial soul (including mindsets, emotions, faith, perceptions, motives, and morality) and the material genome. Molecular psychiatrist Wolfgang Maier submits,

> Psychiatric genetics is a relatively new term for an old research question: "Are behavioral and psychological conditions and deviations inherited?" The systematic empirical inquiries in this field started in the late nineteenth century with the work of Francis Galton and his monograph Talent and Character, **which was motivated by Darwin's theory and the concept of degeneration. During the twentieth century, the methodological standard of the field was improved by the development of epidemiological, biometrical, and clinical research tools.** This was the precondition to perform valid family, twin, and adoption studies. These methods revealed that all psychiatric disorders aggregate in families, and that genes influence the manifestation of these disorders.[504]

The science of psychiatric eugenics rested fully on showing that human tendencies correlated within a family or ethnic group, and Rüdin's and Kallmann's twin and familial studies provided the foundation of scientific exploration toward this end.

---

[503] Francis Galton, "The History of Twins as a Criterion of the Relative Powers of Nature and Nurture," *Journal of the Anthropological Institute of Great Britain and Ireland*, 5 (1875): 391.

[504] Wolfgang Maier, *Psychiatric Genetics: Methods in Molecular Medicine* vol. 77 (Humana Press, 2003), 3.

"Heritability," "genetic predisposition," "hereditary risk," and "fixed genes" were popular phrases that psychiatric eugenicists utilized in the early 1900s—terms that expressed correlations within families and phrases which remain a common psychiatric means to assert perceived genetic degeneracy. Clinical psychologist Jay Joseph, considered by many to be an expert on the psychiatric genetic theory and especially the history and pseudoscience of twin studies, maintains that

> a key psychiatric genetic concept is *heritability* . . . .
> Heritability estimates are derived from correlations among relatives, which include twins, adoptees, siblings, and other types of family relationships. Although heritability assesses the causes of variation in a population, it does not address developmental processes that cause individuals to develop various characteristics and abilities . . . Researchers frequently use "model fitting" statistical analyses (structural equation modeling) to calculate heritability, which attempt to test the "fit" between a model of genetic and environmental relatedness against the observed data.[505]

Dr. Joseph also notes that the statistical approach ("heritability estimates") has never been objective science:

> Heritability estimates apply only to a specific population, at a specific time, and in a specific environment. Estimates can change substantially under different environmental conditions.[506]

One of the important takeaways from Joseph's comments is that "heritability" requires a standard of normalcy or a

[505] Jay Joseph, "Are *DSM* Psychiatric Disorders 'Heritable'? *Mad In America Online* (June 24, 2015): https://www.madinamerica.com/ 2015/06/are-dsm-psychiatric-disorders-heritable/.

[506] Ibid.

group of "fit"/healthy people in order to determine not only who is disordered but also how the disorder allegedly affects genomes.

Since its conception, the psychiatric concept of biological "heritability" has been based upon faith in individual degenerationism, materialism, and bio-determinism—both positive and negative eugenics. Within psychiatry, "heritability" is a means to disguise psychiatric eugenics and present it as a seemingly valid science wrapped in seemingly objective statistics. Historian of medicine Paul Lombardo reveals this fallacy in an educational medical journal:

> **This article reviews the uses of family studies carried out in the early 20th century under the banner of eugenics, a companion discipline to early genetics.** It explores how, in an attempt to analyze and quantify purportedly biologic bases of social problems, the eugenicists constructed pedigree charts of notoriously "defective" families. Investigation of individuals with suspect traits formed the basis for instruction of field workers who linked those traits to larger groups. **The resulting eugenic family studies provided a "scientific" face for a popular hereditarian mythology that claimed to explain all social failure in systematic terms** [emphasis added].[507]

The older version of eugenics was dogmatically claimed to be a field of objective science with big investments and research facilities, with global attention and prominent figures, but without the ability to study genes, let alone provide empirical evidence from poorly conducted and

---

[507] Paul A. Lombardo, "Pedigrees, Propaganda, and Paranoia: Family Studies in a Historical Context," *Journal of Continuing Education in the Health Professions* Vol. 21 (4) (Fall 2001): 247; https://www.ncbi.nlm.nih.gov/pubmed/11803769.

unreliable twin and familial studies.[508] But all of that was about to change—or so it would seem.

Correlates #3: Genes and Statistics

After World War 2— primarily through the work of Kallmann, Slater, and other Kraepelinian-trained psychiatrists, the eugenics theory was transformed from attempting to correlate the human genome with race to attempting to correlate the human genome with other social and descriptive constructs that simply described undesirable or seemingly unexplainable human nature and human phenomena. Most prominent among these constructs was Kraepelin's *premature dementia*, which would become known as the psychiatric construct of *schizophrenia*. Despite the changes in theory and nomenclature, psychiatric researchers still lacked the ability to study the human genome in detail rather than merely theorize about hereditary transmutation. In the 1970s, though, attention turned from studying common familial mindsets and behaviors to discovering and studying specific genes and mapping the human genome.

Today, because genes have been mostly mapped and technology has advanced, scientists are able to observe and measure some structural and molecular changes within individual genes. Rather than being based upon a speculative hereditary theory, modern psychiatric geneticists have the ability to approach the human genome within the scientific method. But the ability to examine the

---

[508] Daniel R. Berger II, *Mental Illness: The Necessity for Dependence* (Taylors, SC: Alethia International Publications, 2016), 54-63.

human genome in detail does not determine that other proposed correlates are approachable with scientific methods, much less caused by the genome. In actuality, many of the popular correlates (other than genes, the nervous system, and observable behavior) are metaphysical realities or phenomena that fall outside of the scientific method (e.g., sorrow, anxiety, trauma). After all, academic psychiatry attempts to explain supposed "mental disorders." This fact led to another alteration to the eugenics theory. Instead of focusing on the social constructs or the alleged symptoms as correlates, psychiatric geneticists turned to a new attempt to correlate genes with perceived psychiatric disorders by focusing on the predicted outcomes in statistical measurements.

Emil Kraepelin was one of the first psychiatrists to propose formally describing and listing symptoms together and constructing syndromes in order to create alleged psychiatric diseases. To Kraepelin, symptoms were only significant in that they could be used as a diagnostic tool to reveal an otherwise invisible disease. In contrast to a symptomatic approach, Kraepelin believed that a person's life history and projected outcome were more significant to understand foundational problems.[509] This Kraepelinian method allowed the notion of predicted hereditary transmission, theorized disease outcomes, and duration of episodes to become factors in determining suggested normalcy and standards in allegedly distinguishing between psychiatric disorders:

---

[509] Edward Shorter, "The History of Nosology and the Rise of the Diagnostic and Statistical Manual of Mental Disorders," *Dialogues in Clinical Neuroscience* 17 (1) (March 2015): 61-62.

> At the foundation of Kraepelin-inspired scientific psychiatry lies the notion of the "clinical study" of disease, as opposed to the "symptomatic" approach (5th edition of the Treatise), whereby it is no longer concerned with the study of mental disorder in terms of symptoms but rather in terms of conditions of occurrence, evolution and outcome thereof.[510]

Kraepelin's approach also permitted the symptoms — though theoretically minimized — to remain the only diagnostic tool. At the same time, it was upon the differing symptoms, durations, and perceived outcomes that Kraepelin hypothesized about varying constructs of mental illness (e.g., schizophrenia and bipolar). It is at this point in history and upon this Kraepelinian theory that psychiatrists would begin to recast the historic belief in unitary-hereditary-madness/psychosis as numerous individual genetic disorders.

Though the true substance of Kraepelinian "diseases," upon which the entire genetic theory rests, are the symptoms themselves, Kraepelin knew that he needed something more substantive to make his case. The creation of the constructs of schizophrenia and bipolar were based upon Kraepelin's own observations, clinical descriptions, and subjective statistical measurements rather than upon actual biology. Moreover, they were based upon his inability to explain these troubling human phenomena with his own worldview. Historian and professor of psychiatry at the University of Toronto, Edward Shorter, explains,

---

[510] M. Geraud, "Emil Kraepelin: A Pioneer of Modern Psychiatry on the occasion of the hundred and fiftieth anniversary of his birth," *L'Encephale* 33 (4) (September 2007): 561; https://www.ncbi. nlm.nih.gov/pubmed/18033143.

The genius of Kraepelin's classification was not that it was biological, but clinical. He used biological concepts, such as "endocrinological," to organize his classification. However, the main disease entities in the Kraepelinian system—manic-depressive insanity and dementia praecox (later "schizophrenia") —were not included for biological, or pseudo-biological, reasons. Rather, it was because Kraepelin had studied the patients in detail and believed that he had discerned two starkly different courses and outcomes .... even though the two great diseases might share some symptoms, it was based on this course that he believed them to differ.[511]

Since the symptoms are regularly alike across most "severe psychiatric disorders," Kraepelin tried to distinguish between his theorized constructs of depression/bipolar and schizophrenia based primarily upon duration and frequency rather than on the actual symptoms themselves. In a similar way, Kraepelin also set out to establish a clinical line demarcating perceived normal and abnormal based upon his own observations, descriptions, and his subjective values. It is upon this speculative belief and approach that the hereditary or genetic "statistical approach," "polygenic risk," and "predictability measurements" were conceived.[512] It is also upon this theory that the *Diagnostic and Statistical Manual of Mental Disorder* (*DSM*) was named. As Dr. Shorter acknowledges, one cannot separate belief in modern psychiatric

[511] Shorter, "The History of Nosology," 62.

[512] Many psychiatric geneticists state that the statistical approach is based upon Darwin's, Mendel's, and Galton's theories, which were systematized under Kraepelin. See Alicia R. Martin, Mark J. Daly, Elise B. Robinson, Steven E. Hyman, and Benjamin M. Neale, "Predicting Polygenic Risk of Psychiatric Disorders," *Biological Psychiatry* vol. 86 (2) (July 15, 2019): 97-109; https://doi.org/10.1016/j.biopsych.2018.12.015.

constructs, the current diagnostic system, and the genetic/hereditary statistical approach from the prominent German eugenicists during the World Wars:

> The current *Diagnostic and Statistical Manual of Mental Disorders (DSM)-5* arose from a tradition filled with haphazard science and politically driven choices. The nosology of modern psychiatry began with the German classifiers of the late 19th century, especially Emil Kraepelin.[513]

Dr. Geraud, French physician and medical researcher, agrees:

> Such an innovative method required special tools capable of exploring not only the symptoms, as had been done previously, but the pathological process per se: therefore, Kraepelin created a systematic method to conduct psychiatric research and founded a Research Establishment divided into different sections (histopathology, topographic histology, serology, genealogy).[514]

Many contemporary clinicians and researchers have attempted to denounce the *DSM*, Kraepelinianism, and the diagnostic process as subjective and invalid while still maintaining the alleged legitimacy of Kraepelinian psychiatric constructs and his statistical genetic/hereditary approach. But as the countless failed attempts to separate these elements of Kraepelinianism have revealed over the centuries, the "science" remains an all or nothing philosophical approach. If statistical manuals (the *DSM*, the *ICD*, and otherwise) and their many categorized

---

[513] Shorter, "The History of Nosology," 59.

[514] Geraud, "Emil Kraepelin: A Pioneer of Modern Psychiatry," 561.

psychiatric constructs are removed, then the statistical approach loses a vital mechanism.

Historian at the University of Toronto Nikolai Krementsov also documents the psychiatric transformation from a focus on symptoms to a search for hereditary or genetic causation (etiology) within Darwinian/Kraepelinian faith:

> The idea that heredity plays a role in pathology, more generally, and in the development of mental illness, in particular, has had a very long history. In psychiatry, empirical observations that certain psychiatric disorders 'run in the family' had cast heredity into the ultimate 'explanation' for those clinical cases in which no obvious cause (either external or internal) for the onset of such disorders could be readily determined. Circa 1900, two independent, but similarly revolutionary, developments – one in psychiatry and another in biology – converged to give this old idea new meanings and new importance. **The novel concepts of inheritance advanced by Darwin, Galton, Weismann, Mendel and their numerous followers had dramatically changed the very notion of heredity. Around the same time, Emil Kraepelin's new nosological and diagnostic approaches displaced the old 'symptomatic' psychiatry and profoundly changed the understanding of mental illness, especially, psychoses. These two 'revolutions' stimulated some psychiatrists' attempts to transform the vague umbrella term 'heredity' into a plausible etiological** [causative] **category that could be not merely invoked but also investigated.**[515]

Modern psychiatric geneticists have capitalized on society's acceptance of Kraepelin's theorized syndromes and hereditary theory, but there still exists no objective means

---

[515] Nikolai Krementsov, "The strength of a loosely defined movement: eugenics and medicine in imperial Russia," *Medical History* vol. 59 (1) (2015): 6-31; doi:10.1017/mdh.2014.68.

to correlate the primary metaphysical symptoms to the human genome. All that exists is the speculative hereditary statistical approach based upon the subjective diagnostic system.

Undoubtedly, Kraepelin's two major contributions to the history of psychiatric eugenics are (1) the provision of the constructs of schizophrenia and bipolar (among several others thereafter) into categorical psychiatric forms of degeneracy and (2) his transformation of the vague hereditary theory of madness into the "scientific field" of psychiatric eugenics based upon subjective statistical measurements, clinical research, and speculative genetic risks. This history is recorded in the *European Archives of Psychiatry and Clinical Neuroscience*:

> Emil Kraepelin is well known due to his development of the psychiatric classification. The *ICD-10* and *DSM-IV* classification is based on the dichotomy of endogenous psychoses into affective psychoses and schizophrenia as early as 1899. **Moreover, besides his classification system he put enormous impact on the development of psychiatry to an empirical field of science.** The research activities of Kraepelin and his coworkers show that he was not only the most active researcher in the field of psychiatry in his time but also that his research activities included a lot of clinical and experimental work in different disciplines of psychiatry, including psychology, pharmacology and natural sciences as 'Hilfswissenschaften.'[516]

Though it is undeniable that Kraepelin's classification system of descriptive constructs was a significant contribution to psychiatric genetics, his establishing a

---

[516] H. Hippius and N. Muller, "The Work of Emil Kraepelin and His research Group in Munchen," *European Archives of Psychiatry and Clinical Neuroscience* 258 (2) (June 2008): 3; doi: 10.1007/s00406-008-2001-6.

research facility, forming research guidelines, and subjecting his theory to the rigors of scientific scrutiny may have done more to sell his theory than anything else Kraepelin offered to psychiatry. It also enabled the statistical approach to flourish as if it were actual empirical science.

Decades later, however, there still exists no empirical evidence to validate Kraepelin's conjecture. Yet, more than ever, people today accept the speculative belief that schizophrenia is a real disease caused by faulty genes and is fully approachable within the scientific method.

Correlates #4: Genotypes and Endophenotypes

After Kraepelin's death, his predecessors narrowed the broad hereditary hypothesis to be primarily focused on the human genome and other somatic correlates. This change has developed in correspondence with geneticists' ability to study the human genome more precisely.

In contrast to categorized metaphysical symptoms for alleged psychiatric disorders, the gene side in the study of genetic correlates has been a history of technological advances. Highly acclaimed psychiatric geneticist and philosopher Kenneth Kendler remarks on the transition:

> Psychiatry has seen massive shifts in our central [philosophical] paradigms in the past 100 years. This is seen in our approach to both etiology and treatment. Popular frameworks have included psychoanalysis, phenomenology, social psychiatry, family systems theory, cross-cultural psychiatry, cognitive science, biological psychiatry, and molecular neuroscience. **Driven in part by exciting advances in neuroscience and molecular genetics, a reductionist "brain-focused" paradigm is**

currently becoming increasingly dominant. Advocates of this paradigm argue vigorously that all "real" explanations for psychiatric illness can be found at the molecular level. Some of this persuasion might tolerate other explanatory approaches (say, at the level of systems of neuroscience or even psychology) but only as a holding pattern until the necessary scientific advances render these perspectives obsolete. We have good reason to be confused [emphasis added]![517]

As Kendler candidly asserts, psychiatric genetics is a "reductionist 'brain-focused' paradigm." The research projects and developments, which Kendler notes, have allowed both discovery of specific genes and the human genome as well as a better understanding of how individual genes function. Though technology has clearly advanced and the human genome is better understood, there remains the critical problem with the psychiatric genetic theory: how to scientifically correlate the immaterial psyche/soul and its metaphysical symptoms with the material genome.

Moreover, geneticists must not just correlate these two; they must also prove with empirical evidence at a molecular level that the human genome causes desires, motives, beliefs, falsehood, consciousness, fears, hopelessness, guilt, and all other metaphysical symptoms that are said to be abnormal. Additionally, they must show how healthy beliefs, motives, fears, etc. are biologically produced at a molecular level. Simply because scientific inquiry can now look more precisely at the gene and better identify somatic correlations does nothing to provide

---

[517] Kenneth S. Kendler edited by Kenneth S. Kendler & Josef Parnas, *Philosophical Issues in Psychiatry: Explanation, Phenomenology, and Nosology* (Johns Hopkins University Press, 2008), 2-3.

empirical evidence that genes cause human mindsets, emotions, and moral behaviors or that psychiatric constructs represent valid forms of mental degeneracy or even valid disease entities.

Despite these realities, the ability to more precisely study the human genome and the nervous system enabled scientists to make another shift in theory and experimentation that focuses not on the metaphysical symptoms, not on the categorized descriptive construct, but on the physical correlates determined by statistical studies. If, for example, there are three correlates, (A, B, and C), and one correlate is metaphysical (C), then modern psychiatric geneticists choose to focus on proving correlations between the proposed somatic correlates (A and B) alone, while assuming that the metaphysical correlate (C) is caused by A and B. But the metaphysical "symptoms" (C) are the core of the syndrome/construct of schizophrenia upon which all diagnoses are made:

> So far, neither imaging [B] nor genetic [A] or clinical markers have sufficient accuracy to be suitable for prognostication at the individual patient level . . . . Schizophrenia is a syndrome that includes several symptom clusters and subclusters [C]. For example, the negative symptom category includes symptoms of amotivation and anhedonia that cluster together and symptoms of affective flattening and poverty of expression that cooccur more frequently with each other than with the amotivation-anhedonic symptoms. Consequently, individual patients may differ markedly in their symptom profiles [C], and it is thus unsurprising that there is heterogeneity in neurobiological findings and treatment response. **One approach proposed to address this is to focus instead on the circuits [B] and processes [A] underlying specific symptoms or symptom clusters**

[C] (for example, the research domain criteria approach).[518]

The *research domain criteria theory* (the RDoC project) follows that if A and B correlate in an empirical way in a large percentage of a specific population, then C must be caused by A and/or B whether or not C can be approached using the scientific method. Such a scientific strategy may be convenient, but it does nothing to validate the genetic hypothesis. The National Institute of Mental Health comments on the RDoC:

> RDoC is not meant to serve as a diagnostic guide, nor is it intended to replace current diagnostic systems. **The goal is to understand the nature of mental health and illness in terms of varying degrees of dysfunction in general psychological/biological systems.** The RDoC framework is a research strategy that is implemented as a matrix of elements . . . . . Constructs are studied along a span of functioning from normal to abnormal with the understanding that each is situated in, and affected by, environmental and neurodevelopmental contexts. Measurements of constructs can be made using several different classes of variables, or units of analysis, which include genetic, physiological, behavioral, and self-report assessments [emphasis added].[519]

Though the NIMH asserts that the RDoC does not replace diagnostic systems, it also claims that it does not rely upon these same subjective "disorder-based categories":

518 Robert A. McCutcheon, Tiago Reis Marques, and Oliver D. Howes, "Schizophrenia—An Overview," *JAMA Psychiatry Online* (October 30, 2019): doi:10.1001/jamapsychiatry.2019.3360.

519 "About RDoC, "NIMH (2020): https://www.nimh.nih.gov/research/research-funded-by-nimh/rdoc/about-rdoc.shtml.

Traditionally, mental illnesses have been conceptualized as disorders that are diagnosed on the basis of the number and type of symptoms, and the presence of distress or impairment. This view of mental disorders – and the resulting diagnostic systems – provides benefits such as reliability and ease of diagnosis across a variety of contexts; however, this approach has come at the cost of numerous tradeoffs . . . . These problems, and others, suggest that in order to understand both the development and treatment of mental disorders, the field needs a comprehensive picture of typical and atypical brain and behavioral development across the lifespan. It is essential to find a way to increase knowledge concerning the biological, physiological, and behavioral components and mechanisms through which multiple and interacting mental-health risk and protective factors operate – a research framework that does not rely on disorder-based categories.[520]

As will be further discerned, this model or "research strategy" of relying significantly on retained subjective diagnostic categories — while at the same time denying this practice — represents the core of modern-day psychiatric genetic theory and the hope of validation.

Scientific Advances

The new psychiatric strategy for establishing correlates and attempting to prove genetic causes depends heavily on the promise of new scientific advancements. Two of the most significant advancements, which virtually resurrected the floundering field of psychiatric genetics and enabled deeper faith in the statistical approach, came in the form of the *Human Genome Project* (HGP) and the *Genome Wide Association Studies* (GWAS). The HGP in particular is the

520 Ibid.

principle project, which "may be considered the single most influential venture in the past decades,"[521] that both allowed scientists to discover specific genes as well as to map most of the human genome. The project's key figures also promised to scientifically provide a complete picture of human nature from which all human problems could be evaluated and potentially remedied:

> The Human Genome Project (HGP) was one of the great feats of exploration in history. Rather than an outward exploration of the planet or the cosmos, the HGP was an inward voyage of discovery led by an international team of researchers looking to sequence and map all of the genes — together known as the genome — of members of our species, *Homo Sapiens*. Completed in April 2003, the HGP gave us the ability, for the first time, to read nature's complete genetic blueprint for building a human being.[522]

"Science" and big business are typically not disconnected enterprises, and psychiatric genetics is no exception, as the field is based upon large financial investments and directly connected to the pharmaceutical industry.[523]

Furthermore, psychiatric genetics is a theory that if discredited would yield tremendous financial loss for its investors as well as those clinicians, researchers, and venders (e.g., pharmaceutical companies) dependent upon its being sustained. In addition, it would significantly

---

[521] Sevilla D. Detera-Wadleigh, Nirmala Akula, and Liping Hou, *Psychiatric Genetics: A Primer for Clinicians and Basic Scientists* edited by Thomas G. Schulze and Francis J. McMahon (New York: Oxford University Press, 2018), 35.

[522] National Human Genome Research Institute, "The Human Genome Project," *National Institutes of Health* (2019): https://www. genome.gov/human-genome-project.

[523] Arribas-Ayllon, Bartlett, and Lewis, *Psychiatric Genetics*, 5.

undermine the secular belief that all of human nature and human phenomena are approachable through scientific means and would open the door for scientists to consider dualism as best explaining human nature. In many ways, the overwhelming financial investment into the HGP demands that psychiatrists and other evolutionary biologists dogmatically hold to genetic determinism with greater resolve than ever before.

But large financial investments have sustained eugenics from its conception.[524] Paul Silverman, who was an early advocate for the HGP and a highly acclaimed professor of genetics before his death, discusses the connection:

> In the mid-and late 1980s, our testimony before the congressional committees controlling HGP purse strings relied upon our old assumptions. In describing the genome's potential medical value, we elevated the status of the gene in human development and by extension, human health. At the same time, the deterministic nature of the gene entered the social consciousness with talk of "designer" babies and DNA police that could detect future criminals. Armed with DNA determinism, scientific entrepreneurs convinced venture capitalists and the lay public to invest in multi-billion-dollar enterprises whose aim was to identify the anticipated 100,000-plus genes in the human genome, patent the nucleotide sequences, and then lease or sell that information to pharmaceutical companies for use in drug discovery. Prominent among these were two Rockville, Md.-based companies, Celera, under the leadership of J. Craig Venter, and Human Genome Sciences, led by William Haseltine. But when the first draft of the human genome sequence was published in the spring of 2001, the

[524] Volker Roelcke, "Mentalities and Sterlization Laws in Europe During the 1930s. Eugenics, Genetics, and Politics in a Historic Context," *Der Nervenarzt* 73 (11) (November 2002): 1019; https://www.ncbi.nlm.nih.gov/pubmed/12430043.

unexpectedly low gene count (less than 30,000) elicited a hasty reevaluation of this business model. On a genetic level, humans, it seems, are not all that different from flies and worms.[525]

Others also recognize non-altruistic motives for upholding the genetic presupposition:

> Biologists have known for a long time that gene expression is complex and DNA does not determine biology, let alone other characteristics of physical and mental health, behavior and intelligence. Nevertheless, over the years, the deterministic model that genes alone define biology has become enshrined as the prevailing paradigm. This dogma was manifested on a large scale in the pursuit of the Human Genome Project. Why do scientists, with the full knowledge that various aspects of the cellular machinery and the environment work in cohort, continue to apply and propagate the DNA mantra? The motivations may be many, but chief among them is the simplicity of the "DNA is everything" model, and the outside commercial and scientific incentives available for such a focus. The application of DNA ideology has led to a problematic construction of race, sexuality, and intelligence, as seen through a lens of genetic determinism and has fostered the belief that for each of us our physical and mental well-being are pre-programmed and reflect the composition of our individual DNA. This scientific interpretation enhances a sense of inevitability and forecloses efforts at promoting social justice by presenting them as futile [emphasis added].[526]

---

[525] Paul H. Silverman, "Rethinking Genetic Determinism," *The Scientist* (May, 2004): https://www.the-scientist.com/ vision/rethinking-genetic-determinism-50020.

[526] The Council for Responsible Genetics "Genetic Determinism," (2010): http://www.councilforresponsiblegenetics.org/ Projects/PastProject.aspx?projectId=11.

As the Council for Responsible Genetics acknowledges, this "DNA ideology" is the eugenics theory based upon the same original philosophies. If, though, psychiatric genetics fails to explain the soul and metaphysical phenomena of human nature, then the philosophy of materialism is also discredited.

While there is certainly value in understanding and studying the human genome within valid medicine, the HGP propelled psychiatric eugenics into a more dogmatic insistence of materialism and genetic determinism:

> The scientists writing about the Genome Project explicitly reject an absolute genetic determinism, but they seem to be writing more to acknowledge theoretical possibilities than out of a conviction. If we take seriously the proposition that the internal and external codetermine the organism, **we cannot really believe that the sequence of the human genome is the grail that will reveal to us what it is to be human, that it will change our philosophical view of ourselves, that it will show how life works.** It is only the social scientists and social critics, such as Kevles, who come to the Genome Project from his important study of the continuity of eugenics with modern medical genetics [emphasis added].[527]

Genetic determinism reduces humanity to be merely a servant of evolutionary forces — those of evolutionary concepts of natural selection. Yet as one scientific journal notes, though the terms and technology are more sophisticated, the HGP and *Genome Wide Association Studies*

---

[527] Lewontin, *Biology as Ideology*, 64.

(GWAS) are important aspects of the same unproven Kraepelinian theory.[528] Bentall and Pilgrim likewise write,

> Genetic theories of schizophrenia were popular in the early part of the 20th century. They were built on 19th century concepts of eugenics that assumed a "tainted" gene pool that underpinned insanity, idiocy, prostitution, alcoholism, epilepsy and all other forms of physical or psychological "deviance". Psychiatric geneticists of the period laid the foundation stones for what is now known as "quantitative genetics", using studies of families, twins and adopted children to estimate the amount of variation in a trait such as schizophrenia that could be attributed to genes. That early work, which was reinforced by that of eminent eugenicist psychiatrists, such as Franz Kallmann and Eliot Slater after World War Two, led ultimately to large estimates of the "heritability" of schizophrenia, typically around 80%, which were assumed to leave little room for social causes of the disorder. The later decoding of the structure of DNA seemed to promise a new era of molecular psychiatry, apparently uninfluenced by eugenic considerations. The development of genome wide association studies (GWAS) in recent years has allowed an enormous number of genetic variations to be measured simultaneously. Using very large samples (tens of thousands of patients and controls), many genes, each with a tiny effect, have been linked to schizophrenia. Their contributions can be added together to create a "polygenic risk score", describing a person's total genetic risk [emphasis added].[529]

The HGP and the GWAS parallel the global impact that German psychiatric eugenics had in the early 1900s, but the

---

[528] S. Cichon and S. Ripke, *The Neurobiology of Schizophrenia* edited by Ted Abel and Thomas Nickl-Jockschat (New York: Academic Press, 2016), 39-49.

[529] Richard Bentall and David Pilgrim, "There Are No 'Schizophrenia Genes': Here's Why," *The Conversation* (April 8, 2016): https://theconversation.com/there-are-no-schizophrenia-genes-heres-why-57294.

advancement in technology and better scientific understanding of human genome still does nothing to validate Kraepelin's genetic theory of mental illness.

What has certainly increased due to the ability to better understand and study the human genome is faith in neo-Kraepelinianism. Still, empirically correlating the metaphysical mind with the physical body remains elusive. Researchers Michael Arribas-Ayloon, Andrew Bartlett, and Jamie Lewis submit that

> for psychiatric genetics, the recent incarnation of Big Biology signifies a stunning transformation of its public visibility, scales of production and global organization. **Though it might be tempting to say that genomics 'saved' the field from controversy and obscurity, we argue that there has been no fundamental change in its core styles of reasoning.** The rapid growth of *-omic* technologies is not a gestalt switch to a new paradigm of 'molecular psychiatry' but a reorganization of its styles of reasoning. The ability to genotype thousands of cases and controls is only a technical 'revolution' insofar as it provides an infrastructure for stabilizing the *clinical, statistical, and laboratory* styles of psychiatric genetics [emphasis added].[530]

As with EEGs and MRIs and the unfulfilled promise of discovering psychiatric disorders in the brain, the ability to closely examine specific genes and better understand the human genome offered geneticists the hope that correlations could be better studied to yield empirical evidence which could theoretically prove Kraepelinianism.

What is troubling and also worth noting is that the man who was originally tasked with heading up the Human

[530] Arribas-Ayloon, Bartlett, and Lewis, *Psychiatric Genetics*, 8.

Genome Project in 1988 and who won the Nobel Prize for discovering the structure of DNA, James Watson, is well-known to be motivated by eugenic belief.[531] Watson has publicly declared that whites are more intelligent than blacks,[532] and he has made several references to aborting babies who have specific genetic disorders which are unique to the Jewish people. As appalling as these assertions are, Watson has also expressed regret for not having aborted his own son who had eventually been diagnosed as having schizophrenia: "I think I would be a monster to want someone to suffer the way he has . . . so, yes, I would have aborted him."[533] Other geneticists, such as the German Peter Propping, who was honored as the Emil Kraepelin Professor for Psychiatry at the Max Planck Institute of Psychiatry for his ongoing effort to sustain Kraepelin's eugenic research, were also key figures in the GWAS. The modern genetic field is still filled with prominent eugenicists, which may be what led Historian Edward Black to assert that

> eugenics was the racist pseudoscience determined to wipe away all human beings deemed "unfit," preserving only those who conformed to a Nordic stereotype . . . . Today we are faced with a potential return to eugenic discrimination, not under national flags or political

[531] Paul Vallely, "James Watson: Genetic Disorder," *The Independent* (October 20, 2007): https://www.independent. co.uk/news/people/profiles/james-watson-genetic-disorder-395100.html.

[532] Ibid.

[533] Ibid.

credos, **but as a function of human genomic science and corporate globalization** [emphasis added].[534]

As long as the eugenic philosophies such as individual degenerationism and materialism are accepted, however, there is not "a potential return to eugenic discrimination." Rather, there is a continuation of eugenic discrimination. Moreover, though the technology behind eugenics and the terms are constantly changing, the underlying philosophies, psychiatric constructs, goals, and many of the barbaric practices remain the same within the neo-Kraepelinian/bio-psycho-social paradigm. While technology has clearly advanced, it has not safeguarded against eugenic ideology or application.

The fact that scientists have mapped the human genome, are able to examine and understand specific genes in more detail, and are able to correlate the human genome with other somatic functions still has not proven Rush, Morel, or Kraepelin's shared biological theory of mental illness. Geneticists have yet to empirically correlate the metaphysical mind/psyche/soul to genetic processes utilizing the scientific method. Despite the inability to correlate the true substance of perceived psychiatric disorders to the body, geneticists continue to propagate the belief that someday they will, while at the same time, they continue to deny humanity's dual nature.

[534] Edwin Black, *War against the Weak: Eugenics and America's Campaign to Create a Master Race* (New York: Four Walls Eight Windows, 2003), preface xvii-iii.

CHAPTER 6
THE SCIENCE OF PSYCHIATRIC GENETICS (2)

———————

"The eminent geneticist, Benno Muller-Hill, described eugenics as 'explosive mixture between something we might call hard science, that is, human genetics, and the sphere of political action. On the one hand, geneticists needed politicians to implement their ideas. On the other hand, Hitler and the Nazis needed scientists who could say that anti-Semitism has scientific theoretical foundations.' For some Polish eugenicists, the Third Reich was not the home of the Nuremberg Laws, but a country that 'boldly embarked on racial hygiene.' This enthusiastic attitude of Polish intellectual circles towards Nazi eugenic laws was characteristic of the status of pre-war science in Poland, which in many areas, such as anthropology and psychiatry, remained strongly influenced by the paradigm of German science."[535] Professor of Medicine, O. Blach

The modern-day psychiatric paradigm—especially the underlying proposed science behind psychiatric genetics—still rests heavily on the pre-war German worldview. The most recent stage in the theory of correlates consists of the same German phenomenology and suggested pathology dating back to the time of Wundt, Kraepelin, and Rüdin.

———————

535 O. Blach, "Eugenics—a Side effect of Progressivism? Analysis of the Role of Scientific and Medical Elites in the Rise and Fall of Eugenics in Pre-War Poland," *Vesalius* vol. 16 (1) (June, 2010): 10-5; https://www.ncbi.nlm.nih.gov/pubmed/20977151.

Sophisticated Terms

As technology has advanced within the field of psychiatric eugenics, so too has the nomenclature that is used to discuss and study correlates as well as to search for potential causes. While there is clearly more scientific insight into the human genome, the metaphysical soul remains a mystery to scientists and is still unapproachable within scientific investigation. Despite this reality, human mindsets, emotions, and moral behaviors which are perceived to be distressful or impairing and persist must be correlated with genes in some way or the Kraepelinian model that sustains the modern mental health system will continue to be substantially undermined.

Upon the vital psychiatric necessity to correlate the metaphysical reality of human nature with the human genome, geneticists introduced new terms into the theory in attempt to study psychiatric "disorders" as if they were valid genetic diseases with proven pathologies. These terms also provided an illusion that the field is advancing beyond merely understanding the human genome and the nervous system.

More specifically, the terms *endophenotypes, phenotypes,* and *genotypes* are the new way to describe the old theory while directly relating to genetic theories of correlation and causation. *Endophenotype,* for example, is defined as

> an epidemiological term used to connect behavioral
> symptoms with more well-understood structural

phenotypes associated with known genetic causes or with abnormal genetic testing.[536]

And proposed endophenotypes must theoretically fall within scientific investigation and be perceived as hereditary:

> There are potentially many kinds of endophenotypes, including various measures of metabolic activity and brain structure or function. But scientists believe that for purposes of preventing and treating psychiatric disorders, endophenotypes should ideally have certain characteristics in common. They should be state-independent — in other words, always present even when a person is not showing symptoms. They should be objectively measurable. They should be heritable — that is, differences in the likelihood of having the endophenotype should be correlated with genetic differences. They should occur at a relatively high rate in the families of people with the disorder (the phenotype), and they should be associated with genetic variants that occur at a relatively high rate in people with the disorder. They should involve brain circuits that are associated with the symptoms of the disorder, such as dopamine neurotransmitter systems in schizophrenia.[537]

At a minimum, there must exist measurable perceived correlations if theorists are to sustain psychiatric genetics and society is to believe the bannered hypotheses. The desire of psychiatric researchers, however, is not just to "connect" phenotypes with genotypes; it is to attempt to prove that genotypes cause phenotypes and to

[536] Mary Lee Gregory, Vera Joanna Burton, and Bruce K. Shapiro, *Neurobiology of Brain Disorders* edited by Michael J. Zigmond, Lewis P. Rowland, and Joseph T. Coyle (Academic Press, 2015), 18.

[537] Harvard Medical School, "Endophenotypes," *Harvard Health Publishing* (September 2007): https://www.health.harvard.edu/newsletter_article/Endophenotypes.

dogmatically insist that this speculated pathology — in this exact order — is true until proven otherwise.

The etymology of *endophenotype* and *phenotype* offers further insight. For example, a *phenotype* is a type of *phenomenon* — "an object or aspect known through the senses rather than by thought or intuition."[538] Conversely, a genotype is simply a specific gene or group of genes.

But the word *phenomenon* has an important and relevant nuance: "a fact or event of scientific interest susceptible to scientific description and explanation."[539] When it comes to psychiatric genetics and alleged mental disorders, this last definition is most accurate. A phenotype is a type of phenomena — a seemingly "scientific description or explanation" — that could be metaphysical or biological but that is of "scientific interest." This nomenclature represents descriptive psychology and permits scientists to present psychiatric constructs and their immaterial symptoms (e.g., hopelessness, false beliefs, and guilt) as if the constructs were tangible empirical realities that can be studied in the body. Harvard University defines the terms further and explains how these words were created in correlation with Kraepelinian eugenics becoming the prominent American psychiatric paradigm in the early 1970s:

> "Pheno-" means showing or appearing. The phenotype of a disorder is its immediately observable signs and symptoms. "Endo-" means internal or inside; an endophenotype, also called an intermediate phenotype, refers to a characteristic that is not easily observed on the

---

[538] "Phenomenon, "*Merriam-Webster's Dictionary*: https://www. merriam-webster.com/dictionary/phenomenon.

[539] Ibid.

surface. People with a given endophenotype are more susceptible to the disorder, and that fact reveals something about the biological processes that underlie the disorder. The concept was introduced in the 1970s, but mental health professionals have become much more interested in it recently, partly because of developments in brain imaging and genetics. More than half of the scholarly articles on endophenotypes have been published since 2004.[540]

As applied to many psychiatric constructs, phenotype is the word psychiatric geneticists use to frame mindsets, emotions, and motives/explanations of moral behavior that fall outside of the scientific method yet are listed as symptoms of psychiatric disorders. Often, these metaphysical symptoms are the only true substance of each created psychiatric construct, and, since the conception of each construct, the observable phenomena (symptoms) have represented the only diagnostic means to claim alleged individual degeneracy.

In contrast to phenotypes, endophenotypes are suggested correlates that are said to exist in the body between genotypes and phenotypes. Some theorists, however, include environments, experiences, and "nurture" as endophenotypes, which they assert are positioned between symptoms and the human genome. As historians record,

[540] Harvard Medical School, "Endophenotypes," *Harvard Health Publishing* (September 2007): https://www.health.harvard.edu/newsletter_article/Endophenotypes.

though, eugenicists have always considered environments to be causative factors.[541]

For these reasons, an endophenotype is often referred to as an "intermediate phenotype."[542] Psychiatrist G.A. Miller and psychologist B.S. Rockstroh comment on the nature of endophenotypes:

> Endophenotypes [B] are biological or psychological phenomena of a disorder believed to be in the causal chain between genetic contributions [genotypes; A] to a disorder and diagnosable symptoms [phenotypes; C] of psychopathology.[543]

The typical claim is made that specific genes (A) cause disorder in the nervous system (B), which in turn produces hallucinations and delusions (C). But endophenotypes are not scientifically established. Professor of psychiatry, L. L. Gottesman, who along with Dr. James Shields coined the term endophenotype in 1967,[544] states that

> endophenotypes, measurable components unseen by the unaided eye along the pathway between disease and

541 "It is important to point out that most eugenicists claimed they realised that environmental factors played a role in determining phenotypes, especially for human personality and social traits" (Garland E. Allen, "Eugenics and Modern Biology: Critiques of Eugenics, 1910-1945," *Annals of Human Genetics* vol. 75 [2011]: 319; doi: 10.1111/j.1469-1809.2011.00649.x).

542 Roberta Rasetti and Daniel R. Weinberger, "Intermediate Phenotypes in Psychiatric Disorders," *Current Opinion in Genetics & Development* Vol. 21 (3) (2011): 342–343; doi:10.1016/j.gde.2011.02.003.

543 G.A. Miller and B.S. Rockstroh, *The Neurobiology of Schizophrenia* (2016), 17.

544 Sadie F. Dingfelder, "The Hunt for Endophenotypes," *Monitor Staff* vol. 37 (10) (November 2006): 20.

distal genotype, have emerged as an important concept in the study of complex neuropsychiatric diseases.[545]

While scientists dogmatically claim that there is a sound pathology from phenotypes (C) to endophenotypes (B) to ending with genotypes as causative (A), there remains the impossible scientific task of correlating metaphysical phenotypes and endophenotypes with physical endophenotypes and genotypes. Simply because somatic variances exist and correlate with other bodily changes and that a person is thinking in a destructive way proves nothing about which phenomena causes the other, how they precisely correlate, or the many factors involved in producing them.

Humanistic Phenomenology

Since psychiatric constructs, which rest upon mostly metaphysical or spiritual phenotypes and "hidden mechanisms" (endophenotypes),[546] are not scientifically approachable entities, psychiatric genetics depends largely upon the field of *phenomenology* — the study and interpretation of human experiences, appearances, phenomena, and consciousness. In fact, phenotypes, endophenotypes, and genotypes in psychiatry are all born out of neo-Kraepelinian phenomenology, which psychiatrists claim enables them to study and consider an

545 L. L. Gottesman, "The Endophenotype Concept in Psychiatry: Etymology and Strategic Intentions," *American Journal of Psychiatry* vol. 160 (4) (April 2003): 636.

546 Sadie F. Dingfelder, "The Hunt for Endophenotypes," *Monitor Staff* vol. 37 (10) (November 2006): 20.

individual's perspective, motives, desires, emotions, volition, faith, morality, etc. — the metaphysical issues of the soul or as some prefer to call it: "human consciousness."[547] Real human struggles, such as sorrow, hopelessness, guilt, deceit, beliefs, fear, and anxiety are internal spiritual struggles that only the individual person can fully understand and experience from his/her own first-person perspective. Though metaphysical in nature, it is clear that these human phenomena are real. Still, these alleged psychiatric issues must be understood, explained, and approached, and often they are the core of psychiatric disorders listed in the *DSM*.

In truth, psychiatric phenomenology is the humanistic attempt to explain the fallen/broken condition of the metaphysical human soul — a person's self-perception of life/awareness/consciousness/personhood — within an allegedly scientific framework. This philosophical approach is less of a scientific endeavor and more of a belief system shrouded in medical authority and statistical data; it is the necessary approach to the post-Genesis 3 human soul and human phenomena within materialistic faith.

Phenomenology — through diagnosis, classifications, descriptive psychology, and utilitarian propaganda is utilized in attempt to establish a new and common way for people to think about themselves, human phenomena, and the world around them. All too often, when a person accepts established psychiatric phenomenology as best

---

[547] David Woodruff Smith, "Phenomenology," *Sandford Encyclopedia of Philosophy* (Summer Edition, 2018): https://plato.stanford.edu/entries/phenomenology/.

explaining his/her struggles and conscious experiences of the soul, that individual's identity and lifestyle are altered accordingly. Such a reality is precisely why phenomenology is considered to be a branch of philosophy that stands alone as well as an aspect of all philosophy:

Phenomenology is commonly understood in either of two ways: as a disciplinary field in philosophy, or as a movement in the history of philosophy. **The discipline of phenomenology may be defined initially as the study of structures of experience, or consciousness. Literally, phenomenology is the study of "phenomena":** appearances of things, or things as they appear in our experience, or the ways we experience things, thus the meanings things have in our experience. **Phenomenology studies conscious experience as experienced from the subjective or first-person point of view.** This field of philosophy is then to be distinguished from, and related to, the other main fields of philosophy: ontology (the study of being or what is), epistemology (the study of knowledge), logic (the study of valid reasoning), ethics (the study of right and wrong action), etc. [emphasis added].[548]

Kraepelinian/humanistic phenomenology has been the central empowering tenet of psychiatric genetics for over the last century.[549] Influential evolutionary professor of psychiatric genetics Kenneth Kendler and professor of psychiatric phenomenology Josef Parnas along with numerous other psychiatric philosophers explain in one of their books how phenomenology undergirds all psychiatric theory and practice:

The second part of this book deals with phenomenological approach to psychiatry. One way to clearly see the

[548] Ibid.

[549] Kendler edited Kendler & Parnas, *Philosophical Issues in Psychiatry*, 3.

interrelationship between our first and second sections is to go back to the question of "explanation" and "understanding" as articulated by Karl Jaspers in his great text General Psychopathology (1963). Explanation—the approach taken to the world by the "natural" science—views all phenomena from the third-person perspective and seeks to comprehend causal processes in a third-person, objective, and therefore verifiable framework. **Understanding, by contrast, is a distinctly human process involving our ability, through empathy, to grasp the phenomena of meaning and connect with our fellow human beings. . . . More than any other philosophical approach, phenomenology has been intertwined with the effort by psychiatrists to develop a detailed understanding of the experiences of the psychiatrically ill** [emphasis added].[550]

Other prominent academic psychiatrists also recognize phenomenology's vital importance to psychiatry. Chair of psychiatry at the University of Massachusetts Medical School and chair of the *DSM* steering committee, Paul Appelbaum, is one such figure. He writes,

Though I can speak firsthand about the value of philosophy for the psychiatrist, I must rely on the judgments of my philosopher-friends regarding the usefulness of the study of psychiatric disorders for the philosopher. **They tell me that the phenomenology of mental disorders, the complex ethical issues that arise, and the dilemmas inherent in the line-drawing process of diagnosis provide challenging opportunities to test and refine philosophical theories** [emphasis added].[551]

[550] Ibid., 5-6.

[551] Paul S. Appelbaum, *Philosophy of Psychiatry: A Companion* edited by Jennifer Radden (New York: Oxford University Press, 2014), foreword viii.

Influential psychiatrist Andrew Sims also discusses phenomenology's centrality in psychiatry, noting how individual degeneracy is created within this perspective:

> *Phenomenology,* **as used in psychiatry, involves observing and categorizing abnormal psychological states, the** *internal* **experiences of the patient and his consequent behavior.** How can one *observe* an *internal* experience? By using *empathy* to explore the patient's subjective state. Empathy is a learned skill and not an inborn intuition; it enables accurate assessment of the subjective state [italics are Sims' original emphasis; other emphasis added].[552]

Despite Sim's claims, however, empathy does not "enable accurate assessment" of a person's soul or consciousness. Rather, one's assessment of both his/her own and others' souls is based upon his/her own presuppositional moral faith and not an ability to understand another's feelings. Empathy is certainly important, but accuracy in discerning a soul's condition depends primarily upon the observer's epistemology (what he/she foundationally believes to be true). The currently accepted psychiatric epistemology is both humanistic and utilitarian, and the championed phenomenology is Emil Kraepelin's, who approached perceived "degenerates" as strictly evolved masses of material rather than as souls in need. If empathy "enables accurate assessment" of the soul, as historians Juri Allik and Erki Tammiksaar attest, then approaching souls from the neo-Kraepelinian perspective explains its failure: "Kraepelin was often portrayed as a rational diagnostic machine without any compassion or empathy towards

---

[552] Sims, *Is Faith Delusion?* 146.

those whom he was supposed to help."[553] Both objective truth and genuine love based upon the character of the Creator God are required to effectively treat the human soul. Approaching people statistically, materially, and apart from establishing transparent, moral, and loving relationships, may explain why many clinicians who hold to the bio-psycho-social model are unable to rightly understand and explain the troubling and distressful phenomena of those seeking their help. It is far easier to fit people into an established phenomenological framework and label them, than it is to truly know and disciple them.

It is beneficial to also understand the various aspects of psychiatric phenomenology and its historic contributors. As with most of the modern theory, Germany is central to the discussion. Psychiatric phenomenology is a philosophical field constructed upon the teachings of several psychologists (known during their lifetime as philosophers) such as Wilhelm Wundt, Fredrich Nietzsche, and Franz Brentano. Nietzsche, for example, wrote in his book *Beyond Good and Evil* (1886) that "there are no moral phenomena at all, but only a moral interpretation of phenomena."[554] Nietzsche's perspective would greatly impact Nazi Germany — including Kraepelin's own development of psychiatric phenomenology.

Moreover, the reality is that psychiatric syndromes (e.g., schizophrenia, bipolar I, borderline personality disorder)

---

[553] Juri Allik and Erki Tammiksaar, "Who was Emil Kraepelin and Why do we Remember Him 160 Years Later?" *TRAMES*, 20 (4) (2016): 332-33; DOI: 10.3176/tr.2016.4.01.

[554] Fredrich Nietzsche *Beyond Good and Evil*, translated by Walter Kaufmann (New York: Vintage, 1966 (1886), 108.

do not actually exist. Instead, what is apparent is the outworking symptoms (e.g., delusions and hallucinations), which are simply described and explained within the established psychiatric phenomenology (phenotypes, endophenotypes, and genotypes). Professor of philosophy at UC Irvine, who is considered by many to be a leader in describing and defining the field of phenomenology, David Smith, relates,

> In its root meaning, then, phenomenology is the study of *phenomena*: literally, appearances as opposed to reality . . . . Originally, in the 18th century, "phenomenology" meant the theory of appearances fundamental to empirical knowledge, especially sensory appearances. The Latin term "Phenomenologia" was introduced by Christoph Friedrich Oetinger in 1736.[555]

Psychiatric constructs are not realities; they are appearances which merely describe and categorize common realities of human nature and consciousness (e.g., mindsets, emotions, and behaviors) within a restricted presuppositional faith. By applying Kraepelinian phenomenology, metaphysical phenomena/symptoms can be constructed into a syndrome that is dogmatically claimed to be a biological problem with medicine as the solution. Other humanistic phenomenologies, such as Freudianism, describe, explain, and seek to approach symptoms within a different presuppositional faith.

The "scientific field" of phenomenology or consciousness was developed and applied in Germany over several decades, but it was formally recognized by psychologist

---

[555] Smith, "Phenomenology."

Edmund Husserl in the early 1900s[556] and considered then as empirically sound, due in large part to psychologists Wilhelm Wundt's and Franz Brentano's corresponding teachings on descriptive psychology.[557] Dr. Smith remarks,

> By 1889 Franz Brentano used the term to characterize what he called "descriptive psychology." From there Edmund Husserl took up the term for his new science of consciousness, and the rest is history.[558]

Thus, psychiatrists established a new way to interpret the phenomena of the human soul within the religion of humanism by describing mental processes, emotions, experiences, and behaviors, etc. (phenomena or things which are apparent in human consciousness), offering an explanation within the restraints of psychiatric philosophy, claiming impairing and destructive phenomena to be biological diseases, and forming a psychiatric construct with a corresponding descriptive label and within a statistical diagnostic system. Professor of clinical psychology Jonathan Shedler discusses how descriptive psychology combined with the statistical approach enables psychiatric constructs to be fashioned, and further, how acceptance of the constructs depends entirely upon circular reasoning:

> Diagnoses listed in the *DSM*—*the Diagnostic and Statistical Manual of Mental Disorders*, the so-called bible of psychiatry—do not cause anything. They are not things.

---

[556] Anna-Teresa Tymieniecka, *Phenomenology World-Wide: Foundations – Expanding Dynamics – Life-Engagements A Guide for Research and Study* (Springer, 2014), 18.

[557] Wundt, *An Introduction to Psychology*, 194.

[558] Smith, "Phenomenology."

They are agreed-upon labels — a kind of shorthand — for describing symptoms. Generalized anxiety disorder means a person has been anxious or worried for six months or longer and it's bad enough to cause problems — nothing else. **The diagnosis is description, not explanation . . . . Here is the circular logic: How do we know a patient has depression? Because they have the symptoms. Why are they having symptoms? Because they have depression** [emphasis added].[559]

The circular reasoning of descriptive psychology is applied in forming and diagnosing all psychiatric constructs.

As another example of how the descriptive method works, the construct of schizophrenia can be considered. If a person is delusional and hallucinating (metaphysical symptoms) in a way that a clinician cannot explain or that is troubling, then they are likely to be diagnosed as having a psychotic disorder. How does one know that a person has a psychotic disorder? Because it can be observed that an individual is delusional and hallucinating. The metaphysical criteria used to make the diagnosis is the only true explanation and justification for the construct's existence. The construct's official name, *schizophrenia* (meaning "split-minded"), is also descriptive not explanatory.

This fact can be observed in most psychiatric labels: *bipolar disorder* describes two different alternating moods, *ADHD* describes a child's struggle to behave and perform as an authority expects, *dissociative identity disorder* describes

[559] Jonathan Shedler, "A Psychiatric Diagnosis Is Not a Disease: Doublethink makes for bad Treatment," *Psychology Today* (July 27, 2019): https://www.psychologytoday.com/us/blog/psychologically-minded/201907/psychiatric-diagnosis-is-not-disease?fbclid=IwAR0HB vie7R1uPUC0XpB2MFws4UinQMKb7mDJRwxmnV23SbugqUPQWnRIeqo.

what was previously termed as *multiple personality disorder*, and substance use disorder simply conveys the obvious fact that a person is consuming dangerous substances. The labels do not explain a valid disease; they only describe a person's struggle and highlight the prevalence of descriptive psychology within humanistic phenomenology.

Former president of the Royal College of Psychiatrists Andrew Sims offers insight into why phenomenology is vital to psychiatric theory and application:

> In psychiatry, examination of the mental state becomes preeminent with the patient describing mental symptoms: what, in his own words, is he actually experiencing? It is this, the subjective experience of patients ["phenomenology"], that is so crucial for making a psychiatric diagnosis, and it all depends upon our allowing our patients to *talk for themselves*, thereby giving vent to symptoms, complaints about their condition, and signs, speech and behavior that indicate the presence of mental illness [italics are Sims' original emphasis].[560]

Psychiatric diseases are not discovered in the body (via biomarkers), but by applying psychiatric phenomenology. Constructs are simply designed according to presuppositional faith and classified as described. People are not diagnosed with a biological disease within psychiatric phenomenology. Instead, their phenomena are simply interpreted and framed as described and according to the established neo-Kraepelinian worldview.

Key to the neo-Kraepelinian psychiatric phenomenology is the combination of Mesmer's, Rush's, and Wundt's agreed upon assertion that the soul is physical (materialism) and

---

[560] Andrew Sims, *Is Faith Delusion? Why Religion is Good for Your Health* (London: Continuum, 2009), 151.

hereditarily fixed (bio-determinism), Nietzsche's teaching that humanity is not itself moral, Wilhelm Wundt's and Franz Brentano's introduction of descriptive psychology into academic psychology and psychiatry, and Kraepelin's formal establishment of genetic, abnormal, social, and descriptive psychologies (eugenics; individual degeneracy) into an agreed upon and seemingly medical and scientific diagnostic/classification/statistical system.

The fact that psychiatric constructs are created and maintained through applied phenomenology also explains why people "diagnosed" as having schizophrenia regularly do not share the same symptoms or have the same genetic and neurological variances.[561] Psychiatrists often explain the subjective nature of the construct of schizophrenia (and other alleged mental disorders) as revealing the "heterogeneous nature of schizophrenia." But in truth, this common utility of explaining the construct of schizophrenia as a "heterogeneous disease" exposes how psychiatrists are essentially forcing symptoms to fit into their established phenomenological categories in attempt to explain and approach the soul within a medical framework. For example, biological psychiatrists have long claimed that schizophrenia is a "neurodegenerative disease" — that a person's problem is somehow rooted in a disordered or malfunctioning brain. But a large controlled study conducted by psychiatrists and biologists worldwide and published in 2020 revealed that people labeled as schizophrenic regularly do not have "abnormal brains." Rather than outright admitting that schizophrenia is a

[561] Will Boggs, "Schizophrenia Linked to Mutations in Genes Critical to Synaptic Function," *Medscape Psychiatry* (February 6, 2020): https://www.medscape.com/viewarticle/924828.

subjective construct, materialists still present the construct's fluidity as "heterogenous" and insist upon interpreting the empirical data according to their biased perspective:

> **Neurobiological heterogeneity in schizophrenia is poorly understood and confounds current analyses** . . . . Two distinct neuroanatomical subtypes were found . . . . Subtype 1 displayed widespread volume reduction correlating with illness duration, and worse premorbid functioning. Subtype 2 had normal and stable anatomy, except for larger basal ganglia and internal capsule, not explained by antipsychotic dose. **These subtypes challenge the notion that brain volume loss is a general feature of schizophrenia and suggest differential aetiologies** [emphasis added].[562]

While the many researchers should be commended for their honesty about their findings, their confusion regarding their own analyses, and their theories of causation, they fail to consider that schizophrenia is not a real thing apart from a philosophical construct; it is simply an attempt at explaining real aspects of human nature which fall outside of materialists' ability to explain otherwise. If there is not even consistent neurodegeneration in those categorized as schizophrenic, though, then psychiatrists cannot continue to claim the

---

[562] Ganesh B Chand, Dominic B Dwyer, Guray Erus, Aristeidis Sotiras, Erdem Varol, Dhivya Srinivasan, Jimit Doshi, Raymond Pomponio, Alessandro Pigoni, Paola Dazzan, Rene S Kahn, Hugo G Schnack, Marcus V Zanetti, Eva Meisenzahl, Geraldo F Busatto, Benedicto Crespo-Facorro, Christos Pantelis, Stephen J Wood, Chuanjun Zhuo, Russell T Shinohara, Haochang Shou, Yong Fan, Ruben C Gur, Raquel E Gur, Theodore D Satterthwaite, Nikolaos Koutsouleris, Daniel H Wolf, Christos Davatzikos, "Two distinct neuroanatomical subtypes of schizophrenia revealed using machine learning," *Brain* awaa025 (Oxford University Press) (February 27, 2020): https://doi.org/10.1093/brain/awaa025.

construct of schizophrenia as a neurodegenerative disease. Likewise, the very real possibility remains that the measurable deterioration in some people's brains and genomes who are labeled as disordered could very well be natural negative effects rather than being the cause.

Since the diagnostic system is at its core phenomenological and not medical, diagnoses of most categorized mental disorders do not require medical training or any knowledge of biology. A group of psychiatric geneticists at Harvard and Cambridge remark:

> In psychiatry, biomarkers are very much needed for both research and treatment, given the heterogenous populations identified by current phenomenologically based diagnostic systems.[563]

Others also comment on this reality concerning the construct of schizophrenia,

> Connecting these symptoms to patterns in the brain has proved extremely difficult, especially since animal models aren't useful in a disorder that is largely diagnosed through self-reporting [phenomenology]. The main message is that the biological underpinnings of schizophrenia — and actually many other neuropsychiatric disorders — are quite heterogeneous.[564]

---

563 Alicia R. Martin, Mark J. Daly, Elise B. Robinson, Steven E. Hyman, and Benjamin M. Neale, "Predicting Polygenic Risk of Psychiatric Disorders," *Biological Psychiatry* vol 86 (2) (July 15, 2019): 97-109; https://doi.org/10.1016/j.biopsych.2018.12.015.

564 Carly Cassella, "Brain Scans Reveal a New Schizophrenia Type that Almost Looks Like a 'Healthy' Brain," *Science Alert* (February 28, 2020): https://www.sciencealert.com/brain-scans-reveal-a-second-type-of-schizophrenia-and-it-looks-surprisingly-normal/amp?fbclid=IwAR0d1h2sF4Rbnez5_9c_-UwV1ht6DmvkwHUZ91KWQqVnN7Y9iofwRr7ZNJk.

As will be established in the next chapter, sleep deprivation, prescribed psychotropic drugs, ways of coping with trauma, religious ceremonies, loss of loved ones, and many other human experiences produce the very categorized "symptoms" upon which all diagnoses of alleged schizophrenia/psychosis are made.

Psychiatric diagnoses are not medically based but are phenomenologically applied through descriptive psychology. Anna-Teresa Tymieniecka writes on this reality, noting how Wundt's, Brentano's, and Husserl's "descriptive psychology" is still the prominent approach: "[Husserl] entrusts this analysis to a pure or phenomenological psychology whose links with Brentano's descriptive psychology are still clearly visible."[565] Today's "bio-psycho-social" model, as the neo-Kraepelinian approach is now commonly called, depends heavily on descriptive psychology. In fact, geneticist Richard Lewontin proposes key steps that must be followed in forming and upholding psychiatrists' bio-psycho-social vision. The first step directly relates to the descriptive approach within psychiatric phenomenology.[566] Philosophical psychologist Jennifer Radden agrees:

> Psychiatry boasts an impressive tradition of meticulous clinical description. In some instances this has been inspired by a thoroughgoing application of empirical method, in others by phenomenological assumptions, and in yet others by no more — or less — than a remarkable ear

[565] Anna-Teresa Tymieniecka, *Phenomenology World-Wide: Foundations — Expanding Dynamics — Life-Engagements A Guide for Research and Study* (New York: Springer, 2014), 18.

[566] Lewontin, *Biology as Ideology*, 89.

for meaning and nuance in spoken and unspoken expression.[567]

Neuropsychiatrists and psychiatric geneticists Heike Tost, Tajvar Alam, and Adnreas Meyer-Lindeberg, working under the direction of the National Institute of Mental Health, also admit that "the operational criteria implemented in modern classification systems are entirely descriptive."[568] Without the Kraepelinian-based *DSM-5*, which systematically describes common impairing mindsets, emotions, and behaviors, people are less likely to relate negative or undesirable aspects of their souls and outworking behavior to the bio-psycho-social faith.[569]

Phenomenology is not merely applied by psychiatrists; every counselor, therapist, and clinician is promoting their own presuppositional belief system to everyone they counsel. The Group for the Advancement of Psychiatry (GAP) does not shy away from this fact, as it encourages psychiatrists to establish a "schema"/phenomenology that directly affects both the individual's sense of consciousness/identity and that also influences the person's family:

> A "story of understanding" that the psychiatrist conveys to the patient at the end of the interview will trigger one of these cultural schemas and social role expectations. A "chemical imbalance in the brain" elicits the "disease"

[567] Radden, *Philosophy of Psychiatry*, 10.

568 Heike Tost, Tajvar Alam, and Andreas Meyer-Lindenberg, "Dopamine and Psychosis: Theory, Pathomechanisms and Intermediate Phenotypes," *Neuroscience and Biobehavioral Reviews* vol. 34 (5) (April 2010): 689–700; doi:10.1016/j.neubiorev.2009.06.005.

[569] Lewontin, *Biology as Ideology*, 89.

schema. A proposal for psychotherapy activates "problem of living" schema. These schemas influence the behavior of patient (and family) thus changing the social brain and course of illness.[570]

The faith of everyone involved in counseling, labeling, treatment outcomes, and related endeavors is of great importance.

As conveyed in the previous chapter, Kraepelinian (eugenic) phenomenology requires that all human nature, experiences, relationships, and so forth be understood and interpreted through an established set of philosophical assumptions: individual degeneracy, materialism, genetic-determinism, utilitarianism, and humanism. Those who place their faith in the combination of these core beliefs must insist that the arrow of causality always point to the human genome or other suggested somatic explanations. It makes logical sense, then, that Lewontin describes the necessity to insist that all human nature be "coded in our genes" as the second step in accepting sociobiology or the bio-psycho-social perspective, as it is referred to in relation to human consciousness. He states that all true sociobiologists believe that "there are genes for religiosity, genes for entrepreneurship, genes for whatever characteristics are said to be built into the human psyche and human social organization."[571] As psychiatrist Paul Minot indicates, the medical model (neo-Kraepelinian or reductionistic model) is an attempt to explain the

---

[570] Johan Verhulst, Russel Gardner, Beverly Sutton, John Beahrs, Fred Wamboldt, Michael Schwartz, Carlo Carandang, Doug Kramer, and John Looney, "The Social Brain in Clinical Practice," *Psychiatric Annals* vol. 35 (2005): 803-811.

[571] Lewontin, *Biology as Ideology*, 89.

"substance" of the human soul while at the same time denying the soul's true metaphysical nature:

> The idea that our thoughts, feelings, and internal struggles can be reduced to mere chemical reactions is IMO indefensible–not just because it's so damned demeaning to our patients and ourselves, but also because this reasoning has *no firm basis in science*. The physiological nature of thought remains an utter mystery to us all–yet our patients are not merely biological entities. They have thoughts, affections, strengths, weaknesses, hopes, fears, struggles, and goals that are just as real as our own. Such abstractions are contributory to most if not all psychiatric disorders, but aren't usually taken into consideration while we're treating those pesky "symptoms"–you know, those things we used to call "feelings," back in the day when we were taught to *listen* to them.[572]

"Feelings" is another term conceived from phenomenology, which many people use to describe their soul's true condition or first-person perspective. One might say that *feelings* are metaphysical phenomena of the soul, which reveal themselves through bodily processes. Too often within psychiatric phenomenology, though, the somatic effects are said to cause the feelings.

Essentially, there are two key components to the "field" of psychiatric genetics, which are both based upon presuppositional philosophies: 1) phenomenology and 2) an insistence upon genetic/hereditary causes or risks. These tenets were promoted by German psychologist Franz Brentano, utilizing the terms "descriptive psychology" and "genetic psychology" in his book, *Vom Ursprung Sittlicher Erkenntnis (The Origin of our Knowledge of Right and*

---

[572] Paul Minot, "About Me," *Straight Talk Psychiatry* (December 31, 2019): https://paulminotmd.com.

Wrong).[573] But these suggestions did not originate with Brentano; he simply observed and recorded their growing acceptance and association in German philosophy/psychology. Psychiatrist Karl Jaspers, "upon whose work much of [psychiatrists'] current descriptive psychology is based,"[574] compares and contrasts psychiatric phenomenology with the field of botany:

> We have detailed knowledge of particular phenomena, of causal connections and meaningful connections, etc., but complex disease entities remain an endless, inextricable web. The individual configurations of disease are not like plants which we can classify in a herbarium. Rather it is just what is a 'plant' – an illness – that is most uncertain. What do we diagnose? . . . Diagnosis is expected to characterize in a comprehensive manner the whole morbid occurrence which has assailed the person and which stands as a well-defined entity among others....But however we devise we realize that it cannot work; that **we can only make temporary and arbitrary classifications; that there are a number of different possibilities which account for the fact that different workers construct entirely different schemata; and that classification is always contradictory in theory and never quite squares with the facts. Why then do we keep on making this vain attempt?** In the first place we want to see properly what this idea of disease-entity has achieved in respect to the *over-all picture* of existing psychic disorders, and particularly where we have failed because it is the basic and radical failure which makes us aware of the actual state of our knowledge. In the second place *every presentation of special psychiatry* requires some classification of psychosis at its base. **Without some such schema [diagnostic system] it cannot order its material. In the third place we need a classification in order to**

[573] Franz Brentano, *Vom Ursprung Sittlicher Erkenntnis* (*The Origin of our Knowledge of Right and Wrong*) (1889).

[574] Sims, *Is Faith Delusion?* 147.

make statistical investigations **of a large case material**
[emphasis added in bold; italics are Jasper's original emphasis].'[575]

In his statement, Jaspers acknowledges that psychiatric nosology or constructs are merely products of descriptive psychology. Likewise, Jaspers insists that a statistical approach (which Kraepelin's theory provided and the *Diagnostic and Statistical Manual* sustains) should always be of premier importance in explaining human phenomena.

As with descriptive psychology, the statistical approach is fundamental to psychiatric genetics and its phenomenology and explains why the genetic theory must continue to be sustained upon hereditary predictability and statistical "risk scores." Professor of Psychiatry Nassir Ghaemi discusses Jasper's perspective:

> To translate: Jaspers is saying that psychiatric nosology is like botany; it is a clinical description of what we observe about persons with mental problems, much like botany is an observational description of the characteristics of plants. The larger question of "What is a mental illness?" is like asking the question "What is a plant?" It is much easier to describe specific plants than to fully explain the nature of being a plant (one might call it "planthood"). Jaspers is, perhaps, taking a stance here on the old philosophical debate about the particular versus the universal, and saying we should stick with the particular. He notes that nosology can never be definitive or absolutely valid (as is the case with everything in his philosophy), but he does not conclude, unlike many critics today, that psychiatric diagnosis is therefore useless. It has three utilities: 1. we need specific diagnoses

575 Karl Jaspers, *General Psychopathology*, Vol. 1 & 2 (Baltimore, MD: Johns Hopkins University Press; 1997 first published in 1959), 604.

by which to judge the larger question of overall mental illness; 2. we cannot engage in any specific aspect of psychiatry (I think this is what he means by "special psychiatry") without having some organizing schema for the whole (a general nosology; for Jaspers defining psychosis forms the basis for his nosology); 3. we need to make diagnoses reliably so we can engage in research (which is necessary for science, and Jaspers values science a great deal) [emphasis added].[576]

As Ghaemi makes clear, "judging" or selecting fully depends upon the organizational schema established, and the schema depends fully upon a subjective agreement, since in the psychiatric perspective, "nosology can never be definitive or absolutely valid." As Ghaemi also notes, without objectively establishing alleged abnormalities through phenomenology, diagnoses cannot be made. Psychiatrists must create and attempt to save concepts of abnormal by applying descriptive psychology.

Psychiatric phenomenology is the combination of descriptive and genetic psychologies:

Brentano distinguished *descriptive* psychology from *genetic* psychology. Where genetic psychology seeks the causes of various types of mental phenomena, descriptive psychology defines and classifies the various types of mental phenomena, including perception, judgment, emotion, etc. According to Brentano, every mental phenomenon, or act of consciousness, is directed toward some object, and only mental phenomena are so directed. This thesis of intentional directedness was the hallmark of Brentano's descriptive psychology. In 1889 Brentano used the term "phenomenology" for descriptive

576 Nassir S. Ghaemi, "Nosologomania: *DSM* & Karl Jaspers' critique of Kraepelin." *Philosophy, Ethics, and Humanities in Medicine* (*PEHM*) vol. 4 (10) (July 23, 2009): doi:10.1186/1747-5341-4-10.

psychology, and the way was paved for Husserl's new
science of phenomenology.[577]

Wundt, Brentano, Husserl, and Nietzsche illustrate well how German psychologists (philosophers) — by utilizing a specific phenomenology and claiming it as scientifically sound — produced both modern clinical psychology and psychiatry. In actuality, these fields are variances of the same phenomenology derived from the same philosophical presuppositions.

By combining social/race, descriptive, and genetic psychologies, as many Germans did after Wundt, Kraepelin was able to construct his eugenic theory in a formal way. Psychiatry is not principally a field of science, but a worldview, anthropological faith, or religion; it is a presuppositional approach to the human soul and its phenomena.

Psychiatric *phenotypes*, then, are established by accepting the belief that all human consciousness is best explained within individual degeneracy, materialism, genetic-determinism, and humanism. Negative, impairing, distressful, destructive, undesirable, frightening, horrific, and other detrimental mindsets, emotions, and behaviors which cannot be easily explained within the evolutionary/humanistic anthropology are theoretically transformed into psychiatric phenotypes in attempt to sustain and potentially prove the eugenic theory. Psychiatric constructs, such as Kraepelin's schizophrenia and bipolar disorders, are based upon humanistic and evolutionary faith and philosophy. Accepting these descriptive constructs as if they were valid diseases is to accept —

---

[577] Smith, "Phenomenology."

knowingly or not — the German humanistic system of faith that is based on the same philosophies and phenomenology which led to the Holocaust.

In fact, in the *Humanist Manifestos I and II*, psychologists (such as John Dewey, who for years served as president of the American Psychology Association and was instrumental in attempting to remove God's wisdom and phenomenology from the public educational system) explain that for the secularist all human experiences must be reduced to humanistic "religious" explanations and descriptions:

> [Humanistic] religion consists of those actions, purposes, and experiences which are humanly significant. Nothing human is alien to the religious. It includes labor, art, science, philosophy, love, friendship, recreation — all that is in its degree expressive of intelligently satisfying human living. The distinction between the sacred and the secular can no longer be maintained.[578]

This humanistic premise not only determines how the human soul and experiences *of* life are explained within psychiatric terms, but also influences how humanists consider play therapy, sex therapy, and music therapy — to name a few — to be religious, empowering, amoral tools that restore the human soul to health. It is in counseling ("psychotherapy" or "talk therapy") where therapists attempt to reshape their counselee's conscious perspective. In essence, psychotherapy — whether Freudian, Skinnerian, Kraepelinian, or otherwise — is a humanistic tool that seeks

---

[578] Raymond Bragg, John Dewey, and Charles Francis Potter, et. al., *Humanist Manifestos I and II* edited by Paul Kurtz (Buffalo, NY: Prometheus Books, 1973), 9.

to make disciples of those who submit themselves to the established humanistic phenomenology.

Moreover, insisting that people consider a phenomenology apart from their current faith (which is precisely what counseling/psychotherapy — religious or secular — attempts to do) undermines the idea that turning inward and furthering self-dependence is the answer. Having such a relationship would undermine humanistic goals and expose human nature as needing something outside of a person's own self for deliverance. Editor-in-chief of the *Psychiatric Times* James Knoll IV explains:

> Most psychiatrists are familiar with the clinical aphorism that one of the highest therapeutic achievements is to assist and guide a patient to that unquantifiable and transcendent point at which they arrive at *their own* insights, *their own* relief from suffering, and *their own* lessening of incapacitation [humanism]. Indeed, our supreme achievement would be to make ourselves — eventually — unnecessary. **Fostering a dependent or otherwise interminable therapeutic relationship is acknowledged among competent psychiatrists as fundamentally problematic**: It is unhelpful to the patient, as well as a signal that the psychiatrist must reevaluate his or her approach. This is because in such situations, it is likely that the patient's subjective experience [phenomenology] has not been meaningfully appreciated and the psychiatrist has not adequately understood his or her own emotional reaction to the patient [emphasis added].[579]

To have empathy, to foster meaningful relationships, and to create a dependence on someone or something apart from one's self in a counseling/discipleship approach

---

[579] James L. Knoll IV, "The Return of the Alienist," *Medscape Psychiatry* (May 10, 2013): https://www.medscape.com/viewarticle/803662.

undermines humanistic phenomenology. Yet, without this discipleship, specific phenomenologies cannot be well-propagated.

Furthermore, within this Kraepelinian humanistic faith—just as within Freudian phenomenology, phenotypes must never be considered as causative; they should only be considered as symptoms/effects of the material nature. This fact explains why genetic mutations must theoretically be firmly established as being causative rather than considered as effects. The first three affirmations of the humanistic religion offer clear reasons why:

> (1): Religious humanists regard the universe as self-existing and not created. (2): Humanism believes that man is a part of nature and that he has emerged as the result of a continuous process. (3): Holding an organic view of life, humanists find that the traditional dualism of mind and body must be rejected.[580]

The philosophies of materialism, humanism, and evolution, as opposed to empirical evidence, demand a rigid adherence to elevating genes to the causative position, as Richard Lewontin maintains:

> It is not that the methods of and institutions of science somehow compel us to accept a material explanation of the phenomenal world, but on the contrary, that we are forced by our *a priori adherence* to material causes to create an apparatus of investigation and a set of concepts that produce material explanations.[581]

---

[580] Ibid., 8.

[581] Richard C. Lewontin, "Billions and Billions of Demons," review of *The Demon-Haunted World: Science as a Candle in the Dark*, by Carl Sagan, *New York Review of Books*, January 7, 1997, 31.

Ironically, holding to materialism is not an embrace of empirical science. On the contrary, the psychiatric genetic theory must sometimes be anti-science in order to sustain its acceptance. As Nassir Ghaemi, influential professor of psychiatry and director of translational medicine at Novartis, reveals, the *DSM*'s descriptive psychology enables continued faith in neo-Kraepelinianism and represents a *priori adherence* or genetic strategy:

> Gerald Klerman, who coined the term 'neo-Kraepelinian', outlined the benefits of *DSM-III* as follows: First, it embodies the concept of multiple disorders, reaffirming psychiatry's acceptance of the modern medical model of disease [materialism]. Second, and for the first time, an official nomenclature has incorporated operational criteria with exclusion and inclusion criteria...**based on manifest descriptive psychopathology rather than on presumed etiology** – psychodynamic, social, or biological. This reliance on descriptive rather than etiological criteria does not represent an abandonment of the ideal of modern scientific medicine that classification and diagnosis should be by causation. **Rather, it represents a strategic mode of dealing with the frustrating reality that, for most of the disorders we currently treat, there is only limited evidence for their etiologies** [emphasis added].[582]

Both the biological changes (genotypes and endophenotypes) and metaphysical/behavioral "phenotypes" that comprise the suggested psychiatric syndromes are real, but the psychiatric constructs, which represent humanistic faith, are not themselves scientific fact. Instead, they represent a presumed neo-Kraepelinian, humanistic, and Darwinian "strategic mode" of upholding eugenic thinking at all costs.

582 Nassir S. Ghaemi, "Nosologomania: *DSM* & Karl Jaspers."

Psychiatric genetics is not a valid scientific or medical field. Rather, this popular but destructive approach to the human soul and interpretation of human phenomena is a humanistic faith from which the "science" of psychiatric genetics is born. But neo-Kraepelinianism only represents one type of phenomenology to approach the soul, and the cognitive and behavioral existence of human consciousness can easily be interpreted apart from this failed humanistic-eugenic faith. Rejecting the neo-Kraepelinian/humanistic constructs of alleged mental disorders allows alternative phenomenologies to be considered in explaining impairing or destructive human mindsets, emotions, and moral behaviors.

Speculated Pathology

In accordance with humanistic phenomenology, a theory of causation must be established. The term "bio-psycho-social," which most modern psychiatrists prefer in describing their phenomenology,[583] highlights the various elements that constitute the construct according to their established priorities and their perceived pathology: 1) biology, 2) the psyche/soul/mind, and 3) relationships/society/environments. Editor in chief emeritus for the *Psychiatric Times* Ronald Pies relates how "academic psychiatry — for at least the past 30 years — has advocated a 'bio-psycho-social' model of mental illness."[584] Elsewhere, Pies expresses his prejudice toward the biological tenet of

[583] Ronald W. Pies, "Debunking the Two Chemical Imbalance Myths, Again," *Psychiatric Times* (April 30, 2019): https://www. psychiatrictimes.com /depression/debunking-two-chemical-imbalance-myths-again/page/0/1.

[584] Ibid.

the BPS model while admitting that at its core, the bio-psycho-social model is simply a worldview:

> I have argued here that the original BPSM is often held to a standard more befitting a true "scientific model" — like the Bohr atom — when, in reality, what George Engel described **is better characterized as a _paradigm_: a world-view with clear implications for practice.** That said, the BPS paradigm needs to be sharpened and "particularized" to specific psychiatric disorders. We need to understand the "scientific and clinical specifics" for all the major psychiatric disorders. For example, when considering schizophrenia, what relative contribution does "biology" make to the etiology of this disease, as distinct from psychological and social risk factors or causes? **(My guess: biology is by far the overwhelming factor)** [emphasis added].[585]

Within this worldview, the agreed upon symptoms, which psychiatrists attempt to correlate to the human genome, consist of either biological phenomena (e.g., catatonia, genetic variances, and atrophied areas of the brain), psychological/spiritual phenomena (e.g., delusions, deep sorrow, trauma, hopelessness, fear, and guilt), and social or relational phenomena (e.g., rejection or abuse). This perspective attempts to eliminate the nature versus nurture argument and accepts that both nature and nurture — as defined within secular phenomenology — might work together to produce disorders.

As previously discussed, psychiatric eugenics/neo-Kraepelinianism is the combination of cultural, social, race, descriptive, genetic, and abnormal psychologies within Darwinian anthropology. No matter how the

---

[585] Ronald Pies, "Can We Salvage the Bio-psycho-social Model?" _Psychiatric Times_ (January 22, 2020): https://www.psychiatrictimes.com/couch-crisis/can-we-salvage-biopsychosocial-model/page/0/1.

phenomenology is framed, it is principally Kraepelin's eugenic approach. Psychiatrist Jaak Panksepp comments on psychiatry's genesis and its new desired image,

> Evolutionary psychiatry emerged from the conceptual successes of sociobiology and evolutionary psychology. It will need to avoid the many mistakes that biology-free Evolutionary Psychology has been prey to. It should not ignore the wealth of information that exists between the phenotypic expression of symptoms and the genotypic sources of core brain/mind processes that are disrupted in psychiatric disorders.[586]

This new way of thinking (the "neo-Kraepelinian approach" or the "bio-psycho-social model") does not entail a search for actual syndromes/disorders in the body (e.g., "major depression"), nor is it an attempt to correlate the metaphysical phenotypes (e.g., sorrow, guilt, delusions, and hopelessness) with the body. Instead, psychiatric theorists persistently choose to focus on the theorized genotypes and the somatic endophenotypes derived from statistical figures, while still using only symptoms (e.g., hopelessness, sorrow, false beliefs, apathy, guilt, atrophied brains, insomnia, weight loss, catatonia, etc.) to make diagnoses from which to obtain those statistics. Whether or not a biological diagnostic test is ever suggested in the future, the fact remains that for decades diagnoses of alleged mental disorder have been almost exclusively based upon fitting people into categories based upon metaphysical phenomena rather than actually discovering diseases.

---

[586] Jaak Panksepp, "Emotional Endophenotypes in Evolutionary Psychiatry," *Progress in Neuropsychopharmacology and Biological Psychiatry* 30 (5) (July, 2006): 774; https://www.ncbi.nlm.nih.gov/pubmed/16554114.

Since neither the actual constructs nor the metaphysical symptoms are tangible certainties that can be empirically found in the body or scientifically studied in a lab, it makes sense within material phenomenology to only consider biological symptoms and to propose those selected variances as the main focus of investigation:

> Syndromal-conceptual thinking has become a barrier to illuminating the biological sources of psychiatric disorders. Endophenotypic-biomarker approaches now offer robust alternatives for generating linkages between psychiatrically relevant psychological changes and the neurobiological infrastructure of disordered mentation.[587]

The International Society of Psychiatric Genetics agrees, yet it highlights how the constructs that are allegedly being validated as genetic diseases are both classified and diagnosed solely on the symptoms:

> **One reason for the difficulties in identification of risk genes is the phenotype-based approach used for classification and diagnosis of psychiatric disorders. Diagnostic tests based on quantitative biomarker levels, imaging results, or tissue pathology do not exist yet.** Instead, diagnoses are typically made via observation and an assessment of the patient's medical history. At the same time, even the classification of psychiatric disorders and the validity of diagnostic boundaries are still subject to intense debate among psychiatrists and psychologists. **As a result, the disorders represent heterogenous and partly overlapping syndromic concepts. This**

---

[587] Ibid.

> heterogeneity and uncertainty in diagnosis lead to
> **decreased power in genetic studies** [emphasis added].[588]

As the International Society of Psychiatric Genetics recognizes, "the disorders represent . . . syndromic concepts."[589] As this group further acknowledges, the phenotypes represent the entire core of the psychiatric constructs, the diagnostic process, and the history of the hereditary theory's existence. Yet, the core substance of all suggested psychiatric disorders is minimized by neo-Kraepelinians when considering etiological theory. This common practice is the consequence of the restrictive nature of the philosophies of materialism and bio-determinism, which demand a rejection of dualism and thus the consideration that the spiritual nature both causes spiritual problems and negatively alters the physical body.

Accordingly, most psychiatric researchers prefer to discuss the correlations between genes in the genome and neurons in the nervous system without consideration that these very real biological variances could be effects of faulty thinking, traumatic experiences, or poor social relationships rather than the theorized causes. Molecular psychiatric researcher Jaak Panksepp explains this new "endophenotypic thinking:"

> Here I summarize recent advances in **endophenotypic thinking in biological psychiatry,** and suggest that various core **emotional-affective processes** may be among the **most important endophenotypes** that need to

---

[588] Till F. M. Andlauer, Bertram Muller-Myhsok, and Stephan Ripke, *Psychiatric Genetics: A Primer for Clinicians and Basic Scientists* edited by Thomas G. Schulze and Francis J. McMahon (New York: Oxford University Press, 2018), 57-58.

[589] Ibid.

be clarified at both neurobiological [B] and genetic [A] levels of analysis. To this end, I discuss **strategies to link basic emotional processes [C] that are commonly imbalanced in psychiatric disorders to neuroanatomical, neurochemical, neurophysiology, and molecular genetic levels of analysis.** Conjoint animal behavioral-genetic and gene expression, microarray analyses can clarify a variety of key emotional endophenotypes and thereby provide a coherent infrastructure for psychiatric systematics. **To further clarify the neurobiological dimensions of psychiatric disorders, we must also focus on psychosocial and environmental stress vectors [B] that converge to create imbalanced emotional and motivational brain activities of psychiatric significance [C].**[590]

In his statement, Panksepp offers a number of correlates or phenotypes and endophenotypes to consider: the nervous system, the genes, emotional processes, psychosocial vectors, motivational brain activities, and environmental stress vectors, which he believes all "converge to create imbalanced emotional and motivational brain activities." In other words, there are many correlates to consider, but the underlying psychiatric way of thinking remains individual degeneracy, materialism, and genetic determinism, which together demand the assumption that genes are ultimately responsible for all human existence and consciousness — even motivations and faith. Acknowledged by many molecular psychiatrists and geneticists, "endophenotypic thinking" — as Panksepp calls it — is yet another way to

---

[590] Panksepp, "Emotional Endophenotypes in Evolutionary Psychiatry," 774.

describe the "neo-Kraepelinian ideology"/"the bio-psycho-social perspective."[591]

The chain or pathology that psychiatric geneticists insist upon is that diagnostic symptoms (phenotypes; C) are caused by neural dysfunctions (intermediate phenotypes; B) which are ultimately caused by genetic risks (genotypes; A) (see table 1).

GENETIC THEORY OF PATHOLOGY - TABLE 1

Genotypes (A)	Endophenotypes (B)	Phenotypes (C)
Genes →	Neural dysfunction & nurture (e.g., trauma)→	Cognitive, emotional, & behavioral symptoms

Psychiatrists C. Feinstein and L. Chahal expose how psychiatrists assume that genes cause perceived symptoms:

> Advances in understanding the human genome and clinical application have led to identification of genetically based disorders that have distinctive behavioral phenotypes and risk for serious psychiatric disorders. Some patients have unrecognized genetic disorders presenting as psychiatric symptoms. Practitioners must be

---

[591] Vikram Patel, et. al., *Mental and Neurological Public Health: A Global Perspective* (San Diego: Academic Press, 2010), 477.

knowledgeable about the association between symptoms and underlying genetic bases.[592]

A large group of German psychiatrists and bioengineers also share their own attempt to link symptoms to the nervous system and the nervous system to the genes (to form a theoretical path), while at the same time admitting that there is no concrete evidence to do so:

> Schizophrenia is increasingly recognized as a disorder of distributed neural dynamics, but the molecular and genetic contributions are poorly understood . . . . Our results identify a potential dynamic network intermediate phenotype related to the genetic liability for schizophrenia that manifests as altered reconfiguration of brain networks during working memory. The phenotype appears to be influenced by NMDA receptor antagonism, consistent with a critical role for glutamate in the temporal coordination of neural networks and the pathophysiology of schizophrenia.[593]

As already noted, the metaphysical phenotypes (C) cannot be empirically correlated to genes. Therefore, psychiatric geneticists seek only to focus on somatic or material endophenotypes (B) and genotypes (A) in establishing both correlations and attempting to prove materialistic theories of causation.

The speculative theory is that if the genome (A) and the nervous system (B) can be shown to correlate scientifically,

[592] C. Feinstein and L. Chahal, "Psychiatric Phenotypes Associated with Neurogentic Disorders," *The Psychiatric Clinics of North America* 32 (1) (March 2009): 15; doi: 10.1016/j.psc.2008.12.001.

[593] U Braun, A. Shafer, and D.S. Bassett et al., "Dynamic Brain Network Reconfiguration as a potential Schizophrenia Genetic Risk Mechanism Modulated by NMDA Receptor Function," *Proceedings of the National Academy of Sciences of the United States* vol. 113 (44) (November 1, 2016): 12568.

then the core symptoms or phenomena of the construct —
though metaphysical — (C) must also correlate:

> Investigating the genetic roots [A] of psychiatric disorders
> is one of the most important potential uses of
> endophenotypes [B]. We know that most psychiatric
> disorders are highly heritable, but the phenotypes [C] of
> these disorders — the signs and symptoms — almost
> always result from combinations of many genes [A] as
> well as their interactions with environmental influences
> [B].[594]

Since humanists reject dualism, the metaphysical is
reduced to material explanations even if no empirical
evidence exists to justify this faith. Psychiatric geneticist
and neuroscientist for the National Institutes of Health
(NIH) Roberta Rasetti and Daniel Weinberger explicate,

> To link a gene effect in brain to the gene effect on risk for
> the syndromal diagnosis, it is necessary to show that the
> brain effect is a biological substrate also linked to illness
> risk, a so-called intermediate phenotype
> [endophenotype]. An intermediate phenotype related to
> mental illness is a heritable trait that is located in the path
> of pathogenesis from genetic predisposition to
> psychopathology. **The path goes from relatively simple
> effects in cells [A], to more complex effects in neural
> circuits in the brain [B], to much more complex effects
> on the emergent phenomenology of these simpler
> effects, i.e. behavior and psychiatric syndromes [C]**
> [emphasis added].[595]

[594] Harvard Medical School, "Endophenotypes," *Harvard Health Publishing*
(September 2007): https://www.health.harvard.edu/ newsletter_article/
Endophenotypes.

[595] Roberta Rasetti and Daniel R. Weinberger, "Intermediate Phenotypes in
Psychiatric Disorders," *Current Opinion in Genetics & Development* Vol. 21 (3)
(2011): 342–343; doi:10.1016/j.gde.2011.02.003.

Neo-Kraepelinian faith asserts that if a path or "pathology" can be empirically established from the genome to the brain, then symptoms or phenotypes are assumed to be caused by the human genome based upon an observable somatic link. Rasetti and Weinberger continue:

> From genes to behavior, Genes encode for molecules, not specific symptoms. **The abnormal behaviors observed in psychiatric disorders (such as delusions, hallucinations and cognitive deficits in schizophrenia) are the product of intermediate steps that occur between genes and behavior, such as cell activity and neural circuits.** An intermediate phenotype is a heritable trait that is located on the pathogenesis path from genetic predisposition to psychopathology and is likely associated with a more basic and proximal etiological process and therefore more amenable to genetic investigation [emphasis added].[596]

German neurobiologists concur, noting the same gene to brain to behavior "strategy" or hypothesized pathology (A to B to C) underlying the Kraepelinian eugenic hereditary theory:

> The search for quantifiable biological mediators of genetic risk or 'intermediate phenotypes' **is an essential strategy in psychiatric neuroscience** and a useful tool for exploring the complex relationships between genes [A], neural circuits [B] and behaviors [C]. In recent years, the examination of connectivity-based intermediate phenotypes has gained increasing popularity in the study of schizophrenia, a brain disorder that manifests in early adulthood and disturbs a wide range of neural network functions. To date, several potential connectivity phenotypes [C] have been identified that link neuroimaging measures of neural circuit [B] interaction to

[596] Ibid.

genetic susceptibility [A] for schizophrenia [emphasis added].[597]

This "strategy" is not objective science, but conjecture, as other neuropsychiatrists indicate:

> The search for the intermediate neural mechanisms of psychiatric risk genes has been a complicated endeavor for several reasons. First, the majority of psychiatric risk genes are not "functional" in the traditional sense of a coding variant, and their effect size is rather small. This implicates that very large sample sizes are necessary in order to characterize the associated neural correlates. Second, **the operational criteria implemented in modern classification systems are entirely descriptive**, but, at the same time, there is no one-to-one mapping between risk gene variants and neural system mechanisms or between neural mechanisms and psychopathology . . . . **The intermediate phenotype strategy takes advantage of the fact that many genetic variants associated with psychiatric disorders are frequently expressed in the normal population** [emphasis added].[598]

Worth repeating is that "genetic susceptibility," "genetic predisposition," "hereditary risk," and "polygenic risk scores" are all phrases that expose the original eugenic bio-deterministic and materialistic philosophies which are utilized to uphold created psychiatric disorders.

597 H. Cao, L. Dixson, A. Meyer-Lindenberg, H. Tost, "Functional Connectivity Measures as Schizophrenia Intermediate Phenotypes: Advances, Limitations, and Future Directions," *Current Opinion in Neurobiology* vol. 36 (February 2016): 7; doi: 10.1016/j.conb.2015.07.008.

598 Heike Tost, Tajvar Alam, and Andreas Meyer-Lindenberg, "Dopamine and Psychosis: Theory, Pathomechanisms and Intermediate Phenotypes," *Neuroscience and Biobehavioral Reviews* vol. 34 (5) (April 2010): 689–700; doi:10.1016/j.neubiorev.2009.06.005.

When studies show how the human genome and brain correlate (studies should reveal somatic correlations in all individuals), the claim is made that the construct of schizophrenia is both real and that the genomic etiological theory edges closer to being validated:

> "For the first time, we were able to identify 10 genes that when disrupted, dramatically increase risk for schizophrenia," said Dr. Singh. He noted that two of the 10 genes coded for glutamate receptors, a type of protein known to be crucial in communication among brain cells. By pinpointing glutamate receptors as genetically involved in disease, **this finding strongly suggests that decreased function of these receptors drives disease symptoms**, and that this system can potentially be a target for future therapies.[599]

Findings such as these can only "strongly suggest" a material cause of metaphysical symptoms (such as delusions) when materialism drives theory, research, and interpretation of somatic variances. In an article published in late 2019 in the *Journal of American Medical Association* (*JAMA*), dozens of psychiatric geneticists provide another example in their conclusions:

> These analyses identified several genomic regions of interest that require further exploration and validation. This data seems to demonstrate the utility of endophenotypes [B] for resolving the genetic [A] architecture of schizophrenia and characterizing the underlying biological dysfunctions. Understanding the molecular basis of these endophenotypes may help to identify novel treatment targets and pave the way for

[599] American Society of Human Genetics, "New insights into biological underpinnings of schizophrenia," *ScienceDaily* (October 15, 2019): www.science daily.com/releases/2019/10/191015192940.htm

precision-based medicine in schizophrenia and related
psychotic disorders [emphasis added].[600]

It cannot be overstated that proving how bodily systems
and experiences (genotypes and endophenotypes) correlate
is not proof that metaphysical phenotypes are caused by
genetic processes. In fact, no one has ever shown at a
molecular level how a gene forces or even influences
someone to believe falsely (delusions) or to have false
sensory perceptions (hallucinations). Several members of
the International Society of Psychiatric Genetics recognize
this truth:

> Even today, most psychiatric disorders lack an
> explanatory molecular or cellular pathology. In most
> cases, they are likely to be the consequence of a
> multifactorial etiology with numerous environmental and
> genetic components.[601]

Though the claims are made somewhat dogmatically that
this psychiatric hope will one day be realized, valid
scientific exploration can never objectively examine or
correlate the metaphysical with the physical. To further
complicate matters, as previously set forth, many people
who are diagnosed as having schizophrenia or other
alleged "severe mental illnesses" have relatively "normal

[600] Tiffany Greenwood, L.C. Lazzeroni, A.X. Maihofer, et al., "Genome-wide Association of Endophenotypes for Schizophrenia from the Consortium on the Genetics of Schizophrenia (COGS) Study," *JAMA Psychiatry Online* (October 9, 2019): doi:10.1001/jamapsychiatry.2019.2850.

[601] Tobias B. Halene, Gregor Hasler, Amanda Mitchell, and Schahram Akbarian, *Psychiatric Genetics: A Primer for Clinicians and Basic Scientists* edited by Thomas G. Schulze and Francis J. McMahon (New York: Oxford University Press, 2018), 144.

brains," which invalidates the speculated pathology of mental disorders.[602]

In actuality, even if it were possible to fully understand and precisely examine the human genome and neural systems on a molecular level, no scientific investigation could ever empirically prove that metaphysical beliefs or first-person perceptions are caused by the body. Such conjecture can only be done in philosophical theory, not in valid science. This reality may be what led the influential chair of the *DSM-IV* and former head of psychiatry at Duke University medical school, Allen Frances, to admonish future psychiatrists in 2019 to

> read the scientific literature with great skepticism and awareness that most studies do not replicate, positive results are always exaggerated, and negative results are usually buried. **Do not be wowed by genetic findings — so far, they have flopped in finding causes and have no place in planning treatments** . . . . **For every complex question, there is a simple, reductionistic answer — and it's wrong.** Don't expect or believe simple answers to complex questions, such as "What causes mental illness and how best to treat it?" [emphasis added][603]

Drs. Rasetti and Weinberger also attest that connecting differing somatic changes does nothing to validate the conjecture that the body causes false beliefs or false perceptions:

---

[602] Chand, Dwyer, et. al., "Two distinct neuroanatomical subtypes of schizophrenia revealed using machine learning," *Brain* awaa025 (Oxford University Press) (February 27, 2020): https://doi.org/10.1093/brain/awaa025.

[603] Allen Frances, "Advice to Young Psychiatrists from a very old one," *Psychiatric Times Online* (October 4, 2019): https://www.psychiatrictimes.com/couch-crisis/advice-young-psychiatrists-very-old-one/page/0/1.

A crucial point in identifying the mechanisms through which genes confer risk for psychiatric disorders is to define whether the brain phenotype that the risk gene modulates is a biological mechanism implicated in the psychiatric disorder and in risk for the psychiatric disorder. **Finding an association between a gene and a brain function does not mean that that association is related to the mechanism of risk for the clinical illness** [emphasis added].[604]

Genetic research into psychiatric constructs will always fall short of objective conclusions, since phenomenology and metaphysical human phenomena cannot be scientifically studied and empirically correlated to the human genome.

Moreover, observable and measurable variances in the genome and nervous system do not prove how those variances occurred. In other words, the reality that there are correlating genotypes and endophenotypes that are negatively altered does not prove that these variances are inherited rather than caused by one's thinking or faith. Realistically, genetic variances are expected within the human race.[605] The "science" of psychiatric genetics, then, rests primarily on believing in the Kraepelinian-hereditary-phenomenology, on assuming that undesirable differences equal fixed individual degeneracy/disorder, and on claiming scientific validity for descriptive and subjective

---

[604] Rasetti and Weinberger, "Intermediate Phenotypes in Psychiatric Disorders,"342-343.

[605] "Because the genes may be different in different individuals and families, clear and useful genetic findings are hard to come by." Harvard Medical School, "Endophenotypes," *Harvard Health Publishing* (September 2007): https://www.health.harvard.edu/ newsletter_article/Endophenotypes.

humanistic constructs based solely on correlating bodily systems and carefully crafted statistical measurements.

Phenotypic Variations

The field of phenomenology also allows those granted social authority to change how human phenomena are interpreted and classified. When suggested psychiatric symptoms manifest differently than listed in the diagnostic system, then new constructs (subconstructs) can be created and stated as "phenotypic variations" (e.g., bipolar I and II). The construct of schizoaffective disorder, for example, is now said to be a phenotypic variation of schizophrenia rather than a separate disorder as published in the *DSM-5*:

> More problematic is a diagnosis of schizoaffective disorder which does not appear to be a stable clinical entity. This would suggest that schizoaffective disorder is not a true clinical syndrome but rather a phenotypic variation.[606]

Consider as another example the psychiatric construct of anorexia or the broader construct of eating disorders. Since the existence of the syndrome of anorexia rests on delusional thinking and presents genetic variances similar to those listed in the construct of schizophrenia, many psychiatric researchers have concluded that only the content of the delusion and the corresponding behavior

---

[606] Y.D. Lapierre, "Schizophrenia and Manic-Depression: Separate Illnesses or a Continuum?" *Canadian Journal of Psychiatry* Vol. 39 (9) (November 1994): 59.

differentiates most severe types of mental illness.[607] Professor of psychiatry at the University of Toronto Mary Seeman compares the two allegedly different psychiatric disorders, revealing that they are only truly different in the content of their delusions and the subsequent behavior:

> Eating disorders and psychotic disorders are both characterized by distorted thoughts, overvalued ideas, depersonalization and derealization phenomena, and delusions. Moreover, auditory hallucinations, considered to be the hallmark of psychosis, can also occur in anorexia nervosa. A basic mistrust of others—a trait that often leads to social isolation, poor therapeutic alliance, and poor treatment adherence—is common to both eating disorders and psychotic disorders. The ability to put oneself in the mindset of the other person (theory of mind) is deficient in both disorders, as are difficulties in shifting sets or being able to pass quickly from one mode of thinking to another.[608]

In late 2019, Dr. Seeman published a follow-up article in which she suggests that anorexia is not a separate disorder from schizophrenia, but a "phenotypic expression":

> The body image disturbance at the heart of anorexia nervosa is a false perception akin to the perceptual disorders found in schizophrenia. Additional psychotic features associated with eating disorders—usually transient—have been attributed to the effects of starvation

---

[607] For further study on how delusional thinking is the basis of all "severe psychiatric disorders," how the historical definition of insanity is rooted in identifying people who are deceived in various ways, and how there exists only one unitary psychosis ("condition of the soul"), see Daniel R. Berger II, *The Insanity of Madness: Defining Mental Illness* (Taylors, SC: Alethia International Publications, 2018).

[608] Mary V. Seeman, "Eating Disorders and Psychosis," *Psychiatric Times Online* (April 28, 2016), 2; https://www.psychiatrictimes.com/special-reports/eating-disorders-and-psychosis/page/0/1.

and electrolyte imbalance. Eating disorders and psychotic disorders are both characterized by distorted thoughts, overvalued ideas, depersonalization and derealization phenomena, and delusions. Moreover, auditory hallucinations, considered to be the hallmark of psychosis, can also occur in anorexia nervosa . . . . Antipsychotics are sometimes used off label for eating disorders. The reason is because clinicians find it difficult to distinguish the firm belief that one is fat (when that is clearly not the case) from a delusion. **Despite several potential explanations for the co-occurrence of eating disorders, it is possible that eating disorders and psychotic disorders are different phenotypic expressions of a similar genetic predisposition** [emphasis added].[609]

When carefully examined, it becomes apparent that these allegedly different psychiatric disorders are in actuality different manifestations of the same human struggle with deceit as are all alleged "severe mental disorders."

The capability that psychiatrists have to decide if human phenomena become categorized as distinct psychiatric syndromes or as phenotypic variations, along with their altering between the two ideas, highlights that these descriptive concepts are socially constructed rather than being stable clinical entities. As symptoms differ and fall outside of psychiatry's established value system, disorders can be recast as "phenotypic expressions," "phenotypic variations," or just eliminated altogether because of a change of heart rather than a scientific discovery — such as

[609] Mary V. Seeman, "When Eating Disorders and Psychosis Co-Exist: 6 Take Home Points," *Psychiatric Times Online* (October 23, 2019): https:// www.psychiatrictimes.com/schizophrenia/when-eating-disorders-and-psychosis-co-exist-6-take-home-points?rememberme=1&elq_mid=9318&elq _cid=893295&GUID=31158D64-F01A-4DEA-AC1A-D3CE843FC9BC.

occurred in the case of homosexuality between the *DSM-II* and *DSM-III.*

By utilizing the terms *endophenotype, phenotype,* and *genotype* — combined with the ability to study specific genes in detail — psychiatrists seem to be more advanced in their theory. But the theory remains the dated and speculative Kraepelinian eugenic hope — founded upon the teachings of the eugenicists of old — of finding hereditary predispositions and risks by describing all of human phenomena within humanistic phenomenology.

In 1938, Karl Menninger — at that time "one of America's leading psychiatrists"[610] — wrote in his book *Man Against Himself,*

> I believe that our best defense against self-destructiveness lies in the courageous application of intelligence to human phenomenology. If such is our nature, it were better that we knew it and knew it in all its protean manifestations. To see all forms of self-destruction from the standpoint of their dominant principles would seem to be logical progress toward self-preservation and toward a unified view of medical science. [Researchers] and others who have consistently applied these principles to the understanding of human sickness and all those failures and capitulations that we propose to regard as variant forms of suicide [sic]. No one is more aware than I of the unevenness of the evidence to follow and of the speculative nature of some of the theory, but in this I beg the indulgence of the read to whom I submit that **to have a theory, even a false one, is better than to attribute events to pure chance.** "Chance"

---

[610] As stated on the cover of his book (Karl A. Menninger, *Man Against Himself* [New York: Harcourt, Brace, and Company, 1938], preface vii-viii).

explanations leave us in the dark; a theory will lead to confirmation or rejection [emphasis added].[611]

Genotypes and phenotypes are symbols of mankind's attempt to apply his own wisdom in explaining human phenomena within a restricted bio-psycho-social faith. It is a false and destructive religion which can never be empirically proven as promised but continues to be sustained despite its pseudoscientific nature. Ironically, this Kraepelinian statistical approach is based entirely upon humanistic evolutionary theory that champions human nature as naturally selected by chance rather than diagnosed within categorical systems developed out of people's faith.

SPECULATED MODELS

Though most evolutionary geneticists agree that genes are responsible for all of human nature, they do not all agree on what that model should look like. Unsurprisingly, when more carefully examined, the dogma of genetic causes is not concrete, and there is wide disagreement among psychiatric geneticists on which genes and how many genes are involved in creating supposed psychiatric disorders. Furthermore, there exists a growing list of "potentially" causative genes that sees no end in sight. Because of both the large number of suggested genes as well as the impossibility of explaining how a gene produces delusions at a molecular level, psychiatric geneticists and academics have suggested three models to

---

[611] Ibid., preface vii-viii.

consider within neo-Kraepelinian thinking: *single gene*, *polygene*, and *omnigene* theories.

Single-Gene Theory

Possibly the most well-known and historic theory of psychiatric genetics is the single-gene theory. This straightforward position hypothesizes that there is a single gene that allegedly causes schizophrenia.

Franz Joseph Kallmann, Kraepelinian eugenicist and friend of Ernst Rüdin, is considered to be the father of the single-gene theory. Renowned Harvard geneticist Richard Lewontin, neuroscientist Steven Rose, and psychologist Leon Kamin express that

> perhaps the most influential psychiatric geneticist in the English-speaking world was a student of Rüdin's, the late Franz Kallmann. The blizzard of statistics published by Kallmann seemed to indicate conclusively that schizophrenia was a genetic phenomenon . . . . These figures led Kallmann to argue that schizophrenia could be attributed to a single recessive gene.[612]

Kallmann's single-recessive-gene hypothesis has sustained the propagation of the eugenics theory ever since WW2. Historian of science Pauline Mazumdar writes,

> By then, most geneticists accepted that eugenic sterilization could not rid society of its undesirables. But paradoxically, eugenics still had supporters even among its scientist critics, whom Kevles called 'reform eugenicists.' **My opinion is that there was no such sharp**

---

[612] Richard C. Lewontin, Steven Rose, and Leon J. Kamin, *Not in Our Genes: Biology, Ideology, and Human Nature 2nd edition* (Chicago: Haymarket Books, 2017), 207-208.

turning point in eugenics. Reliance on simple mendelian inheritance faded away, but eugenics continued much as before until after World War II. In this paper, I consider the history of the eugenics movement in terms of its concepts of the inheritance of 'feeble-mindedness' and **psychosis as single-gene recessives, and sterilization as a means of control** [emphasis added].[613]

But even within the single-gene theory, there are disagreements about which gene "likely" causes the phenotypes claimed as the core of schizophrenia. For example, the National Institutes of Health sees 22q11 as potentially causative in some cases:

> Deletions or duplications of genetic material in any of several chromosomes, which can affect multiple genes, are also thought to increase schizophrenia risk. In particular, a small deletion (microdeletion) in a region of chromosome 22 called 22q11 may be involved in a small percentage of cases of schizophrenia.[614]

One large group of geneticists discuss their own research: "The 22q11.2 deletion is found in one per 100–200 individuals with SCZ, making 22q11DS one of the strongest known genetic risk factors for SCZ."[615] While the claim is made rather dogmatically, the "science" is based largely on

---

[613] Pauline M. Mazumdar, "'Reform' Eugenics and the Decline of Mendelism," *Trends in Genetics* 18 (1) (January 2002): 48; https://www.ncbi.nlm.nih.gov/pubmed/11750701.

[614] Genetics Home Reference, "Schizophrenia," *National Institutes of Health* (2019): https://ghr.nlm.nih.gov/condition/schizophrenia#genes.

615 Tae-Yeon Eom, Seung Baek Han, Jieun Kim, et al., "Schizophrenia-related microdeletion causes defective ciliary motility and brain ventricle enlargement via microRNA-dependent mechanisms in mice," *Nature Communication* 11 (912) (2020): https://doi.org/10.1038/s41467-020-14628-y.

mice studies. What is more, these researchers admit in the same article that "despite this strong linkage, the mechanisms of ventricular enlargement in psychiatric disorders are mostly unknown." True to their faith, these researchers interpret the data to fit into their predisposition of "genetics will explain all of human nature."

Other researchers, however, disagree and pronounce the C4 gene as primarily causative:

> In what has been hailed a "breakthrough" in schizophrenia research, scientists from Harvard Medical School, the Broad Institute and Boston Children's Hospital - all in Massachusetts - have discovered how a gene called complement component 4 (C4) plays a key role in schizophrenia development. The research team - including senior author Steven McCarroll, associate professor of genetics and director of genetics for the Stanley Center at Harvard - says their findings may aid the development of much-needed new treatments and preventive strategies for schizophrenia. Schizophrenia is a mental disorder characterized by hallucinations, delusions, dysfunctional thought processes and agitated body movements.[616]

The C4 model is not a proven fact, however, but a "hypothesis-driven approach."[617] Despite its failure, many theorists and researchers alike still uphold the single-gene theory, though there is a growing trend toward its dismissal.

---

[616] Honor Whiteman, "Schizophrenia breakthrough: Scientists Shed Light on Biological Cause," *Medical News Today* (February 4, 2016): https://www.medicalnewstoday.com/articles/306063.php.

[617] Robert A. McCutcheon, Tiago Reis Marques, and Oliver D. Howes, "Schizophrenia—An Overview," *JAMA Psychiatry Online* (October 30, 2019): doi:10.1001/jamapsychiatry.2019.3360.

The single-gene theory is also not restricted to the psychiatric construct of schizophrenia. There are attempts within psychiatric genetics to locate single genes to explain the etiology of virtually all created psychiatric constructs and human nature. In 2019, for instance, the single gene theory made global headlines as researchers pronounced after extensive research that they could not discover a single gene that could be attributed to causing the mindsets, emotions, and behaviors culturally and descriptively referred to as homosexuality or being "gay." Contributor Megan Brooks reports in the *Medscape Psychiatry*:

> "There is no gay gene that determines whether someone has same-sex partners," lead author Andrea Ganna, PhD, Center for Genomic Medicine, Massachusetts General Hospital and Harvard Medical School, Boston, said during a telebriefing with reporters.

Despite the empirical evidence, geneticists are still unwilling to give up materialism and bio-determinism and continue to assert that human behavior — including moral behavior — has "biological underpinnings:"

> With this study, "we see how large-scale GWAS studies can give insights into the biological underpinnings of behavior, **but at the same time we are warned that behavior phenotypes are complex and we cannot draw simplistic conclusions,**" Valda Vinson, PhD, research editor for Science, said at the briefing [emphasis added].[618]

[618] Megan Brooks, "No Single 'Gay Gene': New Data," *Medscape Psychiatry* (August 30, 2019): https://www.medscape.com/view article/917500?nlid=131348_2051&src=WNL_mdplsnews_190830_mscpedit_psyc&uac=264124BV&spon=12&impID=2078660&faf=1.

Noteworthy is that Valda Vinson identifies mindsets and behavior (in this case homosexuality) as a phenotype. One cannot, however, objectively and reliably study motives, preferences, fears, desires and other metaphysical underpinnings of moral behavior using scientific tools. These human phenomena will always be approached through one's philosophy (phenomenology) and morality.

Homosexuality has historically been a psychiatric construct/syndrome much like the construct of race and thereafter schizophrenia. In fact, homosexuality was one of Kraepelin's original categories of degeneracy, and it was once considered by the APA to be a mental disorder formally categorized in the *DSM* until the publication of the *DSM-III*. Former APA president-elect and head of psychiatry at Columbia University Jeffrey Lieberman briefly describes the APA's ensuing dilemma in considering the removal of the psychiatric construct of homosexuality from the *DSM-III*:

> Like everyone at the APA, [Bob] Spitzer knew these arguments were taking a toll on the reliability of his profession. He believed that mental illnesses were genuine medical disorders rather than social constructs — but now he was about to declare homosexuality to be exactly such a social construct. If he disavowed homosexuality, he could open the door to the antipsychiatrists to argue that other disorders, such as schizophrenia and depression, should also be disavowed.[619]

As Lieberman notes, the issue of homosexuality highlights how psychiatric disorders have been constructed solely upon moral judgment and not upon medicine or science.

---

[619] Lieberman, *Shrinks*, 125.

The remarks made by John Oldham, another former APA president, on the significance of the APA's decision to remove homosexuality affirms how psychiatric degeneracy is constructed subjectively:

> What qualified as an actual, legitimate illness, and what didn't, was really an interesting history. Sexual disorders were classified as personality disorders in *DSM-I*. That is a very different way that we later thought about it when they became viewed as disorders all by themselves. But it was the progress based on the courage of this man, and many others who followed, that led to the recognition that sexual orientation was not something that should be qualified or classified as an illness.[620]

It is also significant that homosexuality was dogmatically claimed to be genetically caused until 2019.[621] In 2018, for instance, one study emphatically suggested four genetic variants on chromosomes 7, 11, 12, and 15, to be causative.[622]

The construct of homosexuality is a good example of how psychiatric constructs are created by theorists within humanistic phenomenology, attributed to single or multiple gene variances, and imposed upon society as empirically sound medical disorders without solid

---

[620] John M. Oldham, "A Brief History of American Psychiatry: From a Founding Father to Dr. Anonymous," *Medscape Psychiatry* (November 7, 2019): https://www.medscape.com/viewarticle/917451?nlid=132561_424&src =WNL_mdplsfeat_191112_mscpedit_psyc&uac=264124BV&spon=12&impID=2 164621&faf=1.

[621] Brooks, "No Single 'Gay Gene.'"

[622] Michael Price, "Giant Study Links DNA variants to Same-sex Behavior," *Science* (October 20, 2018): https://www.sciencemag.org/ news/2018/10/giant-study-links-dna-variants-same-sex-behavior.

evidence to validate such claims.[623] In an interview with fellow Columbia University psychiatrist Lloyd Sederer, Jack Drescher reports on this tendency:

> The history of psychiatry and homosexuality begins in the 19th century in Europe. Most people attribute this to Richard von Krafft-Ebing, a German-Austrian psychiatrist who wrote a very famous catalog of sexual diversity called *Psychopathia Sexualis*. If you were in the book, it meant that there was something psychopathological about you, because that is how it worked in the 19th century. **You just needed a psychiatrist to say you had an illness to have one.** He wrote about homosexuality; he also wrote about transgender presentations but he called that homosexuality too. **He was famous for popularizing the word "homosexuality"** .... **Homosexuality was a sin. The sin of sodomy. And what Krafft-Ebing and many people in psychiatry did afterwards was say, "This is not about religion. This is about science."** In the language of science, many psychiatrists said, "This is what we call illness," or "This is what we call pathological or psychopathological." That became the starting point for many people [emphasis added].[624]

Drescher later exposes that such a pathological position about human phenomena is actually not scientific and that the gay gene theory has failed:

> A lot of my work, particularly with gay men in my psychiatry/psychotherapy practice, has to do with people trying to figure out why they are gay. I'd like [people] to know that today in 2019, we don't know why anybody is

---

[623] Berger, *Mental Illness: The Necessity for Faith and Authority*, 77-81.

[624] Lloyd L. Sederer and Jack Drescher in accordance with Columbia University Psychiatry, "The 'Checkered' History of Psychiatry's Views on Homosexuality," *Medscape Psychiatry* (December 3, 2019): https://www.medscape.com/viewarticle/921143?nlid=132938_424&src=WNL_mdplsfeat_191210_mscpedit_psyc&uac=264124BV&spon=12&impID=2199579&faf=1.

gay. Some people say you are born gay. Some people say
you are converted gay. We don't know why people are
gay. We just know that it's very difficult to change, and
that for many people, it feels intrinsic to who they are. . . .
But everybody comes in [wondering], "Why am I gay?"
Gay gene theories tend to support the view that people
are born gay . . . . There was no finding that there is one
gay gene. Some studies were done in the '90s by Dean
Hamer and his associates, saying they found a gene on the
X chromosome that they thought might be a cause of
homosexuality. But this study says no, there is no one
gene that causes it and we still don't know what causes
it.[625]

Sederer responded to Drescher's insights in their interview
by admitting that there are no objective answers to explain
people's internal perspectives and struggles:

It looks like, even in the whole area of gene studies, we're
discovering that there are no simple answers. Perhaps
people's identity and sexuality are a complex matter of
genes and environment; we just don't know.[626]

Sederer's comments also expose that one's internal
perspective or "identity" (phenomenology) is the main
issue in all that is framed as normal and abnormal within
psychiatry.

Polygenic Theory

As popular as the single gene theory has been, many
psychiatric geneticists and figureheads have begun to reject
the theory in favor of the polygenic position. The polygenic
theory of schizophrenia was first proposed by psychiatrists

[625] Ibid.

[626] Ibid.

L. L. Grottesman and J. Shields in 1967.[627] In some ways, the polygenic theory became necessary, since so many different single genes have been suggested as causative by a variety of researchers.[628] The polygenic model accommodates this dilemma, as it suggests that multiple genes "mutate" through natural selection to cause schizophrenia (or at least a risk for schizophrenia) and other alleged mental illnesses:

> Think of your genes as a blueprint for your body. If there's a change to these instructions, it can sometimes increase your odds for developing diseases like schizophrenia. Doctors don't think there's just one "schizophrenia gene." Instead, they think it takes many genetic changes, or mutations, to raise your chances of having the mental illness.[629]

While the claim is made somewhat dogmatically, there is no actual objective evidence to make the assertion valid. In effect, claiming that mental struggles are caused by many genes further confounds the hereditary theory. These same researchers continue, stating that

> many genes play a role in your odds of getting schizophrenia. A change to any of them can do it. But usually it's several small changes that add up and lead to

[627] L. L. Gottesman & J. Shields, "A polygenic theory of schizophrenia," *Proceedings of the National Academy of Sciences of the United States of America* vol. 58 (1) (July 1967): 199–205; doi:10.1073/pnas.58.1.199.

[628] Douglas M. Ruderfer, Alexander W. Charney, Ben Readhead, Brian A. Kidd, Anna K. Kähler, Paul J. Kenny, Stuart A. Scott, Pamela Sklar, et al., "Polygenic Overlap Between Schizophrenia Risk and Antipsychotic Response: a Genomic Medicine Approach," *The Lancet Psychiatry* Vol. 3 (4) (April, 2016): 350–357; doi:10.1016/S2215-0366(15)00553-2.

[629] "What Causes Schizophrenia?" WebMD (2019): https://www.webmd.com/schizophrenia/what-causes-schizophrenia#1.

a higher risk. **Doctors aren't sure how genetic changes lead to schizophrenia** [emphasis added].[630]

"Genetic odds" "or "polygenic risks" identify this clear eugenic faith that has become the current trend in psychiatric genetics.

Professor of psychiatry at Columbia University Medical School, Jeffrey Lieberman, offers his own testimony of conversion from the single-gene theory to the polygenic belief:

> One of the most promising arenas of research is genetics. It is virtually certain that no single gene alone is responsible for any particular mental illness, but through increasingly powerful genetic techniques we are starting to understand how certain patterns or networks of genes confer levels of risk.[631]

Like Lieberman, there are many psychiatric researchers who have rejected the single-gene theory and prefer the belief that many genes are responsible for mental illnesses:

> Genetic epidemiology has provided consistent evidence over many years that schizophrenia has a genetic component, and that this genetic component is complex, polygenic, and involves epistatic interaction between loci. **Molecular genetics studies have, however, so far failed to identify any DNA variant that can be demonstrated to contribute to either liability to schizophrenia or to any identifiable part of the underlying pathology.** Replication studies of positive findings have been difficult to interpret for a variety of reasons. First, few have reproduced the initial findings, which may be due either to random variation between two samples in the genetic inputs involved, or to a lack of power to replicate an effect

[630] Ibid.

[631] Lieberman, *Shrinks*, 306.

at a given alpha level. Where positive data have been found in replication studies, the positioning of the locus has been unreliable, leading no closer to positional cloning of genes involved. However, an assessment of all the linkage studies performed over the past ten years does suggest a number of regions where positive results are found numerous times. These include regions on chromosomes 1, 2, 4, 5, 6, 7, 8, 9, 10, 13, 15, 18, 22 and the X [emphasis added].[632]

Though the National Institutes of Health asserts 22q11 as possibly causative in some cases, they also list sixteen more genes that are potentially "associated" with schizophrenia.[633] Other psychiatric geneticists, utilizing the GWAS, have suggested that the *CACNA1C, GRIN2A, AKT3,* and *HCN1* genes are associated with schizophrenia.[634] In late 2019, the American Society of Human Genetics added 10 new "potential" genes to this ever-growing list:

Researchers have implicated 10 new genes in the development of schizophrenia using a method called whole exome sequencing, the analysis of the portion of DNA that codes for proteins . . . . Schizophrenia is a severe psychiatric disorder, the risk of which can be

---

[632] Brien P. Riley and Peter McGuffin, "Linkage and associated studies of schizophrenia," *Medical Genetics* Vol 97 (1) (October 23, 2002): https://doi.org /10.1002/(SICI)1096-8628(200021)97:1%3C23::AID-AJMG5%3E3.0.CO;2-K.

[633] Genetics Home Reference, "Schizophrenia," *National Institutes of Health* (2019): https://ghr.nlm.nih.gov/condition/ schizophrenia#genes. Accessed September 2, 2019.

[634] Douglas M. Ruderfer, Alexander W. Charney, Ben Readhead, Brian A. Kidd, Anna K. Kähler, Paul J. Kenny, Stuart A. Scott, Pamela Sklar, et al., "Polygenic Overlap Between Schizophrenia Risk and Antipsychotic Response: a Genomic Medicine Approach," *The Lancet Psychiatry* Vol. 3 (4) (April, 2016): 350–357; doi:10.1016/S2215-0366(15)00553-2.

dramatically increased by the disruption of certain protein-coding genes. Since these changes are so strongly selected against in every generation, Dr. Singh explained, they are rare in the population and researchers need a very large sample size to study them with enough statistical power to draw robust conclusions.[635]

Others like geneticists at Vanderbilt University Genetics Institute speculate that 104 different types of genes somehow cause schizophrenia and that other genes could be potentially identified.[636] Still, more recent studies (2019) suggest "145 loci in total,"[637] while others believe the number of "risk loci" to be over 180:

> Genome-wide association studies (GWASs) have identified over 180 independent schizophrenia risk loci. Nevertheless, how the risk variants in the reported loci confer schizophrenia susceptibility remains largely unknown.[638]

But the estimates do not stop at 180 "risk variants." Prominent German genetic and phenomic researchers, Thomas Schulze and Kristina Adorjan, claim that "more

[635] American Society of Human Genetics, "New insights into biological underpinnings of schizophrenia," *ScienceDaily* (October 15, 2019): www.sciencedaily.com/releases/2019/10/191015192940.htm

[636] Vanderbilt University Medical Center, "Researchers find high-risk genes for Schizophrenia," *Science News* (April 22, 2019): https://www.sciencedaily.com/releases/2019/04/190422170538.htm.

[637] Antonio F. Pardiñas, Peter Holmans, Andrew J. Pocklington, et al., "Common schizophrenia alleles are enriched in mutation-intolerant genes and in regions under strong background selection," *Nature Genetics* vol. 51 (7) (July, 2019): 1193; doi:10.1038/s41588-018-0059-2.

[638] Y. Huo, S. Li, J. Liu, X Li, X. J. Luo, "Functional Genomics Reveal Gene Regulatory Mechanisms Underlying Schizophrenia Risk," *Nature Communications* vol. 10 (1) (February 2019): 670.

than 250 genetic loci have been found for schizophrenia."[639] These "risk loci" and "risks scores," which allegedly identify large numbers of "associated genes," are largely founded upon Kraepelin's, Rüdin's and Kallmann's controversial and discredited twin studies:

> Twin and other studies have consistently shown there is a large genetic component to schizophrenia, with heritability estimated at around 80%. Heritability refers to how much of the variability of the trait in the population is attributable to between-individual genetic variation and does not allow for either the estimation of risk at the individual level or the identification of any specific genetic loci associated with disorder. In recent years, technological advances and falling costs have made genome-wide association studies (GWAS) possible, allowing an unbiased, data-driven approach to identify loci associated with schizophrenia. Genome-wide association studies show that multiple common variants, each of small effect, are associated with schizophrenia. After adjusting for the number of tests, more than 100 loci are significantly associated with schizophrenia. Thus schizophrenia, like many other common conditions, is a polygenic disorder in most patients. The development of GWAS has also enabled the construction of polygenic risk scores, which provide a genetic risk summary of the disorder based on the number of risk alleles an individual has, weighted by the odds ratio associated with each allele.[640]

---

[639] Thomas Schulze and Kristina Adorjan, "Psychiatric Genetics," *Psychiatric Times Online* vol. 35 (8) (August 23, 2018): http://www.psychiatric times.com/genetic-disorders/psychiatric-genetics-2018-genomic-revolution-friendly-data-sharing-and-global-partnerships.

640 Robert A. McCutcheon, Tiago Reis Marques, and Oliver D. Howes, "Schizophrenia—An Overview," *JAMA Psychiatry Online* (October 30, 2019): doi:10.1001/jamapsychiatry.2019.3360.

Though "risk" is asserted, there is no empirical evidence to sustain such conjecture. In another article, published in the *New England Journal of Medicine*, Professor of Neuroscience and Human Behavior at UCLA, Stephen Marder, and professor of psychiatry and psychology at Yale University, Tyrone Cannon, confirm the foundation of "risk factors" by referencing the same twin and familial studies, as well as the eugenic heritable risk figure of 80%:

> On the basis of twin and family studies, heritable factors are estimated to explain 80% of the risk of schizophrenia in a population. However, only a small portion of this heritable component has been shown to be attributable to common disease-associated single-nucleotide variants, each with a small effect on risk, or to larger but rare mutations, each with a putatively greater influence on risk.[641]

Although using twin studies as empirical evidence has been widely discredited by many historians, psychiatrists, and researchers,[642] eugenicists have viewed the statistical approach as seemingly objective and as providing a solid basis for estimates:

> Twin research was initiated in the nineteenth century by the British statistician and founder of the eugenics movement, Francis Galton . . . . Twin research was developed more fully in the 1920s and 1930s by Galton's followers in Germany, the United States, and the United Kingdom, and elsewhere. Many German eugenicists of the first half of the twentieth century preferred the term racial hygiene to eugenics. Early twin studies based on

641 Stephen R. Marder and Tyrone D. Cannon, "Schizophrenia," *NEJM* Vol. 381 (October 31, 2019): 1753-61; DOI: 10.1056/NEJMra1808803.

642 Lewontin, Rose, and Kamin, *Not in Our Genes*, 207-213.

reared-together pairs focused on IQ, criminality, schizophrenia, and several medical conditions.[643]

Bental and Pilgrim likewise note this sobering eugenic concept:

> That early work, which was reinforced by that of eminent eugenicist psychiatrists, such as Franz Kallmann and Eliot Slater after World War Two, led ultimately to large estimates of the "heritability" of schizophrenia, typically around 80%, which were assumed to leave little room for social causes of the disorder.[644]

Kraepelin, who based his hereditary/genetic theory of madness on both Galton's theory of twin studies and eugenic faith and Morel's concept of hereditary degeneration,[645] would provide the groundwork for Rüdin, Kallmann, and Slater to promote their eugenic narrative of 80% estimation for twin studies, which psychiatrists continue to insist upon as objective. The statistical approach in psychiatric genetics, which allegedly produces risk factors today, is the same "science" that was foundational to eugenics in Nazi Germany.

In addition to being based upon the Kraepelinian hereditary theory and Rüdin's and Kallmann's pseudoscientific twin studies, these studies are also conducted from a presuppositional phenomenology of evolutionary natural selection. As a case in point, the clear

---

643 "Twin Jay Joseph, *The Trouble with Twin Studies: A Reassessment of Twin Research in the Social and Behavioral Sciences* (New York: Routledge, 2014), 7-8.

644 Richard Bentall and David Pilgrim, "There Are No 'Schizophrenia Genes': Here's Why," *The Conversation* (April 8, 2016): https://theconversation.com/there-are-no-schizophrenia-genes-heres-why-57294.

645 Lewontin, Rose, and Kamin, *Not in Our Genes*, 223-20.

goal of eugenicists, stated by several researchers, was published in *JAMA Psychiatry* in 2019: "We aimed to explore the hypothesis that some form of natural selection is linked to the maintenance of common genetic risk in schizophrenia."[646] Psychiatric researchers with the International Society of Psychiatric Genetics express their similar view:

> In this review, we consider evolutionary perspectives of schizophrenia and of the empirical evidence that may support these perspectives. Proposed evolutionary explanations include balancing selection, fitness trade-offs, fluctuating environments, sexual selection, mutation-selection balance and genomic conflicts. We address the expectations about the genetic architecture of schizophrenia that are predicted by different evolutionary scenarios and discuss the implications for genetic studies. Several potential sources of "missing" heritability, including gene-environment interactions, epigenetic variation, and rare genetic variation are examined from an evolutionary perspective. **A better understanding of evolutionary history may provide valuable clues to the genetic architecture of schizophrenia and other psychiatric disorders, which is highly relevant to genetic studies that aim to detect genetic risk variants** [emphasis added].[647]

In still another article, published in *Biological Psychiatry*, numerous psychiatrists, psychopharmacologists, and

646 Robert A. McCutcheon, Tiago Reis Marques, and Oliver D. Howes, "Schizophrenia — An Overview," *JAMA Psychiatry Online* (October 30, 2019): doi:10.1001/jamapsychiatry.2019.3360.

647 J. Van Dongen and D.I Boomsma, "The Evolutionary Paradox and the missing Heritability of Schizophrenia," *American Journal of Medical Genetic, Neuropsychiatric Genetics: The Official Publication of the International Society of Psychiatric Genetics* Vol. 162b (2) (March, 2013): 122; doi: 10.1002/ajmg.b.32135.

geneticists express their common belief that schizophrenia is a form of evolutionary degeneracy:

> Why schizophrenia has accompanied humans throughout our history despite its negative effect on fitness remains an evolutionary enigma. It is proposed that schizophrenia is a by-product of the complex evolution of the human brain and a compromise for humans' language, creative thinking, and cognitive abilities . . . . **Our results suggest that there is a polygenic overlap between schizophrenia and NSS score, a marker of human evolution, which is in line with the hypothesis that the persistence of schizophrenia is related to the evolutionary process of becoming human** [emphasis added].[648]

Some researchers utilize an approach called "exome sequencing" (studying only part of the genome), whereas other geneticists employ an evolutionary tactic — "a statistical framework" — that they refer to as "the Neanderthal Selective Sweep (NSS) Score."[649] The Neanderthal tactic is based upon the theory that schizophrenia is a form of individual degeneracy, with schizophrenia representing a process of natural selection which explains a regression to an early evolutionary or Neanderthal stage. Several geneticists discuss this common belief in *Frontiers in Genetics*, one of the world's most influential journals in the field of human genetics:

> Schizophrenia is a psychiatric disorder with a worldwide prevalence of ~1%. The high heritability and reduced fertility among schizophrenia patients have raised an

---

[648] S. Srinivasan, F. Bettella, M. Mattingsdal, Y. Wang, et. al., "Genetic Markers of Human Evolution Are Enriched in Schizophrenia," *Biological Psychiatry* vol. 80 (4) (August 15, 2016): 284; doi: 10.1016/j.biopsych.2015.10.009.

[649] Ibid.

evolutionary paradox: **why has negative selection not eliminated schizophrenia associated alleles during evolution?** To address this question, we examined evolutionary markers, known as modern-human-specific (MD) sites and archaic-human-specific sites, using existing genome-wide association study (GWAS) data from 34,241 individuals with schizophrenia and 45,604 healthy controls included in the Psychiatric Genomics Consortium (PGC). By testing the distribution of schizophrenia single nucleotide polymorphisms (SNPs) with risk and protective effects in the human-specific sites, we observed a negative selection of risk alleles for schizophrenia in modern humans relative to archaic humans (e.g., Neanderthal and Denisovans). **Such findings indicate that risk alleles of schizophrenia have been gradually removed from the modern human genome due to negative selection pressure. This novel evidence contributes to our understanding of the genetic origins of schizophrenia** [emphasis added].[650]

The International Society of Psychiatric Genetics also expresses this popular perspective by suggesting "that these variants effectively escaped natural selection because of their small individual effects."[651] It is evident that the statistical approach in psychiatric genetics is the attempt to scientifically prove the eugenic concept of "negative selection."[652] Professors of psychiatry Roland Littlewood

[650] C. Liu, I. Everall, C. Pantelis, and C Bousman, "Interrogating the Evolutionary Paradox of Schizophrenia: A Novel Framework and evidence Supporting Recent Negative Selection of Schizophrenia Risk Alleles," *Frontiers in Genetics* vol. 30 (10) (April 30, 2019): 389; doi: 10.3389/fgene.2019.00389.

[651] Till F. M. Andlauer, Bertram Muller-Myhsok, and Stephan Ripke, *Psychiatric Genetics: A Primer for Clinicians and Basic Scientists* edited by Thomas G. Schulze and Francis J. McMahon (New York: Oxford University Press, 2018), 63.

[652] Liu, Everall, Pantelis, and Bousman, "Interrogating the Evolutionary Paradox of Schizophrenia," 389.

and Maurice Lipsedge explain how the statistical approach was developed upon Darwinian concepts of race and as an attempt to replace biblical authority:

> The concept of the Great Chain of Being arranged all living organisms in a hierarchy in which the white was the perfect creation. This idea was consolidated in the later theory of evolution. **Darwin and Malthus replaced God as the authority; in an age of enlightenment only science could rationalize inhumanity. Biblical exegesis was replaced by measurement.** To treat humans as objects required objective theories: in 1788 appeared an approach which later became popular – the weighing of brains [412]. **'Both Europeans and Americans sought in the nineteenth century development of somatometry** [the science of comparative body measurements] **a scapegoat for individual conscience.** They saw the function of statistical somatometry as a means of gratifying the desire for certainty. **They would allow the purely statistical experimental and "uninvolved" discipline of somatometry to justify an a priori judgement** [emphasis added].[653]

The statistical approach to human nature is Darwinian/Kraepelinian *somatometry* – also known as *biometry* or *anthropometry*, which was continued through the work of psychiatric eugenicists such as Kallmann and Slater.[654] As these psychiatrists rightly recognize, the statistical genetic approach is an attempt to uphold a presuppositional faith that opposes Scripture while claiming this new faith to be scientific.

---

[653] Roland Littlewood and Maurice Lipsedge, *Aliens and Alienists: Ethnic Minorities and Psychiatry*, 3rd edition (London: Taylor and Francis, 1997), 36-37.

[654] Ian Skottowe, "Somatometry – A second look," *The British Journal of Psychiatry* vol. 111 (470) (January, 1965): 4-9.

In late 2019, a large group of psychiatric geneticists at Harvard and Cambridge University, which included prominent figures such as Steven Hyman,[655] declared this presuppositional faith clearly in an article published in *Biological Psychiatry,*

> Genetic risk prediction is rooted in complex trait theory and biometry (the application of statistics to biological measures), which emerged in the 19th century. Darwin's concepts of selection based on continuous phenotypic variation were reconciled with Mendel's laws of inheritance proposing discontinuous steps, which were initially interpreted as contradictory. In this context, in the mid-1870s Sir Francis Galton promoted use of twin and family studies to investigate inheritance . . . . Ultimately, **this synthesis of statistical and evolutionary theory to complex traits established the fundamental models still used today** [emphasis added].[656]

It cannot be overemphasized that to believe in the genetic theory of mental illness is to embrace at some level — knowingly or not — a presuppositional evolutionary phenomenology that is antithetical to biblical wisdom.

If there are measurable differences perceived to be negative, as the evolutionary theory insists, then selection and the survival of the fittest must be occurring. This perspective points out how bio-determinism, materialism,

---

[655] Hyman is a psychiatrist on faculty at the Stanley Center for Psychiatric Research, Broad Institute of Harvard and MIT, Cambridge, Massachusetts and Department of Stem Cell and Regenerative Biology, Harvard University, Cambridge, Massachusetts.

[656] Alicia R. Martin, Mark J. Daly, Elise B. Robinson, Steven E. Hyman, and Benjamin M. Neale, "Predicting Polygenic Risk of Psychiatric Disorders," *Biological Psychiatry* vol. 86 (2) (July 15, 2019): 97-109; https://doi.org/10.1016/j.biopsych.2018.12.015.

and individual degeneracy undergird both the evolutionary theory of natural selection and the statistical approach:

> This claim strengthens the claim of legitimacy because it goes beyond mere description to assert that the **human nature described is inevitable, given the universal law of the struggle for existence and the survival of the fittest**. In this sense, the sociobiological theory of human nature puts on a mantle of universality and of utter fixity. [emphasis added].[657]

These proposed genetic risks are the result of a "computational approach" that relies on computer-generated statistical comparisons carefully formulated within evolutionary faith. They are not based upon objective molecular studies that prove how delusions and hallucinations are formed by specific genes.[658]

Furthermore, these "risk factors" are drawn from large global gene statistical banks that cannot consider all factors in the individual's life that the statistical numbers represent (e.g., unreported sexual abuse, the effects of psychiatric drugs, life history, insomnia, guilt, etc.). NIH geneticist Roberta Rasetti and neuroscientist Daniel Weinberger recognize one of the serious problems with statistical approaches:

> Phenotype studies of relatives of patients with schizophrenia, however, have potentially serious methodological problems which should be appreciated.

[657] Lewontin, *Biology as Ideology*, 90.

[658] "Scientists Identify Gene as a Master Regulator in Schizophrenia: Finding may offer a key target for future treatments," *Science Daily* (September 11, 2019): https://www.sciencedaily. com/releases/2019/09/190911142806. htm.

Relatives may share environmental or behavioral characteristics (e.g. drug or tobacco use, temperament) that can impact on measures of brain function. Moreover, comparisons of relatives across generations are especially problematic because they involve age and life experience factors that are difficult to control.[659]

Other studies, especially ones conducted on the construct of schizophrenia, rely heavily on animal models — comparing apples with oranges, figuratively speaking.[660] The foremost difference, as even psychiatric geneticists must admit, is that animals do not have a human mind/soul:

> **Animal models are indispensable to translating the findings in psychiatric genetics into basic sciences** such as the elucidation of neurobiological bases of psychiatric disorders, the development of new treatment, and the discovery of new biomarkers . . . . It can be argued which species can have the "mind." However, in that sense, **no animal can have the same higher order mental function as humans. Thus any animal model suffers from this difficulty** . . . . Since the role of copy number variations in schizophrenia was established, model mice of

[659] Rasetti and Weinberger, "Intermediate Phenotypes in Psychiatric Disorders," 342–343.

[660] Richard Bentall and David Pilgrim, "There Are No 'Schizophrenia Genes': Here's Why," *The Conversation* (April 8, 2016): https://theconversation.com/there-are-no-schizophrenia-genes-heres-why-57294. See also Tae-Yeon Eom, Seung Baek Han, Jieun Kim, et al., "Schizophrenia-related microdeletion causes defective ciliary motility and brain ventricle enlargement via microRNA-dependent mechanisms in mice," *Nature Communication* 11 (912) (2020): https://doi.org/10.1038/s41467-020-14628-y.

chromosomal abnormality have been used for the animal models of schizophrenia [emphasis added].[661]

In late 2019, an editorial published in the *Lancet Psychiatry* acknowledged the serious error of comparing mice with humans:

> While this all contributes to very exciting neuroscience, two key points when considering the potential clinical relevance are that these studies are done in animal models, and that they are of behaviour, not disorders or even symptoms . . . . much time and funding is expended on animal models of psychiatric disorders where researchers seem to expect that altering the expression of a single gene produces a valid model of a complex condition, even when the relevant mutation (or even a single nucleotide polymorphism associated with an unknown mutation) occurs in only a small proportion of patients with the disorder in question.[662]

The article goes on to show how this speculative leap from mice to men regularly occurs in psychiatric genetics:

> **We have a summary that jumps from reversing network and cognitive deficits in a mouse to prevention of schizophrenia — a uniquely human disorder.** There are useful mouse models of schizophrenia but they represent only a subset of its features, basically those known in people as negative or cognitive symptoms, and only some of those, for example, reduced social drive, loss of motivation, and inattention. They do not represent poverty of speech and thought, or positive symptoms such as hallucinations and delusions. Psychiatry needs input from neuroscience, but that input will have greater

[661] Tadafumi Kato, *Psychiatric Genetics: A Primer for Clinicians and Basic Scientists* edited by Thomas G. Schulze and Francis J. McMahon (New York: Oxford University Press, 2018), 195-97.

[662] Editorial, "Of Mice and Mental Health," *The Lancet Psychiatry* vol. 6 (11) (November, 2019): 877; https://doi.org/10.1016/S2215-0366(19)30407-9.

credibility if it is reported clearly, accurately, and cautiously . . . . **While animal models will continue to be important tools for scientists to understand the basic biology of the brain, translating that knowledge to human experiences of mental illness is complex and fraught. Translational scientists should avoid the temptation to oversimplify and oversell the potential clinical implications of their work** [emphasis added].[663]

One should be very cautious in reading claims of genetic discovery surrounding the construct of schizophrenia, especially when those claims are based upon statistics derived from animal models.[664]

Even more significant, though, is the certainty that there does not exist an optimal brain or genome from which to suggest psychiatric abnormalities using statistical estimates.[665] In an article published in *Trends in Cognitive Sciences*, Yale psychologists Avram Holmes and Lauren Patrick offer insight into how constructs of psychiatric degeneracy ("illnesses") are always based upon constructs of perceived normalcy — even in neuroscience and genetics:

> Implicit in modern dimensional theories of psychiatric illness is the assumption that population variability and illness vulnerability are interchangeable constructs. **Mounting evidence suggests that healthy variation is ubiquitous in natural populations and must be**

[663] Ibid.

[664] Tae-Yeon Eom, Seung Baek Han, Jieun Kim, et al., "Schizophrenia-related microdeletion causes defective ciliary motility and brain ventricle enlargement via microRNA-dependent mechanisms in mice," *Nature Communication* 11 (912) (2020): https://doi.org/10.1038/s41467-020-14628-y.

[665] Chand, Dwyer, et. al., "Two distinct neuroanatomical subtypes of schizophrenia revealed using machine learning," *Brain* awaa025 (Oxford University Press) (February 27, 2020): https://doi.org/10.1093/brain/awaa025.

interpreted in terms of cost–benefit tradeoffs. Psychiatric illnesses arise through a web of interactions linking brain function, behavior, and a lifetime of experiences. Research on illness etiology will only progress through the collection of comprehensive phenomic-level datasets. Large-scale collaborative efforts have begun to generate broad phenotypic batteries that encompass environmental and contextual factors, brain structure and function, as well as multiple domains of cognition, behavior, and genetics. These datasets hold great potential for clinical researchers seeking to map links across diverse neural and cognitive states [emphasis added].[666]

Though people have come to believe that the "risk" approach is scientifically sound, "no model accounts for all of the alterations associated with schizophrenia."[667] In fact, none of the Polygenic Risk Scores (PRS) approaches explain causes to genetic variances or to categorized psychiatric symptoms from an empirical approach. Prominent psychiatric geneticists at Harvard and Cambridge Universities assert:

> While PRSs are useful for studying the correlation between pairs of genotype-phenotype associations, they cannot be taken as evidence of causality, in part because PRSs are a weak epidemiological instrument.[668]

[666] Avram J. Holmes and Lauren M. Patrick, "The Myth of Optimality in Clinical Neuroscience," *Trends in Cognitive Sciences* vol. 22 (3) (March 1, 2018): 241; DOI: https://doi.org/10.1016/j.tics.2017.12.006.

667 Robert A. McCutcheon, Tiago Reis Marques, and Oliver D. Howes, "Schizophrenia — An Overview," *JAMA Psychiatry Online* (October 30, 2019): doi:10.1001/jamapsychiatry.2019.3360.

668 Alicia R. Martin, Mark J. Daly, Elise B. Robinson, Steven E. Hyman, and Benjamin M. Neale, "Predicting Polygenic Risk of Psychiatric Disorders," *Biological Psychiatry* vol. 86 (2) (July 15, 2019): 97-109; https://doi.org/10.1016/j.biopsych.2018.12.015.

These numerous approaches or "strategies" to the polygenic model, and statistical methods expose that even within the various evolutionary models, there exist conflicting theories, varying methodologies, and subjective means to interpret statistics favorably. In truth, all that psychiatric geneticists will ever possess in regard to objective science concerning the human soul and human phenomena are physical correlations and metaphysical problems, which must be "interpreted" according to one's presuppositional faith/phenomenology.

Omnigenic Theory

Added to the single-gene and polygenic theories is a relatively newer theory that has also emerged. Since the other two theories have only produced correlations and not hard facts, and with the number of suggested associated genes expanding daily, a growing number of geneticists are pronouncing the omnigenic theory as the new eugenic hope. This model indicates that either the entire human genome or any particular gene in the genome can cause alleged disorders.

As genetic theorists and researchers continue to add "potential genes" to their already extensive list, the omnigenic model will inevitably be foremost. In the journal of *Schizophrenia Neuropsychopharmacology*, researchers explain the necessity of this "new" genetic model:

> There are commonalities among both the clinical features and genomics of major psychiatric disorders and a recent cross-disorder mega-analysis GWAS that indicated that common variation predisposing to mental illnesses might be shared to some degree among major psychiatric disorders." This model states that most genes expressed

in cells that are relevant to the biology of an illness contribute to heritability and PRSs [Polygenic Risk Scores] because of the likely interaction of multiple signaling pathways within cells that support their biological functions. In the light of this omnigenic hypothesis, implicating a greater number of SNPs [single nucleotide polymorphisms] than the ordinary polygenic model would suggest, our results support the hypothesis by demonstrating a weak polygenic effect extant in every random subset of genes . . . . Even though most of the genes in these sets are not associated with risk in current GWAS datasets, they may be part of networks of genes that underlie common mechanisms for schizophrenia.[669]

As researchers realize, there are three reasons why the omnigenic model will continue to gain popularity: 1) there already exist far too many people who are said to have various psychiatric disorders, yet they share the same genetic variances claimed to cause allegedly different disorders, 2) there are far too many genes already suggested to manage and arrive at objective and agreed upon conclusions — that is if genes could in fact be empirically correlated to metaphysical human phenomena in the first place, and 3) people who are said to have alleged schizophrenia have different "genetic mutations"; no "mutated gene(s)" has consistently correlated to people said to be schizophrenic. But true to their genetic priori adherence, psychiatrists still suggest that though there is no reliable pattern of genetic mutation or variance (either the entire genome, any gene, or a random combination of

[669] A. Rammos, L.A.N. Gonzalez, D.R. Weinberger, K.J. Mitchell, and K.K. Nicodemus, The Role of Polygenic risk Score Gene-set Analysis in the Context of the Omnigenic Model of Schizophrenia," *Schizophrenia Neuropsychopharmacology* (2019): doi:10.1038/s41386-019- 0410-z.

genes can cause suggested schizophrenia), the fluidity still proves that genes somehow cause the alleged disorder:

> "Each person with schizophrenia in the study had different mutations, and most of the rare damaging mutations occurred in different genes," Dr. Jon M. McClellan of the University of Washington, in Seattle, told Reuters Health by email. "This suggests that most people with the illness have a different genetic cause. This helps explain why there is so much clinical heterogeneity in how the illness presents, and why there is so much variability in how affected persons respond to different medication treatments."[670]

This new perspective undermines the statistical approach that has sustained the eugenic theory since Kraepelin. Yet, this model, as with the single gene and polygenic theories, "fit[s] an evolutionary model of schizophrenia."[671]

While all three genetic models of mental illness are conjecture, the omnigenic theory will enable the hope of validity to be sustained throughout the future; it is a theory that cannot be proved or disproved with empirical evidence. In fact, the omnigenic view is no different than the original theory of hereditary madness, which psychiatrists such as Rush and Morel made popular without any scientific data to support their conjecture. Once again, psychiatrists have returned to the position that no specific gene or group of genes needs to be identified as causative to claim genetic causes; any or all genes, so the

---

[670] Will Boggs, "Schizophrenia Linked to Mutations in Genes Critical to Synaptic Function," *Medscape Psychiatry* (February 6, 2020): https://www.medscape.com/viewarticle/924828.

[671] Ibid.

theory follows, can cause people to be delusional and hallucinate.

Instead of making the broad statement that heredity causes madness, psychiatrists have replaced the assertion with the equally grand and unfounded claim that the human genome causes mental disorder. While the theory seems to have scientifically progressed, it has actually only fundamentally changed terms and accumulated years of expensive research.

The true pathology of the genetic theory, then, is not medical, but historical and philosophical. Theorists have moved from the sweeping hereditary theory (A), to the single gene theory (B), to the polygenic model (C), and back again to the sweeping omnigenic model (A). While the focus seems to be on the human genome or specific genes and appears to be more empirically sound and progressing, the omnigenic model is intrinsically the same hereditary theory of psychiatrists like Rush and Kraepelin reframed into more sophisticated terms, advanced scientific knowledge of the genome, and more costly experiments.

The underlying philosophies or core style of reasoning/phenomenology and the foundational pseudoscience of psychiatric eugenics have not changed, as several researchers convey:

> The recent appearance of Big Biology in psychiatric genetics is an interesting sociological story in itself, but without a strong historical perspective we risk having only a fleeting understanding of its epistemic organizations. For instance, we might assume that the so-called 'omics' revolution of high-throughput technologies has ushered in a new 'paradigm' of molecular genetics. The shift from single-gene determinism to probabilistic

models of systems biology may appear to be a decisive break from the past. Depending on one's historical perspective, or lack of it, we might see more discontinuity and revolution than accumulation in the life sciences.[672]

James Knoll IV, who currently serves as the editor in chief of the *Psychiatric Times* (2020), and his father, James Knoll III, retired clinical professor of psychiatry at the University of Texas Southwestern Medical Center and Medical Director of Presbyterian Hospital of Dallas, may have summed up the discussion best when they warned younger psychiatrists in 2019 to

be aware that over time, people claim to "discover" theories which, upon closer examination, are actually older, well-known psychiatric/psychological principles wrapped in a new package.[673]

Psychiatric genetics is not a new theory or a new scientific field. It is simply the failed eugenic theory repackaged in more sophisticated terms and upheld by technological advances which can never validate the conjecture.

Inevitably, scientific research on somatic variances will continue and there will be future claims with media fanfare pronouncing that the illusive schizophrenia gene(s) has been found or that the theory has been validated. Nonetheless, the eugenic paradigm must still rely upon the acceptance of the Kraepelinian humanistic faith, which

---

[672] Arribas-Ayloon, Bartlett, and Lewis, *Psychiatric Genetics: From Hereditary Madness to Big Biology* (Vanderbilt, New York: Routledge, 2019), 6.

[673] James L. Knoll IV and James L. Knoll III, "Guidance Along the Path: 20 meditations for Psychiatry Residents," *Psychiatric Times Online* (October 15, 2019): https://www.psychiatrictimes.com/couch-crisis/guidance-along-path-20-meditations-psychiatry-residents.

denies dualism and creates individual degenerates utilizing descriptive and genetic psychologies.

When one considers the "science" of psychiatric genetics, he/she should understand that the field is primarily a subjective phenomenology of correlations primarily based not on fact but on faith. No matter how advanced research may become and how the genome is understood, the Kraepelinian faith can never be proven within empirical methods due to the metaphysical reality of the soul/psyche/mind and its phenomena. Moreover, the secular approach to the soul can never explain on a molecular level how genes cause people to believe and perceive falsely or that false beliefs and sensory perceptions are forms of individual genetic degeneracy.

Stated forthrightly, psychiatric genetics is a philosophical pseudoscience and not a legitimate scientific field; it is a faith in the theories of men like Rush, Morel, Darwin, and Kraepelin concerning the understanding and true nature of the soul. And worse, it is a faith that seeks to dismiss faith in Christ, who purposes and desires to deliver and restore the human soul/psyche with His truth.

CHAPTER 7
THE PROBLEMS WITH PSYCHIATRIC GENETICS

The resemblance of parents and children is the observation to be explained. It is not evidence for genes. For example, the two social traits that have the highest resemblance between parents and children in North America are religious sect and political party. Yet even the most ardent biotical determinist would not seriously argue that there is a gene for Episcopalian or voting Social Credit.[674] – Richard Lewontin, Harvard geneticist

Despite the popularity of the neo-Kraepelinian/bio-psycho-social model, hard evidence to support the theory is lacking. In fact, the empirical evidence available consistently undermines the genetic theory and humanistic phenomenology of mental illness. It is necessary, then, to examine the many problems facing the genetic theory which reveal psychiatric genetics to be a pseudo-science — an anthropological faith — rather than a valid scientific theory of human nature and human phenomena.

Whereas the construct of race was central to eugenics at the field's genesis, the construct of schizophrenia/psychosis, since the days of Kraepelin and Rüdin, has become the main focus of genetic studies and research within the bio-psycho-social perspective. It is easily argued that schizophrenia (*dementia praecox*) represents the most

[674] Richard C. Lewontin, *Biology as Ideology: The Doctrine of DNA* (New York: HarperCollins Publishers, 1991), 31-32.

important psychiatric construct Kraepelin created, and the descriptive construct continues to be the point on which psychiatry and the genetic theory are sustained and hopes of validity primarily rest.[675]

Largely based upon Kraepelin's conjecture and Rüdin's and Kallmann's faulty experimentations and publications, many people today believe that schizophrenia is an empirically-proven disease caused by genetic defects:

> The belief that schizophrenia has a clear and important genetic basis is now very widely held. The father of psychiatric genetics, Ernst Rüdin, was so convinced of this that, arguing on the basis of statistics collected by his co-workers, he advocated the eugenic sterilization of schizophrenics. When Hitler came to power in 1933, Rüdin's advocacy was no longer merely academic.[676]

As previously noted, the horrific history and foundation — especially the Nazi era — of psychiatric genetics is certainly a problem that must be acknowledged. But there is a wealth of scientific evidence and facts which exist beyond the neo-Kraepelinian theory's eugenic reality in Nazi Germany which must also be considered.

Currently, many people accept the genetic theory of the mind as true, not because of hard science, but because the two-hundred-year hypothesis is heavily researched and funded, a large number of scientists say it must be true, the human genome has been mapped, the promise of future discovery continues to be propagated, and to some degree,

---

[675] For further study on the construct of Schizophrenia and its importance to modern psychiatry, see Daniel R. Berger II, *The Insanity of Madness: Defining Mental Illness* (Taylors, SC: Alethia International Publications, 2018).

[676] Lewontin, Rose, and Kamin, *Not in Our Genes*, 207.

the genes and neurons can now be studied at the molecular level. Simply because a hypothesis or theory has been scrutinized for centuries within a scientific framework does not validate a social or descriptive construct. Scientists G.A. Miller and B.S. Rockstroh recognize the long history of researching the social construct of schizophrenia in attempt to prove the genetic theory without the result of any validating evidence to prove psychiatrists' dogmatically-held, albeit speculative, theory of genetic psychopathology:

> Decades of psychophysiological research have identified a variety of established and candidate endophenotypes for schizophrenia without offering much insight into genetic contributions to the disorder and without substantially improving the understanding of the complex psychopathology.[677]

Additionally, psychiatric geneticists, writing in 2019 on their own findings, declared that molecular understanding, which is vital to validate the theory and to enable objective clinical diagnoses, is still absent:

> While striatal hyperdopaminergia is a well-established finding in schizophrenia, the molecular mechanisms underlying this remain unclear. Likewise, the exact mechanisms leading to disrupted excitatory-inhibitory balance remain unclear; for example, it remains uncertain whether changes in GABAergic interneurons are best understood as a primary pathology or as a compensatory mechanism for dendritic spine loss. Moreover, while there is evidence that impaired cortical regulation could

---

[677] G.A. Miller and B.S. Rockstroh, *The Neurobiology of Schizophrenia* edited by Ted Abel and Thomas Nickl-Jockschat (New York: Academic Press, 2016), 17.

underlie mesostriatal dopamine dysregulation, causality has yet to be demonstrated in vivo.[678]

Numerous other neuropsychiatrists agree that the dopamine dysregulation theory of schizophrenia — one of the traditional chemical imbalance theories — has not been validated:

> Although disturbances in dopamine neurotransmission have long been postulated, a comprehensive model that links the phenomenology, pathophysiology, and psychopharmacology of psychosis has long been missing.[679]

If the key phenotypes, which allegedly identify the proposed disorder of schizophrenia and are used as the primary diagnostic tools, are considered to be vital empirical elements to understanding the science of schizophrenia, then carefully examining these phenotypes is a necessary exercise.

Metaphysical Phenotypes

Objective researchers will consider that all correlates are potentially causative — not restricting themselves to biased beliefs. Thus, if metaphysical symptoms such as delusions and hallucinations are considered to be valid diagnostic tools and real human phenomena that can be universally

678 Robert A. McCutcheon, Tiago Reis Marques, and Oliver D. Howes, "Schizophrenia — An Overview," *JAMA Psychiatry Online* (October 30, 2019): doi:10.1001/jamapsychiatry.2019.3360.

679 H. Tost, T. Alam, & A. Meyer-Lindenberg, "Dopamine and Psychosis: Theory, Pathomechanisms and Intermediate Phenotypes," *Neuroscience and Biobehavioral Reviews* vol. 34 (5) (April 2010): 689–700; doi:10.1016/j.neubiorev.2009.06.005.

described and formally categorized, then the metaphysical reality of human nature must be considered as potentially causative of somatic negative changes. This consideration, while necessary, poses a tremendous threat to psychiatric genetics and materialism in general. If scientists are only willing within their restricted worldview to consider the physical nature as causative and the metaphysical nature as only effects, then they will overlook the very real possibility that the pathology of mental struggles may actually go the opposite direction than their faith allows them to consider.

The two prominent phenotypes in the construct of schizophrenia are delusions and hallucinations, which psychiatrists assert to be the "hallmark" correlates (phenotypes) to endophenotypes and genotypes.[680] Without people experiencing delusions and hallucinations, Kraepelin would never have been able to construct his concepts of schizophrenia and bipolar, and clinicians would not be able today to diagnose various suggested types of psychosis/historic madness and "severe mental disorders." Renowned psychiatrist Andrew Sims comments on the significance of delusions within psychiatric phenomenology:

> Delusion has now become a psychiatric word . . . . in modern speech it always implies the possibility of psychiatric illness. It has been appropriated by psychiatry and invariably implies at least the suspicion of psychiatric diagnosis. If I am deluded, then I am necessarily mentally ill. In English law, delusion has been the cardinal feature of insanity for the last 200 years. It is a mitigating

[680] David Rosenthal and Olive W. Quinn, "Quadruplet Hallucinations: Phenotypic Variations of a Schizophrenic Genotype," *Archive of General Psychiatry* vol 34 (7) (1977): 817–827.

circumstance and can convey diminished responsibility. **It is within the professional competence of psychiatrists to deem what is, and is not, delusional** [emphasis added].[681]

Moreover, without these primary metaphysical symptoms listed in the construct of schizophrenia and historical hereditary madness, there is neither history of the genetic theory nor decades of psychiatric research that prove the validity of psychosis/schizophrenia as a disease entity.

Despite their centrality to the genetic theory, most prominent geneticists now wish to minimize the role of delusions and hallucinations in understanding psychiatric constructs. However, the core of what is dogmatically claimed to be a psychiatric abnormality must be thoughtfully considered.

By definition delusions are metaphysical/spiritual phenotypes which occur in the soul and are revealed in a person's words and actions:

> Delusions are **false firm ideas** that cannot be corrected by reasoning and are out of keeping with patient's educational and cultural background. **Delusions can also be regarded as a mode of adaptation to stress and may serve a metaphorical or allegorical function in which the patient portrays her problems and experiences** [emphasis added].[682]

---

[681] Andrew Sims, *Is Faith Delusion? Why Religion is Good for Your Health* (London: Continuum, 2009), 117-18.

[682] Tarun Yadav, Yatan Pal Singh Balhara, and Dinesh Kumar Kataria, "Pseudocyesis Versus Delusion of Pregnancy: Differential Diagnoses to be Kept in Mind," *Indian Journal of Psychological Medicine* 34 (1) (Jan.-Mar. 2012): 82–84.

The APA defines this hallmark "phenotype" or "symptom" of psychosis in the *DSM-5* as

> **a false belief based on incorrect inference about external reality** that is firmly held despite what almost everyone else **believes** and despite what constitutes incontrovertible and obvious proof or evidence to the contrary [emphasis added]."[683]

The APA also objectively defines the *hallucination* phenotype, which is another foundational symptom to the concept of psychosis[684] and which occurs in approximately 70% of people diagnosed as having alleged schizophrenia:

> . . . a **perception-like experience** with the clarity and **impact of a true perception but without the external stimulation** of the relevant sensory organ. . . . One hallucinating person may recognize the **false sensory experience**, whereas another may be convinced that the experience is grounded in **reality** [emphases added].[685]

Acclaimed neurologist and materialist Oliver Sacks offers his own understanding of the true nature of hallucinations:

> **Hallucinations are "positive" phenomena,** as opposed to the negative symptoms, the deficits or losses caused by accident or disease, which neurology is classically based on. **The phenomenology of hallucinations** often points to the brain structures and mechanisms involved and can

---

[683] American Psychiatric Association, *Diagnostic and Statistical Manual of Mental Disorders*, 5th ed. (Washington, DC: American Psychiatric Publishing, 2013), 819.

[684] Delusional thinking is the primary symptom and hallucinations are secondary. Kathleen Smith, "Schizophrenia: Hallucinations and Delusions," *PSYCHOM* (July 17, 2019): https://www.psycom.net/schizophrenia-hallucinations-delusions/.

[685] APA, *DSM-5*, 822.

therefore, potentially, provide more direct insight into the workings of the brain . . . . **Hallucination is a unique and special category of consciousness and mental life** . . . . The **power of hallucinations is only to be understood from first-person accounts** [emphasis added].[686]

Clearly, hallucinations are phenomena which occur in the metaphysical soul or consciousness and are not objective realities approachable within scientific investigation. Of course, as Sacks' statements indicate, materialists endeavor to attribute hallucinations to the brain and biological processes. This hypothesis was first suggested by Benjamin Rush, who referred to hallucinations as "illusions." Neurologist C. H. Hughes observes,

> Rush's definition of illusion, "a waking dream," is the briefest on record, and his amplification of it, as "a false perception, in the waking state, from a morbid affection of the brain," is perhaps the best on record.[687]

Rush, who claimed to be a Christian, made some unbiblical assertations during his life, such as suggesting the possibility that the prophecies recorded in the Old and New Testaments could have been hallucinations ("illusions") rather than the actual voice of God that the prophets heard:

> I am aware that this explanation of illusions may be applied to invalidate the accounts that are given in the Old and New Testaments of the supernatural voices and

---

[686] Oliver Sacks, *Hallucinations* (New York: Random House, 2012), preface xii-xii; xiv.

[687] Speech at the annual *American Medical Association* conference presented by C. H. Hughes, "Neurological Progress in America," (June 1-4, 1897), published in *JAMA: Medical Literature of the Period* edited by John B. Hamilton (Chicago, American Medical Association Press, August 1897), 315.

objects, that were heard or seen by individuals.,
particularly by Daniel, Elisha, and St. Paul . . . . But,
admitting the voices or objects that were heard or seen, by
the prophets and apostle above-mentioned, to have been
produced by a change in the natural actions of the brain,
or of the organs of hearing or seeing that change,
considering its design, was no less supernatural, than if
the voices or objects supposed to have been heard, or
seen, had been real.[688]

Rush then argued that, though these biblical accounts fit
the psychiatric definition, these instances were likely not
hallucinations because others heard or saw them too, and
"in all of whom it is scarcely possible for an illusion to have
existed at the same time from natural causes."[689] Modern
psychiatrists disagree and refer to the phenomena of two or
more people sharing delusions or hallucinations as *Folie à
deux* or "shared delusional disorder,"[690] with some
psychiatrists insisting that Jesus Christ and the prophets
were delusional.[691]

Rush's brain dysfunction mantra is still believed today. For
example, the NIH's *Genetic Home Reference* attempts to

---

[688] Benjamin Rush, *Medical Inquiries and Observations Upon the Diseases of the Mind* ed. (Philadelphia: Grigg and Elliot, 1835), 306.

[689] Ibid.

[690] Atefeh Ghanbari Jolfaei, et al., "Folie à deux and delusional disorder by proxy in a family," *Journal of Research in Medical Sciences* vol. 16 (1) (2011): S453-5.

[691] Evan D. Murray, Miles G. Cunningham, and Bruce H. Price, "The Role of Psychotic Disorders in Religious History Considered," *Journal of Neuropsychiatry and Clinical Neurosciences* 24 (2012): 410-26.

claim schizophrenia as a brain disorder while still explaining it as a problem with one's phenomenology:

> Schizophrenia is a brain disorder classified as a psychosis, **which means that it affects a person's thinking, sense of self, and perceptions** [phenomenology]. The disorder typically becomes evident during late adolescence or early adulthood. **Signs and symptoms of schizophrenia include false perceptions called hallucinations.** Auditory hallucinations of voices are the most common hallucinations in schizophrenia, but affected individuals can also experience hallucinations of visions, smells, or touch (tactile) sensations. **Strongly held false beliefs (delusions) are also characteristic of schizophrenia.** For example, affected individuals may be certain that they are a particular historical figure or that they are being plotted against or controlled by others [emphasis added].[692]

Psychiatrists assert that the most prominent phenotypes in the construct of schizophrenia, which they claim to be linked to specific genes, are metaphysical in nature (false beliefs and false perceptions). While the claim is made that genes and neurons cause these human phenomena to occur, there is no empirical means to ever link metaphysical beliefs and perceptions to biological correlates (genotypes or endophenotypes) let alone prove causality.

Interestingly, in 2019 several professors and researchers of psychiatry at Johns Hopkins University School of Medicine discovered in a small study that 45% of people who enter the clinic experiencing psychosis do not receive a diagnosis on the schizophrenia spectrum. Of the ones who are

---

[692] Genetics Home Reference, "Schizophrenia," *National Institutes of Health* (2019): https://ghr.nlm.nih.gov/condition/ schizophrenia#genes. Accessed September 2, 2019.

diagnosed as allegedly having schizophrenia, over half are said to be misdiagnosed:[693]

> "Hearing voices is a symptom of many different conditions, and sometimes it is just a fleeting phenomenon with little significance," says Russell L. Margolis, M.D., professor of psychiatry and behavioral sciences and the clinical director of the Johns Hopkins Schizophrenia Center at the Johns Hopkins University School of Medicine. "At other times when someone reports 'hearing voices' it may be a general statement of distress rather than the literal experience of hearing a voice. The key point is that hearing voices on its own doesn't mean a diagnosis of schizophrenia."[694]

These statistics expose both how many people experience hallucinations and delusions and how psychiatric constructs are subjective concepts that are applied in diagnoses based upon a clinician's personal phenomenology. When someone is diagnosed or categorized as "psychotic," the label simply identifies that an individual is deceived in some way that another finds to be abnormal or is unable to explain with the knowledge available, which makes discovering and discerning why a person is deceived so difficult. This fact also makes the statistical approach subjective and irrelevant since the statistics will always be based on the researchers and

---

693 Chelsey Coulter, Krista K. Baker, Russell L. Margolis, "Specialized Consultation for Suspected Recent-onset Schizophrenia: Diagnostic Clarity and the Distorting Impact of Anxiety and Reported Auditory Hallucinations," *Journal of Psychiatric Practice* vol. 25 (2) (March 2019): 76-81; doi: 10.1097/PRA.0000000000000363.

694 Johns Hopkins Medicine, "Study suggests overdiagnosis of Schizophrenia," *Science News* (April 22, 2019): https://www.sciencedaily.com/releases/2019/04/190422090842.htm.

diagnostician's presuppositional phenomenology and subjective clinical opinions.

These facts alone poses a fatal problem for any claim of scientific validity for psychiatrists' cherished Kraepelinian genetic theory. Metaphysical phenomena of the soul are neither approachable using the traditional scientific method nor are they objective phenomena that can be approached, understood, or attempted to be remedied apart from presuppositional beliefs. Psychiatrist and neuroscientist at the University of Kentucky and the University of Granada, Spain, Jose de Leon, for instance, points out that acclaimed psychiatrist Karl Jaspers

> described psychiatry as a hybrid science and heterogeneous. Berrios affirmed that psychiatric symptoms/signs are hybrid. Some symptoms are in the "semantic space" and cannot be "explained" by neuroscience.[695]

One's "sense of self," beliefs, and perceptions are phenomenological issues that cannot be empirically approached. Psychiatrist Paul Appelbaum comments on how delusions are both normative and descriptive, and how they require philosophical presuppositions, not scientific tools:

> Delusional thinking is a standard criterion for identifying severe mental disorder — a mainstay in diagnosis, research, treatment, and mental health policy. **Yet delusion is far from the simple, descriptive category this suggests. Despite its undeniable importance, the loose characterizations of delusional thinking employed**

---

[695] Jose De Leon, "It is time to awaken Sleeping Beauty? European Psychiatry has been sleeping since 1980," *Review of Psychiatry and Mental Health* vol. 7 (4) (October-December 2014): 186; doi: 10.1016/j.rpsm.2013.12.004.

within psychiatry for decades, all insufficient, went largely unquestioned. It had been maintained that delusions were false beliefs, though not all false beliefs are delusion (we all mistakenly believe something untrue on occasion) and not all delusions are false (sometimes your wife is truly cheating on you); it had been held that delusions were fixed beliefs, though not all fixed beliefs are delusional (religious and moral beliefs are often unshakably fixed, yet they are not usually designated delusions) and not all delusions are held with such tenacity. **Delusion is a complex, nuanced category, recent systematic attention has revealed, with both normative and descriptive elements. Its definition calls for sophisticated philosophical tools and a refined understanding of language and epistemology. As the category of delusion also makes clear, descriptions of psychopathological symptoms and the very idea of mental disorder must contain abiding interest for the philosophically minded.**[696]

In his book, Paul Applebaum rightly delineates that "sophisticated philosophical tools" are necessary to approach delusions and delusional people. Though these phenomena are central to the neo-Kraepelinian construct of schizophrenia and other psychotic disorders — while limited to being framed as only effects, they are not discernibly correlatable to physical phenomenon such as a gene:

> Phenotypic variation is produced through a complex web of interactions between genotype and environment, and such a 'genotype-phenotype' map is inaccessible without the detailed phenotypic data that allow these interactions to be studied. Despite this need, our ability to characterize phenomes - the full set of phenotypes of an individual - lags behind our ability to characterize genomes. Phenomics should be recognized and pursued as an

---

[696] Paul S. Appelbaum, *Philosophy of Psychiatry: A Companion* edited by Jennifer Radden (New York: Oxford University Press, 2014), foreword viii.

independent discipline to enable the development and adoption of high-throughput and high-dimensional phenotyping.[697]

Psychiatric disorders are more the product of the philosophical field of phenomics/phenomenology than they are empirical science. No scientist will ever be able to factually prove that genes at their molecular level cause people to believe falsehood or to construct a false identity about themselves, since no phenotypic empirical data exists. The physical effects can certainly be observed within the scientific method and scientific tools (e.g., neuroimaging and genome studies), but studying the effects are not the same as examining the actual phenomena much less determining their foundational cause. Nevertheless, this futile psychiatric belief and hope drives billions of dollars into research promised to do just that.

But another deleterious circumstance that delusions and hallucinations pose for genetic theorists, as Paul Appelbaum notes, is that delusions and hallucinations are aspects of normal human nature.[698] Eugenicists assume that delusions and hallucinations — when they are impairing, distressful, violent, negative, religious, horrific in nature, seemingly out of the ordinary, or are unexplainable within their worldview — are abnormalities or signs of disorder. But there is no empirical evidence to support this assertion.

697 D. Houle, D.R. Govindaraju, and S. Omholt, "Phenomics: the next challenge," *Nature Reviews Genetics* vol. 11 (12) (December 2010): 855. doi: 10.1038/nrg2897.

698 Appelbaum, *Philosophy of Psychiatry*, foreword viii.

Instead, this viewpoint represents a biased individual degenerative belief rather than an empirically proven fact.

Hallucinations and delusions, though, are normal aspects of human nature, and framing them as abnormalities is at the core of both Rush's diseases of the mind and Kraepelin's original construct of schizophrenia. Neurologist Oliver Sacks states in his book *Hallucinations* that hallucinatory experiences are "an essential part of the human condition."[699] Professor of Psychiatry and Bioethics and Editor in Chief Emeritus of the *Psychiatric Times* Ronald Pies explains how all people fall on a spectrum of deceit:

> All of us need to parse perceived from actual reality every day, in nearly every aspect of our lives . . . . **Some people who voice falsehoods appear incapable of distinguishing real from unreal, or truth from fiction, yet are sincerely convinced their worldview is absolutely correct. And this is our entree into the psychiatric literature. . . . We can think of distortions of reality as falling along a continuum, ranging from mild to severe, based on how rigidly the belief is held and how impervious it is to factual information.** On the milder end, we have what psychiatrists call over-valued ideas. These are very strongly held convictions that are at odds with what most people in the person's culture believe, but which are not bizarre, incomprehensible or patently impossible. A passionately held belief that vaccinations cause autism might qualify as an over-valued idea: it's not scientifically correct, but it's not utterly beyond the realm of possibility. On the severe end of the continuum are delusions. These are strongly held, completely inflexible beliefs that are not altered at all by factual information, and which are clearly false or impossible. **Importantly, delusions are not explained by the person's culture, religious beliefs or ethnicity.** A

[699] Sacks, *Hallucinations*, preface xiv.

patient who inflexibly believes that Vladimir Putin has personally implanted an electrode in his brain in order to control his thoughts would qualify as delusional. When the patient expresses this belief, he or she is not lying or trying to deceive the listener. It is a sincerely held belief, but still a falsehood. Falsehoods of various kinds can be voiced by people with various neuropsychiatric disorders, but also by those who are perfectly "normal." Within the range of normal falsehood are so-called false memories, which many of us experience quite often. For example, you are absolutely certain you sent that check to the power company, but in fact, you never did [emphasis added].[700]

What Pies recognizes is significant: diagnoses of delusions are based upon a clinician's ability or inability to explain why a person is delusional. If clinicians are unable or unwilling to explain, then people who are deceived are viewed and categorized as disordered. Pies also points out that clinicians are prone to not understand the spiritual heart or history of the person that they are diagnosing within the confines of the current diagnostic system, and he later states that a clinician's judgment on what is alleged mental illness (delusional thinking) versus normal but distressful behavior can be wrong:

Sometimes, clinicians can be wildly mistaken in their first impressions. A colleague of mine once described a severely agitated patient who was hospitalized because he insisted he was being stalked and harassed by the FBI. A few days into his hospitalization, FBI agents showed up on the unit to arrest the patient. As the old joke goes, just

[700] Ronald W. Pies, "'Alternative Facts': A Psychiatrist's Guide to Twisted Relationships to Truth," *The Conversation* (March 1, 2017): https://getpocket. com/explore/item/alternative-facts-a-psychiatrist-s-guide-to-twisted-relationships-to-truth?utm_source=pocket-newtab.

because you're paranoid doesn't mean they aren't after you![701]

Diagnosing individuals as psychotic/schizophrenic, more often than not, represents a clinician's inability to understand and rightly discern the life context and character of the person in turmoil.

In late 2019, numerous psychiatric geneticists published their own research in *JAMA Psychiatry* highlighting how delusions are commonplace and how phenomenology rather than biology determines the interpretation and explanation of these phenomena:

> Psychotic experiences, such as hallucinations and delusions, are features of psychiatric disorders (e.g., schizophrenia), but they are also reported by approximately 5% to 10% of the general population. Psychotic experiences are considered to be symptoms of psychiatric illness only if they co-occur with other features of that disorder, including some aspect of psychosocial impairment.[702]

Other studies, however, which provide the opportunity for surveyors to remain anonymous, reveal that 84% of people identify themselves as having experienced

---

[701] Ibid.

[702] Sophie E. Legge, Hannah J. Jones, Kimberley M. Kendall, Antonio F. Pardiñas, Georgina Menzies, Matthew Bracher-Smith, Valentina Escott-Price, Elliott Rees, Katrina A. S. Davis, Matthew Hotopf, Jeanne E. Savage, Danielle Posthuma, Peter Holmans, George Kirov, Michael J. Owen, Michael C. O'Donovan, Stanley Zammit, James T. R. Walters, "Association of Genetic Liability to Psychotic Experiences With Neuropsychotic Disorders and Traits," *JAMA Psychiatry* (September 25, 2019): doi:10.1001/jamapsychiatry.2019.2508.

hallucinations.[703] Several clinicians and researchers report on both the significance and the normalcy of hallucinations in everyone:

> Differences in prevalence can be attributed in part to differences in definitions and methodologies, but also to true variations based on gender, ethnicity and environmental context. The findings support the current movement away from pathological models of unusual experiences and towards **understanding voice-hearing as occurring on a continuum in the general population, and having meaning in relation to the voice-hearer's life experiences** [emphasis added].[704]

As rightly acknowledged, delusions and hallucinations are directly correlated to a person's metaphysical soul and life history. Neurologist David Eagleman remarks on how all people naturally create their own sensory realities — which are apart from objective truth and according to their own desires, fears, and experiences:

> Despite the simplicity of that assembly-line model of vision, it's incorrect. In fact, the brain generates its own reality, even before it receives information coming in from the eyes and the other senses. This is known as the internal model.[705]

703 A. Millham & S. Easton, "Prevalence of auditory hallucinations in nurses in mental health," *Journal of Psychiatric and Mental Health Nursing* vol. 5 (1998): 95–99.

704 Vanessa Beavan, John Read, and Claire Cartwright, "The prevalence of voice-hearers in the general population: A literature review," *The Journal of Mental Health* vol. 20 (3) (2011): 281-292; http://dx.doi.org/10.3109/09638237.2011.562262.

705 David Eagleman, *The Brain: The Story of You* (New York: Pantheon Books, 2015), 51.

One of the most common visual and auditory hallucinations occurs when people have lost a loved one and desire to be with that person.

> According to the National Institutes of Health, hallucinations can be normal in some cases. For example, after a loved one dies, some people hear the person's voice, or briefly think that they see the loved one, which can be part of the grieving process, the NIH says.[706]

The National Library of Medicine discloses this same observation on their *MedlinePlus* website:

> Hallucinations involve sensing things such as visions, sounds, or smells that seem real but are not. **These things are created by the mind . . . Sometimes, hallucinations are normal.** For example, hearing the voice of or briefly seeing a loved one who recently died can be a part of the grieving process [emphasis added].[707]

Hallucinations and delusions make more sense to the observer as the one who is entangled in falsehood reveals his/her spiritual heart's desires, fears, and experiences as delusions and hallucinations — though foundationally falsehood — always reflect truths about that individual.

The hallucinations regularly experienced after a loved one's passing are typically not diagnosed as psychosis (though sometimes they are), since most clinicians can explain these phenomena within the person's life context

---

[706] Racheal Rettner, "How Common are Hallucinations?" *CBS News* (May 28, 2015): https://www.cbsnews.com/news/how-common-are-hallucinations/.

[707] U.S. National Library of Medicine, "Hallucinations," *Medline Plus* (September 11, 2019): https://medlineplus.gov/ency/article/003258.htm.

and desires. The APA also recognizes in the *DSM-5* that hallucinations are common when people face distress:

> Distress may take the form of hallucinations or pseudo-hallucinations and overvalued ideas that may present **clinically similar to true psychosis but are normative** to the patient's subgroup [emphasis added].[708]

It is normal for traumatic experiences to lead people who are unable to understand and move beyond their distressful phenomena into delusional thinking and hallucinations. Similarly, in a study published in *JAMA Psychiatry*,[709] researchers write,

> We used to think that only people with psychosis heard voices or had delusions, but now we know that otherwise healthy, high-functioning people also report these experiences.[710]

Editor in Chief of *JAMA Psychiatry* Albert Powers notes this common human phenomenon in a separate study:

> The lifetime incidence of psychotic experiences among individuals in the general population has been repeatedly estimated to be greater than 5% across large international samples. Many affected individuals do not seek

[708] APA, *DSM-5*, 103.

[709] John J. McGrath, Sukanta Saha, and Ali Al-Hamzawi, et. al., "Psychotic Experiences in the General Population: A Cross-National Analysis Based on 31261 Respondents From 18 Countries," *JAMA Psychiatry* Online vol. 72 (7) (July 2015): doi:10.1001/jamapsychiatry. 2015.0575.

[710] Chris Pash, "Hallucinations and Delusions are More Common Than We Thought," first published on *Business Insider Online* (May 28, 2015): https://www.sciencealert.com/hallucinations-and-delusions-are-more-common-than-we-thought.

psychiatric help and yet report experiences remarkably similar to those seen in classically defined psychosis.[711]

Research professor at the University of Queensland John McGrath also shares this widespread perspective:

> In particular, we are interested in learning why some people recover, while others may progress to more serious disorders such as schizophrenia . . . . We need to understand why it's temporary for some people and permanent for others. We can use these findings to start identifying whether the mechanisms causing these hallucinations are the same or different in both situations. **We need to rethink the link between hearing voices and mental health—it's more subtle than previously thought.** While people may experience a false perception such as mistakenly hearing their name called out in public, hallucinations and delusions are quite detailed, for example hearing voices that no one else can hear or a belief that somebody else has taken over your mind. **People should be reassured that there isn't anything necessarily wrong with them if it happens once or twice,** but if people are having regular experiences, we recommend that they seek help [emphasis added].[712]

Upon realizing that hallucinations are not rare let alone forms of pathological abnormality, Chief of the Hospital Psychiatric Division for the VA Greater L.A. Healthcare Center, Joe Pierre, discusses the problem psychiatrists face

---

[711] Albert R. Powers III, "Psychotic Experiences in the General Population: Symptom Specificity and the Role of Distress and Dysfunction," *JAMA Psychiatry Online* (September 25, 2019): doi:10.1001/jamapsychiatry.2019.2391.

[712] John McGrath for the University of Queensland, "Hallucinations and Delusions more Common than Thought," *ScienceDaily* (May 27, 2015): https://www.sciencedaily.com/releases/2015/05/150527124725.htm.

in attempting to fit this verifiable knowledge into their phenomenology:

> Now that we have a better understanding of the apparent commonality of voice-hearing, how do we make sense of these experiences? **The prevailing approach in psychology now is to conceptualize voice-hearing that is part of mental illness and voice-hearing that isn't as existing on a continuum. In other words, they're fundamentally the same experience – hallucinations – but they differ somehow in terms of severity.** More specifically, studies that have compared voice-hearing among "clinical" (help-seeking patients receiving professional treatment) and non-clinical persons reveal that voice-hearers who seek help tend to have voices that are perceived with greater frequency, more negative content, more associated distress, longer duration, less control, and greater associated interference with their lives and well-being. As expected then, voice-hearers who don't seek help tend to experience voices with more pleasant or neutral content that are more controllable and cause less distress or life interference.[713]

As is becoming more commonly accepted, the true psychiatric diagnostic basis of alleged disorder[714] is not the

713 Joseph M. Pierre, "Is it Normal to 'Hear Voices'? Distinguishing Normality from Pathology within auditory verbal hallucinations," *Psychology Today Online* (August 31, 2015): https://www.psychologytoday.com/us/blog/psych-unseen/201508/is-it-normal-hear-voices. Dr. Pierre expounds further on what he means by hallucinations being more distressful: "Since people with mental illness don't usually just report voice-hearing alone (there is no such thing as "hallucination disorder"), a thorough examination would also carefully explore for other symptoms, such as delusional thinking or evidence of mania or depression, that might lead a clinician to a clearer diagnosis that would guide appropriate treatment" (ibid.).

714 For further study on how the content of the delusions and hallucinations reveals the person's history and spiritual heart, see Daniel R. Berger, *The Insanity of Madness: Defining Mental Illness* (Taylors, SC: Alethia International Publications, 2018).

occurrence but is the content, the "severity," the difficulty in explaining, the frequency, and the determination of whether the content of the delusions and hallucinations are considered to be good or bad/healthy or unhealthy.

Furthermore, if practitioners place their faith in individual degenerationism, then they must ascertain subjectively if a person who is in distress and hallucinating is normal or abnormal. This diagnostic exercise is primarily founded on the content and frequency of the delusions and hallucinations and not on biological mechanisms or reliable objective evidence.[715]

Since its creation, the Kraepelinian model has failed to show scientifically how delusions and hallucinations are forms of degeneracy to begin with—a point on which the disease model of the psyche/soul largely depends. These human phenomena are certainly destructive and distressful by nature, but that reality does not determine them to be forms of abnormality. If delusions and hallucinations are normal—whether or not they are distressful or clinicians can explain them, then the theory that psychosis—the deceived condition of the soul—is a genetic disease is undermined at its principal philosophical level. In fact, a more urgent question is whether or not the human soul is naturally deceived.[716] Such a foundational discussion

---

[715] "In modern Western culture, hallucinations are more often considered to portend madness or something dire happening to the brain—even though the vast majority of hallucinations have no such dark implications" (Sacks, *Hallucinations*, preface xix).

[716] For further study on how human nature is naturally deceived, see Daniel R. Berger II, *The Insanity of Madness: Defining Mental Illness* (Taylors, SC: Alethia International Publications, 2018).

would determine if deceit is created by the body and certain experiences or is simply part of normal human nature and better revealed under psychological and physical stressors.

The Constructs are not Valid or Reliable

Psychiatric geneticists also face the problem of proving causation of alleged disease entities (constructs) that have no reliability and no validity. The boundaries between psychiatric disorders are actually still not objectively established as Kraepelin had hoped to prove. This fact poses a serious problem in claiming that schizophrenia, Bipolar, PTSD, DID, or OCD are separate forms of individual degeneracy let alone legitimate and objective diseases.

The lack of validity in claiming social and descriptive constructs as diseases applies not only to the individual constructs listed in the *DSM-5*, but also to the concept of mental illness in general. As presented in chapter six, even respected geneticists, psychiatrists, and other researchers recognize the *DSM-5* to simply be descriptive and social psychologies based upon Kraepelin's statistical approach rather than on validated scientific categories of discovered diseases.

The *DSM-5* Categories

The diagnostic categories contained in the *DSM-5* are facades that promote Kraepelin's degeneracy theory as a medical concept in exchange for statistically stigmatizing and further ostracizing those who desperately need help. The *DSM-5* is a politically driven pseudoscientific tool of perceived degenerative selection that is sourced in Kraepelin's eugenics. Psychiatrist and historian Ed Shorter describes the *DSM-5's* lack of scientific progress:

> It would be easy to think that the *Diagnostic and Statistical Manual of Mental Disorders (DSM)-5* evolved as a logical and scientific progression from *DSM-IV*. In fact, it evolved in a haphazard and politically driven manner from a century and a half of effort to get the classification of psychiatric illness right. In addition, the disappointing outcome of this entire endeavor is that, today, the field's nosology seems even farther from "cutting nature at the joints," — discerning the true illness entities locked in the brain — than in the days of Emil Kraepelin around 1900.[717]

In an article published in 2019 in the *Journal of Psychiatry Research*,[718] psychiatrists from the University of Liverpool concluded that the psychiatric labels are subjective attempts to explain what materialists cannot explain within their limited worldview:

> **although diagnostic labels create the illusion of an explanation, they are scientifically meaningless and can create stigma and prejudice.** I hope these findings will encourage mental health professionals to think beyond diagnoses and consider other explanations of mental

---

[717] Edward Shorter, "The History of Nosology and the Rise of the Diagnostic and Statistical Manual of Mental Disorders," *Dialogues in Clinical Neuroscience* 17 (1) (March 2015): 59.

[718] John Read, Rhiannon Corcoran, and Peter Kinderman "Heterogeneity in Psychiatric Diagnostic Classification," *Psychiatry Research* vol. 279 (September 2019): 15-22; https://doi.org/10.1016/j._psychres.2019.07.005.

distress, such as trauma and other adverse life experiences [emphasis added].[719]

Diagnoses of alleged mental illnesses represent descriptions and faith-based explanations rather than medical discovery.

Nassir Ghaemi, a psychiatrist, biomedical researcher, and Harvard and Tufts professor of psychiatry and translational medicine, left fulltime academia to enter the psychopharmaceutic industry as the director of translational medicine-neuroscience at Novartis Institutes. Despite his influential positions within the Kraepelinian model, he came to realize the true "unscientific nature" of the psychiatric industry:

> Somewhere in the midst of following the well-established academic psychiatrist career path, I came to believe that the profession itself was off track in important ways. For instance, the **Diagnostic and Statistical Manual of Mental Disorders (DSM), the Holy Bible of the American Psychiatric Association, is mostly false and unscientific.** Standard treatments, like antidepressants, the bread and butter of practicing clinicians, are mostly ineffective, especially for certain depressive states like bipolar depression or mixed states. Most current drugs are me-too variants of those that are either minimally effective or have had their benefit and will not produce much further gain with the same basic biological effects. **The research designs used for some studies are invalid, in my view, and overestimate drug benefits. This leads academics and clinicians to use some agents in scenarios where belief in their efficacy exceeds reality** (like antidepressants for prevention of depression, or

[719] Ibid., 22.

antipsychotics for prevention of bipolar illness) [emphasis added].[720]

There can be no science or discovery of valid diseases within an approach that creates its own subjective-descriptive constructs/syndromes about human phenomenology and insists that these metaphysical human struggles be viewed as medical abnormalities that allegedly identify some people as genetically defective. Only in the field of psychiatry can a group of phenomenologists sit around a table and subjectively decide who should be viewed as healthy and unhealthy while claiming such activity to fall within medicine. Dr. Ghaemi also addresses the unscientific nature of the vital phenotypes listed as symptoms:

> If we don't get our phenotypes right, even if we are looking at the right genes with the right methods, we'll get false negative results . . . . Unfortunately, we can't absolve ourselves of the need to be clinically as precise and accurate as we can, while also conducting genetic and other biological studies. That's the whole problem with *DSM-III, IV,* and *5,* in my view: they are made up professionally for a myriad of "pragmatic" reasons, not scientific ones. Thus they provide scientifically invalid phenotypes which doom genetic studies to failure.[721]

Genetic claims cannot be trusted because psychiatric phenotypes are not scientific. Most traditional "mental illnesses" or forms of "historical madness" are so labeled

---

[720] Nassir Ghaemi, "How Academia Left Me: a psychiatric researcher's mid-career shift to the pharmaceutical industry," *Medscape Psychiatry* (June 13, 2018): https://www.medscape.com/viewarticle/897877 #vp_2.

[721] Nassir Ghaemi, "The Genetic Fallacy in Psychiatry," *Medscape Psychiatry* (August 5, 2013): http://boards.medscape.com/ forums/?128@@.2a590550! comment=1.

because they specifically lack core biological markers; they are metaphysical phenomena. Significantly, as Ghaemi indicates, Kraepelin himself built psychiatric disorders upon faulty phenotypes from the beginning:

> This is what has happened in my view with 30 years of MDD [Major Depressive Disorder] genetic research . . . . Kraepelin didn't get it just right either; he wasn't a god. But at least he tried to move the scientific process along. Our problem is that we stopped following that process in about 1920, when Freud came along to enrapture the profession, like my senior colleague in past years. And in 1980, when we tried to pick up the scientific thread with *DSM-III*, we got misled again by the postmodernist "pragmatism" of American psychiatry; we didn't really care about science and truth, only insurance payments and power.[722]

Whether or not geneticists like the fact that metaphysical symptoms are the true substance of schizophrenia and all psychotic disorders, it remains that the decades of the constructs' existence, diagnostic relevance, and systematic categorization in the *DSM* and other publications, based solely on these alleged phenotypes since Kraepelin, expose this fact as undeniable. As Brazilian research psychiatrist at Tufts Medical School Sivan Mauer recognizes, the concept of psychosis is a description of phenomenological problems (symptoms) and not an actual diagnosis: "What we must understand is that psychosis is an entirely nonspecific diagnosis; actually, it is just a set of symptoms."[723]

---

[722] Ibid.

[723] Sivan Mauer, "'All I've Got are Negative Thoughts': Reflections on *The Joker*," *Medscape Psychiatry* (December 23, 2019): https://www.medscape.com/viewarticle/923045.

The categories that Kraepelin invented and that psychiatric geneticists thereafter have embraced and added to are not scientifically reliable. Others agree and present how the *DSM* diagnostic system "dehumanizes" some people and enables degenerative applications:

> The key problem remains that of the validity of diagnostic criteria. Ideally, these should be based on demonstrable etiologic or pathogenic data, but such information is rarely available in psychiatry. Current classifications rely on the use of extremely diverse elements in differing degrees: descriptive criteria, evolutive criteria, etiopathogenic criteria, psychopathogenic criteria, etc. Certain syndrome-based classifications such as *DSM III* and its successors aim to be atheoretical and pragmatic. Others, such as *ICD-10*, while more eclectic than the different versions of *DSM*, follow suit by abandoning the terms "disease" and "illness" in favor of the more consensual "disorder." The legitimacy of classifications in the field of psychiatry has been fiercely contested, being variously dubbed "a reductive academic exercise of no relevance to patients," "a dehumanizing labelling system, and a potential source of social and political violence," "a destructive prognostic guide," and so on.[724]

Former director of the National Institutes of Mental Health Thomas Insel asserted in 2013 in anticipation of the *DSM-5's* publication,

> While *DSM* has been described as a 'Bible' for the field, it is, at best, a dictionary, creating a set of labels and defining each . . . The weakness [of the *DSM*] is its lack of validity. Unlike our definitions of ischemic heart disease, lymphoma, or AIDS, the *DSM* diagnoses are based on a

---

[724] T. Lemperiere, "The Importance of Classifications in Psychiatry," *L'Encephale* Vol. 5 (21) (December, 1995): 3.

consensus about clusters of clinical symptoms, not any objective laboratory measure.[725]

Psychiatrist Maria Turri also highlights how the diagnostic system, its numerous psychiatric constructs, and its proposed treatments are maintained and applied primarily through circular reasoning:

> **Psychiatric interventions (particularly biological ones) are tested on a large scale on the basis of a diagnostic system which is founded on the standard psychiatric interview. Or shall we say, that the standard psychiatric interview is founded on the official diagnostic system? It's a chicken-and-egg situation.** On this chicken-and-egg is grounded all the evidence that determines whether therapeutic interventions are efficacious or not. And yet there is absolutely no evidence-base for the diagnostic system (and many have written about this), and there is no evidence-base either – and this is the best kept secret in psychiatry – for the standard psychiatric interview. **Most evidence-base in psychiatric research has been built on quicksand** [emphasis added].[726]

Kraepelin's concepts of schizophrenia, bipolar, and mental and racial hygiene were not scientific concepts, but hypotheses based upon presuppositional faith in individual degenerationism, materialism, humanism, bio-determinism, and Darwinianism just as today's expanded psychiatric categories are. Without proving that delusions and hallucinations are both abnormalities and disease entities, the discussion of genetic causes as a scientific

725 Thomas Insel, "Transforming Diagnosis." *National Institute of Mental Health* (April 29, 2013): http://www.nimh.nih.gov/about/ director/2013/ transforming -diagnosis.shtml.

726 Maria Grazi Turri, "The Best Kept Secret in Psychiatry," *Asylum* 26 (2) (Winter 2019): https:// asylummagazine.org/2019/06/the-best-kept-secret-in-psychiatry-by-maria-grazia-turri/.

venture is illogical. Yet, no empirical evidence exists to accept schizophrenia or any other alleged psychotic disorder as a legitimate organic disease. The construct of mental illness is merely descriptive psychology, empowered by circular reasoning, and applied according to a dogmatic secular phenomenology.

The *DSM* Constructs

Not only is the *DSM-5* a subjective diagnostic system, but also the specific categories/constructs presented in the *DSM-5* are not objective themselves and do not possess significant lines of demarcation between any of the "severe mental illnesses." In the book *Psychiatric Genetics: A Primer for Clinical and Basic Scientists*, the authors, writing for the International Society of Psychiatric Genetics, state,

> **The lack of validity of psychiatric phenotypes — the extent to which a diagnostic concept represents a true entity, based solely on clinical manifestations without pathognomonic markers or laboratory tests — has been the chief impediment to our identification of their causes.** Widespread agreement regarding the lack of validity of the psychiatric classification system has led to substantial efforts to study the dimensional manifestations of the core domains underlying psychiatric disorders [emphasis added]. [727]

It is upon claiming psychiatric phenotypes (e.g., delusions and hallucinations) as valid that "diagnostic concepts" or different psychiatric constructs are presented as true. But as admitted, delusions and hallucinations' lack of scientific

[727] Alison K. Merikangas and Kathleen R. Merikangas, *Psychiatric Genetics: A Primer for Clinicians and Basic Scientists* edited by Thomas G. Schulze and Francis J. McMahon (NY: Oxford University Press, 2018), 5.

validity causes a tremendous problem for genetic theorists. Another group of psychiatric researchers also explain in the abstract of their report,

The theory and practice of psychiatric diagnoses are central yet contentious. This paper examines the heterogeneous nature of categories within the *DSM-5*, how this heterogeneity is expressed across diagnostic criteria, and its consequences for clinicians, clients, and the diagnostic model. Selected chapters of the *DSM-5* were thematically analyzed: schizophrenia spectrum and other psychotic disorders; bipolar and related disorders; depressive disorders; anxiety disorders; and trauma- and stressor-related disorders. Themes identified heterogeneity in specific diagnostic criteria, including symptom comparators, duration of difficulties, indicators of severity, and perspective used to assess difficulties. Wider variations across diagnostic categories examined symptom overlap across categories, and the role of trauma. **Pragmatic criteria and difficulties that recur across multiple diagnostic categories offer flexibility for the clinician, but undermine the model of discrete categories of disorder. This nevertheless has implications for the way cause is conceptualised**, such as implying that trauma affects only a limited number of diagnoses despite increasing evidence to the contrary. Individual experiences and specific causal pathways within diagnostic categories may also be obscured. **A pragmatic approach to psychiatric assessment, allowing for recognition of individual experience, may therefore be a more effective way of understanding distress than maintaining commitment to a disingenuous categorical system** [emphasis added].[728]

The APA also concedes in the *DSM-5* that

---

[728] John Read, Rhiannon Corcoran, and Peter Kinderman, "Heterogeneity in Psychiatric Diagnostic Classification," *Psychiatry Research* vol. 279 (September 2019): 15-22; https://doi.org/10.1016/j. psychres.2019.07.005.

although some mental disorders may have well-defined boundaries around symptom clusters, scientific evidence now places many, if not most, disorders on a spectrum with closely related disorders that have **shared symptoms, shared genetic and environmental risk factors, and possibly shared neural substrates . . . . In short, we have come to recognize that the boundaries between disorders are more porous than originally perceived.**[729]

Genetic research verifies the APA's assertion that "the same genetic factors can lead to different disorders."[730] These scientists, however, are not proving genetic causation as suggested. Rather, they discovered that the boundaries between allegedly different disorders are not objectively established or empirically sound. In truth, what researchers are observing is that people who are labeled differently within the bio-psycho-social system and based upon their allegedly different struggles share similar genetic variances and similar life difficulties. Other researchers note this reality, though they interpret the data according to their presuppositional phenomenology:

It should also be recognized that, as with environmental risk factors, many of the genetic variants associated with schizophrenia may also be associated with other psychiatric disorders, suggesting overlap in risk factors and potentially mechanisms.[731]

[729] APA, *DSM-5*, 5-6.

[730] Elliott Rees and George Kirov, *Psychiatric Genetics: A Primer for Clinicians and Basic Scientists* edited by Thomas G. Schulze and Francis J. McMahon (New York: Oxford University Press, 2018), 92.

731 Robert A. McCutcheon, Tiago Reis Marques, and Oliver D. Howes, "Schizophrenia—An Overview," *JAMA Psychiatry Online* (October 30, 2019): doi:10.1001/jamapsychiatry.2019.3360.

Psychiatric geneticists also recognize that there are not significant genetic differences between the original Kraepelinian constructs of bipolar and schizophrenia:[732]

> Bipolar disorder (BD) overlaps schizophrenia in its clinical presentation and genetic liability. Alternative approaches to patient stratification beyond current diagnostic categories are needed to understand the underlying disease processes and mechanisms.[733]

Conclusions to a study published by a number of psychiatric geneticists in late 2019 in *JAMA Psychiatry* confirm the same findings:

> Large genetic association studies of psychotic experiences from the population-based UK Biobank sample found support for a shared genetic liability between psychotic experiences and schizophrenia, major depressive disorder, bipolar disorder, and [ADHD].[734]

If researchers considered that the genetic responses to life's circumstances due to a person's spiritual perspective and lack of sleep better explain normal human reactions than

---

732 Sophie E. Legge, Hannah J. Jones, Kimberley M. Kendall, Antonio F. Pardiñas, Georgina Menzies, Matthew Bracher-Smith, Valentina Escott-Price, Elliott Rees, Katrina A. S. Davis, Matthew Hotopf, Jeanne E. Savage, Danielle Posthuma, Peter Holmans, George Kirov, Michael J. Owen, Michael C. O'Donovan, Stanley Zammit, James T. R. Walters, "Association of Genetic Liability to Psychotic Experiences With Neuropsychotic Disorders and Traits," *JAMA Psychiatry* (September 25, 2019): doi:10.1001/jamapsychiatry.2019.2508.

733 J. Allardyce, G. Leonenko, M. Hamshere, A.F. Pardinas, L. Forty, S. Knott, et al., "Association Between Schizophrenia-Related Polygenic Liability and the Occurrence and Level of Mood-Incongruent Psychotic Symptoms in Bipolar Disorder," *JAMA Psychiatry* vol. 75 (1) (January 1, 2018): 28; doi: 10.1001/jamapsychiatry.2017.3485.

734 Legge, Jones, Kendall, et. al. "Association of Genetic Liability to Psychotic Experiences with Neuropsychotic Disorders and Traits."

alleged degeneracy does, then the shared neurological and genetic variances discovered in research make logical sense.[735] But admitting these physical changes are normal effects — albeit impairing and destructive — rather than etiologies undermines Kraepelinian faith and the historic psychiatric narrative.

Not only are "genetic liabilities" shared among allegedly differing *DSM-5* disorders, but they are also observed in people considered to be "normal." In one journal entry published in *JAMA Psychiatry*, for example, geneticists write that the same alleged genetic predisposition for schizophrenia is observed in the "normal" or general population as well.[736] Numerous other studies such as the one published by the International Society of Psychiatric Genetics reveal that "psychotic-like experiences" are normative in adolescence and "partly share genetic influences with clinically-recognized psychiatric disorders, specifically schizophrenia and major depression."[737] In other words, the alleged abnormal genes themselves are

[735] One example of the shared correlate of sleep deprivation can be observed in children said to have ADHD, who commonly struggle with insomnia (Berger, *The Truth about ADHD*, 107-11).

736 H.J. Jones, E. Stergiakouli, K.E. Tansey, J. Heron, M. Cannon, P. Holmans, G. Lewis, D.E. Linden, P.B. Jones, G. Davey Smith, M.C. O'Donovan, M.J. Owen, J.T. Walters, and Z. Zammit, "Phenotypic Manifestation of Genetic Risk for Shcizophrenia During Adolescence in the General Population," *JAMA Psychiatry* vol. 73 (3) (March 2016): 221-28; doi: 10.1001/jamapsychiatry.2015.3058.

737 O. Pain, F. Dudbridge, A.G. Cardno, D. Freeman, Y. Lu, S. Lundstrom, P. Lichtenstein, and A. Ronald, "*American Journal of Medical Genetic, Neuropsychiatric Genetics: The Official Publication of the International Society of Psychiatric Genetics* vol. 177 (4) (June 2018): 416-25; doi: 10.1002/ajmg.b.32630.

not significantly different across allegedly different psychiatric disease entities or among people both considered normal and abnormal within psychiatric phenomenology.[738] Hallucinations and delusions are common and normal phenomena of human nature, which explains why shared genetic expressions exist in both perceived normal and theorized abnormal people. The Kraepelinian diagnostic system of eugenic degeneracy is simply not a valid or reliable phenomenology.

The results reveal that people — no matter how they are labeled or categorized within psychiatric phenomenology — really are not all that different, as they share the same struggle to live in the post-Genesis three world. Consequently, psychiatrists have developed a "new" philosophical approach to psychiatry. This "dimensional approach," as it has come to be called by psychiatric researchers and even in the *DSM-5*, returns the theory of madness to the time prior to Emil Kraepelin's attempt to split madness into alleged distinct diseases:

> The dimensional model would suggest that psychotic symptoms occurring in different psychiatric disorders such as schizophrenia and bipolar disorder share the same neurobiology and etiological factors. **The hypothesis of an extensive overlap in the phenomenology and etiopathophysiology of psychosis occurring across different disorders is a fundamental challenge to the Kraepelinian conceptualization of major psychotic disorders.** Several lines of evidence support this hypothesis: phenomenological similarities in psychosis across disorders are frequently observed in clinical practice. Slight qualitative differences in reality

---

738 Legge, Jones, Kendall, et. al. "Association of Genetic Liability to Psychotic Experiences with Neuropsychotic Disorders and Traits."

distortions can easily be due to the modulating effects of the other features of the disorder [emphasis added].[739]

Allegedly, the genes are very similar, the neurobiology is essentially the same, and the major symptoms are the same across the spectrum of "severe mental illnesses." Eugenics has in essence returned to Benjamin Rush's theories of hereditary madness and diseases of the mind. In fact, upon discovering this reality, some psychiatric geneticists, including the famed Kenneth Kendler, have been honest enough to admit and list the fatal flaws of Kraepelianism, which still today fully represents the modern psychiatric genetic theory:

> First, Kraepelin's new categories of dementia praecox and manic-depressive insanity were too broad and too heterogeneous. Second, his emphasis on course of illness was misconceived, as the same disease can result in brief episodes or a chronic course. Third, the success of his system was based on the quality of his textbooks and his academic esteem, rather than on empirical findings. Fourth, his focus on symptoms and signs led to neglect of the whole patient and his or her life story. Fifth, Kraepelin's early emphasis on experimental psychology did not bear the expected fruit. **Sixth, Kraepelin was committed to the application of the medical disease model. However, because of the many-to-many relationship between brain pathology and psychiatric symptoms, true natural disease entities may not exist in psychiatry. Most of the ongoing debates about Kraepelin's nosology have roots in these earlier discussions and would be enriched by a deeper appreciation of their historical contexts. As authoritative as Kraepelin was, and remains today, his was only one among many voices, and attention to them would be**

[739] Gunvant K. Thaker, "Boundaries of the Psychosis Phenotype." *Schizophrenia Bulletin* vol. 38 (2) (2012): 205-6; doi:10.1093/schbul/sbs003.

well repaid by a deeper understanding of the
fundamental conceptual challenges in our field
[emphasis added].[740]

As Kendler and Engsrom candidly confess in *American
Journal of Psychiatry*, the metaphysical psychiatric
symptoms and the body cannot be empirically correlated,
thus leaving psychiatry hopeless to prove Kraepelinian
constructs let alone his genetic etiological theory: "True
natural disease entities may not exist in psychiatry."[741]

Toward the end of his life, even Kraepelin realized that the
two constructs of madness (manic depressive insanity and
dementia praecox), which he had created himself, could
not be objectively differentiated:

> We shall have to get accustomed to the fact that our
> much-used clinical checklist does not permit us to
> differentiate reliably manic depressive insanity [now
> called unipolar and bipolar disorders] from dementia
> praecox [now called schizophrenia] in all circumstances;
> and that there is an overlap between the two, which
> depends on the fact that the clinical signs have arisen
> from certain antecedent conditions.[742]

As one psychiatric journal recognizes, there exists no
significant scientific boundary between Kraepelin's created
constructs:

[740] Kenneth S. Kendler and E.J. Engsrom, "Criticisms of Kraepelin's
Psychiatric Nosology: 1898-1927," *American Journal of Psychiatry* vol. 175 (4)
(April 1, 2018): 316.

[741] Ibid.

[742] Kraepelin, Emil Kraepelin, "Clinical Manifestations of Mental Illness,"
History of Psychiatry 3 (1920): 499-529.

Kraepelin tried to bring forward the empirical knowledge in psychiatry, he did not want to have cessation in psychiatry in general and in the classification of psychiatric disorders in particular. He discussed and partly revisited his view and his theoretical approach in the different editions of his textbook according to the state of his empirical knowledge. This is also true for the dichotomy. More than twenty years after the 6th edition of his textbook, he wrote in an essay 'Die Erscheinungsformen des Irreseins' ('The manifestations of insanity') regarding the dichotomy: "No experienced diagnostician would deny that cases where it seems impossible to arrive to a clear decision, despite extremely careful observation, are unpleasantly frequent." . . . **"therefore, the increasingly obvious impossibility to separate the two respective illnesses satisfactorily should raise the suspicion that our question is wrong." This contribution shows that Kraepelin himself questioned his dichotomy of** *dementia praecox* **and** *manic depressive* **insanity,** a discussion which is lively still today. [emphasis added].[743]

Psychiatrist and historian Ed Shorter comments on Kraepelin's conclusions drawn on his own theory:

In 1920 Kraepelin softened slightly the watertight division between affective and nonaffective psychoses by admitting that the prognosis could not always be made on the basis of the presenting symptoms.[744]

Clinical psychologist Richard Bentall agrees: "The most likely explanation for the strong associations observed between schizophrenia, depression, and mania is that these

---

[743] H. Hippius and N. Muller, "The Work of Emil Kraepelin and His research Group in Munchen," *European Archives of Psychiatry and Clinical Neuroscience* 258 (2) (June 2008): 3; doi: 10.1007/s00406-008-2001-6.

[744] Shorter, *A History of Psychiatry*, 356.

diagnoses do not describe separate disorders."[745] In the *Journal of Abnormal Psychology*, dozens of clinical psychologists and psychiatrists jointly explain that there is no reliability between labeling some people as degenerates (psychopathology) and others as "normal" or for justifying a difference between psychiatric constructs:

> The reliability and validity of traditional taxonomies are limited by arbitrary boundaries between psychopathology and normality, often unclear boundaries between disorders, frequent disorder co-occurrence, heterogeneity within disorders, and diagnostic instability. These taxonomies went beyond evidence available on the structure of psychopathology and were shaped by a variety of other considerations, which may explain the aforementioned shortcomings [emphasis added].[746]

Within Kraepelin's original constructs of degeneracy (alleged psychiatric disorders) on which the genetic theory and its cherished statistical approach rests, there is also no substantial objective means to differentiate between psychiatric subconstructs (e.g., between depression and bipolar):

> In its absence, the hunt for mood genes must rely on a diagnostic scheme based solely on patterns of behavior. Unfortunately, it is not easy to draw a sharp line between manic-depression and other mood variations. In fact, as we shall now see, the nature of this boundary has been a

---

[745] Bentall, *Madness Explained*, 71.

[746] R. Kotov, R.F. Kreugar, and D. Watson, et al. "The Hierarchical Taxonomy of Psychopathology (HiTOP): A dimensional alternative to traditional nosologies," *Journal of Abnormal Psychology* Vol. 126 (4) (May 2017): 454; doi: 10.1037/abn0000258.

matter of heated controversy for about a hundred years.[747]

There is no objective difference between these constructs to justify considering them as separate problems and certainly not as valid diseases.[748] Furthermore, there does not exist a significant somatic difference between allegedly normal and abnormal people.

Though the "dimensional approach" or "hiTOP" appears to be more empirically based than Rush's traditional hereditary madness or Kraepelin's eugenic theory, there remains the problems that no objective evidence exists to accept the notion of individual degeneracy and that metaphysical symptoms cannot be scientifically approached to validate such a theory. All that is left in continuing to uphold psychiatric genetics is utilizing Kraepelin's statistical approach and foundational philosophies within a dimensional perspective:

> Implementation of dimensional underpinning of complex disorders has long been recognized in population genetics as represented by models [constructs] . . . . **Thresholds that distinguish disorder from non-disorder are defined by the population prevalence or prevalence in relatives of affected individuals.** The application of these models for family studies of psychiatric disorders has informed the spectra of expression of many psychiatric disorders, including alcoholism, mood disorders, and schizophrenia. **However, whether these dimensional domains are more valid than traditional categorical domains in psychiatry, according to the classic formulation of diagnostic**

[747] Samuel H. Barondes, *Mood Genes: Hunting for Origins of Mania and Depression* (New York: Oxford Press, 1998), 23.

[748] Daniel R. Berger II, *Rethinking Depression: Not a Sickness Not a* Sin (Taylors, SC: Alethia International Publications, 2019).

validity by Robins and Guze, is still to be determined [emphasis added].[749]

The APA has admitted in their "*DSM-5* Integrated Approach to Diagnosis and Classifications" pamphlet that,

> The dimensional approach, which allows a clinician more latitude to assess the severity of a condition and does not imply a concrete threshold between "normality" and a disorder.[750]

There is absolutely no validating science to view people as disordered versus non-disordered or to view schizophrenia as a real disease that differs from the construct of bipolar, anxiety, depression, transgenderism, or eating disorders. Simply because people are struggling in persistent ways, are responding to life's difficulties, evils, or their own guilt, or are turning to their natural deceit does not make some people degenerates.

Transgenderism or *gender dysphoria*, as it is now called, offers one example of how delusional thinking is easily transformed into a content specific psychiatric construct rather than being viewed as a type of schizophrenia. Gender dysphoria (with its impairing, distressful, and destructive behavior) represents a distinct delusion that

[749] Alison K. Merikangas and Kathleen R. Merikangas, *Psychiatric Genetics: A Primer for Clinicians and Basic Scientists* edited by Thomas G. Schulze and Francis J. McMahon (New York: Oxford University Press, 2018), 5.

750 The American Psychiatric Association, "*DSM-5* Integrated Approach to Diagnosis and Classifications" downloadable PDF (2013): https://www. google.com/url?sa=t&rct=j&q=&esrc=s&source=web&cd=&ved=2ahUKEwjIk 4Ljmd3pAhVhnuAKHclNBzUQFjANegQIAxAB&url=https%3A%2F%2Fwww. psychiatry.org%2FFile%2520Library%2FPsychiatrists%2FPractice%2FDSM%2F APA_DSM-5-Integrated-Approach.pdf&usg=AOvVaw2w5JqbUZcxa0Dm0US aR3yq.

could easily be considered as falling within the criteria of alleged schizophrenia — once again exposing the fluid boundaries between allegedly different disorders. But at the same time, gender dysphoria poses a tremendous empirical problem for the psychiatric genetic theory. The delusional thinking that a biological boy falsely identifies himself as a girl opposes the boy's undeniable genetics and obvious, objective evidence. Psychiatrist Perry Wilson describes "transgender girls":

> This means they were born with male genetics and genitalia, but at some point before enrollment in the study, they transitioned socially to living as a girl.[751]

Genes do not predispose people to produce delusional or psychotic thinking. Rather, the strong, deceived desires of the flesh and one's worldview shape a person's identity and drive delusional thinking no matter how these phenomena are categorized. Some psychiatrists such as renowned professor of psychiatry at Johns Hopkins University Paul McHugh believe that what is taking place in hormone treatments and sex changes "amounts to an experiment on these young people without telling them it's an experiment."[752] Rather than lovingly correcting a person's delusions, many clinicians have chosen to support these false fixed beliefs and insist that society agree with

---

[751] F. Perry Wilson, "'No, I'm a Girl: What Influences Gender Identity,'" *Medscape Psychiatry* (November 20, 2019): https://www.medscape.com/view article/921136?nlid=132762_424&src=WNL_mdplsfeat_191126_mscpedit_psyc &uac=264124BV&spon=12&impID=2182659&faf=1.

[752] Paul McHugh, quoted by Maria Lencki, "Johns Hopkins professor on child transgender trend: 'Many will regret this,'" *The College Fix* (September 17, 2019): https://www.thecollegefix.com/johns-hopkins-professor-on-child-transgender-trend-many-will-regret-this/.

this phenomenology that, ironically, contradicts clear genetic evidence to the contrary.

Despite the lack of validity and reliability, many people still believe that bipolar, schizophrenia, and gender dysphoria (to name a few) are real diseases that are distinct from one another rather than merely being Kraepelinian eugenic constructs.[753] Instead of some people being categorized as abnormal because Kraepelin and many others before and after him could not explain distressful, impairing, or frightening behavior and falsehood within their Darwinian faith, the appropriate and scientifically sound perspective of human nature should be to understand that all humanity — not just a few people — are both weak and deceived. Moreover, substantiating evidence shows that the psychiatric constructs framed as disorders are simply normal but impairing reactions to the many difficulties of life and the destructive desires of human nature.

Genes are not Fixed

In addition to the facts that delusions and hallucinations cannot be approached within science nor are they abnormalities and that the psychiatric constructs themselves are subjective descriptions of people's problems rather than actual diseases, there also exists several other devastating problems to the eugenic theory. Chief among

---

[753] John Read, Richard P. Bentall, and Roar Fosse, "Time to abandon the Bio-bio-bio model of psychosis: Exploring the epigenetic and psychological mechanisms by which adverse life events lead to psychotic symptoms," *Cambridge University Press* Vol. 18 (40) (December 2009): 299; https://doi.org/10.1017/S1121189X00000257.

these problems is that the hereditary theory rests on the false notion that genes are fixed and thus predetermine a person's beliefs, risks, behaviors, and life outcomes. In accordance with this belief, psychiatric geneticists suggest that their concept of schizophrenia is currently a hopeless, incurable condition:

> Schizophrenia is a chronic, severe mental disorder characterized by hallucinations and delusions, "flat" emotional expression and cognitive difficulties. Symptoms usually start between the ages of 16 and 30. **Antipsychotic medications can relieve symptoms but there is no cure for the disease** [emphasis added].[754]

Because Kraepelin and countless psychiatrists before and after him have argued that "mental illness" was hereditary, they have insisted that one's genes are fixed. Hence, those diagnosed as individual degenerates were said to have no hope of recovery within eugenic belief:

> Though Kraepelin's views about the course of schizophrenia were found to be unsupported over 30 years ago, many in the general public continue to believe that people diagnosed with schizophrenia cannot recover. In fact, research finds that exposure to information about the biological and genetic contributions to disorders such as schizophrenia is associated with increased support for these negative stereotypes. This is likely the case because many members of the general public struggle to understand that human characteristics can be both "genetically-influenced" and

---

[754] Vanderbilt University Medical Center, "Researchers find high-risk genes for Schizophrenia," *Science News* (April 22, 2019): https://www.sciencedaily.com/releases/2019/04/190422170538.htm.

"changeable" — a nuance that runs counter to the eugenics-derived view that people are born, not made.[755]

Historian Susan Lamb explains why genetic determinism is necessary to sustain faith in psychiatry:

> Unlike general medicine and surgery, moreover, psychiatry possessed no magic bullets, no technological marvels. As a result, the custodial character of mental institutions had remained unchanged as they continued to fill with people popularly perceived as hopeless cases.[756]

German psychiatric researcher and historian Heinz Haefner records the perspective of early psychiatrists regarding forms of degeneracy as evolutionary natural selection and as inherited. He discusses Swiss born Eugen Bleuler, the psychiatrist who renamed Kraepelin's construct of *dementia praecox* to its currently accepted name: *schizophrenia,*:

> The most severely burdened should not propagate themselves . . . . If we do nothing but make mental and physical cripples capable of propagating themselves, and the healthy stocks have to limit the number of children because so much has to be done for the maintenance of others, if natural selection is generally suppressed, then unless we will get new measures our race must rapidly deteriorate.[757]

[755] Philip Yanos, "The Long Shadow of the Eugenics Movement: Its Influence Persists," *Psychology Today Online* (June 02, 2018): https://www.psychologytoday.com/us/blog/written/201806/the-long-shadow-the-eugenics-movement.

[756] Susan D. Lamb, *Pathologist of the Mind: Adolf Meyer and the Origins of American Psychiatry* (Baltimore: Johns Hopkins University Press, 2014), 100.

[757] Paul Eugen Bleuler, *Textbook of Psychiatry*, translated by A. A. Brill (New York: Macmillian Press, 1924), 434.

Bleuler also believed that "hereditary schizophrenia" was hopeless, which led him to consider euthanasia as a seemingly altruistic remedy:

> The idea of preventing incurable mental illness on a large scale by steering the evolutionary process by eugenic measures must have seemed to be very attractive, if not fascinating, to many disillusioned psychiatrists. This background helps us to understand why even a Swiss psychiatrist of such high moral values as Eugen Bleuler (1857–1939), Zurich, wrote in his 1936 "*Article on biological ethics*": **"In the case of incurably mentally ill patients suffering from severe hallucinations and melancholic depression and incapacitated in their functioning I would confer upon a council of doctors the right and in very severe cases the duty to shorten their suffering — often by several years."** It offered a justification and a ready-made program for killing incurably ill people. And there were many more who thought likewise.[758]

The sterilization and euthanasia measures executed in Nazi Germany were founded on the false beliefs that genes are fixed, that social constructs represent valid disease entities, and that eliminating faulty genes (including if necessary their human carriers) is altruistic and necessary for the health of everyone. Accepting the notion that delusions and hallucinations are fixed without remedy both leaves a person helpless and leads to pragmatic and historically horrific approaches to "treating" people who are deeply deceived.

Simply because a gene — such as the C4 gene — is altered or different in people who have typically been through trauma, are not sleeping well, or might be consuming

---

[758] Heinz Haefner, "Comment on E.F. Torrey and R.H. Yolken: "Psychiatric genocide: Nazi attempts to eradicate schizophrenia" *Schizophrenia Bulletin* vol. 36 (1) (2010): 26-32.

prescribed or illicit psychotropic drugs does not determine that the gene has caused delusions and hallucinations or that the construct of schizophrenia has been validated as a real disease or as the underlying problem. Despite this fact, genetic psychiatrists and other eugenicists insist that genes are causative while at the same time admitting the theory is still speculative:

> Schizophrenia is a severe mental disorder with an unclear pathophysiology. Increased expression of the immune gene C4 has been linked to a greater risk of developing schizophrenia; however, **it is unknown whether C4 plays a causative role in this brain disorder** [emphasis added].[759]

Scientists are only able to "link" or "correlate" somatic variances.

The popular trope that genes cause schizophrenia — an allegedly fixed disorder — and most other alleged mental illnesses rests on several false assumptions that need to be examined. When scrutinized with objective scientific evidence, these psychiatric assumptions are shown to be false theories.

Fixity's Necessity

Believing that genes are fixed is an essential presupposition to accepting the psychiatric genetic theory, and such a

---

[759] Ashley L. Comer, Tushare Jinadasa, Lisa N. Kretsge, Thanh P.H. Nguyen, Jungjoon Lee, Elena R. Newmark, Frances S. Hausmann, SaraAnn Rosenthal, Kevin Liu Kot, William W. Yen, Alberto Cruz-Martín, "Increased expression of schizophrenia-associated gene C4 leads to hypoconnectivity of prefrontal cortex and reduced social interaction," *BioRxiv* 598342; doi: https://doi.org/ 10.1101/598342.

position intrinsically leads to believing in genetic fatalism or genetic determinism (that genes cause one's conscious experiences and moral behaviors). But the empirical evidence available undermines the psychiatric notion that people cannot change and, therefore, that they are determined by their genes to be hopeless. The theory of genetic fatalism or the immutability of a person's genome is simply not a valid hypothesis:

> Although genetic fatalism has also become a popular belief in some circles, critical examination of this idea shows that it does not square with modern biology or with commonsense. As an almost trivial example, for genetic fatalism to be true an individual possessing a gene responsible for a specific type of cancer must develop that type of cancer, no matter what he or she does. Clearly, this is not the way the world works.[760]

Essentially, what is claimed to be *genetic determinism* in psychiatry is actually *genetic probabilism*, which bioethicist David Resnik and Daniel Vorhaus affirm:

> While deterministic causation is common in the physical sciences, it is very rare in biology and in medicine. Most explanations and predictions in the biomedical sciences are probabilistic, not deterministic. As we shall soon see, despite assumptions to the contrary, most of the causal claims related to genetic determinism are probabilistic, not deterministic.[761]

Asserting that genes might influence a person's character and behavior is far different than claiming that a person's

---

[760] David B. Resnik and Daniel B Vorhaus, "Genetic Modification and Genetic Determinism." *Philosophy, Ethics, and Humanities in Medicine (PEHM)* vol. 1 (9) (June, 26 2006): doi:10.1186/1747-5341-1-9.

[761] Ibid.

genome causes them to think and behave in specific ways without the hope of changing. When psychiatric geneticists use terms such as "risk scores," "risk factors," "odd ratios," and "vulnerability," they are subjectively theorizing about genetic probability and not actually causation. For example, Peter Propping, an Emil Kraepelin Professor for Psychiatry at the Max Planck Institute of Psychiatry (2005) and acclaimed psychiatric geneticist, recounts the change from genetic determinism (nature and nurture) to genetic risk within the field of psychiatric genetics:

> When the study of human inheritance became a topic of scientific interest more than 100 years ago, brain function and mental disease immediately attracted the interest of researchers. Psychiatric genetics was dominated from its early beginnings by the question of nature and nurture. **Today this problem can be quantitatively approached with odds ratios and attributable risks for certain genotypes.**[762]

These terms identify the psychiatric eugenics theory of hereditary madness reframed in a more believable scientific façade. But as Richard Lewontin acknowledges, this eugenic theory is also a control mechanism:

> One of the major **biological ideological weapons** used to convince people that their position in society is fixed and unchangeable and, indeed, fair is the constant confusion between inherited and unchangeable.[763]

---

[762] Peter Propping, "The Biography of Psychiatric Genetics: From early achievements to Historical Burden, form an Anxious Society to Critical Geneticists," *American Journal of American Genetics: Neuropsychiatric Genetics* 136B (1) (July 5, 2005): 2; https://www.ncbi.nlm.nih.gov/pubmed/15924298.

[763] Lewontin, *Biology as Ideology*, 33.

When it comes to the human soul and its metaphysical phenomena, genetic determinism — based upon fixity — is a "biological ideological weapon" of eugenics that is not empirically sound.

A classic example of psychiatric "genetic risk" can be observed in the common belief that genes cause the human phenomena suggested by Benjamin Rush as "alcoholism" and categorized by the APA as "substance use disorders." The belief follows that since childhood abuse and trauma are correlated with a child growing up to use substances, then those who do not struggle with drugs even though they were abused must have a healthy genome compared to those who do struggle, as reported by Julie Brown in the *Psychiatric Times*:

> Exposure to adversities, such as parental divorce, during childhood and adolescence may increase the risk of substance abuse in persons with a particular gene mutation. Researchers at the University of Oklahoma College of Medicine focused on a common variant of the gene for the enzyme catechol-O-methyltransferase (COMT, Val158Met, rs4680) in their study, which was published in Alcoholism: Clinical and Experimental Research. Persons with this mutation of the COMT gene are more vulnerable to the effects of stress in their early lives. The heightened vulnerability often leads to the consumption of alcohol and drugs before the age of 15 years, which is one of the key independent predictors of addiction. **"Early-life adversity doesn't make everyone an alcoholic,"** said senior study author William R. Lovallo, PhD, Professor of Psychiatry and Behavioral Sciences, OU College of Medicine, Oklahoma City, OK, in a press statement. **"But this study showed that people with this genetic mutation are going to have a higher**

Claiming that someone is at greater risk or predisposed to think a certain way is not the same as claiming that because genes are fixed, they cause people's desires and outworking behaviors. Likewise, one cannot assume that a person's genome is not altered by his/her faith and normal mental struggles after surviving child abuse, for instance. In other words, correlations do not equal evidence of claimed causation.

The fact that genes do not cause people to consume drugs explains the well-documented reality that many "alcoholics" or "addicts" — labels that indoctrinate the philosophies of individual degenerationism, materialism, and bio-determinism — arrive at a place in their lives of abstaining from substances entirely. Actually, the number of people who have overcome or "recovered" from what eugenicists for decades have referred to as "alcoholism" significantly undermines the deterministic theory. These are not merely casual drinkers or users, but people who were heavily enslaved to substances, entrapped in destructive patterns, and said within the psychiatric system to have had no hope of deliverance.

If a person's metaphysical/spiritual nature is considered, however, and not just his/her genes, then the verifiable evidence available that reveals how many people overcome their spiritual predisposition (as observed in behavior)

---

[764] Julie Brown, "Gene Mutation Can Raise Risk of Alcohol and Drug Abuse," *Psychiatric Times* (August 19, 2019): https://www.psychiatrictimes. com/substance-use-disorder/gene-mutation-can-raise-risk-alcohol-and-drug-abuse?rememberme=1 &elq_mid=8312&elq_cid=893295&GUID=31158D64-F01A-4DEA-AC1A-D3CE843FC9BC. Accessed August 25, 2019.

makes logical sense. As Benjamin Rush, who first proposed the psychiatric construct of alcoholism, readily confessed: "The use of strong drink is at **first the effect of free agency**. From habit it takes place and from necessity [emphasis added]."[765] Evolutionary bioethicists David Resnik and Daniel Vorhaus perceptively point out that "an individual with a genetic predisposition toward alcoholism will not develop this disease if he/she never drinks alcohol."[766] Similarly, Marc Lewis states,

> Alternatives to the brain disease model often highlight the social and environmental factors that contribute to addiction, as well as the learning processes that translate these factors into negative outcomes. For example, it has been shown repeatedly that adverse experiences in childhood and adolescence increase the probability of later addiction. Also, exposure to physical, economic, or psychological trauma greatly increases susceptibility to addiction. **Learning models propose that addiction, though obviously disadvantageous, is a natural, context-sensitive response to challenging environmental contingencies, not a disease**. Yet the brain disease model construes addictive learning in terms of pathologic brain changes triggered mainly by substance abuse. Learning models also favor individual solutions for overcoming addiction, facilitated by cognitive modifications and personal agency [emphasis added].[767]

[765] Benjamin Rush quoted by unknown, "Dr. Benjamin Rush and His Views on Alcoholism," *Health* (April 17, 2011): http://www.health.am/psy/more/dr-benjamin-rush-and-his-views-on-alcoholism/#ixzz5y0EnRAea.

[766] Resnik and Vorhaus, "Genetic Modification and Genetic Determinism."

[767] Marc Lewis, "Change in Addiction as Learning, Not Disease," *The New England Journal of Medicine* vol. 379 (16) (2018): 1151; DOI: 10.1056/NEJMra1602872.

What these statements highlight is that genes do not cause people to take a drink of alcohol or consume illicit drugs, much less predetermine them to do so. A person's desires and faith (moral will), however, do. Therefore, how a person's moral will—his or her innate desires and motives—is predisposed is far more relevant to discern than examining and considering the human genome. Behavioral neuroscientist at Becknell University Judith Grisel remarks on the common eugenic perspective taught to most premed students:

> The causes of this public health disaster are complicated, but it is widely accepted that about half of the contribution comes from inherited risk, and the rest an unfortunate confluence of environmental factors interacting with that biologic vulnerability. Either way, addiction has been widely seen as an individual dilemma driven by a derelict nervous system. **The sanguine view that the problem with people like me is in people like me furnishes tidy categories – sick or well; normal or abnormal – making those personally unaffected by the epidemic seem exempt from responsibility.** We'll find the misguided proteins or pathways correlated with aberrant behaviour, translate this knowledge into biomedical interventions and voila! Cured . . . . A clump of abnormal cells may cause a heart attack or melanoma, **but substance use disorders involve large swaths of neural real estate and processes such as motivation and learning. Excising brain cells or chemicals responsible for these sorts of global functions isn't feasible, and the chance of finding a specific gene or chemical**

responsible for addictive behaviours is nil [emphasis added].[768]

People might be predisposed to desire alcohol, but such a predisposition does not determine that they pursue the drug nor that there exists an abnormality. Accepting this fact, though, also determines that a person's spiritual heart (desires, motives, and guiding faith) and not their physical genome is ultimately responsible for the psychiatric descriptive construct referred to as alcoholism or substance abuse disorder.

Without considering the reality of a person's moral will as a part of his or her metaphysical nature, one cannot accurately discuss how the metaphysical soul/psyche and the physical body correlate. Clearly, morality cannot be approached within the field of science, which clarifies why many sociobiologists desire to dismiss human morality as a valid aspect of human nature and as explaining human behavior:

> Advances in behavioral genetics – the study of the genetic basis of behavior – suggest that genetic determinism may have implications for psychological determinism. If an individual has a gene linked to a type of behavior, such as aggression, does this gene undermine the individual's free will when it comes to that behavior? Can an individual with a genetic tendency toward aggression choose to not act aggressively? If he/she has a gene that predisposes him to aggression, should he/she be held legally or morally responsible for his actions? Behavioral genetics has led some legal scholars to raise questions like

768 Judith Grisel, "I studied Neuroscience to understand my addictions. Now I know it's not the cure," *The Guardian* (December 30, 2019): https://www.theguardian.com/commentisfree/2019/dec/30/studied-neuroscience-understand-addictions-not-cure?fbclid=IwAR36TZ41 armCJubOF_F_9AeVBfdZEk3Bbrgrkc8d8e6W03MtjGgwwoscynw.

these . . . . we would like to note that those who are troubled by these questions must assume two different kinds of determinism to get their arguments off the ground: strong genetic determinism *and* psychological determinism. To seriously claim that a gene linked to aggression invalidates the free will of a person with that gene, one would need to show that the gene both strongly determines aggressive tendencies in people and, in addition, that people with these tendencies are not free to act differently. Such a person would truly be a puppet controlled by his/her genes.[769]

What some theorists now refer to as "psychological determinism" or as "free will," the Bible has presented for centuries to be a moral and metaphysical/psychological predisposition toward destructive and habitual values. "Lust" and "depravity" represent the biblical and theological terms most often utilized to describe the inherited and natural spiritual drive that guides everyone's—not just a statistical few—impairing and destructive pursuits and behaviors. Though humanity's propensity to pursue lusts is inherited through Adam and varies between people (not everyone lusts after the same objects), everyone is predisposed toward impairing and destructive pursuits. James 1:14-16 clearly states this aspect of human nature:

> But each person is tempted when he is lured and enticed by his own desire. Then desire when it has conceived gives birth to sin, and sin when it is fully grown brings forth death. Do not be deceived, my beloved brothers.

When deceitful desires (lusts)—which all people inherit and are predisposed to—are pursued, they will impair, enslave, produce distress, bring forth destruction, and alter

---

[769] Resnik and Vorhaus, "Genetic Modification and Genetic Determinism."

the neural pathways to physically correlate to the spiritual drive. Everyone inherits and is thus predisposed to pursue deceitful desires that lead to enslavement (Ephesians 4:20-24). In this way, all people are morally equal. King Solomon the wise presents this truth in Ecclesiastes 9:3b — clearly defining the human condition: "The hearts of the children of man are full of evil, and **madness is in their hearts while they live**, and after that they go to the dead [emphasis added]." The spiritual nature of mankind is naturally vexed with evil, deep destructive deceit, and faced with inevitable death.

Genetic determinism is not sustained logically if spiritual predisposition is considered as causative. As already noted, hundreds of people whom psychiatrists claim to be genetically predisposed to drug abuse and "addictions" do in fact radically change — an empirical observable and repeatable occurrence that cannot be denied. Establishing a desire that is greater and of more value than the desire to pursue a substance is always the driving force behind these successful case studies. Having a predisposition toward desiring and pursuing alcohol does not determine a person's character, lifestyle, or his/her highest values.

The eugenic prejudice has kept many scientists from recognizing that not only do genes change, but also an alternative perspective/worldview/phenomenology exists. Professor of biology Garland Allen recognizes this reality: "Another methodological issue is the failure of eugenicists to consider seriously, and test, alternative explanations for the causes of mental and social behaviors."[770] In his book *Biology as Ideology* Harvard geneticist Richard Lewontin likewise comments on this narrowminded starting point, and stresses how "individual" degeneracy is a key component:

> Modern biology is characterized by a number of ideological prejudices that shape the form of its explanations and the way its researches are carried out. One of those major prejudices is concerned with the nature of causes. Generally, one looks for the cause of an effect, or even if there are a number of causes allowed, one supposes that there is a major cause and the others are only subsidiary. And in any case, these causes are separated from each other, studied independently, and manipulated and interfered with in an independent way. Moreover, these causes are usually seen to be at an individual level, the individual gene or the defective organ or an individual human being who is the focus of internal biological causes and external causes from an autonomous nature. This view of causes is nowhere more evident than in our theories of health and disease.[771]

The correlations between "severe mental illnesses" and cats and dogs provide a great example both how research can be designed to yield evidence that seemingly supports a presuppositional belief and how available data can be manipulated to fit one's philosophical perspective. Chair of the Stanley Division of Pediatric Neurovirology at Johns Hopkins University, Robert Yolken, along with his fellow psychiatrists, claimed in late 2019 that

770 Garland E. Allen, "Eugenics and Modern Biology: Critiques of Eugenics, 1910-1945," *Annals of Human Genetics* vol. 75 (2011): 321; doi: 10.1111/j.1469-1809.2011.00649.x.

771 Lewontin, *Biology as Ideology*, 41.

exposure to household pet dogs may decrease the risk for schizophrenia, whereas exposure to household pet cats was associated with a trend toward an increased risk for schizophrenia and bipolar disorder diagnosis for particular age groups.[772]

True to their genetic presuppositional approach, Yolken and colleagues explain this correlation within a biological/genetic framework:

> There are several plausible explanations for this possible 'protective' effect from contact with dogs — perhaps something in the canine microbiome that gets passed to humans and bolsters the immune system against or subdue a genetic predisposition to schizophrenia.[773]

But more simplistic explanations exist for the correlations apart from the eugenic theory. For example, children who have dogs as pets are often living in stable conditions. Additionally, owning a dog can teach responsibility, sacrifice, and empathy and may provide affection and attachment. Logically, there is no genetic explanation needed to explain such correlations. Yet, making all available evidence fit into the eugenic theory is of great importance to maintain faith in a genetic phenomenology.

The same tendency to maintain a philosophical bias can be observed in how researchers regularly ignore prominent correlations which do not fit into their established

---

[772] Robert Yolken, "Having Dogs as Pets May Decrease Schizophrenia Risk," *Healio Psychiatry* (December 19, 2019): https://www.healio.com/psychiatry/schizophrenia/news/online/%7B3a3f94ca-bae8-4f88-96fc-4fec6926f7bc%7D/having-dogs-as-pets-may-decrease-schizophrenia-risk?fbclid=IwAR1bZ8bCSdRNGWAPtphNJCeOyIFtqGIOITIhLFGfLs YVo7hJ33VNn_0FVEk.

[773] Ibid.

narrative. In 2020, for example, it was discovered in a controlled study that a correlation existed between loss of brain volume and educational levels in those diagnosed as schizophrenic. The studies revealed that 40% of participants who were well-educated had no significant brain atrophy though diagnosed as having schizophrenia, while those who were uneducated consistently showed loss of brain volume. Rather than consider that education and neuroplasticity, which occurs naturally in the learning process, explain brain variances, researchers concluded that there must be two types of schizophrenia.[774] Admitting that another correlate other than the label of schizophrenia is likely to be causative for the observable brain variances (e.g., educational level) would undermine the essential neurobiological theory of schizophrenia.

Clearly, Dr. Lewontin also believes that empirical science is being ignored or outright denied in order to sustain what he calls the "doctrine of DNA":

> There is an extraordinary biological naivete' and
> ignorance of the principles of developmental biology

---

[774] Ganesh B Chand, Dominic B Dwyer, Guray Erus, Aristeidis Sotiras, Erdem Varol, Dhivya Srinivasan, Jimit Doshi, Raymond Pomponio, Alessandro Pigoni, Paola Dazzan, Rene S Kahn, Hugo G Schnack, Marcus V Zanetti, Eva Meisenzahl, Geraldo F Busatto, Benedicto Crespo-Facorro, Christos Pantelis, Stephen J Wood, Chuanjun Zhuo, Russell T Shinohara, Haochang Shou, Yong Fan, Ruben C Gur, Raquel E Gur, Theodore D Satterthwaite, Nikolaos Koutsouleris, Daniel H Wolf, Christos Davatzikos, "Two distinct neuroanatomical subtypes of schizophrenia revealed using machine learning," *Brain* awaa025 (Oxford University Press) (February 27, 2020): https://doi.org/10.1093/brain/awaa025.

involved in assertions that genes make us behave in particular ways in particular circumstances.[775]

Objective evidence is available, but it does not support the bio-psycho-social faith that dominates psychiatric theory. Genes simply do not determine people's character, faith, phenomenological experiences, or their moral behavioral choices.

Genes are Altered

The assumption that genes are fixed is also undermined by the reality that genes themselves are empirically and reliably shown to be altered by many factors rather than being fixed determiners of human nature and outworking behavior. There exist many known human phenomena, which can produce genetic variances and expressions that must be considered. Moreover, the reality that genetic variances exist highlights the fact that no standard of genetic normalcy exists. To insist that a gene or group of genes causes people to believe and embrace falsehood or to be distressed is to ignore available scientific evidence in favor of a reductionistic anthropology and phenomenology in order to uphold theories of individual degeneracy.

Sleep

Insomnia or sleep deprivation not only is heavily correlated with what psychiatrists claim to be severe mental illnesses but also is widely understood in scientific research to alter the human genome and produce negative

[775] Lewontin, *Biology as Ideology*, 97.

somatic changes. Despite this understanding, many psychiatric geneticists choose to view the genomic changes as causes instead of effects.

One example can be observed in how psychiatrists have widely accepted the theory that the C4 gene is primarily responsible for causing alleged hereditary schizophrenia or at least increasing probability. Within this view, the genome is asserted to be the executive governor of human phenomena rather than a controlled agent. The C4 gene, however, is not fixed and is known to be negatively altered by insomnia and sleep deprivation—especially when REM sleep is disturbed or limited. People who are haunted by their past trauma and/or past moral failures, are living through the reality of broken and harmful relationships, or are in deep physical pain will understandably struggle to sleep due to related post-traumatic stress, guilt, or discomfort (as applicable).

Lack of REM sleep is understood to negatively affect both the human genome and the brain:

> Both C-3 and C-4 were significantly associated with REM sleep. This result is striking, given that there is commonality between the rhythm pattern of C-3, C-4, and REM sleep regulation. REM sleep has a predominant circadian regulation, and the serum levels of both C-3 and C-4 have well-characterized circadian patterns.[776]

Since it is also widely recognized that a large percentage of people categorized as psychotic have first endured trauma,

---

[776] M. E. Hussain, A. H. Golam Sarwar, M. S. Alam, M. M. Noohu, W. Zannat, S.R. Pandi-Perumal, ... M.D. Manzar, "Polysomnographic correlates of inflammatory complement components in young healthy males," *Sleep Science* 9 (2) (2016): 123–127; doi:10.1016/j.slsci.2016.04.001.

sleep's direct effects upon the C4 gene is not a minor issue to be overlooked.

During REM sleep, the brain typically cleans itself of debris, but when REM sleep does not occur, negative somatic effects — including those observed in the genome — are inevitable:

> Sleep deprivation disrupts the lives of millions of people every day and has a profound impact on the molecular biology of the brain. These effects begin as changes within a neuron, at the DNA and RNA level, and result in alterations in neuronal plasticity and dysregulation of many cognitive functions including learning and memory.[777]

Other molecular psychiatrists and psychopharmacologists also have shown that genes are negatively altered (a process referred to as epigenetics) when insomnia occurs:

> **Sleep is critical for normal brain function and mental health.** However, the molecular mechanisms mediating the impact of sleep loss on both cognition and the sleep electroencephalogram remain mostly unknown. **Acute sleep loss impacts brain gene expression broadly. These data contributed to current hypotheses regarding the role for sleep in metabolism, synaptic plasticity and neuroprotection. These changes in gene expression likely underlie increased sleep intensity following sleep deprivation (SD).** Here we tested the hypothesis that epigenetic mechanisms coordinate the gene expression response driven by SD. **We found that SD altered the**

[777] Marie E. Gaine, et al., "Sleep Deprivation and the Epigenome." *Frontiers in Neural Circuits* vol. 12 (14) (February 27, 2018): doi:10.3389/fncir.2018.00014.

cortical genome-wide distribution of two major
epigenetic marks ... [emphasis added].[778]

Still, numerous other geneticists note in another study that

insomnia is a common disorder linked with adverse long-
term medical and psychiatric outcomes, but underlying
pathophysiological processes and causal relationships
with disease are poorly understood. We identified 57
genome-wide significant loci for self-reported insomnia
symptoms (n=453,379) and confirmed their impact on
self-reported insomnia symptoms in the HUNT study
(n=14,923 cases, 47,610 controls), physician diagnosed
insomnia in the Partners Biobank (n=2,217 cases, 14,420
controls), and accelerometer-derived measures of sleep
efficiency and sleep duration in the UK Biobank
(n=83,726).[779]

Genetic studies focusing on people diagnosed within
psychiatry as schizophrenic consistently emphasize that

**sleep abnormalities are common in schizophrenia, often
appearing before psychosis onset** .... These molecular
genetic results support recent findings from twin analysis

---

[778] Massart R, Freyburger M, Suderman M, Paquet J, El Helou J, Belanger-
Nelson E, Rachalski A, Koumar OC, Carrier J, Szyf M, Mongrain V., The
genome-wide landscape of DNA methylation and hydroxymethylation in
response to sleep deprivation impacts on synaptic plasticity genes. *Translational
Psychiatry.* 2014 Jan 21;4(1): e347. doi: 10.1038/tp.2013.120.

[779] J.M. Lane S. Jones, H.S. Dashti, A. Wood, V. Van Hees, K. SPiegelhalder,
H. Wang, J. Bowden, S.D. Kyle, D. Ray, T. M. Frayling, D.A. Lawlor, M.K.
Rutter, M. Weedon, and R. Saxena, "Biological and clinical insights from
Genetics of Insomnia Symptoms," SLEEP vol. 41 (1) abstract Supplement (April
27, 2018): https://doi.org/10.1093/sleep/zsy061.014.

that show **genetic overlap between sleep disturbances and psychotic-like experiences** [emphasis added].[780]

While the popular assertion that genetic variances in the C4 gene cause delusions and hallucinations,[781] lack of sleep (caused by understandable ongoing mental turmoil) is more likely the cause of altered genes and neurons, as well as the positive and negative symptoms. As these studies also expose, insomnia regularly precedes alleged psychosis. Several psychiatrists at the University of Oxford published their own findings in the *Schizophrenia Bulletin*:

> **Our view is that insomnia may be a causal factor in the occurrence of psychotic experiences such as paranoia and hallucinations** . . . . After the sleep loss condition, relative to the control condition, participants reported significant increases in paranoia, hallucinations, and cognitive disorganization, with no significant changes in grandiosity. The sleep loss condition was also associated with significant increases in negative affect, negative self and other cognitions, worry, and working memory impairment. Mediation analyses indicated that changes in psychotic experiences were mediated by changes in negative affect and related processes, but not memory impairment. **The overall conclusion is that insomnia has a causal role in the occurrence of certain psychotic**

[780] Z.E. Reed, H.J. Jones, G. Hemani, S. Zammit, and O.S.P. Davis, "Schizophrenia Liability Shares Common Molecular Genetic Risk Factors with sleep duration and nightmares in Childhood," *Wellcome Open Research* vol. 4 (August 20, 2019): https://www.ncbi.nlm.nih.gov/pubmed/31544153.

[781] "Scientists Identify Gene as a Master Regulator in Schizophrenia: Finding may offer a key target for future treatments," *Science News Online* (September 11, 2019): https://www.sciencedaily. com/releases/2019/09/1909 11142806.htm.

experiences, and that a key route is via negative affect [emphasis added].[782]

Whether or not it is well known in the general public, it is widely understood in psychiatric research that all essential criteria listed in the *DSM-5* as diagnostic for schizophrenia and other psychotic disorders ("mood changes, disordered, thoughts, bizarre behavior, dissociation and depersonalization, delusions, distortions in the sense of time, perceptual changes, anxiety and irritability, depression, apathy alternating with euphoria, anger, and hostility") are directly correlated to insomnia.[783] For example, in one article published in early 2020 in *Molecular Psychiatry*, psychiatrists note how "low sleep duration in adults is correlated with psychiatric and cognitive problems."[784] They go on to state that

> dimensional psychopathology in the parents was also correlated with short sleep duration in their children. The brain areas in which higher volume was correlated with longer sleep duration included the orbitofrontal cortex, prefrontal and temporal cortex, precuneus, and supramarginal gyrus. Longitudinal data analysis showed that the psychiatric problems, especially the depressive

[782] S. Reeve, R. Emsley, B. Sheaves, and D. Freeman, "Disrupting Sleep: the Effects of Sleep Loss on Psychotic Experiences Tested in an Experimental Study with Mediation Analysis," *Schizophrenia Bulletin* 44 (3) (April 6, 2018): 662-71.

[783] Flavie Waters, Vivian Chiu, Amanda Atkinson, Jan Dirk Blom, "Severe Sleep Deprivation Causes Hallucinations and a Gradual Progression Toward Psychosis with Increasing Time Awake," *Frontiers in Psychiatry* vol. 9 (July 10, 2018): 303; doi:10.3389/fpsyt.2018.00303.

[784] Wei Cheng, Edmund Rolls, Weikang Gong, Jingnan Du, Jie Zhang, Hiao-Yong Zhang, Fei Li, and Jianfeng Feng, "Sleep duration, brain structure, and psychiatric and cognitive problems in children," *Molecular Psychiatry* (February 3, 2020): https://doi.org/10.1038/s41380-020-0663-2.

problems, were significantly associated with short sleep duration 1 year later . . . . Public health implications are that psychopathology in the parents should be considered in relation to sleep problems in children.[785]

Their findings are also significant in that they explain the hereditary theory to be in parenting techniques and shared behavioral patterns rather than in genetics. Others also report,

Sleep disturbances are common in people with schizophrenia, and severe insomnia is associated with exacerbations of the condition, leading to additional symptoms, but Dr. Ettinger said he was surprised to see the extent of effects of the loss of just 1 night of sleep even among healthy individuals. "A single night of sleep deprivation may not at first seem like a particularly drastic intervention, and can for instance occur with students out partying or people working through the night; therefore, we were surprised to see such statistically significant increases in self-ratings of all 3 dimensions of schizophrenia — thought disorder, perceptual aberrations, and negative symptoms."[786]

Studies have also revealed a "progression of symptoms [correlated] with increasing time spent awake."[787] Symptoms classified as "psychosis" increase proportionally to the degree that a person is deprived of REM sleep.

[785] Ibid.

[786] Nancy A. Melville, "Sleep Deprivation Mimics Psychosis," *Medscape Psychiatry* (July 21, 2014): https://www.medscape.com /viewarticle/828576#vp_2.

[787] Waters, Chiu, Atkinson, Blom, "Severe Sleep Deprivation Causes Hallucinations," 303.

Psychiatric researchers, writing for the journal *Frontiers in Psychiatry*, acknowledge this common finding:

> Psychotic symptoms develop with increasing time awake, from simple visual/somatosensory misperceptions to hallucinations and delusions, ending in a condition resembling acute psychosis. These experiences are likely to resolve after a period of sleep, although more information is required to identify factors which can contribute to the prevention of persistent symptoms.[788]

Don Dexter, a physician in the Neurology Department and Sleep Disorders Center at the Mayo Clinic Health System, remarks, "Prior research shows that prolonged sleep deprivation can actually cause a syndrome indistinguishable from paranoid schizophrenia."[789] Sleep deprivation is not only heavily correlated to the construct of schizophrenia, it is also highly correlated to other psychiatric constructs where delusions and hallucinations are likewise common (e.g., bipolar and dissociative disorders):

> There is also extensive clinical literature describing the link between sleep deprivation and acute psychotic states. **Studies in schizophrenia and bipolar disorder show that sleep problems are among the most prominent correlates of positive symptoms — such as auditory hallucinations and delusions — and illness severity. Studies also show that many psychotic episodes are preceded, if not precipitated, by prolonged insomnia. Insomnia is a well-known clinical stressor, and it is indeed considered a prodromal symptom of psychosis.** Finally, clinical studies have observed the dynamic relationship that exists between sleep and symptoms, with reductions in sleep duration being directly followed

---

[788] Ibid.

[789] Donn Dexter quoted by Melville "Sleep Deprivation Mimics Psychosis."

by increases in psychotic symptom severity with a time lag of approximately 1 day [emphasis added].[790]

It is not, however, that people who are delusional and hallucinating are abnormal. Instead, the normal response to sleepless nights is that people's naturally deceived nature will likely be exposed:

> Perceptual distortions and hallucinations after a period of sleep loss have also been reported in individuals with no history of psychiatric illness. These sleep-loss phenomena offer the opportunity to study the continuum of perception in healthy humans from the point of view of a normally occurring stressor.[791]

It is vital to understand that sleep deprivation does not create deceived thinking in the soul; rather, it exposes the true human condition to be deceived (Jeremiah 17:9), as even the content of an individual's delusions and hallucinations reflect a person's spiritual heart and history.

What is also significant is the fact that lack of sleep, especially REM sleep, is regularly brought on by a person experiencing a traumatic or distressful event(s). It is well known and understandable that lack of sleep and trauma are correlates that naturally produce hallucinations, cognitive impairment, and overall declination and dysregulation of the nervous system:[792]

---

[790] Waters, Chiu, Atkinson, Blom, "Severe Sleep Deprivation Causes Hallucinations," 303.

[791] Ibid.

[792] V. Cheung, V.M. Yuen, G.T.C. Wong, and S.W. Choi, "The Effect of Sleep Deprivation and Disruption on DNA damage and health of doctors," *Anaesthesia* vol. 74 (4) (January 23, 2019): 417.

Traumatic life events can also lead to lack of sleep. Coming back from the theater of war is known to cause sleep deprivation which in turn can produce psychotic behavior and neuroses.[793]

If a person's thinking about his or her traumatic experience or moral failure (as applicable) positively changes, and sleep is restored, then one should expect positive mental and somatic changes to also occur. In these common occurrences, what is needed is not an alteration to the gene or a psychotropic drug, but a change of mind and a proper perspective/phenomenology that will enable a person to sleep well again and that will positively alter the genome.

Targeting genes with psychotropic drugs can only suppress or "manage" symptoms, though "antipsychotics" and "antidepressants" have been shown in short-term to both facilitate sleep and to subsequently minimize delusions and hallucinations. In fact, participants in sleep deprivation studies who receive just one night of sleep (both with people labeled as psychotic and the control group considered to be "healthy") show measurably reduced psychotic symptoms.[794] Sadly, when a person labeled as psychotic is able to sleep due to being drugged, and his/her psychotic symptoms are relieved, materialists choose to depict the drug as specifically healing the body

[793] R. Greenberg, C. A. Pearlman, and D. Gampel, "War Neuroses and the Adaptive Function of REM Sleep," *British Journal of Medical Psychology* 45 (1) (1972): 27-33.

[794] Nancy A. Melville, "Sleep Deprivation Mimics Psychosis," *Medscape Psychiatry* (July 21, 2014): https://www.medscape.com /viewarticle/828576#vp_2.

or "reversing impairments."[795] This reality led the influential psychiatrist, Nassir Ghaemi, to rightly connect psychopharmacology and Kraepelinianism in America:

> Though some have suggested that the rise of the neo-Kraepelinian *DSM-III* occurred independently of the psychopharmacology revolution, contemporaries have observed that the two seemed to play off each other at the time (Ross J. Baldessarini MD, Frederick K. Goodwin MD, personal communications, March 2006). Indeed, **I suggest that the psychopharmacology revolution laid the groundwork for the neo-Kraepelinian restoration** . . . . In the Appendix (written in the 1940s) to *General Psychopathology*, [Jaspers] **specifically also links Kraepelin's work to the incipient rise of psychopharmacology: Kraepelin was responsible for one of the most fruitful lines of research, the investigation of the whole life-history of the patient. [Kraepelin] laid the foundations for psychopharmacology.**...But Kraepelin's basic conceptual world remained a somatic one which in the company of the majority of doctors he held as the only important one for medicine, not only as a matter of preference but in an absolute sense [emphasis added].[796]

The measurable positive changes in symptoms (the "therapeutic effect"), which can be observed in both clinics and research labs and which are directly attributable to sleep, are used as evidence to further faith that psychopharmacology will one day be linked to the genome

---

[795] Ibid.

[796] Nassir S. Ghaemi, "Nosologomania: *DSM* & Karl Jaspers' critique of Kraepelin." *Philosophy, Ethics, and Humanities in Medicine (PEHM)* vol. 4 (10) (July 23, 2009): doi:10.1186/1747-5341-4-10.

and provide a remedy to alleged schizophrenia and other psychotic disorders.[797]

However, these classes of psychotropic drugs typically suppress consciousness, which induces sleep, and the therapeutic benefit that is realized is best explained by the person's ability to sleep rather than in the alleged healing properties of prescribed psychiatric drugs. These drugs' true chemical actions are to perturb and mostly antagonize the nervous system, which in the end can do far more harm. What is truly healing for a person who has endured trauma is to possess a faith/phenomenology that enables right thinking about his/her identity — a faith that cuts to the root of his/her problem and that over time enables him/her to sleep and have peace of mind.

Despite the known facts about insomnia/sleep deprivation, psychiatric geneticists wish to overlook them and regularly attribute the cause of hallucinations and delusions to the genome in order to sustain their eugenic hereditary theory.[798]

---

797 Nadine Petrovsky, Ulrich Ettinger, Antje Hill, Leonie Frenzel, Inga Meyhöfer, Michael Wagner, Jutta Backhaus and Veena Kumari, "Sleep deprivation Disrupts Prepulse Inhibition and Induces Psychosis-Like Symptoms in Healthy Humans," *Journal of Neuroscience* 34 (27) (July 2, 2014): 9134-9140; DOI: https://doi.org/10.1523/JNEUROSCI.0904-14.2014.

798 Amy Ellis Nutt, "Scientists open the 'Black Box' of Schizophrenia with Dramatic Genetic Discovery," *The Washington Post* (January 27, 2016): https://www.washingtonpost.com/news/speaking -of-science/wp/2016/01/27/scientists-open-the-black-box-of schizophrenia-with-dramatic-genetic-finding/?noredirect=on&utm _term=.0fb4574363a7.

Scientists postulate descriptions based on theorized associations that are biased by their presuppositional faith to be either causative or a theorized risk for schizophrenia:

> Recently, C4 mRNA levels in plasma have been correlated with severity of psychopathology in schizophrenia. Another study found correlations between predicted C4A transcription and impairment in memory. Complement proteins were also associated with risk for schizophrenia, and with thinning of superior frontal cortex. Thus, in humans, the complement system serves diverse immune and neural functions and **suggest that abnormal C4A function contributes to schizophrenia pathogenesis** [emphasis added].[799]

These "suggestions" overlook the fact that sleep deprivation/insomnia produces the exact same effects and precedes what is dogmatically claimed to be a mental disorder.

Controlled studies have shown that there are far too many factors involved to objectively approach psychiatric constructs from a statistical vantagepoint.[800] Correlations between the genes and the brain prove nothing, nor do they provide a legitimate arrow of causality. These tools simply show that the genes and the brain are correlated in people who think similarly, have similar life experiences,

---

[799] Knoasale M. Prasad, Kodavali V. Chowdari, Leonardo A. D'Aiuto, Satish Lyengar, Jeffrey A Stanley, and Vishwajit L. Nimgaonkar, "Neuropil Contraction in Relation to Complement C4 Gene Copy Numbers in Independent Cohorts of Adolescent-onset and Young Adult-onset Schizophrenia Patients-a pilot Study," *Translational Psychiatry* vol. 8 (134) (2018): https://www.nature.com/articles/s41398-018-0181-z.

[800] Robin M. Murray, "Mistakes I Have Made in My Research Career," *Schizophrenia Bulletin Online* (December, 2016): doi: 10.1093/schbul/sbw165.

and share like behavioral and sleep patterns, which should all be expected.

Circumstances/Trauma

In addition to lack of REM sleep, a person's internalization and mental struggle through stressful environments and troubling experiences (referred to as trauma) are other influences that produce genetic variances. Many psychiatrists propose *trauma*, for example, to be an endophenotype (determined by alleged genetic predispositions) that produces psychotic symptoms and alters the genome:

> Torsten Klengel, a scientist at the Max Planck Institute of Psychiatry, explains the findings of the study as follows: "Depending on genetic predisposition, childhood trauma can leave permanent epigenetic marks on the DNA, further depressing *FKBP5* transcription. The consequence is a permanent dysregulation of the victim's stress hormone system, which can ultimately lead to psychiatric illness. Decisive for victims of childhood abuse, however, is that the stress-induced epigenetic changes can only occur if their DNA has a specific sequence."[801]

Though it is admitted that the genome is altered by trauma, geneticists — holding true to genetic-determinism/ probability — choose to blame these alterations on

---

[801] Max-Planck-Gesellschaft, "Childhood Trauma Leaves Mark on DNA of Some Victims: Gene-environment interactions causes lifelong dysregulation of stress hormones," *ScienceDaily Online* (December 2, 2012): https://www.sciencedaily.com/releases/2012/12/1212021640 57.htm?utm_medium=cpc&utm_campaign=ScienceDaily_TMD_1&utm_source=TMD.

suggested "genetic predispositions."[802] The logic follows that if a person's genes are altered by trauma, resulting in hallucinations and delusions or ongoing distress and impairment, then evolutionary processes supposedly provided that person with a genome that was predisposed to fail when subjected to stressful environments. Consequently, the same perspective suggests that if a person endures trauma without hallucinations or delusional thinking, then they must not be genetically predisposed — only the "strong survive":

> Another consequence of a simplistic bio-genetic approach is the failure of the mental health community to lobby for primary prevention programs aimed at keeping children securely attached and safe in the first five years of life. (Davies & Burdett, 2004). For example, an environmental enrichment program at age 3-5 years has been shown to reduce schizotypal traits in early adulthood (Raine et al., 2003).[803]

This way of thinking is not empirically derived; it is conjecture that attempts to explain the reality that people differ in how they internalize and react to extreme hardships in life. This fact also exposes that one's normal mental responses to the many distresses and horrible experiences of life directly alter the human genome.

---

[802] It is worth noting from the aforementioned citation that the Max Planck Institute is the new name for Kraepelin's psychiatric eugenic research facility where Rüdin served as director, and it is the institute where Kraepelin's theory is still upheld despite its horrific history.

[803] John Read, Richard P. Bentall, and Roar Fosse, "Time to abandon the Bio-bio-bio model of psychosis: Exploring the epigenetic and psychological mechanisms by which adverse life events lead to psychotic symptoms," *Cambridge University Press* vol. 18 (40) (December 2009): 299; https://doi.org/10.1017/S1121189X00000257.

Clearly, trauma and distress correlate to the phenomena of delusions and hallucinations, but such correlations do not explain causality. One's faith in response to life's most difficult circumstances and experiences is just as plausible of an explanation for a person's negative cognitive responses and correspondingly negative genetic expressions. In one published case study, while still attempting to maintain the genetic predisposition theory, researchers admit that a person's "psychological" processes following a distressful/traumatic event should be considered:

> The patient in the Clinical Challenge is a member of a racial/ethnic minority and grew up in a densely populated city. These factors and several other later environmental risk factors are associated with an increased risk of developing schizophrenia. Research indicates that these associations are unlikely to result from genetic differences between members of different races/ethnicities or biases among clinicians and instead exert their influence via **aberrant reactions** within the stress-response circuitry, particularly the amygdala and frontal cortex, **which are thought to lead** to sensitization of the subcortical dopamine system. **Other stressful psychosocial factors, such as life events, also increase the risk of developing schizophrenia. This is evident in the patient in the Clinical Challenge, with the death of her father preceding the onset of the first episode of psychosis** [emphasis added].[804]

In this particular study, the lady used as a case study by the authors was reacting to her father's death. Instead of considering how one's faith elicits a response to life's circumstances, these materialists and bio-determinists

---

804 Robert A. McCutcheon, Tiago Reis Marques, and Oliver D. Howes, "Schizophrenia—An Overview," *JAMA Psychiatry Online* (October 30, 2019): doi:10.1001/jamapsychiatry.2019.3360.

choose only to consider somatic variances and "risks." In fact, one's worldview or personal phenomenology is typically never mentioned in genetic studies or considered as relevant in psychiatric research. Yet, as established, with beliefs and perspectives at the core of the issue, traumatic events are known to test and alter one's faith and phenomenology. As psychologists at Wake Forest recognize, "Post Traumatic Stress Disorder may have the potential to change the way you think about yourself and others, as a result of trauma."[805] Much of trauma counseling/therapy centers around offering the survivors a potentially healing phenomenology.

How people think and behave is largely determined by their faith, and their faith and desires establish their concepts of hope and directly affect their bodies and their relationships. (Hebrews 11:1). In his book, *The End of Faith, Religion, Terror, and the Future of Reason*, neuroscientist and atheist Sam Harris attempts to exult scientific pursuit above faith, but he begins his book by undermining his very premise, as he recognizes that faith is at the core of everything that it means to be human:

> Your beliefs define your vision of the world; they dictate your behavior; they determine your emotional responses to other human beings. . . . They become part of the very apparatus of your mind, determining your desires, fears, expectations and subsequent behavior. [806]

805 Wake Forest University "The Critical Role of Counselors in PTSD Counseling Treatment," *WFU Online* (December 5, 2019): https://counseling.online.wfu.edu/blog/the-critical-role-of-counselors-in-ptsd-treatment/.

806 Sam Harris, *The End of Faith: Religion, Terror, and the Future of Reason* (New York: Norton and Company, 2005), 12.

Staunch materialists insist that even metaphysical faith is produced by one's genetic predisposition, and geneticists choose to frame these traumatic events as genetic triggers lest one's faith be considered as causative. Within Kraepelinian phenomenology, genes must be rigidly reduced to the primary etiological explanation at all costs.

But if a person goes through a traumatic event, then his/her subsequent mental struggles and biological negative changes — even delusions and hallucinations — should qualify as post-traumatic stress rather than as alleged psychosis. Psychiatrist Raphael van Riel explains in the journal *Frontiers in Psychiatry* that interpreting anyone's mental struggles and discerning their true problems is dependent upon a presuppositional belief system or phenomenology:

> Consider a person who has been diagnosed with PTSD and is, based on this diagnosis, classified as suffering from a mental disorder. This will, on the side of the patient, involve (a) PTSD itself, with its specific history, including the etiology or the trigger of PTSD, (b) a specific subjective experience and, possibly, a specific phenomenology, and a set of symptoms that are indicative of PTSD. **Note that depending on the view one adopts regarding the nature of mental disorders, these may ultimately collapse into one single target, if the phenomenology, the subjective experience and particular symptoms enter the individuating criteria for the disorder itself;** but even if this were the case, talk about symptoms, phenomenology, experience, and the disorder would still be acceptable. Drawing the

terminological distinction appears to be innocent [emphasis added].[807]

As previously noted in this chapter, boundaries between allegedly different psychiatric disorders are not objectively established and expose that these proposed differing mental disorders are simply descriptive constructs derived from Kraepelinian phenomenology. The mental and behavioral struggles are real, but the constructs are not valid. Dr. Charles Whitfield expresses his own conclusions:

> I have found post-traumatic stress disorder (PTSD) to be the most accurate, inclusive and potentially useful of all the *DSM* diagnostic categories. Its accuracy begins with the fact that many of the common mental disorders are strongly associated with, and in some cases possibly caused by, repeated childhood and other trauma.[808]

The natural tendency to struggle internally in one's soul after a traumatic event, in accordance with his/her faith, explains why over 90% of people who enter counseling in a public mental health facility have experienced a traumatic event.[809] A person who endures a traumatic event will most likely receive either a diagnosis of PTSD, Bipolar I, Schizophrenia, or any number of other suggested psychotic disorders, depending upon the clinicians phenomenology and the content of the individual's delusions,

[807] Raphael van Riel, "What Is Constructionism in Psychiatry? From Social Causes to Psychiatric Classification." *Frontiers in Psychiatry* vol. 7 (57) (April 18, 2016): doi:10.3389/fpsyt.2016.00057.

[808] Charles Whitfield, *The Truth about Mental Illness*, 9.

809 National Counsel for Behavioral Health, "Trauma," *SAMHSA-HRSA Center for Integrated Health Solutions* (December 5, 2019): https://www.integration.samhsa.gov/clinical-practice/trauma.

hallucinations, and behavioral reactions,[810] as psychiatrist Robert Berezin points out:

> Different combinations of temperament and trauma create the entire fabric of psychiatric nosology: obsessive, compulsive, anxiety, depression, paranoia, panics, phobias, and delusions.[811]

Psychiatric researchers at the University of Liverpool not only agree that trauma is significant, but they also point out that the context of a person's trauma can be observed in the content of his or her delusions and hallucinations:

> For many years research in mental health has focused on the biological factors behind conditions such as schizophrenia, bipolar disorder and psychotic depression, **but there is now increasing evidence to suggest these conditions cannot be fully understood without first looking at the life experiences of individual patients** . . . . The Liverpool team also conducted a new study which looked at the relationship between specific psychotic symptoms and the type of trauma experienced in childhood. **They found that different traumas led to different symptoms.** Childhood sexual abuse, for example, was associated with hallucinations, whilst being brought up in a children's home was associated with paranoia. The research further suggests a strong relationship between environment and the development

[810] E.g., "Bipolar disorder has been linked to traumatic childhood experience and to the potential for violence," (Allison M. R. Lee, Igor I. Galynker, Irina Kopeykina, Hae-Joon Kim, and Tasnia Khatun, "Violence in Bipolar Disorder," *Psychiatric Times Online* [December 16, 2014]: http://www.psychiatrictimes. com/bipolar-disorder/violence-bipolar-disorder?GUID=3115 8D64-F01A-4DEA-AC1A-D3CE843FC9BC&rememberme=1&ts= 21042017).

[811] Robert A. Berezin, "How Our Genomes Shape Psychiatric Symptoms," *Medscape Psychiatry Online* (November 9, 2018): https://www.medscape.com/viewarticle/904589?nlid=126054_424&src=WNL_mdplsfeat_181113_mscpedit_psyc&uac=264124BV&spon=12&impID=1799736&faf=1#vp_3.

of psychosis, and provides clues about the mechanisms leading to severe mental illness [emphasis added].[812]

The content of delusions and hallucinations have significant meaning and help to explain a person's struggle rather than being signs of degeneracy. Clinical psychologist Richard Bentall also comments on the significance of delusions' and hallucinations' content:

> The causes of psychotic disorders, particularly schizophrenia, are a source of controversy amongst psychiatrists, psychologists and doctors. There is also disagreement about how the disorders are defined. It's not unusual, for example, for a patient to be diagnosed with schizophrenia by one psychiatrist, but as bipolar by another. Our findings suggest that studies on the neurological and genetic factors associated with these conditions, which are not yet fully understood, are more likely to advance our knowledge if we take into account a patient's life experiences.[813]

Both the Kraepelinian genetic theory and his established borders between claimed psychiatric disorders are fluid and not objective as advertised.

While psychiatric categories and labels are controversial, one thing is sure: a person's phenomenology will determine how he/she judges and approaches others who are mentally struggling. The factors involved in psychiatric constructs are socially, philosophically, and morally constructed in one's phenomenology rather than

---

[812] University of Liverpool, "Childhood Trauma Linked to Schizophrenia," *ScienceDaily* (April 19, 2012): https://www.sciencedaily.com/releases/2012/04/120419102440.htm.

[813] Richard Bentall quoted in *ScienceDaily*, Ibid.

representing actual diseases. Raphael van Riel offers several social factors, which illustrate this actuality:

> The classification of PTSD as a mental disorder will involve (c) a specific aspect of PTSD in virtue of which it counts as a mental disorder (rather than, say, a stressful episode of minor importance) and becomes clinically relevant. Finally, being diagnosed with and treated for PTSD typically requires that the patient interact with a clinician. She will (d) express her experiences and **inner perspective** as well as report symptoms in a particular way. **On the side of the clinician, (e) an interpretation of the observed and reported (verbal and non-verbal) behavior of the patient is required. For each of these targets, one can subscribe to the view that it is shaped by social facts. We have thus identified five candidate targets for social constructivism, all of which may give rise to a form of social constructivism about psychiatry, or at least may go together with some constructivist rhetoric** [emphasis added].[814]

The phenomenologies of both the person being evaluated and the clinician become relevant to the diagnosis and relationship. Their own presuppositional faith, not empirical evidence, explains how people choose to propose explanations and theories of causation, interpret their own experiences and those of others, and attempt remediation of mental distress and deceit. Furthermore, their respective phenomenology (their faith) and not their own biology determines how they react to life's distressful and difficult realities.

As geneticist Richard Lewontin asserts, to accept that a person's genes and nervous system predispose him/her to

---

[814] Raphael van Riel, "What Is Constructionism in Psychiatry? From Social Causes to Psychiatric Classification." *Frontiers in Psychiatry* vol. 7 (57) (April 18, 2016): doi:10.3389/fpsyt.2016.00057.

react to trauma in a certain way, in itself requires immense faith that rests outside of scientific exploration:

> It takes an enormous set of assumptions to suppose that the human central nervous system, with thousands of times more nervous connections than in an ant, has completely stereotyped and fixed genetic responses to circumstance.[815]

It is possible that some researchers — holding rigidly to their genetic phenomenology — believe that they themselves are genetically predisposed to believe in the delusion that is entirely Kraepelinian eugenics.

Other psychiatrists, though, are beginning to denounce the narrow-minded Kraepelinian eugenics perspective. For example, Aaron Levin reported for the American Psychiatric Association in 2019:

> "Early life adversity is the single biggest determinant of psychiatric illness, greater even than genetics," Charles Nemeroff, M.D., Ph.D., said to attendees of a presidential symposium at the APA Annual Meeting in May . . . The effect of these adverse childhood experiences is becoming clearer, Nemeroff said. Studies show that children who are abused are at a greater risk of posttraumatic stress disorder (PTSD), anxiety, depression, and substance use disorder later in life. Early life adversity is also a risk factor for diabetes, stroke, and premature mortality and for worse financial and educational outcomes.[816]

If genes are altered by a person's mental struggle rather than cause a person's impairment and distress, then an

---

[815] Lewontin, *Biology as Ideology*, 98.

[816] Aaron Levin, "Early Life Trauma Changes Biology of Brain," *Psychiatric News* (American Psychiatric Association) (July 18, 2019): https://doi.org/10.1176/appi.pn.2019.6b19.

entirely new perspective and corresponding hope emerges. With estimates ranging from 70% to 90% of the adult population having survived trauma,[817] it becomes apparent that a person's faith must be considered as a strong and potentially primary correlate to how people respond to life's fallen reality and the somatic changes that inevitably follow. In the *Quick Guide for Clinicians*, published by the U.S. Department of Health and Human Services, the centrality of faith and reason is discussed:

> Often, individuals report that they no longer see life the same way after a traumatic experience. **Trauma can alter core beliefs and assumptions about life — beliefs and assumptions that provide meaning and a way to organize one's life and one's interactions with the world and others.** Consider asking whether a client's core beliefs about life (e.g., about safety, perception of others, fairness, purpose of life, future dreams) were challenged or disrupted during or after the traumatic event [emphasis added].[818]

Such a view is not only empirically sound, but it is also logical.

Rather than being the primary cause of an alleged disease called schizophrenia, it makes more sense — considering the wealth of available validated evidence — to understand that those who have been through a traumatic experience (s),

817 Wake Forest University "The Critical Role of Counselors in PTSD Counseling Treatment," *WFU Online* (December 5, 2019): https://counseling. online.wfu.edu/blog/the-critical-role-of-counselors-in-ptsd-treatment/.

818 Department of Health and Human Services, *Quick Guide for Clinicians: Trauma-Informed Care in Behavioral Health Services, Substance Abuse and Mental Health Services and Administration* (US Government, 2015), 28.

who are diagnosed as psychotic, who have measurable negative variances/expressions in their C4 gene or numerous other genes, and who are not sleeping well are reacting in a normal but impairing way to distressful and trying life events according to their faith. Though they are traumatized in a way that forever alters their lives — an unfortunate, vexing, impairing, and common human phenomena, they are entirely normal for struggling internally.

In these cases, lack of sleep, the absence of solid faith and meaningful help to get one through the expected stress of trauma, and possibly unhealthy relationships rather than an alleged malady is causative. What all people need is meaningful relationships that can offer a healthy and truthful perspective/faith, which can provide a restorative phenomenology based upon God's wisdom that explains their traumatic experience truthfully, enables them to understand their shared distressful human condition, and offers a hope-filled path forward (John 16:33; Acts 14:22; James 1:1-3).

Substantiated evidence consistently reveals that those who endure trauma and receive comfort from others who have endured the same or similar tragedy have high rates of recovery and are not genetically defective or predisposed to struggle apart from normal human nature.[819] A person's faith and his/her established relationships within a like-

---

819 Hope Hodge Seck, "This Squad PTSD Therapy Runs Just 2 Weeks. And It's Changing Vet's Lives," *Military* (November 14, 2019): https://www. military.com/daily-news/2019/11/14/squad-style-ptsd-therapy-runs-just-2-weeks-and-its-changing-vets-lives.html?fbclid=IwAR0Y0xsfAX0-xUvS6eZrMGc-RVQjjGZy--ytN-e9zBO7_wgnyvQGEAcWxnE. See also 2 Corinthians 1:1-5.

minded, faith-based community must be considered as central to caring for the souls of those who have endured trauma (Acts 14:22).

Drugs

But there are also other alleged phenotypes, which, instead of being caused by genes, directly alter the genome and the nervous system through their chemical properties. Both prescribed and illicit psychotropic drugs, for instance, not only alter gene expressions and take control of or attack the nervous system, but they also produce delusions and hallucinations.

Despite this reality, some psychiatric eugenicists insist on explaining substance consumption as a comorbidity (occurring as another suggested parallel psychiatric disease) to schizophrenia/psychosis rather than as a causation of somatic effects that induces delusions and hallucinations. In other words, a person's desire to pursue and use mind-altering drugs is the primary pathological problem (the cause), and the negative physical changes to the genome and the brain along with delusions and hallucinations are the effects:

> Detrimental effects on brain structure and function were shown for patients for whom alcohol is the main substance of abuse. . . . Alcohol and cannabis abuse have been associated with more frontal lobe and thalamus abnormities and increased risk for developing psychosis

in individuals with high familial risk for developing schizophrenia.[820]

Since deceitful desires ("lusts") cannot be examined within science, there is no objective means of proving that a gene or group of genes causes people to desire specific things or are the genesis of corresponding behavior. Theory of causation as it relates to substance abuse and desires is principally a religious/moral/philosophical discussion even if it is framed as a scientific and medical issue.

As with modern scientific discovery, the Bible also declared thousands of years ago that when the amount consumed enables the substance to control a person, psychotropic substances (e.g., alcohol) have the expected potential to produce hallucinations and delusions. Proverbs 23:31-34 states,

> Do not look at wine when it is red, when it sparkles in the cup and goes down smoothly. In the end it bites like a serpent and stings like an adder. Your eyes will see strange things [hallucinations], and your heart utter perverse things [delusions]. You will be like one who lies down in the midst of the sea, like one who lies on the top of a mast. "They struck me," you will say, "but I was not hurt; they beat me, but I did not feel it. When shall I awake? I must have another drink [dependency]."

The very substance (the deceitful quality of all human nature) of the phenomena referred to as psychosis/schizophrenia is shown in the Bible to be

[820] P. Thoma and I. Daum, "Comorbid Substance Use Disorder in Schizophrenia: a Selective Overview of Neurobiological and Cognitive Underpinnings," *Psychiatry and Clinical Neurosciences* 67 (6) (September 2013): 367; doi: 10.1111/pcn.12072.

exposed by consuming mind-altering drugs that are compared to the poison of a snake — emphasizing the destructive nature of mind-altering substances. Elsewhere in Scripture (Ephesians 5:18), the Bible states more precisely: "And do not get drunk with wine, for that is debauchery [literally "a condition as if not saved" or "a return to the naturally deceived nature apart from Christ"], but be filled [controlled] with the Spirit." What a person allows to control his/her mind impacts whether he/she lives in deceit or in truth.

There is a great deal of research available that verifies the Bible's assertion, similar to that which was published in *Psychiatry and Clinical Neurosciences*:

> **All drugs of abuse act on neurotransmitter systems implicated in the pathophysiology of schizophrenia, either directly or indirectly.** The three neurotransmitter systems most frequently found to be involved in schizophrenia are dopamine, GABA and glutamate. In particular, hyperactivity of the mesolimbic dopamine system has been linked to the positive symptoms and hypoactivity of the mesocortical dopamine system to the negative symptoms of schizophrenia [emphasis added].[821]

Megan Brooks reports in *Medscape Psychiatry* on similar findings in regard to high quality cannabis:

> Daily use of cannabis, particularly high potency cannabis, is associated with higher rates of psychosis, new research shows. In the first study to show the impact of cannabis use at a population level, investigators found daily users of high potency cannabis were up to five times more

---

[821] Thoma and Daum, "Comorbid Substance Use Disorder in Schizophrenia," 369.

likely to have a first episode of psychosis than noncannabis users.[822]

Numerous other studies reveal the same consistent findings:

> Studies show that taking certain mind-altering drugs called psychoactive or psychotropic drugs, such as methamphetamine or LSD, can make you more likely to get schizophrenia. Some research has shown that marijuana use has a similar risk. The younger you start and the more often you use these drugs, the more likely you are to have symptoms like hallucinations, delusions, inappropriate emotions, and trouble thinking clearly. Scientists are looking at possible differences in brain structure and function in people with and people without schizophrenia. In people with schizophrenia, they found: 1) Spaces in the brain, called ventricles, were larger. 2) Parts of the brain that deal with memory, known as the medial temporal lobes, were smaller. 3) There were fewer connections between brain cells.[823]

These observable-neural-differentials that sometimes occur are known effects of psychotropic drugs.

Despite the objective evidence, which shows how *psychotropic drugs* (mind-altering substances) produce said psychosis, materialists frame delusions and hallucinations as a disorder or abnormality. Some of these psychiatric researchers, instead of accepting the fact that these drugs' actions naturally expose humanity's deceived nature, insist

[822] Megan Brooks, "High Potency Cannabis Tied to 50% of New Psychosis Cases," *Medscape Psychiatry* (March 20, 2019): https://www.medscape.com/viewarticle/910658?nlid=128841_2051&src=WNL_mdplsnews_190322_mscpedit_psyc&uac=264124BV&spon=12&impID=1915227&faf=1.

[823] "What Causes Schizophrenia?" *WebMD* (2019): https://www.webmd.com/schizophrenia/what-causes-schizophrenia#1.

that psychotropic drugs "trigger schizophrenia:" "The risk of transition to schizophrenia was highest for cannabis (34%), hallucinogens (26%), and amphetamines (22%) and lowest for alcohol (9%) and sedatives (10%)."[824]

Whether or not prescribed psychotropic drugs (e.g., "antipsychotics") are acknowledged to be factors in gene expression and neurological variances, there is mounting evidence that the body is harmed by their ingestion. In 2020, researchers discovered that the brain's thickness and both gray and white matter were negatively altered when antipsychotic drugs were consumed as treatments:

> The primary outcome measure was cortical thickness in gray matter and the secondary outcome measure was microstructural integrity of white matter . . . antipsychotic medication was shown to change brain structure.[825]

Psychotropic drugs, which are claimed to be medicinal for those diagnosed as psychotic, work by attacking the nervous system rather than healing it. These powerful drugs are influential in most genetic studies and statistical reviews, yet the large worldwide genetic databases cannot fully factor in neuroleptic dosages and duration of use, histories, relationships, and religious views in their statistical analysis—let alone genetic polymorphisms that react differently to ingested substances. Because most

[824] Brian Miller, "Drug Psychosis May Pull the Schizophrenia trigger," *Psychiatric Times Online* (February 4, 2020): https://www.psychiatrictimes.com/article/drug-psychosis-may-pull-schizophrenia-trigger.

[825] A.N. Voineskos, B. H. Mulsant, E. W. Dickie, et al., "Effects of Antipsychotic Medication on Brain Structure in Patients With Major Depressive Disorder and Psychotic Features: Neuroimaging Findings in the Context of a Randomized Placebo-Controlled Clinical Trial," *JAMA Psychiatry* (February 26, 2020): doi:10.1001/jamapsychiatry.2020.0036 .

antipsychotics are psychotropic antagonists,[826] these powerful drugs naturally alter the human body in negative ways.

For this reason, psychopharmacologists often refer to these specific drugs as neuroleptics ("taking hold of the neuron").[827] In the journal of *Biological Psychiatry*, researchers assert their belief that brain variances are not caused by "antipsychotics." But these same researchers acknowledge that "whether such changes reflect processes associated with the pathophysiology of schizophrenia or exposure to antipsychotic drugs is unknown."[828] Subha Subramanian and James Potash, writing on behalf of the International Society of Psychiatric Genetics, also maintain that "mood stabilizers and antidepressants alter epigenetic marks to influence gene function."[829] The drugs' chemical effects on the genome and the brain cannot be discounted, and hallucinations and delusions—the true substance of psychosis—are known to be brought on by both prescribed

---

[826] See Daniel R. Berger II, *The Chemical Imbalance Delusion* (Taylors, SC: Alethia International Publications, 2019).

[827] Trevor Turner, "Chlorpromazine: Unlocking Psychosis," *British Medical Journal* 007 (January 6, 2007): 334.

[828] T.D. Cannon, Y. Chung, G. He, D. Sun, A. Jacobson, T. G. Van Erp, S. McEwen, J. Addignton, CE Bearden, K. Cadenhead, B Comblatt, DH Mathalon, T. McGlashan, D. Pekins, C. Jeffries, L. J. Seidman, M. Tsuang, E. Walker, S. W. Woods, R. Heinsen, "Progressive Reduction in Cortical Thickness as Psychosis Develops: a multisite longitudinal neuroimaging study of youth at elevated clinical risk," *Biological Psychiatry* 15 (2) (January 2015): 147-57: doi: 10.1016/j.biopsych.2014.05.023.

[829] Subha Subramanian and James B. Potash, *Psychiatric Genetics: A Primer for Clinicians and Basic Scientists* edited by Thomas G. Schulze and Francis J. McMahon (New York: Oxford University Press, 2018), 167.

psychiatric drugs and illicit psychotropic drugs. Lewontin, Rose, and Kamin remark on how one prescribed "antipsychotic" is known to create the very suggested disorder it allegedly treats:

> There is still another twist to the spiral of interdependence of the drug industry and the diagnosis of mental illness. **With prolonged use of drugs, a whole new range of disorders has become apparent.** Substances intended to cure one problem generate another, and the growth in such iatrogenic (medically induced) disorders is serious and disturbing. This is particularly the case for the major tranquilizers like chlorpromazine.[830]

One must consider that alleged "fixity" claimed as normative within the construct of psychosis is regularly produced by the dependence upon psychiatrists' suggested chemical remedy rather than from a person's genome. Simply stated, abnormal states are all too often created and sustained by ingesting mind-altering/controlling drugs.

Other researchers have also arrived at the same conclusions, though they claim that delusions and hallucinations seem to be alleviated by the consumption of "antipsychotics:"

> The traditional typical and atypical antipsychotics demonstrate clinical efficacy in treating positive symptoms, such as hallucinations and delusions, while [they] **are largely ineffective and may worsen negative symptoms, such as blunted affect and social withdrawal, as well as cognitive function. The inability to treat these latter symptoms may contribute to social function impairment associated with schizophrenia.** The

---

[830] Richard C. Lewontin, Steven Rose, and Leon J. Kamin, *Not in Our Genes: Biology, Ideology, and Human Nature* 2nd edition (Chicago: Haymarket Books, 2017), 204.

dysfunction of multiple neurotransmitter systems in schizophrenia suggests that drugs selectively targeting one neurotransmission pathway are unlikely to meet all the therapeutic needs of this heterogeneous disorder [emphasis added].[831]

Psychiatrist Peter Breggin also comments on "chemical lobotomy":

The pioneers of the first "antipsychotic drugs" were well aware that they had moved from surgical lobotomy to chemical lobotomy; and they never claimed that they had a specific antipsychotic effect. Calling them "antipsychotics" was a later and highly misleading approach to promoting the drugs. **With the exception of clozapine, all antipsychotic drugs cause a functional lobotomy by blockading dopamine neurotransmission, which is the main conduit to the frontal lobes. This fact is confirmed in the FDA-approved labels (package inserts) for antipsychotic drugs** [emphasis added].[832]

A professor of psychiatry at the University of Toronto, Mary Seeman, writes similarly in 2019, describing how prescribed antipsychotic medication may directly stir delusional thinking in regard to how one sees his/her own

---

[831] Li Peng, et al., "Dopamine Targeting Drugs for the Treatment of Schizophrenia: Past, Present and Future," *Current Topics in Medicinal Chemistry* vol. 16 (29) (2016): 3385-3403; doi:10.2174/1568026616666160608084834.

[832] Breggin, "Psychopharmacology for Therapists," 3.

body and how he/she relates to food — referred to as an eating disorder within psychiatric phenomenology.[833]

After years of both clinical practice and teaching psychiatry at the University level, psychiatrist Joanna Moncrieff concluded that "the occurrence of tardive dyskinesia confirms that antipsychotics can irreversibly alter the way the brain functions."[834] Antipsychotics may temporarily suppress hallucinations and delusions (so-called positive symptoms of psychosis) from being expressed by partially shutting down the nervous system through intoxication — thus suppressing the metaphysical mind. They also can enable a person to sleep. But over time, the drugs so perturb the body that they can and regularly do induce the very symptoms they allegedly treat.[835]

Still other studies have shown that when psychotropic drugs are eventually stopped and after the severe withdrawal symptoms have worn off, a person diagnosed as psychotic recovers better. Psychiatrists M. Harrow and T.H. Jobe concluded in their own research that

> a larger percent of schizophrenia patients not on antipsychotics showed periods of recovery and better global functioning (p < .001). The longitudinal data

[833] Mary V. Seeman, "When Eating Disorders and Psychosis Co-Exist: 6 Take Home Points," *Psychiatric Times Online* (October 23, 2019): https://www.psychiatrictimes.com/schizophrenia/when-eating-disorders-and-psychosis-co-exist-6-take-home-points?rememberme=1&elq_mid=9318&elq_cid=893295&GUID=31158D64-F01A-4DEA-AC1A-D3CE843FC9BC.

[834] Joanna Moncrieff, *The Bitterest Pills: The Troubling Story of Antipsychotic Drugs* (London: Palgrave Macmillan, 2013), 152.

[835] For further study on the drugs' action and effects, see Berger, *The Chemical Imbalance Delusion.*

identify a subgroup of schizophrenia patients who do not immediately relapse while off antipsychotics and experience intervals of recovery. **Their more favorable outcome is associated with internal characteristics of the patients,** including better premorbid developmental achievements, favorable personality and attitudinal approaches, less vulnerability, greater resilience, and favorable prognostic factors [emphasis added].[836]

As these psychiatric researchers recognize, a person's character is an important factor often not discussed in conversations about mental struggles or considered in psychiatric research. In late 2019, as another example, dozens of psychiatrists and researchers concluded from a worldwide-long-term study that those labeled as schizophrenic had a higher recovery rate when mind-altering drugs (illicit in this case) were stopped.[837] Director of a "medication-free" facility in Norway, Ole Andreas Underland, reports his clinic's own findings:

I am a psychiatric nurse by profession, and I had been working for decades in this field and I had never heard about this, that the long-term recovery rate for patients

---

[836] M. Harrow, "Factors Involved in Outcome and Recovery in Schizophrenia Patients Not on Antipsychotic Medications: a 15-year multifollow-up study," *Journal of Nervous and Mental Disease* 195 (5) (2007): 406-14.

[837] M. A. Wiebell, et al., "Early Substance Use Cessation Improves Cognition-10 Years Outcome in First-Episode Psychosis Patients," *Frontiers in Psychiatry* 10 (July 12, 2019): 495; doi: 10.3389/fpsyt.2019.00495.

suffering from schizophrenia was far better without medication than with medication.[838]

Regrettably, many genetic theorists and researchers only present the pursuit of psychotropic substances as a symptom of an alleged disease lest correlations be reconsidered outside of a eugenic framework.[839]

Among those who agree that illicit drugs like cannabis should be viewed as a phenotype of schizophrenia are psychiatrists Caroly Asher and Linda Gask. In one study, they note that cannabis usage is five times higher in people diagnosed with schizophrenia than it is in the general population.[840] Other studies show much higher numbers:

> The link between the use of substances and the development of psychoses is demonstrated by the high prevalence of substance abuse in schizophrenia. Apart from alcohol misuse, substances commonly abused in this patient group include nicotine, cocaine, and cannabis. In particular, heavy cannabis abuse has been reported to be a stressor eliciting relapse in schizophrenic patients. In general, substance use in psychosis is associated with

[838] Ole Andreas Underland quoted by Robert Whitaker, "Medication-Free Treatment in Norway: A private Hospital Takes Center Stage," *Mad in America* (December 8, 2019): https://www.madinamerica.com/2019/12/medication-free-treatment-norway-private-hospital/.

[839] Genetics Home Reference, "Schizophrenia," *National Institutes of Health* (2019): https://ghr.nlm.nih.gov/condition/ schizophrenia#genes.

[840] Carolyn J. Asher, and Linda Gask, "Reasons for illicit drug use in people with schizophrenia: Qualitative study," *BMC Psychiatry* vol. 10 (94) (November 22, 2010): doi:10.1186/1471-244X-10-94.

poorer outcomes, including increased psychotic symptoms and poorer treatment compliance.[841]

Here is a case where what is framed as schizophrenia or as psychosis is naturally produced by a person's deceitful pursuits and subsequent behavior rather than by his/her genome. But thanks in large part to Benjamin Rush, psychiatrists illogically continue to claim that predisposed genetic risk factors cause a person to crave and consume mind-controlling drugs.

When the data is gathered for statistical analysis in psychiatric genetic studies, the consumption of both illicit and prescribed psychotropic drugs in those diagnosed with psychotic disorders is not a point of serious consideration as to why the genome and brain are both perturbed and negatively altered. Such consideration of this obvious correlate would not only be extremely expensive (as each person diagnosed has a different drug history, life history, and biological response to these drugs), but it would also undermine the very genetic theory psychiatrists desire to prove — that all of human nature is sourced in the human genome. Moreover, the number of people who consume alcohol (one of the most commonly consumed mind-altering drugs) on a daily basis would require its own in-depth study. Rather than being considered a comorbidity to psychosis, researchers would need to honestly consider how alcohol destroys the nervous system and other bodily functions, as well as address how psychotic episodes are

[841] Bernadette Winklbaur, Nina Ebner, Gabriele Sachs, Kenneth Thau, and Gabriele Fischer, "Substance Abuse in Patients with Schizophrenia," *Dialogues in Clinical Neuroscience*, 8 (1) (2006): 37.

expected effects of consuming these mind-controlling drugs — as both the Bible and science attest.

The psychiatric constructs of "schizophrenia" and "drug usage disorder" are not diseases a person is born with or that individuals contract. Instead, heterogeneous constructs (fluid and malleable descriptions), such as alleged "schizophrenia," are an evolutionary explanation of a person's naturally deceived and fallen nature. Sometimes these constructs describe the heart's deceitful pursuits, while other times they explain a normal and expected negative response to sleep deprivation or traumatic events which the person's faith/phenomenology is not adequate to explain. Nonetheless, the issues at hand in the construct of schizophrenia/psychosis are, in fact, faith, deceit, and perceptions as delusions and hallucinations affirm and which mind-controlling drugs, insomnia, and traumatic experiences expose and can exacerbate.

Genes Are Controlled

Fortunately, there is an alternative explanation to humanity's deceived nature, which is supported by consistent evidence. That perspective is *epigenetics*, a field that undermines the theory of psychiatric genetics by exposing that the human genome is not fixed but is altered by stimuli. Genes are not the primary determiner of a person's character/soul and metaphysical phenomena — though genes do produce a person's physical traits and are sometimes responsible for valid physical diseases.

The term *epigenetics* means above or over the genes. Former professor at Stanford University's School of Medicine and cellular biologist Bruce Lipton shares,

Epigenetics, the study of the molecular mechanisms by which environment controls gene activity, is today one of the most active areas of scientific research. . . . I came to the conclusion that we are not victims of our genes, but master of our fates, able to create lives overflowing with peace, happiness, and love.[842]

The Group for the Advancement of Psychiatry (GAP) also suggests a concept of the "social brain" in accordance with epigenetic changes to both the genome and the brain:

Brains, including human brains, derive from ancient adaptations to diverse environments and are themselves repositories of phylogenetic adaptations. In addition, individual experiences shape the brain through epigenesis; that is, the expression of genes is shaped by environmental influences. Thus, the social brain is also a repository of individual development . . . The social brain concept allows psychiatry to utilize pathogenesis in a manner parallel to practice in other specialties.[843]

While psychiatrists focus on environments and insist upon the social brain concept in order to maintain the medical model of mental illness, it is not environments that control and shape a person's genome. Instead, a person's soul and specifically his/her faith/phenomenology govern his/her reactions to life's circumstances. Expressing his own take on the concept of the social brain, chair of the committee on

---

[842] Bruce H. Lipton, *The Biology of Belief: Unleashing the Power of Consciousness, Matter and Miracles* (New York: Hay House, 2005), preface xxiv-v.

[843] Johan Verhulst, Russel Gardner, Beverly Sutton, John Beahrs, Fred Wamboldt, Michael Schwartz, Carlo Carandang, Doug Kramer, and John Looney, "The Social Brain in Clinical Practice," *Psychiatric Annals* vol. 35 (2005): 803-811.

research for the GAP, Douglas Kramer, highlights the centrality of phenomenology and epigenetics:

> The social brain consists of structures and processes in the nervous system that incorporate embodied interactional knowledge, which is the result of social learning at different levels. Thus, the social brain includes: (a) the effects of evolutionary **learning** exemplified in the genetically encoded adaptations to living in social groups, subject to **epigenetic changes**, (b) the effects of **basic developmental learning** in early childhood through engagement in specific interaction patterns that **help form a first sense of self, others, and interpersonal context**, and (c) the effects of **socio-cultural learning** through on-going discourse in the family, society, and the broader culture; **through these interactions one acquires schemas of one's social role** and that of others in various contexts; **these schemas further develop one's sense of self and may be modified with new interpersonal experiences** [emphasis added].[844]

People's faith/phenomenology — especially as it relates to personal identity and relationships with God and others — is key to understanding mental struggles and somatic changes.

If, however, metaphysical phenotypes, such as faith or beliefs, cannot be scientifically approached to prove or disprove causation or potentially accepted as causative, then they also cannot be scientifically approached to prove or disprove them as empirical genetic effects or as diagnostic tools. Other professionals agree:

---

844 Douglas A. Kramer, "Remembering: A Gentleman and a Psychiatrist," *Psychiatric Times Online* (December 9, 2019): https://www.psychiatrictimes. com/couch-crisis/remembering-gentleman-and-psychiatrist/page/0/1 ?rememberme=1&elq_mid=10030&elq_cid=893295&GUID=31158D64-F01A-4DEA-AC1A-D3CE843FC9BC.

> Mental health services and research have been
> dominated for several decades by a rather simplistic,
> reductionistic focus on biological phenomena, with
> minimal consideration of the social context within
> which genes and brains inevitably operate. This
> 'medical model' ideology, enthusiastically supported by
> the pharmaceutical industry, has been particularly
> powerful in the field of psychosis, where it has led to
> unjustified and damaging pessimism about recovery.
> The failure to find robust evidence of a genetic
> predisposition for psychosis in general, or 'schizophrenia'
> in particular, can be understood in terms of recently
> developed knowledge about how epigenetic processes
> turn gene transcription on and off through mechanisms
> that are highly influenced by the individual's socio-
> environmental experiences [emphasis added].[845]

Not only are genes not fixed, but they also express themselves according to a person's faith, cognition, relationships, reactions to experiences, and patterns of behavior. John Perritano, writing for *National Geographic*, discusses the field of epigenetics:

> Geneticists used to think humans were stuck with the
> genes that our parents gave us. We now know we can
> change them without changing our DNA sequence. This
> insight has given rise to a new science — epigenetics. The
> word comes from the Greek prefix epi-, which means
> "above" or "over," plus genetics. So, epigenetics means
> above or on top of genetics and refers to changes to DNA

---

[845] John Read, Richard P. Bentall, and Roar Fosse, "Time to abandon the Bio-bio-bio model of psychosis: Exploring the epigenetic and psychological mechanisms by which adverse life events lead to psychotic symptoms," *Cambridge University Press* vol. 18 (40) (December 2009): 299; https://doi.org/10.1017/S1121189X00000257.

that turn genes on or off. To put it more clearly, it's about how genes are used or expressed.[846]

Genes are not immutable, nor do they contain predetermined expressions that control or produce human faith, character, and moral behavior, as psychiatric geneticists Tobias Halene, Gregor Hasler, and Amanda Mitchell indicate:

> One promising direction in neuroscience research is epigenetics, which has—for at least 15 years—piqued the interest of neuroscientists and psychiatrists, so that even popular scientific literature has caught on to the trend. Epigenetics is the tempting proposition that environment and experience can leave a lasting mark in our bodies, a welcome alternative to the rather dull prospect of genetic determinism.[847]

As rightly noted, the field of epigenetics undermines the theory of fixity or genetic determinism. But unlike what these geneticists suggest, environments and experiences do not "leave lasting marks," which is still belief in bio-determinism. Many people actually can and do experience positive genomic and neural changes after enduring the negative somatic changes regularly incurred after traumatic experiences. The common thread of recovery in these cases is both enduring faith and the establishment of caring relationships.

---

[846] John Perritano, *Your Genes: 100 Things You Never Knew* (Washington, DC; National Geographic, 2019), 102-104.

[847] Tobias B. Halene, Gregor Hasler, Amanda Mitchell, and Schahram Akbarian, *Psychiatric Genetics: A Primer for Clinicians and Basic Scientists* edited by Thomas G. Schulze and Francis J. McMahon (New York: Oxford University Press, 2018), 145.

Halene, Hasler, and Mitchell further consider how both the human genome and brain are "plastic" and respond to stimuli rather than merely determining physical traits:

> On a more concrete level, this is because human and animal brain studies have shown that many epigenetic markings, including DNA methylation and various histone modifications, remain "plastic" throughout the human lifespan, with ongoing dynamic regulation even in neurons and other differentiated cells once believed to be set in stone after birth. Changing neuronal activity, learning and memory, and numerous other processes all have been shown to be associated with DNA methylation and histone modification and histone variant changes at specific genomic sequences in brain chromatin.[848]

They later expound this point:

> Most, or perhaps all, epigenetic markings are likely to be reversible even in post-mitotic cells, and subject to bidirectional regulation. There is no *a priori* reason for a specific epigenetic mark to only accumulate while the brain is maturing and aging. Instead, chromatin markings appear to remain plastic throughout the lifespan of the human brain, with implications for the neurobiology of psychiatric diseases.[849]

Stated differently, the human genome and the brain (structurally and in the functional nervous system) are constantly changing according to the spiritual, behavioral, relational, and environmental factors in a person's life. Dr. Perritano also comments on how genes are controlled:

> **Genes don't work by themselves. They have to be told what to do, where to do it, and when to do it. Epigenetic modifications, so-called tags, give each gene their**

[848] Ibid.

[849] Ibid., 148.

instructions. These chemical tags sit on top of and outside the genome, telling genes to turn on or off, like a light switch. Other tags act more like a dimmer, telling genes to increase or decrease in intensity. Our genome contains at least four million of these "switches" that can be turned on or off, dimmed, or made brighter, often by what we do in our daily lives and by our environment. Smoking, sleep, exercise, diet, and exposure to toxins, among many other things, can affect the behavior of these epigenetic markers [emphasis added].[850]

Terms like *polymorphism* reveal that genes do in fact vary and can be altered, though terms such as epigenetics and polymorphisms are typically only utilized by psychiatric geneticists in attempt to prove the eugenic theory and not to undermine the false philosophy of bio-determinism.

In epigenetics, the genes are shown to be altered by one's thoughts/phenomenology (how a person perceives various environments and experiences) rather than governing them. Cognitive neuroscientist Caroline Leaf is one who emphasizes the mind's control over the human genome in relation to character formation and personality:

> Thoughts collectively form your attitude, which is your state of mind, and it's your attitude and not your DNA that determines much of the quality of your life. This state of mind is a real, physical, electromagnetic, quantum, and chemical flow in the brain that switches groups of genes on or off in a positive or negative direction based on your choices and subsequent reactions. Scientifically, this is called epigenetics.[851]

[850] Perritano, *Your Genes*, 104.

[851] Caroline Leaf, *Switch on Your Brain: The Key to Peak Happiness, Thinking, and Health* (Grand Rapids: Baker, 2013), 14.

Leaf's remarks on "choices" and "reactions" not only reveal the importance of epigenetics, but they also expose that the suggested eugenic pathology, which dogmatically insists upon genetic causes and that produce alterations in the brain, is not accurate. Actually, the brain itself acts upon the genome as well. Other biological researchers confirm epigenetics' significance to scientific theory and research:

> **The complex interaction and interdependence of genes and environments, a fundamental and frequently ignored reality of biology, undermines the notion that genotypes alone determine (or cause) phenotypes.** There are several reasons why strong genetic determinism turns out to be rare. First and foremost, the environment plays a very important role in the expression of most genes. An individual with the genetic potential to be six feet tall will not reach this height if he/she lacks a proper diet during childhood . . . . Second, most traits are epistatic: they are determined not by a single gene but by many different genes. Dozens or even hundreds of genes may play a causal role in the genesis of complex traits such as intelligence, personality, or athletic ability. So, a single gene may only have a small influence on the development of the trait. Third, **development (or epigenesis) has a significant impact on gene expression, i.e. how organisms convert genetic information into traits.** Because developmental patterns and processes influence gene expression, two organisms with identical genomes and substantially similar environments may still express different phenotypes [emphasis added].[852]

Though it is theorized that people are products or "victims" of their genes, in truth, their genes are altered by their metaphysical souls.

---

[852] Resnik and Vorhaus, "Genetic Modification and Genetic Determinism."

ALTERNATIVE EXPLANATION OF PATHOLOGY - TABLE 2

Phenotypes	Endogenotypes	Phenotypes
Faith, cognition, habits, substances, desires, & behaviors →	Genetic Variances→	←Neural dysfunction, delusions, hallucinations . . .

If genes are indeed altered by proposed phenotypes, then the Rushian, Morelian, and Kraepelinian arrow of causality must be considered as inaccurate and should be denounced. Paul Silverman, an early advocate of the Human Genome Project, professor at University of California Irvine, and the founder of the Human Genome Center, concedes that the arrow of causality could certainly go the other way:

> **Indeed, the gene may not be central to phenotype at all,** or at least it shares the spotlight with other influences. Environmental, tissue, and cytoplasmic factors clearly dominate the phenotypic expression processes, which may, in turn, be affected by a variety of unpredictable protein-interaction events. The cell-signaling process heavily depends on extracellular stimuli to trigger nuclear DNA transduction . . . . On the medical front, epidemiologists have long known that diet, exercise, antioxidants, and environmental factors may affect gene expression . . . . **"Phenotype overrides genotype."** Yet despite these many observations, the DNA deterministic

model continues to dominate molecular biology
[emphasis added].[853]

As Silverman acknowledges, the empirical evidence available undermines the eugenic faith. Psychiatrists, writing for the International Society of Psychiatric Genetics, also remark on both the lack of validity of classifying mindsets, emotions, and behaviors as disorders as well as how the theoretical "path" is not as established as it is promoted to be:

> **The major impediments to gene identification for psychiatric disorders are the lack of validity of the classification of psychiatric disorders (e.g., phenotypes, or observable aspects of disease) and the complexity of the pathways from genotypes to psychiatric phenotypes.** Recent studies have attempted to identify more valid phenotypical constructs for genetic studies. Phenotypical traits or markers that may represent intermediate forms of expression between the output of underlying genes and the broader disease phenotypes have been termed endophenotypes. Studies of the role of genetic factors involved in these systems may be more informative than studies of the aggregate psychiatric phenotypes because they may more closely represent expression of underlying biological systems. However, **a recent meta-analysis of psychiatric endophenotypes and a review of the genetic architecture of traits in model organisms do not provide evidence that currently identified endophenotypes are superior to current phenotypical disease definitions** [emphasis added].[854]

[853] Paul H. Silverman, "Rethinking Genetic Determinism," *The Scientist* (May 24, 2004): https://www.the-scientist.com/vision/ rethinking-genetic-determinism-50020. Accessed August 24, 2019.

[854] Alison K. Merikangas and Kathleen R. Merikangas, *Psychiatric Genetics: A Primer for Clinicians and Basic Scientists* edited by Thomas G. Schulze and Francis J. McMahon (New York: Oxford University Press, 2018), 5.

Other psychiatric geneticists agree that no genetic model has been proven and that biological variances may very well be individual responses rather than causes:

> No model accounts for all of the alterations associated with schizophrenia, and, for many of them, it remains unknown if they are causal or potentially compensatory reactions to upstream dysfunction.[855]

Additionally, psychiatrist Niall McLaren states:

> In case anybody should think that dismissing biological theories on theoretical grounds is a little hasty, it remains the case that there is no extant reductionist model of mental disorder. No psychiatrist has ever written anything that could possibly count as an articulated theory or model of mental disorder as biology. The proposition "All Mental Disorder is Brain Disorder" is metaphysical, purely an ideological claim, and not of a form that empirical science can investigate.[856]

The genetic theory — founded upon bio-determinism — is a weak, unvalidated anthropological faith that is used to explain character traits — especially as applied to metaphysical aspects of human nature:

> Genetic determinism can be loosely defined as the view that genes (genotypes) cause traits (phenotypes). This definition is almost trivially true, because most traits have some type of genetic basis. Strong genetic determinism is

855 Robert A. McCutcheon, Tiago Reis Marques, and Oliver D. Howes, "Schizophrenia — An Overview," *JAMA Psychiatry Online* (October 30, 2019): doi:10.1001/jamapsychiatry.2019.3360.

856 Niall McLaren, "Pies' Polemic and the Question of Theories in Psychiatry, Again," *Mad in America* (September, 4, 2019): https://www.madinamerica.com/2019/09/pies-polemic-and-the-question-of-theories-in-psychiatry-again/.

not very common: the vast majority of traits are either moderately or weakly determined by genetics.[857]

Psychiatric genetics, an ideological strategy, is faith driven and not objective science; it is faith that exults genes to the causative role in explaining human nature at all costs despite the clear evidence to the contrary.

Many scientists recognize that the construct of schizophrenia (and all forms of suggested psychosis) is itself a fluid concept and not an objective reality to begin with. As previously noted but worth repeating, the term "heterogeneous" is regularly utilized in acknowledging the subjective nature of Kraepelinian descriptive constructs.[858] But this fact makes it nearly impossible to objectively assert etiological claims or statistical predictabilities in the first place.

> The construct of 'schizophrenia' is indeed heterogeneous. It is also disjunctive and has little reliability or validity (Bentall, 2003; 2009; Read, 2004a), rendering it very difficult to identify any specific cause, genetic or otherwise.[859]

Paul Silverman declares that if available objective evidence in the field of epigenetics is considered apart from

---

[857] Resnik and Vorhaus, "Genetic Modification and Genetic Determinism."

[858] Kenneth S. Kendler and E.J. Engsrom, "Criticisms of Kraepelin's Psychiatric Nosology: 1898-1927," *American Journal of Psychiatry* 175 (4) (April 1, 2018): 316.

[859] John Read, Richard P. Bentall, and Roar Fosse, "Time to abandon the Bio-bio-bio model of psychosis: Exploring the epigenetic and psychological mechanisms by which adverse life events lead to psychotic symptoms," *Cambridge University Press* Vol. 18 (40) (December 2009): 299-300; https://doi.org/10.1017/S1121189X00000257.

dogmatic bio-deterministic assumptions, then the genetic (eugenic) model should not continue to be promoted:

> For more than 50 years scientists have operated under a set of seemingly incontrovertible assumptions about genes, gene expression, and the consequences thereof. Their mantra: One gene yields one protein; genes beget messenger RNA, which in turn begets protein; and most critically, the gene is deterministic in gene expression and can therefore predict disease propensities. Yet during the last five years, data have revealed inadequacies in this theory. Unsettling results from the Human Genome Project (HGP) in particular have thrown the deficiencies into sharp relief. Some genes encode more than one protein; others don't encode proteins at all. These findings help refine evolutionary theory by explaining an explosion of diversity from relatively little starting material. We therefore need to rethink our long-held beliefs: A reevaluation of the genetic determinism doctrine, coupled with a new systems biology mentality, could help consolidate and clarify genome-scale data, enabling us finally to reap the rewards of the genome sequencing projects.[860]

As Silverman correctly insists, the genetic theory of mental illness is a "long-held belief" that is not supported by valid science and needs to be reconsidered.

Regardless of one's presuppositional faith, the field of epigenetics continues to expose that genes are not fixed — a reality that undermines the fixity theory of hereditary madness that is vital to sustain psychiatric genetics. Instead of stopping at the genes, objective researchers must consider what alters the human genome and produces both variant genetic expressions and neurological differences. If only somatic factors can be considered as causative,

---

[860] Silverman, "Rethinking Genetic Determinism."

however, then metaphysical phenotypes (such as delusions and hallucinations), should likewise not be considered as valid organic diseases or valid diagnostic symptoms. But if delusions and hallucinations are considered to be valid phenotypes upon which diagnoses can be made (and have been made since psychiatric constructs were introduced), then the metaphysical deceived human nature that operates on faith and meaningful relationships must also be considered as valid etiologies which can negatively alter a person's biology.

Changes are Constant

Yet another problem that psychiatric genetic theorists must also face in maintaining their false theory of genetic fixity is the reality that the human genome, the nervous system, and people's characters are constantly changing as they learn, experience life, mature, and form new relationships. Simply put, people are in a constant state of spiritual/mental, behavioral, and biological change. Whether for good or for bad, spiritual and physical changes and variances are part of normal human nature, and just because someone's life changes drastically toward distress, does not mean that he/she is disordered.

People Change

While schizophrenia and other psychiatric constructs are framed as fixed genetic predispositions or hereditary risks, people regularly recover from the negative phenomena framed as psychosis. Several psychiatrists share their own findings:

... This 'enriched' sample of severely ill patients with poor outcome represents only a fraction of the broader phenotype that includes a variety of psychosis spectrum diagnostic categories such as schizophreniform disorder, delusional disorder, brief psychotic disorder and so on (Perala et al. 2007) .... **Patients with better outcome either never enter, or eventually drop out of mental health care: They either recover and do not necessitate mental health treatment or display a favourable illness course and thus no longer fit into the schizophrenia definition per current classification systems.** [emphasis added].[861]

Research scientist at the UCLA Neuropsychiatric Institute, Robert Liberman, also comments:

Our findings join a growing body of research that flies in the face of the long-held notion that individuals diagnosed with schizophrenia are doomed to a life of disability with little expectation for productive involvement in society, a fatalistic view that in itself is damaging to prospects for recovery.[862]

In 2014, Allen Frances interviewed James Hickman, who not only recovered from "schizophrenia" by "thinking logically" through his problems but also went on to become a licensed social worker. In the article, the influential Frances emphasizes that schizophrenia is a fluid or heterogeneous construct:

[861] Courtenay Harding, Joseph Zubin, and John S. Strauss, "Chronicity in Schizophrenia: Fact, Partial Fact, or Artifact?" *Hospital Community Psychiatry* 38 (5) (1987): 47; available from DOI: 10.1176/ps. 38.5.477.

[862] Robert P. Liberman quoted by Jeanie Lerche Davis, "Keys to Recovery from Schizophrenia: Patients Need More Help, Hope from Psychiatrists, Family, Friends," *WebMD* (December 6, 2002): https://www.webmd.com/schizophrenia/news/20021206/keys-to-recovery-from-schizophrenia#1.

"Schizophrenia" is a name, not a disease. It presents in many different ways and has many different outcomes. There is certainly not one cause of "schizophrenia."[863]

Larry Davidson, writing in the *Journal of Personality*, also documents similar findings and notes how a person's identity/faith is a core phenomenology of the construct of schizophrenia:

> Objective Diverse theoretical orientations on psychopathology, including most recently phenomenological and neuroscientific approaches, **consistently have viewed a core component of schizophrenia to be the loss, or distortion, of a person's sense of self as an effective agent in a shared, social world.** How such a sense of self becomes lost or distorted, and the questions of whether or not, and if so, how it can be recovered have received considerably less attention. These questions are taken up in the present paper. **Method Review of a substantial body of longitudinal research, enhanced by a growing trove of recovery narratives, provide ample evidence that many people recover a sense of self over time** [emphasis added].[864]

If one's faith enables a person to have a realistic view of self even through the difficult circumstances of life which test one's faith, recovery is both possible and proven. Establishing vital truth that can help people rightly perceive themselves, their souls, their purpose, and their

---

[863] Allen Frances, "Recovery From "Schizophrenia": One Man's Journey from Patient to Therapist," *Psychiatric Times Online* (October 30, 2014): https://www.psychiatrictimes.com/schizophrenia/recovery-schizophrenia-one-mans-journey-patient-therapist.

[864] Larry Davidson, "Recovering a Sense of Self in Schizophrenia," *Journal of Personality* (February 2019): DOI: 10.1111/jopy.12471.

hopes becomes vital for truly helping people overwhelmed with falsehood.

With this evidence available (as will be discussed further in the next chapter), it seems more plausible to understand that the possibility of improvement for those who are diagnosed as schizophrenic and confined to the neo-Kraepelinian eugenic system is diminished, while those who remain in meaningful relationships and improve their phenomenology (sense of self, relationships, and life) apart from psychiatric treatment regularly recover from what is claimed to be psychosis.

Since schizophrenia is a subjective construct (heterogeneous), those who hold to fixity can withdraw diagnoses and claim these cases as "misdiagnoses" after people recover. Such practices highlight how those who believe that they have authority over matters of the soul can manipulate their concepts of degeneracy in order to maintain their control over society and sustain their false narrative.

People try to Change People

While promoting the idea that people are products of their fixed genes, psychiatric geneticists, neuropsychiatrists, psychotherapists, psychopharmacologists, and many other professionals seek to produce changes in people. If people cannot change mentally and behaviorally apart from how their genes have allegedly predisposed them to function, then it is insanity/futility to insist upon such practices as psychotherapy and psychopharmacology.

Still, these popular humanistic means of dealing with degeneracy focus on and produce hope for changes in individuals, families, and societies, while regularly claiming to be efficient means of producing change even in brain structure and neurological activity. For example, psychotherapy is said to positively alter the brain physically.[865] Several researchers discuss their own findings concerning *cognitive behavioral therapy* (CBT) in the journal, *Translational Psychiatry*:

> These findings show that reorganisation occurring at the neural level following psychological therapy can predict the subsequent recovery path of people with psychosis across 8 years . . . . Our previous investigation provided evidence that CBTp leads to substantial reorganisation of functional connectivity supporting social affective processing, relatively little of which is captured by measures of symptom change. The present findings extend this work by providing initial evidence that it is the degree to which this reorganisation takes place that determines sustained gains in the long-term recovery of people with psychosis.[866]

They further express,

> It seems plausible to conclude that being better able to cognitively regulate negative emotion, especially in

[865] See Hasse Karlsson, "How Psychotherapy Changes the Brain," *Psychiatric Times Online* vol. 28 (8) https://www.psychiatrictimes.com/ psychotherapy/how-psychotherapy-changes-brain. (August 12, 2011): see also Paquette V, Lévesque J, Mensour B, et al. "Change the mind and you change the brain": effects of cognitive-behavioral therapy on the neural correlates of spider phobia," *Neuroimage* 18 (2003): 401-409.

[866] L. Mason, E Peters, S.C. Williams, and V. Kumari, "Brain Connectivity Changes Occuring Following Cognitive Behavioural Therapy for Psychosis Predict Long-term Recovery," *Translational Psychiatry* vol. 7 (August 15, 2017): doi:10.1038/tp.2016.263.

response to potential threat, is an important CBTp outcome that determines personally perceived recovery in the long run. This is concordant with service user-focused research, which has highlighted that the ability to better manage negative emotions is an important feature of recovery for people with psychosis. Overall, these findings highlight that neural changes following CBTp confer a long-lasting benefit.[867]

If genetic and neural fixity are valid explanations of human nature, then psychotherapy should not produce positive changes, and "recovery" from psychosis should not ever occur. However, if faith and relationships are both considered as central to being human and the interpretation of human phenomena, then the observable somatic changes make sense as effects. In early 2020, the American Psychiatric Association published an article exposing that the brain does react both to empathetic relationships in counseling and to new ways to understand and perceive negative life experiences:

> Psychotherapy, or talk therapy, is an effective treatment for many mental health disorders. Advances in brain imaging are increasingly allowing researchers to observe the changes in the brain resulting from psychotherapy treatment . . . . A 2017 study by researchers in London found that CBT strengthens specific connections in the brains of people with schizophrenia. These changes were associated with reduced symptoms and recovery many years later. People in the study who had received medication treatment only did not show similar brain changes. The authors point out that people with schizophrenia are often not offered psychotherapies . . . . While they are two distinct types of therapy, they have some core elements in common, including re-elaborating

[867] Ibid.

traumatic events or memories and building new positive attitudes and behaviors.[868]

Likewise, Psychiatrist Daniel Collerton discusses that the changes in thinking/consciousness (phenomenology) directly alter the brain:

> **For the last century or so, psychotherapy has aimed to change the mind. And if it has been effective in doing so, it must have led to lasting changes in conscious content, and potentially in the process of consciousness itself [phenomenology].** Few other human endeavors seek so systematically to produce predictable enduring variation in emotion, cognition, behavior and somatic perceptions; changes which can persist for many years beyond the end of therapy. **Over the last few decades, as methods have become available for measuring brain structure and function, it has provided a potential real-life method by which meaningful changes in consciousness can be related to measures of brain function** [emphasis added].[869]

One must question why change in others is desired if evolutionary theory is held and no standard of optimality is established for mindsets, emotions, behaviors, neural networks, or the human genome. Nonetheless, there exists a great deal of evidence that people can and regularly do change from relationships formed in "talk therapy."

[868] APA Staff, "Brain Imaging Shows the Impacts of Psychotherapy," *American Psychiatric Association* (January 6, 2020): https://www.psychiatry.org/news-room/apa-blogs/apa-blog/2020/01/brain-imaging-shows-the-impacts-of-psychotherapy?fbclid=IwAR35JbV rrzfdW2nwdv8at4MI-7SAtKbloOdIfCBk7-xAzno1Djj6afCvrlM.

[869] Daniel Collerton, "Psychotherapy and Brain Plasticity," *Frontiers in Psychology* 4 (September 6, 2013): 548; doi:10.3389/fpsyg.2013.00548.

Eugenicists have as a lofty goal to not only change individual's character and identity through understanding the genome, but to change society as a whole at every level. Harvard Geneticist Richard Lewontin explains this absurdity:

> Some of the wonder-workers and their disciples see even beyond the major causes of death and disease. They have an image of social peace and order emerging from the DNA data bank at the National Institutes of Health. The editor of the most prestigious general American scientific journal, *Science*, and energetic publicist for large DNA sequencing projects, in special issues of his journal filled with full-page multicolored advertisements from biotechnology equipment manufacturers, has visions of genes for alcoholism, unemployment, domestic and social violence, and drug addiction. What we had previously imagined to be messy moral, political, and economic issues turn out, after all, to be simply a matter of an occasional nucleotide substitution. While the notion that the war on drugs will be won by genetic engineering belongs to Cloud Cuckoo Land, it is a manifestation of a serious ideology that is continuous with the eugenics of an earlier time.[870]

Significantly, Nathaniel Scharping, a contributor for the *Genetic Literacy Project* as well as for *Discover Magazine*, advises that

> **framing our genes in this deterministic way vastly oversimplifies the way they work and grants genes powers they simply don't have.** Just like there's no one "gene for speed," there's no "gene for crime." "It's not like you have one mutation and now you're a serial killer," says Paige Harden, an associate professor of psychology at the University of Texas at Austin. Instead, thousands of genes each influence in a minuscule way the probability that a given person might develop a trait, like

---

[870] Lewontin, *Biology as Ideology*, 72.

impulse control or poor literacy, that in turn is correlated with committing a crime. And that's not even taking the environment into account. The set of circumstances that surrounds us as we develop into adults also plays an integral role in who we turn out to be — it's why identical twins can end up so different. Our experiences shape the influence our genes have on us. And our genes help determine what kinds of environments we seek out, which in turn shapes how our genes are expressed, and so on. The interactions are extraordinarily complex, and we're nowhere near understanding the majority of them. "Be very wary of claims to genetic exceptionalism, that genes are somehow special, that they play a causal role that nothing else does," says Leslie Francis, a professor of law and philosophy at the University of Utah. **If anything, research is showing that genes may play a lesser role than we think** [emphasis added].[871]

Dr. Joe Dispenza agrees,

> The genetic-determinism concept still reigns in the general public's mind. Most people believe the common misconception that our genetic destiny is predetermined . . . . The news media reinforce this by repeatedly suggesting that specific genes cause this condition or that disease. They've programmed us into believing that we're victims of our biology and that our genes have the ultimate power over our health, our well-being, and our personalities—and even that our genes dictate our human affairs, determine our interpersonal relationships, and forecast our future. But are we who we are, and do we do what we do, because we're born that way? This concept implies that genetic determinism is deeply entrenched in our culture and that there are genes for schizophrenia,

[871] Nathaniel Scharping, "Can We Blame Our Genes for Our Decisions?" *Discover Magazine* (December 10, 2018): http://blogs.discovermagazine.com/ crux/2018/12/10/genetic-determinism-genes-blame/#.XWHpBy3MyfU. Accessed August 24, 2019.

genes for homosexuality, genes for leadership, and so on. These are all dated beliefs built on yesterday's news.[872]

Further, geneticist Paul Silverman calls to attention that molecular psychiatry was formed based on the false belief in biodeterminism and hereditary transmission:

> For more than 50 years the simplistic DNA deterministic model of hereditary transmission has provided a useful and satisfying context for the development of molecular biology. Yet though it cannot account for the increased complexity and plasticity being discovered for gene expression, the model continues to receive strong support among molecular biologists who have been reluctant to alter or abandon it without a viable alternative.[873]

Similarly, Peter Breggin writes,

> Clearly, proving an association between a particular state of mind and a particular reaction in the brain doesn't indicate which came first. Yet the biopsychiatrists, without discussing it, usually assume that the brain is the egg from which the chicken — mental disorder — is born. They search for signs of hyperactivity in the dopamine system of schizophrenics without acknowledging that if they find it, it could be the normal response of a normal brain to the prolonged expression of an intense emotional state.[874]

The true nature of psychiatric genetics led former president of the American Psychiatry Association Dr. Sharfstein to state about his profession that "we have allowed the bio-

---

[872] Joe Dispenza, *You are the Placebo: Making Your Mind Matter* (New York: Hay House, 2014), 83.

[873] Silverman, "Rethinking Genetic Determinism."

[874] Breggin, *Toxic Psychiatry*, 112.

psycho-social model to become the bio-bio-bio model."[875] To open the possibility that a metaphysical soul is part of human nature would not only cause a significant paradigm shift, but it would also replace the foundational philosophies and explain the pathology of human nature that the genetic theory and the medical model have failed to do. Moreover, having a right worldview/ phenomenology would reveal the remedy to the metaphysical aspects of human nature, and a true and healthy view of self, others, and the world in which people live would replace delusional phenomenologies that have proved to be destructive.

But it must be emphasized that bio-determinism and "risk" factors are vital to sustain the philosophy of individual degenerationism and molecular, genetic, and neuropsychiatry. The concept of psychiatric determination and individual degenerationism rests on the idea that one's genes, and thus one's "poor" mindsets, emotions, and behaviors, are fixed and immutable — unless, as in some people's view, psychiatry is able to intervene through molecular mechanisms. These beliefs are not just dated; they are the foundational doctrines of Kraepelin's psychiatric eugenics which sustain today's established construct of mental illness:

> The nonsense propagated by ideologues of biological determinisms that the lower classes are biologically inferior to the upper classes, that all the good things in European culture come from the Nordic groups, is precisely nonsense. **It is meant to legitimate the structures of inequality in our society by putting a**

---

[875] Steven S. Sharfstein, "Big Pharma and American Psychiatry: The Good, the Bad, and the Ugly," *Psychiatric News* August 19, 2005), 3; https://doi.org/10.1176/pn.40.16.00400003.

> biological gloss on them and by propagating the
> continual confusion between what may be influenced
> by genes and what may be changed by social and
> environmental alterations.[876]

The genetic theory—and its philosophy of genetic determinism—is one of the primary means of social control and the creating of degenerates. Convincing people through neo-Kraepelinian phenomenology that their genes cause their entire personhood and consciousness and that this random choice of mother nature is fixed unless medically addressed is perverted, destructive, and opposed to the empirical science that is available.

Genetic determinism may be a necessary theme for eugenicists to explain their inability to help people within their faith, but it is not an accurate or necessary. According to geneticist Richard Lewontin, the propagation of bio-determinism is purposeful as a means to control the "system" that maintains "inequality":

> The vulgar error that confuses heritability and fixity has been, over the years, the most powerful single weapon that biological ideologues have had in legitimating a society of inequality. Since as biologists they must know better, one is entitled to at least a suspicion that the beneficiaries of a system of inequality are not to be regarded as objective experts.[877]

It is not that biologists are unaware that people change. Rather, genetic determinism—a foundational philosophy of psychiatric eugenics—enables degenerates to be made and social control to be maintained. Sadly, bio-determinism

[876] Lewontin, *Biology as Ideology*, 37.

[877] Ibid.

leaves individuals and society in a hopeless phenomenological state.

Evolutionary Theory is all about Change

Ironically, the evolutionary theory rests on the belief that life, including human consciousness, is constantly adapting, and only those species that positively change (advancing rather than degenerating) survive:

> The rule of life, according to Darwin, is "adapt or die." Those organisms whose properties enabled them to cope with the problems set by the external world would survive and leave offspring, and the others would fail to do so.[878]

If evolutionary adaptation is true, then only degeneracy — a regression to a lesser state of humanity — can explain maladaptive or negative character and relational, behavioral, and phenomenological problems. However, the evolutionary concepts of adaptation and fixed genes are antithetical theories, as a large group of psychiatrists and researchers, writing for the World Psychiatric Association, realize:

> One approach to understand psychiatric disorders in an evolutionary perspective builds upon Nobel laureate Nikolaas Tinbergen's ideas, suggesting that, for a full understanding of any given phenotypic trait, one needs to detect the development and nature of its mechanisms, construed as the "proximate causes", and, in addition, its evolutionary (or phylogenetic) history and adaptive value. Studying the proximate mechanisms is standard in psychiatry and the clinical neurosciences, but the questions pertaining to the phylogeny of traits have

[878] Ibid.

512

largely been ignored. **Admittedly, placing dysfunctional cognitive, emotional and behavioral processes in the context of possible adaptation is not straightforward at first sight. The clinical directive requires that "disorder" represent the appropriate focus. However, a "disorder" – by definition – is counter-intuitive in the context of adaptation** [emphasis added].[879]

The same authors continue,

Important to the understanding of a particular phenotype is the evolutionary concept of variation. Without variation, no evolution by natural selection could take place. **Mainstream psychiatry has largely ignored the fact that variation is the rule, not the exception, and this creates conceptual tensions. Psychiatry conceptualizes "disorder" as a statistical deviation from a normative statistical mean, yet handles it as a category. In other words, both "normalcy" as well as "disorder" with regard to psychological or behavioral functioning are burdened with the connotation of low variation.** Phenotypic variation is the result of a complex interplay of genotype and environment, including epigenetic mechanisms that are decisively shaped by experience over the individual lifespan [emphasis added].[880]

These psychiatrists explain further that variation rather than adaptation becomes necessary within evolutionary thinking if psychiatric theory is to be sustained. Additionally, they insist that the same genes which allegedly cause psychiatric disorders can also enable a

[879] Martin Brüne, Jay Belsky, Horacio Fabrega, Jay R. Feierman, Paul Gilbert, Kalman Glantz, Joseph Polimeni, John S. Price, Julio San Juan, Roger Sullivan, Alfonso Troisi, Daniel R. Wilson, "The Crisis of Psychiatry—insights and prospects from evolutionary theory," *World Psychiatry* 11 (1) (February 2012): 55-57.

[880] Ibid.

person's "enhanced coping" mechanisms if placed in the right environments. In this theory, environments supersede the human genome as the primary controlling evolutionary agent:

> One presumption of how to explain the nature and causes of psychiatric conditions pertains to the idea that individuals carry variations of genes that make them vulnerable to develop a disorder, commonly referred to as the "diathesis-stress-model". **Evolutionarily informed research into the genetics of psychiatric disorders now demonstrates that while such alleles can predispose to developing a psychiatric condition under adverse environmental conditions such as childhood maltreatment, they can also protect, and in fact can allow enhanced coping upon encountering favorable environmental conditions during early stages of development.** For example, the "short" allele of the serotonin transporter coding gene is associated with greater risk for depression if linked with early childhood adversities, yet the same version of the gene is associated with reduced risk for depression if carriers grow up in emotionally secure conditions. This suggests that selection favored plasticity or "open programs" that render individuals more susceptible to environmental contingencies – for better and worse [emphasis added].[881]

These evolutionists are not dismissing genetic determinism. Instead, they are adding environmental determinism to the hypothesis to explain why people with the alleged same genetic predisposition react differently to the same environments. Such a perspective not only shows that genes are not fixed, but that evolutionists must exclude, at all costs, a person's faith and phenomenology as determining how he/she responds to environments in

[881] Ibid.

order to sustain the idea of evolved fixity. Dr. Lewontin realizes, however, that fixity and change are antithetical:

> Psychiatry must either accept that human nature is constantly changing and adapting or that it is fixed based upon individual genomes. If a person believes that genes are fixed and inherited, then adaptation cannot occur and evolution makes no sense. If adaptation is not occurring and the human genome is more similar than different, then there should be no differences in mindsets, emotions and behaviors and abnormalities cannot be suggested . . . . There are deep contradictions in simultaneously asserting that we are all genetically alike in certain respects, that our genes are all-powerful in determining our behavior, and at the same time observing that people differ.[882]

Evolutionists must either believe that genes are fixed and adaptation cannot occur or they must establish that genes are naturally varied and change both individually and corporately, and therefore, degeneration cannot exist. If evolutionary theory were true, then variances in human mindsets, emotions, behaviors, and even somatic differences should be understood to rest on an expected spectrum of adaptation. If, however, variances within the human genome are not allowed — thus opening the door for the existence of abnormalities — then evolution and doctrines of adaptation cannot be valid.

Lewontin proceeds to relate the dilemma of how the existence of variations in human nature and in individual genomes undermine an insistence upon a normative standard of genomic material from which degeneracy is allegedly measured:

---

[882] Lewontin, *Biology as Ideology*, 97.

But if we all share these genes, if evolution has made us all alike in this human nature, then in principle there would be no way to investigate the heritability of the brains. On the other hand, if there is genetic variation among human beings in these respects, then on what basis do we declare that or another manifestation is universal human nature.[883]

What is believed to be normal—even when it comes to the human genome—determines what is believed to be abnormal.

The same logic must be applied in considering not only the human genome but also the nervous system. Yale psychologists Avram Holmes and Lauren Patrick discuss how the absence of brain optimality—a consistent standard of health and function—undermines the currently accepted Kraepelinian diagnostic system for determining perceived individual degeneracy:

Clear evidence supports a dimensional view of psychiatric illness. Within this framework the expression of disorder-relevant phenotypes is often interpreted as a breakdown or departure from normal brain function. Conversely, health is reified, conceptualized as possessing a single ideal state. We challenge this concept here, arguing that there is no universally optimal profile of brain functioning. The evolutionary forces that shape our species select for a staggering diversity of human behaviors. To support our position, we highlight pervasive population-level variability within large-scale functional networks and discrete circuits.[884]

[883] Ibid.

[884] Avram J. Holmes and Lauren M. Patrick, "The Myth of Optimality in Clinical Neuroscience," *Trends in Cognitive Sciences* vol. 22 (3) (March 1, 2018): 242; DOI: https://doi.org/10.1016/j.tics.2017 .12.006.

Many other psychiatrists have also come to realize that Kraepelin's theory, so widely held today, is counterintuitive to the evolutionary theory:

> We present factual anatomical, physiological and clinical data critical of the platonic Kraepelinean classification of mental diseases, and claim that this classification is contrary to modern ideas on the evolution of nervous systems. We argue against the view of mainstream evolutionary psychiatrists that mental diseases are adaptations. We do so on two accounts. One is methodological; authors in this position do not ask whether every disease has evolutionary causes, but assume this in order to explain all diseases in such terms. The other mistake is biological; it is their belief that adaptation is the driving force of evolution while in fact it is just an outcome of evolution . . . These data, taken together, plus arguments derived from the high degree of plasticity of nervous systems, lead us to suggest a different approach to classification of mental diseases.[885]

Within evolutionary belief, mental and behavioral differences, which are blamed on adaptations or genetic variances, should be the expected norm and not forms of degeneracy/disorders/diseases. Whether or not one holds to an intelligent designer or an evolutionary faith regarding origins, the eugenics theory is not logically sustainable.

If there does not exist a standard of a normal/healthy genome or standard brain size and function, then there cannot be an objective standard of abnormality. If there is no abnormal, then psychiatry and the construct of mental disorder ceases to exist as a valid anthropology and

---

[885] B. Dubrovsky, "Evolutionary Psychiatry. Adaptationist and Nonadaptationist Conceptualizations," *Progress in Neuropsychopharmacology and Biological Psychiatry* 26 (1) (January, 2002): 1-19; https://www.ncbi.nlm.nih.gov/pubmed/11853097.

phenomenology. Academic psychiatrists must save concepts of abnormal at all cost, though, as a means to perpetuate their field's existence, even if it is illogical within the evolutionary theory from which psychiatry was conceived and destructive to the society in which it is applied.

Genes are not the Core of Human Nature

What is also important to understand is that the largest and most horrific psychiatric experiment ever conducted on alleged schizophrenia, bipolar, alcoholism and other forms of created psychiatric degeneracy disproves and discredits Kraepelin's genetic/hereditary theory rather than validating it. The empirical evidence the experiment produced proved that people who struggle with delusions and hallucinations are normal, though they are impaired and are rightfully struggling with traumatic distress. Esteemed psychiatrists E. Fuller Torry and Robert Yolken estimate that between 70-100 percent of people thought to have schizophrenia and their relatives were euthanized in Nazi Germany, but even so, "postwar rates of the incidence of schizophrenia in Germany were unexpectedly high."[886] If the construct of schizophrenia were a valid genetic disease, then minimizing or eliminating the faulty genes would have had a significant effect on its prevalence in the near future.

---

[886] E. Fuller Torrey and Robert H Yolken, "Psychiatric genocide: Nazi attempts to eradicate schizophrenia." *Schizophrenia Bulletin* vol. 36,1 (2010): 26-32; doi:10.1093/schbul/sbp097.

518

What is also relevant to the discussion is that survivors of the Holocaust—not diagnosed within the psychiatric classification—were found to have had the stress-sensitive gene fK506 negatively altered.[887] Something other than genes, then, should be considered as explaining delusions and hallucinations which are persistent and distressful, especially following traumatic experiences, such as the Holocaust was even for the German citizens.

Another example of how faith, desires, and relationships and not genes are at the core of a person's soul can be observed in marriages. The International Society of Psychiatric Genetics published a clinical primer in 2018, which revealed that married couples are more prone to be fit into the same or similar psychiatric construct and assigned the same of type psychiatric label:

> Systematic family studies of both clinical and community samples have shown that spouses of people with mental disorders often manifest either the same or another mental disorder . . . . studies of genetic risk should incorporate the tendency for assortative mating, which may influence the distribution of susceptibility alleles in both clinical and population samples. The importance of assortative mating in recent polygenic analyses (as described later) has received increasing attention.[888]

In this case, psychiatric geneticists speculate that a genetic predisposition causes people with the same mental

[887] Tobias B. Halene, Gregor Hasler, Amanda Mitchell, and Schahram Akbarian, *Psychiatric Genetics: A Primer for Clinicians and Basic Scientists* edited by Thomas G. Schulze and Francis J. McMahon (New York: Oxford University Press, 2018), 149.

[888] Alison K. Merikangas and Kathleen R. Merikangas, *Psychiatric Genetics: A Primer for Clinicians and Basic Scientists* edited by Thomas G. Schulze and Francis J. McMahon (New York: Oxford University Press, 2018), 11.

disorders to search out each other — a phenomena that evolutionary geneticists call *assortative mating*. "Assortative mating has been associated with numerous psychiatric disorders, including depression, alcoholism, and schizophrenia."[889] Despite the clear relational/social correlations of human struggles and the reality that beliefs and behaviors are commonly shared within families, intimate relationships, and communities based upon fellowship, bio-psycho-socialists persist in demanding that biology be considered as the premier and unquestionable explanation of all human nature:

> Most genetic and brain researchers, however, have either ignored the psycho-social causes of psychosis or relegated them to the role of triggers or exacerbators of a vulnerability which they assumed to be genetic. Meanwhile brain researchers identified abnormalities in 'schizophrenics' without considering what might have happened in their lives to have caused them.[890]

Psychiatric geneticists have promoted faith in conjecture simply by establishing statistics that are neither reliable nor valid and demanding that statistics be interpreted according to neo-Kraepelinian phenomenology.

Still, other studies, such as the famous study conducted and published by David Rosenhan in the 1970's, reveal that the construct and diagnostic process of schizophrenia has been entirely subjective since Kraepelin first proposed its consideration as a possible disease. Moreover, these types of studies show that genes are not the valid determiner of

---

[889] Ibid.

[890] Read, Bentall, and Fosse, "Time to abandon the Bio-bio-bio model of psychosis."

statistical occurrences of alleged schizophrenia. But it is socially accepted moral standards, relationships, and one's faith that play the primary roles, significantly influencing behavior and therapeutic outcomes. Lewontin, Rose, and Kamin note that when Rosenhan's study that exposed the subjective/heterogenous nature of the construct of schizophrenia was published in the prestigious *Science* magazine,[891] there was a significant drop in numbers of people struggling with the alleged disorder and entering the hospital in that area to be diagnosed.[892] As the general population lost faith in schizophrenia as an organic disease entity, the amount of people believing themselves to be diseased also decreased proportionally. To summarize, as eugenic phenomenologies are shown to be false, informed people are less likely to accept these beliefs as part of their own identity, as accurately describing them, and to submit themselves to the eugenic diagnostic system. Whether or not eugenicists wish to acknowledge that a person's faith and social factors are far more influential than genes, the available evidence reveals otherwise.

If there is no valid biological marker and pathology to objectively determine that an alleged form of illness actually exists beyond being a social/descriptive construct, if there is no empirical means to differentiate between one psychiatric disorder (construct) and another, and if these constructs contained in the *DSM-5* have no unique genetic and environmental risk factors to distinguish them from each other or from those of the alleged general public, then the entire genetic theory of mental illness that Kraepelin

[891] Berger, *Mental Illness: The Necessity for Faith and Authority*, 88-90.

[892] Lewontin, Rose, and Kamin, *Not in our Genes*, 229.

first formalized is shown to be pseudoscience. Eugenics/ psychiatric genetics is not a medical or scientific field, but a humanistic anthropology and phenomenology based upon the unproven theory of Darwinian evolution.

The available scientific evidence and knowledge about human nature points to the reality that genes, neural patterns, mindsets, emotions, behaviors, and relationships — all aspects of the bio-psycho-social model — are not fixed. What determines how these changes are interpreted/framed, explained, and approached is a person's presuppositional faith.

Psychiatric constructs that attempt to explain phenotypes, endophenotypes, and genotypes are merely one commonly accepted Darwinian anthropology and phenomenology. Yet, this faith in Kraepelin's construct of mental illness — as in Germany pre-WW2 — has come to dominate much of the world's medicine, science, education, and politics.

Empirical science, however, does not validate neo-Kraepelinianism. Instead, it reveals that though there are clear variances among people, people are not all that different from one other, and the psychiatric assertion of individual degenerationism is not a valid anthropology or phenomenology to be upheld, whether someone holds to biblical dualism or to evolutionary materialism. While some outworking observations can be made within the scientific method, the soul must primarily be approached through faith. Failure to accept the human soul's true nature and needs best explains why Kraepelinians of all sorts have historically failed to help souls in great need.

CHAPTER 8

THE REPLACEMENT OF PSYCHIATRIC GENETICS

---

*"There has been **no fulfillment** of the hope that clinical observation of psychic phenomena, of the life-history and of the outcome might yield **characteristic groupings** which would **subsequently be confirmed in the cerebral findings**, and thus pave the way for the brain-anatomists . . . . The original question: are there only **stages and variants** of one unitary psychosis [historic madness] or is there **a series of disease-entities** which we can delineate, now finds its answer: **there are neither**. The latter view is right in so far that the idea of disease-entities has become a fruitful orientation for the investigations of special psychiatry. The former view is right in so far that no actual disease-entities exist in scientific psychiatry [emphasis is original to Jasper]."[893] - Karl Jaspers, acclaimed psychiatric phenomenologist*

The available evidence has shown not only that Kraepelinianism/psychiatric genetics is a pseudoscience, but also that the theory of and approach to human nature and human phenomena are consistently destructive to individuals, families, and societies. Psychiatric eugenics simply does not save lives, nor does the belief system

893 Karl Jaspers, *General Psychopathology* vol. 1 & 2 (Baltimore, MD: Johns Hopkins University Press; 1997 first published in 1959), 568-70.

deliver on the promises which many have claimed for centuries that the theory will one day fulfill. This reality was true during Benjamin Rush's life and much later in Nazi Germany, just as it is in modern times.

It must be clearly stated, however, that most psychiatrists are not willfully attempting to stigmatize some people in order to bring about another Holocaust; it is more likely far from that scenario. Rather, many psychiatrists and society in general have ignorantly accepted the very philosophical system that incited the Holocaust by falsely believing that neo-Kraepelinian theory is an altruistic, credible, and scientific approach to human struggles.

Exposing the psychiatric theory to be eugenic is not an attack on individuals who have dedicated their lives in attempt to help people. It is, instead, rightly denouncing the false, destructive, and "anarchist" Kraepelinian or bio-psycho-social paradigm,[894] and graciously challenging society at large to reconsider their philosophies of anthropology, epistemology, phenomenology, and theology.

Moreover, it might be argued that most modern clinical psychiatrists and primary care physicians today genuinely desire to help people and are merely following the pseudoscientific paradigm they were taught in their

---

[894] S. Nassir Ghaemi, "The Postmodern Assumptions of Biopsychosocial Approach," *Psychiatric Times* (January 27, 2020): https://www.psychiatrictimes.com/couch-crisis/postmodern-assumptions-biopsychosocial-approach?rememberme=1&elq_mid=10664&elq_cid=893295&GUID=31158D64-F01A-4DEA-AC1A-D3CE843FC9BC.

universities—just as occurred in Nazi Germany, as historian Rael Strous reveals:

> In the absence of firm and unbending timeless ethical underpinnings to the practice of psychiatry, many felt that what they were doing was correct from a moral and scientific standpoint; therefore, they were not the demons and "paradigms of evil" that we perceive them to be. Their actions were a colossal misjudgment based on what today we may term "pseudoscience", but which at the time was deemed correct by many. Although actions based on "scientific theories" of mental illness in the past have led to patient deaths . . . . . the extent and scale of the German psychiatrists' actions during the Nazi era remains unprecedented. These rationalizations based on faulty scientific theory and unethical medical practice were difficult to accept and therefore the nature and extent of these activities remained on the backbenches of the academic literature until more recently, when these issues have begun to be faced in an era of openness and transparency.[895]

In the same way that the general public trusts in so-called scientific academic experts, physicians too rely on academic figureheads and published information, which doctors too often assume to be validated and empirically sound. Many modern psychiatrists, clinicians, and psychologists are not purposely trying to hurt people; their error is not in their motives or their desire to help people in need. Instead, the problem remains their underlying faith in the "science" of Kraepelinianism, just as occurred in Nazi Germany. Strous later states,

> Much of the early involvement by psychiatric clinicians and researchers in the process of "racial purification"

[895] Rael D. Strous, "Psychiatry During the Nazi Era: Ethical Lessons for the Modern Professional," *Annals of General Psychiatry* vol. 6 (8) (February 27, 2007): doi:10.1186/1744-859X-6-8.

arose from a genuine desire to improve mankind and not necessarily from the perspective of racist genocide. **While no direct parallel can be drawn, today many continue in a sincere scientific effort towards the "enhancement" of man through molecular biology and genetic engineering.** Appropriate dialogue is required in order to ensure that the desire for "improving man," creating a "better human," does not come at the expense of the individual patient [emphasis added].[896]

Society's acceptance of both the eugenics worldview and its companion diagnostic system depends fully on claims that they are "scientifically sound" and carried out under the auspice of altruistic medical care. In Nazi Germany, the T4 project, which "involved virtually the entire German psychiatric community"[897] and which psychiatrists convinced Hitler to commission, was even framed as "mercy killings."[898] While the Nazi euthanasia program began in the psychiatric wards, many parents were deceived into admitting their children into these facilities in order for them to receive "altruistic medical help." Tragically, these families, who typically paid for the "medical" treatments, never saw their children again.[899]

If people can identify with a created construct that describes their problems within a medical framework and

[896]Ibid.

[897] Michael Berenbaum, "T4 Progam: Nazi Poloicy," Encyclopaedia Britannica (September 10, 2018): https://www.britannica.com/event/T4-Program.

[898] Ibid.

[899] Rael Strous, "Extermination of the Jewish Mentally-ill during the Nazi era — the "doubly cursed," *Israel Journal of Psychiatry and Related Sciences* vol. 45 (4) (2008): 247-56.

receive treatment from a caring physician who is unaware of the true nature of his/her underlying theory and treatments, then people are more likely to view their problems as medical issues and believe that they are abnormal. This reality is especially true if said theories and practices are dogmatically claimed to be scientifically sound by the medical community at large and propagated by the media. Starting with Rush's blood-letting, spinning chairs, and bilious pills and continuing until today, the eugenic paradigm has historically failed to genuinely help the souls of individuals or societies.

Biological psychiatry's failures over the last two centuries have provided ample evidence to cause some leading psychiatric theorists to understand the pressing need for a significant paradigm shift away from the neo-Kraepelinian/bio-psycho-social faith. Professors of psychiatry at Cambridge and Harvard Universities, Caleb Gardner and Arthur Kleinman are examples of this trend:

> We believe that a fundamental rethinking of psychiatric knowledge creation and training is in order . . . . It seems clear that psychiatry needs to be rebuilt, and academics can lead the way.[900]

Recognizing this same reality, dozens of influential psychiatrists and psychologists, including Nasir Ghaemi and Thomas Fuchs, published the *Oxford Handbook of Philosophy and Psychiatry* to address their own concerns:

> **Of one thing at least we can be confident: by the end of the century the problems of philosophy, the "big**

900 Caleb Gardner and Arthur Kleinman, "Medicine and the Mind — The Consequences of Psychiatry's Identity Crisis," *NEJM* vol. 381 (October 31, 2019): DOI: 10.1056/NEJMp1910603.

questions" of mind and brain, of freedom and
determinism, of what is and of what ought to be, will
remain unresolved**. In an earlier model of philosophy, it
would have been assumed that the role of philosophers in
psychiatry is to solve problems of just this kind and
thereby to provide foundations on which empirical
research and practice might securely build. The search for
foundations is natural enough. Consistently with the
philosophy of Jasper's time, there is something of this
Philosophy-as-the-Queen-of-the-Sciences model in
General Psychopathology, and latter day claims to having
established a new philosophical foundation for psychiatry
will no doubt continue to be made in years to come. **But if
there is a lesson from twentieth-century philosophy for
psychiatry today, it is that (post-Godel, Wittgenstein,
Quine, and others) foundations are not to be had**
[emphasis added].[901]

It is evident that the anthropology and phenomenology of
psychiatry past, present, and future is a hopeless faith that
expects answers to remain hidden from mankind.

In 2020, the Society for Humanistic Psychology wrote an
open letter to figureheads within the neo-Kraepelinian
system calling for reform:

> In 2011, the British Psychological Society (BPS) and the
> Society for Humanistic Psychology responded to the
> American Psychiatric Association's proposals for what
> would become the fifth edition of its *Diagnostic and
> Statistical Manual of Mental Disorders* (DSM-5). Both
> professional bodies expressed concern that: *"...clients and
> the general public are negatively affected by the continued and
> continuous medicalisation of their natural and normal
> responses to their experiences; responses which undoubtedly*

---

[901] Nasir Ghaemi, Thomas Fuchs, et. al., edited by K.W.M. Fulford, Martin
Davies Richard G.T. Gipps, George Graham, John Z. Sadler, Giovanni
Stanghellini, and Tim Thornton, *The Oxford Handbook of Philosophy and
Psychiatry* (Oxford University Press, 2015), 2.

*have distressing consequences which demand helping responses, but which do not reflect illnesses so much as normal individual variation..."*That concern, among others, appeared in an *Open Letter to the DSM-5* that was endorsed by over 15,000 mental health professionals and other individuals, as well as by over 50 professional organizations, including 15 additional divisions of the American Psychological Association. . . . Whilst there is much to be welcomed in these initiatives, we have scientific, conceptual and ethical concerns about each of them. The diagnostic categories proposed by these frameworks — the *DSM*, the *ICD* and newly proposed models such as the *RDoC* project — are based largely on social norms about what constitutes "normal" or desirable behavior or experience. Their definitions inevitably rely on subjective judgments, which are themselves grounded in cultural norms. As Thomas Insel has pointed out, despite billions of dollars of research investment, no biomarkers, confirmatory physical "signs" or pathognomonic evidence of biological causation have been discovered for the putative pathologies represented by the category labels within these systems. Many researchers have pointed out that psychiatric diagnoses are plagued by problems of reliability, validity, prognostic value and comorbidity.[902]

In the letter, the authors jointly called for the elimination of the Kraepelinian worldview:

> We therefore recommend a paradigmatic revision of the empirical and conceptual frameworks used to think about mental health. **A classification approach that pursues the neo-Kraepelinian goal (now nearly half a century old) of establishing biomarkers for individual conditions or symptoms would not constitute such a paradigm shift**

902 Peter Kinderman, Sarah Kamens, Brent Dean Robbins, and Frank Farley, "Regarding the Reform and Revision of Diagnostic Systems: An open letter from Div. 32 (Society for Humanistic Psychology)," *The Society of Humanistic Psychology* (February 12, 2020): https://www.apadivisions. org/division-32/leadership/task-forces/diagnostic-alternatives.

but rather an attempt to revitalize the current paradigm. A true paradigm shift would start with recognition of the overwhelming empirical evidence that the experiences we call mental illness are understandable and essentially "normal" human responses, and that psychosocial and structural factors such as inequity, abuse, poverty, housing insecurity, unemployment and trauma are the most robustly evidenced social determinants. Rather than applying preordained diagnostic categories to clinical populations, we believe that any empirical classification system should begin from the bottom up – starting with the specific concerns expressed by those seeking mental health services about their experiences, behaviour, problems, "symptoms" or "complaints" [emphasis added].[903]

As even these prominent humanistic psychiatrists and psychologists recognize, the time has come to reconsider currently held dogmatic beliefs about the human soul. But it is not enough to merely tweak practices and slightly alter existing theories. Rather, the time has come to fully replace failed theories of the soul at their foundational philosophical level. The foundational issue is faith.

If the underlying Kraepelinian ideology has not changed, then neither has the "fundamental thinking." Thus, modern-day psychiatrists, psychologists, and geneticists cannot help but maintain the same horrific-historic practices that the ideology demands. Dr. Ghaemi and numerous other psychiatrists acknowledge that psychiatric philosophies are, in fact, responsible for the history of "abuses of psychiatric care":

This is an important lesson for psychiatric science. The German historian and psychiatrist Paull Hoff (2005) has neatly summarized the history of psychiatric science as a

903 Ibid.

history of repeated collapses into "single message mythologies" reflecting this or that influential school's or individual's view of the "true" nature of psychiatry. **But it is an important lesson also for psychiatry practice: It has been the misguided conviction that this or that model provided "foundations" that have been the basis of some of the worst abuses of psychiatry care** [emphasis added]."[904]

Psychiatrist Mary Seeman at the University of Toronto contemplates this sobering reality:

The otherwise laudable concept of holistic health (that is, biological integrity, social well-being, and spiritual right-mindedness) led first to the sterilization and ultimately to the "euthanization" of not only the handicapped but, eventually, of the socially and spiritually unworthy — persons with mental illness, the socially wayward, criminals, Gypsies, homosexuals, and Jews. Psychiatrists helped in the selection. Can this happen ever again? Can this happen today? In a one-payer government system, are Canadian physicians sufficiently independent of the ideology of the government in power? Can we, like German psychiatrists from 1920 to 1940, come to value the health of Canadian society sufficiently to remove from that society those who threaten its health?[905]

Dr. Seeman answers her own questions by exposing that psychiatrists already practice the Kraepelinian eugenic theory in some of the very same ways as originally applied:

In one sense, we do it now when we impose involuntary hospitalization on those with mental illness; will our

[904] Nasir Ghaemi, Thomas Fuchs, et. al., edited by K.W.M. Fulford, Martin Davies Richard G.T. Gipps, George Graham, John Z. Sadler, Giovanni Stanghellini, and Tim Thornton, *The Oxford Handbook of Philosophy and Psychiatry* (Oxford University Press, 2015), 2.

[905] Mary V. Seeman, "Psychiatry in the Nazi Era," *Canadian Journal of Psychiatry* vol. 50 (4) (March 2005): 219.

motives for doing so be questioned by history? We currently prescribe large amounts of tranquilizing drugs that sometimes inadvertently impair our patients' health. Are we being hoodwinked into acquiescence by a profit-driven pharmaceutical industry? After all, this is the industry that supports our meetings, whose advertisements sustain our journals, whose backing partly pays for our continuing education, whose funding often assists our clinical projects, whose deep pockets sometimes reimburse individual psychiatrists for recruitment into drug studies. Pressed by internal and external demands of career advancement, do we straightjacket our patients into *DSM-IV*–defined diagnostic categories? Can we, in other words, resist the pressure to close ranks behind our ideological leaders?[906]

In an article published in 2020, psychiatrist Steven Starks, writing for the American Psychiatric Association (APA), remarks on how the Kraepelinian construct of schizophrenia is still utilized to target African Americans:

Institutional racism extended beyond the realm of social injustice and the struggle for civil rights. It also permeated American medical education, medical practice, and scientific research **that remains to impact the community today. Research shows that African American or black patients are**: more likely to receive treatment for mental health in emergency and hospital settings; **misdiagnosed at a higher rate with schizophrenia spectrum disorders** [emphasis added]. . . [907]

---

[906] Ibid.

[907] Steven Starks, "Working with African American/Black Patients," *The American Psychiatric Association* (February 2020): https://www.psychiatry.org/psychiatrists/cultural-competency/education/best-practice-highlights/best-practice-highlights-for-working-with-african-american-patients?fbclid=IwAR0e0yedfsVDHrgr5TuufbUTi8bRtI_s_sPBKximxYbfUP-cWhH5uUodFd0.

On its website, the APA states further that "blacks are 20%
more likely to experience serious mental health problems
than the general population."[908] But if psychiatrists'
"misdiagnoses" of severe mental disorders among African
Americans are prevalent, then blacks are still being
targeted today rather than being diagnosed. Since
schizophrenia has been a subjective or "heterogeneous"
concept from its creation, those who possess societal
authority can impose the construct upon anyone.

It must be emphasized that unless the underlying
anthropology/philosophies of human nature are
denounced, the "science" of mental illness and its
application will continue to produce atrocities upon
humanity:

> Almost no one stopped to think that something could be
> wrong with psychiatry, with anthropology, or with
> behavioral science. The international scientific
> establishment reassured their German colleagues that it
> had indeed been the unpardonable misconduct of a few
> individuals, but that it lay outside the scope of science.
> **The pattern of German anthropology, psychiatry and
> behavioral science continued essentially unchanged,
> and it will continue so, unless a substantial number of
> scientists begin to have doubts and to ask questions**
> [emphasis added].[909]

Other psychiatrists also note that the eugenic applications
have not been abandoned; they have simply gone from
being applied actively to being applied passively or

---

[908] Ibid.

[909] B. Muller-Hill, Murderous Science: Elimination by Scientific Selection of
Jews, Gypsies, and Others, Germany, 1933- 1945 (New York: Oxford University
Press, 1988), 87.

ignorantly. For example, influential psychiatrist Peter Breggin lists seven "fundamental principles of Western Psychiatry"/Kraepelinian eugenics that were in place before the Holocaust and which mirror today's psychiatric practices:[910] 1) involuntary treatment; 2) the state mental hospital system; 3) applying medical "diagnoses" to psychological, spiritual, social and political problems; 4) the biological or medical model for human differences (individual degeneration and selection); 5) damaging biological interventions/treatments that enable psychiatrists to control or minimize behavior by dehumanizing people; 6) involuntary or active eugenics that minimizes or prevents reproduction of alleged defective people; and 7) mass murder/euthanasia. These fundamentals are applications of degenerationism, materialism, bio-determinism, and utilitarianism more than they are underlying principles. Nonetheless, as Dr. Breggin reveals, the Kraepelinian model of mental illness that increasingly dominates American health care — whether realized or not — is structured around the same applications of Nazi eugenics.

Typically, such as in suicidal ideation and completions caused by prescribed psychiatric drugs, the practitioner's intention in prescribing them is most likely not to cause death. Still, the taking of life frequently occurs, and both the FDA and most physicians are well aware that the drugs they prescribe are known to regularly induce suicidal

[910] Peter Breggin, Psychiatry's Role in the Holocaust," *International Journal of Risk and Safety in Medicine* 4 (1993), [133-148] 142-45.

ideation.[911] In the *International Review of Psychiatry*, for instance, Drs. David Healy and Graham Aldred report how the drastic rise in suicide attempts and completions are best explained by the parallel rise in psychiatric prescriptions:

> Investigative Medication Routine translates such findings into estimates of likely adverse outcomes, and explains why apparently increasing consumption of antidepressants would not be expected to lead to increased national suicide rates. From this data, we conclude that there is a clear signal that suicides and suicidal acts may be linked to antidepressant usage. It would seem likely that explicit warnings and monitoring in the early stages of treatment could greatly minimize these hazards.[912]

Another study, published in the journal of *Social Psychiatry and Psychiatric Epidemiology* concluded that

> the results of a study in this issue of the *Journal* cast further doubt on the appropriateness of suicide risk assessment when patients receive hospital-based psychiatric care. **They also raise the disturbing possibility that psychiatric care might, at least in part, cause suicide** [emphasis added].[913]

Psychiatrists Matthew Large and Christopher Ryan went on to point out in the same journal entry a chilling correlation between the level of psychiatric care a person

[911] Daniel R. Berger II, *The Chemical Imbalance Delusion* (Taylors, SC: Alethia International Publications, 2019), 69-71.

[912] David Healy and Graham Aldred, "Antidepressant Drug Use and the Risk of Suicide," International Review of Psychiatry vol. 17 (3) (June 2005): 163.

[913] Matthew M. Large and Christopher J. Ryan, "Disturbing Findings about the Risk of Suicide and Psychiatric Hospitals," *Journal of Social Psychiatry and Psychiatric Epidemiology* vol. 49 (June 2014): 1353-55; DOI: 10.1007/s00127-014-0912-2.

receives and the proportional rise in the percentages of attempted suicides:

> The study found that, compared to those who had no psychiatric treatment in the previous year and after adjustment for other risk factors: those who only received psychiatric medication had 5.8 times the risk of suicide those with at most outpatient psychiatric treatment had 8.2 times the risk of suicide; non-admitted patients who had contact with emergency departments had 27.9 times the risk of suicide. And admitted patients had 44.3 times the risk of suicide. Particularly striking are the strength of the associations between emergency room treatment and suicide and between inpatient treatment and suicide. The magnitude of risk rations of nearly 30 or more for whole groups of patients who have contact with hospital-based services exceed both the risk of suicide associated with major psychiatric disorders and the strength of clinical risk factors of suicide among hospitalized patients by about an order of magnitude.[914]

Clinical psychiatrist Paul Minot also highlights how psychiatric phenomenology and its reductionistic approach have not helped lessen suicidal ideation, but have increased it:

> With more people carrying psychiatric diagnoses and receiving treatment than we ever could have imagined, you would expect to see improved psychiatric health and decreased suicide. But the opposite has occurred. The percentage of Americans on psychiatric disability benefits more than doubled from 1987 to 2007. And from 1999 to 2016, in the midst of this Age of Prozac, the incidence of suicide in America has increased by 30%.[915]

[914] Ibid.

[915] Paul Minot, "About Me," *Straight Talk Psychiatry* (December 31, 2019): https://paulminotmd.com/about-me/.

In 2020, a group of psychiatric researchers reexamined whether or not the FDA's black box warning, which is required to be printed on the labels of all "antidepressants," was legitimate. After conducting thorough double-blind studies, these psychiatrists published their conclusions in *Frontiers in Psychiatry*:

> **Based on the sum of this evidence, regulatory warnings regarding antidepressant-linked suicidality are clearly warranted.** When a clear body of evidence points to increased treatment-linked risk, patients and healthcare providers should be made aware of these risks. To suggest otherwise both breaches the ancient injunction of *primum non nocere* (first, do no harm) and is not aligned with the practice of evidence-based medicine [emphasis added].[916]

To deny or to ignore the regular negative effect of suicidal ideation that are induced by ingesting psychotropic drugs is both to deny empirical evidence and the Hippocratic Oath itself. Breggin also comments,

> Since antidepressants are now the drugs most commonly implicated in successful suicides, it would seem far more appropriate to designate them as "suicide drugs" rather than anti-suicide drugs. Yet psychiatrists persist in giving them to depressed patients who are suicidal.[917]

[916] Glen I. Spielmans, Tess Spence-Sing, and Peter Parry, edited by Michael P. Hengartner, Maurizio Pompili, and Sami Timimi, "Duty to Warn: Antidepressant Black Box Suicidality Warning is Empirically Justified," *Frontiers in Psychiatry* (February 13, 2020): https://doi.org/10.3389/fpsyt.2020.00018.

[917] Breggin, *Toxic Psychiatry*, 158.

Many Nazi psychiatric treatments, such as psychopharmacology[918] and shock treatment,[919] continue today from their origins within the Kraepelinian model. These measures are not healing practices, but control mechanisms, which by nature inflict psychological and physiological damage upon the one who is categorized as abnormal and is treated within psychiatric eugenics. Logically, it makes little sense to inflict abnormal circumstances on people who are perceived to be abnormal (if that were in fact the case), while claiming that these practices are medicinal and empirically sound.

In similar fashion to drug-induced suicides, psychiatrists and all clinicians who prescribe psychotropic drugs to patients for a length of time passively sterilize consumers who are often unaware that "sexual dysfunction is a known adverse effect of psychotropic medications."[920] It is also widely recognized within medical research that "antipsychotic drugs" used to address people labeled as schizophrenic, for example, antagonize the nervous system

---

[918] Valenstein, *Blaming the Brain,* 10.

[919] "They called doctors who were showing how to use electric aversive treatments to cure homosexuality 'Nazi' doctors" (Jack Drescher in accordance with Columbia University Psychiatry, "The 'Checkered' History of Psychiatry's Views on Homosexuality," *Medscape Psychiatry* [December 3, 2019]: https://www.medscape.com/viewarticle/ 921143?nlid=132938_424&src =WNL_mdplsfeat_191210_mscpedit_psyc&uac=264124BV&spon=12&impID=2 199579&faf=1). See also Robert Lifton, *Nazi Doctors: Medical Killing and the Psychology of Genocide* (New York: Basic Books, 1986), 299.

[920] V.N. Shetageri, G.S. Bhogale, N.M. Patil, R.B. Nayak, and S.S. Chate, "Sexual Dysfunction among Females Receiving Psychotropic Medication: a Hospital-based Cross-sectional Study," *Indian Journal of Psychological Medicine* vol. 38 (5) (September-October 2016): 447.

and atrophy the brain rather than heal it.[921] A number of studies conducted have consistently yielded this same finding, as reported in such journals as *Biological Psychiatry*:

> Eighteen studies involving 1155 patients with schizophrenia and 911 healthy control subjects were included. **Over time, patients with schizophrenia showed a significantly higher loss of total cortical GM volume. This was related to cumulative antipsychotic intake during the interval between scans in the whole study sample.** Subgroup meta-analyses of studies on patients treated with second-generation antipsychotics and first-generation antipsychotics revealed a different and contrasting moderating role of medication intake on cortical GM changes: more progressive GM loss correlated with higher mean daily antipsychotic intake in patients treated with at least one first-generation antipsychotic and less progressive GM loss with higher mean daily antipsychotic intake in patients treated only with second-generation antipsychotics [emphasis added].[922]

Other psychiatrists have written entire books dedicated to exposing with empirical evidence and real-life case studies

[921] See S. Weinmann, V. Aderhold, C. Haegele, and A. Heinz, "Brain Atrophy and Antipyschotic Medication — a Systematic Review," European Psychiatry vol. 30 (1) (March 2015): 65; https://doi.org/10. 1016/S0924-9338(15)30055-9. See also University of Cambridge, "Antipsychotic Drugs linked to slight decrease in brain volume," *Science Daily* (July 18, 2014): https://www.sciencedaily.com/releases /2014/07/140718172039.htm.

[922] Antonio Vita, Luca De Peri, Giacomo Deste, Stefano Barlati, and Emilio Sacchetti, "The Effect of Antipsychotic treatment on Cortical Gray Matter Changes in Schizophrenia: Does the Class Matter" A Meta-Analysis and Meta-regression of Longitudinal Magnetic Resonance Imaging Studies," *Biological Psychiatry* vol. 78 (6) (September 15, 2015): 403-412; http://dx.doi.org /10.1016/j.bio psych.2015.02.008.

how and why psychotropic drugs create abnormal states rather than heal proposed degeneracy.[923]

But instead of rethinking currently held psychiatric perspectives and treatments, which have shown to increase suicidal ideation and somatic decline, new legislation has been passed that increasingly removes patient rights and creates environments that further isolate those seeking help. In fact, some people perceive these changes as returning psychiatric facilities to the asylums of old by creating abnormal circumstances for those classified as abnormal. Beresford Wilson, who co-chairs the Connecticut Behavioral Health Partnership, shares his own concern:

> I think to make the experience as normal as possible when the person is under that distress, what they are looking for is normalcy as much as possible, not restriction or confinement.[924]

Many people who have been hospitalized have claimed that their stay in psychiatric care was the most severe trauma that they have experienced. Psychiatrist Charles Herrick tells how an established environment — even in a psychiatric ward — can influence one's identity by shaping his/her phenomenology:

> If you perceive the environment as a prison — and prisons are a place of punishment — then you can't help

---

[923] Peter R. Breggin, *Medication Madness: The Role of Psychiatric Drugs in Cases of Violence, Suicide, and Crime* (New York: St. Martin's Griffin, 2008).

[924] Beresford Wilson quoted by Chris Ehrmann, "Hospital Psychiatric Wards Now Feel Like Prisons, Some Say," *AP News Online* (November 19, 2019): https://apnews.com/066d55e71c6a4b3f9ec088e91fa4b32d?fbclid=Iw AR10MNXIzHveootTyRtp5u7bMq9srEV63p73C82BI42_37PNGQFKSR50eHE.

but think you are being punished, whether consciously or unconsciously.[925]

Since Kraepelinianism was introduced and established in American culture, the mental health crisis has not been helped. Rather, individuals and societies as a whole have been further damaged by the eugenic phenomenology. The asserted best Kraepelinian treatments for alleged abnormal human conditions destroy people's minds, bodies, relationships, families, and cultures in measurable, repeatable, and observable ways. More damaging, however, is not what Kraepelinianism does, but what it seeks to deny or keep from humanity: the genuine and proven remedy to the human soul coupled with the false identity and anthropology this false faith imposes upon individuals and societies.

But to dismiss God as the creator of and authority over the human soul is to grant power to a human or group of people. Unless individuals, families, and societies accept God's declaration of human nature to be morally equal and return to God's design and understanding of the metaphysical soul, then systems of inequality and control will continue to arise, and constructs of disorders and subsequent categories of degenerates will be created by humans who seek and gain the most power. Worse still, the only empirically proven remedy for the human soul will continue to be disregarded and denied as viable.

Not only has the time come to expose psychiatric eugenics for the failed theory it truly is, but also the time has come to replace it at its foundational philosophical and phenomenological levels. It is not enough to merely

[925] Charles Herrick quoted by Chris Ehrmann, Ibid.

attempt "saving normal." Rather, both the creation of pseudo-scientific categories of perceived degenerates and all efforts in "saving abnormal" must cease. This necessary paradigm shift begins with reconsidering anthropology (e.g., where did man come from, what is his purpose, where is he headed, and is he dual natured?), epistemology (e.g., what/who is the authority on what is true about the human soul and human phenomena?), phenomenology (how do we perceive and approach the soul and its spiritual/metaphysical phenomena?), and theology (e.g., how does mankind relate to the Creator God or is humanity its own god?). The presuppositional faith that society chooses to accept will always determine where and how that society goes from any point in time.

One might also consider that even the humanists, who formally affirmed the *Humanistic Manifesto II* and denied the existence of God, advocated the "principle of moral equality." Signers such as B.F. Skinner and Francis Crick state:

> We deplore racial, religious, ethnic, or class antagonisms. Although we believe in cultural diversity and encourage racial and ethnic pride, we reject separations which promote alienation and set people and groups against each other; we envision an integrated community where people have a maximum opportunity for free and voluntary association.[926]

For alienation — based upon subjective constructs — to be eliminated, the alienists and their belief system that creates and maintains individual degeneracy must be completely

---

[926] Francis Crick, B.F. Skinner, and Thomas Greening, et. al., *Humanist Manifestos I and II* edited by Paul Kurtz (Buffalo, NY: Prometheus Books, 1973), 20.

discounted and assigned to history as a failure. Psychiatrists, "known archaically as alienists,"[927] must truly denounce the underlying faith of eugenics which sustains modern psychiatry. While physical alienation may be rare today, spiritual and phenomenological alienation continues. Humanity's continued attempts to sustain concepts of abnormal souls under the guise of science and without empirical evidence to do so must stop.

Those who expose the sordid history of psychiatry, the underlying faith, the destructive applications, and its pseudoscientific reality position themselves to be unofficially diagnosed by psychiatrists as "antipsychiatrists." Many prominent psychiatrists, such as former APA president Jeffrey Lieberman, regularly utilize the term,[928] which is intended to stigmatize anyone (especially other psychiatrists) who speak out against neo-Kraepelinianism. Another influential psychiatrist, Ronald Pies, created his own social construct and label in 2020 so that he could unofficially diagnose anyone within his own moral system who questions or exposes the pseudoscience of materialism:

> As an ethicist and physician, I have been struggling to come up with a term that summarizes the potent combination of ignorance and immorality that characterizes certain elements in American society today . . . . I have settled on the portmanteau word, *immoronic*: a combination of *immorality* and *moronic*. Examples of the immoronic are not hard to find in modern American

[927] Michael Arribas-Ayloon, Andrew Bartlett, and Jamie Lewis, *Psychiatric Genetics: From Hereditary Madness to Big Biology* (Vanderbilt, New York: Routledge, 2019), 23.

[928] Lieberman, *Shrinks*, 125.

culture, and they transcend any one political party or ideology.[929]

In the article, Pies offers a list of *"immoronics,"* which includes alleged antivaxxers, anti-global warmers, and antipsychiatrists.[930] Pies states his concern to be that

> there are worrisome societal trends at work that may be contributing to immoronic claims and behavior in this country (and perhaps elsewhere). In our post-modern age, the role of the "expert" has been severely undermined and discredited . . . . Driving the surge of immoronic ideas is a culture drowning in "alternative facts;" misleading internet websites; and a general distrust of science itself.[931]

But it is not a distrust in science that is driving people to do their own research and to not accept blindly the published conclusions. There have been so many false and harmful claims made by "experts" over the last several decades under the banner of science that people have begun to rightly question the presuppositional faith and subsequent conclusions and applications of the established scientists. Ironically, what Pies really suggests is that people should not apply the scientific method or place trust in the scientific process themselves, but they should just accept by faith what they are told by others who insist that they apply the scientific method according to their own established like-minded belief system. The label

---

[929] Ronald W. Pies, "Have We Entered the Age of the Immoronic?" The *Psychiatric Times Online* (January 2, 2020): https://www.psychiatrictimes.com/couch-crisis/have-we-entered-age-immoronic?fbclid=IwAR3EA7hRRaBo PCxSroWhyU0RvgrVh9SGPitkpyXHF0WEbiVVCz9nJMiQ_bI.

[930] Ibid.

[931] Ibid.

"antipsychiatry" helps to reveal the true moral nature of psychiatry and the religion that it has established. The term "antipsychiatrist" (and "immoronics") also highlights how influential psychiatrists label and set aside anyone they find to be undesirable or judge to be deceived/delusional within their worldview/moral system. Nonetheless, the failure of psychiatric phenomenology must be discussed honestly and the destructive beliefs denied thereafter.

Thankfully, there is an alternative approach available that has been proven over the centuries to be reliable, valid, and empirically effective. The Christian or biblical phenomenology/worldview continues to help people despite the evolutionary assertion that the Christian faith is outdated. But if the truth about the human soul and its moral and metaphysical nature and phenomena is objective rather than evolving, then God's perspective contained in Scripture should be understood as consistent and reliable rather than as being outdated and irrelevant. Even on this point, it can be observed that one's presuppositional view of origins and epistemology will dictate how that person approaches the human soul and interprets mindsets, emotions, behaviors, and available empirical data.

At its core, Christianity is an approach to human nature and human phenomena that demands that empathy/love/ right relationships and equality be central to helping others, and it establishes a healthy phenomenology for those mentally and emotionally struggling. Though Benjamin Rush's beliefs about the soul, his eugenic theories, and his suggested remedies were all barbaric and continue to negatively impact the world today, he himself acknowledged that having a right understanding of

Scripture was healing and preventative — even to those he wrongly perceived to be abnormal:

> Let not religion be blamed for these cases of insanity. The tendency of all its doctrines and precepts is to prevent it from most of its mental causes; and even the errors that have been blended with it, produce madness less frequently than love, and many of those common and necessary pursuits, which constitute the principal enjoyments and business of life.[932]

Many contemporary psychiatrists and neuroscientists also note that religious faith, practically lived out, guards people against delusional thinking. "People who have a spiritual understanding of life in the absence of a religious framework are vulnerable to mental disorder."[933] One specific example of how the Christian faith is important to guard against substance use can be seen in the research of psychiatrists Louise Hope and Christopher Cook:

> The findings suggest that for church affiliated young people it is initially the socialization of religion that acts as a prohibitor against substance use, though, as age increases, a greater internalization of Christian commitment becomes more important.[934]

[932] Benjamin Rush, *Medical Inquiries and Observations Upon the Diseases of the Mind* 5th ed. (Philadelphia: Grigg and Elliot, 1835), 43.

[933] Michael King, Louise Marston, Sally McManus, Terry Brugha, Howard Meltzer, and Paul Bennington, "Religion, Spirituality and Mental health: Results from a National Study of English Households," *The British Journal of Psychiatry* vol. 202 (1) (January 2013), 68-73.

[934] Louise C. Hope and Christopher C.H. Cook, The Role of Christian Commitment in Predicting Drug Use Amongst Church Affiliated Young People," *The Journal of Mental Health, Religion and Culture* vol. 4 (2) (2001): 109.

Other studies such as that published in the *Journal of Drug and Alcohol Dependence* found the same overwhelming results:

> The relationship of religion to lower levels of alcohol abuse merits further study, such as investigating religious denominations with healthy patterns of abstention and moderate drinking, to learn how these norms are initiated and maintained. Such knowledge has promise of application in programs for prevention and treatment of alcohol problems.[935]

Like other prominent contemporary psychiatrists, Andrew Sims points out that

> there are many individual accounts of dramatic release from alcohol or drug addiction resulting from conversion to Christian faith and followed by abstinence. A critic would claim that that [sic] is a gift or a grace and cannot be prescribed; the believer would say, "try it, you will not know otherwise". In the field of preventing drug and alcohol dependence the effect of religious belief is overwhelmingly positive. It is a mystery why, when we have such a massive drug and alcohol misuse problem in our society and we know that the church and faith have so much to contribute in this area, government and other authorities are opposed to seeking help from religious organization to lessen this exploding disaster.[936]

[935] Laurence Michalak, Karen Trocki, and Jason Bond, "Religion and Alcohol in the U.S. National Alcohol Survey: How important is religion for abstention and drinking?" *The Journal of Drug and Alcohol Dependence* vol. 87 (2-3) (March 16, 2007): 268-280.

[936] Andrew Sims, *Is Faith Delusion? Why Religion is Good for Your Health* (London: Continuum, 2009), 108.

Still other psychiatrists have found that considering and approaching the soul as spiritual rather than as material has shown beneficial results in addressing psychosis:

> Spiritual assessment appears to be useful for patients with psychosis. This is in accordance with the recommendations of the World Psychiatric Association which promotes considering the whole person in clinical care.[937]

Several psychiatrists remark in the *New England Journal of Medicine* on the growing evidence that one's spiritual nature directly alters a person's physical nature:

> Today, meditation and other mind–body practices, such as yoga and mindfulness, are growing in popularity, with 14% of the U.S. adult population reporting having used these techniques within the previous year. Historically, these tools have been used to promote human flourishing, insight, peace, enlightenment, and connection to something larger than oneself. Today, many people are drawn to these practices for their perceived physical and mental health benefits and stress relief. All religious traditions and cultures have some form of meditative or other mind–body practice, but the current explosion of interest in these practices has largely occurred within a secular context. **Concurrent with this growing public interest is emerging research describing various neurobiologic, physiological, and genomic changes associated with mind–body practices, particularly meditation, including activation of specific brain regions, increased heart-rate variability, and**

---

[937] P. Huguelet, P.Y. Brandt, and S. Mohr, "The Assessment of Spirituality and religiousness in Patients with Psychosis," *Encephale* vol. 42 (3) (June 2016): 219.

suppression of stress-induced inflammatory pathways, among others [emphasis added].[938]

When John M. Galt attempted to end Benjamin Rush's eugenic/hereditary ideas and practices in the early 1800s, Galt was met with great opposition despite his success in helping people find hope to resolve their mental and behavioral struggles. Galt's right view of mankind and his applications were based upon Scriptural truth in both principle and in practice.

Today, there are hundreds of churches, mission houses, counseling organizations, and counseling centers around the world that are seeing the same efficacy in establishing biblical faith and practices with those struggling in all degrees and types of mental, emotional, and behavioral impairments and distresses (e.g., The Addiction Connection or TAC).[939] Of course, though no one can change another's faith (whether true or false beliefs), offering the only truth that can set people free is vital to addressing the most destructive human deceits.

A paradigm shift back to biblical phenomenology has already begun within the church. But the sobering reality is that a critical paradigm shift must progress on a massive scale if society is to be genuinely helped through the many struggles of life. This radical change must start with denouncing the failed underlying beliefs on which the

---

[938] Michelle L. Dossett, Gregory L. Fricchione, and Herbert Benson, "A New Era for Mind—Body Medicine," *NEJM* 382 (April 9, 2020): 1390-91; DOI: 10.1056/NEJMp1917461.

[939] For more information on a biblical phenomenology of "addictions" and the many mission houses and churches that regularly see lives positively changed, visit https://www.theaddictionconnection.org.

eugenic/Kraepelinian theory survives and, thereafter, reinstating the right perspective on origins and anthropology which the Bible teaches.

Origins

As revealed throughout this book, psychiatric eugenics was partially built and remains dependent upon faith in the Darwinian evolutionary theory (both the concepts of adaptation and Darwinian natural selection). Degenerationism, materialism, genetic-determinism, humanism, and utilitarianism are all tenets of eugenic faith that are derived from rejecting God as Creator and deliverer and thereby trusting in mankind to deliver themselves from all their own problems.

The anthropological and phenomenological struggles being discussed, explained, approached, and attempted to be remedied in psychiatry are precisely the same issues of the soul/psyche/human consciousness which the Christian Bible explores in detail. In any discussion about "psychosis/madness" (deceit), hopelessness, anxiety, guilt, self-centeredness, false-identities, destructive habitual behaviors, etc., both Scripture and psychiatry represent faith-based approaches to human nature. Psychiatrists Michael King and Simon Dein explain,

> Psychiatrists concern themselves with human mental suffering. Behind the consulting room door they reflect with their patients on questions of meaning and existence, issues that concern philosophy and religion as much as psychiatry. It is striking, therefore, that psychiatrists regard spirituality and religion as, at best, cultural noise to be respected but not addressed directly,

or at worst pathological thinking that requires modification [delusions] (Larson et al. 1993).[940]

Though it is apparent that psychiatric genetics has failed on a foundational philosophical level, the eugenic theory has far too often insisted that the very truth which has historically been shown to free people from the grip of delusional thinking should be viewed by society as itself a delusion.[941]

Though it may be difficult for some scientists to consider and still harder to embrace, the necessary starting point of change must begin with believing that the order and truths found in nature and which researchers seek to discover and to explain were created by an immutable and powerful God. The alternative to theorizing about human nature and demanding that others accept the manmade "religion of humanism"[942] from which psychiatry and psychology were constructed is to accept that the God of consciousness, life, love, holiness, truth, order, and all that is good made mankind in His own immaterial image with designed purpose, mindfulness, justice, identity, and moral consciousness. Without this right starting point, a true perception of human nature and how to fix the universal problems of human fragility and depravity will never be

[940] Michael B. King and Simon Dein, "The Spiritual Variable in Psychiatric Research," *Psychological Medicine* vol. 28 (6) (November 1998): 1259-1262.

[941] Andrew Sims refutes fellow psychiatrists' assertions that religious faith is delusional (*Is Faith Delusion? Why Religion is Good for Your Health* [London: Continuum, 2009], 146).

[942] Raymond Bragg, John Dewey, and Charles Francis Potter, et. al., *Humanist Manifestos I and II* edited by Paul Kurtz (Buffalo, NY: Prometheus Books, 1973).

properly understood, accurately applied, nor accepted by those in need.

If there is disorder, then there must be designed order. If God is not the designer and thus the authority of mankind — which He claims to be, then humanity is left on its own, trusting in its own ways, devises, and theories to survive human struggles within the soul and to overcome those who gain power, assert their own authority, and seek to control the world by controlling ideas of mental hygiene/health. If God is not the designer of humanity's spiritual nature, then humanists must still establish a concept of normal from which to assert alleged abnormalities. Establishing a right anthropology, epistemology, theology, and phenomenology are essential to discovering valid solutions, as these philosophies establish identity, authority, and the potential for fulfilled hope.

Universal Degenerationism

In addition to exchanging the false belief of evolution for the creation account of Scripture, the next vital change of mind in eliminating eugenics is to return to the biblical understanding that all men are morally equal and responsible for their thoughts and moral behaviors. As noted in chapter one, even early psychiatrists Phillip Pinel and John Galt recognized to some degree that this right moral approach to human nature was vital to help fellow humans in need.

Universal Degenerationism does not claim the false notion that some individuals become degenerates (individual degenerationism). Rather, the biblical perspective recognizes that everyone struggles with mental fragility and depravity, behavioral problems, and deceived feelings. No matter the severity or persistent nature of a person's struggle, the Bible describes all people as deeply and naturally deceived (e.g., Jeremiah 17:9; Ephesians 4:20-25; Romans 1) and makes clear that all people are created morally equal and in mental turmoil. "Madness" is universal and resides in the spiritual heart rather than in the physical body (Ecclesiastes 9:3b). *Universal degeneration* is an anthropological position which explains humanity as normally both weak and wicked, and it is an essential tenet of faith that must replace the false psychiatric eugenic belief in individual degenerationism.

Until the influence of Rush, Darwin, Wundt, Kraepelin, Morel, Rüdin, and Kallmann (to name a few) upon their own societies, individual degeneracy was not traditionally accepted. Instead, the historic position was acknowledging universal degeneracy. Eugenics was introduced as an antithetical anthropology — an attempt to redefine humanity apart from the Creator God, to remove His moral law from society, and to declare mankind's sovereignty and sufficiency to judge, explain, and solve all human struggles. Psychiatry is an attempt to replace the Christian concepts of universal degenerationism, dualism, and God's sovereignty with its own secular faith and subsequent phenomenology. Psychiatrist Robert Lifton notes this historic transition in writing about the "Nazification of German medicine":

> A Nazi version of holistic medicine that would "put in the foreground . . . questions of the psyche that had been neglected . . . " **This worldview replaced two false doctrines — that of Christianity, which understood human beings "only in a spiritual sense"; and that of the French Revolution, which claimed that "all human**

beings are equal" — both of which, according to [Dr. Johann] **S.,** "came into conflict with biological experience. That is, it was all a matter of scientific biology and of community [emphasis added].[943]

While Lifton acknowledges that secularists (such as Wundt, Kraepelin, and Rüdin) had clearly desired to replace Christianity with materialism and individual degenerationism, he missed the reality that the anthropological approach which affirms that all human beings are created equal was not a concept developed by Philip Pinel during the French Revolution or by John Galt in the United States. Instead, moral equality is a historically Christian perspective if the Bible is taken literally and applied graciously as God intended.[944] Likewise, the Bible teaches a dualistic or psychosomatic view of man rather than reducing all of human nature to being only spiritual as Lifton also suggests. Nonetheless, Lifton rightly recognizes that Kraepelinianism (eugenics) was a rejection of true biblical Christianity and a purposeful installment of individual degenerationism and materialism. Professors of psychiatry Roland Littlewood and Maurice Lipsedge add their own considerations:

> **Modern medicine encourages us to regard emotional difficulties as illnesses rather than as spiritual questions** . . . . Different societies have their own way of describing

[943] Robert Lifton, *Nazi Doctors: Medical Killing and the Psychology of Genocide* (New York: Basic Books, 1986), 129-30.

[944] Throughout history there have been numerous people and religious groups who claimed to be Christian but ignored or denied the biblical truth that all men are created equal and are of the same moral value. Benjamin Rush illustrates this fact well. This unfortunate reality does not discredit the Bible as true; it exposes the deceptive nature of people who do not truly understand or accept Scripture.

what we usually call mental illness. It may be thought of, as it is by most psychiatrists, as analogous to physical illness or it may be perceived as a religious phenomenon—spirit possession or the consequence of witchcraft—or even in terms of abnormal or anti-social behaviour . . . . **Is it possible that religion and mental illness may both be alternative responses to the same situation** [emphasis added]? [945]

As respected psychiatrist Karl Jaspers made clear, "the idea of disease-entities has become a fruitful orientation for the investigations of special psychiatry."[946] One may choose to either accept a biblical phenomenology or a psychiatric orientation. Yet, faith undergirds both positions.

Souls are Created Morally Equal

If all souls are created morally equal and deeply deceived, then those diagnosed as disordered within the established Kraepelinian social and descriptive constructs are being stigmatized by its application. The stigma of mental illness is derived not from an individual's struggles or society's opinions or reactions, but from the categories, labels, and constructed diagnoses that create and maintain perceived degeneracies. It is disingenuous, then, for the American Psychiatric Association, which currently creates and controls constructs of theoretical abnormalities, to assert in

[945] Roland Littlewood and Maurice Lipsedge, *Aliens and Alienists: Ethnic Minorities and Psychiatry*, 3rd edition (London: Taylor and Francis, 1997), 21-23.

946 Jaspers, *General Psychopathology*, 70.

its published *DSM-5* a desire to end the stigma it has significantly helped to produce.[947]

Along with the acceptance of individual degeneracy also comes prejudice and contempt. In an article published in the *Schizophrenia Bulletin*, several psychiatrists concluded from their own research that psychiatrists themselves regularly share a distain for those they diagnose as having a "severe mental illness."[948] In the same study, they also discovered that at least 25% of clinicians saw "normal" people in a clinical setting as falling within a psychiatric diagnosis:

> A survey was conducted of the attitudes of mental health professionals (n = 1073) and members of the public (n = 1737) toward mental illness and their specific reaction toward a person with and without psychiatric symptoms ("non-case" as a reference category). Psychiatrists had more negative stereotypes than the general population. Mental health professionals accepted restrictions toward people with mental illness 3 times less often than the public. **Most professionals were able to recognize cases of schizophrenia and depression, but 1 in 4 psychiatrists and psychologists also considered the non-case as mentally ill.** The social distance toward both major depression and the non-case was lower than toward schizophrenia. However, in this regard, there was no difference between professionals and the public. The study concludes that the better knowledge of mental health professionals and their support of individual rights neither entail fewer stereotypes nor enhance the

[947] APA, *DSM-5*, 6.

[948] Carlos Nordt, Wulf Rössler, & Cristoph Lauber, "Attitudes of mental health professionals toward people with schizophrenia and major depression," *Schizophrenia Bulletin* vol. 32 (4) (2006): 709–714; doi:10.1093/schbul/sbj065.

willingness to closely interact with mentally ill people [emphasis added].[949]

These statistics highlight how accepting psychiatric phenomenology as truth forces individuals to evaluate people and most of human nature through a restricted lens, and they also expose just how fluid the concepts of individual degeneracy truly are.

But it is not only the one who insists upon the psychiatric eugenic phenomenology who views life through this philosophical lens. What also occurs with most every psychiatric diagnosis is the creation of a new and damaging identity for the one who is set aside and categorized. This phenomenon is an internal stigma created by the "disease schema."[950] Historian of madness Roy Porter remarks,

> **Stigmatizing — the creation of spoiled identity — involves projecting onto an individual or group judgments as to what is inferior, repugnant, or disgraceful.** It may thus translate disgusting and fears into the fearful, first by singling out difference, next by calling it inferiority, and finally by blaming 'victims' for their otherness. This demonizing process may be regarded as psychologically driven, arising out of deep-seated and perhaps unconscious needs to order the world by demarcating self from other, as in the polarized distinctions we draw between Insiders and Outsiders, Black and White, Natives and Foreigners, Gay and Straight, Pure and Polluted, and so forth. The construction of such "them-and-us" oppositions reinforces our fragile

[949] Ibid., 709–14.

[950] Johan Verhulst, Russel Gardner, Beverly Sutton, John Beahrs, Fred Wamboldt, Michael Schwartz, Carlo Carandang, Doug Kramer, and John Looney, "The Social Brain in Clinical Practice," *Psychiatric Annals* vol. 35 (2005): 803-811.

sense of self-identity and self-worth through the **pathologization of pariahs** [emphasis added].[951]

It is well recognized that when a person is categorized as disordered within psychiatric nosology, he/she regularly takes on a "self-stigma," which creates a new false identity and often a disdain for one's own life.[952] Other psychiatrists state, "The outsider is always conscious of a precarious identity. When rejected he may attempt to reaffirm or rephrase his original identity."[953] The American Psychiatric Association defines "self-stigma":

> Self-stigma is when people internalize these negative stereotypes about themselves, often leading to lowered feelings of self-worth, greater isolation and more difficulty coping and recovering.[954]

Psychiatrist Sivan Mauer agrees: "The stigma of mental illness is related to the act of labelling and associating different people with negative stereotypes. The loss of

---

[951] Roy Porter, *Madness: A Brief History* (New York: Oxford University Press, 2002), 62-63.

[952] Qi Yuan, Esmond Seow, Edimansyah Abdin, Boon Yiang Chua, Hui Lin Ong, Ellaisha Samari, and Mythily Subramaniam, "Direct and moderating effects of personality on stigma towards mental illness," *BMC Psychiatry*, vol. 18 (1) (2018): 358.

[953] Roland Littlewood and Maurice Lipsedge, *Aliens and Alienists: Ethnic Minorities and Psychiatry*, 3rd edition (London: Taylor and Francis, 1997), 31.

[954] APA Staff, "Knowing about Mental Health Concerns of Friends and Fmaily Members Reduces Stigma and Encourages People to Seek Help," The American Psychiatric Association (December 20, 2019): https://www.psychiatry.org/news-room/apa-blogs/apa-blog/2019/12/knowing-about-mental-health-concerns-of-friends-and-family-members-reduces-stigma-and-encourages-people-to-seek-help.

status in society is part of the concept."[955] Since a person's struggle with his/her own identity is almost always a factor in his/her being diagnosed within psychiatry, delusions and other mental struggles are often only worsened upon receiving a descriptive psychiatric label.

Many contemporary psychiatrists have begun to realize that individual degeneracy is a dangerous and subjective philosophical approach to human nature. The influential Allen Frances, the psychiatrist who wrote the book *Saving Normal* and chaired the *DSM-IV* task force, edges ever closer to espousing some of the views expressed by Philip Pinel and John Galt. In an article published in the *Psychiatric Times*, Dr. Frances explains what he believes needs to occur to destigmatize mental illness:

> Everyone talks about ending the stigma attached to mental illness, but almost no one does anything meaningful about it. Recurring anti-stigma campaigns rely on empty rhetoric and never have any lasting impact. It takes decisive action, not words, to really end stigma . . . **As Harry Stack Sullivan (1894 – 1949) put it, "We are all much more simply human than otherwise." This is by far the best way to kill stigma. In contrast, our neglectful dehumanization and exclusion of the severely ill makes them much sicker than they need be. Social inclusion is by itself a powerful healing force . . . . It is not just more humane but also far cheaper to promote recovery in the community than to isolate people in costly institutions. Better emotionally, but**

[955] Sivan Mauer, "'All I've Got are Negative Thoughts': Reflections on *The Joker*," *Medscape Psychiatry* (December 23, 2019): https://www.medscape.com/viewarticle/923045.

> also economically, for patients to earn a paycheck than
> to receive a disability check [emphasis added].[956]

Viewing people as created beings with purpose and as having equal moral value, seeing social inclusion and deinstitutionalizing as healing, and encouraging people to fulfill their God-given responsibilities in society closely echo Galt's and Pinel's moral therapy. Conversely, labeling people as disordered inevitably creates further mental struggles and shapes how individuals view themselves. Other respected evolutionary psychiatrists admonish society to return to approaching struggling individuals as people instead of as amoral material degenerates:

> The issues are not some brain thing, but human issues. People with schizophrenia and manic-depression are no different from you and me . . . . The real source of human suffering is not, nor ever has been, the brain.[957]

Drs. David Pilgrim and Anne Rogers realize that both psychiatric theory and practice have created stigma, and that psychiatrists' "anti-stigma" campaigns have led society to view psychiatrists as "social engineers."[958]

---

[956] Allen Frances, "Restoring Respect to People with Mental Illness," *Psychiatric Times Online* (July 31, 2019): https://www. psychiatrictimes.com /articles/restoring-respect-people-mentally-illness.

[957] Robert Berezin, "Psychiatric Drugs are False Prophets with Big Profits. Psychiatry has been Hijacked," (July 5, 2015): http://robertberezin.com/ psychiatric-drugs-are-false-prophets-with-big-profits-psychiatry-has-been-hijacked/.

[958] David Pilgrim and Anne E. Rogers, "Psychiatrists as social Engineers: A study of an anti-stigma campaign," *Social Science and Medicine* vol. 61 (12) (December 2005): 2546-56; https://doi.org/10.1016/j.socscimed.2005.04.042.

Many psychiatrists and clinicians consider Peter Breggin to be a modern reformer of psychiatric theory, as he both exposes the neo-Kraepelinian model as a historic agent of social and political control and condemns the model's eugenic goals and harmful practices.[959] Similar to Pinel's and Galt's moral therapy, Dr. Breggin suggests that clinicians embrace an "empathic therapeutic approach," which focuses on treating people as souls rather than as soulless biological machines on which to be experimented and biologically manipulated.

In fact, as Dr. Breggin points out, prior to individual degenerationism being accepted and applied in theory to the human soul and its many struggles, people recovered from what is today presented as hopeless cases of "severe mental illnesses" within religious, empathetic, and moral environments:

> The individual in a *euphoric or manic state* is an extreme challenge to clinicians who do not want to involuntarily hospitalize patients or to use drugs as chemical restraints. **In the era of Moral Therapy in the 18th and 19th century, these individuals were successfully treated** without resort to drugs in genuine asylums that provided round-the-clock monitoring, caring social interactions, and moral support, **often in the form of religious persuasion** [emphasis added].[960]

While these evolutionary psychiatrists attest to the truth, they regularly overlook the fact that healing truth is sourced in the Bible. It is not the Christian faith—a faith

---

[959] Peter Breggin, "Psychiatry as an Instrument of Social and Political Control," https://breggin.com/social-page/.

[960] Peter Breggin, *Psychiatric Drug Withdrawal* (New York: Springer Publishing, 2013), 177.

which teaches that every person is both weak and wicked—that has created the hopelessness of mankind and stigmatized many people. Instead, it is the false faith in individual degeneracy, materialism, bio-determinism, and humanism that has furthered humanity's hopeless condition, hidden the remedy to fallen human nature, created a phenomenology that itself is destructive and stigmatizing, and has limited society's thinking to narrow strictures rather than allowing healing hope in Christ to flourish.

In reality, approaching other people altruistically is illogical if the biblical anthropology of the soul's moral equality (as explained in Scripture) is not foundationally understood, accepted, and applied. Even the notion of continuing to fulfill responsibilities—such as working, which Rush, Galt, Pinel, and contemporary psychiatrists like Frances and Breggin support, originates in and is best understood from the creation mandate of Genesis 1-2. Whether realized or not, that which is good originates in God's wisdom.

Rather than depicting just some people as being genetically predisposed to be deceived and to embrace falsehood, Scripture presents everyone as naturally deceived, impaired, and in a destructive state of mind that opposes God's moral law. The apostle Paul writes in Romans 7:10-25, for example, that the natural inherited predisposition of all people is to be lawbreakers and to be delusional in their thinking. Paul describes his own condition, which is representative of human nature:

> The very commandment that promised life proved to be death to me. **For sin, seizing an opportunity through the commandment, deceived me and through it killed me. So the law is holy, and the commandment is holy and**

righteous and good. . . . For I know that nothing good
dwells in me, that is, in my flesh. For I have the desire to
do what is right, but not the ability to carry it out. For I do
not do the good I want, but the evil I do not want is what I
keep on doing. Now if I do what I do not want, it is no
longer I who do it, but sin that dwells within me. So I find
it to be a law that when I want to do right, evil lies close at
hand. For I delight in the law of God, in my inner
being, but I see in my members another law waging war
against the law of my mind and making me captive to the
law of sin that dwells in my members. Wretched man that
I am! Who will deliver me from this body of
death? Thanks be to God through Jesus Christ our Lord!
So then, I myself serve the law of God with my mind, but
with my flesh I serve the law of sin [emphasis added].

According to Scripture, everyone who is descended from
Adam is hereditarily predisposed to be a lawbreaker, to be
deceived, to be somatically inclined to impairing and
destructive sin, and to be spiritually dead (separated from
fellowship with Christ and His sound mind). As Paul also
establishes, deceit is by nature destructive, whereas God's
moral law/truth is healing. Yet, the human tendency is to
despise the moral law as if it were the underlying problem.
When people understand that Christ is the fulfillment of
the law, that He alone is holy, and that in Him there is
genuine hope (the good news), then the true human
condition (the bad news of human depravity and fragility)
can be understood, better accepted, and the stigma of
mental struggles rejected. Having a right phenomenology
requires that people first confess wrong views of
themselves, others, and their Creator, and accept a new
identity in Jesus Christ, which alone can restore the soul.

When a person receives Christ and pursues restoring
his/her mind to Christ's mind, these naturally destructive
fleshly urges do not go away. Thus, 1 Peter 2:11 warns of

the conflict: "Beloved, I urge you as sojourners and exiles to abstain from the desires of the flesh, which war against your soul (ψυχῆς; *psyches*)." Fleshly desires, and not the body, destroy the human psyche. John makes the point clear in 1 John 2:15-17 that it is false desire and false high self-esteem that are the central problems of the soul:

> Do not love the world or the things in the world. If anyone loves the world, the love of the Father is not in him. For all that is in the world — **the desires of the flesh and the desires of the eyes and pride of life — is not from the Father but is from the world.** And the world is passing away along with its desires, but whoever does the will of God abides forever.

The natural bodily desires — with which all people struggle and which all people inherit from Adam — impair, attack, and take away life from the human soul and body (Genesis 3). The battle is not the body versus the soul/psyche, but rather, the true battle is the destructive and deceitful desires of the heart versus the restorative values and pursuits that reflect the perfect mind of Jesus Christ.

Scripture also conveys that though everyone is the same in regard to the human condition and the deception of one's self, each individual is deceived differently. In other words, though there is variation in mankind's inherited deceived or "lustful" natures, everyone struggles. One person might naturally desire illicit drugs, whereas another might naturally desire to be sexually satisfied whenever and however he/she pleases. Still others may desire life to be almost perfect — to go according to their own plans and wishes. James 1:14-15 declares this important truth:

> But each person is tempted when he is lured and enticed by his own desire. Then desire when it has conceived

gives birth to sin, and sin when it is fully grown brings forth death.

As Ephesians 4:17-32 makes clear, these are "deceitful desires" at their foundation that destroy both body and soul and that must be replaced by "healthy" pursuits.[961]

"Alcoholism" provides just one example of the result of deceitful desires that many people naturally lust after, which the body craves, and which attack a person's soul. From a secular perspective, Dr. Marc Lewis of the University of Toronto reveals how one's moral choices naturally produce vices and biological conformity:

> The shift from impulsive (operant, reward-driven) actions to compulsive (automatic, Pavlovian) associations is a case in point. When drug taking is found to be highly rewarding, the ventral striatum (including the nucleus accumbens) focuses attention on the desired goal, activates a behavioral sequence to achieve that goal, and produces a motivational urge to energize that behavior. Over time, however, as behavior becomes more compulsive and less impulsive (less reward-driven), activation increases in the dorsal striatum, the region most associated with automatic responses. This progression is thought to eradicate willpower, because conscious choice is no longer driving the behavior.[962]

961 There is an abundance of case studies available which show how a person's unfulfilled or crushed desires have led them to be diagnosed with "severe mental illnesses." (e.g., Maria Grazi Turri, "The Best Kept Secret in Psychiatry," *Asylum* 26 [2] [Winter 2019]: https://asylummagazine.org/2019/06/the-best-kept-secret-in-psychiatry-by-maria-grazia-turri/).

962 Marc Lewis, "Change in Addiction as Learning, Not Disease," *The New England Journal of Medicine* vol. 379 (16) (October, 2018): 1553; DOI: 10.1056/NEJMra1602872.

Dr. Lewis continues, relating that biological changes are still guided and determined by spiritual desires and not vice versa:

> Not only is normal behavior partly automatic, but also addictive behavior, even in its later stages, remains partly operant (reward-driven). Supporting evidence comes from numerous studies in which the reward value of the addictive goal (e.g., the amount of drug offered) shifts in relation to the reward value of an alternative goal (e.g., money). **In fact, these studies show that the probability of abstaining is proportional to the relative reward value of the two choices; this sensitivity to environmental contingencies is the hallmark of operant learning. Contingency management programs, based on these principles, have shown a consistent effect in the reduction of drug use.** The ventral striatum continues to be involved in reward seeking in later-stage addiction, even when the dorsal striatum dominates behavior control. **In sum, a combination of deliberate and automatic neurobehavioral mechanisms characterizes both addiction and "normal" habitual behavior** [emphasis added].[963]

By nature, everyone's normal human desires and outworking behaviors, which are inherited from Adam, are deceitful, impairing, destructive, and distressing. Only by finding moral values apart from the desires of their corrupted flesh can people find remedies to their deceived nature and subsequent pursuits.

Though there is variation in humanity's individual deceitful desires, everyone is facing the serious, normal, and destructive disorder of the human soul/psyche apart from the Creator's restoration and designed order. What all

---

963 Ibid., 1555.

people need is to be restored to the Creator's original design and to value Him above all other pursuits.

Christ is the Standard of Normal

Although many people – including religious figures – have attempted to reduce Christianity to merely a religion, true Christianity can only be properly understood when the Bible is accepted literally within context, applied relationally as required, and not perverted primarily into being rules and regulations (a religion), as Scripture warns against. Tragically, depraved people have perverted Christianity throughout history and seemingly transformed the message of grace into a twisted control mechanism (e.g., the crusades, the inquisition, cults, political institutions, and many other unbiblical applications) that presents a phenomenology apart from the truth of Scripture.

When right relationships with the one true God and people are not the substance/focus and quality of supposed Christianity, then the rituals and rules propagated are just another dead religion and not truly biblical. Religions (whether secular or claimed to be based upon Scripture but are apart from God's grace and truth) have been historically applied by selfish and/or deceived human powers – much like psychiatrists who have accepted individual degeneracy, and these false applications have consistently been destructive.

But the Bible clearly teaches that the two related commands which fully govern genuine Christianity are these: love the one true God and love others (Matthew 22:36-40). To be a genuine Christian is to embrace God's grace, holiness, wisdom, sovereignty, love, etc., and to denounce the perverted and unbiblical applications of Scripture that are dictatorial, controlling, destructive, and primarily self-advancing — those that seek to fulfill deceitful lusts (e.g., 1 Peter 5:3).

Love and truth are central to true Christianity because these vital needs of human nature are central to the person of Jesus Christ as recorded in Scripture. Jesus is the way, the truth, and the life, and no man can have a mentally abundant life in his/her fallen condition or be restored to fellowship with God apart from knowing Him (John 14:6). The only one that can mend the broken relationship between God and humanity and offer truth that sets mankind free from deceit is the holy one of Israel, Jesus Christ, who is both fully God and fully man. Moreover, Jesus is the standard of mental normalcy/health, which humanity must gratefully accept, intimately know, and practically apply in restoring the soul/psyche to real joy, peace, hope, and a sound mind.

But to be clear, studying the natural world will not supply this remedy for the mind. Deliverance can only be obtained by God's grace through one's personal faith in Christ as presented in the Word of God. Isaiah 26:3-4 assures,

> You keep him in perfect peace whose mind is stayed on
> you, because he trusts in you. Trust in the LORD forever,
> for the LORD GOD is an everlasting rock.

Faith in the one true God and not in scientific discovery (scientism) or in unproven human theory brings about mental health and stability. It is not in studying the natural world that one finds transformational answers to the soul's deepest needs, but it is in studying and intimately knowing the Creator of the natural world that a person finds deliverance.

Furthermore, the Bible teaches that an undeserved relationship with Jesus Christ by grace (no one has a right to know God) through faith is restorative. Stated otherwise, mental health does not come about from intellectual knowledge about God or by following rules. Rather, mental restoration comes through a covenant relationship with Christ based upon proper faith in God's character, Word, and work, as John 17:2-3 points out, saying that

> since you have given [Christ] authority over all flesh, to give eternal life to all whom you have given him. And this is eternal life, that they know you [intimately and covenantly], the only true God, and Jesus Christ whom you have sent.

Scripture clearly pronounces that rules and regulations (religion) are not restorative to the human soul or life giving and neither is simply creating a false god to worship and depend upon. By entering into a covenant relationship with the one true God, Jesus Christ, through faith, a person begins to be restored to life and mental health. This change of mind and behavior is a progressive occurrence through a person's life, though, rather than being a magic bullet that occurs overnight.

For some, placing faith in a figure who claims to have created the world, to be God incarnate, to be virgin born, and to have died and rose again is too much to believe. This common position, which rejects or denies Jesus as the one true God, is based upon the realities that faith rests on what is not seen rather than what is seen, and human nature would rather accept what can be observed, measured, and repeated. It is easier to trust that science is the highest or only form of truth, since it seemingly does not require faith. Yet, the existence of the metaphysical soul, whether it is reduced to material explanations or not, demands that a metaphysical reality be accepted as real, and faith becomes the primary vehicle for anyone to both understand and approach the soul/consciousness and attempt to explain the natural world.

Thus, placing one's faith in science, as with trusting in Christ, requires implicit faith. Trusting in a seemingly scientific hypotheses about the soul, such as the genetic theory of mental illness, is itself a religious faith.

A Standard of Health

No matter one's faith—whether in biblical creation or in evolution—every person must establish a standard of normalcy or "mental health" in order to suggest (or not) mental abnormalities/disorders. The World Health Organization defines mental health as "a state of complete physical, mental, and social well-being and not merely the absence of infirmity."[964] Such a standard of mental health, from which alleged psychiatric deviances arise and to which the alleged disordered can supposedly be restored, requires an empirical example of perfection. Without a standard of normalcy, there can be no abnormality, and without a standard, there can also be no ethical or practical direction in restoring a person to mental health, whether through counseling or by utilizing biological means.

---

[964] World Health Organization, http://www.who.int/trade/glossary/story046/en/.

However, secularists possess no scientific/objective standard of mental health.

Because of this fact, many materialists/reductionists recognize the need to establish a tangible standard of normalcy/perfection from which suggested abnormality can be declared and to which mankind can be theoretically restored. In accordance, secularists are attempting to create a "virtual perfect human" based solely on physical matter and theoretical constructs. Head of bioengineering at the University of Washington, J.B. Bassingthwaighte, explains the need for evolutionists to have an ideal specimen of human mental and physical health — what they refer to as the "physiome project":

> The physiome is the quantitative description of the functioning organism in normal and pathophysiological states. The human physiome can be regarded as the virtual human. It is built upon the morphome, the quantitative description of anatomical structure, chemical and biochemical composition, and material properties of an intact organism, including its genome, proteome, cell, tissue, and organ structures up to those of the whole intact being. The Physiome Project is a multicentric integrated program to design, develop, implement, test and document, archive and disseminate quantitative information, and integrative models of the functional behavior of molecules, organelles, cells, tissues, organs, and intact organisms from bacteria to man. A fundamental and major feature of the project is the databasing of experimental observations for retrieval and evaluation. . . . The Physiome Project will provide the integrating scientific basis for the Genes to Health initiative, and make physiological genomics a reality applicable to whole organisms, from bacteria to man.[965]

[965] J.B. Bassingthwaighte, "Strategies for the Physiome Project," *Annals of Biomedical Engineering* (8) (August 2000): 1043.

Since evolutionists do not have a tangible standard of mental normalcy to measure degeneracy, since they reduce the soul to be the product of humanity's material nature, and since they largely reject the mental, emotional, and behavioral perfection of Christ, they must both base all human nature on physical explanations and at the same time create a virtual or conceptual standard of normalcy.

Conversely, psychiatrists also attempt to base psychiatric "diseases" on a theoretical ideal or perfect model of individual disorders. Their reasoning follows that if no empirical example of perfect mental health exists, then a perfect model of imperfection/disorder must be hypothetically developed from which to measure deviances. Sandford University discusses philosopher of psychiatry Dominic Murphy's perspective:

> Murphy (2006) argues that the variety in mental illness requires us to explain psychiatric phenomena not by looking for stable regularities but by constructing exemplars. Murphy sees the exemplar as an imaginary patient who has the ideal textbook form — something like Thagard's network, and the narrative it provides — of a disorder, and only that disorder, although the textbook needs to thought of as a statement of the final theory, and not any current work in psychiatry . . . . They are not formal relations but the sort of comparisons between imaginary and real states of affairs that we all perform effortlessly. If there is a general theory, then, it is likely to be found not by philosophers but by cognitive scientists studying analogical thought (e.g. Hummel and Holyoak 2005). And because it is instrumental concerns that drive our search for explanations in psychiatry, as in medicine more generally, the clinically significant relations between disease, model and patient are likely to be highly context-specific; they will be determined in part by whether they offer opportunities for successful therapeutic interventions, which depend not just on how the world is

arranged, but also on what our resources and opportunities are.[966]

Murphy goes on to show both that this type of modeling is conjecture and that it attempts to establish a hypothesis about the perfectly diseased individual:

> The exemplar lets us identify robust processes that are repeatable or systematic in various ways, rather than the actual processes that occur as a disorder unfolds in one person. But we do not stop there: the ultimate goal is causal understanding of a disease. We build a model to serve this end. It aims to represent the pathogenic process that accounts for the observed phenomena in the exemplar. To explain an actual history in a patient is to show how the processes unfolding in the patient resemble those that are assumed to occur in the exemplar. **Exemplars provide an idealized form of the disorder that aims to identify the factors that remain constant despite all the individual variation. Not every patient instantiates every feature of an exemplar, and so not every part of a model will apply to a given patient. Once we understand the resemblance relations that exist between parts of the model and the exemplar, we can try to manipulate the model so as to change or forestall selected outcomes in the real world** . . . [emphasis added].[967]

But as Murphy also acknowledges, there are problems with such idealistic thinking about human nature and about constructed theoretical diseases. Chief among these issues is that attempting to establish a perfect degenerate from which to measure all other alleged subcategories of this created degeneracy contradicts the "category" style

---

[966] Dominic Murphy, "Philosophy of Psychiatry," *Stanford Encyclopedia of Philosophy* (March 21, 2015): https://plato.stanford .edu/entries/psychiatry/.

[967] Ibid.

Kraepelin invented and which psychiatry is attempting to prove:

> One argument that might be made against zooming-out is that it assumes that mental disorders are categorical, rather than dimensional. The neo-Kraepelinian approach is often faulted for assuming that disorder is an all or nothing affair, whereas it might mark an extreme point on a dimension that is present to a greater or lesser degree throughout the population (Kendell 1975, McHugh and Slavney 1998, Poland et. al 1994, Widiger and Sankis 2000). **So, schizophrenia might be seen either as condition that is present or not — just as one either is of voting age or not. But we might also see it as like having high blood pressure — marking a point on one or more dimensions where normal psychological traits become aggravated enough to constitute a population of clinical concern.** Some psychiatrists have supported one approach or the other. Others, like Ghaemi (203), have argued that some conditions, like the major psychoses and mood disorders, are probably categorical, whereas other conditions, especially the personality disorders, are dimensional. This is clearly an empirical issue in the end, so if the zooming-out approach is committed to a categorical approach it is a cause for concern [emphasis added].[968]

However, if everyone is on a spectrum rather than falling into specific constructed categories, then determining where suggested normalcy ends and where theorized abnormality begins are left to the subjective opinion of the holder of the psychiatric construct. Whether one chooses to focus on theoretical ideal concepts of abnormality or to search for a specimen who exhibits perfect mental health and behavior, a standard of perfection must be established

[968] Ibid.

from which to suggest degeneracy. Otherwise, theories of abnormality can never be considered as valid and reliable.

All psychiatric models, including the bio-psycho-social paradigm key to psychiatric genetics, have serious flaws in establishing concepts of normalcy:

> The composite "biopsychosocial" theory, which attempts to amalgam of several of these types of explanations, has fared no better when subjected to a careful analysis; it is not a model in any scientific sense (McLaren 1998). The quest for explanation in psychiatry appears to be far from ended. Yet the importance of finding a successful explanatory model or explanatory models for psychiatry can hardly be overestimated.[969]

Other influential psychiatrists such as Nassir Ghaemi have written books like *The Rise and Fall of the Biopsychosocial Model* in which they point out how the BPS model has failed. In early 2020, Dr. Awais Aftab, a member of the executive council of Association for the Advancement of Philosophy and Psychiatry, states in a bit of irony how the BPS model is itself degenerative:

> BPS framework has failed to move psychiatry forward beyond that original insight. For a framework that [prominent psychiatrists] consider to be the solid center of psychiatry and the predominant guide to psychiatric diagnosis and treatment, it appears to have become largely irrelevant as a guiding force for the advances in the field of psychiatry . . . . It no longer helps to generate and test new knowledge, and by Engel's own criteria, needs either to be modified or discarded. To borrow terminology from philosopher of science Imre Lakatos,

---

[969] Grant Gillett, *Philosophy of Psychiatry: A Companion* edited by Jennifer Radden (New York: Oxford University Press, 2014), 12.

BPS framework has become a *degenerative* rather than *progressive* research program.[970]

It is worth reiterating that an objective standard of mental health must be real and not just hypothesized about through utilitarianism or derived from imperfect statistical analysis of large groups of people. If real mental health is non-existent, then objective abnormalities cannot logically exist either. Stated differently, without a standard of normalcy, proposing and then attempting to uphold psychiatric abnormalities is illogical and an exercise in futility.

In the same way as the created constructs, the soul's symptoms (e.g., delusions, hallucinations, anxiety, hopelessness, etc.) cannot be discerned to be abnormal in themselves without an established objective understanding of normal human nature. Professor of Medical Ethics Grant Gillett submits,

> The nature of psychotic irrationality and the cognitive dynamics of a psychotic break in the sense of self are both hotly debated. **In entering this debate, it seems obvious that any account of these phenomena in the context of psychosis ought to draw on an adequate understanding of our normal thinking and its role in informing our contact with the world** [emphasis added].[971]

Whether one chooses to place his/her faith in the physiome project or in Christ, faith is the foundational approach to all anthropological perspectives that suggest either individual

---

[970] Awais Aftab, "The Nine Lives of the Biopsychosocial framework," *Psychiatric Times Online* (January 23, 2020): https://www.psychiatrictimes.com/couch-crisis/nine-lives-biopsychosocial-framework.

[971] Gillett, *Philosophy of Psychiatry*, 21.

or universal degeneration of mankind. Director of the Virginia Institute for Psychiatric and Behavioral Genetics and professor of psychiatric genetics Kenneth Kendler discusses the influence of one's faith in clinical settings:

> **Psychiatry treats a subject matter—human behavior—that is very close to home. We deal in both our research and our clinical work with fundamental questions about the nature of human behavior and the human experience.** Of love and hate, suffering and exhilaration, meaning and hopelessness, responsibility and the perception of reality. Because these issues touch so intimately on our ideas of what it means to be human, it is difficult to view them as dispassionately as we might questions about the nature of light, chemical bonds, or the origins of earthquakes. **Indeed, people often come to these psychiatric issues with their own deeply held personal system of beliefs. It is a challenge to keep these personal viewpoints from being mixed up with the science and clinical practice of psychiatry** [emphasis added].[972]

It is not, though, that some people some of the time approach mental struggles from their personal faith as Kendler suggests. Rather, no one can approach alleged normalcy and abnormality apart from presuppositional faith. Psychiatry is at its core existence a "deeply held personal system of beliefs"; psychiatry is a religion/phenomenology about humanity's broken condition, a form of discipleship that asserts a dogmatic interpretation of the soul and that attempts to restore the soul, and a faith that suggests a hypothetical savior claimed

[972] Kenneth S. Kendler edited by Kenneth S. Kendler & Josef Parnas, *Philosophical Issues in Psychiatry: Explanation, Phenomenology, and Nosology* (Johns Hopkins University Press, 2008), 3.

to renew the soul/psyche/mind to mental health —
whatever that standard might be.

Choosing a Standard

Much like early America's choice between accepting Galt's
or Rush's approach to the soul/mind, each person today
has the privilege and responsibility of choosing a standard
of normalcy and subsequent beliefs. Those choices, though,
determine that everyone does establish a presuppositional
faith concerning human nature and human phenomena.

The Bible Provides a Clear Standard

The Bible claims to be the one true faith/phenomenology
that timelessly addresses humanity's greatest problems,
and it declares its full sufficiency to do so (e.g., 2 Peter 1:3-
4). Unlike psychiatry, however, the Bible clearly establishes
a standard of normalcy.

The Bible teaches three key truths in regard to mental
normalcy and corresponding faith: 1) Christ is the perfect
standard of mental health, stability, and behavior; God is
Holy and true, and therefore, He is of a unique sound
mind; 2) all of mankind enters the world morally
delinquent in reference to this immutable standard. One
might say that everyone has degenerated from God's
original design after Adam, which produces as a
consequence both wickedness and weakness in the human
soul; and 3) Jesus is not only the standard but also the only
remedy to restore humanity back to God's original design
of spiritual life, healthy relationships, truth, and mental
wholeness. In other words, every degenerated soul needs

to be regenerated and have his/her mind restored to God's original design, and only Christ fulfills and enables others to participate in His divine nature as they know Him and identify with Him in a covenant relationship. This regeneration, progressive mental restoration, and relationship by faith is made effective through the sacrificial death of Christ. Accepting the doctrine of universal degeneration as Scripture presents in Genesis 3 and in more detail throughout its pages is vital to begin the mind's renewal. There is clearly bad news about human nature that the good news of Jesus Christ directly addresses, and which provides deliverance to all those who believe in Him. This change of faith is an exchange of pursuing deceitful desires for pursuing immutable and vital truth, and it is a faith that establishes vital hope. Only God, who is truth, can set the captives free.

It must be emphasized, though, that the Bible does not teach that some individuals are special and deserve to be delivered. Scripture does teach that Christ alone is holy, gracious, and merciful, so no person is worthy of being restored to His perfect image or deserves His love. When people enter into a saving covenant relationship with Christ, they are not genetically predisposed to place their faith in Jesus or to think in a healthy way that produces hope, nor have they earned God's favor because of their moral superiority or "good" behavior. Instead, there is a supernatural regeneration that occurs through God's grace and mercy alone and not through mankind's efforts or innate abilities. Ephesians 2:1-16 explicitly reveals,

> And you were dead in the trespasses and sins in which
> you once walked, following the course of this world,
> following the prince of the power of the air, the spirit that
> is now at work in the sons of disobedience — **among**

whom we all once lived in the passions of our flesh, carrying out the desires of the body and the mind, and were by nature children of wrath, like the rest of mankind. But God, being rich in mercy, because of the great love with which he loved us, even when we were dead in our trespasses, made us alive together with Christ—by grace you have been saved— and raised us up with him and seated us with him in the heavenly places in Christ Jesus, so that in the coming ages he might show the immeasurable riches of his grace in kindness toward us in Christ Jesus. For by grace you have been saved through faith. And this is not your own doing; it is the gift of God, not a result of works, so that no one may boast. For we are his workmanship, created in Christ Jesus for good works, which God prepared beforehand, that we should walk in them. Therefore remember that at one time you Gentiles in the flesh, called "the uncircumcision" by what is called the circumcision, which is made in the flesh by hands— remember that you were at that time separated from Christ, alienated from the commonwealth of Israel and strangers to the covenants of promise, having no hope and without God in the world. But now in Christ Jesus you who once were far off have been brought near by the blood of Christ. For he himself is our peace, who has made us both one and has broken down in his flesh the dividing wall of hostility by abolishing the law of commandments expressed in ordinances, that he might create in himself one new man in place of the two, so making peace, and might reconcile us both to God in one body through the cross, thereby killing the hostility [emphasis added].

Faith in Christ is required to receive this right anthropology, this new identity, and this unique and genuine supernatural remedy for the soul that alone establishes transformational hope.

It cannot be overstated that faith is also required in accepting any view of the metaphysical soul/psyche's condition which opposes Scriptures' teachings. Individual degenerationism, materialism, bio-determinism, humanism, and evolutionism are just as much faith-based explanations and approaches to the soul as are the doctrines of biblical Christianity. The evolutionary doctrines are antithetical to the biblical teachings of universal degenerationism, dualism, God's sovereignty, theocentricity, and divine creation. The person who rejects Jesus Christ as the perfect embodied soul must still establish a standard of normalcy/ideal human nature, and from this philosophical point, that individual can then pursue concepts of perceived degeneracy.[973]

Evolution is Not an Objective Standard

As previously noted, secularists most often claim evolution to be the alleged standard of normalcy (e.g., Wakefield[974]). Yet, no standard or ordered design can exist within evolutionary faith which holds to chance, adaptation, natural selection, and the strongest organisms surviving. Still, it is helpful to reexamine more carefully what factors or philosophical concepts are considered within evolutionary thinking for categorizing someone within the bio-psycho-social model as being disordered.

In the textbook of *Abnormal Psychology*, the authors assert that there are three general axioms on which the secular concepts of individual degeneracy rest. These potential

---

[973] For further study on establishing normalcy, see Daniel R. Berger II, *Mental Illness: The Necessity for Faith and Authority* (Taylors, SC: Alethia International Publications, 2016), 30-42.

[974] Jerome C. Wakefield, "The Concept of Mental Disorder," *American Psychologist* 47 (1992): 373.

standards are 1) statistical rarity; 2) distress and impairment; and 3) socially unacceptable, maladaptive, or morally reprehensible thoughts, emotions, and behavior.[975]

Statistical Rarity

The eugenic theory's "risk score" and "hereditary predisposition" concepts rest on the statistical analysis and predictability axiom. As observed in chapter three, "the quantitative methodologies" originated with Francis Galton and Kraepelin.[976] Within this approach, secularists search for statistical rarities in the general population and in genetic databases rather than searching for a perfect person:

> **From a statistical point of view, abnormality is any substantial deviation from a statistically calculated average.** Those who fall within the "golden mean" — those, in short, how do what most other people do — are normal, while those whose behavior differs from that of the majority are abnormal . . . . One has only to measure the person's performance against the average performance. If it falls outside the average range, it is abnormal. **There are obvious difficulties with this approach, however. As we saw earlier, the norm-violation approach can be criticized for exalting the shifting value to social groups. Yet the major weakness of the statistical-rarity approach is that it has no values; it lacks any system for differentiating between desirable and undesirable behaviors . . . . Such a point of view is**

[975] Lauren B. Alloy, Joan Acocella, and Richard R. Bootzin, *Abnormal Psychology: Current Perspectives* 7th edition (New York: McGraw-Hill, 1996), 6.

[976] Eric J. Engstrom and Matthias M. Weber, "Emil Kraepelin (1856-1926)," *The Encyclopedia of Clinical Psychology* (2015): DOI: 10.1002/9781118625392.wbecp090.

potentially very dangerous, since it discourages even valuable deviations [emphasis added].[977]

Having no values means that someone or a group of people must decide what is morally and statistically normal/ acceptable and what should be considered as statistical degeneracy.

Furthermore, this approach assumes that "normal" people are not mentally unstable for long periods of time. Though it is regularly denied, this approach requires a presuppositional moral standard to determine the values — what is bad or mad/evil or ill. Professor of psychiatry John Sadler discloses this reality concerning diagnosis: "This most apparently scientific activity of sorting and labeling disorders is imbued with moral, social, and political meaning."[978]

If the content of the delusions determines how people are categorized and whether they are viewed as degenerates or normal, then a person's subjective opinion and not scientific fact is the basis of every diagnoses. For example, a young girl who has been repeatedly molested will rightly think and behave differently from her peers. But such post-traumatic struggle should be expected and discerned to be normal rather than viewed as a disorder. Simply because people are statistically different does not provide an objective standard to determine perceived abnormality or help to explain their human struggles. Rarity, whether desirable or not, does not determine degeneracy.

[977] Alloy, Acocella, and Bootzin, *Abnormal Psychology*, 6.

[978] John Sadler, *Philosophy of Psychiatry: A Companion* edited by Jennifer Radden (New York: Oxford University Press, 2014), 15.

Otherwise, gold medalists would be considered degenerates based on statistical rarity. Instead, a moral system founded on perceived truth about the soul/psyche determines which mental and behavioral tendencies are framed as abnormalities.

Moreover, it has been shown statistically, for instance, that all people are delusional and hallucinate; deceit is a fundamental problem of all humanity and not just of a few. When delusions and hallucinations occur, these phenomena are not signs of abnormality. Rather, they are phenomena which reveal true human nature. The statistical approach must treat people as soulless objects — as numbers that fit into subjectively created categories rather than as moral souls which depend upon values, faith, and relationships.

An illustration of how the statistical approach is commonly applied in psychiatric genetics can be observed in the construct of Attention Deficit Hyperactivity Disorder (ADHD). "Hyperactivity" implies that a deviance from a speculative normal energy level has occurred, and therefore, the child should be viewed as a degenerate. The argument is made that high energy and inattentiveness are detrimental and are also genetically caused. But who decides that having high energy is detrimental, and what is the standard of normal energy that psychiatrists use to measure "hyper"? Are there not millions of people who wish they had more energy, and do not levels of energy fluctuate between people throughout a day, a week, and over the course of their lives? Furthermore, when children learn self-control, does hyperactivity not become an asset?

Simply because a human phenomenon is statistically rare or a social group is a minority does not determine a statistical rarity to be an abnormality or a physical disease. The statistical axiom appears to be objective and reliable on paper, but most people do not take the time to realize its morally subjective and pseudoscientific nature. Chair of psychiatry at the University of Massachusetts Medical School and chair of the *DSM* steering committee Paul Appelbaum comments,

> The phenomenological tradition of careful description of mental function and dysfunction often reveals unexpected diversity among presentations grouped under a common rubric and raises questions regarding theories of etiology. Both of these enterprises may have direct, practical implications for diagnosis and treatment. Similarly, **from long philosophical experience with the development of typologies come important critiques of the dominant diagnostic schemata, especially regarding the difficult task of defining the boundary between the pathological and the normal** [emphasis added].[979]

By constructing any seemingly rare or undesirable human phenomena into descriptive categories, psychiatrists can subjectively create individual degeneracy at will and in accordance with their own moral values. But as Appelbaum rightly discusses, theories of etiology cannot be objective within the subjective nature of descriptive psychology and psychiatric phenomenology.

The statistical rarity standard attempts to cover the fact that evolutionists have no standard of mental health in the natural world from which to base abnormality. The theory proposes that by looking at humanity in general and indirectly suggesting ideas of normalcy, perfection can theoretically be established. In truth, such logic establishes

---

[979] Paul S. Appelbaum, *Philosophy of Psychiatry: A Companion* edited by Jennifer Radden (New York: Oxford University Press, 2014), foreword viii.

means and averages based upon values and morals rather than on a perfect empirical specimen of mental health.

Far from proving individual degeneracy and establishing alleged normalcy, such a practice exposes that people vary at many levels, even from day to day and season to season in their own lives. Whether from a biblical or secular perspective, change is expected within human nature, personalities, and relationships with some drastic negative changes being a part of human nature as well. Statistical approaches cannot bring people to genuine mental health since no standard of mental health's appearance exists within evolutionism and humanism.

Discomfort, Distress, or Impairment

In addition to statistical rarity, a person's personal discomfort, impairment, or distress that persists are also considered within eugenic and humanistic thinking to be forms of individual degeneracy. In essence, if life does not go a person's way and he or she cannot mentally endure via his or her own internal abilities, then psychiatry declares and categorizes the negative results and responses to be abnormalities:

> Another criterion for defining abnormality is personal discomfort. If people are content with their lives, then their lives are of no concern to the mental health establishment. If, on the other hand, they are distressed over their thoughts or behavior, then they require treatment.[980]

[980] Alloy, Acocella, and Bootzin, *Abnormal Psychology*, 6.

This approach is established upon teaching people to interpret their personal phenomena and experiences through a specific humanistic moral lens, and it encourages self-diagnosis when discontentment or stress cannot be resolved from one's own efforts. Essentially, any psychiatric construct that is not considered to be classic "madness" or "severe mental illness" is accepted by society upon this philosophical standard:

> [This axiom] makes people the judge of their own normality, rather than subjecting them to the judgment of the society or diagnostician. This is the approach that is probably the most widely used in the case of less severe psychological disorders. Most people in psychotherapy are there not because anyone has declared their behavior abnormal but because they themselves are unhappy with some aspect of their lives.[981]

As already established, this humanistic standard of perceived abnormality is represented in the *DSM-5* under "the definition of mental disorder."[982] However, it is helpful to recognize that this particular basis of determining degeneracy is derived from the teachings of Fredrich Nietzsche in the 1800s.[983] Psychiatrist Heinz Haefner refers to the present-day scientific presuppositional faith within psychiatry — which he claims was formed by combining the theories of Darwin, Morel,

[981] Ibid.

[982] APA, *DSM-5*, 20.

[983] Heinz Haefner, "Comment on E.F. Torrey and R.H. Yolken: ("Psychiatric genocide: Nazi attempts to eradicate schizophrenia" *Schizophrenia Bulletin* vol. 36 1 (2010): 26-32.) *Schizophrenia Bulletin* vol. 36 3 (2010): 450-4. doi:10.1093/schbul/sbq034.

and Nietzsche—as the "Neo-Darwinian outlook on human life":

> The theory of evolution together with Friedrich Nietzsche's (1844–1900) morality of strength and power helped to spread the conviction that modern medicine and the welfare of the disabled had stalled human evolution ultimately preventing the rise of a new and fitter human race.[984]

Modern psychiatric application of individual degeneracy as published in the *DSM-5* becomes functional by combining Darwin's, Kraepelin's (with Morel's), and Nietzsche's teachings.

Nietzsche formally introduced the widely accepted humanistic ideas of self-actualization, self-realization, and self-esteem into philosophy—including psychology and psychiatry. Thereafter, Abraham Maslow and other humanistic psychologists would champion Nietzsche's concept of esteeming self as the highest good, the most worthy pursuit, and as an important "human need." Professor of philosophy Dale Wilkerson explains that

> Nietzsche claimed the exemplary human being must craft his/her own identity through self-realization and do so without relying on anything transcending that life—such as God or a soul.[985]

Nietzsche called this self-reliance and self-realization apart from God the "will to power," and this worldview became a central theme in Nietzsche's writings. In place of the one true God, *Zarathustra* and the *Übermensch* (two of

[984] Ibid.

[985] Dale Wilkerson, "Friedrich Nietzsche (1844-1900)," *The Internet Encyclopedia of Philosophy* (2016): https://www.iep.utm.edu/nietzsch/.

Nietzsche's favorite metaphors for human self-dependence and self-actualization) became the highest good and standard of normalcy in the universe. Nietzsche's humanistic worldview helped to shape Wundt's, Kraepelin's, and Freud's theories of the human soul/psyche as an aspect of human nature apart from God and designed by "mother nature" (evolution) to fulfill whatever the individual's heart desires. Still, this phenomenology did not bring about mental healing for Nietzsche. Instead, it led him into further deceit until he himself was deemed to be insane and confined to an asylum. How ironic that today's most popular theory of mental disorder has a philosophical basis in an allegedly psychotic man's own internal struggle.

As with Nietzsche, Abraham Maslow presented self-actualization, self-esteem, and self-fulfillment as vital

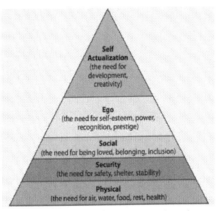

Figure 3 - Maslow's Hierarchy of Needs

needs. Accordingly, Maslow suggested his now famous "hierarchy of needs," as psychiatrist Neel Burton shares,

In his influential paper of 1943, *A Theory of Human Motivation*, the American psychologist **Abraham**

> **Maslow proposed that healthy human beings have a certain number of needs**, and that these needs are arranged in a hierarchy, with some needs (such as physiological and safety needs) being more primitive or basic than others (such as social and ego needs). Maslow's so-called 'hierarchy of needs' is often presented as a five-level pyramid, with higher needs coming into focus only once lower, more basic needs are met [emphasis added].[986]

If mental health means that life goes according to one's desires, dreams, and self-perceptions, then those who face the reality that life's hardships regularly oppose the fulfillment of one's deceived desires, and he or she falsely believes that it does the same for everyone else, then sorrow, anxiety, hopelessness, guilt, envy, anger, bitterness, etc. will inevitably follow. When the humanistic bio-psycho-social model has been embraced, people begin to perceive within their own souls that their distressful condition is a form of degeneracy and that they are not like everyone else. The two highest levels of Maslow's hierarchy are self-actualization and self-esteem, and these humanistic goals become the hope for all who believe in them until the false humanistic belief in self fails to deliver what it promised.

What is also important to understand, as Wilkerson notes, is that how people perceive themselves and their innate desires is key to their own identity. Psychiatric labels, derived from psychiatric phenomenology, not only stigmatize people as individual degenerates, but they also

---

[986] Neel Burton, "Our Hierarchy of Needs: True Freedom is a luxury of the mind. Find out Why," *Psychology Today* (June 21, 2019): https://www.psychologytoday.com/us/blog/hide-and-seek/201205/our-hierarchy-needs.

create a new negative identity and self-fulfilling prophecy. Dr. Allen Frances recognizes this far-too-common reality:

> Having a mental disorder label "marks" someone in ways that can cause much secondary harm. . . . A great deal of the trouble comes from a change in how you see yourself—the sense of being damaged goods, feeling not normal or worthy, not a full-fledged member of the group. . . . Labels can also create self-fulling prophecies. If you are told you are sick, you feel and act sick, and others treat you as if you are sick. . . . The sick role can be extremely destructive when it reduces expectations, truncates ambitions, and results in a loss of personal responsibility.[987]

What Frances states also illuminates (whether realized or not) the fact that faith is an important factor of human nature regarding people's mental struggles and health as well as their identities.

Nonetheless, the impairment and distress standards presuppose that people choose how their lives should unfold and that if life does not unfold as they wish and they cannot move past those disappointments and tragedies within their own "will to power," then there must be something wrong with them. In the *Humanist Manifesto I and II*, figures like former president of the American Psychology Association John Dewey explain this key humanistic anthropology:

> Man will learn to face the crises of life in terms of his knowledge of their naturalness and probability. Reasonable and manly attitudes will be fostered by education and supported by custom. **We assume that**

---

[987] Allen Frances, *Saving Normal: An Insider's Revolt against Out-of-Control Psychiatric Diagnosis, DSM-5, Big Pharma, and the Medicalization of Ordinary Life* (New York: HarperCollins, 2013), 109.

humanism will take the path of social and mental
hygiene and discourage sentimental and unreal hopes
and wishful thinking [emphasis added].[988]

In effect, humanists believe that human nature will correct
delusional thinking and false hopes rather than naturally
produce them. "Mental hygiene" is a key psychiatric
eugenic term — coined by Kraepelin's American student
Adolf Meyer and popularized by Clifford Beers.[989] As
discussed in previous chapters, the term represents
positive eugenics that was so instrumental in ushering in
the Holocaust. The authors of *Humanist Manifesto I and II*,
then, offer a philosophical nod to Nietzsche's concept of
"will to power":

> Though we consider the religious forms and ideas of our
> fathers no longer adequate [Christianity], the quest for the
> good life is still the central task for mankind. Man is at
> last becoming aware that he alone is responsible for the
> realization of the world of his dreams, that **he has within
> himself the power for its achievement.** He must set
> intelligence and **will to task** [emphasis added].[990]

This humanistic standard for judging normalcy and
degeneracy offers society a situation in which psychiatry
creates the constructs to describe how people react when
false hope is exposed and the heart is made sick, and where
psychiatrists — under the directed changes instated by the

---

[988] Raymond Bragg, John Dewey, and Charles Francis Potter, et. al.,
Humanist Manifestos I and II edited by Paul Kurtz (Buffalo, NY: Prometheus
Books, 1973), 9.

[989] Jose Bertolote, "The roots of the concept of mental health," *World
Psychiatry: official journal of the World Psychiatric Association* vol. 7 (2) (2008): 113–
116.

[990] Bragg, Dewey, and Potter, et. al., *Humanist Manifestos I and II*, 10.

chair of *the DSM-III* task force, Bob Spitzer — have established a false standard of normalcy — a psychiatric phenomenology — from which people learn to judge/diagnose themselves and form an identity.

Whereas Kraepelin focused on people who were judged to be deceived (delusional and hallucination), Spitzer introduced a new form of degeneracy based upon Nietzsche's concepts of humanism and relativism that categorizes persistent mental distress and impairment as abnormalities. Both of these alleged types of degeneracy were conceived in secular phenomenology, which attempts to explain the deceitful nature, destructive desires, and fragility of the normal human soul.

Psychiatrists have also discovered in their research that "among females, strong humanistic beliefs were associated with internalizing problems."[991] Not surprisingly, people who "internalize" their problems are known to be more susceptible to suicidal thinking and dismissive of counseling from others.[992] But humanism encourages both freedom to commit suicide and freedom to euthanize. Signers of the *Humanist Manifesto II*, which included

[991] W. Van der Jagty-Jelsma, M. de Vries-Schot, P. Scheepers, Pam van Deurzen, H. Klip, and J.K. Buitelaar, "Longitudinal Study of Religiosity and Mental Health of Adolescents with Psychiatric Problems. The TRAILS Study," *The Journal of European Psychiatry* vol. 45 (September 2017): 65-71; doi: 10.1016/j.eurpsy.2017.05.031.

[992] Matthew Sunderland and Tim Slade, "The Relationship between internalizing psychopathology and suicidality, treatment seeking, and disability in the Australian population," *Journal of Affective Disorders* (171) (January 15, 2015): 6; doi: 10.1016/j.jad.2014.09.012.

psychologists such as B.F. Skinner and the former president of Planned Parenthood, Alan F. Guttmacher, assert that

> to enhance freedom and dignity the individual must experience a full range of civil liberties in all societies . . . . It also includes a recognition of an individual's right to die with dignity, euthanasia, and the right to suicide.[993]

Labeling someone as abnormal who struggles with turning inward and is encouraged in counseling to do so often worsens their mental state, teaches them to accept their own deceived self-concepts of life and their own failing wisdom, and discourages them from denying themselves in favor of loving God and others.

Suicidal ideation does not explain a person who has lost hope, because suicidal people are best understood as those who falsely believe that they are responsible to deliver themselves from their own broken state and the many vexations in life. Such false hope is only encouraged by the delusional thinking of "will to power"/"will to task."

The impairment and distress axiom are based upon the false idea that human nature and the world in general are getting better rather than declining and that human nature is intrinsically good and strong rather than morally wicked and weak. Within this thinking, psychiatric theorists see the "mentally healthiest" as those people who pursue their own natural desires and achieve their fullest human potential. Basically, with society's acceptance of the bio-psycho-social model, psychiatrists have convinced people that life is great, and everyone should expect to both fulfill

---

[993] Francis Crick, B.F. Skinner, and Thomas Greening, et. al., *Humanist Manifestos I and II* edited by Paul Kurtz (Buffalo, NY: Prometheus Books, 1973), 19.

his or her dreams and fully enjoy living however one prefers. But Scripture offers a different perspective. As an example, Job 14:1 declares, "Man who is born of a woman is few of days and full of trouble." One's worldview/phenomenology truly determines a person's mental state and his or her interpretations and reactions to the harsh realities of life.

Thus, the teaching of self-dependence, self-actualization, self-esteem, and self-realization within humanistic psychology creates degenerates out of people who come to realize that life is not going according to their plan or their false concepts of reality. Ironically, it is a psychiatric system where those who denounce the delusion of life's happy state and come to realize life's fallen reality are categorized and approached as degenerates. Clinical therapist Tania Glyde illustrates how many people who are labeled as depressed, thus being further stigmatized, arrive at a place of depression based upon their comparing their own lives with others according to their own false ideas about the world:

> Feeling indefinably different from others is often a sign of depression, which is why therapists encounter it so often. Some people live their entire lives never feeling what they perceive to be normal. The seeming ability of other people to live their lives without apparent effort feels like an impossibility. You walk through life as if pushing at thickened glass. Some people with depression use alcohol and drugs in response, some self-harm, some withdraw, and some overcompensate. Depression, similarly to anxiety, parks itself like an extra layer of awareness on top of ordinary consciousness.[994]

---

[994] Tania Glyde, "Wanting to be Normal," *The Lancet Psychiatry* vol. 1 (3) (August 1, 2014): 179-180.

It is easy for people to recognize their own sorrow, anxiety, and hopeless condition of life when they are told that life should be in their control and go according to their plans and it does not. When reality does not fit the humanistic narrative of the strong surviving, those who have accepted this false teaching are left feeling disordered within their souls.

Indubitably, humanistic teaching based upon evolutionary principles creates psychiatric degenerates by convincing people to accept the delusional thinking that encourages them to turn inward for joy, peace, satisfaction, mental stability, and hope and by transforming persistent impairment and distress into disorders that describe their human condition. Humanism is not a belief system that heals, offers genuine hope, or provides true lasting joy. The opposite is true, as humanism is a worldview that empowers psychiatrists to create and maintain degenerates out of normal people by promoting delusional ideas about normal life, human nature, and human phenomena. Sadly, humanistic faith produces the very distress and hopeless conditions which are constructed into disease entities and loosely defined in the *DSM-5* as mental disorders.

Maladaptive or "Bad"

There also exists a third standard which psychiatrists regularly utilize in creating and asserting constructs of abnormality. This diagnostic tool is the maladaptive rule, an axiom that first requires establishing a standard of morality or acceptable performance:

> Here the question is whether the person, given that
> behavior pattern, is able to meet the demands of his or her

> life—hold down a job, deal with friends and family, pay
> the bills on time, and the like. If not, the pattern is
> abnormal. . . . The maladaptiveness standard is also
> favored by many professionals for its elasticity: because it
> focuses on behavior relative to life circumstances, it can
> accommodate many different styles of living. But as with
> the personal-discomfort criterion, this liberalism is
> purchased at the cost of values.[995]

Both forming ideas of maladaptive behavior or "bad" behavior and establishing the idea that some people are disordered while others are not require a presuppositional and subjective value system. This value system can be either personal, familial, or communal, but a standard of normal behavior and acceptable production is necessary.

A child, for example, who is misbehaving can be judged as either morally "bad" or as genetically defective, depending upon one's presuppositional faith. Within this thinking, a man who daily drinks alcohol may not be viewed as disordered unless the drinking is associated with decreased production or unacceptable societal interactions. Some people are even praised for the volume of alcohol that they can consume at one time, unless the consumption leads to undesirable, impairing, or dangerous behavior. A mother, who after giving birth struggles to return to work and is far less productive than before, may be perceived as disordered rather than as struggling in a normal and expected way, because her life has drastically changed as she assumes more stress and responsibility and has less sleep and free time. In these cases, the standard of normalcy is based on the individual and not on humanity as a whole. But negative changes—even if they are not initially understood—are expected within human nature.

---

[995] Alloy, Acocella, and Bootzin, *Abnormal Psychology*, 6.

Simply because emotions or moral behavior are out of character for an individual does not mean there are no reasonable explanations to be found within the person's character, relationships, faith, and history. In these cases, a psychiatric diagnosis represents a clinician's inability or unwillingness to understand why the individual is struggling. Fitting people into categories is much easier than trying to understand their situations and struggles.

Family vacations provide one example of how drastic changes in behavior regularly occur among people, but which believers in the bio-psycho-social model do not judge to be abnormal. Visiting the beach for a week is drastically different than the mundane 40- hour work week for the majority of the year. Yet, this unusual statistical change is not categorized as an abnormality, since so many people take family vacations and the motive/desire for such atypical behavior is understood. Additionally, this behavior is typically not impairing. Within purported psychiatric disorders, there are millions of people thinking and behaving in the same way. So, rarity is not the issue in these cases nor is the sudden change in behavior. But it is the inability of psychiatric theorists to explain a person's condition (rather than considering the drastic changes from their typical lifestyle) as well as the negative quality of the changes that results in a person's being classified as mentally disordered.

When the three axioms of statistical rarity, distress, and maladaptive behavior are considered together, it becomes clear that any standard of individual degenerationism suggested to distinguish abnormality from normalcy based upon one or all of these standards will always be subjective and fluid. Moreover, any alleged standard of normalcy and proposed deviances are based upon established values. Simply because people are unique, are statistical minorities, are in distress, or do not meet the established social standards does not determine them to be disordered.

Along the same line of reasoning, persistent human distress and impairments should be understood as normal aspects of human nature. Furthermore, falling short of societal standards, turning to deceit to deal with trauma, and making poor moral choices according to an established value system should be viewed as issues of faith and morality rather than as medical concerns.

Regeneration

Accepting the anthropological truth that all men are mental degenerates when compared to Christ not only provides the right and necessary starting point for mental, emotional, and behavioral restoration, but also illuminates the fact that being restored to fellowship with Christ and to His sound mind is the only viable remedy to the human condition. In the Bible, Christ uses the metaphor of "new birth" (lit. regeneration) to express the new life that people long for apart from the normal degenerative state of humanity (Revelation 22:17) — the process of mental restoration that Christ provides. John 3:3-7 states:

> Jesus answered him, "Truly, truly, I say to you, unless one is born again he cannot see the kingdom of God." Nicodemus said to him, "How can a man be born when he is old? Can he enter a second time into his mother's womb and be born?" Jesus answered, "Truly, truly, I say to you unless one is born of water and Spirit, he cannot enter the kingdom of God. That which is born of the flesh is flesh, and that which is born of the Spirit is Spirit. Do not marvel that I said to you, You must be born again."

Though the physical body will continue to degenerate and will eventually die, the spiritual psyche/soul can become new through faith in Jesus Christ and progressively reverse the destructive consequences of Adam's sin.

By nature, people are spiritually/metaphysically dead, but Christ alone is mercifully able to make people alive together in a personal relationship with Christ (Ephesians 2:4-5). 1 Peter 1:3 declares the same truth, while emphasizing that regeneration or "new birth" is the only hope for degenerates:

> Blessed be the God and Father of our Lord Jesus Christ! According to his great mercy, he has caused us to be born again to a living hope through the resurrection of Jesus Christ from the dead.

It is not science or medicine that can return people to mental normalcy, but faith in the supernatural birth of Christ, His atoning death, and His supernatural resurrection, which delivers degenerates from normalcy in a fallen world, overcomes death, and provides genuine hope.

It is worth noting that both John 3:3-7 and 1 Peter 1:3 focus on the immaterial nature of mankind and assign the physical body to a secondary concern. The body is not the principle issue when considering the mind's health, though a person's physical nature is clearly affected by the spiritual nature, as physical death confirms (Romans 6:23).

Rather than presenting the false notion that most people normally have it together, Scripture teaches that no one other than Christ is naturally mentally healthy since the fall of the first man Adam as recorded in Genesis 3. This right anthropology is commonly referred to in theology as the doctrine of original sin, and it is a clear teaching found in Genesis 3, Romans 5, and 1 Corinthians 15:22. Romans 5 expresses well the inherited, destructive, and universal realities of the sin nature imputed to all mankind from the first man Adam — with the exception of Christ who was conceived apart from the hereditary transmutation of depravity/degeneracy:

> Therefore, just as sin came into the world through one man, and death through sin, and so death spread to all men because all sinned — for sin indeed was in the world before the law was given, but sin is not counted where there is no law. Yet death reigned from Adam to Moses, even over those whose sinning was not like the transgression of Adam, who was a type of the one who was to come. But the free gift is not like the trespass. For if many died through one man's trespass, much more have the grace of God and the free gift by the grace of that one man Jesus Christ abounded for many. And the free gift is not like the result of that one man's sin. For the judgment following one trespass brought condemnation, but the free gift following many trespasses brought justification. For if, because of one man's trespass, death reigned through that one man, much more will those who receive the abundance of grace and the free gift of righteousness reign in life through the one man Jesus Christ. Therefore, as one trespass led to condemnation for all men, so one act of righteousness leads to justification and life for all men. For as by the one man's disobedience the many were made sinners, so by the one man's obedience many will be made righteous. Now the law came in to increase the trespass, but where sin increased, grace abounded all the more, so that, as sin reigned in death, grace also might reign through righteousness leading to eternal life through Jesus Christ our Lord.

As this passage highlights, the deterioration in the human genome, which researchers observe and attempt to explain within the limited strictures of materialism, is the very real effect of the fall of the first man Adam and his wife Eve in the Garden of Eden. The deceitful false beliefs, destructive desires, and false perceptions recorded in Genesis 3:6 produced hereditary declination in all of humanity — not just in some. What this text also makes clear is that what every degenerative soul needs is Jesus Christ's grace.

It is also significant that even Christ Himself, while sinless and excluded from inheriting the degenerative or depraved nature of Adam, was in a state of intense distress as He lived in a fallen world and interacted with fallen people. Universal degeneracy places everyone into the same fallen condition of both wicked and weak; all have sinned and all face destruction apart from a reversal of Adam's original sin. Being restored to a relationship with Christ and returning to His wisdom, which He graciously designed for mankind before the fall of Adam, becomes the only vital means to being restored to genuine mental health.

Instead of man fulfilling his own temporal will (to power) or "self-actualization" in order to live life abundantly and eternally, what people desperately need is to return to knowing and doing God's will. 1 John 2:15-17 is one passage of Scripture that imparts this important truth:

> Do not love the world or the things in the world. If anyone loves the world, the love of the Father is not in him. For all that is in the world — the desires of the flesh and the desires of the eyes and pride of life — is not from the Father but is from the world. And the world is passing away along with its desires, but whoever does the will of God abides forever.

Psalm 34:7 presents the same truth: "Delight yourself in the LORD, and he will give you the desires of your heart." Christ-actualization (His person and will be realized) and Christ-esteemed and not self-actualization or self-esteem are restorative and satisfying. God's plan of regeneration and sanctification, therefore, is the only viable remedy to human degeneracy and restoring the metaphysical mind/psyche to health as God designed it. As people see themselves as God sees them, and they exchange failed human phenomenology for God's divine wisdom and will, mental peace and stability, even in the midst of the troubles of this difficult and fallen world, can be their reality.

A Spirit Embodied

If eugenics is to be fully abandoned, then a return to viewing human nature dualistically rather than reducing all of human nature to material explanations must also occur. Dr. Breggin seems to understand at some level the need for this important paradigm shift:

> If people who express seemingly irrational ideas are best understood mechanistically, then these people are broken, disordered, or defective devices. If we take the viewpoint that they are persons, beings, or souls in struggle, then an infinite variety of more subtle possibilities comes to mind for understanding and helping those who seem mad, crazy, or deranged.[996]

Christian neurosurgeon Michael Egnor began his career as a staunch materialist, but he could not deny the empirical evidence which revealed a powerful unseen nature in humanity that was apart from biological mechanisms or explanations. Dr. Egnor now believes that valid neuroscience points people to three important truths about the metaphysical nature of mankind, often referred to as the mind, soul, consciousness, or psyche:

---

[996] Breggin, *Toxic Psychiatry*, 25.

Remarkably, neuroscience tells us three things about the mind: [1] the mind is metaphysically simple, [2] the intellect and will are immaterial, and [3] free will is real [individual desires and corresponding behavior]. Materialism has limited the kinds of questions that we're allowed to ask, but neuroscience, pursued without a materialist bias, points towards the reality that we are *chimeras* [a single entity with a dual nature]: material beings with immaterial souls.[997]

It is not enough, however, to just insist that man is both a body and soul—that mankind is both metaphysical and physical or dual-natured. Understanding the exact nature of mankind as God designed it to function and as recorded in the Bible is also vital to help people in need.

What Humanity Is

Some of the most significant differences between the creation account and Darwinian faith are the asserted origins of mankind and humanity's true substance. Evolution contends that from nothing everything was created by chance; whereas the Bible declares that from God, who is a spirit, comes all metaphysical life and material matter as orderly designed. Evolutionists focus on and worship the material matter while creationists exult the Creator. Creationists also recognize both the Creator's image in mankind as well as the bodily form the Creator designed to house the metaphysical nature in this temporal material world and to be animated by a person's soul. One's faith in the origins of human nature and the universe

[997] Michael Egnor, "More Than Material Minds," *Christianity Today Online* (September 14, 2018): https://www. christianitytoday.com/ct/2018/september-web-only/more-than-material-minds-neuroscience-souls.html.

is of the upmost importance, superseding and establishing all other philosophical and phenomenological beliefs.

Moreover, evolutionists teach that material order (from which alleged disorder is theorized) occurred by random processes, but creationists recognize that human order is logically derived from a powerful designer and the source of life. It requires more faith, then, to believe that a metaphysical "mother nature" randomly designed humanity by chance and mutation into an amoral life-form with order and consistency than it does to accept the biblical account of the Creator God of life designing and producing life to reflect His own image. The empirical evidence that does exist reveals that the creation account is valid and the pattern repeated through human creativity. Whereas, mutations consistently create disorder rather than an advancement in creation or further order as the evolutionary theory suggests.

If mankind was, in fact, created in the image of God, then understanding God's image is vital to understanding human nature and human phenomena. Furthermore, if that image is marred and all humanity is born degenerated from the designed standard as Scripture reveals, then pursuing mental restoration apart from this vital standard of health and in accordance with the Creator's original design becomes futile. Thus, when anyone — secular or Christian — discusses psychological/spiritual change, that person must base the goal of change, the means of change, and the object of change upon the concept of original design and a corresponding standard of normalcy. If human nature was created by chance/random processes and chaos, then claiming that aspects of human nature are disordered is a logical fallacy.

The Bible is clear about the image of God from which mankind was created. John 4:24 says that "God is a spirit, and those who worship him must worship in spirit and truth." God is a unique spirit who exists apart from any physical limitation, time restriction, or any disorder and imperfection. The rules of nature pursued and discovered in the fields of science were created by God, and as the miracles recorded in Scripture affirm, the rules of the natural world do not restrict God's presence and work in this world. In other words, God — who is metaphysical — is not bound by the rules which He created to govern the material and temporal world.

In Christ, "The Incarnate One," it can also be observed that God, the Holy Spirit, took upon Himself the form of a man and became flesh in order to deliver humanity from its degenerative state. Philippians 2:5-11 states,

> **Have this mind among yourselves**, which is yours in Christ Jesus, who, though he was in the form of God, did not count equality with God a thing to be grasped, but emptied himself, **by taking the form of a servant, being born in the likeness of men. And being found in human form,** he humbled himself by becoming obedient to the point of death, even death on the cross. Therefore God has highly exalted him and bestowed on him the name that is above very name, so that at the name of Jesus every knee should bow in heaven and on earth and under the earth, and every tongue confess that Jesus Christ is Lord, to the glory of God the Father [emphasis added].

By taking on flesh, Christ provided humanity with the only measurable, observable, and true relational means of knowing the one true God and of being delivered after the fall of the first man Adam.

Positive and restorative changes to the soul/psyche, which occur in biblical counseling/discipleship, are based upon mankind being created by God in His own metaphysical image. 2 Corinthians 3:17-18 explains this important truth:

> Now the Lord is the Spirit, and where the Spirit of the
> Lord is, there is freedom. And we all, with unveiled face,
> beholding the glory of the Lord, are being transformed
> into the same image from one degree of glory to another.
> For this comes from the Lord who is the Spirit.

Biblical change pivots upon God's design in fashioning man in His own image — a spirit — and man's beholding God's glorious image as the unique standard, direction, and enabler of transformation. Those who understand and confess this reality in this life begin a process of change and restoration toward God's original design for mankind. Addressing or remedying human degeneracy, then, can only occur in referencing the Designer God's spiritual image and being restored to this liberating standard of created order. Though the process of change begins at regeneration, fully knowing God in His glory cannot occur until the sinful nature (the flesh) is completely dead and the believer is in God's presence. This hope of full restoration by knowing God fully allows progressive restoration in this life and remedies the soul. 1 John 3:2-3 writes:

> Beloved, we are God's children now, and what we will be
> has not yet appeared; but we know that when he appears
> we shall be like him, because we shall see him as he is.
> And everyone who thus hopes in him purifies himself as
> he is pure.

According to Scripture, positive change and obtaining freedom from the universal degenerative state is directly related to a person's relationship with the Creator and related self-concepts of identity (phenomenology). The destructive deceit of the human soul can only be remedied through the immutable and healing truth of God's wisdom contained in His Word. The more that a person intimately knows Christ from His Word and accepts His wisdom in his/her temporal life, the more he/she is progressively freed from the naturally disordered state of deceit and destructive desires. When believers see Christ face to face in eternity, they will finally then be perfectly/completely restored to mental health (Revelation 21:3-4). Simply stated, the only phenomenology that is both restorative and fully explains the human condition is God's wisdom contained in His Divine Word.

Additionally, the means and method of change (not just the object) must also follow the Creator's counsel/wisdom/phenomenology. Therefore, biblical counseling/"soul care"/discipleship is not a man-made therapy that is focused on symptomatic behaviors or human goals and materialistic gimmicks. But it is a God-provided solution, for the soul has the vital need to be restored to the only known mental health: the mind of Jesus Christ through relationship with God the Father.

Since Nietzsche and Freud, humanists have taken the biblical concept of discipleship and secularized its content, goals, and relationships. "Psychotherapy" or "talk therapy" are the most popular terms used to describe human attempts and methods to change people or to return them to alleged normalcy. As countless books attest, psychotherapy is founded upon relationships that encourage like-minded faith in a specific humanistic phenomenology.[998]

But beyond the secular version, psychotherapy is foremost a biblical concept focused on biblical phenomenology. *Psychotherapy* comes from the combining of the Greek words *psyche* (soul) and *therapia* (therapy). *Therapia* has three nuances in Scripture: 1) Christ as a servant attending to others' needs (e.g., Luke 12:42); 2) Christ miraculously healing physical ailments/diseases with his words (e.g., Luke 9:11); and 3) Christ fully restoring his created order in human nature (e.g., Revelation 22:2). The last usage in Scripture is the concept upon which humanistic psychotherapy (apart from Christ and His gospel) is based. Stated otherwise, humanists see humanity as its own Savior and the only means of beneficial discipleship toward this end. In contrast, Scripture reveals that restoring humanity to God's created original state and design is primarily God's work in which believers participate together, as Revelation 22:1-4 acknowledges:

> Then the angel showed me the river of the water of life, bright as crystal, flowing from the throne of God and of the Lamb through the middle of the street of the city; also, on either side of the river, **the tree of life** with its twelve kinds of fruit, yielding its fruit each month. **The leaves of the tree were for the healing** [*therapia*] **of the nations. No longer will there be anything accursed,** but the throne of God and of the Lamb will be in it, and his servants will worship him. They will see his face, and his name will be on their foreheads. And night will be no more [emphasis added].

[998] John Norcross et al., *Psychotherapy Relationships That Work: Therapist Contributions and Responsiveness to Patients* (New York: Oxford University Press, 2002).

The tree of life is a direct reference to the fall of Adam recorded in Genesis 3:22-24 and the universal degenerative state and hopelessness of all mankind thereafter. Biblical "psychotherapy" — literally the healing or restoring of the soul — is a lifelong process of knowing and depending upon God, receiving counsel (a right phenomenology of life; wisdom) from God's Word and God's people (Psalm 19:7; Psalm 23:3), helping others along the same path (discipleship), and hoping in the full deliverance that is to come. Biblical discipleship is the foundation of hope, as genuine *psychotherapy* will not be completed until Christ is known in the fullness of His glory, though the Christian can see Him, as it were, through a dim glass now.

If deceit — what has been historically framed as madness or insanity[999] — and deceitful desires are the foundation of universal human degeneracy that needs to be changed, then the gospel — the good news and truth about God and mankind that enables regeneration and the soul's restoration — is the only remedy. Biblical discipleship/ biblical counseling offers God's wisdom to the soul in need so that God's truth, in accordance with God's Spirit, can restore the soul to health and set the captive free (John 8:31-32).

A right perspective of human nature, then, is not merely that humanity is dual-natured or psychosomatic — though there is truth in this statement. Clearly, a more precise anthropology must be taught, accepted, and applied within the church, family unit, and society as a whole. That specific truth is, as the Bible teaches, that each person is a

---

[999] For further study on the history of madness and the deceived nature of humanity, see Berger, *The Insanity of Madness: Defining Mental Illness.*

metaphysical soul created in the image of God, is granted a temporal and degenerating physical shell (a temple which the soul animates while it lives in this material world), and is placed under the mental/spiritual degenerative and hereditary curse of the first man Adam.[1000] It is not that some people are genetically defective and struggle with falsehood and destructive desires. Rather, everyone is born in a degenerative state apart from the mental health of and hope in Jesus Christ alone.

Materialism is not a minor false doctrine on which Kraepelinianism and Darwinianism rest; it is a major doctrine—as with individual degenerationism, that forms a false gospel which does not liberate the human soul. The false doctrine of materialism further impairs and destroys humanity with greater deceit and keeps the struggling soul from genuine deliverance.

What Drives Humanity

Accepting the right created order/design of human nature enables people to discover not only a right remedy but also the "cause" of degeneracy. What drives people reveals as much about who they are as does their faith or philosophies. A person's metaphysical goals, desires, motives—what secularists regularly explain as an aspect of human consciousness—all expose the core of human nature to be spiritual. Because the problems of psychiatry are problems of the metaphysical soul/psyche/

1000 For further study on the doctrine of imputation, see Gary Robert Reimers, *The Significance of the Visitation of the Sins of Fathers on Children for the Doctrine of Imputation* (Bob Jones University, 1984), Tren ID# 003-0026.

consciousness is precisely why these phenomena are primarily framed as "mental disorders," though they are theorized to be neurological diseases.[1001]

The "mind-brain gap" — how the spiritual and physical natures relate — poses a tremendous problem for psychiatric geneticists and secular theorists alike within a materialistic framework. Rather than acknowledging humanity's true dual nature and accepting necessary faith, most psychiatrists resort to reducing the metaphysical mind to only metaphysical explanations (e.g., the genome and nervous system). Stated differently, secularists must reduce the very core of human existence to an effect so that they can sustain their false worldview. Writing in the *New England Journal of Medicine*, professors of psychiatry Caleb Gardner and Arthur Kleinman make clear their anthropological views:

> Our mind arises from brain function, and both conscious and unconscious mind processes feedback continuously to shape that function. Over the past century, both the psychodynamic tradition and basic neuroscience have painted pictures of a brain-mind that is fundamentally dynamic and plastic, in which cognition is inseparable from emotion and feeling, and where conscious awareness is a porous vessel on a sea of unconscious processes. The influence of the wider social world on well-being and illness has also been systematically elaborated by fields such as social psychology and anthropology. Interpersonal relations, from family dynamics to cultural practices and political constraints, affect our brain-minds. And in all our interventions (whether medications, cognitive techniques, or insight-

---

[1001] Lieberman, *Shrinks*, 26.

oriented therapy), the power and centrality of the clinician–patient relationship are clear.[1002]

They continue, submitting that

> if advances in modern neuroscience have taught us anything, it's that the brain-mind and its emotional and cognitive processes are even more complicated and mysterious than previously thought. It is crucial that this work continue. At the same time, we are learning more and more about the interconnections of mind, body, and society, and the interdependence of mental, medical, and social health. This interdependence has profound and practical implications for the practice of general medicine as well as psychiatry. In many ways, the unknown continent of the mind looms even larger now than it did in Jaspers' day — a reality that is both humbling and inspiring.[1003]

Psychiatrist Ronald Pies also clarifies this common reductionistic position:

> I don't like the term "mental disorder," because it makes it seem as if there's a huge distinction between the mind and the body — and most psychiatrists don't see it that way. I wrote about this recently, and used the term "brain-mind" to describe the unity of mind and body. So, for lack of a better term, I'll just refer to "psychiatric illnesses."[1004]

1002 Caleb Gardner and Arthur Kleinman, "Medicine and the Mind — The Consequences of Psychiatry's Identity Crisis," *NEJM* vol. 381 (October 31, 2019): DOI: 10.1056/NEJMp1910603.

1003 Ibid.

1004 Ronald W. Pies, et. al, "Doctor, Is My Mood Disorder Due to a Chemical Imbalance?" *Psychiatric Times Online* (August 12, 2011): http://www.psychiatrictimes.com/blogs/doctor-my-mood-disorder-due-chemical-imbalance.

In another article, Pies admits that the currently accepted bio-psycho-social (BPS) model will not answer the philosophical mind-brain problem:

> The BPS paradigm imposes no need to solve the ancient "mind-body" conundrum that has bedeviled philosophy for millennia (e.g., "What is the mind? Is it distinct from brain? How does mind interact with the brain?). **Those issues, though philosophically important, are at a different epistemic level than that of the BPS paradigm** [emphasis added].[1005]

As Pies rightly recognizes, the mind-brain "conundrum" is a matter of epistemology — the study of what is true and from where truth is derived. Professor of psychiatry Diogo Telles-Correia and like-minded psychiatrists also admit that some form of philosophical system — whether acknowledged or not — is required to bridge the tremendous gap between the metaphysical mind and the biological brain:

> A problem underlying the mind brain gap is the complex integration among the disciplines involved in it: neurosciences, clinical psychiatry and psychology, and philosophy of science. Research in neurosciences and clinical psychiatry requires a positioning in relation to some conceptual/philosophical aspects. These are related to the models of interrelationship of the brain and the mind, to explanatory approaches in psychiatry, and to conceptual issues such as dimensionality versus categories, symptoms versus disorders, and

---

[1005] Ronald Pies, "Can We Salvage the Bio-psycho-social Model?" *Psychiatric Times Online* (January 22, 2020): https://www.psychiatrictimes.com/couch-crisis/can-we-salvage-biopsychosocial-model/page/0/1.

neurobiological correlates versus clinical determination of mental disorder.[1006]

As Telles-Correia also acknowledges in the same journal entry, because the mind and brain are not the same, there is also a gap between the fields of neuroscience and psychiatry/psychology.

Other psychiatrists and clinicians, however, believe that such philosophical discussions, which attempt to resolve how the mind and brain are both connected and different, "will remain unsolved."[1007] Still others such as the influential psychiatrist Paul Appelbaum are skeptical, but they do realize that reductionism without empirical evidence is a threat to the notion that psychiatry is a scientific field that is advancing:

> Whether or not mental phenomena will ever be reducible to cellular interactions in the brain, and hence explicable at the molecular level, it is clear that a premature reductionism is one of the greatest threats to progress in our field.[1008]

Psychiatrist Paul Minot agrees:

> For centuries psychiatry has seesawed between two opposing models of assessment and treatment. One

---

[1006] Diogo Telles-Correia, "The mind-brain gap and the neuroscience-psychiatry gap," *Journal of Evaluation in Clinical Practice* vol. 24 (4) (March 2, 2018): 797; https://doi.org/10.1111/jep.12891.

[1007] Nasir Ghaemi, Thomas Fuchs, et. al., edited by K.W.M. Fulford, Martin Davies Richard G.T. Gipps, George Graham, John Z. Sadler, Giovanni Stanghellini, and Tim Thornton, *The Oxford Handbook of Philosophy and Psychiatry* (Oxford University Press, 2015), 9.

[1008] Paul S. Appelbaum, *Philosophy of Psychiatry: A Companion* edited by Jennifer Radden (New York: Oxford University Press, 2014), foreword viii.

is **biological**, focused on the obscure physiology of the brain; the other is **psychological**, focused on the even hazier functions of the mind . . . . There are two driving forces that have led to this philosophical divide in our profession. One is academic: **To date we have no scientific explanation as to how these two realms intersect.** The other is economic: Throughout its history, **psychiatry's prevailing treatment model has been dictated by its marketability.** And we've never had more customers than we do in this biological era, now that we're able to deal in pills–you know, real medicine. The side effects thereof have included the elevation of a psychiatrist's status to "real doctor" at last–a title rarely conferred on any of the psychoanalysts in their bygone era . . . . The dogma of contemporary psychiatry drives me crazy. **Its reductionist model is inane; its science is institutionally corrupt.** But what bugs me most of all is that it lays claim to an understanding of human thought and behavior, of happiness and healthy function–and yet it doesn't exhibit one shred of wisdom [original emphasis].[1009]

Since materialism insists that all human function be reduced to material explanations, all speculative causes to alleged psychiatric disorders — problems of human consciousness or the soul/psyche — are also reduced to material etiologies. Materialism is not an empirical fact that can be proven or disproven; it is simply a narrowminded limitation — a restriction — to explaining spiritual/metaphysical human nature and phenomena.

But as psychologist Sharon Hewitt Rawlette discusses, even approaching and interpreting the material world — a scientific approach — is largely dependent upon the metaphysical "consciousness" of human nature:

[1009] Paul Minot, "Bringing Psyche Back to Psychiatry," *Straight Talk Psychiatry* (December 31, 2019): https://paulminotmd.com.

The key to resolving the hard problem of consciousness lies in the following observation. **While physical properties cannot explain consciousness, consciousness is needed to explain physical properties** . . . . In the same way, if the universe is to actually exist, its properties can't be exclusively relational/dispositional. Something in the universe has to have some kind of quality in and of itself to give all the other relational/dispositional properties any meaning. Something has to get the ball rolling. That something (at least in our universe) is consciousness.[1010]

If human consciousness was created by God based on His own personhood, then God, and not humanity, is the rightful measure of meaning in the Universe. Therefore, desires, faith, motives, morality, etc. — the metaphysical core of human nature — becomes central to explaining mental distress, deceit, and destructive pursuits and impairing habitual behaviors.

Such commonsense understanding of human nature can be observed in how mankind creates and constructs in the physical world. A building, for instance, is first conceived in a person's or group of people's minds based upon desire, and then the building process is carried out in the physical world by the purposeful and intelligent creation of blueprints and utility schematics. Scientific hypothesis, theory, and experimentation, likewise, begin in the metaphysical mind before they are ever subjected to the scientific method. As already indicated, many of the scientific studies are crafted in accordance with one's

---

[1010] Sharon Hewitt Rawlette, "What if Consciousness Comes First?: Bridging the Mind-body gap will require a fundamental shift in perspective," *Psychology Today* (July 22, 2019): https://www.psychologytoday.com/us/blog/mysteries-consciousness/201907/what-if-consciousness-comes-first?fbclid=IwAR2Ya-lU8HjE2NeA4eSRiW4crwt52a3wL0PawjmC5kaA0TcH3DaDdq28_TE.

presuppositional belief and manipulated to produce desired outcomes.

Kraepelinianism itself was conceived in the humanistic minds of several key figures before it was attempted to be applied in the physical world or upheld in society. Humanity does not sit around and wait for creation to occur by chance out of nothing. Instead, intelligent people willfully — out of desire or necessity — create things in the metaphysical realm before they appear in their physical form, just as God declares how the creation of the world occurred (Hebrews 11:3; Proverbs 3:19-27).[1011]

Moreover, Proverbs 3:19-27 connects accepting God's wisdom to having mental health and adorning behavior:

> The LORD by wisdom founded the earth; by understanding he established the heavens; by his knowledge the deeps broke open, and the clouds drop down the dew. **My son, do not lose sight of these — keep sound wisdom and discretion, and they will be life for your soul and adornment for your neck.** Then you will walk on your way securely, and your foot will not stumble. If you lie down, you will not be afraid; when you lie down, your sleep will be sweet. Do not be afraid of sudden terror or of the ruin of the wicked, when it comes, for the LORD will be your confidence and will keep your foot from being caught [emphasis added].

Mental struggles such as anxiety and life dominating sins, as well as human experiences like insomnia caused by mental turmoil, can all be overcome through knowing and sincerely accepting God's phenomenology/perspective of

---

[1011] Hebrews 11:3 states, "By faith we understand that the universe was created by the word of God, so that what is seen was not made out of things that are visible."

life. Both Scripture and observable human patterns expose that the spiritual nature governs moral mankind and is the executive over the human soul's function.

Yet, when it comes to human mental struggles, many people have chosen to ignore the basic principle of human nature: the metaphysical precedes the physical effect. In exchange, materialists have attempted to reduce humanity's core to be explained as amoral biological processes. Secular philosophers such as Tim Thornton, however, have concluded that the mind and the brain can no longer be reduced in this way. Grant Gillett comments on Thornton's understanding:

> Philosophical naturalism and the doctrine of the unity of science, Tim Thornton illustrates, have provided a powerful impetus for a sweeping reductionism by which the mind, including the disordered mind, is nothing more than the brain. But, as Thornton goes on to point out in a creative and original discussion, there is a long tradition that can be traced from Jaspers through Wittgenstein to the contemporary philosophers. John McDowell's contrast between the space of reasons and the realm of law, in which mind, meaning and mental content, and mental disorder, are importantly irreducible.[1012]

If humanity is understood as having a metaphysical embodied soul — not simply as psychosomatic and certainly not only material or only spiritual, then both the direction of pathology and the appropriate and necessary remedy can be discovered and then effectively applied. Clearly, there are somatic differences. But the questions remain whether these measurable differences in the genome and nervous system are effects or causes, and answers to these

---

[1012] Grant Gillett, *Philosophy of Psychiatry: A Companion* edited by Jennifer Radden (New York: Oxford University Press, 2014), 15.

questions will always be derived from a person's presuppositional faith.

Materialists' wrong approach to human cognition, emotion, and moral behavior would also explain why psychiatric eugenics has failed miserably since it was first conceived in the minds of men like Benjamin Rush, Wilhelm Wundt, and Emil Kraepelin and why the methods suggested and applied to allegedly change the mind continue to be mostly harmful and to further hopelessness. Psychiatric biological treatments have only served to suppress symptoms — typically by attacking healthy bodily function — rather than genuinely treating the soul and restoring the spiritual mind to health.

But what if the narrow-minded faith that all human phenomena must be explained through only material causes is denounced and the metaphysical nature considered as its own legitimate reality and the primary core of human personality, pursuit, and consciousness? Such a change in position would allow false faith, false desires, hopelessness, anxiety, and other impairing mindsets to be considered the primary problems rather than being reduced to mere symptoms. Just as a desire to construct a building precedes the physical manifestation, so too, false fixed beliefs (delusions), as an example, could be understood to be the causative agent of negative genomic and neural alterations rather than merely being considered as symptoms. If the soul is actually considered as causative rather than reduced to effects, then an entirely different approach emerges. If faith, however, cannot be considered as empirically approachable or causative, then beliefs and perceptions cannot be considered as empirically sound symptoms let alone valid correlates, legitimate diagnostic tools, or the primary basis of categorizing people as degenerates, as Kraepelinians have done for decades. If scientists and clinicians are not willing to consider such human phenomena as faith and desires to be causing somatic changes, then the "bio-bio-bio model"[1013] will continue to produce a history of saving abnormal at the expense of losing souls.

At a minimum, neo-Kraepelinian psychiatrists and researchers should stop pretending to practice science when the core of their alleged descriptive psychiatric disorders, such as schizophrenia and bipolar, are metaphysical in nature and cannot be approached empirically. The sobering reality of the pseudoscience of the Kraepelinian genetic theory led Emil Kraepelin himself to admit in his memoirs that no scientific explanation exists to explain humanity's deceived nature, which psychiatrists continue to transform into psychiatric disorders:

> The first impressions of my new job were discouraging. The confusing throng of demented, sometimes unapproachable, sometimes obtrusive patients with their ridiculous or repellent, pitiable or dangerous oddities, the futility of the medical treatment ... **the complete helplessness against these types of insanity, for which there was no scientific explanation, made me feel the entire rigour of my chosen profession.** As they had done in Würzburg, the chaotic and repulsive pictures of the

[1013] Read, Bentall, and Fosse, "Time to abandon the Bio-bio-bio model of psychosis," 299.

day's work also followed me into the nights [emphasis added].[1014]

Today, there still exists no scientific explanation — only conjecture based upon a presuppositional faith. Having a wrong philosophical starting point to explain anthropology and phenomenology leaves not just the primary author of the failed psychiatric eugenic theory (Kraepelin) hopeless, but also everyone else who believes it.

What must occur is the replacement of the "bio-psycho-social model" (neo-Kraepelinianism) with the biblical model. The biblical worldview/phenomenology fully explains the causes to deep impairing deceit, destructive desires, and bad behavior (e.g., Genesis 3; Romans 5). Furthermore, Scripture discusses how the metaphysical mind and faith alter the body, and it also emphasizes right relationships as helpful to the soul (e.g., Proverbs 3:7-8, "Be not wise in your own eyes [a shared universal delusion]; fear the LORD, and turn away from evil. It will be healing to your flesh and refreshment to your bones"). At the same time, Scripture relates throughout how many aspects of life positively and negatively influence the soul (e.g., Romans 10:17; "Faith comes from hearing, and hearing from the Word of God") and how they may provide help or increase distress.

Whether or not people accept Scripture's phenomenology and anthropology, the Bible explains within a cohesive and practical worldview all of human phenomena claimed by

---

[1014] H. Hippius, G. Peters, D. Ploog, editors, *Emil Kraepelin Memoirs* (Berlin, Germany: Springer-Verlag; 1983).

secularists to be mental disorders; all issues of life and godliness are understood when the one true God who designed mankind in His own image is accepted and intimately known (2 Peter 1:3-4). Of course, Scripture does not utilize psychiatric descriptive constructs or ever-changing psychiatric labels. But the Bible does depict human nature precisely and describes the "symptoms" of claimed psychiatric syndromes in careful detail.

Cause	Effects	Influences on the Soul
False faith and desires which attempt to explain and save the fragile and depraved soul existing in a broken world (Genesis 3)→	Mindsets, emotions, behavior, somatic changes→	Relationships, diseases, the body, environments/experiences, behavioral patterns, etc.

Figure 4: The Biblical Model

In contrast to the religion of humanism, the Bible presents humanity as dual-natured and attributes mental turmoil or the "vexation of the soul" (e.g., Ecclesiastes 2;17; 22) to the fall of the first man Adam as recorded in Genesis 3. The two primary causes to mental turmoil which the fall produced are 1) the degeneration of all humanity from God's design—both moral depravity in relation to God and others and amoral fragility; and 2) the fallen and deteriorating condition of the created material world itself. According to Scripture, people experience the mental struggle of their own degenerated condition, others' degenerated souls and behaviors, and the curse of sin upon the world that is degenerating (as even the first and second laws of thermodynamics affirm). All people, and not just a few, are naturally in mental turmoil. Simply stated, Solomon expresses this reality in Ecclesiastes 2:22-23:

> What has a man from all the toil and *striving of heart* ["vexation of soul"] with which he toils beneath the sun? For all his days are full of sorrow, and his work is a vexation. Even in the night his heart does not rest. This also is vanity.

Humanity desperately needs to be delivered from its degenerative and distressed state. Whereas Genesis 3 first explains the cause of mental turmoil for humanity, other passages of the Scriptures point out that many factors influence and press upon the human soul. Disease, death, natural disasters, relational problems, drugs, sin, insomnia, etc., all reveal humanity's true nature rather than being the cause of weaknesses and wickedness.

There is a necessary distinction that must be made between what influences the human soul and what causes the soul's condition. For instance, Christ Himself, though sinless and mentally healthy (the perfect soul), rightly experienced intense sorrow most of His life as He interacted with broken people in a broken world. Christ willfully came into this broken state in order to both comfort the afflicted and to fix what was hopelessly broken in humanity (Isaiah 53). The fallen nature of the world and those around Him influenced Jesus but did not cause Him to enter into a depraved condition or think or behave in a destructive and impairing way.

The cause of universal mental degeneracy occurred in Genesis 3 at the fall of the first man Adam and universally affects all of humanity thereafter. Universal degeneracy teaches hereditary causes for the wicked and weak state of humanity, but that corrupt condition is not a disease that can be traced to physical DNA or specific genes, nor is it a theory that applies to only certain people. Romans 5:12-17 elucidates,

> Therefore, just as sin came into the world through one man, and death through sin, and so death spread to all men because all sinned — for sin indeed was in the world before the law was given, but sin is not counted where these is no law. Yet death reigned from Adam to Moses, even over those whose sinning was not like the transgression of Adam, who was a type of the one who was to come. But the free gift is not like the trespass. For if many died through one man's trespass, much more have the grace of God and the free gift by the grace of that one man Jesus Christ abounded for many. And the free gift is not like the result of that one man's sin. For the judgment following one trespass brought condemnation, but the free gift following many trespasses brought justification. For if, because of one man's trespass, death reigned through that one man, much more will those who receive the abundance of grace and the free gift of righteousness reign in life through the one man Jesus Christ.

The endless attempt both to find causes of alleged psychiatric disorders and to prove materialistic etiologies for the metaphysical soul's deceit and distress is based upon the rejection of the Scriptural account of Creation — including dualism, universal degeneracy, and the sovereignty of God over His creation. Any theory which opposes this Scriptural teaching of universal degeneracy is a false gospel which hinders people — all of whom are degenerates — from the only means of regeneration.

If the cause of mental turmoil and moral behavioral struggles are the soul's condition and not the body's measurable effects, then faith, desires/pursuits, hopes, and identity become primary issues in counseling and helping others to be restored to mental health. Discussing the importance of hope and treatments in counseling makes no logical sense if faith is not of primary importance (Hebrews 11:1). Conversely, if the body is causative for mental struggles, then counseling and psychotherapy can only treat symptoms or suppress human consciousness.

A cursory overview of medical treatments both past and present, though, reveal that medicinal somatic treatments are widely known to only be symptomatic approaches[1015] — with the exception of the existence of the placebo effect. In other words, even the materialistic treatments reveal that the true cause of mental turmoil is not the body.

To truly help people who endure crises would mean that society begins to teach them a right faith/worldview/ phenomenology that enables them to endure through every level of hardship they encounter and to understand in a truthful and comforting way the horrific phenomena they have experienced. Such practical help does not wait until there is a crisis to attempt teaching moral and relational truth by which people can find freedom. Children must be taught at an early age how God has specifically designed them, who they are in Christ, and how the fallen nature of both all humanity and the world in which they live affects them (e.g., Acts 14:22). This faith or phenomenology denounces self-realization and the world's system that encourages pursuing destructive desires and which

---

[1015] Robert L. Taylor, *Finding the Right Psychiatrist: A Guide for Discerning Consumers* (2014), 40-45. For further study on psychopharmacology, see Berger, *Mental Illness: The Necessity for Dependence*, and Berger, *The Chemical Imbalance Delusion*.

promises to deliver souls into joy, peace, and satisfaction, but cannot.

While it is antithetical to humanistic faith, children must be taught that setting aside their natural and deceived desire to please self over loving God and others is vital to each of their heart's ability to endure every level of trial/trauma (James 1:1-2) that each one will inevitably encounter. In many ways, teaching children a right worldview that explains the true fallen condition of this world before trauma occurs will also require a paradigm shift. By not waiting until they are in distress and traumatized, each person – child or adult – will be better prepared and mentally equipped with proper faith that can enable endurance when trials inevitably come.

Without God's wisdom, trials of faith will leave people "split-minded" and unstable in all their ways (James 1:1-13). People cannot dogmatically believe the humanistic doctrine that their desires should be fulfilled in this life, then encounter the undeniable, harsh, and very real vexations of life, and still expect to be mentally stable. In contrast, God's wisdom, discovered in His Word, is fully sufficient to explain the human soul and life itself. Such an education not only helps prepare people who undoubtedly will face tragedy and trauma in life, but it also helps to minimize the evil that many people turn to and by which others are traumatized. The gospel is not only healing to the soul; it is also preventative of mental ruin.

Of course, no one can change others' false beliefs and perceptions or convince them to overcome their deceitful desires by manipulation or human efforts. Delivering faith only comes from a person's acknowledging the only one who is mentally healthy and who took upon Himself the curse of Adam to provide the way of mental restoration and eternal life.

There does exist an alternative faith to that of the failed bio-psycho-social worldview; a faith that is both reliable and valid, and a faith that provides genuine hope. When people choose to approach the human soul from a truly biblical perspective, then mental/spiritual healing, hope, and progressive positive change can all be realized.

CHAPTER 9

CONCLUSION

"The wit of man has rarely been more exercised than in the attempt to classify the morbid mental phenomena covered by the term insanity. The result has been disappointing."[1016] *- Daniel Tuke, lecturer in psychological medicine*

At its birth America was faced with a choice of approaching human nature and human phenomena from either a dualistic or a materialistic worldview. While many of America's founding fathers were Deists or Christians, some still chose to uphold and propagate a perspective of human nature that was antithetical to the Word of God. Yet, the signers of the Declaration of Independence both acknowledged that mankind was created by God and that people were created with souls that are morally equal.

One of these founding fathers, Dr. Benjamin Rush, who is also known historically as the father of American psychiatry, profoundly shaped American thinking by asserting philosophies which opposed the wisdom of God. More specifically, Rush's key hypotheses of a material soul, hereditary degeneration, and race psychology, coupled with his many descriptive constructs (e.g., alcoholism and

---

1016 Daniel Hack Tuke, *A Dictionary of Psychological Medicine* vol 1 (London, UK: Churchill, 1892), 229.

negritude), his psychiatric textbook, and his material attempts to treat mental struggles would profoundly shape psychiatric theory and practices for over two centuries following his death.

Since the days of Rush (including psychiatrists such as Mesmer, Morel, and numerous others who followed like Wundt, Kraepelin, Rüdin, and Kallmann), the philosophies of eugenics have increasingly subverted the biblical concept of the metaphysical soul. Rush's introduction of the doctrines of individual degenerationism, materialism, and biodeterminism remain today the foundational beliefs undergirding psychiatric theory and psychiatric genetics in particular.

In accordance with this worldview/phenomenology, many have chosen to view struggling, distressed, deceived, impaired, and even sinful souls as defective products of evolution and to flood people's bodies with chemicals and material treatments that do not fix the soul's problems or restore people's lives. Sadly, the notion has been accepted that classifying some people as abnormal, subjecting those people to abnormal circumstances, and insisting upon a phenomenology that worsens the soul's struggles are all somehow altruistic and represent the best approaches to help people who need soul care.

Moreover, society in general has denied that Jesus is the perfect standard of mental health and has insisted instead upon the delusional idea that humanity must turn inward to find deliverance. This popular perspective is based upon the claims that mental health can be found in one's own natural phenomenology and that psychiatric phenomenology is authoritative and empirically sound.

This paradigm is not only destructive, but in the end, this faith regularly leaves people in a hopeless state.

The hallmark of empirical science is the human ability to observe, measure, and replicate discovered results. These important features of approaching the natural/material world, however, still require subjective interpretations of the data available. Scientific hypothesis and conclusions about the natural world are primarily the products of one's faith, especially if scientists' motive is to prove belief rather than to objectively understand the natural world and human nature. Psychiatric genetics/eugenics is foremost a religion that teaches the doctrines of materialism, individual degenerationism, bio-determinism, and humanism as unquestionably true and which demands that the metaphysical and physical realities of human nature be interpreted and approached accordingly. Ironically, it is a faith that must regularly deny the available scientific evidence in order to be sustained.

One of the hallmarks of Hippocratic medicine is to reject false theories which have proven through controlled studies to be false and/or harmful. The genetic theory of mental illness has over the last two centuries consistently shown itself to be an empirically failed and harmful theory — a pseudoscience that creates and sustains constructs of abnormal rather than restoring the human soul and remedying mental turmoil. It is time that society allows science to truly advance beyond the destructive and controlling false faith of psychiatric phenomenology — a faith which was first applied by Benjamin Rush and made popular thereafter by the influential German psychiatrist Emil Kraepelin. Treating the soul as if it were a material object within the realm of medicine has only deepened

631

humanity's struggles; it has not delivered people from their often profound troubling mental and emotional conditions. Instead of restoring humanity to struggling people, the neo-Kraepelinian approach has dehumanized them. In turn, this secular phenomenological approach has made a mockery of the scientific method and genuine altruistic medicine. Still, many academic psychiatrists and physicians continue to claim this eugenic system as falling under the banner of empirical science and medicine.

Even more sobering is the reality that denying humanity's true dual nature is an affront to the Creator's image in whom mankind was fashioned, and dogmatically rejecting this truth keeps humanity from the only available remedy for the soul. While it may be convenient to view only some people as degenerates or disordered, it is a false belief held despite empirical evidence otherwise. Everyone is deceived and impaired at his or her core, and each has a great need to accept the Creator God's truth in order to be restored, comforted, and mentally and behaviorally liberated.

Though many people in today's society may reject Jesus as the only standard of normal and true mental health, these same individuals lack an alternative model of mental health from which to base alleged mental abnormalities. It is a logical fallacy, however, to assert that people are disordered when a standard of order has not yet been objectively established and ideas of man's existence are said to be the result of chance. If Jesus is the immutable standard and his Word is true, then all human souls must be understood as fragile and depraved degenerates in need of regeneration and restoration—everyone is in a state of madness. When compared to this standard of mental health, all people must be viewed as naturally abnormal—

mentally, emotionally, and behaviorally. Along this same line of reasoning, those who are deeply deceived, impaired, distressed, hopeless, etc. should be understood as being normal when compared to others. Fragility and depravity, rather than strength and goodness, best explain the normal human condition.

As Scripture established thousands of years ago, hereditary degenerationism must be understood as universal, as spiritual, as a result of humanity's inability to meet the Creator's designed order, and as a condition in accordance with the history first recorded in Genesis 1-3. Moreover, corresponding somatic effects of the spiritual soul and outworking behavior, which are both observable and measurable, should be expected and understood as normal symptoms of the human condition rather than as causes of mental struggles. Whether one chooses to view negative somatic variances and deterioration as causes or as effects of the soul/psyche's condition largely depends upon a person's presuppositional faith.

Early America and the world since then have had an opportunity to either accept Rush's race psychology or Galt's moral therapy. Regrettably, America first chose to establish faith in fallible mankind, which continues today to consistently fail to deliver the human soul/psyche.

Modern America and the world at large are once again faced with the same choice. But it is not enough to return to Galt's or Pinel's moral therapy. Rather, we must move beyond psychiatric ideas/phenomenologies of moral therapy and return to God's precise description and understanding of the human soul, His wisdom, and His original moral design.

Simply accepting some elements of the gospel (such as altruism, ethics, the creation mandate, and the universality of degeneracy), while at the same time denying God's character, covenantal promises, His wisdom, and His relational design for humanity to be in right fellowship with God and others, will continue to mislead humanity down the path of further destruction. Until we accept the unfortunate bad news about human nature, we will never realize the good news that delivers the human soul. What is needed is a return to biblical phenomenology and discipleship.

In this light, without establishing Christ as the perfect standard of mental health to which the soul needs to be restored and the only enabler to restore a disordered mind to God's original design, the remedy to the soul will remain elusive. Healing, altruism, true "mental health," and destigmatizing can only occur as people reestablish right faith in the one true God. It is God alone who is perfectly able to describe and approach human nature and fully explain human phenomena such as trauma, hopelessness, delusions, and anxiety and who is entirely capable to ultimately restore the human soul to health. It is through applying biblical anthropology, epistemology, theology, and phenomenology that all the soul's troubling conditions can make sense and positive changes can begin to occur.

The only proven faith observed throughout history demands that people themselves stop attempting to save abnormal and turn instead to the only one who is mentally healthy, Jesus Christ. It is well past time that society return the care of the soul to God's plan of deliverance. Only Jesus, the great soul physician and standard of normalcy, can genuinely save abnormal.

APPENDIX A

DEFINITIONS OF KEY TERMS

---

1. *Allele* – one of two or more mutated genes that are found at the same place on a chromosome.

2. *Alienist* – one of the first titles given to psychiatrists, which described their job of alienating people from the rest of society.

3. *Anthropometry* – also knowns as *somatometry* or *biometry* – is an approach that focuses biological processes that can be measured, compared, and fit into statistics.

4. *Dimensional Approach* – the "new" approach to the classification and diagnoses of alleged mental disorders, which attempts to dismiss objective delineating lines between *DSM* disorders. This perspective arose from the realization that there are not significant differences between the symptoms of supposedly different psychiatric constructs. The dimensional approach sets psychiatry in the direction of returning to the historic concept of unitary madness (only one type of insanity that manifests in different ways among different people).

5. *Endophenotype* – the invisible alleged connection between a gene and the phenotype.

6. *Epigenetics* – "above or over the genes." Genes are not fixed, and they can be altered positively or negatively by habitual mindsets, behaviors, and life events.

7. *Eugenics* – the unscientific classification of people according to social or descriptive constructs, which subjectively determine them to be healthy or unhealthy. Eugenics typically claims to be medicinal, as well as scientifically founded.

8. *Gene* – a unit of heredity which carries biological information from parents to children. A gene is a sequence of nucleotides in DNA or RNA that encodes and determines the gene product.

9. *Genome* – an organism's entire set of genes.

10. *Mental hygiene* – a movement popularized in Nazi Germany along with "racial hygiene," but both movements were part of the global eugenic perspective. Today, the term "mental hygiene" has been replaced with the preferred and less offensive "mental health."

11. *Race Psychology* – the false belief that different races exist and produce different mental capabilities, mental and emotional struggles, and intellects. Race psychology is one of the foundational teachings on which psychiatry was formed and eugenics is based (e.g., racial hygiene).

12. *Schizophrenia* – ("premature dementia" as it was first called) the most important psychiatric construct Emil Kraepelin created. The category allows delusions and hallucinations, which a clinician is

either unable or unwilling to explain, to be theoretically explained as an alleged biological illness that has no biological markers or validated pathology. If, however, a the life history and spiritual heart of a person who is diagnosed as having schizophrenia, is revealed, then the individual's struggle is easily explained apart from the stigmatizing label. For example, people have been diagnosed as schizophrenic who have used both prescribed and illicit drugs, who have lost a loved one or survived a traumatic experience, who are deprived of sleep for an extended period of time, who are nearing death, who have valid physical ailments (e.g., brain tumors), and who carry heavy burdens of guilt. The construct of schizophrenia was the catalyst to the Holocaust and remains the central descriptive construct (along with "alcoholism") that sustains the eugenic worldview.

13. *Phenomenology* – the study of and teaching about human consciousness (first person perspective), the human soul, and the metaphysical phenomena of human nature. A person's phenomenology is ultimately based upon their accepted worldview and is applied to interpret experiences and establish identity.

14. The four underlying doctrines of the eugenic theory:

   a. *Individual degeneracy* – the belief that some people mentally, emotionally, and behaviorally degenerate from an alleged standard of normalcy, making them within the established diagnostic system "unhealthy," "abnormal," or "disordered."

637

b. *Materialism* – the belief that human nature consists entirely of material and is fully approachable and explainable through science. Materialism is antithetical to the biblical teaching of dualism (that mankind is created with both metaphysical/spiritual and physical natures) and is a belief that attempts to reduce even metaphysical phenomena into material explanations or causes. Materialism is also referred to as reductionism, scientism, and positivism.

c. *Bio-determinism* – the belief that every aspect of human nature and human phenomena are determined/fixed by a person's biology. Genetic-determinism is one type of bio-determinism.

d. *Utilitarianism* – the belief that truth must be established based upon its utility. This doctrine treats truth as if it is subjective and variable. Utilitarianism depends upon a group of people agreeing upon what is truth.

15. *Phenotype* – the observable "symptoms" of a person. Within bio-determinism, the phenotype is said to be determined by how a person's genotype and the environment interact.

16. The three psychiatric genetic models:

a. *Single-gene model* — a model which hypothesizes that there is a single gene that allegedly causes schizophrenia. Historically, the single gene model has been the most popular, and originated with Ernst Rüdin and Franz Joseph Kallmann in Nazi Germany.

b. *Polygenic model* — a model which suggests that multiple genes "mutate" through natural selection to cause schizophrenia (or at least cause a risk for schizophrenia) and other alleged mental illnesses. "Genetic odds" or "polygenic risk scores" identify this clear eugenic faith that has become the current trend in psychiatric genetics.

a. *Omnigenic model* — is a model which asserts that either the entire human genome or any particular gene in the genome can cause alleged disorders.

APPENDIX B

KEY EUGENIC FIGURES THROUGHOUT HISTORY

----

1. **Benjamin Rush (1746-1813)** is the father of American psychiatry, the father of the hereditary theory of mental illness, the father of race psychology, and one of the first psychiatrists to assert in writing that the metaphysical soul and human morality should be reduced to material explanations. Rush was also one of the first psychiatrists to construct and categorize alleged disorders based upon social and descriptive observations, and he authored one of the first influential psychiatric textbooks to transmit his theories. Because of his concepts of hereditary madness and his materialistic approach to the soul, Rush's face is also the image chosen to represent the American Psychiatric Association on their official seal.

2. **Charles Darwin (1809-1882)** is the father of the *Evolutionary theory*, the concept of natural selection, and the *pangenesis theory*.

3. **Augustin Morel (1809-1873)** is the psychiatrist who is most noted for his theory of individual or hereditary degeneracy.

4. **Francis Galton (1822-1911)** is historically considered to be the father of eugenics, since he coined the term. Rush and Darwin, however, had already presented the worldview within race psychology prior to the field's formalization.

5. **Wilhelm Wundt (1832-1920)** is the father of modern, descriptive, and experimental psychology. Wundt globally popularized the material theory of the soul and the idea of "mental sciences"/"psychologies." Both Kraepelin and Freud studied under Wundt.

6. **Emil Kraepelin (1856-1926)** is the father of the brain dysfunction theory, the statistical approach, Nazi eugenics, and the formalization of psychiatry as a perceived medical and scientific field. Kraepelin also popularized the idea of psychopharmacology as a potential remedy, and his published book of alleged disorders became the standard on which psychiatric diagnostic systems have been founded since his lifetime. Kraepelin is arguably the most significant figure in modern psychiatric genetic theory, and his invented psychiatric constructs of premature dementia (now referred to as schizophrenia) and depression (now split into unipolar and bipolar depressions) remain central to upholding the bio-psycho-social model. Kraepelin's list of alleged degenerates and his genetic theory became the philosophical basis of the experimentations, sterilizations, and euthanasia that occurred during the Holocaust.

7. **Ernst Rüdin (1874-1952)** is the protégé to Emil Kraepelin and considered historically as the father of Nazi eugenics. Rüdin is also credited with asserting the single gene theory, and he was the psychiatrist whom Hitler asked to write the legislation on sterilization. Rüdin was also appointed as head over all German medicine and was the one who ensured that the Kraepelinian eugenic theory was implemented and upheld in Germany. Rüdin's most noted contribution to the genetic theory of mental illness was his pseudo-scientific work on twin studies that is still cited today.

8. **Franz Joseph Kallmann (1897-1965)** is the father of modern American psychiatric genetics. Kallmann introduced Nazi eugenics to America under the new label of psychiatric genetics. As many historians record, Kallmann was more of a eugenicist than even his good friend Ernst Rüdin was.

9. **Eliot Slater (1904-1983)** was to Europe what Kallmann was to America post WW2. Thanks in large part to the work of Slater and Kallmann, Kraepelinian eugenics continues today under the new name of *psychiatric genetics*.

SELECTED BIBLIOGRAPHY

Because of the vast number of sources referenced or quoted in this book, the bibliographic information for each work cited can be found in every chapter that a source is used.

Made in the USA
Columbia, SC
04 November 2020